D1276517

MACHINE LEARNING

An Artificial Intelligence Approach

MACHINE LEARNING

An Artificial Intelligence Approach

Contributing authors:

John Anderson
Ranan Banerji
Gary Bradshaw
Jaime Carbonell
Thomas Dietterich
Norman Haas
Frederick Hayes-Roth
Gary Hendrix
Patrick Langley
Douglas Lenat
Ryszard Michalski
Tom Mitchell
Jack Mostow
Bernard Nudel
Michael Rychener
Ross Quinlan
Herbert Simon
Derek Sleeman
Robert Stepp
Paul Utgoff

Editors:

Ryszard S. Michalski
University of Illinois
at Urbana-Champaign, IL

Jaime G. Carbonell
Carnegie-Mellon University
Pittsburgh, PA

Tom M. Mitchell
Rutgers University
New Brunswick, NJ

MORGAN KAUFMANN
PUBLISHERS, INC.

Library of Congress Cataloging-in-Publication Data

Machine learning.

Reprint. Originally published: Palo Alto, Calif. : Tioga Pub. Co., © 1983.
Bibliography: p.
Includes index.
1. Machine learning. 2. Artificial intelligence.
I. Anderson, John R. (John Robert), 1947– .
II. Michalski, Ryszard Stanislaw, 1937– .
III. Carbonell, Jaime G. (Jaime Guillermo) IV. Mitchell, Tom M. (Tom Michael), 1951– .
Q325.M32 1986 006.3′1 86-2953
ISBN 0-934613-09-5

© 1983 by Morgan Kaufmann

All rights reserved. No part of this publication may be reproduced, stored in a retrieval system, or transmitted, in any form or by any means, electronic, mechanical, photocopying, recording, or otherwise, without the prior written permission of the publisher. Printed in the United States of America, Library of Congress Catalog Card Number 86-2953.

This book was set in Times Roman by *Fast* on a Mergenthaler Omnitech™/2000 phototypesetter driven by the Scribe™ document production system.

ISBN 0-934613-09-5
(Previously published by Tioga Publishing Company under ISBN 0-935382-05-4)
DEFG-DO-8

PREFACE

The ability to learn is one of the most fundamental attributes of intelligent behavior. Consequently, progress in the theory and computer modeling of learning processes is of great significance to fields concerned with understanding intelligence. Such fields include cognitive science, artificial intelligence, information science, pattern recognition, psychology, education, epistemology, philosophy, and related disciplines.

The recent observance of the silver anniversary of artificial intelligence has been heralded by a surge of interest in machine learning—both in building models of human learning and in understanding how machines might be endowed with the ability to learn. This renewed interest has spawned many new research projects and resulted in an increase in related scientific activities. In the summer of 1980, the First Machine Learning Workshop was held at Carnegie-Mellon University in Pittsburgh. In the same year, three consecutive issues of the *International Journal of Policy Analysis and Information Systems* were specially devoted to machine learning (No. 2, 3 and 4, 1980). In the spring of 1981, a special issue of the *SIGART Newsletter* No. 76 reviewed current research projects in the field.

This book contains tutorial overviews and research papers representative of contemporary trends in the area of machine learning as viewed from an artificial intelligence perspective. As the first available text on this subject, it is intended to fulfill several needs. For researchers in artificial intelligence, computer science, and cognitive psychology, it provides an easily accessible collection of state-of-the-art papers presenting current results, which will hopefully spur further research. For students in artificial intelligence and related disciplines, this volume may serve as a supplementary textbook for a course in artificial intelligence, or as a primary text for a specialized course devoted to machine learning. Finally, due to the potential impact of machine learning on a variety of disciplines, this book may be of interest to a diverse range of readers, including computer scientists, robotics experts, knowledge engineers, educators, philosophers, data analysts, psychologists and electronic engineers.

The major contemporary research directions in machine learning covered in this book include: learning from examples, modeling human learning strategies, knowledge acquisition for expert systems, learning heuristics, learning from instruction, learning by analogy, discovery systems, and conceptual data analysis. A glossary of selected terminology and an extensive up-to-date bibliography are provided to facilitate instruction and suggest further reading.

—Ryszard S. Michalski, Jaime G. Carbonell, Tom M. Mitchell

ACKNOWLEDGMENTS

The editors wish to express a deep gratitude to all the authors whose efforts made this book possible, and to the reviewers whose ideas and criticism were indispensable in refereeing and improving the contributions. They are most grateful to the Office of Naval Research for supporting the First Machine Learning Workshop, where the idea of publishing this book originated.

The following people provided invaluable assistance in preparing the book: Margorie Ast, Trina and Nathaniel Borenstein, Kitty Fischer, Edward Frank, Jo Ann Gabinelli, Joan Mitchell, June Wingler and Jan Zubkoff. Their hard work and perseverance are gratefully acknowledged. The editors also acknowledge the support and access to technical facilities provided by the Computer Science Departments of Carnegie-Mellon University, the University of Illinois at Urbana-Champaign, and Rutgers University.

CONTENTS

Preface **v**

PART ONE **GENERAL ISSUES IN MACHINE LEARNING** **1**

Chapter 1 **An Overview of Machine Learning** **3**
Jaime G. Carbonell, Ryszard S. Michalski, and Tom M. Mitchell

1.1 Introduction 3
1.2 The Objectives of Machine Learning 3
1.3 A Taxonomy of Machine Learning Research 7
1.4 An Historical Sketch of Machine Learning 14
1.5 A Brief Reader's Guide 16

Chapter 2 **Why Should Machines Learn?** **25**
Herbert A. Simon

2.1 Introduction 25
2.2 Human Learning and Machine Learning 25
2.3 What is Learning? 28
2.4 Some Learning Programs 30
2.5 Growth of Knowledge in Large Systems 32
2.6 A Role for Learning 34
2.7 Concluding Remarks 35

PART TWO **LEARNING FROM EXAMPLES** **39**

Chapter 3 **A Comparative Review of Selected Methods for Learning from Examples** **41**
Thomas G. Dietterich and Ryszard S. Michalski

3.1 Introduction 41
3.2 Comparative Review of Selected Methods 49

3.3 Conclusion 75

Chapter 4 A Theory and Methodology of Inductive Learning **83**
Ryszard S. Michalski

4.1 Introduction 83
4.2 Types of Inductive Learning 87
4.3 Description Language 94
4.4 Problem Background Knowledge 96
4.5 Generalization Rules 103
4.6 The Star Methodology 112
4.7 An Example 116
4.8 Conclusion 123
4.A Annotated Predicate Calculus (APC) 130

PART THREE LEARNING IN PROBLEM-SOLVING AND PLANNING **135**

Chapter 5 Learning by Analogy: Formulating and Generalizing Plans from Past Experience **137**
Jaime G. Carbonell

5.1 Introduction 137
5.2 Problem-Solving by Analogy 139
5.3 Evaluating the Analogical Reasoning Process 149
5.4 Learning Generalized Plans 151
5.5 Concluding Remark 159

Chapter 6 Learning by Experimentation: Acquiring and Refining Problem-Solving Heuristics **163**
Tom M. Mitchell, Paul E. Utgoff, and Ranan Banerji

6.1 Introduction 163
6.2 The Problem 164
6.3 Design of LEX 167
6.4 New Directions: Adding Knowledge to Augment Learning 180
6.5 Summary 189

Chapter 7 Acquisition of Proof Skills in Geometry **191**
John R. Anderson

7.1 Introduction 191
7.2 A Model of the Skill Underlying Proof Generation 193
7.3 Learning 201
7.4 Knowledge Compilation 202

7.5	Summary of Geometry Learning	217
Chapter 8	**Using Proofs and Refutations to Learn from Experience** *Frederick Hayes-Roth*	**221**
8.1	Introduction	221
8.2	The Learning Cycle	222
8.3	Five Heuristics for Rectifying Refuted Theories	225
8.4	Computational Problems and Implementation Techniques	234
8.5	Conclusions	238
PART FOUR	**LEARNING FROM OBSERVATION AND DISCOVERY**	**241**
Chapter 9	**The Role of Heuristics in Learning by Discovery: Three Case Studies** *Douglas B. Lenat*	**243**
9.1	Motivation	243
9.2	Overview	245
9.3	Case Study 1: The AM Program; Heuristics Used to Develop New Knowledge	249
9.4	A Theory of Heuristics	263
9.5	Case Study 2: The Eurisko Program; Heuristics Used to Develop New Heuristics	276
9.6	Heuristics Used to Develop New Representations	282
9.7	Case Study 3: Biological Evolution; Heuristics Used to Generate Plausible Mutations	286
9.8	Conclusions	302
Chapter 10	**Rediscovering Chemistry With the BACON System** *Pat Langley, Gary L. Bradshaw, and Herbert A. Simon*	**307**
10.1	Introduction	307
10.2	An Overview of BACON.4	309
10.3	The Discoveries of BACON.4	312
10.4	Rediscovering Nineteenth Century Chemistry	319
10.5	Conclusions	326

Chapter 11	**Learning From Observation: Conceptual Clustering** *Ryszard S. Michalski and Robert E. Stepp*	**331**
11.1	Introduction	332
11.2	Conceptual Cohesiveness	333
11.3	Terminology and Basic Operations of the Algorithm	336
11.4	A Criterion of Clustering Quality	344
11.5	Method and Implementation	345
11.6	An Example of a Practical Problem: Constructing a Classification Hierarchy of Spanish Folk Songs	358
11.7	Summary and Some Suggested Extensions of the Method	360
PART FIVE	**LEARNING FROM INSTRUCTION**	**365**
Chapter 12	**Machine Transformation of Advice into a Heuristic Search Procedure** *David Jack Mostow*	**367**
12.1	Introduction	367
12.2	Kinds of Knowledge Used	370
12.3	A Slightly Non-Standard Definition of Heuristic Search	374
12.4	Instantiating the HSM Schema for a Given Problem	378
12.5	Refining HSM by Moving Constraints Between Control Components	384
12.6	Evaluation of Generality	398
12.7	Conclusion	399
12.A	Index of Rules	403
Chapter 13	**Learning by Being Told: Acquiring Knowledge for Information Management** *Norm Haas and Gary G. Hendrix*	**405**
13.1	Overview	405
13.2	Technical Approach: Experiments with the KLAUS Concept	408
13.3	More Technical Details	413
13.4	Conclusions and Directions for Future Work	418
13.A	Training NANOKLAUS About Aircraft Carriers	422

Chapter 14 **The Instructible Production System: A Retrospective Analysis** **429**
Michael D. Rychener

14.1 The Instructible Production System Project 430
14.2 Essential Functional Components of Instructible Systems 436
14.3 Survey of Approaches 443
14.4 Discussion 453

PART SIX **APPLIED LEARNING SYSTEMS** **461**

Chapter 15 **Learning Efficient Classification Procedures and their Application to Chess End Games** **463**
J. Ross Quinlan

15.1 Introduction 463
15.2 The Inductive Inference Machinery 465
15.3 The Lost N-ply Experiments 470
15.4 Approximate Classification Rules 474
15.5 Some Thoughts on Discovering Attributes 477
15.6 Conclusion 481

Chapter 16 **Inferring Student Models for Intelligent Computer-Aided Instruction** **483**
Derek H. Sleeman

16.1 Introduction 483
16.2 Generating a Complete and Non-redundant Set of Models 488
16.3 Processing Domain Knowledge 503
16.4 Summary 507
16.A An Example of the SELECTIVE Algorithm: LMS-I's Model Generation Algorithm 510

Comprehensive Bibliography of Machine Learning **511**
Paul E. Utgoff and Bernard Nudel

Glossary of Selected Terms In Machine Learning **551**

About the Authors **557**

Author Index **563**

Subject Index **567**

PART ONE

GENERAL ISSUES IN MACHINE LEARNING

1

AN OVERVIEW OF MACHINE LEARNING

Jaime G. Carbonell
Carnegie-Mellon University

Ryszard S. Michalski
University of Illinois at Urbana-Champaign

Tom M. Mitchell
Rutgers University

1.1 INTRODUCTION

Learning is a many-faceted phenomenon. Learning processes include the acquisition of new declarative knowledge, the development of motor and cognitive skills through instruction or practice, the organization of new knowledge into general, effective representations, and the discovery of new facts and theories through observation and experimentation. Since the inception of the computer era, researchers have been striving to implant such capabilities in computers. Solving this problem has been, and remains, a most challenging and fascinating long-range goal in artificial intelligence (AI). The study and computer modeling of learning processes in their multiple manifestations constitutes the subject matter of machine learning.

1.2 THE OBJECTIVES OF MACHINE LEARNING

At present, the field of machine learning is organized around three primary research foci:

- **Task-Oriented Studies**—the development and analysis of learning systems to improve performance in a predetermined set of tasks (also known as the "engineering approach")

- **Cognitive Simulation**—the investigation and computer simulation of human learning processes
- **Theoretical Analysis**—the theoretical exploration of the space of possible learning methods and algorithms independent of application domain

Although many research efforts strive primarily towards one of these objectives, progress towards one objective often leads to progress towards another. For instance, in order to investigate the space of possible learning methods, a reasonable starting point may be to consider the only known example of robust learning behavior, namely humans (and perhaps other biological systems). Similarly, psychological investigations of human learning may be helped by theoretical analysis that may suggest various plausible learning models. The need to acquire a particular form of knowledge in some task-oriented study may itself spawn new theoretical analysis or pose the question: "How *do* humans acquire this specific skill (or knowledge)?" This trichotomy of mutually challenging and supportive objectives is a reflection of the entire field of artificial intelligence, where expert systems research, cognitive simulation, and theoretical studies provide cross-fertilization of problems and ideas.

1.2.1 Applied Learning Systems: A Practical Necessity

At present, instructing a computer or a computer-controlled robot to perform a task requires one to define a complete and correct algorithm for that task, and then laboriously program the algorithm into a computer. These activities typically involve a tedious and time-consuming effort by specially trained personnel.

Present-day computer systems cannot truly learn to perform a task through examples or by analogy to a similar, previously-solved task. Nor can they improve significantly on the basis of past mistakes, or acquire new abilities by observing and imitating experts. Machine learning research strives to open the possibility of instructing computers in such new ways, and thereby promises to ease the burden of hand-programming growing volumes of increasingly complex information into the computers of tomorrow. The rapid expansion of applications and availability of computers today makes this possibility even more attractive and desirable.

When approaching a task-oriented knowledge acquisition task, one must be aware that the resultant computer systems must interact with humans, and therefore should closely parallel human abilities. The traditional argument that an engineering approach need not reflect human or biological performance is not truly applicable to machine learning. Since airplanes, a successful result of an almost pure engineering approach, bear little resemblance to their biological counterparts, one may argue that applied knowledge acquisition systems should be equally divorced from any consideration of human capabilities. This argument does not apply here because airplanes need not interact with or understand birds. Learning machines, on the other hand, will have to interact with the people who make use of them, and consequently the concepts and skills they acquire—if not necessarily their internal mechanisms—must be understandable to humans.

1.2.2 Machine Learning as a Science

The question of what are the genetically-endowed abilities in a biological system (versus environmentally-acquired skills or knowledge) has fascinated biologists, psychologists, philosophers and artificial intelligence researchers alike. A clear candidate for a cognitive invariant in humans is the learning mechanism—the innate ability to acquire facts, skills and more abstract concepts. Therefore, understanding human learning well enough to reproduce aspects of that learning behavior in a computer system is, in itself, a worthy scientific goal. Moreover, the computer can render substantial assistance to cognitive psychology, in that it may be used to test the consistency and completeness of learning theories, and enforce a commitment to fine-structure process-level detail that precludes meaningless, tautological or untestable theories.

The study of human learning processes is also of considerable practical significance. Gaining insights into the principles underlying human learning abilities is likely to lead to more effective educational techniques. Thus, it is not surprising that research into intelligent computer-assisted instruction, which attempts to develop computer-based tutoring systems, shares many of the goals and perspectives with machine learning research. One particularly interesting development is that computer tutoring systems are starting to incorporate abilities to infer models of student competence from observed performance. Inferring the scope of a student's knowledge and skills in a particular area allows much more effective and individualized tutoring of the student.

An equally basic scientific objective of machine learning is the exploration of alternative learning mechanisms, including the discovery of different induction algorithms, the scope and limitations of certain methods, the information that must be available to the learner, the issue of coping with imperfect training data, and the creation of general techniques applicable in many task domains. There is no reason to believe that human learning methods are the only possible means of acquiring knowledge and skills. In fact, common sense suggests that human learning represents just one point in an uncharted space of possible learning methods—a point that through the evolutionary process is particularly well suited to cope with the general physical environment in which we exist. Most theoretical work in machine learning has centered on the creation, characterization and analysis of general learning methods, with the major emphasis on analyzing generality and performance rather than psychological plausibility.

Whereas theoretical analysis provides a means of exploring the space of possible learning methods, the task-oriented approach provides a vehicle to test and improve the performance of functional learning systems. By constructing and testing applied learning systems, one can determine the cost-effectiveness trade-offs and limitations of particular approaches to learning. In this way, individual data points in the space of possible learning systems are explored, and the space itself becomes better understood. Many of the chapters of this book can be viewed from this perspective.

1.2.3 Knowledge Acquisition versus Skill Refinement

There are two basic forms of learning: *knowledge acquisition* and *skill refinement*. When we say that someone learned physics, we mean that this person acquired significant concepts of physics, understood their meaning, and understood their relationship to each other and to the physical world. The essence of learning in this case is the acquisition of new knowledge, including descriptions and models of physical systems and their behaviors, incorporating a variety of representations—from simple intuitive mental models, examples and images, to completely tested mathematical equations and physical laws. A person is said to have learned more if his knowledge explains a broader scope of situations, is more accurate, and is better able to predict the behavior of the physical world. This form of learning is typical in a large variety of situations and is generally termed *knowledge acquisition*. Hence, knowledge acquisition is defined as learning new symbolic information coupled with the ability to apply that information in an effective manner.

A second kind of learning is the gradual improvement of motor and cognitive skills through practice, such as learning to ride a bicycle or to play the piano. Acquiring textbook knowledge on how to perform these activities represents only the initial phase in developing the requisite skills. The bulk of the learning process consists of refining the learned skills, whether mental or motor coordination, by repeated practice and by correcting deviations from desired behavior. This form of learning, often called *skill refinement*, differs in many ways from knowledge acquisition. Whereas the essence of knowledge acquisition may be a conscious process whose result is the creation of new symbolic knowledge structures and mental models, skill refinement occurs at a subconscious level by virtue of repeated practice. Most human learning appears to be a mixture of both activities, with intellectual endeavors favoring the former, and motor coordination tasks favoring the latter.

This book focuses on the knowledge acquisition aspect of learning, although some chapters, specifically those concerned with learning in problem-solving and transforming declarative instructions into effective actions, touch on aspects of both types of learning. Whereas knowledge acquisition clearly belongs in the realm of artificial intelligence research, a case could be made that skill refinement comes closer to non-symbolic processes, such as those studied in adaptive control systems. It may indeed be the case that skill acquisition is inherently non-symbolic in biological systems, but an interesting symbolic model capable of simulating gradual skill improvement through practice has been proposed recently by Newell and Rosenbloom [Newell, 1981]. Hence, perhaps both forms of learning can be captured in artificial intelligence models.

1.3 A TAXONOMY OF MACHINE LEARNING RESEARCH

This section presents a taxonomic road map to the field of machine learning with a view towards presenting useful criteria for classifying and comparing most artificial intelligence-based machine learning investigations. Later sections survey the main directions actually taken by research in machine learning over the past twenty years, and introduce each major research approach corresponding to subsequent chapters in this book.

One may classify machine learning systems along many different dimensions. We have chosen three dimensions as particularly meaningful:

- Classification on the basis of the *underlying learning strategies* used. The processes themselves are ordered by the amount of inference the learning system performs on the available information.
- Classification on the basis of the *representation of knowledge* or skill acquired by the learner.
- Classification in terms of the *application domain* of the performance system for which knowledge is acquired.

Each point in the space defined by the above dimensions corresponds to a particular learning strategy, employing a particular knowledge representation, applied to a particular domain. Since existing learning systems employ multiple representations and processes, and many have been applied to more than one domain, such learning systems are characterized by several points in the space.

The subsections below describe explored values along each of these dimensions. Future research may well reveal new values and dimensions. Indeed, the larger space of all possible learning systems is still only sparsely explored and partially understood. Existing learning systems correspond to only a small portion of the space because they represent only a small number of possible combinations of the values.

1.3.1 Classification Based on the Underlying Learning Strategy

Since we distinguish learning strategies by the amount of inference the learner performs on the information provided, we first consider the two extremes: performing no inference, and performing a substantial amount of inference. If a computer system is programmed directly, its knowledge increases, but it performs no inference whatsoever; all cognitive effort is on the part of the programmer. Conversely, if a system independently discovers new theories or invents new concepts, it must perform a very substantial amount of inference; it is deriving organized knowledge from experiments and observations. An intermediate point in the spectrum would be a student determining how to solve a mathematics problem by analogy to worked-out examples in the textbook—a process that requires inference, but much less than discovering a new branch of mathematics without guidance from teacher or textbook.

As the amount of inference that the learner is capable of performing increases, the burden placed on the teacher or external environment decreases. It is much more difficult to teach a person by explaining each step in a complex task than by showing that person the way that similar tasks are usually handled. It is more difficult yet to program a computer to perform a complex task than to instruct a person to perform the task; as programming requires explicit specification of all requisite detail, whereas a person receiving instruction can use prior knowledge and common sense to fill in most mundane details. The taxonomy below captures this notion of trade-offs in the amount of effort required of the learner and of the teacher.

1. **Rote learning and direct implanting of new knowledge**—No inference or other transformation of the knowledge is required on the part of the learner. Variants of this knowledge acquisition method include:
   - Learning by being programmed, constructed or modified by an external entity, requiring no effort on the part of the learner (for example, the usual style of computer programming).
   - Learning by memorization of given facts and data with no inferences drawn from the incoming information (for example, as performed by primitive database systems). The term "rote learning" is used primarily in this context.
2. **Learning from instruction** (or, learning by being told)—Acquiring knowledge from a teacher or other organized source, such as a textbook, requiring that the learner transform the knowledge from the input language to an internally-usable representation, and that the new information be integrated with prior knowledge for effective use. Hence, the learner is required to perform some inference, but a large fraction of the burden remains with the teacher, who must present and organize knowledge in a way that incrementally augments the student's existing knowledge. Learning from instruction parallels most formal education methods. Therefore, the machine learning task is one of building a system that can accept instruction or advice and can store and apply this learned knowledge effectively. This form of learning is discussed in Chapters 12, 13 and 14.
3. **Learning by analogy**—Acquiring new facts or skills by transforming and augmenting existing knowledge that bears strong similarity to the desired new concept or skill into a form effectively useful in the new situation. For instance, a person who has never driven a small truck, but who drives automobiles, may well transform his existing skill (perhaps imperfectly) to the new task. Similarly, a learning-by-analogy system might be applied to convert an existing computer program into one that performs a closely-related function for which it was not originally designed. Learning by analogy requires more inference on the part of the learner than does rote learning or learning from instruction. A fact or skill analogous in relevant parameters must be retrieved from memory; then the retrieved knowledge must be transformed, applied to the new situation, and stored for future use. This form of learning is discussed in Chapters 5 and 7.

4. **Learning from examples** (a special case of inductive learning)—Given a set of examples and counterexamples of a concept, the learner induces a general concept description that describes all of the positive examples and none of the counterexamples. Learning from examples is a method that has been heavily investigated in artificial intelligence. The amount of inference performed by the learner is much greater than in learning from instruction, as no general concepts are provided by a teacher, and is somewhat greater than in learning by analogy, as no similar concepts are provided as "seeds" around which the new concept may be grown. Learning from examples can be subcategorized according to the *source* of the examples:

    - The source is a *teacher* who knows the concept and generates sequences of examples that are meant to be as helpful as possible. If the teacher also knows (or, more typically, infers) the knowledge state of the learner, the examples can be selected to optimize convergence on the desired concept (as in Winston's system [Winston, 1975]).
    - The source is the *learner itself*. The learner typically knows its own knowledge state, but clearly does not know the concept to be acquired. Therefore, the learner can generate instances (and have an external entity such as the environment or a teacher classify them as positive or negative examples) on the basis of the information it believes necessary to discriminate among contending concept descriptions. For instance, a learner trying to acquire the concept of "ferromagnetic substance", may generate as a possible candidate "all metals". Upon testing copper and other metals with a magnet, the learner will then discover that copper is a counterexample, and therefore the concept of ferromagnetic substance should not be generalized to include all metals.
    - The source is the *external environment*. In this case the example generation process is operationally random, as the learner must rely on relatively uncontrolled observations. For example, an astronomer attempting to infer precursors to supernovas must rely mainly upon unstructured data presentation. (Although the astronomer knows the concept of a supernova, he cannot know *a priori* where and when a supernova will occur, nor can he cause one to exist.)

    One can also classify learning from examples by the *type* of examples available to the learner:

    - *Only positive examples available*. Whereas positive examples provide instances of the concept to be acquired, they do not provide information for preventing overgeneralization of the inferred concept. In this kind of learning situation, overgeneralization might be avoided by considering only the minimal generalizations necessary, or by relying upon *a priori* domain knowledge to constrain the concept to be inferred.

- *Positive and negative examples available.* In this kind of situation, positive examples force generalization whereas negative examples prevent overgeneralization (the induced concept should never be so general as to include any of the negative examples). This is the most typical form of learning from examples.

Learning from examples may be one-trial or incremental. In the former case, all examples are presented at once. In the latter case, the system must form one or more hypotheses of the concept (or range of concepts) consistent with the available data, and subsequently refine the hypotheses after considering additional examples. The incremental approach more closely parallels human learning, allows the learner to use partially learned concepts (for performance, or to guide the example generation process), and enables a teacher to focus on the basic aspects of a new concept before attempting to impart less central details. On the other hand, the one-step approach is less apt to lead one down garden paths by an injudicious choice of initial examples in formulating the kernel of the new concept. Various aspects of learning from examples are discussed in Chapters 3, 4, 5, 6, 7, 8, 15 and 16.

5. **Learning from observation and discovery** (also called unsupervised learning)—This is a very general form of inductive learning that includes discovery systems, theory-formation tasks, the creation of classification criteria to form taxonomic hierarchies, and similar tasks without benefit of an external teacher. This form of unsupervised learning requires the learner to perform more inference than any approach thus far discussed. The learner is not provided with a set of instances of a particular concept, nor is it given access to an oracle that can classify internally-generated instances as positive or negative instances of any given concept. Moreover, rather than focusing on a single concept at a time, the observations may span several concepts that need to be acquired, thus introducing a severe focus-of-attention problem. One may subclassify learning from observation according to the *degree of interaction* with an external environment. The extreme points in this dimension are:

   - *Passive observation*, where the learner classifies and taxonomizes observations of multiple aspects of the environment.
   - *Active experimentation*, where the learner perturbs the environment to observe the results of its perturbations. Experimentation may be random, dynamically focused according to general criteria of interestingness, or strongly guided by theoretical constraints. As a system acquires knowledge, and hypothesizes theories it may be driven to confirm or disconfirm its theories, and hence explore its environment applying different observation and experimentation strategies as the

need arises. Often this form of learning involves the generation of examples to test hypothesized or partially acquired concepts.

Learning from observation is discussed in Chapters 4, 9, 10 and 11.

The above classification of learning strategies helps one to compare various learning systems in terms of their underlying mechanisms, in terms of the available external source of information, and in terms of the degree to which they rely on pre-organized knowledge.

1.3.2 Classification According to the Type of Knowledge Acquired

A learning system may acquire rules of behavior, descriptions of physical objects, problem-solving heuristics, classification taxonomies over a sample space, and many other types of knowledge useful in the performance of a wide variety of tasks. The list below spans types of knowledge acquired, primarily as a function of the representation of that knowledge.

1. **Parameters in algebraic expressions**—Learning in this context consists of adjusting numerical parameters or coefficients in algebraic expressions of a fixed functional form so as to obtain desired performance. For instance, perceptrons [Rosenblatt, 1958; Minsky & Papert, 1969] adjust weighting coefficients for threshold logic elements when learning to recognize two-dimensional patterns.
2. **Decision trees**—Some systems acquire decision trees to discriminate among classes of objects. The nodes in a decision tree correspond to selected object attributes, and the edges correspond to predetermined alternative values for these attributes. Leaves of the tree correspond to sets of objects with an identical classification.
3. **Formal grammars**—In learning to recognize a particular (usually artificial) language, formal grammars are induced from sequences of expressions in the language. These grammars are typically represented as regular expressions, finite-state automata, context-free grammar rules, or transformation rules.
4. **Production rules**—A production rule is a condition-action pair $\{C \Rightarrow A\}$, where C is a set of conditions and A is a sequence of actions. If all the conditions in a production rule are satisfied, then the sequence of actions is executed. Due to their simplicity and ease of interpretation, production rules are a widely-used knowledge representation in learning systems. The four basic operations whereby production rules may be acquired and refined are:

    - *Creation:* A new rule is constructed by the system or acquired from an external entity.
    - *Generalization:* Conditions are dropped or made less restrictive, so that the rule applies in a larger number of situations.

- *Specialization:* Additional conditions are added to the condition set, or existing conditions made more restrictive, so that the rule applies to a smaller number of specific situations.
- *Composition:* Two or more rules that were applied in sequence are composed into a single larger rule, thus forming a "compiled" process and eliminating any redundant conditions or actions.

5. **Formal logic-based expressions and related formalisms**—These general-purpose representations have been used to formulate descriptions of individual objects (input to a learning system) and to formulate resultant concept descriptions (output from a learning system). They take the form of formal logic expressions whose components are propositions, arbitrary predicates, finite-valued variables, statements restricting ranges of variables (such as "a number between 1 and 9"), or embedded logical expressions.
6. **Graphs and Networks**—In many domains graphs and networks provide a more convenient and efficient representation than logical expressions, although the expressive power of network representations is comparable to that of formal logic expressions. Some learning techniques exploit graph-matching and graph-transformation schemes to compare and index knowledge efficiently.
7. **Frames and schemas**—These provide larger units of representation than single logical expressions or production rules. Frames and schemas can be viewed as collections of labeled entities ("slots"), each slot playing a certain prescribed role in the representation. They have proven quite useful in many artificial intelligence applications. For instance, a system that acquires generalized plans must be able to represent and manipulate such plans as units, although their internal structure may be arbitrarily complex. Moreover, in experiential learning, past successes, untested alternatives, causes of failure, and other information must be recorded and compared in inducing and refining various rules of behavior (or entire plans). Schema representations provide an appropriate formalism.
8. **Computer programs and other procedural encodings**—The objective of several learning systems is to acquire an ability to carry out a specific process efficiently, rather than to reason about the internal structure of the process. Most automatic programming systems fall in this general category. In addition to computer programs, procedural encodings include human motor skills (such as knowing how to ride a bicycle), instruction sequences to robot manipulators, and other "compiled" human or machine skills. Unlike logical descriptions, networks or frames, the detailed internal structure of the resultant procedural encodings need not be comprehensible to humans, or to automated reasoning systems. Only the external behavior of acquired procedural skills become directly available to the reasoning system.
9. **Taxonomies**—Learning from observation may result in global structuring

of domain objects into a hierarchy or taxonomy. Clustering object descriptions into newly-proposed categories, and forming hierarchical classifications require the system to formulate relevant criteria for classification.

10. **Multiple representations**—Some knowledge acquisition systems use several representation schemes for the newly-acquired knowledge. Most notably, some discovery and theory-formation systems that acquire concepts, operations on those concepts, and heuristic rules for a new domain must select appropriate combinations of representation schemes applicable to the different forms of knowledge acquired.

1.3.3 Classification by Domain of Application

A useful dimension for classifying learning systems is their area of application. The list below specifies application areas to which various existing learning systems have been applied. Application areas are presented in alphabetical order, not reflecting the relative effort or significance of the resultant machine learning system.

1. Agriculture
2. Chemistry
3. Cognitive Modeling (simulating human learning processes)
4. Computer Programming
5. Education
6. Expert Systems (high-performance, domain-specific AI programs)
7. Game Playing (chess, checkers, poker, and so on)
8. General Methods (no specific domain)
9. Image Recognition
10. Mathematics
11. Medical Diagnosis
12. Music
13. Natural Language Processing
14. Physical Object Characterizations
15. Physics
16. Planning and Problem-solving
17. Robotics
18. Sequence Prediction
19. Speech Recognition

The Bibliography provides an index to the literature organized around several criteria including some of the more commonly explored application areas. Now that we have a basis for classifying and comparing learning systems, we turn to a brief historical outline of machine learning.

1.4 AN HISTORICAL SKETCH OF MACHINE LEARNING

Over the years, research in machine learning has been pursued with varying degrees of intensity, using different approaches and placing emphasis on different aspects and goals. Within the relatively short history of this discipline, one may distinguish three major periods, each centered around a different paradigm:

- neural modeling and decision-theoretic techniques
- symbolic concept-oriented learning
- knowledge-intensive learning systems exploring various learning tasks

The distinguishing feature of the first paradigm was the interest in building general purpose learning systems that start with little or no initial structure or task-oriented knowledge. The major thrust of research based on this *tabula rasa* approach involved constructing a variety of neural model-based machines, with random or partially random initial structure. These systems were generally referred to as *neural nets* or *self-organizing systems*. Learning in such systems consisted of incremental changes in the probabilities that neuron-like elements (typically threshold logic units) would transmit a signal.

Due to the primitive nature of computer technology at that time, most of the research under this paradigm was either theoretical or involved the construction of special purpose experimental hardware systems, such as perceptrons [Rosenblatt, 1958], pandemonium [Selfridge, 1959] and adelaine [Widrow, 1962]. The groundwork for this paradigm was laid in the forties by Rashevsky and his followers working in the area of mathematical biophysics [Rashevsky, 1948], and by McCulloch and Pitts [1943], who discovered the applicability of symbolic logic to modeling nervous system activities. Among the large number of research efforts in this area, one may mention works such as [Ashby, 1960; Rosenblatt, 1958, 1962; Minsky & Papert, 1969; Block, 1961; Yovits, 1962; Widrow, 1962; Culberson, 1963; Kazmierczak, 1963]. Related research involved the simulation of evolutionary processes, that through random mutation and "natural" selection might create a system capable of some intelligent behavior (for example, [Friedberg, 1958, 1959; Holland, 1980]).

Experience in the above areas spawned the new discipline of pattern recognition and led to the development of a decision-theoretic approach to machine learning. In this approach, learning is equated with the acquisition of linear, polynomial, or related forms of discriminant functions from a given set of training examples (for example, [Nilsson, 1965; Koford, 1966; Uhr, 1966; Highleyman, 1967]). One of the best known successful learning systems utilizing such techniques (as well as some original new ideas involving non-linear transformations) was Samuel's checkers program [Samuel, 1959, 1963]. This program was able to acquire through learning a master level of performance. Somewhat different, but closely related, techniques utilized methods of statistical decision theory for learning pattern recognition rules (for example, [Sebestyen,

1962; Fu, 1968; Watanabe, 1960; Arkadev, 1971; Fukananga, 1972; Duda & Hart, 1973; Kanal, 1974]).

In parallel to research on neural modeling and decision-theoretic techniques, researchers in control theory developed adaptive control systems able to adjust automatically their parameters in order to maintain stable performance in the presence of various disturbances (for example, [Truxal, 1955; Davies, 1970; Mendel, 1970; Tsypkin, 1968, 1971, 1973; Fu, 1971, 1974]).

Practical results sought by the neural modeling and decision theoretic approaches met with limited success. High expectations articulated in various early works were not realized, and research under this paradigm began to decline. Theoretical studies have revealed strong limitations of the "knowledge-free" perceptron-type learning systems [Minsky & Papert, 1969].

A second major paradigm started to emerge in the early sixties stemming from the work of psychologists and early AI researchers on models of human learning [Hunt *et al.*, 1963, 1966]. The paradigm utilized logic or graph structure representations rather than numerical or statistical methods. Systems learned symbolic descriptions representing higher level knowledge and made strong structural assumptions about the concepts to be acquired.

Examples of work in this paradigm include research on human concept acquisition (for example, [Hunt & Hovland, 1963; Feigenbaum, 1963; Hunt *et al.*, 1966; Hilgard, 1966; Simon & Lea, 1974]), and various applied pattern recognition systems ([Bongard, 1970; Uhr, 1966; Karpinski & Michalski, 1966]).

Some researchers constructed task-oriented specialized systems that would acquire knowledge in the context of a practical problem. For instance, the META-DENDRAL program [Buchanan, 1978] generates rules explaining mass spectrometry data for use in the DENDRAL system [Buchanan *et al.*, 1971].

An influential development in this paradigm was Winston's structural learning system [Winston, 1975]. In parallel with Winston's work, different approaches to learning structural concepts from examples emerged, including a family of logic-based inductive learning programs (AQVAL) [Michalski, 1972, 1973, 1978], and related work by Hayes-Roth [1974], Hayes-Roth & McDermott [1978], Vere [1975], and Mitchell [1978]. More details on this paradigm are included in Chapters 3, 4 and 6. (See also [Michie, 1982].)

The third paradigm represents the most recent period of research starting in the mid-seventies. Researchers have broadened their interest beyond learning isolated concepts from examples, and have begun investigating a wide spectrum of learning methods, most based upon knowledge-rich systems. Specifically, this paradigm can be characterized by several new trends, including:

1. **Knowledge-Intensive Approaches:** Researchers are strongly emphasizing the use of task-oriented knowledge and the constraints it provides in guiding the learning process. One lesson from the failures of earlier *tabula rasa* and knowledge-poor learning systems is that to acquire new knowledge a system must already possess a great deal of initial knowledge.

2. **Exploration of alternative methods of learning:** In addition to the earlier research emphasis on learning from examples, researchers are now investigating a wider variety of learning methods such as learning from instruction (Chapters 12, 13, and 14 in this book), learning by analogy ([Winston, 1979], and Chapter 5 of this book), and discovery of concepts and classifications ([Lenat, 1976] and Chapters 4, 10, and 11 of this book).
3. **Incorporating abilities to generate and select learning tasks:** In contrast to previous efforts, a number of current systems incorporate heuristics to control their focus of attention by generating learning tasks, proposing experiments to gather training data, and choosing concepts to acquire ([Lenat, 1976] and Chapter 6 of this book).

The research presented in this book is concerned primarily with the last, knowledge-intensive paradigm of learning.

1.5 A BRIEF READER'S GUIDE

The chapters in this book are organized according to the major thrust of each investigation, whether that thrust is the development of a general method, the application of various learning techniques to a particular domain, or the theoretical analysis of existing methods. The progression of chapters roughly corresponds to the sequence:

- Basic principles
- General-purpose systems
- Task-oriented applications

Although there is much overlap among the objectives of different chapters, the specific content differs substantially. For instance, the four papers listed under the general category "Learning in problem-solving and planning," share a common top-level objective, but differ substantially in terms of the learning methods employed, the type of knowledge acquired, and the range of applicability of the described systems.

The reader not familiar with the field of machine learning is encouraged to read the first few chapters, omitting technical detail, in order to acquire a general understanding. Later, these chapters and any others that are of special interest may be studied in more detail with an appropriate perspective on the field as a whole. Readers are encouraged to use our chapter descriptions below, as well as the abstracts in the individual chapters, to focus on areas of interest. The topics of the individual chapters range from cognitive modeling and discussion of underlying principles to applications in general problem-solving, chemistry, mathematics, music, education and game playing.

At the Carnegie-Mellon Machine Learning Workshop in July, 1980, Herbert Simon was asked to deliver the keynote address, where he chose to play the role of devil's advocate and ask the question "Why Should Machines Learn?" His analysis concluded that, with the exception of cognitive modeling, some rethinking of long-term objectives was in order. After dispelling some common myths, Simon concluded with a clarified and more appropriate set of reasons why one ought to pursue machine learning research. Chapter 2 is based almost entirely on that rather controversial keynote address.

In Chapter 3, Dietterich and Michalski analyze some well-known work in concept acquisition from a unified perspective. After developing some requisite formalism, they examine the range of possible concept descriptions that may be acquired via a set of basic generalization and discrimination operators applied to logic-based representations of instances and concepts. Then, they describe the work of Winston, Hayes-Roth, Vere, and Michalski's earlier work as particular combinations of learning operators applied to different restrictions on the representation language. Chapter 3, therefore, provides a general framework for comparison of different concept-acquisition systems.

In Chapter 4, Michalski describes a general theory and methodology for inductive learning of structural descriptions from examples. The theory unifies and clarifies various types of inductive learning, and demonstrates that such learning can be viewed as a process of applying *generalization inference rules* (and conventional deductive inference rules) to initial and intermediate descriptions. This process is guided by problem-oriented background knowledge provided to the learning system. Various generalization rules are presented and discussed. The methodology developed is illustrated by a problem from the area of conceptual data analysis.

In Chapter 5, Carbonell examines the issue of learning from experience, a common phenomenon among humans, but heretofore a nemesis to machines that could not transfer planning knowledge to new but similar situations, or otherwise analyze their past behavior. A general planning and problem-solving paradigm is proposed based on a computationally-effective model of analogical reasoning. In essence, the planner exploits prior experience in solving new problems that bear strong similarity to past situations by transforming solutions of past problems into potential plans that solve new, externally or internally generated problems. The analogical paradigm interfaces with a learning-from-examples method, enabling the learner to formulate generalized plans for recurring situations, as well as to accumulate and classify more specific experiences for less common situations.

In Chapter 6, Mitchell, Utgoff and Banerji investigate the issue of acquiring and refining problem-solving heuristics by examining solutions to symbolic integration problems. Like Carbonell's approach, learning is based on past problem-solving experience, but Mitchell *et al.* focus on acquiring heuristics for applying known strategies, rather than generalizing recurring behaviors into reusable plans. Their approach also generates problems internally for the purpose of testing and refining existing heuristics, and uses the version-space approach to keep track of viable generalizations of current heuristics. Unlike Carbonell's analogical approach to problem-solving, Mitchell *et al.* rely on heuristic search guided by the constantly updated domain heuristics to solve new problems. After describing the LEX program for learning heuristics, they consider ways in which the system's learning abilities could be improved by giving it new knowledge about heuristic search, the problem domain, and the goals of the learner.

In Chapter 7, Anderson examines human problem-solving in the context of providing justifications to geometric proofs. He relies entirely upon a production system framework to encode domain knowledge, learning heuristics, and problem-solving strategies. Anderson reviews the basic mechanisms for production-rule knowledge acquisition and demonstrates how they apply to a progression of tasks in Geometry. The major significance of this chapter is the explanation and illustration of learning methods in the context of a performance system implemented as a set of production rules.

In Chapter 8, Hayes-Roth investigates the issue of improving flawed or incomplete theories that guide plan formation in a given domain. His primary thrust is on refining and restructuring theories based upon the way in which observed consequences of one's behavior differ from theoretical predictions. In short, Hayes-Roth views empirical disconfirmation not as a mechanism for rejecting existing theories, but rather as input to various methods of modifying theoretical concepts to accord with past and present observations. He presents five heuristic methods and applies them to problem-solving in playing the card game hearts.

In Chapter 9, Lenat focuses on methods for learning from observation and discovery. He analyzes three domains in which heuristics play a dominant role in guiding search through the space of possible concepts or processes one may acquire. First, Lenat examines his AM system, where heuristic rules that measure intrinsic "interestingness" help the system rediscover essential concepts in number theory, such as the notion of a prime number. Then, the EURISKO system is discussed, which acquires and modifies learning heuristics, as well as formulating task-specific heuristics and concept representations. Finally, Lenat discusses the conjecture that evolution is a heuristically-driven learning engine in constant operation.

In Chapter 10, Langley, Simon and Bradshaw discuss their BACON system and its application to rediscovering some basic laws of Chemistry. BACON applies the principles of scientific inquiry first elucidated by Sir Francis Bacon to find the simplest numerical relations that hold invariant across sets of measurements. In this manner, it postulates meaningful combinations of independent measurements and intrinsic properties of objects (such as specific heat), and searches for the simplest relationship among measured and derived quantities that summarizes all observations. Although not able to design its own experiments, given the unanalyzed results of appropriate chemical experiments, BACON has rediscovered such laws as Gay-Lussac's law and Proust's law of definite proportions.

In Chapter 11, Michalski and Stepp investigate the problem of automated construction of taxonomies of observed events in a manner that is meaningful to a human. That is, given sets of object or process descriptions, plus an *a priori* set of descriptive concepts, they develop a method of grouping observations into meaningful classes that represent selected concepts. They present an algorithm that implements this "conceptual clustering" operation and demonstrate its utility for the tasks of formulating descriptions of plant diseases from observed symptoms and taxonomizing Spanish songs in a manner meaningful to musicologists. In contrast with statistical clustering techniques, the conceptual clustering algorithm produces characteristic descriptions of the concepts defined by each cluster. Both the Michalski and Stepp approach and the Langley *et al.* approach exemplify learning from passive observations, whereas Lenat's approach stresses the role of active experimentation.

In Chapter 12, Mostow discusses the process of learning by taking advice. Declaratively stated advice must be transformed into operational procedures effective in a given task domain. The transformation process can be quite complex, as implicit domain knowledge must be accessed, the advice must be restated in terms consistent with the existing procedural knowledge base, and plausible reasoning heuristics must be consulted in deciding how to make best use of the incoming advice. Mostow focuses on the general issue of providing advice to a heuristic search mechanism, as applied to playing the game of hearts and composing a *cantus firmus*.

In Chapter 13, Haas and Hendrix investigate the issue of automatically extending a natural language interface by acquiring domain semantics, dictionary entries and syntactic patterns from the user. The most significant aspect of their KLAUS system is that the user need not be a computational linguist, but rather is guided by the system into providing exemplary information that is later transformed into effective grammar and dictionary representations. This form of learning by being told, where the student (that is, the KLAUS system) is in control and the teacher provides information only when asked, constitutes an interesting variation on more traditional versions of the learning-from-instruction paradigm.

In Chapter 14, Rychener provides a retrospective analysis of the instructable production system project, in which many different instructional techniques for learning by being told were tried, different organizations of the knowledge were considered, and different problem-solving strategies were investigated. Although many combinations of representational schemes and instructional methods proved infeasible, other approaches proved much more promising. Hence the field of machine learning can learn from its own experience—false starts as well as successful approaches. Rychener concludes his chapter with an analysis of the organizational and instructional principles that a production-system based instructional learner should adhere to in order to maximize chances for successful knowledge acquisition.

In Chapter 15, Quinlan presents a method for generating efficient decision trees for classifying given exemplars, and applies his method to the analysis of king-and-rook versus king-and-knight chess endgames. Chess authorities had previously believed that all but a few special positions of this type were inherently drawn (with best play for both sides). Due to the size of the search space, a systematic analysis was not performed until Quinlan applied his efficient method of learning classifications, whereupon it became clear that a very large fraction of king-and-rook versus king-and-knight positions were forced wins for the side with the rook. Therefore, the Quinlan paper illustrates not only an efficient classification method, but demonstrates the utility of at least one application of machine learning.

In Chapter 16, Sleeman investigates the application of machine learning to infer models of students learning algebra. Student modeling is becoming a recognized necessity in intelligent computer-assisted instruction (ICAI). The difficult task of formulating viable student models requires that the system infer a student's knowledge from his performance (plus general knowledge of the instructional material). A general model must be inferred that can generate all observed student behavior, as well as account for the lack of any expected but unobserved behavior. The search space of possible student models is large, and the number of trials one may require of each student is proportionately small. Therefore the problem becomes one of searching this space quickly and without requiring large amounts of student testing. Sleeman provides and analyzes algorithms that fit these requirements. An interesting aspect of Sleeman's work is that the teacher, in order to be effective, must learn to adapt to the student's needs, indicating that machine learning can help to make computer-assisted human education more effective.

Finally, the book concludes with a comprehensive bibliography of past and present research in machine learning, a glossary of selected terms, and a brief note about each author. The bibliography is indexed according to several criteria (methods, applications, and so on) in order to provide guidance to the reader who desires additional background in the field.

REFERENCES

Arkadev, A. G. and Braverman, E. M., *Learning in Pattern Classification Machines*, Nauka, Moscow, 1971.

Ashby, W. Ross, *Design for a Brain, The Origin of Adaptive Behavior*, John Wiley and Sons, Inc., 1960.

Block, H. D., "The Perceptron: A Model of Brain Functioning, I," *Rev. Math. Physics*, Vol. 34, No. 1, pp. 123-135, 1961.

Bongard, N., *Pattern Recognition*, Spartan Books, New York, 1970, (Translation from Russian original, published in 1967).

Buchanan, B. G. and Mitchell, T. M., "Model-Directed Learning of Production Rules," *Pattern-Directed Inference Systems*, Waterman, D. A. and Hayes-Roth, F. (Eds.), Academic Press, New York, 1978.

Buchanan, B. G., Feigenbaum, E. A. and Lederberg, J., "A heuristic programming study of theory formation in sciences," *Proceedings of the Second International Joint Conference on Artificial Intelligence*, International Joint Conferences on Artificial Intelligence, London, pp. 40-48, 1971.

Culberson, J. T., *The Minds of Robots*, University of Illinois Press, Urbana, Illinois, 1963.

Davies, W. D. T., *System Identification for Self-Adaptive Control*, Wiley-Interscience, Wiley and Sons, Ltd., 1970.

Duda, R. O. and Hart, P. E., *Pattern Classification and Scene Analysis*, Wiley, New York, 1973.

Feigenbaum, E. A., "The Simulation of Verbal Learning Behavior," *Computers and Thought*, Feigenbaum, E. A. and Feldman, J. (Eds.), McGraw-Hill, New York, pp. 297-309, 1963, (originally in Proceedings Western Joint Computer Conference, 1961).

Friedberg, R. M., "A Learning Machine: Part 1," *IBM Journal*, Vol. 2, pp. 2-13, 1958.

Friedberg, R., Dunham, B. and North, T., "A Learning Machine: Part 2," *IBM Journal of Research and Development*, Vol. 3, No. 3, pp. 282-287, 1959.

Fu, K. S., *Sequential Methods in Pattern Recognition and Machine Learning*, Academic Press, New York, 1968.

Fu, K. S., *Pattern Recognition and Machine Learning*, Plenum Press, New York, 1971.

Fu, K. S. and Tou, J. T., *Learning Systems and Intelligent Robots*, Plenum Press, 1974.

Fukanaga, K., *Introduction to Statistical Pattern Recognition*, Academic Press, 1972.

Hayes-Roth, F., "Schematic Classification Problems and their Solution," *Pattern Recognition*, Vol. 6, pp. 105-113, 1974.

Hayes-Roth, F. and McDermott, J., "An interference matching technique for inducing abstractions," *Communications of the ACM*, Vol. 21, No. 5, pp. 401-410, 1978.

Highleyman, W. H., "Linear Decision Functions, with Applications to Pattern Recognition," *Proceedings of IRE*, No. 50, pp. 1501-1504, 1967.

Hilgard, E. R. and Bower, G. H., *Theories of Learning - Third Edition*, Appleton-Century-Grofts, New York, 1966.

Holland, J. H., "Adaptive Algorithms for Discovering and Using General Patterns in Growing Knowledge Bases," *Policy Analysis and Information Systems*, Vol. 4, No. 3, September 1980.

Hunt, E. B. and Hovland, C. I., "Programming a Model of Human Concept Formation," *Computers and Thought*, Feigenbaum, E. A. and Feldman, J. (Eds.), McGraw-Hill, New York, pp. 310-325, 1963.

Hunt, E. B., Marin, J. and Stone, P. T., *Experiments in Induction*, Academic Press, New York, 1966.

Kanal, L., "Patterns in Pattern Recognition: 1968-1974," *IEEE Transactions on Information Theory*, Vol. IT-20, No. 6, pp. 697-722, 1974.

Karpinski, J. and Michalski, R. S., "A System that Learns to Recognize Hand-written Alphanumeric Characters", Technical Report 35, Proce Institute Automatyki, Polish Academy of Sciences, 1966.

Kazmierczak, H. and Steinbuch, K., "Adaptive Systems in Pattern Recognition," *IEEE Transactions of Electronic Computers*, Vol. EC-12, No. 5, pp. 822-835, 1963.

Koford, T. S. and Groner, G. F., "The Use of an Adaptive Threshold Element to Design a Linear Optimal Pattern Classifier," *IEEE Transactions-Information Theory*, Vol. 1T-12, pp. 42-50, 1966.

Lenat, D. B., *AM: an artificial intelligence approach to discovery in mathematics as heuristic search,* Ph.D. dissertation, Stanford University, Stanford, California, 1976.

McCulloch, W. S. and Pitts, W., "A Logical Calculus of Ideas Imminent in Nervous Activity," *Bull. Math. Biophysics*, Vol. 5, pp. 115-133, 1943.

Mendel, T. and Fu, K. S., *Adaptive Learning and Pattern Recognition: Theory and Applications*, Spartan Books, New York, 1970.

Michalski, R. S., "A Variable-Valued Logic System as Applied to Picture Description and Recognition," *Graphic Languages*, Nake, F. and Rosenfeld, A. (Ed.), North-Holland, 1972.

Michalski, R. S. and Larson, J. B., "Selection of Most Representative Training Examples and Incremental Generation of VL1 Hypotheses: The Underlying Methodology and Description of Programs ESEL and AQ11", Report 867, University of Illinois, 1978.

Michalski, R. S., "AQVAL/1 - Computer implementation of a variable valued logic system VL1 and examples of its application to pattern recognition," *Proceedings of the First International Joint Conference on Pattern Recognition*, Washington, D. C., pp. 3-17, 1973b.

Michie, "The State of the Art in Machine Learning," *Introductory Readings in Expert Systems*, D. Michie (Ed.), Gordon and Breach, UK, 1982.

Minsky, M. and Papert, S., *Perceptrons*, MIT Press, Cambridge, Mass., 1969.

Mitchell, T. M., *Version Spaces: An approach to concept learning,* Ph.D. dissertation, Stanford University, December 1978, (also Stanford CS report STAN-CS-78-711, HPP-79-2).

Newell, A. and Rosenbloom, P., "Mechanisms of Skill Acquisition and the Law of Practice," *Cognitive Skills and Their Acquisition*, Anderson, J. R. (Ed.), Erlbaum Associates, Hillsdale, New Jersey, 1981.

Nilsson, N. J., *Learning Machines*, McGraw-Hill, New York, 1965.

Rashevsky, N., *Mathematical Biophysics*, University of Chicago Press, Chicago, IL, 1948.

Rosenblatt, F., "The Perceptron: A Probabilistic Model for Information Storage and Organization in the Brain," *Psychological Review*, Vol. 65, pp. 386-407, 1958.

Rosenblatt, F., *Principles of Neurodynamics and the Theory of Brain Mechanisms*, Spartan Books, Washington, D. C., 1962.

Samuel, A. L., "Some Studies in Machine Learning Using the Game of Checkers," *IBM Journal of Research and Development*, No. 3, pp. 211-229, 1959.

Samuel, A. L., "Some Studies in Machine Learning using the Game of Checkers," *Computers and Thought*, Feigenbaum, E. A. and Feldman, J. (Eds.), McGraw-Hill, New York, pp. 71-105, 1963.

Sebestyen, G. S., *Decision-Making Processes in Pattern Recognition*, Macmillan, New York, 1962.

Selfridge, O. G., "Pandemonium: A Paradigm for Learning," *Proceedings of the Symposium on Mechanization of Thought Processes*, Blake, D. and Uttley, A. (Eds.), HMSO, London, pp. 511-529, 1959.

Simon, H. A. and Lea, G., "Problem Solving and Rule Induction: A Unified View," *Knowledge and Cognition*, Gregg, L. W. (Ed.), Lawrence Erlbaum Associates, Potomac, Maryland, pp. 105-127, 1974.

Truxal, T. G., *Automatic Feedback Control System Synthesis*, McGraw-Hill, New York, 1955, (New York).

Tsypkin, Y. Z., "Self Learning - What is it?," *IEEE Transactions on Automatic Control*, Vol. AC-18, No. 2, pp. 109-117, 1968.

Tsypkin, Ya Z., *Adaptation and Learning in Automatic Systems*, Academic Press, New York, 1971.

Tsypkin, Y. Z., *Foundations of the Theory of Learning Systems*, Academic Press, New York, 1973, (Translated by Z. L. Nikolic).

Uhr, L., *Pattern Recognition*, John Wiley and Sons, New York, 1966.

Vere, S. A., "Induction of concepts in the predicate calculus," *Proceedings of the Fourth International Joint Conference on Artificial Intelligence*, IJCAI, Tbilisi, USSR, pp. 281-287, 1975.

Watanabe, S., "Information-Theoretic Aspects of Inductive and Deductive Inference," *IBM Journal of Research and Development*, Vol. 4, No. 2, pp. 208-231, 1960.

Widrow, B., *Generalization and Information Storage in Networks of Adelaine 'Neurons,'*, Spartan Books, Washington, D. C., pp. 435-461, 1962, (Yovitz, M. C.; Jacobi, G. T.; Goldstein, G. D., editors).

Winston, P. H., "Learning structural descriptions from examples," *The Psychology of Computer Vision*, Winston, P. H. (Ed.), McGraw Hill, New York, ch. 5, 1975, (Original version published as a Ph.D. dissertaition, at MIT AI Lab, September, 1970).

Winston, P. H., "Learning and Reasoning by Analogy," *CACM*, Vol. 23, No. 12, pp. 689-703, 1979.

Yovits, M. C., Jacobi, G. T. and Goldstein, G. D., *Self-Organizing Systems*, Spartan Books, Washington, D. C., 1962.

2

WHY SHOULD MACHINES LEARN?

Herbert A. Simon
Carnegie-Mellon University

2.1 INTRODUCTION

When I agreed to write this chapter, I thought I could simply expand a paper that I wrote for the Carnegie Symposium on Cognition, since the topic of that symposium was also learning. The difficulty with plagiarizing that paper is that it was really about psychology, whereas this book is concerned with machine learning. Now although we all believe machines can simulate human thought—unless we're vitalists, and there aren't any of those around any more—still, I didn't think that was what was intended by the title of the book. I didn't think it was appropriate to write about psychology.

When my chapter finally was outlined and written, it surprised me a bit; whether it will surprise you or not, we can leave to the event. My chapter turned out to propose a thesis to which perhaps the other chapters in this volume will serve as antitheses. That will allow us to arrive at the great Hegelian synthesis that we all wish for.

2.2 HUMAN LEARNING AND MACHINE LEARNING

I must begin, after all, by saying something about human learning, because I want to compare and contrast what is involved in human learning with what is involved in machine learning. Out of the synthesis of that contrast—in itself a thesis and antithesis—will come my thesis.

2.2.1 Tediousness of Human Learning

The first obvious fact about human learning is that it's horribly slow. It takes decades for human beings to learn anything. It took all of us six years just to get up to starting speed for school, and then twenty more years to become cognitive scientists or computer scientists. That is the minimum—some of us took even longer than that. So, we're terribly slow learners. We maintain big expensive educational systems that are supposed to make the process effective, but with all we've been able to do with them—to say nothing of computer aided instruction—it remains a terribly slow process.

I can still remember, although it was 45 years ago, trying to learn how to do multiple regressions by the Gauss-Doolittle method with the aid of a desk calculator. There's nothing complicated about the method except when you're learning it. And then it seems terribly mysterious. You wonder why this gets multiplied by that, and after a long while it gradually dawns on you. As a matter of fact you can carry out the calculations long before you understand the rationale for the procedure.

Learning the linear programming simplex method also illustrates this point and another one as well. Even after you've learned it, even after you've understood it, even after (in principle) you can do it, you still can't *really* do it because you can't compute fast enough. I don't know of any humans who calculate solutions of LP problems by the simplex method; as far as I know it's all done by computers. The human doesn't even have to know the simplex method; he just has to know the program library—cookbook statistics, or cookbook computing, which we all do most of the time.

So human learning is a long, slow process. It should give us some pause, when we build machine learning systems, to imagine what can possibly be going on during all the time a human being is mastering a "simple" skill. We should ask whether we really want to make the computer go through that tedious process, or whether machines should be programmed directly to perform tasks, avoiding humanoid learning entirely.

Of course we might discover a trick: a method of machine learning that was orders of magnitude faster than human learning. Whether such tricks exist depend on whether the inefficiencies of human learning derive from peculiar properties of the human information processing system or whether they will be present in any system that tries to extract patterns or other kinds of information from complex, noisy situations and to retain those patterns in a manner that makes them available for later use. The search for such tricks that manage to escape the tediousness of human learning, however, provides a strong motivation for research in machine learning.

2.2.2 Learning and Copying

The second distinctive feature about human learning is that there's no copy process. In contrast, once you get a debugged program in the computer you can have as many copies as you want (given equivalence in operating systems and hardware). You can have these copies free, or almost free. When one computer has learned it, they've all learned it—in principle. An algorithm only has to be invented once—not a billion times.

I've been involved a little bit in tutoring someone during the last few weeks in beginning calculus. I think I know the calculus pretty well—I haven't used it much for years, but it comes back. Yet I find it terribly frustrating trying to transfer my knowledge and skill to another human head. I'd like to open the lid and stuff the program in. But for one thing, I don't know where it is in *my* head, I don't even know what language it's encoded in. For another thing, I have no way of transferring it to the other head. That, of course, is why we humans go through the slow learning process—because we can't copy and transfer programs.

2.2.3 Why Machine Learning?

Contrast this with the machine learning task. In machine learning, the minute you have the debugged program you read it into the computer and it runs. The computer does what the psychologists call "one-trial learning". And, as I've already indicated, what is learned can be copied *ad nauseam*. So, if one thinks about that a little, one says, "What's all this about machine learning? Why are we interested in it—if by machine learning we mean anything that's at all like human learning? Who—what madman—would put a computer through twenty years of hard labor to make a cognitive scientist or a computer scientist out of it? Let's forget this nonsense—just program it." It would appear that, now that we have computers, the whole topic of learning has become just one grand irrelevancy—for computer science.

I have already qualified that conclusion in one respect: we do have reason to search for machine learning programs that will avoid the inefficiencies of human learning, although we must be alert to the possibility that such programs cannot, in principle, be constructed. The difficulty may be intrinsic in the task; human learning, though slow, may be close to optimally efficient.

I must also enter another caveat because you'll ask me, "What were you saying in that talk you gave two months ago? Why were you talking about learning?" The caveat is: Even in a world in which there are lots of computers it still may be important for us to understand human learning. Artificial intelligence has two goals. First, AI is directed toward getting computers to be smart and do smart things so that human beings don't have to do them. And second, AI (sometimes called cognitive simulation, or information processing psychology) is also directed at using computers to simulate human beings, so that we can find out how humans work and perhaps can help them to be a little better in their work.

None of the doubts I have just raised about computer learning apply to this second application of AI. Anybody who is interested in machine learning because he wants to simulate human learning—because he wants to understand human learning and thinking, and perhaps improve it—can pursue his interest in good conscience. But what about those who have other goals?

2.3 WHAT IS LEARNING?

When I had arrived at this point and surprised myself by writing down these notes, I asked myself, "What can we talk about legitimately for the next three days, other than cognitive psychology?" But I looked at the names of the people who were going to be here and at some of the titles of papers in the program, and I decided that a good deal of what we were talking about wasn't really learning anyway, so it was all right.

Let me elaborate on that remark. The term "learning", like a lot of other everyday terms, is used broadly and vaguely in the English language, and we carry those broad and vague usages over to technical fields, where they often cause confusion. I just saw a notice of a proposed special issue of SIGART, with a list of kinds of learning. It's a long list, and I'd be astonished if all of the items on it denote the same thing. Maybe it is just a list of the different species of learning, but I suspect that it also reflects the great ambiguity of the term "learning".

2.3.1 A Definition of Learning

The only partially satisfactory definition I've been able to find is that learning is any change in a system that allows it to perform better the second time on repetition of the same task or on another task drawn from the same population. The change should be more or less irreversible—not irreversible in the sense that you can't unlearn (although that sometimes is hard, especially unlearning bad habits) but irreversible in that the learning doesn't go away rapidly and autonomously. *Learning denotes changes in the system that are adaptive in the sense that they enable the system to do the same task or tasks drawn from the same population more efficiently and more effectively the next time.*

Since we may want the same task done over and over and over again, tuning a system so that it runs very fast is a great thing. Human beings seem to have some tuning capabilities, often called automating task performance. But more often, particularly in the university, we're interested in learning, not so that the same task can be done over and over again, but so that we acquire the ability to perform a wide range of tasks (for example, solving problems that appear on examinations, or performing similar tasks that may occur afterwards in real life).

2.3.2 Learning and Discovery

There are relations between learning and some other activities. For one thing, learning is related to discovery. By discovery I mean finding new things. Very little human learning is discovery. Most of what we know somebody told us about or we found in a textbook. At the very best we acquired it by working out some very carefully selected exercises, which guided us nicely in the right direction and provided most of the selective heuristics for our search. There can be all kinds of learning without discovery, and there usually are. Most of the things we know were discovered by other people before we knew them, and only a few were even reinvented by us.

Nevertheless, there is a relation between learning and discovery, because if you do discover something and it's good, you'd like to retain it. So, if you have a discovery system, you would like (somehow or other) to associate a learning system with it, even a simple memorization and indexing scheme. That doesn't quite get us off the hook. If you have a computer that discovers the proof for Goldbach's Theorem or the Four Color Theorem, you don't have to have a separate learning program, for you can simply get the proof out of the computer and transport it around on paper in the usual way. But, it would be very convenient if the computer could store the proof so that it could be used in subsequent work.

One of the first learning programs for computers was the little learning routine in the Logic Theorist (LT) [Newell & Simon, 1956]. When the Logic Theorist had the good fortune to prove a theorem in *Principia Mathematica* it had the good sense to keep the theorem around. On the next problems, it didn't start from the axioms alone but could use the new theorem along with the axioms. It wasn't any great feat to program this learning program. It did what we teachers call (pejoratively) "rote learning"—just memorizing. LT memorized only the theorem, not the proof; but giving it the latter capability also would have been a trivial matter.

In the Artificial Intelligence literature, the distinction I have been maintaining here between discovery and learning is not usually observed. That is to say, a great many machine "learning" systems are also discovery systems; they discover new knowledge that they subsequently retain. Most of the skeptical arguments I have raised about machine learning do not apply to the discovery process. Hence, I think it quite appropriate that a large part of the research effort in the domain of "machine learning" is really directed at "machine discovery". As long as we are not ourselves confused by the terminology, I do not even see a strong reason to object to this substitution of terms.

2.3.3 Learning and Understanding Natural Language

So, there's a connection here between learning and discovery. There is also a connection between learning and understanding. Understanding includes the whole natural language problem. In human life (and I'll try later to connect this up with computers) most of what we learn we get from other people, communicated to us in natural language. A good many of the tasks that people have undertaken for machine learning have involved a natural language front end as an important part of the task. It is also a very annoying part of the task, eating up all of your time and energy when you wish you were doing something else.

2.3.4 Learning and Problem-Solving

Additionally, some things we might call "learning" could also be called "problem-solving". I've heard "automatic programming" called "learning". The aim of automatic programming is to be able to say the same brief vague things to a computer you'd say to a good human programmer in defining a task for him and to come out with a program on the other end. What the automatic programming program does is not really learning; it is solving the problem of getting from the sloppy ill-structured input statement of the programming problem to a well-structured program in the programming language. This kind of "learning" could readily come under the usual heading of "problem-solving".

Nevertheless, traditionally at least, the tasks of discovery, of natural language understanding, and of self-programming have often been intermingled with, or even identified as, learning tasks. If you want to call it learning you won't get an argument from me. It really isn't learning but ...

2.4 SOME LEARNING PROGRAMS

I'm going to back off one step further from my unkind words about machine learning and look at some "classical" examples ("classical" in the field of computer science is anything twenty years old) of learning programs, to see whether they really justify my harsh judgment.

2.4.1 Learning to Play Checkers

The first that I ought to mention is surely Arthur Samuel's checker program [Samuel, 1959]. Here was a program that, in the morning, wasn't very much of a checker player. But after you switched on its learning process and gave it games to play and other training exercises, by evening it was a State-champion-level checker player. That is a lot better than any of us could do. So there's a very impressive example of a learning program going back twenty-five years.

Let me submit that however fine this program was from an AI standpoint, it only made sense if we really didn't understand checkers. If Samuel had understood checkers well, he could have put the final evaluation function in right at the beginning. (You may recall that he used two kinds of learning, but the only one I want to mention at the moment is tuning the evaluation function for positions on the basis of outcomes. When good things happened, items that were heavily weighted in the evaluation function got additional weight, and when bad things happened they lost some of their weight.) If Samuel had known the right evaluation function at the outset, he would have put it in the program; he would not have gone through all the learning rigamarole. It cost only one day of computing time, to be sure, but computers were expensive then, even for one day.

It does make sense to provide for such learning in a task where you don't know enough to do the fine tuning. We might think of this as an area of machine learning (or, more accurately, machine discovery) where we can get the system to behave better than it would behave if we just sat down and programmed it. Nobody writing chess programs has had this feeling yet. They all think they know more chess than a computer could acquire just by tuning itself. As far as I know, none of the successful chess-playing programs have had any learning ability.

So there are cases where the computer can learn some things that we didn't know when we programmed it. But if you survey the fields of AI and knowledge engineering today, you will find very few cases where people have had the feeling this could or should be done, or have had any ideas of how to do it. Nevertheless, this potential application of learning procedures is certainly one further qualification on my general stricture against such programs.

I've already mentioned learning by the Logic Theorist, but that was just convenience, unless LT had reached the point where it was discovering genuinely new things. If Doug Lenat had let AM [Lenat, 1977] run for another two hours—as I kept telling him he should—and it had discovered something completely new, then the learning would make sense, for you would want to save what had been discovered.

2.4.2 Automatic Indexing

There's something to be said (again, largely on convenience grounds) for systems that are capable at least of learning discrimination nets—EPAM nets, if you like [Feigenbaum, 1963]. If you're building up a big data base and adding information to it all the time, you want easy access to that information, and so you want an index. It's a lot more convenient to have the system index itself as it goes along, than to index it by hand.[1] Or if you're building a large production system and don't want to search it linearly, you're going to incorporate an index in the production system to select the order in which it performs the tests. There is no difficulty in automating that; we have known for twenty-five years how to do it. So why not?

So there's some room for learning there. I don't know whether there's much room for learning *research*, since the technology of growing discrimination

[1]By "indexing" I mean building up a tree or network of tests so that you can access a data store in ways other than by linear search.

nets, alias indexes, is already pretty well developed, but someone may find a great new way of doing it.

2.4.3 Perceptrons

A final "classical" example (this is a negative example to prove my point) is the whole line of Perceptron research and nerve net learning [Rosenblatt, 1958]. A Perceptron is a system for classifying objects (that is, a discovery and learning system) that computes features of the stimulus display, then attempts to discriminate among different classes of displays by computing linear additive functions of these features. Functions producing correct choices are reinforced (receive increased weight), those producing incorrect choices have their weights reduced. I have to conclude (and here I don't think I am in the minority) that this line of research didn't get anywhere. The discovery task was just so horrendous for those systems that they never learned anything that people didn't already know. So they should again strengthen our skepticism that the problems of AI are to be solved solely by building learning systems.

2.5 GROWTH OF KNOWLEDGE IN LARGE SYSTEMS

In the remainder of my remarks, I would like to focus attention on large knowledge-based AI systems, particularly systems that can be expected to continue to grow and accumulate over a period of years of use. We may find in such systems some reasons to qualify a general skepticism about the role of learning in applied AI. Medical diagnosis systems like INTERNIST [Pople, 1977] and MYCIN [Shortliffe, 1976], and the venerable DENDRAL program [Feigenbaum *et al.*, 1971] are examples of the kinds of systems I have in mind.

There has been attention (as in TEIRESIAS [Davis, 1981] and other such efforts) to designing an effective programming interface between these knowledge-based systems and the humans who are supposed to improve them, and you can call that learning (or instruction). Most of the work has been aimed at making the job of the human easier. (Perhaps that's unfair, for it's a mutual job for the two of them.) So one might think of the man-machine interface as a good locus for learning research.

2.5.1 The ISAAC Program

To make my remarks more concrete, I would like to discuss for a bit Gordon Novak's well-known ISAAC system, which solves English-language college physics problems of the sorts found in textbooks [Novak, 1977]. Although ISAAC is primarily a performance or problem-solving program, one can think of some interesting ways of complementing it with a learning program.

ISAAC has a data bank containing schemas that describe various kinds of simple objects that physicists talk about—levers, masses, pivots, surfaces, and the like. A schema is just what you'd expect—a description list of an object with slots that you can fill in with information about its characteristics. In addition, ISAAC has, of course, some productions and a control structure.

When you give ISAAC a physics problem in natural language out of the physics textbook, it uses its schemas and productions to produce an internal representation of the problem. The representation is another node-link structure, which you can think of as a super-schema made up by assembling and instantiating some of the basic schemas. ISAAC will assemble some levers, and some masses, and a pivot or two, and a surface in the way the problem tells it, and make a problem schema out of them. At the outset it parses the sentences stating the problem, using its schemas to extract structure and meaning from them, and builds its internal representation, a problem schema.

This internal representation contains so much information about the problem that ISAAC uses a little subsidiary program to depict the problem scene on a CRT. Of course the real reason ISAAC wants this internal representation is not to draw a picture on a scope, but to use it to set up an appropriate set of equations and solve them.

Notice that ISAAC doesn't try to translate the natural language problem directly into equations, as Bobrow's STUDENT program did for algebra [Bobrow, 1968]. It first builds up an internal representation—what I think a physicist would call a physical representation (a "mental picture") of the situation. It then uses that intermediate representation to build the equations, which it ultimately solves. The internal representation does a lot of work for ISAAC because it identifies the points where forces have to be equilibrated and therefore identifies which equations have to be set up.

2.5.2 A Learning Extension of ISAAC

We can enlarge ISAAC by adding to it an UNDERSTAND program [Hayes & Simon, 1974]. Now you're going to say, "Ah ha! ISAAC already has an understanding program, because ISAAC can understand the problems it is given." That is true. But to do this, ISAAC must already have in memory a rich set of schemas describing physical devices, and it must already have the set of productions that allow it to organize these schemas into an internal representation. So ISAAC already knows all the physics it's going to know. While it understands problems, how about understanding *physics*? This would require the ability to use natural language information to construct new schemas and new productions. This is what the UNDERSTAND program does—not for physics, but for slightly simpler domains. UNDERSTAND creates, from the natural language, schemas for the kinds of objects being talked about and their relations. (In fact, Novak is presently exploring similar lines of investigation.)

What I want to ask about this whole amalgam of ISAAC and UNDERSTAND is, what is the place here for learning research in AI? (I know what the place is here for learning research in psychology. I think this is a very important area.

But let's continue to talk about the AI side of it.) If we understand the domain ourselves, if we understand physics, why don't we just choose an internal representation and provide the problems to the system in that internal representation? What's all this learning and natural language understanding about? Or, if we still want to give the system a capability of doing the problems in the back of the textbook, which are in natural language, then lets build Novak's ISAAC system. Why go through all the rigamarole of an UNDERSTAND program to learn the schemas and the productions painstakingly instead of just programming them? Before you launch into such a project as an AI effort (as distinct from a psychological research project), you have to answer that question.

2.6 A ROLE FOR LEARNING

Since you have listened very patiently to my skeptical challenge to learning as the road to the future in AI, I think I should own up to one more important qualification that needs to be attached to my thesis—a little fragment of the more complete antithesis that the other papers of this volume develop.

I began by running down the human species—emphasizing how stupid we all are as revealed by our agonizingly slow rates of learning. It is just possible that the complexity of the learning process is not an accident but is, instead, an adaptive product of evolution. The human brain is a very large collection of programs that cumulates over a lifetime or a large part of a lifetime. Suppose that we were allowed to open up the lid and program ourselves directly. In order to write debugged programs, modifications of our present programs, we would have to learn a lot about the internal code, the internal representations of the knowledge and skills we already possess.

Perhaps you know how knowledge is organized in your brain; I don't know how it is organized in mine. As a consequence, I think it would be exceedingly difficult for me to create a new, debugged code that would be compatible with what is already stored. This is, of course, a problem that we already encounter with our time-shared computers today. As we add new utility programs, or modify the monitors or operating systems, we encounter all sorts of interactions that make these modifications cumulatively harder to effect. At best, we encapsulate knowledge in hosts of separate programs that can operate independently of each other, but by the same token, cannot cooperate and share their knowledge effectively. Old programs do not learn, they simply fade away. So do human beings, their undebuggable programs replaced by younger, possibly less tangled, ones in other human heads. But at least until the state of undebuggability is reached, human programs are modified adaptively and repeatedly by learning processes that don't require a knowledge of the internal representation.

It may be that for this kind of system (a human brain or the memory of a very large time-shared computing system) the *only* way to bring about continual modification and improvement of the program is by means of learning procedures that don't involve knowing the detail of the internal languages and programs. It is a salient characteristic of human learning procedures that neither teacher nor learner has a detailed knowledge of the internal representation of data or process. It may turn out that there aren't procedures more efficient than these very slow ones that human beings use. That's just a speculation, but we ought to face the grim possibilities as well as the cheery possibilities in the world.

Even if we had to accomplish our complex programming in this indirect way, through learning, computers still would have a compensation—the costless copying mechanism that is not shared by human beings. Only one computer would have to learn; not every one would have to go to school.

2.7 CONCLUDING REMARKS

By now you are aware that my case against AI research in learning is a very qualified case with several important exceptions—exceptions you may be able to stretch until they become the rule. Let me put the matter in a positive way, and rephrase these exceptions as priorities for learning research. They are five in number.

1. I would give a very high priority to research aimed at simulating, and thereby understanding, human learning. It may be objected that such research is not AI but cognitive psychology or cognitive science or something else. I don't really care what it is called; it is of the greatest importance that we deepen our understanding of human learning, and the AI community possesses a large share of the talent that can advance us toward this goal.
2. I would give a high priority, also, to basic research aimed at understanding why human learning is so slow and inefficient, and correspondingly, at examining the possibility that machine learning schemes can be devised that will avoid, for machines as well as people, some of the tediousness of learning.
3. I would give a high priority to research on the natural language interface between computer systems and human users. Again, it does not matter whether you call it research on learning or research on understanding. We do want systems, particularly in the knowledge engineering area, in which we don't have to know the internal language or representation in order to interact with them. This is especially true, as I have just argued, if the systems are to be cumulative over many years.
4. I think there is an important place for research on programming from incomplete instructions (automatic programming), which is not unrelated to the preceding item. Giving instructions to a skilled programmer is different from writing the program yourself—else why hire the programmer? It is a very important research question to ask whether we can get the computer to be the skilled programmer.

5. My final priority is research on discovery programs—programs that discover new things. We may regard discovery itself as a form of learning, but in addition we will want to give a discovery system learning capabilities because we will want it to preserve and to be able to use all the new things it finds.

So now, I guess, I have come full circle, and have made a strong case for machine learning. But I do not think the effort in addressing my initial skepticism has been wasted. Research done in the right area for the wrong reasons seldom achieves its goals. To do good research on machine learning, we must have clear targets to aim at. In my view, the usual reasons given for AI learning research are too vague to provide good targets, and do not discriminate with sufficient care the learning requirements for people and computers, respectively.

Perhaps the deepest legitimate reason for doing machine learning research is that, in the long run for big knowledge-based systems, learning will turn out to be more efficient than programming, however inefficient such learning is. Gaining a deeper understanding of human learning will continue to provide important clues about what to imitate and what to avoid in machine learning programs. If this is true, then it follows that among the most important kinds of learning research to carry out in AI are those that are oriented toward understanding human learning. Here as elsewhere, Man seems to be the measure of all things.

ACKNOWLEDGMENTS

This research was supported by Research Grant MH-07722 from the National Institute of Mental Health, and a grant from the Alfred P. Sloan Foundation.

REFERENCES

Bobrow, D. G., "Natural language input for a computer problem-solving system," *Semantic Information Processing*, Minsky, M. (Ed.), MIT Press, Cambridge, MA, 1968.

Davis, R., "Applications of meta level knowledge to the construction and use of large knowledge bases," *Knowledge-Based Systems in Artificial Intelligence*, Davis, R. and Lenat, D. (Eds.), McGraw-Hill Book Company, New York, NY, 1981.

Feigenbaum E. A., "The simulation of verbal learning behavior," *Computers and Thought*, Feigenbaum, E. A. and Feldman, J. (Eds.), McGraw-Hill Book Company, New York, NY, 1963.

Feigenbaum, E. A., Buchanan, B. G. and Lederberg, J., "On generality and problem solving: A case study using the DENDRAL program," *Machine Intelligence*, Meltzer, B. and Michie, D. (Eds.), Edinburgh University Press, Edinburgh, Scotland, 1971.

Hayes, J. R. and Simon, H. A., "Understanding written problem instructions," *Knowledge and Cognition*, Gregg, L. W. (Ed.), Lawrence Erlbaum Associates, Potomac, MD, 1974.

Lenat, D. B., "Automated theory formation in mathematics," *Proceedings of the Fifth International Joint Conference on Artificial Intelligence*, IJCAI, Cambridge, MA, pp. 833-842, August 1977.

Newell, A. and Simon, H. A., "The logic theory machine," *IRE Transactions on Information Theory*, Vol. IT-2, No. 3, pp. 61-79, September 1956.

Novak, G. S., "Representations of knowledge in a program for solving physics problems," *Proceedings of the Fifth International Joint Conference on Artificial Intelligence*, IJCAI, Cambridge, MA, pp. 286-291, August 1977.

Pople, H., "The formation of composite hypotheses in diagnostic problem solving," *Proceedings of the Fifth International Joint Conference on Artificial Intelligence*, IJCAI, Cambridge, MA, pp. 1030-1037, August 1977.

Rosenblatt, F., "The perceptron: A probabilistic model for information storage and organization in the brain," *Psychological Review*, Vol. 65, pp. 386-407, 1958.

Samuel, A. L., "Some studies in machine learning using the game of checkers," *IBM Journal of Research and Development*, No. 3, pp. 210-220, 1959.

Shortliffe, E., *Computer-Based Medical Consultations: MYCIN*, American Elsevier Publishing Company, New York, NY, 1976.

PART TWO

LEARNING FROM EXAMPLES

3

A COMPARATIVE REVIEW OF SELECTED METHODS FOR LEARNING FROM EXAMPLES

Thomas G. Dietterich
Stanford University

Ryszard S. Michalski
University of Illinois at Urbana-Champaign

ABSTRACT

Research in the area of learning structural descriptions from examples is reviewed, giving primary attention to methods of learning characteristic descriptions of single concepts. In particular, we examine methods for finding the maximally-specific conjunctive generalizations (MSC-generalizations) that cover all of the training examples of a given concept. Various important aspects of structural learning in general are examined, and several criteria for evaluating structural learning methods are presented. Briefly, these criteria include *(i)* adequacy of the representation language, *(ii)* generalization rules employed, *(iii)* computational efficiency, and *(iv)* flexibility and extensibility. Selected learning methods developed by Buchanan, *et al.*, Hayes-Roth, Vere, Winston, and the authors are analyzed according to these criteria. Finally, some goals are suggested for future research.

3.1 INTRODUCTION

3.1.1 Motivation and Scope of Chapter

The purpose of this chapter is to introduce some of the important issues affecting the design of learning programs—particularly programs that learn from examples. This chapter begins with a survey of these issues. From the survey, four criteria are developed for evaluating learning methods. The remainder of the chapter describes and evaluates five existing learning systems according to these criteria.

We do not attempt to review all of the work on learning from examples (also known as *learning by induction*). Instead, we focus on one particular problem: the problem of learning structural descriptions from a set of positive training instances. Specifically, we survey methods for finding the maximally-specific conjunctive generalizations (called MSC-generalizations) that characterize a given class of entities. This is one of the simplest learning problems that has been addressed by AI researchers. The problem of finding MSC-generalizations lends itself to comparative analysis because several different methods have been developed. This is unusual in current research on machine learning, which is currently investigating a wide variety of learning problems and learning methods. Particular methods reviewed in this chapter include those developed by Buchanan *et al.* [1971, 1976, 1978], , Hayes-Roth [1976a, 1976b, 1977, 1978] Vere [1975, 1977, 1978, 1980], Winston [1970, 1975], and the authors. This chapter is based on the article by Dietterich and Michalski [1981].

Before proceeding any further, let us explain our terminology. The chapter deals first of all with *structural descriptions*. Structural descriptions portray objects as composite structures consisting of various components. For instance, a structural description of a building could represent the building in terms of the floors, the walls, the ceilings, the hallways, the roof, and so forth, along with the relations that hold among these various components. Structural descriptions can be contrasted with *attribute descriptions*, which specify only global properties of an object. An attribute description of a building might list its cost, architect, height, total square-footage and so forth. No internal structure is represented. Attribute descriptions can be expressed using propositional logic—that is, null-ary predicates.[1] Structural descriptions, however, must be expressed in predicate logic. Each subcomponent is described globally using variables and unary predicates, and relations between components are expressed as k-ary predicates and functions.[2] In this chapter, variables, predicates, and functions are all referred to as *descriptors*.

The second item of terminology that requires explanation is the notion of a maximally-specific conjunctive generalization. A *conjunctive generalization* is a description of a class of objects obtained by forming the conjunction (AND) of a group of primitive statements. For example, the class of houses might be described as the set of all objects such that:

---

[1]This is a slight simplification. With multi-valued attributes such as color, one must either create a separate predicate for each color or else employ some form of multiple-valued logic, such as VL_1.

[2]This is also a slight simplification. In principle, it is always possible to convert a structural description into an attribute description, but such a conversion leads to a combinatorial explosion in the number of attributes.

the number of floors is less than four AND the purpose of the building is to be used as a dwelling

We write this symbolically as a VL_1 expression:

[#-of-floors < 4] & [purpose-of-building = dwelling]

An example of a description that is *not* conjunctive is the definition of "not married for tax purposes" as:

[marital status = single] $\vee$ [marital status = married] [filing status = separate returns]

This is a *disjunctive* description.

A *maximally-specific* conjunctive generalization is the most detailed (most specific) description that is true of all of the known objects in the class. Since specific descriptions list many facts about the class, the maximally-specific conjunctive generalization is the longest conjunctive generalization that still describes all of the training instances.

Now that we have described the scope of this chapter, we introduce several issues that are important in learning from examples. From these issues, we will later develop four criteria for evaluating learning systems and apply these criteria to the comparison of five existing learning methods.

3.1.2 Important Aspects of Learning From Examples

The process of inductive learning can be viewed as a search for plausible general descriptions (inductive assertions) that explain the given input data and are useful for predicting new data. In order for a computer program to formulate such descriptions, an appropriate description language must be used. For any set of input data and any non-trivial description language, a large number of inductive assertions can be formulated. These assertions form a set of descriptions partially ordered by the relation of relative generality [Mitchell, 1977]. The minimal elements of this set are the most specific descriptions of the input data in the given language, and the maximal elements are the most general descriptions of these data. The elements of this set can be generated by starting with the most specific descriptions and repeatedly applying rules of generalization to produce more general descriptions.

The view of induction as a search through a space of generalized descriptions draws attention to the following aspects of learning:

- **Representation.** What description language is employed for expressing the input examples and formulating the inductive assertions? What are the possible forms of assertions that a method is able to learn? What operators are used in these forms?
- **Type of description sought.** For what purpose are the inductive assertions being formulated? What assumptions does the induction method make about the underlying process(es) that generated the data?
- **Rules of generalization.** What kinds of transformations are performed on

the input data and intermediate descriptions in order to produce the inductive assertions?

- **Constructive induction.** Does the induction process change the description space; that is, does it produce new descriptors that were not present in the input events?
- **Control strategy.** What is the strategy used to search the description space: bottom-up (data-driven), top-down (model-driven), or mixed?
- **General versus problem-oriented approach.** Is the method oriented toward solving a general class of problems, or is it oriented toward problems in some specific application domain?

We now discuss each of these aspects in more detail.

3.1.3 Representation Issues

Many representational systems can be used to represent events and generalizations of events—for example, predicate calculus, production rules, hierarchical descriptions, semantic nets, frames, and scripts. Much AI work on inductive learning (the exceptions include the AM system [Lenat, 1976], and work by Winston [1970]) has employed predicate calculus (or some closely related system), because of its well-defined syntax and semantics. (An important study of theoretical problems of induction in the context of predicate calculus was undertaken by Plotkin [1970, 1971].)

The mere statement that some learning method "uses predicate calculus" does not tell us very much about that method. Most learning methods place further restrictions on the forms of inductive assertions. For example, although a learning system might in principle be able to represent disjunctive descriptions, in practice it may have no mechanisms for actually discovering such descriptions. One way to capture this distinction between "representable forms" and "learnable forms" is to indicate which operators can actually be used in each. The most common operators are conjunction (&), disjunction ($\vee$), exception, and the existential and universal quantifiers.

3.1.4 Types of Descriptions

Since induction is a search through a description space, one must specify the goal of this search—that is, one must provide criteria that define the goal description. These criteria depend upon the specific domain in question, but some regularities are evident. We distinguish among characteristic, discriminant, and taxonomic descriptions.

A *characteristic description* is a description of a class of objects (or situations, events, and so on) that states facts that are true of all objects in the class. It is usually intended to discriminate objects in the given class from objects in all other possible classes. For example, a characteristic description of the set of all tables would discriminate any table from all things that are non-tables. In this way, the description *characterizes* the concept of a table. The task of discovering a characteristic description is a single-concept acquisition task (see Chapter 4 of this book). Since it is impossible to examine all objects in a given class (or *not* in a given class), a characteristic description is usually developed by specifying all characteristics that are true for all *known* objects of the class (positive examples). In some problems, negative examples (counterexamples) are available that represent objects known to be outside the class. Negative examples can greatly help to circumscribe the desired conceptual class. Even more helpful are counterexamples that are "near misses"—that is, negative examples that just barely fail to be positive examples (see Winston [1970, 1975]).

A *discriminant description* is a description of a class of objects in the context of a *fixed* set of other classes of objects. It states only those properties of the objects in the given class that are necessary to distinguish them from the objects in the other classes. A characteristic description can be viewed as an extreme kind of discriminant description in which the given class is discriminated against infinitely many alternative classes.

A *taxonomic description* is a description of a class of objects that subdivides the class into subclasses. In constructing such a description, it is assumed that the input data are not necessarily members of a single conceptual class. Rather it is assumed that they are members of several different classes (or produced by several different processes). An important kind of taxonomic description is a description that determines a *conceptual clustering*—a structuring of the data into object classes corresponding to distinct concepts. Taxonomic descriptions can be "flat"—with all object classes stated at the same level of abstraction—or hierarchical—with object classes arranged in an abstraction tree. A taxonomic description is fundamentally disjunctive. The overall class is described by the disjunction of the subclass descriptions. Taxonomic description is a kind of descriptive generalization rather than concept acquisition (see Chapter 4 of this book).

Determination of characteristic and discriminant descriptions is the subject of learning from (pre-classified) examples, while determination of taxonomic descriptions (conceptual clustering) is the subject of learning from observation or "learning without teacher". This distinction between these two forms of learning is examined in detail in Chapter 4 of this book.

In this chapter we restrict ourselves to the problem of determining characteristic descriptions. The problem of determining discriminant descriptions has been studied by Michalski and his collaborators [Larson & Michalski, 1977; Larson, 1977; Michalski, 1973, 1975, 1977, 1980a, 1980b] (see also Chapters 4 and 15 of this book.). A general method and computer program, CLUSTER/2, for conceptual clustering is described by Michalski and Stepp in Chapter 11 of this book.

3.1.5 Rules of Generalization

The partially-ordered space of descriptions of different levels of generality can be described by indicating what transformations are being applied to change less general descriptions into more general ones. Consequently, determination of inductive assertions can be viewed as a process of consecutive application of certain "generalization rules" to initial and intermediate descriptions. A generalization rule is a transformation rule that, when applied to a classification rule S_1 ::> K , produces a more general classification rule S_2 ::> K .[3] This means that the implication $S_1 \Rightarrow S_2$ holds. A generalization rule is called *selective* if S_2 involves no descriptors other than those used in S_1. If S_2 does contain new descriptors, then the rule is called *constructive* (see section 3.1.6). Selective rules of generalization do not change the space of possible inductive assertions, while constructive rules *do* change it.

The concept of rules of generalization provides further insight into the view of induction as a heuristic search of description space. The rules of generalization specify the operators that the search uses to move from one node to another in this space. The concept of generalization rules is also useful for comparing different learning methods because these rules abstract from the particular description languages used in the methods. In this chapter, we briefly outline the concept of a generalization rule and present a few examples. Chapter 4 presents a much more detailed discussion of the subject and an extensive list of generalization rules.

One of the simplest generalization rules is the *dropping condition* rule, which states that to generalize a conjunction, you may drop any of its conjunctive conditions. For example, the class K of "red apples" can be generalized to the class of all "apples" of any color by dropping the "red" condition. This can be written as:

red(v) & apple(v) ::> K can generalize to apple(v) ::> K

This is a selective rule of generalization because it does not introduce any new descriptors. An example of a constructive rule is the *find extrema of partial orders* rule. This rule augments a structural description by adding new descriptors for objects that are at the end points of ordered chains. For example, in a description of a four-storey office building, we might have the statement that "the second floor is on top of the first floor, the third floor is on top of the second, and so on." The find extrema rule would generate the fact that "the first floor is the bottom-most and the fourth floor is the top-most floor." The "on top of" relations form an ordered chain. Symbolically, this is written as:

ontop(f2,f1) & ontop(f3,f2) & ontop(f4,f3) |< most-ontop(f4) & least-ontop(f1)

[3]The notation S_1 ::> K means that all objects for which S_1 is true are classified as belonging to class K.

where the |< sign is interpreted as "can be generalized to". Other selective rules of generalization needed for this chapter include:

- the turning constants to variables rule
- the adding internal disjunction rule
- the closing interval rule
- the climbing generalization tree rule

These rules are explained in Chapter 4 of this book.

We also employ one rule of specialization. Any of the above rules of generalization can become rules of specialization by using them in reverse. However, one important rule of specialization is the introducing exception rule. It can be applied to a description in order to specialize it to take into account a counterexample. Suppose, for example, that a program is attempting to learn the concept of a "fish". Its initial hypothesis might be that a fish is anything that swims. However, it then is told about a dolphin that swims and breathes air but is not a fish. At this point, the program might guess that a fish is anything that swims and does not breathe air. This can be written as:

```
current description: swims(v)  ::>  K                  |
                                                        |> swims(v) & ~breathes-air(v)  ::>  K
negative example: swims(v) & breathes-air(v)  ::>  ~K   |
```

The |> sign is interpreted as meaning "can be specialized to".

3.1.6 Constructive Induction

As we have mentioned above, constructive induction is any form of induction that generates new descriptors not present in the input data. It is important for learning programs to be able to perform constructive induction, since it is well known that many AI problems cannot be solved without a change of representation. Many existing methods of induction (for example, [Hunt *et al.*, 1966; Hayes-Roth, 1976a, 1976b; Vere, 1975, 1980; Mitchell, 1977, 1978]) do not perform constructive induction. We say that these methods perform *selective induction*, since the descriptors present in the generalizations produced by the program are selected from those present in the input data.

There are several existing systems that perform some form of constructive induction. Soloway's BASEBALL system [Soloway, 1978], for example, applies several rules of constructive induction to convert raw snapshots of a simulated baseball game into high-level episode descriptions that can be generalized to discover such concepts as "run", "hit", and "out". In this system, the constructive induction takes place first, followed by selective induction.

Larson's INDUCE-1 system [Larson, 1977; Larson & Michalski, 1977], on the other hand, performs constructive and selective induction simultaneously. INDUCE-1 implements the "find extrema of partial orders" rule of generalization described above, along with a few other constructive induction rules. New descriptors are tested for discriminatory ability before they are added to all of the training instances.

Unfortunately, most existing systems have not implemented constructive induction rules in any general way. Instead, specific procedures are written to generate the new descriptors. This is an important problem for future research. In Chapter 4 of this book, Michalski presents more rules of constructive induction.

3.1.7 Control Strategy

Induction methods can be divided into bottom-up (data-driven), top-down (model-driven), and mixed methods depending on the strategy that they employ during the search for generalized descriptions. Bottom-up methods process the input events one at a time, gradually generalizing the current set of descriptions until a final conjunctive generalization is computed:

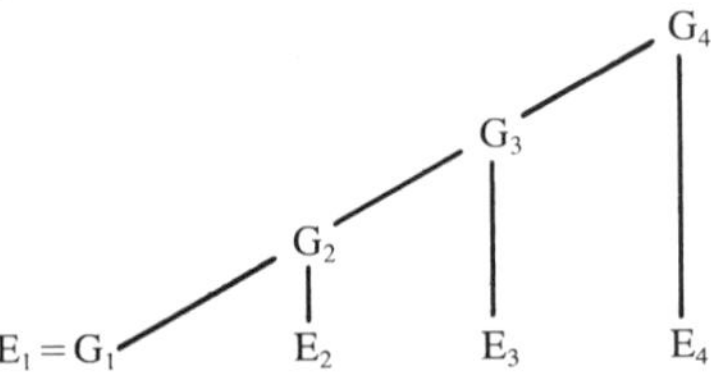

G_2 is the set of conjunctive generalizations of E_1 and E_2. G_I is the set of conjunctive generalizations obtained by taking each element of G_{I-1} and generalizing it with E_I.

Methods described by Winston, Hayes-Roth, and Vere are reviewed in this chapter. Other bottom-up methods include the candidate elimination approach described by Mitchell [1977, 1978], the ID3 technique of Quinlan [1979a, 1979b] (see also Chapter 15 of this book), and the Uniclass method described by Stepp [1970].

Top-down methods search a set of possible generalizations in an attempt to find a few "best" hypotheses that satisfy certain requirements. The two methods discussed in this chapter (Buchanan, *et al.* and Michalski) search for a small number of conjunctions that together cover all of the input events. The search proceeds by choosing as the initial working hypotheses some elements from the partially-ordered set of all possible descriptions. If the working hypotheses satisfy certain criteria, then the search halts. Otherwise, the current hypotheses are modified by slightly generalizing or specializing them. These new hypotheses are then checked to see if they satisfy the termination criteria. The process of modifying and checking continues until the criteria are met. Top-down techniques typically have better noise immunity and can be easily extended to discover disjunctions. The principal disadvantage of these techniques is that the working hypotheses must be checked repeatedly to determine whether they subsume all of the input events.

3.1.8 General versus Problem-oriented Methods

It is a common view that general methods of formal induction, although mathematically elegant and theoretically applicable to many problems, are in practice very inefficient and rarely lead to any interesting solutions. This opinion has led certain workers to abandon (at least temporarily) work on general methods and concentrate on learning problems in some specific domains (for example, Buchanan, *et al.* [1978] in chemistry or Lenat [1976] in elementary number theory). Such an approach can produce novel and practical solutions. On the other hand, it is difficult to extract general principles of induction from such problem-specific work. It is also difficult to apply such special-purpose programs to new areas.

An attractive possibility for solving this dilemma is to develop methods that incorporate various general principles of induction (including constructive induction) together with mechanisms for using exchangeable packages of problem-specific knowledge. This idea underlies the development of the INDUCE programs [Larson, 1977; Larson & Michalski, 1977; Michalski, 1980a] and the Star methodology described by Michalski in Chapter 4 of this book.

3.2 COMPARATIVE REVIEW OF SELECTED METHODS

3.2.1 Evaluation Criteria

The selected methods of induction are evaluated in terms of several criteria considered especially important in view of our discussion in Section 3.1.

1. *Adequacy of the representation language:* The language used to represent input data and output generalizations determines to a large extent the quality and utility of the output descriptions. Although it is difficult to assess the adequacy of a representation language out of the context of some specific problem, recent work in AI has shown that languages that treat all phenomena uniformly must sacrifice descriptive precision. For example, researchers who are attempting to build systems for understanding natural language prefer rich knowledge representations, such as frames, scripts, and semantic nets, to more uniform and less structured representations, such as attribute-value lists and PLANNER-style representations. Although languages with many syntactic forms do provide greater descriptive precision, they also lead to combinatorial increases in the complexity of the induction process. In order to control this complexity, a compromise must be sought between uniformity and richness of representational forms. In the evaluation of each method, a review of the operators and syntactic forms of each description language is provided.

2. *Rules of generalization implemented:* The generalization rules implemented in each algorithm are listed.

3. *Computational efficiency:* To get some approximate measure of computational

efficiency, we have hand simulated each algorithm on the test problem shown in Figure 3-2. In the simulation, we have measured the total number of times an inductive description was generated and the total number of times one inductive description was compared to another (or compared to a training instance). These provide good measures of computational effort, since generation and comparison of structural descriptions are expensive operations. We have also computed the ratio of the number of final descriptions output by the algorithm to the total number of descriptions generated by the algorithm. This provides a measure of overall efficiency, since a ratio of 1 indicates that every description generated by the algorithm was correct, while a ratio of 0 indicates that none of the generated descriptions were correct.

Our evaluation of these induction methods is not based entirely on these numerical measures, however (particularly since they are derived from only one test problem). An additional value of the simulation is that it gives some general idea of how the algorithms behave and shows the kinds of descriptions that the algorithms are able to discover. The reader is admonished to treat the efficiency measurements as highly approximate.

4. *Flexibility and extensibility:* Programs that can only discover conjunctive characteristic descriptions have limited practical application. In particular, they are inadequate in situations involving noisy data or in which no single conjunctive description can describe the phenomena of interest. Consequently, as one of the evaluation criteria, we consider the ease with which each method could be extended to:

- discover descriptions with forms other than conjunctive generalizations, for example, disjunctions and exceptions (see Section 3.1.4)
- include mechanisms that facilitate the detection of errors in the input data
- provide a general facility for incorporating externally-specified domain knowledge into the induction process as an exchangeable package
- perform constructive induction

Two sample learning problems will be used to explain these methods. The first problem (Figure 3-1) is made up of two examples (E1 and E2). Each example consists of objects (geometrical figures) that can be described by:

- attributes *size* (small or large) and *shape* (circle or square)
- relationships *ontop* (which indicates that one object is above another) and *inside* (which indicates that one object lies inside another)

The second sample problem (Figure 3-2) contains three examples of constructions made of simple geometrical objects. These objects can be described by:

- attributes *shape* (box, triangle, rectangle, ellipse, circle, square, or diamond), *size* (small, medium, or large), and *texture* (blank or shaded)
- relationships *ontop* and *inside* (the same as in the first sample problem)

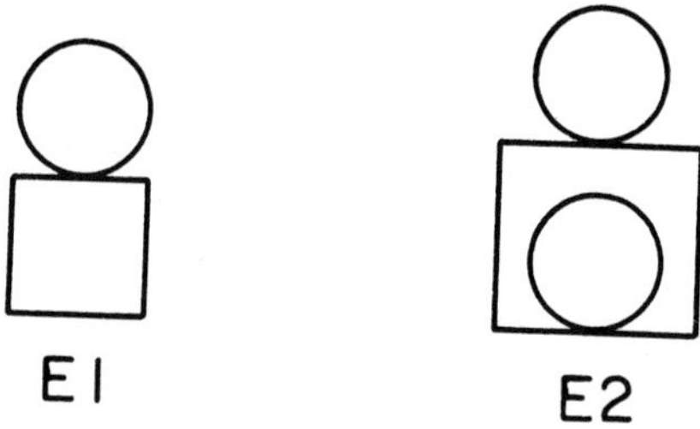

Figure 3-1: Sample problem for illustrating representation languages.

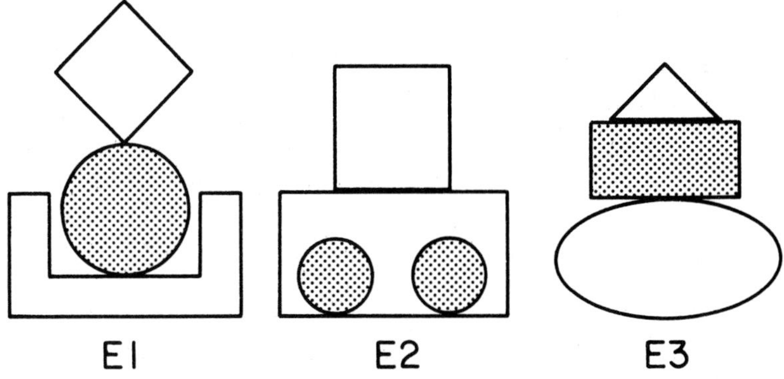

Figure 3-2: Sample problem for comparing the performance of the methods.

In each sample problem, the task is to determine a set of maximally-specific conjunctive generalizations (MSC-generalizations) of the examples. No negative examples are supplied in either problem. In the discussion below, the first problem is used to illustrate the representational formalism and the generalization process implemented in each method. The second, more complex, problem is used to compare the computational efficiency and representational adequacy of each method. This comparison is based on a hand simulation of each method.

3.2.2 Data-driven Methods: Winston, Hayes-Roth, and Vere

3.2.2.1 Winston: Learning Blocks World Concepts

Winston's well known work [Winston, 1970, 1975] deals with learning concepts that characterize simple toy block constructions. Although his method uses no precise criterion to define the goal description, the method usually develops MSC-generalizations of the input examples. The method assumes that the examples are provided to the program by an intelligent teacher who carefully chooses both the kinds of examples used and their order of presentation. The program uses so-called "near miss" negative examples to rapidly determine the correct generalized description of the concept. A near-miss example is a negative example that differs from the desired concept in only one significant attribute. Winston also uses the near-misses to develop "emphatic" conditions such as "must support" or "must not support". These *Must-* type descriptors indicate which conditions in the concept description are necessary to eliminate negative examples.

As Knapman has pointed out in his review of Winston's work [Knapman, 1978], many parts of the exposition in Winston's thesis [Winston, 1970] and subsequent publication [Winston, 1975] are not entirely clear. Although the general ideas in the thesis are well-explained, the exact implementation of these ideas is difficult to extract from these publications. Consequently, our description of Winston's method is necessarily a reconstruction. We begin by discussing the knowledge representation employed by Winston. Then, we turn our attention to his learning algorithm.

A semantic network is used to represent the input events, the background blocks-world knowledge, and the concept descriptions generated by the program (see Figures 3-3 and 3-4). The representation is quite general although the implemented programs appear to process the network in domain-specific ways (see Knapman [1978]; Winston [1970, page 196]).

Nodes in the network are used for several different purposes. We will illustrate these purposes by referring to the corresponding concepts in first-order predicate logic (FOPL). The first use of nodes is to represent various primitive concepts that are properties of objects or their parts (such as *small*, *size*, *circle*, *shape*). Nodes in this case correspond to constants in first-order predicate logic expressions. There is no distinction between attributes and values of attributes in Winston's network representation, and consequently, there is no representational equivalent of the one-argument predicates and functions of FOPL.

Another use of nodes is to represent individual examples and their parts. Thus, in Figure 3-3, we have the node E1 and two nodes A and B that make up E1. These can be regarded as quantified variables in predicate calculus. Distinct variable nodes are created for each training example.

Labeled links connecting these nodes represent various binary relationships among the nodes. The links correspond to two-argument predicates. The first two uses of nodes as constants and variables, plus the standard use of links as predicates, constitute the basic semantic network representation used by Winston.

There is, however, a third use of nodes. Each link type (analogous to a predicate symbol) is also represented in the network as a node. Thus, in addition to the numerous *On-Top* links that may appear in the network, there is an *On-Top* node that describes the link type *On-Top* and its relationship to other link types. For example, there might be a *Negative-Satellite* link that joins the *On-Top* node to the *Beneath* node. Such a link indicates that *On-Top* and *Beneath* are semantically opposite predicates. Similarly, there is a Must-be-Satellite link connecting the *Must-Be-On-Top* node to the *On-Top* node.

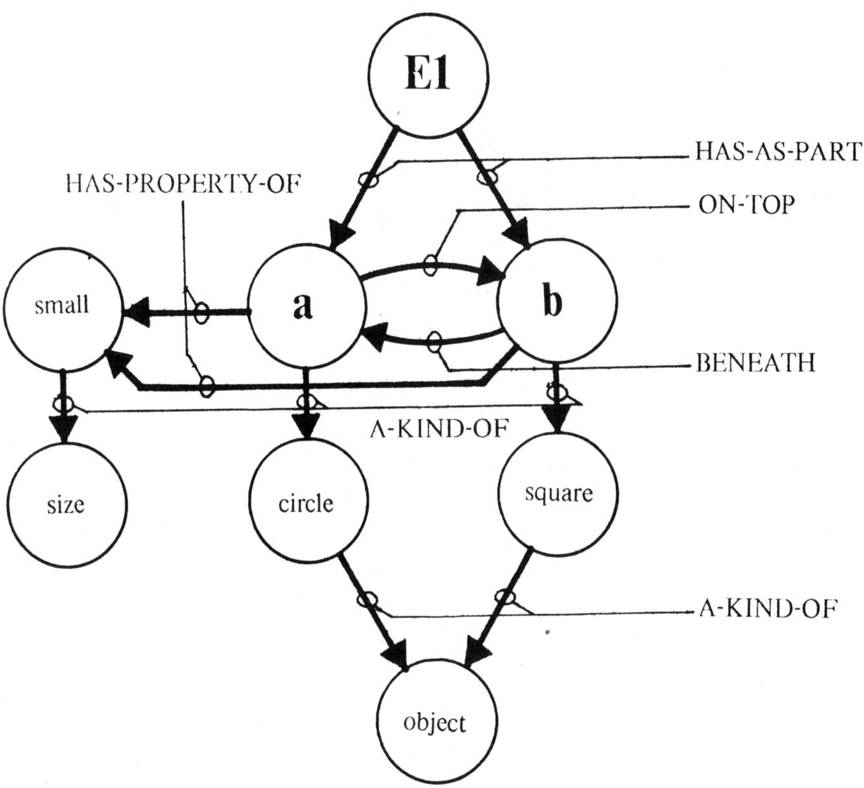

Figure 3-3: Network representing example E1 in Figure 3-1.

All of the nodes in the network are joined into one generalization hierarchy through the *A-Kind-Of* links. This hierarchy is used to implement the climbing generalization tree rule.

Now that we have described the network representation, we turn our attention to the learning algorithm. The learning algorithm proceeds in two steps. First, the current concept description is compared to the next example, and a difference description is developed. Then this difference description is processed to obtain a new, generalized concept description. Often, the second step results in several possible generalized concept descriptions. In such a case, one generalized concept is selected for further refinement and the remaining possibilities are placed on a backtrack list. The program backtracks when it is unable to consistently generalize its current concept description.

The first step of the algorithm (the development of the difference

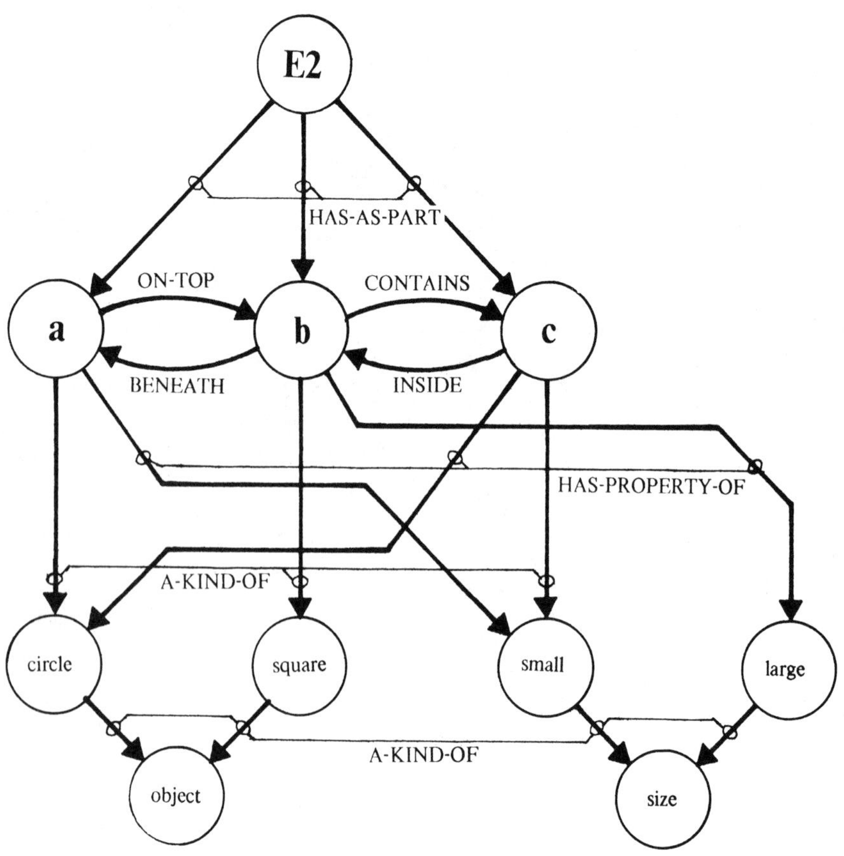

Figure 3-4: Network representing example E2 in Figure 3-1.

description) is accomplished by graph-matching the current concept description against the example supplied by the teacher, and annotating this match with comment notes (C-NOTES). These C-NOTES describe conditions in the concept description and example that partially matched or did not match. Winston's description of the graph-matching algorithm is sketchy [Knapman, 1978; Winston, 1970, pages 254-263]. The algorithm apparently finds one "best" match between the training example and the current concept description. The method does not address the important problem of multiple graph sub-isomorphisms, that is, the problem arising when the training example matches the current concept description in more than one way. This problem was apparently avoided by assuming that the teacher will present training instances that can be unambiguously matched to the current concept description.

Once this match between the concept description and the example is obtained, a generalized skeleton is created containing only those links and nodes that matched exactly. The C-NOTES are then attached to this skeleton. Each C-NOTE is a sub-network of nodes and links that describes a particular type of match. There are several types of C-NOTES corresponding to partially-matching or mismatching nodes and partially-matching or mismatching links. The different types are summarized in Table 3-1. In detail, there are the following types of C-NOTES:

- For nodes:
    - *Intersection* C-NOTES indicate that two nodes match exactly.
    - *A-Kind-of-Merge* and *A-Kind-Of-Chain* C-NOTES indicate that two nodes match partially. The *A-Kind-Of-Merge* C-NOTE handles the case when two nodes are different but share a common *A-Kind-Of* link, for example, when *square* partially matches *triangle* (since they are both polygons). The *A-Kind-Of-Chain* C-NOTE handles the case when a node matches a more general node, for example, when *square* matches *polygon*.
    - *Exit* C-NOTES indicate that two nodes do not match at all.
- For links:
    - *Negative-Satellite-Pair* C-NOTES indicate that two semantically opposite links mismatched, for example, *Marries* and *Does-Not-Marry*.
    - *Must-Be-Satellite-Pair* C-NOTES indicate that a normal link, such as *Supports*, matches an emphatic link, such as *Must-Support*.
    - *Must-Not-Be-Satellite-Pair* C-NOTES indicate that a normal link matches a *Must-Not* form of the same link.
    - *Supplementary Pointer* C-NOTES indicate that two links do not match at all.

Table 3-1: Winston's C-NOTE Categories

	Match	Partially match	Mismatch
Node	Intersection	A-Kind-Of-Merge A-Kind-Of Chain	Exit
Link		Negative-Satellite-Pair Must-Not-Be-Satellite-pair	Supplementary pointer

The network diagram of Figure 3-5 shows the difference description that results from matching the two networks of Figures 3-3 and 3-4 to each other.

The generalization phase of the algorithm is fairly simple. Each C-NOTE is handled in a way determined by the C-NOTE type and whether the example is a positive or negative training example. Winston provides a table that indicates what actions his program takes in each case [Winston, 1970, pages 145-146].

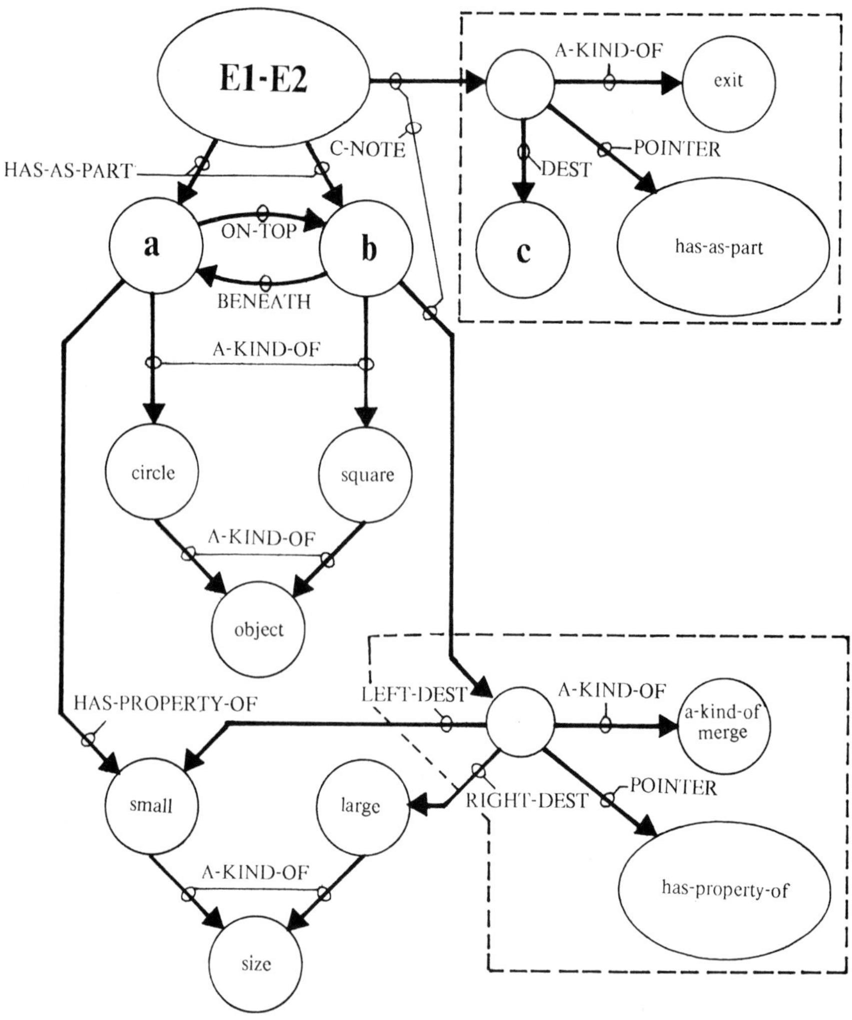

Figure 3-5: Difference description obtained by comparing E1 and E2 from Figure 3-1 and annotating the comparison with two C-NOTES.

Some C-NOTES can be handled in multiple ways. For positive examples, only one C-NOTE causes problems: the *A-Kind-Of-Merge*. In this case, the program can either climb the *A-Kind-Of* generalization tree or else drop the condition altogether. The program develops both possibilities but only pursues the former (leaving the latter on the backtrack list). The concept description that results from generalizing the difference description of Figure 3-5 is shown in

Figure 3-6. The alternative generalization would drop the *Has-Property* link from node *b*.

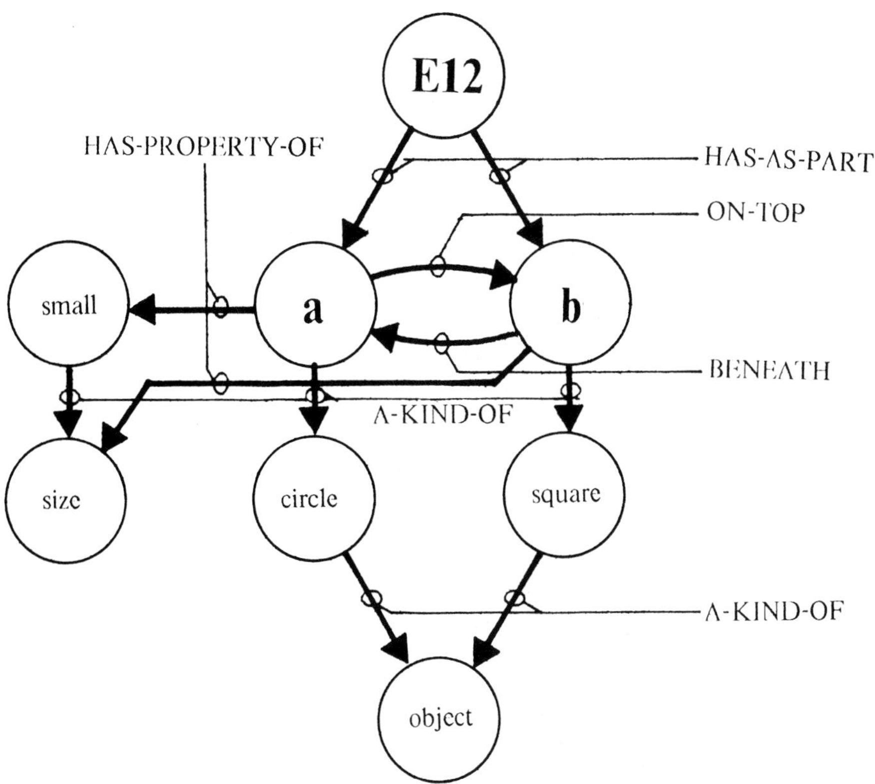

Figure 3-6: Network representing the generalized concept resulting from generalizing the difference description of Figure 3-5.

Evaluation:

1. *Representational adequacy.* The semantic network is used to represent properties, object hierarchies (using *A-Kind-Of*), and binary relationships. As in most semantic networks, n-ary relationships cannot be represented directly. The conjunction operator is implicit in the structure of the network, since all of the conditions represented in the network are assumed to hold simultaneously. There is no mechanism indicated for representing disjunction or internal disjunction. The *Not* and *Must-Not* links implement a form of the exception operator. An interesting feature of Winston's work is the use of the emphatic *Must-* relationships.

The program works in a depth-first fashion and produces only one generalized concept description for any given order of the training examples. Permuting the training examples may lead to a different generalization. Two generalizations obtained by simulating Winston's learning algorithm on the examples of Figure 3-2 are shown in Figures 3-7 and 3-8.

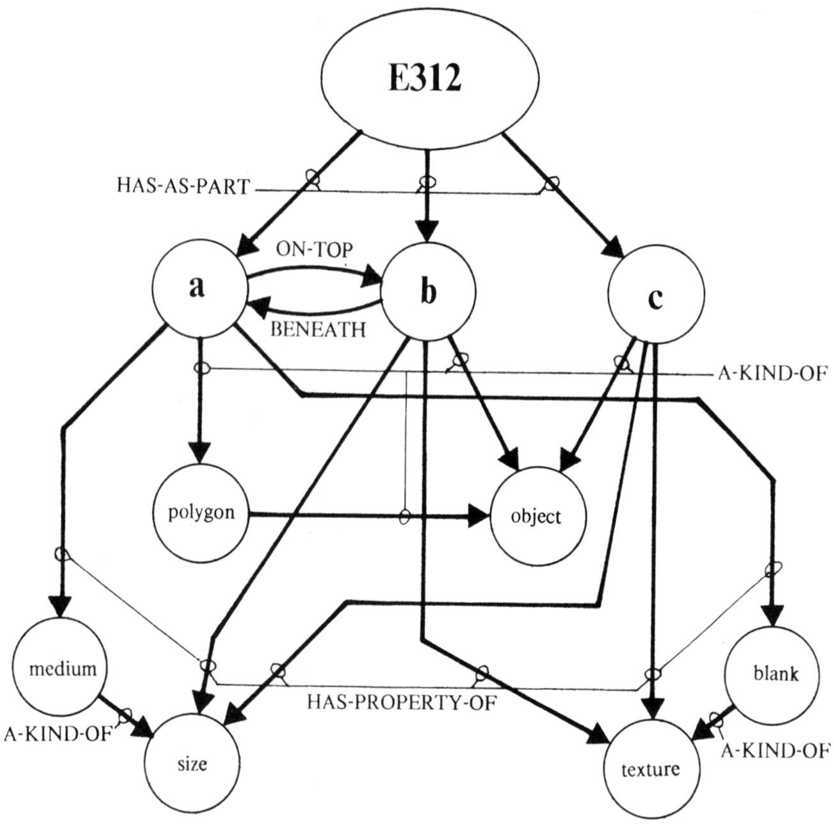

Figure 3-7: The first generalization obtained by simulating Winston's learning algorithm on the examples of Figure 3-2 (in the order E3, E1, E2). An English paraphrase is: "There is a medium, blank polygon on top of another object that has a size and texture. There is also another object with size and texture."

The second generalization (Figure 3-8) is not maximally specific since it does not mention the fact that all training examples also contain a small- or medium-sized shaded object. The algorithm cannot discover this generalization

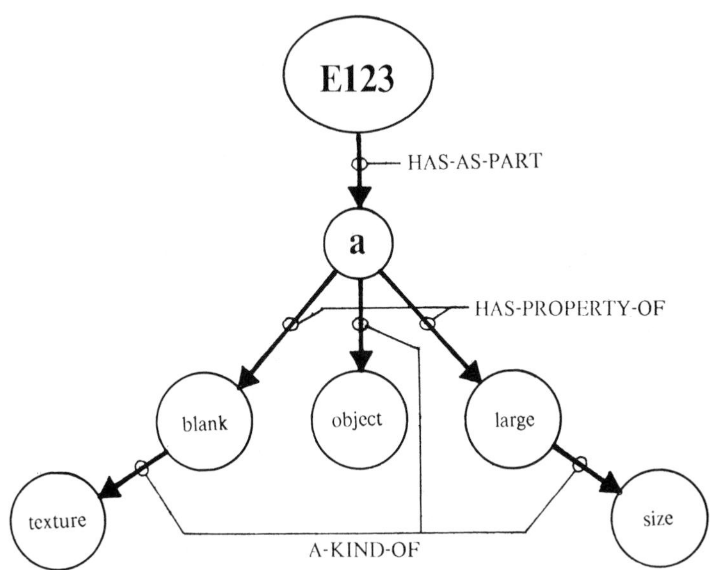

Figure 3-8: The second generalization obtained by simulating Winston's learning algorithm on the examples of Figure 3-2 (in the order E1, E2, E3). An English paraphrase is: "There is a large, blank object."

due to the fact that the graph-matcher finds the "best" match of the current concept with the example. When the order of presentation of the examples is E1 followed by E2 followed by E3, the "best" match of the first two examples eliminates the possibility of discovering the maximally-specific conjunctive generalization when the third example is matched.

2. *Rules of Generalization*. The program uses the dropping condition rule (for generalizing exit C-NOTES), the turning constants to variables rule (when creating the generalized skeleton), and the climbing generalization tree rule (for the *A-Kind-Of-Merge*). It also uses the introducing exception specialization rule (for the *A-Kind-Of-Merge* C-NOTE with negative examples).

3. *Computational efficiency*. The algorithm is quite fast: it requires only two graph comparisons to handle the examples of Figure 3-2. However, the algorithm does use a lot of memory to store intermediate descriptions. The first graph comparison produces eight alternatives, of which only one is pursued. The second graph comparison leads to four more alternatives from which one is selected as the "best" concept description. This inefficient use of memory is reflected in our figure for computational efficiency (the number of output descriptions / the number of examined descriptions), which is 1/11 or 9%.

The performance of the algorithm can be much worse in certain situations. When "poor" negative examples are used—those which do not match the current concept description well—the number of intermediate descriptions explodes combinatorially. Such situations are also likely to cause extensive backtracking.

Since the algorithm produces only one generalization for any given order of the input examples, it must be executed repeatedly if several alternative generalizations are desired.

4. *Flexibility and Extensibility*. Iba [1979] has successfully extended this algorithm to discover some disjunctive descriptions. His solution is not entirely general, however. The main difficulty seems to be that Winston's algorithm operates under the assumption that there is one conjunctive concept characterizing the examples, so the development of disjunctive concepts is not consistent with the spirit of the work.

Since the program behaves in a depth-first manner, noisy training events cause it to make serious errors from which it cannot recover without extensive backtracking. This is not surprising since Winston assumes that the teacher is intelligent and does not make any mistakes in training the student. It seems to be very difficult to extend this method to handle noisy input data.

The inductive generalization portion of the program does not contain much problem-specific knowledge. However, many of the techniques used in the program, such as building complete difference descriptions and using a backtracking search, may become combinatorially infeasible in real-world problem domains. The *A-Kind-Of* generalization hierarchy can be used to represent problem-specific knowledge.

The system of programs described by Winston performs some types of constructive induction. The original inputs to the system are noise-free line drawings. Some knowledge-based algorithms convert these line drawings into the network representation. Winston describes an algorithm for combining a group of objects into a single concept and subsequently using this concept in other descriptions. The "arcade" concept ([Winston, 1970], page 183) is a good example of such a constructive induction process.

3.2.2.2 Hayes-Roth: Program SPROUTER

Hayes-Roth's work on inductive learning [Hayes-Roth, 1976a, 1976b; Hayes-Roth & McDermott, 1977, 1978] is concerned with finding MSC-generalizations of a set of input positive examples (he calls such generalizations *maximal abstractions* or *interference matches*). *Parameterized structural representations* (PSR's) are used to represent both the input events and their generalizations. The PSR's for the two events of Figure 3-1 are:

E1: {{circle:a}{square:b}{small:a}
{small:b}{ontop:a, under:b}}

E2: {{circle:c}{square:d}{circle:e}
{small:c}{large:d}{small:e}
{ontop:c, under:d}{inside:e, outside:d}}

E1: {{circle:a}{square:b}{small:a}
{small:b}{ontop:a, under:b}}

E2: {{circle:c}{square:d}{circle:e}
{small:c}{large:d}{small:e}
{ontop:c, under:d}{inside:e, outside:d}}

In Hayes-Roth's terminology, the expressions such as {small:a} are called case frames. They are composed of case labels (such as small, circle) and parameters (such as a, b, c, d). The PSR can be interpreted as a conjunction of predicates of the form case-label(parameter-list). For example, {small:a} can be interpreted as small(a), and {ontop:c, under:d} can be interpreted as ontop(c,d). The parameters can be viewed as existentially-quantified variables denoting distinct objects.

The induction algorithm works in a purely bottom-up fashion. The first set of conjunctive generalizations, G_1, is initialized to contain only the first input example. Given a new example and the set of generalizations, G_i, obtained in the ith step, a new set of generalizations, G_{i+1}, is obtained by performing a partial match between each element in G_i and the current training example. It is not clear from publications [Hayes-Roth, 1976b; Hayes-Roth, 1976a; Hayes-Roth & McDermott, 1977; Hayes-Roth & McDermott, 1978] whether or not these sets G_i are pruned during this process. Hayes-Roth calls each of the partial-matching operations an *interference match*.

The interference match attempts to find the longest one-to-one match of parameters and case frames (that is, the longest common subexpression). This is accomplished in two steps. First the case frames in E1 and E2 are matched in all possible ways to obtain the set M. Two case frames match if all of their case labels match. Each element of M is a case frame and a list of parameter correspondences that permit that case frame to match in both events:

M = {{circle:((a/c)(a/e))},
{square:((b/d))},
{small:((a/c)(b/c)(a/e)(b/e))},
{ontop,under:((a/c b/d))}}

The second step involves selecting a subset of the parameter correspondences in M such that all parameters can be bound consistently. This is conducted by a breadth-first search of the space of possible bindings with pruning of unpromising nodes. The search can be visualized as a node-building process. Here is one such (pruned) search graph:

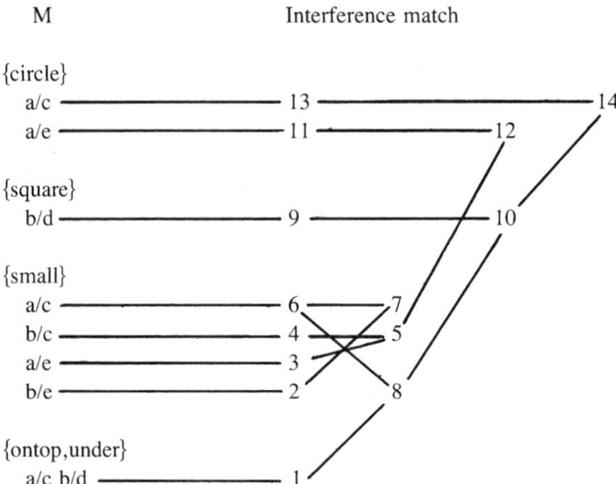

The nodes are numbered in order of their generation. One at a time, a pair of corresponding parameters is selected from M and a new node is created for them. Then this new node is compared with all previously generated nodes. Additional nodes are created for each case in which the new parameter correspondence node can be consistently merged with a previously existing node. In the search graph above, when the parameter binding {small: (a/c)} is selected, node 6 is created. Then node 6 is compared to nodes 1 through 5 and two new nodes are created: node 7, which is created by merging node 6 (a/c) with node 2 (b/e), and node 8, which is created by merging node 6 (a/c) with node 1 (a/c b/d). Node 6 cannot be merged with node 3, for instance, because parameter a would be inconsistently bound to both parameters c and e.

When the search is completed, nodes 7, 12, and 14 are bindings that lead to conjunctive generalizations. Node 14, for example, binds a to c (to give v1) and b to d (to give v2) to produce the conjunction:

{{circle:v1}{square:v2}{small:v1}{ontop:v1, under:v2}}

The node-building process is guided by computing a utility value for each candidate node to be built. The nodes are pruned by setting an upper limit on the total number of possible nodes and pruning nodes of low utility when that limit is reached.

Evaluation:

1. *Representational adequacy*. The algorithm discovers the following conjunctive generalizations of the example in Figure 3-2:

a. {{ontop:v1, under:v2}{medium:v1}{blank:v1}}
   There is a medium blank object ontop of something.
b. {{ontop:v1, under:v2}{medium:v1}{large:v2}{blank:v2}}
   There is a medium object ontop of a large, blank object.
c. {{medium:v1}{blank:v1}{large:v3}{blank:v3}{shaded:v2}}

There is a medium sized blank object, a large sized blank object, and a shaded object.

PSR's provide two symbolic forms: parameters and case labels. The case labels can express ordinary predicates and relations easily. Symmetric relations may be expressed by using the same label twice as in {same!size:a, same!size:b}. The only operator is the conjunction. The language has no disjunction or internal disjunction. As a result, the fact that each event in Figure 3-2 contains a polygon on top of a *circle or rectangle* cannot be discovered.

2. *Rules of generalization.* The method uses the dropping condition and turning constants to variables rules.

3. *Computational efficiency.* On our test example, the algorithm requires 22 expression comparisons and generates 20 candidate conjunctive generalizations of which 6 are retained. This gives a figure of 6/20 or 30% for computational efficiency. Four separate interference matches are required since the first match of E1 and E2 produces three possible conjunctive generalizations.

4. *Flexibility and extensibility.* An attempt has been made (Hayes-Roth, personal communication) to extend this method to produce disjunctive generalizations and to detect errors in data. Hayes-Roth has applied this method to various problems in the design of the speech understanding system HEARSAY II. However, no facility has been developed for incorporating domain-specific knowledge into the generalization process.

Also, no facility for constructive induction has been incorporated although Hayes-Roth has developed a technique for converting a PSR to a lower-level, finer-grained uniform PSR. This transformation permits the program to develop descriptions that involve a many-to-one binding of parameters.

3.2.2.3 Vere: Program Thoth

Vere's earlier work on inductive learning [Vere, 1975] was also directed at finding the MSC-generalizations of a set of input positive examples (in his work such generalizations are called *maximal conjunctive generalizations* or *maximal unifying generalizations*). Each example is represented as a conjunction of *literals*. A *literal* is a list of constants called *terms* enclosed in parentheses. For example, the objects in Figure 3-1 would be described as:

E1: (circle a)(square b)(small a)(small b)(ontop a b)

E2: (circle c)(square d)(circle e)(small c) (large d)(small e)(ontop c d)(inside e d)

Although these resemble Hayes-Roth's PSR's, they are quite different. There are no distinguished symbols. All terms (such as "small" and "e") are treated uniformly.

As in Hayes-Roth's work, Vere's method operates in a purely bottom-up fashion in which the input examples are processed one at a time in order to build the set of conjunctive generalizations. The algorithm for generalizing a pair of events operates in four steps. First, the literals in each of the two events are matched in all possible ways to generate the set of matching pairs MP. Two literals match if they contain the same number of constants and they share at least one common term in the same position. For the sample problem of Figure 3-2, we have:

MP= {((circle a),(circle c)),
((circle a),(circle e)),
((square b),(square d)),
((small a),(small c)),
((small a),(small e)),
((small b),(small c)),
((small b),(small e)),
((ontop a b),(ontop c d))}

The second step involves selecting all possible subsets of MP such that no single literal of one event is paired with more than one literal in another event. Each of these subsets eventually forms a new generalization of the original events.

In the third step, each subset of matching pairs selected in step 2 is extended by adding to the subset additional pairs of literals that did not previously match. A new pair p is added to a subset S of MP if each literal in p is related to some other pair q in S by a common constant in a common position. For example, if S contained the pair ((square b),(square d)) then we could add to S the pair ((ontop a b),(inside e d)) because the third element of (ontop a b) is the second element of (square b) and the third element of (inside e d) is the second element of (square d) (Vere calls this a 3-2 relationship). New indirectly-related pairs are merged into S until no more can be added.

In the fourth, and final, step, the resulting set of pairs is converted into a new conjunction of literals by merging each pair to form a single literal. Terms that do not match are turned into new terms, which may be viewed formally as variables. For example, ((circle a),(circle c)) would be converted to (circle v1).

Evaluation:

1. *Representational adequacy.* When applied to the test example (Figure 3-2) this algorithm produces many generalizations. A few of the significant ones are listed below:

- (ontop v1 v2)(medium v1)(large v2)(blank v2)(blank v3)(shaded v4) (v5 v4)

  There is a medium object on top of a large blank object. Another object is blank. There is a shaded object. (The literal (v5 v4) is *vacuous* since it contains only variables. Variable v5 was derived by unifying circle and triangle).

- (ontop v1 v2)(blank v1)(medium v1)(v9 v1)(v5 v3 v4)(shaded v3) (v7 v3)(v6 v3)(blank v4)(large v4)(v8 v4)

  There is a medium, blank object on top of some other object and there are two objects related in some way (v5) such that one is shaded and the other is large and blank.

- (ontop v1 v2)(medium v1)(blank v2)(large v2)(v5 v2)(shaded v3)(v7 v3) (blank v4)(v6 v4)

  There is a medium object on top of a large blank object. There is a shaded object and there is a blank object.

The representation is basically an uninterpreted list structure and, consequently, has very little logical structure. By convention the first symbol of a literal can be interpreted as a predicate symbol. The algorithm, however, treats all terms uniformly. This absence of semantic constraints creates difficulties. One difficulty is that the algorithm generates vacuous literals in certain situations. For instance, step 3 of the algorithm allows (circle a) to be paired with (triangle b) to produce the vacuous literal (v5 v4) as in generalization 1 above. Although these vacuous literals could easily be removed after being generated, the algorithm would perform more efficiently if it did not generate them in the first place. A second difficulty resulting from the relaxation of semantic constraints is that the algorithm creates generalizations involving a many-to-one binding of variables. While such generalizations may be desirable in some situations, they are usually meaningless, and their uncontrolled generation is computationally expensive.

The description language contains only the conjunction operator. No disjunction or internal disjunction is included.

2. *Rules of generalization.* The algorithm implements the dropping condition rule and the turning constants to variables rule.

3. *Computational efficiency.* From the published articles [Vere, 1975, 1977, 1978, 1980] it is not clear how to perform steps 2 and 3. The space of possible subsets of MP (computed in step 2) is very large, and the space of possible extensions to that set (computed in step 3) is even larger. An exhaustive search could not possibly give the computation times that Vere has published.

4. *Flexibility and extensibility.* Vere has published algorithms that discover descriptions with disjunctions [Vere, 1978] and exceptions (which he calls counterfactuals, see [Vere, 1980]). He has also developed techniques to generalize relational production rules [Vere, 1977, 1978]. The method has been demonstrated using the traditional AI toy problems of IQ analogy tests and blocks-world sequences. A facility for using background information to assist the induction process has also been developed. It uses a spreading activation technique to extract relevant relations from a knowledge base and add them to the input examples prior to generalizing them. The method has been extended to discover disjunctions and exceptions. It is not clear how well the method would work in noisy environments.

3.2.3 Model-driven Methods: Buchanan, *et al.*, and Michalski

In addition to acquiring context-free concept descriptions, some systems use models of the underlying domain to constrain the search for viable structural descriptions.

3.2.3.1 Buchanan, *et al.*: Program META-DENDRAL

META-DENDRAL is a program that discovers cleavage rules to explain the operation of a mass spectrometer. A mass spectrometer is a device that bombards small chemical samples with accelerated electrons, causing the molecules of the sample to break apart into many charged fragments. The masses of these fragments can then be measured to produce a *mass spectrum*—a histogram of the number of fragments (also called the *intensity*) plotted against their mass-to-charge ratio.

Analytic chemists can use the mass spectrum to guess the three-dimensional structure of the molecules in the sample. An expert system has been developed—the Heuristic DENDRAL program—that can also perform this structure elucidation task. It is supplied with the chemical formula (but not the three-dimensional structure) of the sample and its mass spectrum. Heuristic DENDRAL first examines the spectrum to obtain a set of constraints. These constraints are then given to CONGEN, a program that can generate all possible chemical structures satisfying the constraints. Finally, each of these generated structures is tested by running it through a mass-spectrometer simulator. The simulator applies a set of *cleavage rules* to predict which bonds in the proposed structure will be broken. The result is a simulated mass spectrum for each candidate structure. The simulated spectra are compared with the actual spectrum, and the structure whose simulated spectrum best matches the actual spectrum is ranked as the most likely structure for the unknown sample. The purpose of the META-DENDRAL system is to learn cleavage rules for use by the mass-spectrometer simulator.

The cleavage rules employed by the simulator are written as condition-action rules in which the condition part describes—in common ball-and-stick language—a portion of the molecular structure, and the action part indicates (by **) one or more bonds that will break (see Figure 3-9). The simulator applies these rules by matching the condition part against the molecular structure of the molecule being bombarded. Whenever the condition part matches, the simulator predicts that the bonds corresponding to those mentioned in the action part will break.

Figure 3-9 shows a typical cleavage rule. The atom descriptors have the following meanings. *Type* is the atomic element of the atom. *Nhs* is the number of hydrogen atoms bound to that atom. *Nbrs* is the number of non-hydrogen atoms bound to the atom. *Dots* counts the number of unsaturated valence electrons of the atom. This rule says that whenever a molecule containing the four atoms w, x, y, and z (connected as shown in the molecule graph and with the indicated atom descriptors) is placed in a mass spectrometer, then the bond joining w to x will be broken.

How can META-DENDRAL discover these rules? META-DENDRAL is given as input a set of molecules whose three-dimensional structures and mass spectra are known. We can view these training instances as condition-action rules of the form:

CONDITION PART (BOND ENVIRONMENT):

Molecule graph:	w—x—y—z—				
Atom descriptors:	atom	type	nhs	nbrs	dots
	w	carbon	3	1	0
	x	carbon	2	2	0
	y	nitrogen	1	2	0
	z	carbon	2	2	0

ACTION PART (CLEAVAGE PREDICTION):

w ** x—y—z—

Figure 3-9: Typical Cleavage Rule.

<whole molecular structure> $\Rightarrow$ <mass spectrum>

The first step in META-DENDRAL (carried out by subprogram INTSUM) is to apply background knowledge and rules of constructive induction to convert these training instances into the form of highly-specific cleavage rules:

<whole molecular structure> $\Rightarrow$ <one designated broken bond>

To achieve this transformation, INTSUM must hypothesize, for each fragment appearing in the mass spectrum, which bonds could have broken to produce that fragment. INTSUM employs a very simple theory of mass spectrometry (the so-called *half-order theory*) to propose these hypotheses. The result is one or more highly-specific cleavage rules for every fragment that appeared in any of the mass spectra in the original training instances.

These highly-specific cleavage rules are given to the second and third subprograms in the META-DENDRAL system: RULEGEN and RULEMOD. These two programs seek to find a small set of generalized cleavage rules that cover *most* of these highly-specific training rules. Notice that in this learning problem, no single generalized cleavage rule (or equivalently, no conjunctive generalization) can be expected to explain all of the training rules. In fact, since the INTSUM interpretation process can produce incorrect training instances, there is no reason to expect that even a set of cleavage rules will cover all of the training rules. Consequently, RULEGEN and RULEMOD do not search for MSC-generalizations. Instead, they develop a taxonomic description of the mass spectrometry data in the form of a *set* of cleavage rules that together cover the most important of the training rules.

The generalization process is done in two steps. First, RULEGEN conducts a model-driven generate-and-test search of the space of possible cleavage rules. This is a fairly coarse search from which redundant and approximate rules may result. The second phase of the search is conducted by the RULEMOD program, which cleans up the rules developed by RULEGEN to make them more precise and less redundant. We will concentrate on the description of the RULEGEN program, since it employs a top-down, model-driven algorithm that can be compared, in part, to the other learning methods described in this chapter.

The RULEGEN algorithm chooses as its starting point the most general cleavage pattern (x ** y) with no properties specified for either atom. Since this pattern matches every bond in every molecule, it predicts that every bond will break. RULEGEN generates successively more refined rules by specializing this pattern. The algorithm performs a sort of breadth-first search. At each iteration (each level of the search tree) it specializes a parent cleavage pattern by making a change to all atoms at a specified distance (radius) from the ** bond—the bond designated to break. The change can involve either adding new neighbor atoms or specifying an atom feature. All possible specializations are made for which there are supporting training instances. The technique of modifying *all* atoms at a particular radius causes the RULEGEN search to be coarse.

After each cycle of specialization, the resulting bond patterns are tested against the training instances, and a heuristic measure of "improvement" is computed that indicates whether a newly specialized bond pattern is more plausible than its parent pattern. If a pattern is determined to be an improvement, it is retained, and the specialization process continues. If all specializations of a parent pattern are less plausible than their parent, the parent pattern is output as a new cleavage rule, and no more specializations of that pattern are considered.

The improvement criterion states that a child pattern graph is more plausible than its parent if:

- It predicts fewer fragmentations per training molecule (that is, it is more specific).
- It still predicts fragmentations for at least half of all of the training molecules (that is, it is sufficiently general).
- It predicts fragmentations for as many molecules as its parent—unless the parent graph was "too general" in the sense that the parent predicts more than 2 fragmentations in some single training molecule or on the average it predicts more than 1.5 fragmentations per molecule.

Thus, RULEGEN can be viewed as following paths of increasing specialization through the space of possible bond patterns until the improvement criterion achieves a local maximum. The result of this process is a set of such plausible bond patterns. RULEMOD improves this set by performing detailed hill-climbing searches in the region immediately around each generated bond pattern. For the detailed searches, negative training instances are employed as part of the plausibility criterion. Negative training instances are bond patterns for which the actual spectrum shows that the designated bond did *not* break. RULEMOD also compares the generated bond patterns with one another and removes bond patterns that are redundant. The result of the RULEMOD processing is a smaller set of more precise bond patterns. Each of these bond patterns is converted into a cleavage rule and printed out.

Evaluation:

It is somewhat difficult to compare META-DENDRAL to the other methods described in this chapter since it is such a complex system and since even the RULEGEN subprogram is not searching for MSG-generalizations. However, we have included META-DENDRAL because it is such an important and powerful learning system.

1. *Representational adequacy*. The bond-pattern representation was adequate for the task of developing cleavage rules. It was specifically designed for use in chemical domains and is not general. The descriptions can be viewed as conjunctions. Individual rules developed by the program can be considered to be linked by disjunction.

2. *Rules of generalization*. The dropping condition and turning constants to variables rules are used "in reverse" during the specialization process. META-DENDRAL also uses the generalization by internal disjunction rule. For example, it can learn that the number of non-hydrogen neighbors (*nbrs*) of an atom is "greater-than one." In related work on nuclear magnetic resonance (NMR), Schwenzer and Mitchell [1977] present an example in which the value of *nhs* is listed as "greater than or equal to one" (which indicates an internal disjunction).

3. *Computational efficiency*. The comparison of computational efficiency is not provided for META-DENDRAL because it is not possible to hand simulate its operation on the sample problem of Figure 3-2. First of all, it is impossible to represent the sample problem as a chemical graph because the problem uses *two* different connecting relationships (*ontop* and *inside*) whereas META-DENDRAL only allows one (chemical bonding). Secondly, as mentioned above, the algorithm seeks a taxonomic—not characteristic—description of the input examples. Thirdly, the termination criteria for the RULEGEN algorithm are stated in purely chemical terms that have no counterpart in the domain of geometric figures. The current program is considered to be relatively inefficient [Buchanan *et al.*, 1976].

4. *Flexibility and extensibility*. META-DENDRAL has been extended to handle NMR spectra [Schwenzer & Mitchell, 1977]. The program works well in an error-laden environment. It uses domain-specific knowledge extensively. However, there is no strict separation between a general-purpose induction component and a special-purpose knowledge component. It is not clear whether the methods developed for META-DENDRAL could be easily applied to any non-chemical domain.

5. META-DENDRAL has extensive constructive induction facilities. In particular, program INTSUM performs sophisticated transformations of the input spectrum in order to develop the bond-environment descriptions. Unfortunately, this part of the program is highly procedural. None of the rules of constructive induction have been made explicit nor is there a general facility for accepting additional rules of constructive induction from the user. The user can alter some of the parameters of the half-order theory, however.

3.2.3.2 Michalski and Dietterich: Program INDUCE 1.2

Michalski and his collaborators have worked on many aspects of inductive learning. Most relevant here are works by Larson and Michalski [Larson & Michalski, 1977; Larson, 1977; Michalski, 980a]. These articles describe a general method (and program) for determining disjunctive structural descriptions that can also be used (somewhat inefficiently) to discover MSC-generalizations. The method presented here is different from previous work and is specially designed for finding MSC-generalizations.

The language used to describe the input events is VL_{21} [Michalski, 980a], an extension to first-order predicate logic (FOPL) that was developed specifically for use in inductive inference.[4] Each event is represented as a conjunction of *selectors*. A *selector* is a relational statement that typically contains a function or predicate descriptor (with variables as arguments) and a list of values that the descriptor may assume. For example, the selector [size(v1) = small, medium] asserts that the size of v1 may take the values small or medium. Another form of selector is an n-ary predicate in brackets, which is interpreted in the same way as in FOPL. For example, the selector [ontop(v1,v2)] asserts that object v1 is ontop of object v2. A conjunction of selectors is denoted by their concatenation. The events in Figure 3-1 are represented as:

E1: ∃v1, v2 [size(v1) = small][size(v2) = small] &
[shape(v1) = circle][shape(v2) = square][ontop(v1,v2)]

E2: ∃v1, v2, v3 [size(v1) = small][size(v2) = large] &
[size(v3) = small][shape(v1) = circle] &
[shape(v2) = square][shape(v3) = circle] &
[ontop(v1,v2)][inside(v3,v2)]

In this method, we attempt to accelerate the search for plausible generalizations by using techniques similar to those of hierarchical planning [Sacerdoti, 1973] . First, we separate all descriptors into two classes, unary and non-unary. We call the unary descriptors *attribute descriptors* since they are typically used to represent attributes such as size or shape. Non-unary descriptors are called *structure-specifying descriptors* since they are typically used to specify structural information (for example, relationships ontop and inside).

The basic idea of the method is to first search the description space that is defined by the structure-specifying descriptors. Once plausible generalizations are found in this abstract *structure-only space*, attribute descriptor space is searched to fill out the detailed generalizations. There are several advantages to this two-phase approach as compared to a standard search of the entire description space:

The first is representational. As we have seen above, it is usually neces-

---

[4]A somewhat modified and generalized form of VL_{21}, called the annotated predicated calculus, is described in Chapter 4 of this book.

sary to use a graph (or equivalent data structure) to represent an event in a structural learning problem. This is due to the fact that a graph is the most compact way to represent binary relationships among *n* objects when the number of such relationships is substantially less than the *n(n-1)* possible relationships (that is, when the relationship matrix is sparse). Thus, in our method, the structure-only events are represented as graphs. But once we have located plausible points in this structure-only space, we can continue the search in attribute space. Attribute (or unary) descriptors can be represented as vectors that are substantially more compact and more efficiently manipulated than graphs.

The second advantage of this hierarchical approach is computational. The task of comparing two graph structures is NP-complete. Any decrease in the size of these graph structures leads to large decreases in the cost of a graph comparison. Furthermore, we can confine graph comparisons to the first phase of the algorithm.

A third advantage of this approach is that we can take "large steps" during the search for plausible descriptions by conducting much of the search in a sparse, abstract space. This is similar in spirit to the coarse search employed in RULEGEN.

There are also several disadvantages to this approach. Firstly, no speedup will be obtained unless the learning problem uses both unary and non-unary descriptors. There are some learning problems in which attributes play almost no role at all. In such cases, the structure-only search space is the same as the complete search space, so no computational savings will be obtained. There are also learning problems that require only unary descriptors (as in [Hunt *et al.*, 1966]). These are not structural learning problems, and the structure-only space is empty.

A second disadvantage of this approach involves the problem of defining "plausible" descriptions in structure-only space. One fact that can be used is the following: If g is a MSC-generalization in structure-only space, then there exists a full description G, such that g is the structure-only portion of G and G is a MSC-generalization in the complete space.

Thus, if we find all MSC-generalizations of the input events in structure-only space, then we can use these to find MSC-generalizations in the complete space. However, we will not necessarily find all possible MSC-generalizations in this fashion, since there may exist MSC-generalizations in the complete space whose structure-only component is *not* maximally specific in structure-only space. To avoid this problem, the algorithm may accept less than maximally-specific generalizations in the structure-only space (that is, more general descriptions) and terminate the search using some problem-oriented knowledge.

Another difficulty concerns how to conduct the attribute search once plausible structure-only descriptions have been located. Our approach is to use each structure-only description to define a new attribute-only space into which all of the input events are translated. Unfortunately, an input event can be mapped to more than one attribute-only description as shown below. This complicates the search.

The algorithm searches structure-only space using a "beam search"—a form of best-first search in which a *set* of best candidate descriptions is maintained during the search (see [Rubin & Reddy, 1977]). First, all unary descriptors are removed from the input events (thus abstracting them into structure-only space). Then a random sample of these events is taken to form set B_0, the initial set of generalizations (the initial beam set). In each step, B_i is first pruned to a fixed sized *beam width* by removing unpromising generalizations. (Promise is determined by the application of the heuristic evaluation functions described below). Then B_i is checked to see if any of its generalizations covers all of the input examples. If any do, they are removed from B_i and placed in the set C of candidate conjunctive generalizations. Lastly, B_i is generalized to form B_{i+1} by taking each element of B_i and generalizing it in all possible ways by dropping single selectors. When the set of candidates C reaches a prespecified size, the search halts. The set C contains conjunctive generalizations of the input data, some of which are maximally specific. The size limit on C determines how deeply the algorithm searches.

The program allows the user to employ simultaneously several criteria for evaluating the promise of intermediate generalizations. These criteria are combined to form a lexicographic evaluation functional with tolerances [Michalski, 1973]. Some of the criteria presently included in the program are:

- maximize the number of input events covered by a generalization.
- maximize the number of selectors in a generalization.
- minimize the total "cost" of the descriptors in a generalization. Different descriptors can be given costs according to their difficulty of measurement and other domain-dependent properties.

The user creates the evaluation functional by selecting criteria from a list of available criteria and ordering them in decreasing order of importance. Each criterion is accompanied by a tolerance that specifies the allowed departure of the associated criterion from the optimum value (see [Michalski, 1973]).

Once the structure-only candidate set C has been built, each candidate generalization in C must be filled out by finding values for its attribute descriptors. Each candidate generalization g in C is used to define an attribute-only space that is then searched using a beam search technique similar to that used to search the structure-only space. The attribute-only space is defined as follows. Let $\{v_1, v_2, ..., v_k\}$ be the existentially quantified variables used in the candidate structure-only generalization g. The attribute-only space generated by g is the space of all $m \times k$-tuples consisting of the values of the m attributes describing the k objects denoted by the quantified variables $\{v_1, v_2, ..., v_k\}$. In cases where some of the m attributes are not applicable to some of the objects, the attribute-only space will be correspondingly smaller.

In order to search this space, all of the input events must first be translated into this attribute-only space. This is accomplished by matching g against all input events and extracting the attributes of the variables in the input events that match v_1, v_2, ..., v_k in g. The values of these attributes form a single $m \times k$-tuple. For example, if g = [ontop(v1, v2)] and the variables v1 and v2 have two attributes, size and shape, then the attribute-only space generated by g is the space of all 4-tuples of the form:

$<$ size(v1), size(v2), shape(v1), shape(v2) $>$

Let E_1 be the following input event:

E_1: ∃p1, p2, p3 [ontop(p1, p2)][ontop(p2, p3)] &
[size(p1) = 1][size(p2) = 3][size(p3) = 5] &
[color(p1) = red][color(p2) = green][color(p3) = blue]

Then we can translate E_1 into this attribute-only space in two different ways—since g matches E_1 in two distinct ways.

When g is matched to E_1 so that v1 is matched with p1 and v2 with p2, the resulting attribute-only 4-tuple is:

$<$ 1, 3, red, green $>$

When v1 is matched to p2 and v2 to p3, then the resulting event is:

$<$ 3, 5, green, blue $>$

During the search of this attribute-only space, the goal is to find an MSC-generalization that covers at least one of these two translated events (and thus covers E_1). Such an MSC-generalization is in the form of an $m \times k$-tuple as above, except that each position in the tuple may contain a *set* of values of the corresponding attribute. This set of values is expressed by an internal disjunction in the final corresponding formula.

The beam search of attribute-only space is similar to the search of structure-only space. A random sample of events is selected and generalized step-by-step by extending the internal disjunctions in the events. The generalization process is guided by a means-ends analysis to detect relevant differences between the current generalizations and events that have not yet been covered. Heuristic criteria are used to prune the beam set to a fixed beam width. Candidate generalizations that cover all of the input events (that is, at least one of the attribute-only events translated from each input event) are removed from the beam set and added to the candidate set C'. Each candidate in C' provides possible settings of the attribute descriptors that, when combined with the structure-specifying descriptors in g, produces an output conjunctive generalization G.

Among all conjunctive generalizations produced by this algorithm, there may be some that are not maximally specific. This occurs when the search of structure-only space is permitted to produce candidate structure-only generalizations that are not maximally specific. In most observed cases such candidate generalizations become maximally specific when their attribute descriptors are filled in during the second phase of the algorithm.

Evaluation:

1. *Representational adequacy*. Using only selective rules of generalization, the algorithm discovers, among others, the following generalizations of the events in Figure 3-2:

- ∃v1, v2 [ontop(v1,v2)] [size(v1) = medium]
  [shape(v1) = polygon] [texture(v1) = blank]
  [size(v2) = medium∨large] [shape(v2) = rectangle∨circle]

  There exist two objects (in each event), such that one is a blank, medium-sized polygon on top of the other, a medium or large circle or rectangle.
- ∃v1, v2 [ontop(v1,v2)] [size(v1) = medium]
  [shape(v1) = circle∨square∨rectangle] [size(v2) = large]
  [shape(v2) = box∨rectangle∨ellipse] [texture(v2) = blank]

  There exist two objects such that one of them is a medium-sized circle, rectangle, or square on top of the other, a large, blank box, rectangle, or ellipse.
- ∃v1, v2 [ontop(v1,v2)] [size(v1) = medium] [shape(v1) = polygon]
  [size(v2) = medium∨large] [shape(v2) = rectangle∨ellipse∨circle]
  v

  There exist two objects such that one of them is a medium-sized polygon on top of the other, a large or medium rectangle, ellipse, or circle.
- ∃v1 [size(v1) = small∨medium]
  [shape(v1) = circle∨rectangle] [texture(v1) = shaded]

  There exists one object, a medium or small shaded circle or rectangle.

A few simple constructive induction rules have been incorporated into the current implementation. These include rules that count the number of objects possessing certain characteristics and rules that locate the top-most and bottom-most parts of an object (or more generally, extremal elements in a linearly-ordered set defined by any transitive relation, such as *On-top*). Other constructive induction rules can be specified by the user. Using the built-in constructive induction rules, the program produces the following conjunctive generalization of the input events in Figure 3-2:

- [# v's = 3,4] [# v's with texture blank = 2] &
  ∃v1, v2 [top-most(v1)] [ontop(v1,v2)]
  [size(v1) = medium] [shape(v1) = polygon]
  [texture(v1) = clear] [size(v2) = medium, large]
  [shape(v2) = circle, rectangle]

  There are either three or four objects in each event. Exactly two of these objects are blank. The top-most object is a medium-sized, clear polygon and it is on top of a large or medium-sized circle or rectangle.

This algorithm implements the conjunction, disjunction, and internal disjunction operators. The representation distinguishes among descriptors, variables, and values. Descriptors are further divided into structure-specifying descriptors and attribute descriptors. The current method discriminates among three types of descriptors:

- nominal—which have unordered value sets
- linear—which have linearly ordered value sets
- structured—which have tree-ordered value sets

This variety of possible representational forms is intended to provide a better "fit" between the description language and any specific problem.

2. *Rules of generalization*. The algorithm uses all rules of generalization mentioned in Section 3.1.5 and also a few constructive induction rules. It does not implement the introducing exception specialization rule. The effect of the turning constants to variables rule is achieved as a special case of the generalization by internal disjunction rule.

3. *Computational efficiency*. The algorithm requires 28 comparisons and builds 13 rules during the search to develop the descriptions listed above. Four rules are retained so this gives an efficiency ratio of 4/13 or 30%.

4. *Flexibility and extensibility*. The algorithm can be modified to discover disjunctions by altering the termination criteria for the search of structure-only space to accept structure conjuncts that do not necessarily cover all of the input events. The same general two-phase approach can also be applied to problems of determining discriminant descriptions. (See papers by Larson and Michalski [1977], Larson [1977], Michalski [1975, 1980a,b] and Chapter 4 of this book.)

The algorithm has good noise immunity. Noise events can be discovered because the algorithm tends to place them in separate terms of a disjunction.

Domain-specific knowledge can be incorporated into the program by defining the types and domains of descriptors, specifying the structures of these domains, specifying certain simple production rules (for domain constraints on legal combinations of variables), specifying the evaluation functional, and by providing constructive induction rules. These forms of knowledge representation are not always convenient, however. Further work should provide other facilities for knowledge representation.

As mentioned above, this method does perform a few general kinds of constructive induction. The method provides mechanisms for adding more rules of constructive induction.

The comparison of the above methods in terms of the criteria of Section 3.2.1 is summarized in Table 3-2.

3.3 CONCLUSION

This chapter has discussed various aspects of inductive learning of structural descriptions and has presented several criteria for evaluating learning methods. These criteria have been applied to the evaluation of five selected methods for learning structural descriptions. The main features revealed by this analysis are:

Table 3-2: Comparison of different learning methods

Criterion:	Method: Winston	Hayes-Roth	Vere	Buchanan *et al.*	Michalski
Intended application	Learning toy block concepts	General	General	Discovering mass spectrometry rules	General
Language	Semantic net	Parameterized structural representation	Quantifier-free FOPL	Chemical model	Variable-valued Logic system VL_{21}
Syntactic concepts	Nodes and links of many types	Case frames parameters case labels	Literals constants	Molecule graph attributes constants in value sets	Selectors descriptors variables value sets
Operators	&, exception	&	&	&, $\vee$, internal $\vee$	&, $\vee$, internal $\vee$
Generalization and specialization rules:					
Dropping condition?	Yes	Yes	Yes	Yes	Yes
Constants to variables?	Yes	Yes	Yes	Yes	Yes
Generalizing by internal $\vee$?	No	No	No	Yes	Yes
Climbing tree?	Yes	No	No	No	Yes
Closing intervals?	No	No	No	No	Yes
Introducing exceptions?	Yes	No	No	No	No
Efficiency:					
Graph comparisons	2	22	Complete algorithm not known	Not applicable	28
Graph generations during search	11	20		Not applicable	13
Ratio of output to total	1/11 = 9%	6/20 = 30%		Not applicable	4/13 = 30%
Extensibility:					
Applications	None	Speech analysis	None	Mass spectrometry, NMR	Soybean disease diagnosis
Disjunctive forms?	No	No	Yes	Yes	Yes
Noise immunity?	Very low	Low	Probably good	Excellent	Very good
Domain knowledge?	Yes, built-in to program	No	Yes	Yes, built-in to program	Yes
Constructive induction?	Limited facility	No	No	Extensive problem-specific facility	Few general rules

- *Top-down and bottom-up methods present a trade-off between computational efficiency on the one hand, and flexibility and extensibility on the other.* Bottom-up methods tend to be faster, but have lower noise immunity and less flexibility. Top-down methods have good noise immunity and can be easily modified to discover disjunctive and other forms of generalization. They do tend to be computationally more expensive.
- *The description language employed by a learning method is critically important.* A learning method that uses a language with little structure (that is, that has few operators and few types of operands) tends to be relatively efficient and easy to implement but may not be able to learn descriptions that are most useful in real-world applications. On the other hand, a method that uses a language that is too rich will lead to enormous implementation problems that will be detrimental to successful research in machine learning.
- *A significant problem in current research on inductive learning is that each research group is using a different notation and terminology.* This not only makes the exchange of research results difficult, but it also makes it hard for new researchers to enter the field. This chapter has attempted to develop a set of concepts and criteria that abstract from these differences in notation and terminology.

The analysis raises some important problems to be addressed in future research:

- *Further work on representations.* Present learning programs are limited by the kinds of operators and variable types they allow, and also by the forms of descriptions they can produce. Methods for handling additional operators, variable types, and forms of descriptions need to be designed and implemented. Rules of generalization corresponding to these operators, types, and forms should also be developed. Among the forms that are particularly desirable are hierarchical and related forms in which a name of one description is used to build other, more complex descriptions. Some initial work in this area has been done by Winston [1970, 1975], Cohen and Sammut [1978], and in the area of grammatical inference in general (for example, Biermann [1972]).
- *The Principle of Comprehensibility.* In applications where people will need to use the generalizations produced by a learning program, it is important that the learning method produce generalizations that are easy to understand and close to corresponding natural language descriptions. This means that the descriptions developed by an inductive method must be structured to take into consideration human information processing *limitations*. As a rough guideline, conjunctions should involve no more than three or four conditions, full descriptions should involve only two or three disjunctive terms, and there should be no more than two quantifiers in the description. Descriptions should correspond to single "chunks" of infor-

mation. Hierarchically-structured descriptions may provide a way to meet these guidelines. For more details, see Chapter 4 of this book.

- *Constructive induction.* The constructive induction techniques developed to date are very limited. New rules of constructive induction need to be identified and implemented. An important problem is the development of efficient mechanisms for guiding the process of constructive induction through the potentially immense space of possible derived descriptors.
- *Integration of problem-specific knowledge.* Further work should be done on the problem of when and how to use problem-specific knowledge in a general induction method. The use of typed variables is a good example of a general way to incorporate problem-specific knowledge.
- *Extension to discriminant and taxonomic descriptions.* Much work has been done on characteristic generalization. Discriminant and taxonomic descriptions are very important, especially in noisy environments. More work on this subject is needed.
- *User interface.* As AI learning programs become more powerful, their functions will become more opaque. Learning programs should provide explanation facilities for justifying their generalizations.
- *Handling errors and missing data.* Very little attention has been paid to the problem of developing methods that work well in noisy environments. There is need for research on methods of learning from uncertain input information, from incomplete information, and from information containing errors.

ACKNOWLEDGMENTS

The authors gratefully acknowledge the support of the National Science Foundation under grants MCS-79-06614 and MCS-82-05166. This chapter is a descendant and an extension of a paper that first appeared in IJCAI-79. Since that time, reviewers from the AI Journal, where the initial version of the paper was subsequently published, and the editors of this volume have carefully read and criticized this work. The authors are grateful for these comments and criticisms, which significantly helped to improve the presentation and the readability of this chapter.

REFERENCES

Biermann, A. and Feldman, J., *A survey of results in grammatical inference*, Academic Press, New York, 1972.

Buchanan, B. G. and Feigenbaum, E. A., "DENDRAL and Meta-DENDRAL: their applications dimension," *Artificial Intelligence*, Vol. 11, pp. 5-24, 1978.

Buchanan, B. G., Feigenbaum, E. A. and Lederberg, J., "A heuristic programming study of theory formation in sciences," *Proceedings of the Second International Joint Conference on Artificial Intelligence*, International Joint Conferences on Artificial Intelligence, London, pp. 40-48, 1971.

Buchanan, B. G., Smith, D. H., White, W. C., Gritter, R. J., Feigenbaum, E. A., Lederberg, J., and Djerassi, C., "Applications of artificial intelligence for chemical inference XXII. Automatic rule formation in mass spectrometry by means of the Meta-DENDRAL program," *Journal of the American Chemical Society*, Vol. 98, pp. 6168, 1976.

Cohen, B. L. and Sammut, C. A., "Pattern recognition and learning with a structural description language," *Proceedings of the Fourth International Joint Conference on Artificial Intelligence*, IJCPR, Kyoto, Japan, pp. 394, 1978.

Dietterich, T. and Michalski, R., "Inductive Learning of Structural Descriptions," *Artificial* Intelligence, Vol. 16, 1981.

Hayes-Roth, F., "Collected papers on the learning and recognition of structured patterns", Technical Report technical report, Carnegie-Mellon Department of Computer Science, Pittsburgh, PA., May 1976.

Hayes-Roth, F., "Patterns of induction and associated knowledge acquisition algorithms", Technical Report, Carnegie-Mellon University, May 1976.

Hayes-Roth, F. and McDermott, J., "Knowledge acquisition from structural descriptions," *Proceedings of the Fifth International Joint Conference on Artificial Intelligence*, IJCAI, Cambridge, Mass., pp. 356-362, August 1977.

Hayes-Roth, F. and McDermott, J., "An interference matching technique for inducing abstractions," *Communications of the ACM*, Vol. 21, No. 5, pp. 401-410, 1978.

Hunt, E. B., Marin, J. and Stone, P. T., *Experiments in Induction*, Academic Press, New York, 1966.

Iba, G. A., "Learning disjunctive concepts from examples," Master's thesis, M.I.T., Cambridge, Mass., 1979, (also AI memo 548).

Knapman, J., "A critical review of Winston's learning structural descriptions from examples," *AISB Quarterly*, Vol. 31, pp. 319-320, September 1978.

Larson, J., *Inductive inference in the variable-valued predicate logic system VL21: methodology and computer implementation*, Ph.D. dissertation, University of Illinois, Urbana, Illinois, May 1977.

Larson, J. and Michalski, R. S., "Inductive inference of VL decision rules," *Proceedings of the Workshop on Pattern Directed Inference Systems, SIGART Newsletter 63*, pp. 38-44, June 1977.

Lenat, D. B., *AM: an artificial intelligence approach to discovery in mathematics as heuristic search*, Ph.D. dissertation, Stanford University, Stanford, California, 1976.

Michalski, R. S., "Discovering classification rules using variable-valued logic system VL1," *Proceedings of the Third International Joint Conference on Artificial Intelligence*, IJCAI, pp. 162-172, 1973.

Michalski, R. S., "Discovering classification rules using variable-valued logic system VL1," *Proceedings of the Third International Joint Conference on Artificial Intelligence*, IJCAI, pp. 162-172, 1973a.

Michalski, R. S., "Variable-Valued Logic and its Applications to Pattern Recognition and Machine Learning," *Multiple-Valued Logic and Computer Science*, Rine, D. (Ed.), North-Holland, pp. 506-534, 1975a.

Michalski, R. S., "Pattern recognition as rule-guided inductive inference," *IEEE Transactions on Pattern Analysis and Machine Intelligence*, Vol. PAMI-2, No. 4, pp. 349-361, 1980a.

Michalski, R. S. and Chilausky, R. L., "Learning by being told and learning from examples: an experimental comparison of the two methods of knowledge acquisition in the context of developing an expert system for soybean disease diagnosis," *Policy Analysis and Information Systems*, Vol. 4, No. 2, pp. 125-160, June 1980, (Special issue on knowledge acquisition and induction).

Mitchell, T. M., "Version Spaces: A candidate elimination approach to rule learning," *Proceedings of the Fifth International Joint Conference on Artificial Intelligence*, IJCAI, Cambridge, Mass., pp. 305-310, 1977.

Mitchell, T. M., *Version Spaces: An approach to concept learning*, Ph.D. dissertation, Stanford University, December 1978, (also Stanford CS report STAN-CS-78-711, HPP-79-2).

Plotkin, G. D., "A note on inductive generalization," *Machine Intelligence*, Meltzer, B. and Michie, D. (Eds.), Edinburgh University Press, Edinburgh, pp. 153-163, 1970.

Plotkin, G. D., "A further note on inductive generalization," *Machine Intelligence*, Meltzer, B. and Michie, D. (Eds.), Elsevier, Edinburgh, pp. 101-124, 1971.

Quinlan, J. R., "Discovering rules from large collections of examples: a case study," *Expert Systems in the Micro Electronic Age*, Michie, D. (Ed.), Edinburgh University Press, Edinburgh, 1979.

Quinlan, J. R., "Induction over large data bases", Technical Report Report HPP-79-14, Heuristic Programming Project, Stanford University, 1979.

Rubin, S. M., and Reddy, R., "The locus model of search and its use in image interpretation," *Proceedings of the Fifth International Joint Conference on Artificial Intelligence*, IJCAI, pp. 590-595, 1977.

Sacerdoti, E., "Planning in a hierarchy of abstraction spaces," *Proceedings of the Third International Joint Conference on Artificial Intelligence*, IJCAI, pp. 412-422, 1973.

Schwenzer, G. M., and Mitchell, T. M., *Computer-assisted structure elucidation using automatically acquired carbon-13* NMR *rules*, American Chemical Society, 1977.

Soloway, E. M., *Learning interpretation + generalization: a case study in knowledge-directed learning*, Ph.D. dissertation, University of Massachusetts at Amherst, 1978, (Computer and Information Science Report COINS TR-78-13).

Stepp, R., "Learning without negative examples via variable-valued logic characterizations: the Uniclass inductive program AQ7UNI", Technical Report 982, Department of Computer Science, University of Illinois at Urbana-Champaign, July 1979.

Vere, S. A., "Induction of concepts in the predicate calculus," *Proceedings of the Fourth International Joint Conference on Artificial Intelligence*, IJCAI, Tbilisi, USSR, pp. 281-287, 1975.

Vere, S. A., "Induction of relational productions in the presence of background information," *Proceedings of the Fifth International Joint Conference on Artificial Intelligence*, IJCAI, Cambridge, Mass., pp. 349-355, 1977.

Vere, S. A., "Inductive learning of relational productions," *Pattern-Directed Inference Systems*, Waterman, D. A. and Hayes-Roth, F. (Eds.), Academic Press, New York, 1978.

Vere, S. A., "Multilevel counterfactuals for generalizations of relational concepts and productions," *Artificial Intelligence*, Vol. 14, No. 2, pp. 138-164, September 1980.

Winston, P. H., "Learning structural descriptions from examples", Technical Report AI-TR-231, MIT, Cambridge, Mass., September 1970.

Winston, P. H., "Learning structural descriptions from examples," *The Psychology of Computer Vision*, Winston, P. H. (Ed.), McGraw Hill, New York, ch. 5, 1975, (Original version published as a Ph.D. dissertaition, at MIT AI Lab, September, 1970).

4

A THEORY AND METHODOLOGY OF INDUCTIVE LEARNING

Ryszard S. Michalski
University of Illinois at Urbana-Champaign

ABSTRACT

The presented theory views inductive learning as a heuristic search through a space of symbolic descriptions, generated by an application of various inference rules to the initial observational statements. The inference rules include generalization rules, which perform generalizing transformations on descriptions, and conventional truth-preserving deductive rules. The application of the inference rules to descriptions is constrained by problem background knowledge, and guided by criteria evaluating the "quality" of generated inductive assertions.

Based on this theory, a general methodology for learning structural descriptions from examples, called *Star*, is described and illustrated by a problem from the area of conceptual data analysis.

4.1 INTRODUCTION

> "*...Scientific knowledge through demonstration*[1] *is impossible unless a man knows the primary immediate premises ... We must get to know the primary premises by induction; for the method by which even sense-perception implants the universal is inductive...*"—Aristotle, Posterior Analytics, Book II, Chapter 19 (circa 330 B.C.)

The ability of people to make accurate generalizations from a few scattered

[1]That is, what we now call "deduction".

facts or to discover patterns in seemingly chaotic collections of observations is a fascinating research topic of long-standing interest. The understanding of this ability is now also of growing practical importance, as it holds the key to an improvement of methods by which computers can acquire knowledge. A need for such an improvement is evidenced by the fact that knowledge acquisition is presently the most limiting "bottleneck" in the development of modern knowledge-intensive artificial intelligence systems.

The above ability is achieved by a process called *inductive learning*, that is, inductive inference from facts provided by a teacher or the environment. The study and modeling of this form of learning is one of the central topics of machine learning. This chapter outlines a theory of inductive learning and then presents a methodology for acquiring general concepts from examples.

Before going further into this topic, let us first discuss the potential for applications of inductive learning systems. One such application is an automated construction of knowledge bases for expert systems. The present approach to constructing knowledge bases involves a tedious process of formalizing experts' knowledge and encoding it in some knowledge representation system, such as production rules [Shortliffe, 1976; Davis & Lenat, 1981] or a semantic network [Brachman, 1979; Gaschnig, 1980]. Inductive learning programs could provide both an improvement of the current techniques and a basis for developing alternative knowledge acquisition methods.

In appropriately selected small domains, inductive programs are already able to determine decision rules by induction from examples of expert decisions. This process greatly simplifies the transfer of knowledge from an expert into a machine. The feasibility of such inductive knowledge acquisition has been demonstrated in the expert system PLANT/DS, for the diagnosis of soybean diseases. In this system, the diagnostic rules were developed in two ways: by formalizing experts' diagnostic processes and by induction from examples. In an experiment where both types of diagnostic rules were tested on a few hundred disease cases, the inductively-derived rules outperformed the expert-derived ones [Michalski & Chilausky, 1980]. Another example is an inductive acquisition of decision rules for a chess end-game [Michalski & Negri, 1977; Quinlan, 1979; Shapiro & Niblett, 1982; O'Rorke, 1982]. (See also Chapter 15 of this book.)

A less direct, but potentially promising, use of inductive learning is for the refinement of knowledge-bases initially developed by human experts. Here, inductive learning programs could be used to detect and rectify inconsistencies, to remove redundancies, to cover gaps, and to simplify expert-derived decision rules. By applying an inductive inference program to the data, consisting of original rules and examples of correct and incorrect results of these rules' performance in new situations, the rules could be incrementally improved with little or no human assistance.

Another important application of inductive programs is in various experimental sciences, such as biology, chemistry, psychology, medicine, and genetics. Here they could assist a user in detecting interesting conceptual patterns or in revealing structure in collections of observations. The widely used traditional mathematical and statistical data analysis techniques, such as regression analysis, numerical taxonomy, or factor analysis, are not sufficiently powerful for this task. Methods for *conceptual* data analysis are needed, that generate not merely mathematical formulas but logic-style descriptions, characterizing data in terms of high-level, human-oriented concepts and relationships. An early example of such an application is the META-DENDRAL program [Buchanan & Feigenbaum, 1978], which infers cleavage rules for mass-spectrometer simulation. (See its analysis in Chapter 3 of this book.)

There are two basic modes in which inductive programs can be utilized: as interactive tools for acquisition of knowledge from specific facts or examples, or as parts of machine-learning systems. In the first mode, a user supplies learning examples and exercises strong control over the way the program is used (for example, [Michalski, 975a; Quinlan, 1979; Michalski & Chilausky, 1980] and Chapter 15 of this book).

In the second mode, an inductive program is a component of an integrated learning system whose other components generate the needed learning examples [Buchanan *et al.*, 1979]. Such examples—positive and negative—constitute the feedback from the system's attempts to perform a desired task. An example of the second mode is the learning system LEX for symbolic integration (see Chapter 6 of this book), where a "generalizer" module performs inductive inference on instances provided by a "critic" module. Another example is discussed in Chapter 5 of this book, in the context of analogy-based learning.

From the viewpoint of applications, such as aiding the construction of expert systems or conceptual analysis of experimental data, the most relevant is *conceptual inductive learning*. We use this term to designate a type of inductive learning whose final products are symbolic descriptions expressed in high-level, human-oriented terms and forms (more details are given in Section 4.3.1). The descriptions typically apply to real world objects or phenomena, rather than abstract mathematical concepts or computations. This paper is concerned specifically with conceptual inductive learning.

The most frequently studied type of such learning is *concept learning from examples* (called also *concept acquisition*), whose task is to induce general descriptions of concepts from specific instances of these concepts. The early studies of this subject go back to the fifties, for example, [Hovland, 1952; Bruner *et al.*, 1956; Newell *et al.*, 1960; Amarel, 1960; Feigenbaum, 1963; Kochen, 1960; Banerji, 1962; Simon & Kotovsky, 1963; Hunt *et al.*, 1966; Håjek *et al.*, 1966; Bongard, 1970]. Among more recent contributions there are, for instance, [Winston, 1970; Waterman, 1970; Michalski, 1972; Hayes-Roth, 1973; Simon & Lea, 1974; Stoffel, 1974; Vere, 1975; Larson & Michalski, 1977; Mitchell, 1978; Quinlan, 1979; Moraga, 1981]. An important variant of concept learning from examples is the *incremental concept refinement*, where the input information includes, in addition to the training examples, previously-learned hypotheses, or human-provided initial hypotheses that may be partially incorrect or incomplete [Michalski & Larson, 1978]. Chapter 3 of this book discusses various evaluation criteria and several methods for concept learning from examples.

Another type of conceptual inductive learning is *concept learning from* observation (or *descriptive generalization*), concerned with establishing new concepts or theories characterizing given facts. This area includes such topics as automated theory formation (for example, [Lenat, 1976] and Chapter 9 of this book), discovery of relationships in data (for example, [Hájek & Havránek, 1978; Pokorny, 1980; Zagoruiko, 1981] and Chapter 10 of this book), or an automatic construction of taxonomies (for example, Chapter 11 of this book). Differences between concept learning from examples and concept learning from observation are discussed in more detail in the next section.

Conceptual inductive learning has a strong cognitive science flavor. Its emphasis on inducing human-oriented, rather than machine-oriented descriptions, and its primary interest in nonmathematical domains distinguishes it from other types of inductive learning, such as grammatical inference and program synthesis. In grammatical inference, the task is to determine a formal grammar that can generate a given set of symbol strings (for example, [Solomonoff, 1964; Biermann & Feldman, 1972; Yau & Fu, 1978; Gaines, 1979]). In program synthesis the objective is to construct a computer program from I/O pairs or computational traces, or to transform a program from one form to another by applying correctness-preserving transformation rules (for example, [Shaw *et al.*, 1975; Burstall & Darlington, 1977; Case & Smith, 1981; Biermann, 1978; Jouannaud & Kodratoff, 1980; Smith, 1980; Pettorossi, 1980]). The final result of such learning is a computer program, in an assumed programming language, destined for machine rather than human "consumption". For example, the method of "model inference" by Shapiro [1981] constructs a PROLOG program characterizing a given set of mathematical facts.

Recent years have witnessed the development of a number of task-oriented inductive learning systems that have demonstrated an impressive performance in their specific domain of application. Major weaknesses, however, persist in much of the research in this area. Most systems lack generality and extensibility. The theoretical principles upon which they are built are rarely well explained. Lack of common terminology and an adequate formal theory makes it difficult to compare different learning methods.

In the following sections we formulate logical foundations of inductive learning, define various types of such learning, present inference rules for generalizing concept descriptions, and finally describe a general methodology, called Star, for learning structural descriptions from examples. To improve the readability of this chapter, Table 4-1 provides a list of basic symbols used, with a short explanation. The Appendix gives the details of the description language used (the annotated predicate calculus).

Table 4-1: A Table of Basic Symbols

$\sim$	negation
&	conjunction (logical product)
$\vee$	disjunction (logical sum)
$\Rightarrow$	implication
$\Leftrightarrow$	logical equivalence
$\leftrightarrow$	term rewriting
$\setminus$	exception (symmetric difference)
F	a set of facts (formally, a predicate that is true for all the facts)
H	a hypothesis (an inductive assertion)
$\vert>$	specialization
$\vert<$	generalization
$\vert=$	reformulation
$\exists\ v_i$	existential quantifier over v_i
$\exists(I)\ v_i$	numerical quantifier over v_i (I is a set of integers)
$\forall v_i$	universal quantifier over v_i
D_i	a concept description
K_i	a predicate asserting the name of a concept (a class)
::>	the implication linking a concept description with a concept name
e_i	an event (a description of an object or a situation)
E_i	a predicate that is true only for the training events of concept K_i
x_i	an attribute (zero- or one-argument descriptor)
LEF	a lexicographic evaluation functional
DOM(p)	the domain of descriptor p

4.2 TYPES OF INDUCTIVE LEARNING

4.2.1 Inductive Paradigm

As mentioned before, inductive learning is a process of acquiring knowledge by drawing inductive inferences from teacher- or environment- provided facts. Such a process involves operations of generalizing, specializing, transforming, correcting and refining knowledge representations. Although it is one of the most common forms of learning, it has one fundamental weakness: except for special cases, the acquired knowledge cannot, in principle, be completely validated. This predicament, observed by the Scottish philosopher David Hume in the 18th century, is due to the fact that inductively-acquired assertions are hypotheses with a potentially infinite number of consequences, while only a finite number of confirming tests can be performed.

Traditional inquiries into inductive inference have therefore dealt with questions of what are the best criteria for guiding the selection of inductive assertions, and how these assertions can be confirmed. These are difficult problems, permeating all scientific activities. The search for answers has turned inductive inference into a battlefield of philosophers and logicians. There was even doubt whether it would ever be possible to formalize inductive inference and perform it on a machine. For example, philosopher Karl Popper [1968] believed that inductive inference requires an irrational element. Bertrand Russell [1946] stated:

"So far no method has been found which would make it possible to invent hypotheses by rule." George Polya [1954] in his pioneering and now classic treatise on plausible inference (of which inductive inference is a special case) observed: "A person has a background, a machine has not; indeed, you can build a machine to draw demonstrative conclusions for you, but I think you can never build a machine that will draw plausible inferences."

The above pessimistic prospects are now being revised. With the development of modern computers and subsequent advances in artificial intelligence research, it is now possible to provide a machine with a significant amount of background information. Also, the problem of automating inductive inference can be simplified by concentrating on the subject of hypothesis generation, while ascribing to humans the question of how to adequately validate them. Some successful inductive inference systems have already been built and a body of knowledge is emerging about the nature of this inference. The rest of this section will analyze the logical basis for inductive inference, and then Section 4.5 will present various generalization rules, which can be viewed as inductive inference rules.

In contrast to deduction, the starting premises of induction are specific facts rather than general axioms. The goal of inference is to formulate plausible general assertions that explain the given facts and are able to predict new facts. In other words, inductive inference attempts to derive a complete and correct description of a given phenomenon from specific observations of that phenomenon or of parts of it. As mentioned earlier, of the two aspects of inductive inference—the generation of plausible hypotheses and their validation (the establishment of their truth status)—only the first is of primary interest to inductive learning research. The problem of hypothesis validation, a subject of various philosophical inquiries (for example, [Carnap, 1962]) is considered to be of lesser importance, because it is assumed that the generated hypotheses are judged by human experts, and tested by known methods of deductive inference and statistics.

As described in Chapter 1 of this book, there are several different methods by which a human (or a machine) can acquire knowledge, such as rote learning (or learning by being programmed), learning from instruction (or learning by being told), learning from teacher-provided examples (concept acquisition), and learning by observing the environment and making discoveries (learning from observation and discovery).

Although all of these ways except the first involve some amount of inductive inference, in the last two, that is, in learning from examples and in learning from observation, this inference is the central operation. These two forms are therefore considered to be the major forms of inductive learning. In order to explain them, let us formulate a general paradigm for inductive inference:

Given:

- *Observational statements* (facts), F, that represent specific knowledge about some objects, situations, processes, and so on,

- A *tentative inductive assertion* (which may be null),
- *Background knowledge* that defines the assumptions and constraints imposed on the observational statements and generated candidate inductive assertions, and any relevant problem domain knowledge. The last includes the *preference criterion* characterizing the desirable properties of the sought inductive assertion.

Find:

- An *inductive assertion* (hypothesis), H, that tautologically or weakly implies the observational statements, and satisfies the background knowledge.

A hypothesis H tautologically implies facts F if F is a logical consequence of H, that is, if the expression H $\Rightarrow$ F is true under all interpretations ("$\Rightarrow$" denotes logical implication). This is expressed as follows:

H |> F (read: H specializes to F) (1)

or

F |< H (read: F generalizes to H) (2)

Symbols |> and |< are called the *specialization* and *generalization* symbols, respectively. If H $\Rightarrow$ F is valid, and H is true, then by the law of detachment (*modus ponens*) F must be true. Deriving F from H (deductive inference), is, therefore, truth-preserving. In contrast, deriving H from F (inductive inference) is not truth-preserving, but falsity-preserving; that is, if some facts falsify F, then they also must falsify H. (More explanation on this topic is given in Section 4.5.)

The condition that H *weakly implies* F means that facts F are not certain but only plausible or partial consequences of H. By allowing weak implication, this paradigm includes methods for generating "soft" hypotheses, which hold only probabilistically, and partial hypotheses, which account for some but not all of the facts (for example, hypotheses representing "dominant patterns" or characterizing inconsistent data). In the following we will limit our attention to hypotheses that tautologically imply facts.

For any given set of facts, a potentially infinite number of hypotheses can be generated that imply these facts. Background knowledge is therefore necessary to provide the constraints and a preference criterion for reducing the infinite choice to one hypothesis or a few most preferable ones.

A typical way of defining such a criterion is to specify the preferable properties of the hypothesis—for example, to require that the hypothesis is the shortest or the most economical description consistent with all the facts (as, for example, in [Michalski, 1973]). Such a "biased-choice" criterion is necessary when the description language is complete, that is, able to express any possible hypothesis. An alternative is to use a "biased-language" criterion [Mitchell, 1978], restricting the description language in which hypotheses are expressed (that is, to use an incomplete description language). Although in many methods the background knowledge is not explicitly stated, the authors make implicit assumptions serving the same purpose. More details on the criteria for selecting hypotheses are given in Section 4.4.7.

4.2.2 Concept Acquisition versus Descriptive Generalization

As mentioned in the Introduction, one can distinguish between two major types of inductive learning: *learning from examples* (concept acquisition) and *learning from observation* (descriptive generalization). In concept acquisition, the observational statements are characterizations of some objects (situations, processes, and so on) preclassified by a teacher into one or more classes (concepts). The induced hypothesis can be viewed as a concept recognition rule, such that if an object satisfies this rule, then it represents the given concept. For example, a recognition rule for the concept "philosopher" might be:

> "A person who pursues wisdom and gains the knowledge of underlying reality by intellectual means and moral self-discipline is a philosopher."

In descriptive generalization the goal is to determine a general description (a law, a theory) characterizing a collection of observations. For example, observing that the philosophers Aristotle, Plato, and Socrates were Greek, but that Spencer was British, one might conclude:

> "Most philosophers were Greek."

Thus, in contrast to concept acquisition that produces descriptions for classifying objects into classes on the basis of the objects' properties, descriptive generalization produces descriptions specifying properties of objects belonging to a certain class. Here are some example problems belonging to the above two categories:

1. Concept Acquisition:
    - Learning a *characteristic description* of a class of objects, that specifies all common properties of known objects in the class, and by that defines the class in the context of an unlimited number of other object classes (for example, [Bongard, 1967; Winston, 1970; Stoffel, 1974; Vere, 1975; Cohen, 1977; Hayes-Roth & McDermott, 1978; Mitchell, 1978; Stepp, 1978; Michalski, 1980a] and Chapter 3 of this book).
    - Learning a *discriminant description* of a class of objects that distinguishes the given class from a limited number of other classes (for example, [Michalski, 1973; Quinlan, 1979; Michalski, 1980a] and Chapter 15 of this book).
    - Inferring *sequence extrapolation rules* (for example, [Simon & Kotovsky, 1963; Dietterich, 1979]) able to predict the next element (a symbol, a number, an object, and so on) in a given sequence.

2. Descriptive Generalization:
   - Formulating a theory characterizing a collection of entities (for example, a number theory, as in [Lenat, 1976] and Chapter 9 of this book).
   - Discovering patterns in observational data (for example, [Soloway & Riseman, 1977; Hájek & Havránek, 1978; Pokorny, 1980; Zagoruiko, 1981] and Chapter 10 of this book).
   - Determining a taxonomic description (classification) of a collection of objects (for example, [Michalski, 980c; Michalski *et al.*, 1981] and Chapter 11 of this book).

This paper is concerned primarily with problems of concept acquisition. In this case, the set of observational statements F can be viewed as a collection of implications:

$$F : \{e_{ik} \; ::> \; K_i\}, \; i \in I \quad (3)$$

where e_{ik} (a *training event*) denotes a description of the kth example of *concept* (class) asserted by predicate K_i (for short, class K_i) and I is a set indexing classes K_i. It is assumed here that any given event represents only one concept. Symbol ::> is used here, and will be used henceforth, to denote the implication linking a concept description with a predicate asserting the concept name (in order to distinguish this implication from the implication between arbitrary descriptions). The inductive assertion H can be characterized as a set of concept recognition rules:

$$H : \{D_i \; ::> \; K_i\}, \; i \in I \quad (4)$$

where D_i is a concept description of class K_i, that is, an expression of conditions, such that when they are satisfied by an object, the object is considered an instance of class K_i.

According to the definition of inductive assertion, we must have:

$$H \; |> \; F \quad (5)$$

By substituting (3) and (4) for F and H, respectively, in (5), and making appropriate transformations, one can derive the following conditions to be satisfied in order that (5) holds:

$$\forall \; i \in I \; (E_i \Rightarrow D_i) \quad (6)$$

and

$$\forall i,j \in I \; (D_i \Rightarrow \sim E_j), \text{ if } j \neq i \quad (7)$$

where E_i, $i \in I$, is a description satisfied by all training events of class K_i, and only by such events (the logical disjunction of training events).

Expression (6) is called the *completeness condition*, and (7) the *consistency condition*. These two conditions are the requirements that must be satisfied for an inductive assertion to be acceptable as a concept recognition rule. The completeness condition states that every training event of some class must satisfy the description D_i of the same class (since the opposite does not have to hold, D_i is equivalent to, or more general than, E_i). The consistency condition states that if an event satisfies a description of some class, then it cannot be a member of a training set of any other class. In learning a concept from examples and counter-examples, the latter constitute the "other" class.

The completeness and consistency conditions provide the logical foundation of algorithms for concept learning from examples. We will see in Section 4.5 that to derive D_i satisfying the completeness condition one can adopt some inference rules of formal logic.

4.2.3 Characteristic versus Discriminant Descriptions

The completeness and consistency conditions allow us to clearly explain the distinction between the previously mentioned characteristic and discriminant descriptions. A characteristic description of a class of objects (also known as *conjunctive generalization*) is an expression that satisfies the completeness condition or is the logical product of such expressions. It is typically a conjunction of some simple properties common to all objects in the class. From the applications viewpoint, the most interesting are *maximal characteristic descriptions* (maximal conjunctive generalizations) that are the most specific (that is, the longest) logical products characterizing all objects in the given class, using terms of the given language. Such descriptions are intended to discriminate the given class from all other possible classes (for illustration see Section 4.7.2).

A discriminant description is an expression that satisfies the completeness and consistency condition, or is the logical disjunction of such expressions. It specifies one or more ways to distinguish the given class from a fixed number of other classes. The most interesting are *minimal discriminant descriptions* that are the shortest (that is, have the minimum number of descriptors) expressions distinguishing all objects in the given class from objects of the other classes. Such descriptions are intended to specify the minimum information sufficient to identify the given class among a fixed number of other classes (for illustration see Section 4.7.1).

4.2.4 Single- versus Multiple-concept Learning

It is instructive to distinguish between learning a single concept, and learning a collection of concepts. In *single concept learning*, one can distinguish two cases: *(i)* when observational statements are just examples of the concept to be learned (learning from "positive" instances only); and *(ii)* when they are examples and counter-examples of the concept (learning from "positive" and "negative" instances).

In the first case, because of the lack of counter-examples, the consistency condition (7) is not applicable, and there is no natural limit to which description D_i (here, $i = 1$) can be generalized. One way to impose such a limit is to specify restrictions on the form and properties of the sought description. For example, one may require that it be the maximal characteristic description, that is, the longest conjunctive statement satisfying the completeness condition (for example, [Vere, 1975; Hayes-Roth & McDermott, 1978]). Another way is to require that the description not exceed a given degree of generality, measured, for example, by the ratio of the number of all distinct events which could potentially satisfy the description to the number of training instances [Stepp, 1978].

In the second case, when the teacher also provides counter-examples of the given concept, the learning process is considerably simplified. These counter-examples can be viewed as representing a "different class", and the consistency condition (7) provides an obvious limit on the extent to which a hypothesis can be generalized. The most useful counter-examples are the so-called "near misses" that only slightly differ from positive examples [Winston, 1970, 1977]. Such examples place stronger constraints on the generalization process than randomly-generated examples.

In *multiple-concept learning* one can also distinguish two cases: *(i)* when descriptions D_i of different classes are required to be mutually disjoint, that is, no event can satisfy more than one description; and *(ii)* when they are overlapping. In an overlapping generalization an event may satisfy more than one description. In some situations this is desirable. For example, if a patient has two diseases, his symptoms should satisfy the descriptions of both diseases, and in this case the consistency condition is not applicable.

An overlapping generalization can be interpreted in such a way that it always indicates only one decision class. For example, the concept recognition rules, D_i ::> K_i, can be applied in a linear order, and the first rule satisfied generates the decision. In this case, if a concept description D_i for class K_i contains a conjunctively-linked condition A, and precedes the rule for class K_j that contains condition ~A, then the condition ~A is superfluous and can be removed. As a result, the linearly-ordered recognition rules can be significantly simplified. For example, the set of linearly-ordered rules:

$$D_1 \ ::> \ K_1$$
$$D_2 \ ::> \ K_2$$
$$D_3 \ ::> \ K_3$$

is logically equivalent to the set of (unordered) rules:

$$D_1 \ ::> \ K_1$$
$$\sim D_1 \ \& \ D_2 \ ::> \ K_2$$
$$\sim D_1 \ \& \ \sim D_2 \ \& \ D_3 \ ::> \ K_3$$

There are also other ways to derive a single decision from overlapping rules, such as those given in [Davis & Lenat, 1981].

The above forms of multiple-concept learning have been implemented in inductive programs AQVAL/1 [Michalski, 1973] and AQ11 [Michalski & Larson, 1978].

4.3 DESCRIPTION LANGUAGE

4.3.1 Bias Toward Comprehensibility

In concept acquisition, the main interest is in derivation of symbolic descriptions that are human-oriented, that is, that are easy to understand and easy to use for creating mental models of the information they convey. A tentative criterion for judging inductive assertions from such a viewpoint is provided by the following *comprehensibility postulate*:

> *The results of computer induction should be symbolic descriptions of given entities, semantically and structurally similar to those a human expert might produce observing the same entities. Components of these descriptions should be comprehensible as single "chunks" of information, directly interpretable in natural language, and should relate quantitative and qualitative concepts in an integrated fashion.*

As a practical guide, one can assume that the components of descriptions (single sentences, rules, labels on nodes in a hierarchy, and so on) should be expressions that contain only a few (say, less than five) conditions in a conjunction, few single conditions in a disjunction, at most one level of bracketing, at most one implication, no more than two quantifiers, and no recursion (the exact numbers may be disputed,[2] but the principle is clear). Sentences are kept within such limits by substituting names for appropriate subcomponents. Any operators used in descriptions should have a simple intuitive interpretation. Conceptually related sentences are organized into a simple data structure, preferably a shallow hierarchy or a linear list, such as a frame [Minsky, 1975]. (See also Chapter 9 of this book.)

The rationale behind this postulate is to ensure that descriptions generated by inductive inference bear similarity to human knowledge representations [Hintzman, 1978], and therefore, are easy to comprehend. This requirement is very important for many applications. For example, in developing knowledge bases for expert systems, it is important that human experts can easily and reliably verify the inductive assertions and relate them to their own domain knowledge. Satisfying the comprehensibility postulate will also facilitate debugging or improving the inductive programs themselves. When the complexity of problems undertaken by computer induction becomes very great, the comprehensibility of the generated descriptions will likely be a crucial criterion. This research orientation fits well within the role of artificial intelligence envisaged by Michie [1977] to study and develop methods for man-machine conceptual interface and knowledge refinement.

---

[2]The numbers mentioned seem to apply to the majority of human descriptive sentences.

4.3.2 Language of Assertions

One of the difficulties with inductive inference is its open-endedness. This means that when one makes an inductive assertion about some aspect of reality there is no natural limit to the level of detail in which this reality may be described, or to the richness of forms in which this assertion can be expressed. Consequently, when conducting research in this area, it is necessary to circumscribe very carefully the goals and the problem to be solved. This includes defining the language and the scope of allowed forms in which assertions will be expressed, as well as the modes of inference which will be used. The description language should be chosen so that crucial features can be easily encoded while peripheral or irrelevant information ignored.

An instructive criterion for classifying inductive learning methods is therefore the type of language used to express inductive assertions. Many authors use a restricted form of predicate calculus or closely related notation (for example, [Plotkin, 1971; Fikes *et al.*, 1972; Morgan, 1975; Vere, 1975; Banerji, 1980; Michalski, 1980a; Sammut, 1981; Zagoruiko, 1981]). Some other formalisms include decision trees [Hunt *et al.*, 1966; Quinlan, 1979] (see also Chapter 15 of this book), production rules (for example, [Waterman, 1970; Hedrick, 1974] (see also Chapter 16 of this book), semantic nets (Chapter 13), and frames (Chapter 9). In his earlier work (for example, [Michalski, 1972, 1973, 1975a, 1975b] this author used a multiple-valued logic propositional calculus with typed variables, called VL_1 (the variable-valued logic system one). Later on an extension of the predicate calculus, called VL_2, was developed, that was especially oriented to facilitate inductive inference [Michalski, 980a].

Here we will use a somewhat modified and extended version of the latter language, to be called the *annotated predicate calculus* (APC). The APC adds to predicate calculus additional forms and new concepts that increase its expressive power and facilitate inductive inference. The major differences between the annotated predicate calculus and the conventional predicate calculus can be summarized as follows:

1. Each predicate, variable and function (referred to collectively as a *descriptor*) is assigned an *annotation* that contains relevant problem- oriented information. The annotation may contain the definition of the concept represented by a descriptor, a characterization of its relationship to other concepts, a specification of the set over which the descriptor ranges (when it is a variable or a function), a characterization of the structure of this set, and so on (see Section 4.4).
2. In addition to predicates, the APC also includes *compound predicates*. Arguments of such predicates can be *compound terms*, composed of two or more ordinary terms.
3. Predicates that express relations $=$, $\neq$, $\geq$, $>$, $\leq$ and $<$ between terms or between compound terms are expressed explicitly as *relational statements*, also called *selectors*.

4. In addition to the universal and existential quantifiers, there is also a *numerical quantifier* that expresses quantitative information about the objects satisfying an expression.

The concept of annotation is explained in more detail in the next section. Other aspects of the language are described in the Appendix. (The reader interested in a thorough understanding of this work is encouraged to read the Appendix at this point.)

4.4 PROBLEM BACKGROUND KNOWLEDGE

4.4.1 Basic Components

As we mentioned earlier, given a set of observational statements, one may construct a potentially infinite number of inductive assertions that imply these statements. It is therefore necessary to use some additional information, *problem background knowledge*, to constrain the space of possible inductive assertions and locate the most desirable one(s). In this section, we shall look at various components of the problem background knowledge employed in the inductive learning methodology called Star, described in Section 4.6. These components include:

- Information about descriptors (i.e., predicates, variables, or functions) used in observational statements. This information is provided by an annotation assigned to each descriptor (Section 4.4.3).
- Assumptions about the form of observational and inductive assertions.
- A preference criterion that specifies the desirable properties of inductive assertions sought.
- A variety of inference rules, heuristics, and specialized procedures, general and problem-dependent, that allow a learning system to generate logical consequences of given assertions and new descriptors.

Before we examine these components in greater detail, let us first consider the problem of how the choice of descriptors in the observational statements affects the generated inductive assertions.

4.4.2 Relevance of the Initial Descriptors

A fundamental problem underlying any machine inductive learning task is that of what information is provided to the machine and what information the machine is expected to produce or learn. As specified in the inductive paradigm, the major component of the input to a learning system is a set of observational statements. The descriptors used in those statements are observable characteristics and available measurements of objects under consideration. These descriptors are selected as relevant to the learning task by a teacher specifying the problem.

Determining these descriptors is a major part of any inductive learning problem. If they capture the essential properties of the objects, the role of the learning process is simply to arrange these descriptors into an expression constituting an appropriate inductive assertion. If the selected descriptors are completely irrelevant to the learning task (as the color, weight, or shape of men in chess is irrelevant to deciding the right move), no learning system will be able to construct a meaningful inductive assertion.

There is a range of intermediate possibilities between the above two extremes. Consequently, learning methods can be characterized on the basis of the degree to which the initial descriptors are relevant to the learning problem.

Three cases can be distinguished:

1. **Complete relevance**—In this case all descriptors in the observational statements are assumed to be directly relevant to the learning task. The task of the learning system is to formulate an inductive assertion that is a mathematical or logical expression of some assumed general form that properly relates these descriptors (for example, a regression polynomial).
2. **Partial relevance**—Observational statements may contain a large number of irrelevant or redundant descriptors. Some of the descriptors, however, are relevant. The task of the learning system is to select the most relevant ones and construct from them an appropriate inductive assertion.
3. **Indirect relevance**—Observational statements may contain no directly-relevant descriptors. However, among the initial descriptors there are some that can be used to construct derived descriptors that are directly relevant. The task of the learning system is to construct those derived descriptors and formulate an appropriate inductive assertion. A simple form of this case occurs, for example, when a relevant descriptor is the volume of an object, but the observational statements contain only the information about the object's dimensions (and various irrelevant facts).

The above three cases represent problem statements that put progressively less demand on the relevance of the initial descriptors (that is, that require less work from the person defining the problem) and more demand on the learning system. Early work on adaptive control systems and concept formation represents case 1. More recent research has dealt with case 2, which is addressed in *selective inductive learning*. A method of such learning must possess efficient mechanisms for determining combinations of descriptors that are relevant and sufficient for the learning task. Formal logic provides such mechanisms, and therefore it has become the major underlying formalism for selective methods.

An example of a selective learning method is the one implemented in program AQ11 [Michalski & Larson, 1978] that inductively determined soybean disease diagnostic rules for the system PLANT/DS, mentioned in the Introduction. A different type of selective method was implemented in program ID3 (Chapter 15) that determines a decision tree for classifying a large number of events. A comparison between these two programs is described by O'Rorke [1982].

Case 3 represents the task of *constructive inductive learning*. Here, a method must be capable of formulating new descriptors (that is, new concepts, new variables, and the like), of evaluating their relevance to the learning task and of using them to construct inductive assertions. There has been relatively little done in this area. The "automated mathematician" program AM (Chapter 9) can be classified as a domain-specific system of this category. Some constructive learning capabilities have been incorporated in system BACON that automatically formulates mathematical expressions encapsulating chemical and other laws [Langley *et al.*, 1980] (see also Chapter 10). The general-purpose INDUCE program for learning structural descriptions from examples incorporates several constructive generalization techniques [Larson, 1977; Michalski, 1980a]. Sections 4.5 and 4.6 give more details on this subject.

4.4.3 Annotation of Descriptors

An *annotation* of a descriptor (that is, of a predicate, variable, or function) is a store of background information about this descriptor tailored to the learning problem under consideration. It may include:

- A specification of the *domain* and the *type* of the descriptor (see below).
- A specification of operators applicable to it.
- A specification of the constraints and the relationships between the descriptor and other descriptors.
- For numerical descriptors, the mean, the variance, or the complete probability distribution of values for the problem under consideration.
- A characterization of objects to which the descriptor is applicable (such as a characterization of its possible arguments).
- A specification of a descriptor class containing the given descriptor, that is, the parent node in a generalization hierarchy of descriptors (for example, for descriptors "length", "width", and "height", the parent node would be the "dimensions").
- Synonyms that can be used to denote the descriptor.
- A definition of a descriptor (when it is derived from some other descriptors).
- If a descriptor denotes a class of objects, typical examples of this class can be specified.

Let us consider some of the above components of the annotation in greater detail.

4.4.4 The Domain and Type of a Descriptor

Given a specific problem, it is usually possible to specify the set of values each descriptor could potentially adopt in characterizing any object in the population under consideration. Such a set is called the *domain* (or the *value set*) of the descriptor. The domain is used to constrain the extent to which a descriptor can be generalized. For example, the information that the temperature of a living human being may vary, say, only between 34°C and 44°C prevents the system from considering inductive assertions in which the descriptor "body temperature" would assume values beyond these limits.

Other important information for conducting the generalization process is concerned with the structure of the domain, that is, with the relationship existing among the elements of the domain. For numerical descriptors, such relationships are specified by the measurement scale. Depending on the structure of the descriptor domain, we distinguish among three basic types of descriptors:

1. **Nominal (categorical) descriptors**—The value set of such descriptors consists of independent symbols or names, that is, no structure is assumed to relate the values in the domain. For example, "blood-type(person)" and "name(person)" are unary nominal descriptors. Predicates, that is, descriptors with the value set {True, False}, and n-ary functions whose ranges are unordered sets, are also nominal descriptors. An example of a two-argument nominal descriptor is "license-plate-number(car, owner)", which denotes a function assigning to a specific car of the given owner a license plate number.
2. **Linear descriptors**—The value set of linear descriptors is a totally ordered set. For example, a person's military rank or the temperature, weight, or number of items in a set is such a descriptor. Variables measured on ordinal, interval, ratio, and absolute scales are special cases of a linear descriptor. Functions that map a set into a totally-ordered set are also linear descriptors, for example, "distance(P_1,P_2)".
3. **Structured descriptors**—The value set of such descriptors has a tree-oriented graph structure that reflects the generalization relation between the values, that is, is a *generalization hierarchy*. A parent node in such a structure represents a more general concept than the concepts represented by its children nodes. For example, in the value set of descriptor "place", "U.S.A." would be a parent node of the nodes "Indiana", "Illinois", "Iowa", and so on. The domain of structured descriptors is defined by a set of inference rules specified in the problem background knowledge (see, for example, descriptor "shape(B_i)" in Section 4.7.

Structured descriptors can be further subdivided into ordered and unordered structured descriptors (see Chapter 11).

Sometimes, descriptors themselves can also be organized into a generalization hierarchy. For example, as already mentioned, the descriptors "length", "width", and "depth" belong to a class of "dimensions". Information about the type of a descriptor is useful as it determines the operations applicable to a descriptor.

4.4.5 Constraints on the Description Space

For a given induction problem there may exist a variety of constraints on the space of the acceptable concept descriptions, due to the specific properties and relationships among descriptors. Here are a few examples of such relationships:

- **Interdependence among values**—In many practical problems some variables specify a state of an object, and some other variables characterize the state. Depending on the values of the state-specifying variables, the variables characterizing a state may or may not be needed. For example, if a descriptor "state(plant's leaf)" takes on value "diseased", then a descriptor "leaf discoloration" will be used to characterize the change of the leaf's color. When the descriptor "state(plant's leaf)" takes on value "normal", then obviously the "leaf discoloration" descriptor is irrelevant. Such information can be represented by an implication:

  $$[\text{state(plant's leaf)} = \text{normal}] \Rightarrow [\text{discoloration(plant's leaf)} = \text{NA}]$$

  where NA is a special value meaning "not applicable".
- **Properties of descriptors**—Descriptors that are relations between objects may have certain general properties—they can be reflexive, symmetric, transitive, and so on. All such properties are defined as assertions in the annotated predicate calculus (see the Appendix). For example, the transitivity of relation "above(P_1,P_2)" can be defined as:

  $$\forall\, P_1, P_2, P_3, (\text{above}(P_1,P_2)\ \&\ \text{above}(P_2,P_3)) \Rightarrow \text{above}(P_1,P_3)$$
- **Interrelationships among descriptors**—In some problems there may exist relationships between descriptors that constrain their values. For example, the length of an object is assumed always to be greater than or equal to its width:

  $$\forall\, P,\ \text{length}(P) \geq \text{width}(P)$$

  Also, descriptors may be related by known equations. For example, the area of a rectangle is the arithmetic product of its length and width:

  $$\forall\, P, ([\text{shape}(P) = \text{rectangle}] \Rightarrow [\text{area}(P) = \text{length}(P) \times \text{width}(P)])$$

  The infix operator "$\times$" is used to simplify notation of the term multiply(length(P), width(P)).

4.4.6 The Form of Observational and Inductive Assertions

The basic form of assertions in the Star methodology is a *c-expression*, defined as a conjunctive statement:

<quantifier form><conjunction of relational statements> (8)

where <quantifier form> stands for zero or more quantifiers, and <relational

statements> are predicates in a special form, as defined in the Appendix. The following is an example of a c-expression:

$\exists$. P_0,P_1,P_2,P_3([contains(P_0,P_1,P_2,P_3)][ontop(P_1&P_2,P_3)][length(P_1)=3..5] [weight(P_1) > weight(P_2][color(P_1)=red $\vee$ blue][shape(P_1 & P_2 & P_3)=box]

that can be paraphrased in English:

> An object P_0 contains parts P_1, P_2 and P_3 and only these parts. Parts P_1 & P_2 are on top of part P_3, length of P_1 is between 3 and 5, the weight of P_1 is greater than that of P_2, the color of P_1 is red or blue, and the shape of all three parts is box.

An important special case of a c-expression is an *a-expression* (an atomic expression), in which there is no "internal disjunction" (see the Appendix).

Note that due to the use of internal disjunction a c-expression represents a more general concept than a universally quantified conjunction of predicates, used in typical production rules.

Progressively more complex forms of expressions are described below:

- A *case expression* is a logical product of implications:

  $$[L = a_i] \Rightarrow Exp_i, \; i = 1,2,...$$

  where a_i are single elements or disjoint subsets of elements from the domain of descriptor L, and Exp_i are c-expressions.

  A case expression describes a class of objects by splitting it into separate cases, each represented by a different value(s) of a certain descriptor.

- An *implicative expression* (i-expression):

  $$C \; \& \; (C_1 \Rightarrow C_2) \tag{9}$$

  where C, C_1 and C_2 are c-expressions.

  This form of description is very useful when the occurrence of some properties (defined in C_2) depends on the occurrence of some other properties (defined in C_1). Typical production rules used in expert systems are a special case of (9), where C is omitted and no internal logical operators are used. When ($C_1 \Rightarrow C_2$) is omitted, then the conditional expression becomes a c-expression.

- A *disjunctive expression* (d-expression), defined as a disjunction of implicative expressions.

- An *exception-based expression* (e-expression). In some situations it is simpler to formulate a somewhat overgeneralized statement and indicate exceptions than to formulate a precise statement. The following form is used for such purposes:

  $$D_1 \setminus D_2$$

  where D_1 and D_2 are d-expressions. This expression is equivalent to ($\sim D_2 \Rightarrow D_1$) & ($D_2 \Rightarrow \; \sim D_1$).

Observational assertions are formulated as a set of rules:

$$\{\text{a-expression} \;\; ::> \;\; K_i\} \tag{10}$$

Inductive assertions are expressed as a set of rules:

$$\{\text{EXP} \;\; ::> \;\; \text{c-expression}\} \tag{11}$$

where EXP is a c-expression or any of the more complex expressions described above. It is also assumed that the left side and the right side of (11) satisfy the principle of comprehensibility described in Section 4.2.

4.4.7 The Preference Criterion

In spite of the constraints imposed by the above components of the background knowledge, the number of inductive assertions consistent with observational statements may still be unlimited. The problem then arises of choosing the most desirable inductive assertion(s). In making such a choice, one must take into consideration the aspects of the particular inductive learning problem; therefore the definition of a "preference criterion" for selecting a hypothesis is a part of the problem background knowledge. Typically, the inductive assertions are chosen on the basis of some simplicity criterion (such as given in [Kemeni, 1953; Post, 1960]).

In the context of scientific discovery, philosopher Karl Popper [1968] has advocated constructing hypotheses that are both simple and easy to refute. By generating such hypotheses and conducting experiments aimed at refuting them, he argues, one has the best chance of ultimately formulating the true hypothesis. In order to use this criterion for automated inductive inference, it is necessary to define it formally. This, however, is not easy because there does not seem to exist any universal measure of hypothesis simplicity and refutability.

Among more specific measures for evaluating the "quality" of inductive assertions one may list:

- An overall simplicity for human comprehension, measured, for example, by the number of descriptors and number of operators used in an inductive assertion.
- The degree of "fit" between the inductive and observational assertions (measured, for example, by the degree of generalization, defined as the amount of uncertainty that any given description satisfying the inductive assertion corresponds to some observational statement [Michalski, 980c]).
- The cost of measuring values of descriptors used in the inductive assertion.
- The computational cost of evaluating the inductive assertion.
- The memory required for storing the inductive assertion.
- The amount of information needed for encoding the assertion using predefined operators [Coulon & Kayser, 1978].

The importance given to each such measure depends on the ultimate purpose of constructing the inductive assertions. For that reason, the Star methodology allows a user to build a global preference criterion as a function of such measures, tailored to a specific inductive problem. Since some of the above measures are computationally costly, simpler measures are used, called *elementary criteria*. Among such criteria are: the number of c-expressions in the assertion, the total number of relational statements, the ratio of possible but unseen events implied by an assertion to the total number of training events (a simple measure of generalization), and the total number of different descriptors. The global preference criterion is formulated by selecting from the above list those elementary criteria that are most relevant to the problem, and then arranging them into a *lexicographic evaluation functional* (LEF). A LEF is defined as a sequence of criterion-tolerance pairs:

$$\text{LEF: } (c_1, \tau_1), (c_2, \tau_2)... \tag{12}$$

where c_i is an elementary criterion selected from the available "menu", and τ_i is a *tolerance threshold* for criterion c_i ($\tau_i \in [0..100\%]$).

Given a set of inductive assertions, the LEF determines the most preferable one(s) in the following way:

In the first step, all assertions are evaluated from the viewpoint of criterion c_1, and those which score best, or within the range defined by the threshold τ_1 from the best, are retained. Next the retained assertions are evaluated from the viewpoint of criterion c_2 and reduced similarly as above, using tolerance τ_2. This process continues until either the subset of retained assertions contains only one assertion (the "best" one) or the sequence of criterion-tolerance pairs is exhausted. In the latter case, the retained set contains assertions that are equivalent from the viewpoint of the LEF.

An important and somewhat surprising property of such an approach is that the same learning system can generate either characteristic or discriminant descriptions of object classes by properly defining the preference criterion (see Section 4.7).

4.5 GENERALIZATION RULES

4.5.1 Definitions and an Overview

Constructing an inductive assertion from observational statements can be conceptually characterized as a heuristic state-space search [Nilsson, 1980], where:

- *states* are symbolic descriptions; the initial state is the set of observational statements.
- *operators* are inference rules, specifically, *generalization*, *specialization* and *reformulation* rules, as defined below.
- the *goal* state is an inductive assertion that implies the observational state-

ments, satisfies the problem background knowledge and maximizes the given preference criterion.

A generalization rule is a transformation of a description into a more general description, one that tautologically implies the initial description. A specialization rule makes an opposite transformation: given a description, it generates a logical consequence of it. A reformulation rule transforms a description into another, logically-equivalent description. A reformulation rule can be viewed as a special case of a generalization and a specialization rule.

Specialization and reformulation rules are the conventional truth-preserving inference rules used in deductive logic. In contrast to them, the generalization rules are not truth-preserving but falsity preserving. This means that if an event falsifies some description, then it also falsifies a more general description. This is immediately seen by observing that $H \Rightarrow F$ is equivalent to $\sim F \Rightarrow \sim H$ (the law of contraposition). To illustrate this point, suppose that a statement "some water birds in this lake are swans" has been generalized to "all water birds in this lake are swans." If there are no water birds in the lake that are swans, then this fact falsifies not only the first statement but also the second. Falsifying the second statement, however, does not imply the falsification of the first.

In concept acquisition, as explained in Section 4.2.2, transforming a rule $E \;\; ::> \;\; K$ into a more general rule $D \;\; ::> \;\; K$ means that description E must imply description D:

$$E \Rightarrow D \tag{13}$$

(recall expression (6)). Thus, to obtain a generalization rule for concept acquisition, one may use a tautological implication of formal logic. The premise and consequence of such an implication must, however, be interpretable as a description of a class of objects. For example, the known law of simplification:

$$P \;\&\; Q \Rightarrow P \tag{14}$$

can be turned into a generalization rule:

$$P \;\&\; Q \quad ::> \quad K \quad |< \quad P \quad ::> \quad K \tag{15}$$

If P stands for "round objects", Q for "brown objects" and K for "balls", then rule (15) states that the expression "round and brown objects are balls" can be generalized to "round objects are balls." Thus, in concept acquisition, the generalization operation has a simple set-theoretical interpretation: a description is more general if it is satisfied by a larger number of objects. (Such an interpretation does not apply, however, to descriptive generalization, as shown below.)

In order to obtain a rule for descriptive generalization, implication (14) is reversed, and P and Q are interpreted as properties of objects of some class K:

$$P(K) \quad |< \quad P(K) \;\&\; Q(K) \tag{16}$$

If P(K) stands for "balls are round" and Q(K) for "balls are brown," then according to rule (16), the statement "balls are round and brown" is a generalization of the statement "balls are round" (because from the former one can deduce the latter). We can see that the notion "the number of objects satisfying a description" is not applicable here. Generalizing means here adding (hypothesizing) properties that are ascribed to a class of objects.

After this informal introduction we shall now present various types of generalization rules, concentrating primarily on the rules for concept acquisition. These rules will be expressed using the notation of the annotated predicate calculus (see the Appendix). The reverse of these rules are specialization rules and, as special cases, reformulation rules. With regard to other specialization and reformulation rules we shall refer the reader to a standard book on predicate calculus (such as [Suppes, 1957]). Some reformulation rules of the annotated predicate calculus that do not occur in ordinary predicate calculus are given in the Appendix.

We will restrict our attention to generalization rules that transform one or more statements into a single more general statement:

$$\{D_i \;::>\; K\}_{i \in I} \;\;|\!<\;\; D \;::>\; K \qquad (17)$$

Such a rule states that if an event (a symbolic description of an object or situation) satisfies any description D_i, $i \in I$, then it also satisfies description D (the reverse may not be true). A basic property of the generalization transformation is that the resulting description has "unknown" truth-status, that is, is a hypothesis that must be tested on new data. A generalization rule does not guarantee that the obtained description is useful or plausible.

We distinguish between two types of generalization rules, *selective* and *constructive*. If every descriptor used in the generated concept description D is among descriptors occurring in the initial concept descriptions D_i, $i=1,2,\ldots$, then the rule is selective, otherwise it is constructive.

4.5.2 Selective Generalization Rules

In the rules presented below, CTX, CTX_1 and CTX_2 stand for some arbitrary expressions (context descriptions) that are augmented by additional components to formulate a concept description.

• The *dropping condition* rule—This rule is a generalized version of the previously described rule (15):

$$CTX \;\&\; S \;::>\; K \;\;|\!<\;\; CTX \;::>\; K \qquad (18)$$

where S is an arbitrary predicate or logical expression.

This rule states that a concept description can be generalized by simply removing a conjunctively-linked expression. This is one of the most commonly-used rules for generalizing information.

• The *adding alternative* rule:

$$CTX_1 \;::>\; K \;\;|\!<\;\; CTX_1 \vee CTX_2 \;::>\; K \qquad (19)$$

A concept description can be generalized by adding, through the use of logical disjunction, an alternative to it. An especially useful form of this rule is when the alternative is added by extending the scope of permissible values of one specific descriptor. Such an operation can be expressed very simply by using the internal disjunction operator of the annotated predicate calculus. For example, suppose that a concept description is generalized by allowing objects to be not only red but also blue. This can be expressed as follows:

$$\text{CTX} \ \& \ [\text{color}=\text{red}] \ ::> \ \text{K} \ \mid< \ \text{CTX}\&[\text{color}=\text{red} \vee \text{blue}] \ ::> \ \text{K} \quad (20)$$

(Forms in brackets are selectors; the expressions on the right of '=' are called references—see the Appendix)

Because of the importance of this special case, it will be presented as a separate general rule.

- The *extending reference* rule:

$$\text{CTX} \ \& \ [\text{L}=\text{R}_1] \ ::> \ \text{K} \ \mid< \ \text{CTX} \ \& \ [\text{L}=\text{R}_2] \ ::> \ \text{K} \qquad (21)$$

where $R_1 \subseteq R_2 \subseteq$ DOM(L) and DOM(L) denotes the domain of L.

In this rule, L is a term, and R_1 and R_2 (references) are internal disjunctions of values of L. References R_1 and R_2 can be interpreted as sets of values that descriptor L can take in order to satisfy the concept description.

The rule states that a concept description can be generalized by enlarging the reference of a descriptor ($R_2 \supseteq R_1$). The elements added to R_2 must, however, be from the domain of L.

If R_2 is extended to be the whole domain, that is, R_2 = DOM(L), then the selector [L = DOM(L)] is always true, and therefore can be removed. In this case, the extending reference rule becomes the dropping condition rule. There are two other special cases of the extending reference rule. They take into consideration the type of the descriptor L [defined by the structure of DOM(L)]. They are presented as separate rules below.

- The *closing interval rule*:

$$\left.\begin{array}{l}\text{CTX} \ \& \ [\text{L}=\text{a}] \ ::> \ \text{K} \\ \text{CTX} \ \& \ [\text{L}=\text{b}] \ ::> \ \text{K}\end{array}\right| < \ \text{CTX} \ \& \ [\text{L}=\text{a..b}] \ ::> \ \text{K} \qquad (22)$$

where L is a linear descriptor, and a and b are some specific values of descriptor L. The two premises are assumed to be connected by the logical conjunction (this convention holds for the remaining rules as well).

The rule states that if two descriptions of the same class (the premises of the rule) differ in the values of only one linear descriptor, then the descriptions can be replaced by a single description in which the reference of the descriptor is the interval linking these two values.

To illustrate this rule, consider as objects two states of a machine, and K as a class of *normal* states. The rule says that if a machine is in the normal state for two different temperatures, say a and b, then a hypothesis is made that all states in which the temperature falls into the interval [a,b] are also normal.

Thus, this rule is not only a logically-valid generalization rule, but expresses also some aspect of plausibility.

- The *climbing generalization tree* rule

$$\begin{array}{ll|l} & \text{CTX \& [L = a]} \quad ::> \quad \text{K} & \\ & \text{CTX \& [L = b]} \quad ::> \quad \text{K} & \\ \text{(one or} & \quad . \quad . & < \text{CTX \& [L = s]} \quad ::> \quad \text{K} \qquad (23) \\ \text{more} & \quad . \quad . & \\ \text{statements)} & \quad . \quad . & \\ & \text{CTX \& [L = i]} \quad ::> \quad \text{K} & \end{array}$$

where L is a structured descriptor, and s represents the lowest parent node whose descendants include nodes a, b, ... and i, in the generalization tree domain of L.

The rule is applicable only to descriptions involving structured descriptors, and is used in various forms in, for example [Winston, 1977; Hedrick, 1974; Lenat, 1976] (see also Chapters 11 and 6 of this book). The following example illustrates the rule:

$$\begin{array}{l|l} \exists\ \text{P, CTX \& [shape(P) = triangle]} \quad ::> \quad \text{K} & \\ & < \exists\ \text{P, CTX \& [shape(P) = polygon]} \quad ::> \quad \text{K} \\ \exists\ \text{P, CTX \& [shape(P) = rectangle]} \quad ::> \quad \text{K} & \end{array}$$

Paraphrasing this rule in English: if an object of class K is triangular and another object of this class is rectangular, then the rule generates a statement that objects of class k are polygonal.

- The *turning constraints into variables* rule—This rule is best known for the case of descriptive generalization:

$$\begin{array}{ll|l} & F[a] & \\ \text{(one or} & F[b] & \\ \text{more} & . & < \quad \forall\ v, F[v] \qquad (24) \\ \text{statements)} & . & \\ & . & \\ & F[i] & \end{array}$$

where F[v] stands for some description (formula) dependent on variable v, and *a*, *b*, ... are constants.

If some description F[v] holds for v being a constant *a* or constant *b*, and so on, then the rule generalizes these observations into a statement that F[v] holds for every value of v. This is the rule used most often in methods of inductive inference employing predicate calculus.

A corresponding rule for concept acquisition is:

$$F[a] \ \& \ F[b] \ \& \ \ldots \quad ::> \quad K \quad |< \ \exists\ v, F[v] \quad ::> \quad K \qquad (25)$$

To illustrate this version, assume that *a*, *b*, and so on, are parts of an object of class K that have a property F. Rule (25) generalizes these facts into an assertion that if any part of an object has property F then the object belongs to class K.

• The *turning conjunction into disjunction* rule:

$$F_1 \ \&\ F_2 \quad ::> \quad K \quad |< \quad F_1 \vee F_2 \quad ::> \quad K \tag{26}$$

where F_1 and F_2 are arbitrary descriptions.

A concept description can be generalized by replacing the conjunction operator by the disjunction operator.

• The *extending the quantification domain* rule—In the simplest case, the rule changes the universal quantifier into the existential quantifier:

$$\forall\ v,\ F[x] \quad ::> \quad K \quad |< \quad \exists\ v,\ F[v] \quad ::> \quad K \tag{27}$$

This rule can be viewed as a generalization of the previous rule (26). Using the concept of numerical quantifier (see the Appendix) this rule can be expressed in an even more general way:

$$\exists(I_1)v,\ F[v] \quad ::> \quad K \quad |< \quad \exists\ (I_2)v,\ F[v] \quad ::> \quad K \tag{28}$$

where I_1, I_2 are the quantification domains (sets of integers) satisfying relation $I_1 \subseteq I_2$.

For example, the statement "if an object has two parts ($I_1=\{2\}$) with property F, then it belongs to class K" can be generalized by rule (28) to a statement "if an object has two or more parts ($I_2=\{2,3,...\}$) with property F then it belongs to class K."

• The *inductive resolution* rule

(i) As applied to concept acquisition

The deductive inference rule, called the resolution principle, widely used in automatic theorem proving, can be adopted as a rule of generalization for concept acquisition. In propositional form, the resolution principle can be expressed as:

$$(P \Rightarrow F_1)\ \&\ (\sim P \Rightarrow F_2) \quad |> \quad F_1 \vee F_2 \tag{29}$$

where P is a predicate and F_1 and F_2 are arbitrary formulas. By interpreting both sides of (29) as concept descriptions, and making appropriate transformations we obtain:

$$\left.\begin{array}{l} P\ \&\ F_1 \quad ::> \quad K \\ \sim P\ \&\ F_2 \quad ::> \quad K \end{array}\right| < \quad F_1 \vee F_2 \quad ::> \quad K \tag{30}$$

To illustrate this rule, assume that K is the set of situations when John goes to a movie. Suppose that it has been observed that he goes to a movie when he has company (P) and the movie has high rating (F_1), or when he does not have company ($\sim$P), but has plenty of time (F_2). Rule (30) generalizes these two observations to a statement "John goes to a movie when either the movie has high rating or he has plenty of time."

(ii) As applied to descriptive generalization

By applying logical equivalence $(Q \mid> P) \Leftrightarrow (\sim P \mid> \sim Q)$ (the law of contraposition) to expression (29), then reversing the obtained rule and substituting the negative literals by the positive, we obtain:

$$P\&F_1 \vee \sim P \& F_2 \quad |< \quad F_1 \& F_2 \tag{31}$$

This version has been formulated by Morgan (1975).

Both versions, *(i)* and *(ii)*, can be generalized by applying the full-fledged resolution principle that uses predicates with arguments, and the unification algorithm to unify these arguments (for example, [Chang & Lee, 1973]).

- The *extension against* rule:

$$\left.\begin{array}{l} CTX_1 \ \& \ [L=R_1] \quad ::> \quad K \\ \\ CTX_2 \ \& \ [L=R_2] \quad ::> \quad \sim K \end{array}\right| < \quad [L \neq R_2] \quad ::> \quad K \tag{32}$$

where sets R_1 and R_2 are assumed to be disjoint.

Given a description of an object belonging to class K (a positive example), and a description of an object not belonging to this class (a negative example), the rule produces the most general statement consistent with these two descriptions. It is an assertion that classifies an object as belonging to class K if descriptor L does not take any value from the set R_2, thus ignoring context descriptions CTX_1 and CTX_2. This rule is the basic rule for learning discriminant descriptions from examples used in the previously-mentioned inductive program AQ11 [Michalski & Larson, 1978]. Various modifications of this rule can be obtained by replacing reference R_2 in the output assertion by some superset of it that does not intersect with R_1.

4.5.3 Constructive Generalization Rules

Constructive generalization rules generate inductive assertions that use descriptors not present in the original observational statements. This means that the rules perform a transformation of the original representation space. The following is a general constructive rule that makes such a transformation by applying the knowledge of a relationship between different concepts. It is assumed that this relationship is known to the learning system as background knowledge, as a previously-learned concept, or that it is computed according to user-defined procedures.

$$\left.\begin{array}{l} CTX \ \& \ F_1 \quad ::> \quad K \\ \\ \quad F_1 \Rightarrow F_2 \end{array}\right| < \ CTX \ \& \ F_2 \quad ::> \quad K \tag{33}$$

The rule states that if a concept description contains a part F_1 (a concept, a subdescription, and so on) that is known to imply some other concept F_2, then a more general description is obtained by replacing F_1 by F_2. For example, suppose a learning system is told that if an object is black, wide and long, then it belongs to class K (for example, it is a blackboard). This can be expressed in the annotated predicate calculus:

$$\exists\ P,\ [color(P) = black][width(P)\ \&\ length(P) = large]\ \ ::>\ \ K$$

Suppose the learner already knows that:

$$\forall\ P,\ ([width(P)\ \&\ length(P) = large] \Rightarrow [area(P) = large])$$

Then rule (33) produces a generalization:

$$\exists\ P,\ [color(P) = black][area(P) = large]\ \ ::>\ \ K$$

As another example, suppose the system is given a description of an object classified as an arch. This description states that a horizontal bar is on top of two equal objects placed apart, B_1 and B_2, having certain color, weight, shape, and so on. Suppose now that characterizations of B_1 and B_2 in this description satisfy a previously-learned concept of a block. Then rule (33) generates an assertion that an arch is a bar on top of two blocks placed apart. This rule is the basis for an interactive concept learning system developed by Sammut [1981].

Specific constructive generalization rules can be obtained from (33) by evoking procedures computing new descriptors in expression F_2 as functions of initial or previously-derived descriptors (contained in F_1). Here are some examples of rules for generating new descriptors.

- *Counting arguments* rules

  (i) The CQ rule (count quantified variables)—If a concept description is in the form:

  $$\exists.\ v_1,v_2,...,v_k,\ F[v_1,v_2,...,v_k]$$

  then the rule generates descriptors "#v-COND" representing the number of v_i's that satisfy some condition COND. This condition expresses selected properties of v_i's specified in the concept description. Since many such COND's can usually be formulated, the rule allows the system to generate a large number of such descriptors.

  For example, if the COND is "[attribute$_1$(v_i) = R]", then the generated descriptor will be "#v_i-attribute$_1$-R" counting the number of v_i's that satisfy this condition. If the attribute$_1$ is, for instance, length, and R is [2..4], then the derived descriptor is "#v_i-length-2..4" (that is, it measures the number of v_i's whose length is between 2 and 4, inclusively).

  (ii) The CA-rule (count arguments of a predicate)—If a descriptor in a description is a relation with several arguments, REL(v_1,v_2,...), the rule generates descriptors "#v-COND", measuring the number of arguments in REL that satisfy some condition COND. As above, many such descriptors can be generated, each with different COND.

  The annotation of a descriptor provides information about its properties. Such a property may be that a descriptor is, for instance, a transitive relation, such as relation "above", "inside", "left-of", and "before". For example, if the relation is "contains(A,B_1,B_2,...)", stating that object A contains objects B_1,B_2,..., and COND is "large and red", then the derived descriptor "#B-large-red-A-contains" measures the number of B_i-s contained in A that are large and red.

• The *generating chain properties* rule—If the arguments of different occurrences of a transitive relation in a concept description form a chain (that is, form a sequence of consecutive objects ordered by this relation), the rule generates descriptors characterizing some specific objects in the chain. Such objects may be:

LST-object	the "least object",or the object at the beginning of the chain (for example, the bottom object in the case of the relation "above").
MST-object	the object at the end of the chain (for example, the top object).
MID-object	the objects in the middle of the chain.
N^{th}-object	the object in the Nth position in the chain (starting from LST-object).

After identifying these objects, the rule investigates all known properties of them (as specified in the observational statements) in order to determine potentially relevant new descriptors. The rule also generates a descriptor characterizing the chain itself, namely:

REL-chain-length: the length of the chain defined by relation REL.

For example, if the REL is ON-TOP, then descriptor ON-TOP-chain-length would specify the height of a stack of objects. When a new description is generated and adopted, an annotation for it is also generated and filled out, as in Lenat [1976]. This rule can be extended to a partial order relation. In such a case it becomes the "find extrema of a partial order" rule.

• The *detecting descriptor interdependence* rule—Suppose that given is a set of objects exemplifying some concept, and that attribute descriptions are used to characterize these objects. Such descriptions specify only attribute values of the objects; they do not characterize the objects' structure. Suppose that the values a linear descriptor x takes on in all descriptions (events) are ordered in increasing order. If the corresponding values of another linear descriptor y exhibit an increasing or decreasing order, then a two-place descriptor:

M(x,y)

is created, signifying that x and y have a monotonic relationship. This descriptor has value $\uparrow$ when y values are increasing and value $\downarrow$ when they are decreasing.

The idea of the above M-descriptor can be extended in two directions. The first is to create M-descriptors dependent on some condition COND that must be satisfied by the events under consideration:

M(x,y)-COND

For example, descriptor:

M(length,weight)-red

states that length and weight have a monotonic relationship for red objects.

The second direction of extension is to relax the requirement for the monotonic relationship; that is, not to require that the order of y values is strictly increasing (or decreasing), but only approximately increasing (or decreasing). For example, the coefficient of statistical correlation between x and y can be measured, and when its absolute value is above a certain threshold, a descriptor R(x,y) is created. The domain of this R- descriptor can also be $\{\uparrow, \downarrow\}$, indicating the positive or negative correlation, respectively, or it can have values representing several subranges of the correlation coefficient. Similarly, as in the case of M- descriptors, R-descriptors can be extended to R-COND descriptors.

The M- or R-descriptors can be used to generate new descriptors. For example, if [M(x,y) = ↑], then a new descriptor z = x/y can be generated. If z assumes a constant or nearly-constant value, then an important relationship has been discovered. Similarly, if [M(x,y) = ↓] then a new descriptor $z = x \times y$ can be generated. These two techniques for generating new descriptors have been successfully used in the BACON system for discovering mathematical expressions representing physical or chemical laws, as described in Chapter 10 of this book.

The above ideas can be extended to structural descriptions. Such descriptions involve not only global properties of objects, but also properties of objects' parts and the relationships among the parts. Suppose that in a structural description of an object, existentially-quantified variables $P_1,P_2,\ldots,P_m$ denote its parts. If $x(P_i)$ and $y(P_i)$ are linear descriptors of P_i (for example, numerical attributes characterizing parts P_i, $i=1,2,\ldots$), the above-described techniques for generating M- and R- descriptors can be applied.

4.6 THE STAR METHODOLOGY

4.6.1 The Concept of a Star

The methodology presented here for learning structural descriptions from examples receives its name from the major concept employed in it, that of a *star*. In the most general sense, a *star of an event* e *under constraints* E is a set of all possible alternative non-redundant descriptions of event e that do not violate constraints E. A somewhat more restrictive definition of a star will be used here. Let e be an example of a concept to be learned and E be a set of some counterexamples of this concept. A star of the event e *against* the event set E, denoted G(e|E), is defined as the set of all maximally general c-expressions that cover (that is, are satisfied by) event e and that do not cover any of the negative events in E.

The c-expressions in a star may contain *derived* descriptors, that is, descriptors not present in the observational statements. In such a case, testing whether event e satisfies a given description requires that appropriate transformations be applied to the event. Such a process can be viewed as proving that the event implies the description, and therefore methods of automatic theorem proving could be used.

In practical problems, a star of an event may contain a very large number of descriptions. Consequently, such a theoretical star is replaced by a *bounded star* G(e|E,m) that contains no more than a fixed number, m, of descriptions. These m descriptions are selected as the m most preferable descriptions, among the remaining ones, according to the preference criterion defined in the problem background knowledge. Variable m is a parameter of the learning program, defined either by the user or by the program itself, as a function of the available computational resources.

Chapter 11 of this book gives an illustration and an algorithm for generating a bounded star with c-expressions restricted to attribute expressions (that is,expressions involving only object attributes). Section 4.6.3 presents an algorithm for generating a bounded star consisting of regular c-expressions. The concept of a star is useful because it reduces the problem of finding a complete description of a concept to subproblems of finding consistent descriptions of single positive examples of the concept.

Since any single example of a concept can always be characterized by a conjunctive expression (a logical product of some predicates), elements of a star can always be represented by conjunctive descriptions. One should also notice that if the concept to be learned is describable by a c-expression, then this description clearly will be among the elements of a (non-bounded) star of any single positive example of the concept. Consequently, if there exists a positive example not covered by any description of such a star, then the complete concept description must be disjunctive, that is, must include more than one c-expression.

4.6.2 Outline of the General Algorithm

It is assumed that every observational statement is in the form:

a-expression ::> K (34)

where a-expression is an atomic expression describing an object (recall Section 4.4.6) and K is the concept exemplified by this object.

It is also assumed that inductive assertions are in the form of a single c-expression or the disjunction of c-expressions. For simplicity we will restrict our attention to only single-concept learning. In the case of multiple-concept learning, the algorithm is repeated for each concept with modifications depending on the assumed interdependence among the concept descriptions (Section 4.2.4).

Let POS and NEG denote sets of events representing positive and negative examples of a concept, respectively. A general and simplified version of the Star methodology can be described as follows:

1. Randomly select an event e from POS.
2. Generate a bounded star, G(e|NEG,m), of the event e against the set of negative examples NEG, with no more than m elements. In the process of star generation apply generalization rules (both selective and constructive), task-specific rules, heuristics for generating new descriptors supplied by problem background knowledge, and definitions of previously-learned concepts.
3. In the obtained star, find a description D with the highest preference according to the assumed preference criterion LEF.
4. If description D covers set POS completely, then go to step 6.
5. Otherwise, reduce the set POS to contain only events not covered by D, and repeat the whole process from step 1.
6. The disjunction of all generated descriptions D is a complete and consistent concept description. As a final step, apply various reformulation rules (defined in the problem background knowledge) and "contracting" rules [equations (8) and (9) in the Appendix] in order to obtain a possibly simpler expression.

This algorithm is a simplified version of the general covering algorithm A^q [Michalski, 1975b]. The main difference is that algorithm A^q selects the initial events (if possible) from events not covered by any of the descriptions of generated stars, rather than not covered by only the selected descriptions D. This way the algorithm is able to determine a bound on the maximum number of separate descriptions in a disjunction needed to define the concept. Such a process may, however, be computationally costly.

The above algorithm describes only single-step learning. If, after generating a concept description, a newly-presented training event contradicts it, specialization or generalization rules are applied to generate a new consistent concept description. A method for such incremental learning is described in [Michalski & Larson, 1978]. (See also Chapter 8 of this book.)

The central step in the above methodology is the generation of a bounded star. This can be done using a variety of methods. Thus, the above Star methodology can be viewed as a general schema for implementing various learning methods and strategies. The next section describes one specific method of star generation.

4.6.3 Star Generation: The INDUCE Method

This method generates a bounded star G(e|NEG,m) by starting with a set of expressions that are single selectors, either extracted from the event for which the star is generated or inferred from the event by applying constructive generalization rules or inference rules provided by background knowledge. These expressions are then specialized by adding other selectors until consistency is achieved (that is, until each expression does not intersect with set NEG).

Next, the obtained consistent expressions are generalized so that each achieves the maximum coverage of the remaining positive training examples. The best consistent m so obtained and the generalized c-expressions (if some are also complete, then they are alternative solutions) constitute the bounded star sought, G(e|NEG,m). Specifically, the steps of the procedure are:

1. In the first step individual selectors of event e are put on the list called PS. This list is called a *partial star*, because its elements may cover some events in NEG. These initial elements of PS (single selectors from e) can be viewed as generalizations of event e obtained by applying in all possible ways the dropping condition generalization rule (each application drops all selectors except one). Elements of the partial star PS are then ordered from the most to the least preferred according to a preference criterion:

   $$LEF_1 = \langle(\text{-negcov},\tau_1), (\text{poscov}, \tau_2)\rangle \qquad (35)$$

   where negcov and poscov are numbers of negative and positive examples, respectively, covered by an expression in the star, and τ_1 and τ_2 are tolerances (recall Section 4.4.7).

   The LEF_1 minimizes the negcov (by maximizing the -negcov) and maximizes poscov.

2. The list PS is then expanded by adding new selectors obtained by applying the following inference rules to the event e:

   a. the constructive generalization rules (Section 4.5.3)

   b. the problem-specific heuristics defined in the background knowledge

   c. the definitions of the previously-learned concepts (to determine whether parts of e satisfy some already known concepts)

3. Each new selector is inserted in the appropriate place in list PS, according to preference criterion LEF_1. The size of PS is kept within the limit defined by parameter m by removing from PS all but the m most preferred selectors.

4. Descriptions in PS are tested for consistency and completeness. A description is consistent if negcov = 0 (that is, if it covers no events in NEG) and is complete if poscov is equal to the total number of positive examples. Consistent and complete descriptions are removed from PS and put on the list called SOLUTIONS. If the size of the list SOLUTIONS is greater than a parameter #SOL, then the algorithm stops. Parameter #SOL determines the number of desired alternative concept descriptions. Incomplete but consistent descriptions are removed from the list PS and put on the list called CONSISTENT. If the size of the CONSISTENT list is greater than a parameter #CONS, then control is transferred to step 6.

5. Each expression in PS is specialized in various ways by appending to it a single selector from the original list PS. Appended selectors must be of lower preference than the last selector in the conjunctive expression

(initially, the expression has only one selector). Parameter %BRANCH specifies the percentage of the selectors ranked lower (by the preference criterion) than the last selector in the current conjunction. If %BRANCH = 100%, all lower preference selectors are singly appended—that is, the number of new expressions generated from this conjunction will be equal to the total number of selectors having lower preference than the last selector in the conjunction. All newly-obtained expressions are ranked by LEF_1 and only the m best are retained. This "expression growing" process is illustrated in Figure 4-1.

Steps 4 and 5 are repeated until the CONSISTENT list contains the number of expressions specified by parameter #CONS, or until the time allocated for this process is exhausted.

6. Each expression on the CONSISTENT list is generalized by applying the *extension against*, *closing the interval*, and *climbing generalization tree* generalization rules. An efficient way to implement such a process is to transform the original structural-description space into an attribute-description space. Attributes (that is, descriptions with zero arguments) defining this space are created from the descriptors in the given expression on the CONSISTENT list in a manner such as that described in Section 3.2.3.2 of Chapter 3 in this book. The generalization of the obtained attribute descriptions is accomplished by the star generation procedure, analogous to the one described in Chapter 11 of this book. Details of this process of transforming structural descriptions into attribute descriptions are described by Larson [1977]. The reason for such a transformation is that structural descriptions are represented as labeled graphs while attribute descriptions are represented as binary strings. It is computationally much more economical to handle binary strings than labeled graphs.
7. The obtained generalizations are ranked according to the global preference criterion LEF defined in the background knowledge. To obtain a discriminant description, a typical LEF is to maximize the number of events covered in POS set and to minimize the complexity of the expression (measured, for example, by the number of selectors it contains). The m best expressions so determined constitute the bounded star G(e|NEG,m).

The Star algorithm and a somewhat restricted version of the above-described star generation algorithm has been implemented in various incarnations of the INDUCE learning program [Larson, 1977; Dietterich, 1978; Michalski, 1980a; Hoff *et al*, 1982].

4.7 AN EXAMPLE

To illustrate the inductive learning methodology just presented, let us consider a simple problem in the area of conceptual data analysis. Suppose we are

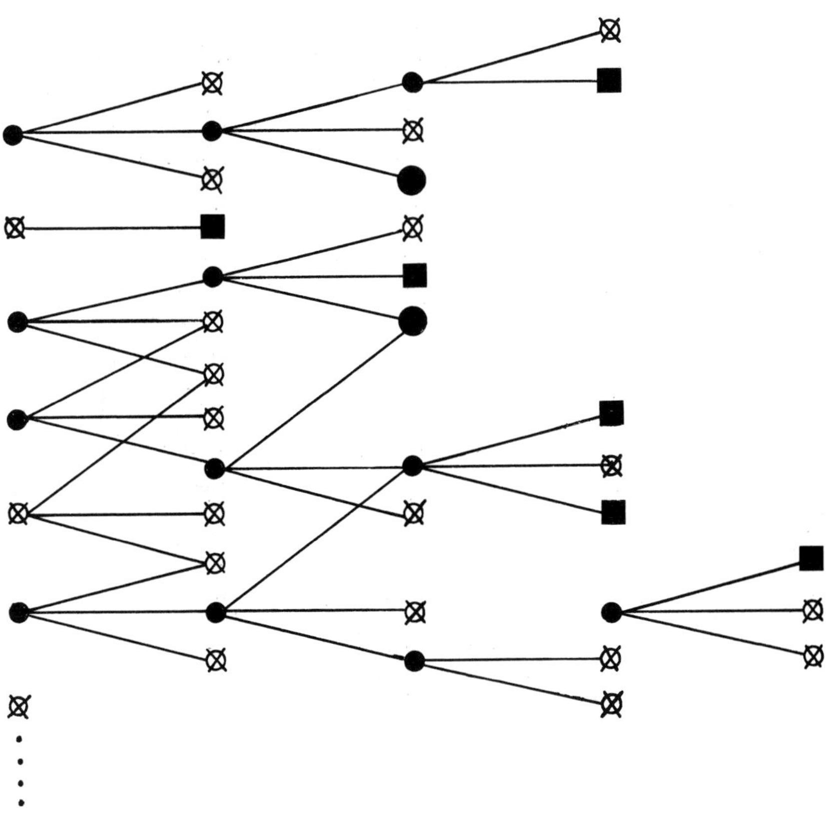

- a disregarded rule

- an active rule

- a terminal node denoting a consistent c-expression

- a terminal node denoting a consistent and complete c-expression (a solution)

The nodes in the first column are selectors extracted from the event e or derived from e by applying inference rules. Each arc represents an operation of adding a new selector to the current c-expression.

Figure 4-1: Illustration of the process of generating a reduced star RG(e|NEG,m).

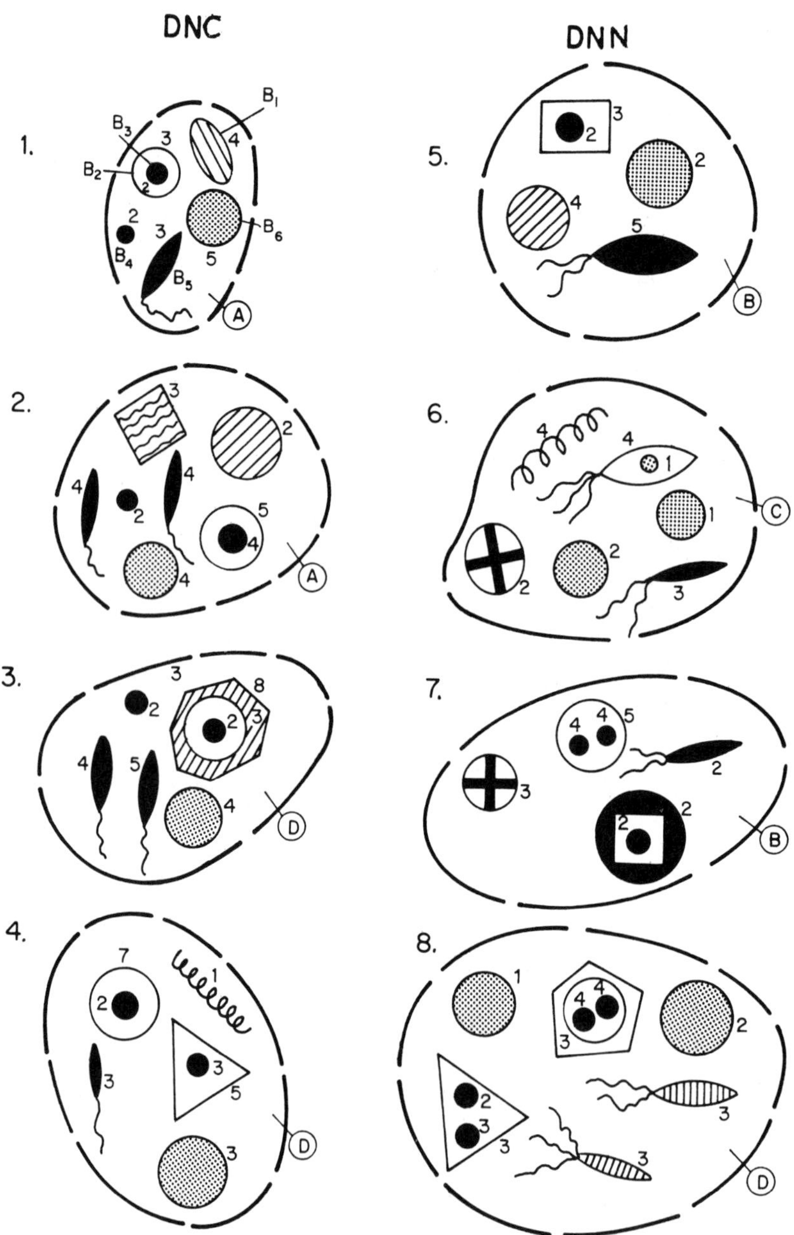

Figure 4-2: "Cancerous" and "Normal" cells.

given examples of "cancerous" and "normal" cells, denoted DNC and DNN, respectively, in Figure 4-2, and the task of the analysis is:

- to determine properties differentiating the two classes of cells (that is, to find discriminant descriptions of each class)
- to determine important common properties of the cancerous and the normal cells (that is, to find characteristic descriptions of each class).

An assumption is made that the properties to be discovered may involve both quantitative information about the cells and their components, and qualitative information, expressed by nominal variables and relationships existing among the components.

The solution to the problem posed (or similar problems) can be obtained by a successive repetition of the "focus attention→hypothesize→test" cycle described below.

The "focus attention" phase is concerned with defining the scope of the problem under consideration. This includes selecting descriptors appearing to be relevant, specifying underlying assumptions, and formulating the relevant problem knowledge. This first phase is performed by a researcher; it involves his/her technical knowledge and informal intuitions. The third, the "test" phase, examines the hypotheses and tests them on new data. This phase may require collecting new samples, performing laboratory experiments, and/or critically analyzing the hypotheses. This phase is likely to involve knowledge and abilities that go beyond currently-feasible computer systems.

It is the second, the "hypothesize" phase, in which an inductive learning system may play a useful role: the role of an assistant for conducting a search for the most plausible and/or most interesting hypotheses. This search may be a formidable combinatorial task for a researcher, if the data sample is large and if each item of the data (in this case, a cell) is described by many variables and/or relations.

Individual steps are as follows:

1. The user determines the set of initial descriptors and provides an annotation for each descriptor. We will assume that the annotation specifies the type, the domain, and any special properties of each descriptor (for example, the transitivity of a relation). In the case of structured descriptors, the annotation also specifies the structure of the domain. The specification of the annotation constitutes the first part of the problem background knowledge.

Suppose that for our simple example problem, the following descriptors are selected:

a. Global descriptors (those characterizing a whole cell)

- circ—the number of segments in the circumference of the cell

  Type: linear Domain: {1..10}

- pplasm—the type of protoplasm in the cell (marked by encircled capital letters in Figure 4-2)

Type: nominal Domain: {A,B,C,D}

Local descriptors (those characterizing cell bodies and their relationships)

- shape (B_i)—the shape of body B_i

  Type: structured
  Domain: a tree structure with a set of leaves {triangle, circle, ellipse, heptagon, square, boat, spring}
  Non-leaf nodes are defined by rules:
  [shape = circle $\vee$ ellipse] $\Rightarrow$ [shape = oval]
  [shape = triangle $\vee$ square $\vee$ heptagon] $\Rightarrow$ [shape = polygon]
  [shape = oval $\vee$ polygon] $\Rightarrow$ [shape = regular]
  [shape = spring $\vee$ boat] $\Rightarrow$ [shape = irregular]

- texture(B_i)—the texture of body B_i

  Type: nominal
  Domain: {blank, shaded, solid-black, solid-grey, stripes, crossed, wavy}

- weight (B_i)—the weight of body B_i

  Type: linear Domain: {1,2,...,5}

- orient (B_i)—the orientation of B_i

  Type: linear-cyclic (the last element is followed by the first)
  Domain: {N, NE, E, SE, S, SW, W, NW}
  Condition of applicability: if [shape (B_i) = boat]

- contains (C, B_1, B_2, ...)—C contains B_1, B_2, ...

  Type: nominal Domain: {True,False}
  Properties: transitive relation

- hastails (B, L_1, L_2, ...)—a body B has tails L_1, L_2, ...

  Type: nominal Domain: {True,False}
  Condition of applicability: if [shape (B) = boat]

Note that the descriptors "contains" and "hastails" are predicates with a variable number of arguments. Descriptor "contains" is characterized as a transitive relation. Descriptors "hastails" and "orient" are applicable only under certain conditions.

2. The user formulates observational statements which describe cells in terms of selected descriptors and specify the class to which each cell belongs. For example, the following is an observational statement for the DNC cell 1:

$\exists$.CELL$_1$, B$_1$,B$_2$,...,B$_6$ [contains(CELL$_1$,B$_1$,...,B$_6$)] [circ(CELL$_1$) = 8] &
[pplasm(CELL$_1$) = A][shape(B$_1$) = ellipse] [texture(B$_1$) = stripes] &
[weight(B$_1$) = 4] [orient(B$_1$) = NW][shape(B$_2$) = circle] &
[contains(B$_2$,B$_3$)][texture(B$_2$) = blank][weight(B$_2$) = 3]... &
[shape(B$_6$) = circle][texture(B$_6$) = shaded][weight(B$_6$) = 5]
::> [class = DNC]

3. To specify the second part of the problem background knowledge the user indicates which general rules of constructive induction (Section 4.5.3) are applicable, and also formulates any problem-specific rules.

The constructive rules will generate various derived descriptors. For example, the counting rule CQ will generate, among others, a descriptor:

- #B-black-boat—the number of bodies whose shape is "boat" and texture is "solid-black" (that is, assuming COND:
[texture(B) = solid-black] & [shape(B) = boat])

(For simplicity of notation, the name of this descriptor, as well as other descriptors below, has been abbreviated, so it does not follow strictly the naming convention described in Section 4.5.3.) The counting rule CA will generate such descriptors as:

- total-B—the total number of bodies in a cell (no COND is used)
- indep-B—the number of independent bodies in a cell (assuming the COND "bodies not contained in another body")
- #contained-in-B—the number of smaller bodies contained in the body B
- #tails-boat-B—the number of tails in a body B, whose shape is "boat"

As advice to the system, the user may formulate arbitrary arithmetic expressions for generating possibly relevant descriptors. For example, the user may suggest a descriptor:

$$\text{weight(CELL)} = \sum_i \text{weight}(B_i)$$

where B_i, i = 1,2,... denote bodies in a cell.

The background knowledge may also contain special concepts, such as even or odd numbers, the definitions of the area and perimeter of a circle or rectangle, and so on.

4. Finally, as the last part of the background knowledge, the user specifies the type of description sought and the hypothesis preference criterion. Let us assume that both characteristic descriptions and discriminant descriptions are sought. We therefore choose as the preference criterion for constructing characteristic descriptions "maximize the length of the complete c-expressions," and for constructing discriminant descriptions, "minimize the length of consistent and complete c-expressions."

As illustration, we shall present here samples of discriminant descriptions and characteristic descriptions of the DNC "cells", obtained by the INDUCE program.

4.7.1 Discriminant Descriptions of DNC Cells

Each of these descriptions is sufficient to discriminate all DNC cells from DNN cells. A concept description for class DNC can thus be any one of these descriptions or the disjunction of two or more of these descriptions.

- $\exists(1)$B [texture(B) = shaded][weight(B) $\geq$ 3]
  Paraphrasing in English: "Every DNC cell, as opposed to DNN, has exactly one body with 'shaded' texture and weight at least 3."
- [circ = even]
  "The number of segments in the circumference of every DNC cell is even." (The concept of "even" was determined by "climbing the generalization tree" rule.)
- $\exists(\geq 1)$B [shape(B) = boat][orient(B) = N $\vee$ NE]
  "Every DNC cell has at least one 'boat' shape body with orientation N or NE."
- $\exists(\geq 1)$B [<u>#tails-boat-B</u> = 1]
  "Every DNC cell has at least one body with number of tails equal to 1."
- $\exists(1)$B [shape(B) = circle][<u>#contains-B</u> = 1]
  "Every DNC cell has a circle containing a single object."

Underscored descriptors are derived descriptors obtained through constructive generalization rules.

4.7.2 Characteristic Descriptions of DNC Cells

Every description below is a characterization of some pattern common to all DNC cells. Some of these patterns taken separately may cover one or more DNN cells. The length of each description has been maximized, rather than minimized, as in the case of discriminant descriptions.

- $\exists(1)$B [weight(B) = 5]
  Paraphrasing in English: "In every DNC cell there is one and only one body with weight 5."
- $\exists.B_1, B_2$ [contains(B_1, B_2)] [shape(B_1) & shape(B_2) = circle] & [texture(B_1) = blank] [weight(B_1) = odd] [texture(B_2) = solid-black] & [weight(B_2) = even] [<u>#contained-in-B_1</u> = 1]
  "In every cell there are two bodies of circle shape, one contained in another, of which the outside circle is blank and has 'odd' weight, the inside circle is solid-black and has 'even' weight. The number of bodies in the outside circle is only one." (This is also a non-minimal discriminant description.)
- $\exists(1)$B [shape(B) = circle][texture(B) = shaded][weight(B) $\geq$ 3]
  "Every cell contains a circle with 'shaded' texture, whose weight is at least 3." (This is also a non-minimal discriminant description.)

- $\exists(\geq 1)$B [shape(B) = boat][orient(B) = N $\vee$ NE][#tails-boat(B) = 1]
  "Every cell has at least one body of 'boat' shape with N or NE orientation, which has one tail." (This is also a non-minimal discriminant description.)
- $\exists(2)$B [shape(B) = circle][texture(B) = solid-black], or, alternatively, [#B-circle-solid-black = 2]
  "Each cell has exactly two bodies that are solid black circles." (This is also a non-minimal discriminant description.)
- [pplasm = A $\vee$ D]
  "The protoplasm of every cell is of type A or D."

The above example is too simple for really unexpected patterns to be discovered. But it illustrates well the potential of the learning program as a tool for searching for patterns in complex data, especially when the relevant properties involve both numerical and structural information about the objects under consideration. An application of this program to a more complex problem [Michalski, 980a] did generate unexpected patterns.

4.8 CONCLUSION

A theory of inductive learning has been presented that views such learning as a heuristic search through a space of symbolic descriptions, generated by an application of certain inference rules to the initial observational statements (teacher-generated examples of some concepts or environment-provided facts). The process of generating the goal description—the most preferred inductive assertion—relies on the universally intertwined and complementary operations of specializing or generalizing the currently-held assertion in order to accommodate new facts. The domain background knowlege has been shown to be a necessary component of inductive learning, which provides constraints, guidance, and a criterion for selecting the most preferred assertion.

Such a characterization of inductive learning is conceptually simple, and constitutes a theoretical framework for describing and comparing learning methods, as well as developing new methods. The Star methodology for learning structural descriptions from examples, described in the second part of this chapter, represents a general approach to concept acquisition which can be implemented in a variety of ways and applied to different problem domains.

There are many important topics of inductive learning that have not been covered here. Among them is learning from incomplete or uncertain information, learning from descriptions containing errors, learning with a multitude of forms of observational statements, as well as multimodel-based inductive assertions, and learning general rules with exceptions. The problem of discovering new concepts, descriptors and, generally, various many-level transformations of the initial description space (that is, the problem of constructive inductive learning) has been covered only very superficially.

These and related topics have been given little attention so far in the field of machine learning. There is no doubt, however, that as the understanding of the fundamental problems in the field matures, these challenging topics will be given increasing attention.

ACKNOWLEDGMENTS

In the development of the ideas presented here the author benefited from discussions with Tom Dietterich and Robert Stepp. Proofreading and comments of Jaime Carbonell, Bill Hoff and Tom Mitchell were helpful in shaping up the final version of the chapter. Comments and suggestions of the reviewers of *Artificial Intelligence Journal*, where the original version of this chapter was submitted and accepted for publication, helped to improve its clarity and organization.

The author gratefully acknowledges the partial support of the research by the National Science Foundation under grant MCS 82-05166, and the Office of Naval Research under grant N00014-82-K-0186.

REFERENCES

Amarel, S., "An approach to automatic theory formation," *Illinois Symposium on Principles of Self-Organization*, H. von Foerster (Ed.), 1960.

Banerji, R. B., "The description list of concepts," *J.A.C.M*, 1962.

Banerji, R. B., *Artificial Intelligence: A Theoretical Perspective*, Elsevier North Holland, New York, 1980.

Biermann, A. W., "The inference of regular LISP programs from examples," *IEEE Transcations on Systems, Man, and Cybernetics*, Vol. SMC-8, No. 8, pp. 585-600, August 1978.

Biermann, A. and Feldman, J., *A survey of results in grammatical inference*, Academic Press, New York, 1972.

Bongard, N., *Pattern Recognition*, Spartan Books, New York, 1970, (Translation from Russian original, published in 1967).

Brachman, R. J., "On the epistemological status of semantic networks," *Associative Networks*, N. V. Findler (Ed.), New York: Academic Press, 1979.

Bruner, J. S., Goodnow, J. J. and Austin, G. A., *A Study of Thinking*, Wiley, New York, 1956.

Buchanan, B. G. and Feigenbaum, E. A., "DENDRAL and Meta-DENDRAL: their applications dimension," *Artificial Intelligence*, Vol. 11, pp. 5-24, 1978.

Buchanan, B. G., Mitchell, T. M., Smith, R. G. and Johnson, C. R. Jr., "Models of Learning Systems", Technical Report STAN-CS-79-692, Stanford University, Computer Science Dept., January 1979.

Burstall, R. M. and Darlington, J., "A transformation system for developing recursive programs," *Journal of the ACM*, Vol. 24, No. 1, pp. 44-67, 1977.

Carnap, R., "The aim of inductive logic," *Logic, Methodology and Philosophy of Science*, Nagel, E., Suppes, P. and Tarski, A. (Eds.), Stanford University Press, Stanford, pp. 303-318, 1962.

Case, J. and Smith, C., "Comparison of identification criteria for mechanized inductive inference", Technical Report TR-154, Dept. Computer Science., State U. of New York at Buffalo, 1981.

Chang, C., and Lee, R. C., *Symbolic Logic and Mechanical Theorem Proving*, Academic Press, New York, 1973.

Cohen, B. L., "A powerful and efficient structural pattern recognition system," *Artificial* Intelligence, Vol. 9, No. 3, December 1977.

Coulon, D. and Kayser, D., "Learning criterion and inductive behavior," *Pattern Recognition*, Vol. 10, No. 1, pp. 19-25, 1978.

Davis, R. and Lenat, D. B., *Knowledge Based Systems in Artificial Intelligence*, McGraw Hill, New York, 1981.

Dietterich, T., "Description of inductive program INDUCE 1.1", Technical Report (Internal), Department of Computer Science, University of Illinois, Urbana-Champaign, October 1978.

Dietterich, T. G., "The methodology of knowledge layers for inducing descriptions of sequentially ordered events," Master's thesis, University of Illinois, Urbana, October 1979.

Feigenbaum E. A., "The simulation of verbal learning behavior," *Computers and Thought*, Feigenbaum, E. A. and Feldman, J. (Eds.), McGraw-Hill Book Company, New York, NY, 1963.

Fikes, R. E., Hart, P. E. and Nilsson, N. J., "Learning and executing generalized robot plans," *Artificial Intelligence*, Vol. 3, pp. 251-288, 1972.

Gaines, B. R., "Maryanski's grammatical inferencer," *IEEE Trans on Computers*, Vol. C-28, pp. 62-64, 1979.

Gaschnig, J., "Development of Uranium Exploration Models for Prospector Consultant System", Internal, SRI International, March 1980.

Hájek, P. and Havránek, T., *Mechanizing Hypothesis Formation: Mathematical Foundations for a General Theory*, Springer-Verlag, 1978.

Hájek, P., Havel, I., and Chytil, M., "The GUHA method of automatic hypothesis determination," *Computing*, No. 1, pp. 293-308, March 1966.

Hayes-Roth, F., "A structural approach to pattern learning and the acquisition of classificatory power," *Proceedings of the First International Joint Conference on Pattern Recognition*, Washington, D. C., pp. 343-355, 1973.

Hayes-Roth, F. and McDermott, J., "An interference matching technique for inducing abstractions," *Communications of the ACM*, Vol. 21, No. 6, pp. 401-410, 1978.

Hedrick, C. L., *A Computer Program to Learn Production Systems Using a Semantic Net,* Ph.D. dissertation, Carnegie-Mellon University, July 1974, (Department of Computer Science).

Hintzman, D. L., *The Psychology of Learning and Memory*, W. H. Freeman and Company, 1978.

Hoff, B., Michalski, R. S., and Stepp, R., "INDUCE 2 - a program for learning structural descriptions from examples", Technical Report 82-5, Intelligent Systems Group, October 1982.

Hovland, C. I., "A 'Communication Analysis' of Concept Learning," *Psychological Review*, pp. 461-472, November 1952.

Hunt, E. B., Marin, J. and Stone, P. T., *Experiments in Induction*, Academic Press, New York, 1966.

Jouannaud, J. P., and Kodratoff, Y., "An automatic construction of LISP programs by transformations of functions synthesized from their input-output behavior," *International Journal of Policy Analysis and Information Systems*, Vol. 4, No. 4, pp. 331-358, December 1980.

Kemeni, T. G., "The use of simplicity in induction," *Psychological Review*, Vol. 62, No. 3, pp. 391-408, 1953.

Kochen, M., "Experimental study of hypothesis formation by computer," *Proc. 1960 London Symp. on Information Theory*, 1960.

Langley, P. W., Neches, R., Neves, D. and Anzai, Y., "A domain-independent framework for procedure learning," *Journal of Policy Analysis and Information Systems*, Vol. 4, No. 2, pp. 163-197, June 1980.

Larson, J., *Inductive inference in the variable-valued predicate logic system VL21: methodology and computer implementation,* Ph.D. dissertation, University of Illinois, Urbana, Illinois, May 1977.

Larson, J. and Michalski, R. S., "Inductive inference of VL decision rules," *Proceedings of the Workshop on Pattern Directed Inference Systems, SIGART Newsletter 63*, pp. 38-44, June 1977.

Lenat, D. B., *AM: an artificial intelligence approach to discovery in mathematics as heuristic search,* Ph.D. dissertation, Stanford University, Stanford, California, 1976.

Michalski, R. S., "A Variable-Valued Logic System as Applied to Picture Description and Recognition," *Graphic Languages*, F. Nake and A. Rosenfeld (Ed.), North-Holland Publishing Co., pp. 20-47, 1972.

Michalski, R. S., "AQVAL/1 - Computer implementation of a variable valued logic system VL1 and examples of its application to pattern recognition," *Proceedings of the First International Joint Conference on Pattern Recognition*, Washington, D. C., pp. 3-17, 1973b.

Michalski, R. S., "Variable-Valued Logic and its Applications to Pattern Recognition and Machine Learning," *Multiple-Valued Logic and Computer Science*, Rine, D. (Ed.), North-Holland, pp. 506-534, 1975a.

Michalski, R. S., "Synthesis of optimal and quasi-optimal variable-valued logic formulas," *Proceedings of the 1975 International Symposium on Multiple-Valued Logic*, Bloomington, Indiana, pp. 76-87, May 1975b.

Michalski, R. S., "Pattern recognition as rule-guided inductive inference," *IEEE Transactions on Pattern Analysis and Machine Intelligence*, Vol. PAMI-2, No. 4, pp. 349-361, 1980a.

Michalski, R. S., "Knowledge Acquisition Through Conceptual Clustering: A Theoretical Framework and an Algorithm for Partitioning Data into Conjunctive Concepts," *Policy Analysis and Information Systems*, Vol. 4, No. 3, pp. 219-244, 1980c, (A Special Issue on Knowledge Acquisition and Induction).

Michalski, R. S. and Chilausky, R. L., "Learning by being told and learning from examples: an experimental comparison of the two methods of knowledge acquisition in the context of developing an expert system for soybean disease diagnosis," *Policy Analysis and Information Systems*, Vol. 4, No. 2, pp. 125-160, June 1980, (Special issue on knowledge acquisition and induction).

Michalski, R. S. and Larson, J. B., "Selection of most representative training examples and incremental generation of VL_1 hypotheses: the underlying methodology and the description of programs ESEL and AQ11", Technical Report 867, Computer Science Department, University of Illinois, 1978.

Michalski, R. S., and Negri, P., "An Experiment on Inductive Learning in Chess End Games," *Machine Representation of Knowledge, Machine Intelligence 8*, E. W. Elcock and D. Michie (Ed.), Ellis Horwood, pp. 175-192, 1977.

Michalski, R. S., Stepp, R., and Diday, E., "A recent advance in data analysis: clustering objects into classes characterized by conjunctive concepts," *Progress in Pattern Recognition*, L. Kanal and A. Rosenfeld (Ed.), North-Holland, Amsterdam, pp. 33-56, 1981.

Michie, D., "New face of AI", Technical Report 33, University of Edinburgh, 1977.

Minsky, M., "A framework for representing knowledge," *The Psychology of Computer Vision*, P. H. Winston (Ed.), McGraw-Hill, New York, ch. 6, pp. 211-277, 1975.

Mitchell, T. M., *Version Spaces: An Approach to Concept Learning*, Ph.D. dissertation, Stanford University, December 1978.

Moraga, C., "A didactic experiment in pattern recognition", Technical Report AIUD-PR-8101, Dartmund University, 1981.

Morgan, C. G., "Automated hypothesis generation using extended inductive resolution," *Advance Papers of Fourth International Joint Conference on Artificial Intelligence*, Tbilisi, USSR, pp. 351-356, September 1975.

Newell, A., Shaw, J. C. and Simon, H. A., "A variety of intelligent learning in a general problem solver," *Self Organizing Systems*, Yovits and Cameron (Eds.), Pergamon Press, New York, 1960.

Nilsson, N. J., *Priciples of Artificial Intelligence*, Tioga Publishing Co., 1980.

O'Rorke, P., "A comparative study of inductive learning systems AQ11 and ID3", Intelligent Systems Group Report 82-2, Department of Computer Science, University of Illinois at Urbana-Champaign, 1982.

Pettorossi, A., "An Algorithm for Reducing Memory Requirements in Recursive Programs Using Annotations," *International Workshop on Program Construction*, September 1980.

Plotkin, G. D., "A further note on inductive generalization," *Machine Intelligence*, Meltzer, B. and Michie, D. (Eds.), Elsevier, Edinburgh, pp. 101-124, 1971.

Pokorny, D., "Knowledge Acquisition by the GUHA Method," *International Journal of Policy Analysis and Information Systems*, Vol. 4, No. 4, pp. 379-399, 1980, (A special issue on knowledge acquisition and induction).

Polya, G., *Mathematics and Plausible Reasoning*, Princeton University Press, Princeton, N.J., 1954.

Popper, K., *The Logic of Scientific Discovery*, Harper and Row, New York, 1968, (2nd edition).

Post, H. R., "Simplicity of Scientific Theories," *British Journal for the Philosophy of Science*, Vol. 11, No. 41, 1960.

Quinlan, J. R., "Discovering rules from large collections of examples: a case study," *Expert Systems in the Micro Electronic Age*, Michie, D. (Ed.), Edinburgh University Press, Edinburgh, 1979.

Russell, B., *History of Western Philosophy*, George Allen and Unwin, London, 1946.

Sammut, C., *Learning Concepts by Performing Experiments,* Ph.D. dissertation, University of New South Wales, November 1981.

Shapiro, Ehud Y., "Inductive Inference of Theories From Facts", Research Report 192, Yale University, February 1981.

Shapiro, A. and Niblett, T., "Automatic Induction of classification rules for a chess endgame," *Advances in Computer Chess, volume 3*, Clarke, M.R.B. (Ed.), Edinburgh University Press, 1982.

Shaw, D. E., Swartout, W. R. and Green, C. C., "Inferring LISP programs from examples," *Fourth International Joint Conference on Artificial Intelligence*, Tbilisi, USSR, pp. 351-356, September 1975.

Shortliffe, E., *Computer Based Medical Consultations: MYCIN*, New York: Elsevier, 1976.

Simon, H. A. and Kotovsky, K., "Human acquisition of concepts for sequential patterns," *Psychological Review*, Vol. 70, pp. 534-546, 1963.

Simon, H. A. and Lea, G., "Problem solving and rule induction: A unified view," *Knowledge and Cognition*, L. Gregg (Ed.), Lawrence Erlbaum Associates, Hillsdale, N.J., 1974.

Smith, D. R., "A Survey of the Synthesis of LISP Programs from Examples", Technical Report, Duke University, Bonas, France, September 1980.

Solomonoff, R. J., "A Formal Theory of Inductive Inference," *Information and Control*, Vol. 7, 1964.

Soloway, E. M. and Riseman, E. M., "Levels of pattern description in learning," *Fifth International Joint Conference on Artificial Intelligence*, Cambridge, Mass., pp. 801-811, 1977.

Stepp, R., "The investigation of the UNICLASS inductive program AQ7UNI and User's Guide", Technical Report 949, Department of Computer Science, University of Illinois, Urbana, Illinois, November 1978.

Stoffel, J. C., "The theory of prime events: data analysis for sample vectors with inherently discrete variables," *Information Processing 74*, North-Holland, Amsterdam, pp. 702-706, 1974.

Suppes, P., *Introduction to Logic*, Van Nostrand Co., Princeton, 1957.

Vere, S. A., "Induction of concepts in the predicate calculus," *Proceedings of the Fourth International Joint Conference on Artificial Intelligence*, IJCAI, Tbilisi, USSR, 1975.

Waterman, D. A., "Generalized learning techniques for automating the learning of heuristics," *Artificial Intelligence*, Vol. 1, No. 1-2, pp. 121-170, Spring 1970.

Winston, P., *Learning Structural Descriptions from Examples*, Ph.D. dissertation, MIT, September 1970.

Winston, P. H., *Artificial Intelligence*, Addison-Wesley, 1977.

Yau, K. C., and Fu, K. S., "Syntactic shape recognition using attributed grammars," *Proceedings of the Eighth Annual EIA Symposium on Automatic Imagery Pattern Recognition*, 1978.

Zagoruiko, N. G., *Mietody obnaruzhenia zakonomiernostiej (Methods for revealing regularities in data)*, Izd. Nauka, Moscow, 1981.

APPENDIX: ANNOTATED PREDICATE CALCULUS (APC)

This appendix presents definitions of the basic components of the annotated predicate calculus and some rules for equivalence-preserving transformations of APC expressions (rules that are nonexistent in the ordinary calculus).

1. **Elementary and Compound Terms**—*Terms* can be elementary or compound. An *elementary term* (an *eterm*) is the same as a term in predicate calculus, that is, a constant, a variable, or a function symbol followed by a list of arguments that are eterms. A *compound term* (*cterm*) is a *composite* of elementary terms or is an eterm in which one or more arguments are such composites. The composite of eterms is defined as the *internal conjunction* (&) or *internal disjunction* ($\vee$) of eterms. (The meaning of these operators is explained later.) The following are examples of compound terms:

$$\text{RED} \vee \text{BLUE} \tag{1}$$

$$\text{height}(\text{BOX}_1 \ \& \ \text{BOX}_2) \tag{2}$$

where RED, BLUE, BOX_1, BOX_2 are constants. Expression (1) and the form in parentheses in (2) are composites. Note that expressions (1) and (2) are not logical expressions that have a truth-status (that is, can be true or false); they are terms to be used only as arguments of predicates. A compound term in which arguments are composites can be transformed (expanded) into a composite of elementary terms. Let f be an n-argument function whose n-1 arguments are represented by list A, and let t_1 and t_2 be elementary terms. The rules for performing such a transformation, that is, term rewriting rules, are:

$$f(t_1 \vee t_2, A) \leftrightarrow f(t_1, A) \vee f(t_2, A) \tag{3}$$

$$f(t_1 \ \& \ t_2, A) \leftrightarrow f(t_1, A) \ \& \ f(t_2, A) \tag{4}$$

Thus, term (2) can be transformed into a composite:

$$\text{height}(\text{BOX}_1) \ \& \ \text{height}(\text{BOX}_2) \tag{5}$$

If list A itself contains composites, then it is assumed that the internal disjunction is expanded first, followed by the internal conjunction (that is, the conjunction binds stronger than the disjunction).

2. **Elementary and Compound Predicates**—Predicates also can be elementary or compound. An *elementary predicate* is the same as a predicate in the predicate calculus, that is, a predicate symbol followed by a list of arguments that are eterms. In a *compound predicate* one or more arguments is a compound term. For example, the following are compound predicates:

$$\text{Went}(\text{Mary} \ \& \ \text{Mother}(\text{Stan}), \text{Movie} \vee \text{Theater}) \tag{6}$$

$$\text{Inside}(\text{Key}, \text{Drawer}(\text{Desk}_1 \vee \text{Desk}_2)) \tag{7}$$

The meaning of a compound predicate is defined by rules for transforming it into an expression made of elementary predicates and ordinary "external" logic operators of conjunction (&) and disjunction (V). We denote the internal and external operators identically, because they can be easily distinguished by the context (note that there is no distinction between them in natural language). If an operator connects predicates, then it is an external operator; if it connects terms, then it is an internal operator.

Let t_1 and t_2 be eterms and P an n-ary predicate whose last n-1 arguments are represented by a list A. We have the following reformulation rules (that is, equivalence-preserving transformations of descriptions):

$$P(t_1 \vee t_2, A) \quad |= \quad P(t_1, A) \vee P(t_2, A) \qquad (8)$$

$$P(t_1 \,\&\, t_2, A) \quad |= \quad P(t_1, A) \,\&\, P(t_2, A) \qquad (9)$$

If an argument of a predicate is a compound term that is not a composite of elementary terms, then it is transformed first into a composite by rules (3) and (4). If A contains a composite of terms, then the disjunction is expanded first before conjunction (similarly as in expanding compound terms).

Rules (3), (4), (8) and (9) can be used as bidirectional transformation rules. By applying them forward (from left to right), a compound predicate can be *expanded* into an expression containing only elementary predicates, and by applying them backward, an expression with elementary predicates can be contracted into a compound predicate.

For example, by applying forward rule (8) and then (9), one can expand the compound predicate (6) into

$$\text{Went(Mary,movie) \& Went(Mother(Stan),movie)} \vee$$
$$\text{Went(Mary,theater) \& Went(Mother(Stan),theater)} \qquad (10)$$

Comparing logically-equivalent expressions (6) and (10), one can notice that expression (6) is considerably shorter than (10), and in contrast to (10), represents explicitly the fact that Mary & Mother(Stan) went to the same place. Also, the structure of (6) is more similar to the structure of the corresponding natural language expression.

3. **Relational Statements**—A simple and often used way of describing objects or situations is to state the values of selected attributes applied to these objects or situations. Although such information can be represented by predicates, this is not the most readable or natural way. The APC uses for this purpose a statement:

$$\text{eterm}_i = a \qquad (11)$$

stating that eterm_i evaluates to a constant a. Such a statement is called an *atomic relational statement* (or an *atomic selector*). Expression (11) is a special case of a *relational statement* (also called *selector*), defined as:

$$\text{Term}_1 \; rel \; \text{Term}_2 \qquad (12)$$

where Term_1 and Term_2 are elementary or compound terms, and *rel* stands for one of the relational symbols: $=, \geq, >, \leq, <$.

If Term_1 and Term_2 are both elementary, then expression (12) states that the value of the function represented by Term_1 is in relation *rel* to the value of function represented by Term_2. For example, the expression:

$$\text{distance(Boston,Tampa)} = \text{distance(Washington,Dallas)} \qquad (13)$$

states that the distance between Boston and Tampa is the same as the distance between Washington and Dallas. If Term_2 is a constant, then it evaluates to itself.

Expression (12) can be represented by a predicate:

$$rel(\text{Term}_1, \text{Term}_2) \qquad (14)$$

If Term_1 and/or Term_2 is compound, then the meaning of expression (12) is defined by expanding it into a form containing only relational statements with elementary terms. The expansion is performed by transforming expression (12) into (14), applying transformation rules (3), (4), (8), and (9), and then converting the elementary predicates into relational statements.

For example, a relational statement:

$$\text{color}(P_1 \vee P_2) = \text{Red} \vee \text{Blue} \qquad (15)$$

can be expanded into an expression:

$$(\text{color}(P_1) = \text{Red} \vee \text{Blue}) \vee (\text{color}(P_2) = \text{Red} \vee \text{Blue}) \qquad (16)$$

and finally to an expression consisting of only atomic selectors:

$$(\text{color}(P_1) = \text{Red}) \vee (\text{color}(P_1) = \text{Blue}) \vee$$
$$(\text{color}(P_2) = \text{Red}) \vee (\text{color}(P_2) = \text{Blue}) \qquad (17)$$

The two selectors in the disjunction (16) are examples of a *referential selector*, defined as a form:

$$\text{Term}_1 \; rel \; \text{Term}_2 \qquad (18)$$

where Term_1 (called *referee*) is a nonconstant elementary term and Term_2 (called *reference*) is a constant or the internal disjunction of constants from the domain of Term_1. If relation *rel* is "=" and Term_2 is the disjunction of some constants, then the referential selector (18) states that the function represented by Term_1 evaluates to one of the constants in Term_2. The referential selector is very useful for representing concept descriptions.

If the reference of a referential selector contains a sequence of consecutive constants from the domain of a linear descriptor, then the range operator ".." is used to simplify the expression. For example:

$$\text{size (P)} = 2 \vee 3 \vee 4$$

can be written:

$$\text{size (P)} = 2..4$$

The negation of a selector:

$$\sim(\text{Term}_1 = \text{Term}_2)$$

can be equivalently written:

$$\text{Term}_1 \neq \text{Term}_2 \qquad (20)$$

An arbitrary predicate $P(t_1,t_2,...)$ can be written in the form of a referential selector:

$$P(t_1,t_2,...) = \text{True} .$$

Therefore, for the uniformity of terminology, a predicate will be considered a special form of a selector.

To facilitate the interpretation and readability of individual selectors in expressions, they are usually surrounded by square brackets and their conjunction is expressed by concatenating the bracketed forms (see Section 4.7).

APC expressions are created from selectors (relational statements) in the same way as predicate calculus expressions are created from predicates, that is, by using logic connectives ($\sim$, &, $\vee$, $\Rightarrow$, $\Leftrightarrow$) and quantifiers. One additional useful connective is the *exception operation* ("$\setminus$"), defined as:

$$S_1 \setminus S_2 \;\; |= \;\; (\sim S_2 \Rightarrow S_1) \;\&\; (S_2 \Rightarrow \sim S_1) \qquad (21)$$

where S_1 and S_2 are APC expressions. ($S_1 \setminus S_2$ reads: S_1 *except when* S_2.) It is easy to see that the exception operator is equivalent to the symmetrical difference.

In addition to ordinary quantifiers there is also a *numerical quantifier*, expressed in the form:

$$\exists(I)\ v,\ S[v] \qquad (22)$$

where I, the *index set*, denotes a set of integers, and S[v] is an APC expression having v as a free variable.

Sentence (22) evaluates as true if the number of values of v for which expression S[v] is true is an element of the set I. For example, formula:

$$\exists(2..8)\ v,\ S[v] \qquad (23)$$

states that there are two to eight values of v for which the expression S[v] is true. The following equivalences hold:

$$\exists v,\ S[v] \text{ is equivalent to } \exists(\geq 1)\ v,\ S[v]$$

and

$$\forall v,\ S[v] \text{ is equivalent to } \exists(k)\ v,\ S[v]$$

where k is the number of possible values of variable v.

To state that there are k and only k distinct values for variables $v_1,v_2,...,v_k$ for which expression $S[v_1,v_2,...,v_k]$ is true, we write:

$$\exists .v_1,v_2,...,v_k,\ S[v_1...,v_k] \qquad (24)$$

For example, the expression:

$$\exists .P_0,P_1,P_2\ [\text{contains}(P_0,P_1\&P_2)]\ \&\ [\text{color}(P_1\&P_2) = \text{red}] \Rightarrow$$
$$[\text{two-red-parts}(P_0)]$$

states that predicate two-red-parts(P_0) holds if P_0 has two, and only two, distinct parts in it that are red.

Section 4.7 presents an example of the usage of the APC for formulating observational statements and concept descriptions.

PART THREE

LEARNING IN PROBLEM-SOLVING AND PLANNING

5

LEARNING BY ANALOGY: FORMULATING AND GENERALIZING PLANS FROM PAST EXPERIENCE

Jaime G. Carbonell
Carnegie-Mellon University

ABSTRACT

Analogical reasoning is a powerful mechanism for exploiting past experience in planning and problem solving. This chapter outlines a theory of analogical problem solving based on an extension to means-ends analysis. An analogical transformation process is developed to extract knowledge from past successful problem-solving situations that bear a strong similarity to the current problem. Then, the investigation focuses on exploiting and extending the analogical reasoning model to generate useful exemplary solutions to related problems from which more general plans can be induced and refined. Starting with a general analogical inference engine, problem-solving experience is, in essence, compiled incrementally into effective procedures that solve various classes of problems in an increasingly reliable and direct manner.

5.1 INTRODUCTION

Analogical reasoning has been a sparsely-investigated phenomenon in artificial intelligence [Kling, 1971; Moore & Newell, 1974; Korf, 1980; Winston, 1979]. Nonetheless, analogy is one of the central inference methods in human cognition as well as a powerful computational mechanism. This chapter discusses a computational model of problem-solving by analogy based on an extension of means-ends analysis (MEA). My central hypothesis (based in part on Schank's theory of memory organization [Schank, 1980; Schank & Carbonell, 1979; Schank, 1979]) is the following: When encountering a new problem situation, a person is reminded of past situations that bear strong similarity to the present problem (at different levels of abstraction). This type of reminding experience serves to retrieve behaviors that were appropriate in earlier problem-solving episodes, whereupon past behavior is adapted to meet the demands of the current situation.

Commonalities among previous and current situations, as well as successful applications of modified plans can serve as the basis for generalization. Similarly, performing an inappropriate action in a new situation can provide information useful in reorganizing episodic memory. If the inappropriate action resulted from the application of a recently-acquired general plan, an analysis of the type of error may trigger a discrimination process that constrains the range of applicability for that plan. In either case, a *reactive environment* that informs the problem solver of success, failure, or partial success is an absolute requirement for any generalization or discrimination process to apply.

Whereas humans exhibit a universal ability to learn from experience no matter what the task [Newell & Rosenbloom, 1981], AI systems are seldom designed to model this adaptive quality. Concept acquisition, that is, inducing structural or attribute descriptions of non-procedural objects from examples, has received substantial attention in the AI literature [Hayes-Roth & McDermott, 1977; Dietterich & Michalski, 1981; Mitchell, 1978; Waterman & Hayes-Roth, 1978; Winston, 1970], but with few exceptions, the techniques developed therein have not been transferred to learning in problem-solving scenarios.[1] Since the process of acquiring and refining problem-solving and planning skills is indisputably a central component in human cognition, its investigation from an AI perspective is clearly justified.

This chapter presents an analogical inference engine and investigates two fundamental hypotheses:

> **Hypothesis:** *Problem-solving and learning are inalienable aspects of a unified cognitive mechanism.*

In other words, one cannot acquire the requisite cognitive skills without solving problems—and, the very process of solving problems provides the information necessary to acquire and tune problem-solving skills. The second hypothesis postulates a unified learning mechanism.

> **Hypothesis:** *The same learning mechanisms that account for concept formation in declarative domains, operate in acquiring problem-solving skills and formulating generalized plans.*

One method of verifying the second hypothesis is to develop a problem-solving mechanism into which one can integrate the techniques developed in concept

[1]Exceptions include Anzai and Simon's Learning-by-Doing Paradigm [Anzai & Simon, 1979], Mitchell's LEX system (Chapter 6 of this book), STRIPS with MACROPS [Fikes & Nilsson, 1971], and indirectly Lenat's AM [Lenat, 1977].

formation—with a resultant system that learns from problem-solving experience. The analogical problem-solving method discussed below provides a framework for automated example generation that enables one to apply learning-from-examples techniques in order to acquire generalized plans. In essence, the objective is akin to Anzai and Simon's learning-by-doing method [Anzai & Simon, 1979]. First, the basic analogical problem-solving method is discussed, and subsequently an experiential learning component is incorporated as an integral part of the general analogical inference process.

5.2 PROBLEM-SOLVING BY ANALOGY

Traditional AI models of problem-solving (such as GPS [Newell & Simon, 1972], STRIPS [Fikes & Nilsson, 1971], and NOAH [Sacerdoti, 1977]) approach every problem almost without benefit of prior experience in solving other problems in the same or similar problem spaces.[2] Consider, for instance, two related problems:

> **The monkey-and-bananas problem:** A (hungry) monkey is placed in a room with bananas suspended from the ceiling beyond its reach. A wooden box of sufficient size to serve as a platform from which the monkey can reach up to the bananas is placed elsewhere in the room.
>
> **The experimenter-and-bananas problem:** An experimenter wishes to set up the monkey-and-bananas problem. He has some bananas, a hook in the ceiling just beyond his reach, and a wooden box elsewhere in the experimental room, and, of course, a monkey.

A means-ends analysis problem solver, such as GPS, will solve either problem, given sufficient time and a reasonable encoding of the permissible actions and their consequences. However, solving one problem does not provide any information useful in solving the other. One would think that practice solving a given type of problem should help in solving similar future problems. For instance, an intelligent monkey observing the experimenter move the box beneath the hook, hang the bananas, and return the box to its original location, may infer which parts of the experimenter's behavior it should replicate in order to reach the bananas. Similarly, if the experimenter tires of watching an unenlightened

---

[2]A *problem space* encodes the information necessary to solve a problem, including goals, initial state, and legal actions that may be taken in solution attempts. *Means-ends analysis* is a problem-solving method that consists of selecting actions that reduce known differences between the current situation and a desired state. Both of these concepts are elaborated in the course of the present discussion. However, the reader not familiar with means-ends analysis is encouraged to review the technique in any standard AI text, such as Winston's *Artificial Intelligence* [Winston, 1977] or Nilsson's *Principles of Artificial Intelligence* [Nilsson, 1980], or read the much more thorough treatment in [Newell & Simon, 1972].

monkey repeatedly fail in its attempts to solve the problem, he should know how to take down the bananas by modifying parts of his earlier plan, rather than replanning from ground zero. In general, transfer of experience among related problems appears to be a theoretically significant phenomenon, as well as a practical necessity in acquiring the task-dependent expertise necessary to solve more complex real-world problems. Indeed, the premise that humans transfer problem-solving expertise between closely related situations is inextricably woven into the pedagogical practices of our educational institutions.

The bulk of human problem-solving takes place in problem spaces that are either well known or vary only slightly from familiar situations. It is rare for a person to encounter a problem that bears no relation to similar problems solved or observed in past experience. New abstract puzzles (such as Rubik's magic cube) are such exceptional problems, where initially the only tractable solution procedure is the application of standard weak methods [Newell & Simon, 1972] without benefit of (non-existent) past experience. Therefore, my investigations center on simplified versions of real-world problems, rather than more abstract, self-contained puzzles.

Now, let us turn to problem-solving in familiar problem spaces. What makes a problem space "familiar"? Clearly, a major aspect consists of memory of past problems and their corresponding solutions that bear strong similarity to the new problem. Such knowledge, once acquired, can be exploited in the problem-solving process. There is no other way to account for the fact that humans solve problems in familiar situations much faster, and with more self-assurance than in unfamiliar abstract situations. A computer model should exhibit the same skill-acquisition process; that is, it should learn to adapt its problem-solving behavior by relying on past experience when available—falling back on the application of standard weak methods when more direct recall-and-modification of existing solutions fails to provide an answer. How might a problem solver be augmented to exhibit such adaptive behavior? First, let us review the standard MEA process; then we will see how the analogical transformation process augments MEA to exploit prior experience.

5.2.1 The Plan-Transformation Problem Space

Consider a traditional means-ends analysis (MEA) problem space [Newell & Simon, 1972], consisting of:

- A set of possible problem states.
- One state designated as the *Initial State*
- One or more state(s) designated as *goal states*—for simplicity, assume there is only one goal state.
- A set of operators with known preconditions that transform one state into another state in the space.
- A difference function that computes differences between two states

(typically applied to compute the difference between the current state and the goal state).

- A method for indexing operators as a function of the difference(s) they reduce (such as the table of differences in GPS).
- A set of global path constraints that must be satisfied in order for a solution to be viable.[3] A path constraint is essentially a predicate on a partial solution sequence, rather than on a single state or operator. The introduction of path constraints in this manner constitutes a slight modification of the standard MEA problem space.

Problem-solving in this space consists of standard MEA:

1. Compare the current state to the goal state
2. Choose an operator that reduces the difference
3. Apply the operator if possible—if not, save the current state and apply MEA to the subproblem of establishing the unsatisfied precondition(s) of that operator.
4. When a subproblem is solved, restore the saved state and resume work on the original problem.

How can one exploit knowledge of solutions to previous problems in this type of problem space? First, consider the simplest case: knowledge consists only of solutions to previous problems. Each solution consists of a sequence of operators and intermediate states, including the initial and final states, together with the path constraints that the solution was designed to satisfy. One rather simple idea is to create *macro-operators* from sequences and sub-sequences of atomic operators that have proven useful as solutions to earlier problems. For instance, STRIPS with MACROPS exploited this idea [Fikes & Nilsson, 1971] using its *triangle table* to store all partial sequences of operators encountered in a solution to a previous problem. However, the simple creation of macro-operators suffers three serious shortcomings. First, the combinatorics involved in storing and searching all possible subsequences of all solutions ever encountered becomes rapidly unmanageable. Searching for applicable macro-operators can become a more costly process than applying MEA to the original problem. Second, path constraints are ignored in this process. If the new problem must satisfy a different set of path constraints, most previous macro-operators may prove invalid. Third, no provision is made for substituting, deleting, or inserting additional operators into recalled solution sequences. These operations prove crucial in the analogical transform process described below. Therefore, let us think not in terms of creating more and more powerful operators that apply to fewer and

[3]For instance, a path constraint may disallow particular subsequences of operators, or prevent an operator that consumes K amount of a resource from applying more than N times, if there is only N×K amount of the resource available to the problem solver.

fewer situations, but rather think in terms of gradually transforming an existing solution into one that satisfies the requirements of the new problem.

Consider a reminding process (a search for solutions to problems similar to the one at hand) that compares differences among the following:

1. The initial state of the new problem and the initial state of previously-solved problems
2. The final state of the new problem and the final state of previously-solved problems
3. The path constraints under which the new problem must be solved and path constraints present when previous similar problems were solved.
4. The proportion of operator preconditions of the retrieved operator sequence satisfied in the new problem situation. This measure is called the applicability of a candidate solution.

The difference function used in comparing initial and final states may be the very same function used for difference reduction in standard MEA. Here, I advocate using the difference function as a *similarity metric* to retrieve the solution of a previously-solved problem closely resembling the present problem. The difference function applied to path constraints is an augmented version of the problem-state difference function, as it must address operator-sequence differences in addition to state information. Hence, *reminding* in our problem-solving context consists of recalling a previously-solved problem whose solution may transfer to the new problem under consideration. A more sophisticated method of computing similarities among episodic memory structures is based on a *relative-invariance hierarchy* among different components of recalled problem solutions, as discussed in [Carbonell, 1982a].

Reminding is only the first phase in analogical problem-solving. The second phase consists of transforming the old solution sequence into one satisfying the criteria for the new problem. How does this transformation process proceed? I submit that it is equivalent to problem-solving in the space of solutions.[4]

Finding an appropriate analogical transformation is itself a problem-solving process, but in a different problem space. The states of the transform problem space are solutions to problems in the original problem space. Thus, the initial state in the transform space is the retrieved solution to a similar problem, and the goal state is a solution satisfying the criteria for the new problem. The operators in the transform problem space are the atomic components of all solution trans-

---

[4]Here I apply my previous definition of a solution to be a sequence of operators and intermediate states together with the set of path constraints that sequence is known to satisfy. Thus, I advocate applying MEA to the space of potential solution sequences rather than the original problem space. However, the reminding process should generate an initial solution sequence close to the goal solution sequence, where closeness is determined by the difference metric above.

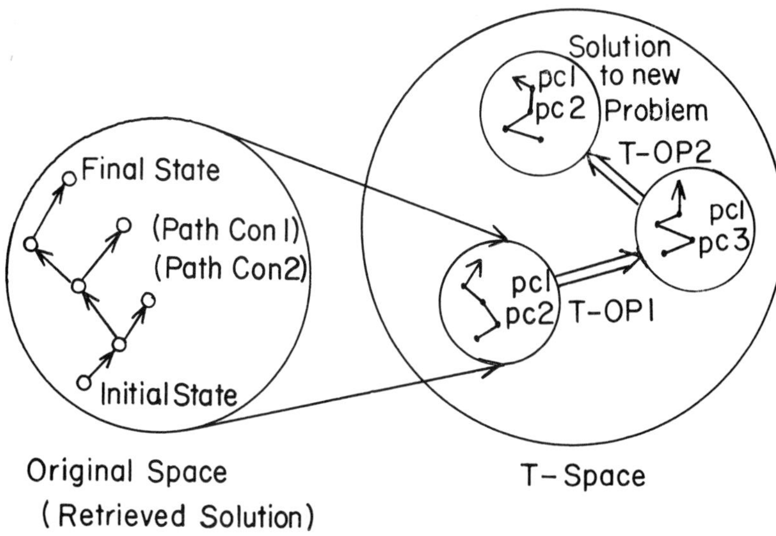

Figure 5-1: A solution path in the original problem space becomes a state in the *analogy transform problem space*.

formations (for example, substitute an operator in the solution sequence for another operator that reduces the same difference, but requires a different set of preconditions or entails different side effects, and so on—see below). The differences that the problem solver attempts to reduce in the new problem space are precisely those computed by the similarity metric in the reminding process. In other words, progress towards a goal is determined by transitions in the solution space towards "solution sequences" corresponding to problems increasingly similar to the new problem. Intermediate states in the transform space need not correspond to *viable* solutions in the original (object) space, in that intermediate solution sequences may not be executable due to unsatisfied operator preconditions. The diagram in Figure 5-1 gives an intuitive flavor of this problem-solving process. More precisely, the *analogy transform problem space* (T-space) is defined as follows:

- States in the transform space are potential solutions to problems in the original problem space (that is, sequences of states and operators including the initial and final states, plus the path constraints under which those solutions were computed.)
- The initial state in the transform space is the solution to a similar problem retrieved by the reminding process.
- A goal state in the transform space is the specification of a solution that solves the new problem, satisfying its path constraints.

- An operator in the transform space (labeled a "T-operator" to avoid confusion) maps an entire solution sequence into another potential solution sequence. The following is a list of the most useful T-operators:
  - **General Insertion**. Insert a new operator into the solution sequence.
  - **General deletion**. Delete an operator from the solution sequence.
  - **Subsequence Splicing**. Splice a solution to a new subproblem into the larger established solution sequence. This T-operator is useful in the following situation: If an operator in the original problem sequence cannot be applied under the new problem specification because one of its preconditions is not satisfied, solve the subproblem of establishing that precondition. This subproblem may be solved either in T-space or in the original (object) space. If successful, splice the precondition-fulfilling subsequence into the original solution sequence.
  - **Subgoal-preserving substitution**. Substitute an operator in the original solution sequence by another operator (or sequence of operators) that reduces the same difference. This T-operator is particularly useful if either a precondition of an operator in the original sequence cannot be satisfied, or if the presence of a particular operator in the solution sequence violates a path constraint.[5]
  - **Final-segment concatenation.** Treat the solution sequence as a macro-operator in the original problem space and apply MEA to reduce the difference between the old final state and the new final state. If successful, concatenate the solution to this subproblem at the end of the original solution sequence.
  - **Initial-segment concatenation.** Apply the process above to find a path in the original problem space from the new initial state to the old initial state. If successful, concatenate the solution to this subproblem at the beginning of the original solution. (Note that in this case we *start* with the initial state for the new problem and seek a path to the initial state for the retrieved solution, whereas in the final segment-concatenation operator the inverse process applies.)
  - **Sequence meshing.** Merge the operator sequences of two complementary solutions retrieved in the reminding process. The resultant solution sequence should differ from a complete solution to the new problem by the intersection of the differences between each

[5]Note that a subgoal-preserving substitution is much more restrictive than a general delete T-operator followed by a general insert T-operator. Therefore, this T-operator is more apt to yield useful transformations, a fact reflected in the ordering of operators under each appropriate entry in the difference table.

retrieved solution and the new problem specification.[6] If the differences between the two retrieved solutions and the new problem specification form disjoint sets, sequence meshing yields a complete solution.

- **Operator reordering**. Reorder the operators in a solution sequence. Often a path constraint in the new problem specification can be satisfied by simple reordering of operators (when allowed by their preconditions) in the retrieved solution.
- **Parameter substitution**. Substitute the objects to which operators were applied in the retrieved solution by the corresponding objects in the new problem specification.
- **Solution-sequence truncation**. Eliminate unnecessary operators. Two significant special cases of this T-operator are **initial-segment truncation** and **final-segment truncation**. For instance, if the final state of an operator subsequence of the retrieved solution exhibits a smaller difference to a goal state of the new problem, use this subsequence as the new basis for mapping into the desired solution sequence.
- **Sequence inversion**. Reverse the operator sequence, inverting each individual operator, if a problem formulation is such that its goal state matches the initial state of a solved problem, and its initial state matches the goal state of that same previously solved problem. Inverting a process is not always possible, and seldom directly achievable. In the present case, the inverse of each operator must be found, and its preconditions satisfied, in order to apply global inversion. However, the general notion is attractive—consider solving the problem of driving between two points in an unknown city. Once this problem is solved, the subsequent problem of returning to the departure site is easily solved by operator sequence inversion (barring travel on one-way streets and other non-invertible operations).

- The *difference metric* in the transform space (D_T) is a combination of the difference measures between initial states (of the retrieved and desired solution sequences), final states, path constraints, and degree of applicability of the retrieved solution in the new problem scenario. Hence, the values of D_T are 4-vectors, with the interpretation that all four component differences must be reduced (independently or jointly) in the transform space (T-space) problem-solving process.

---

[6]Merging two partial operator sequences is an interesting and potentially complex problem in itself. Procedural networks, developed in the NOAH system [Sacerdoti, 1977], facilitate computations of operator interactions when meshing two plans. It is not always the case that two partial solution sequences can be merged effectively (for example, each subsequence may violate necessary preconditions for the other subsequence). Non-algorithmic T-operators, such as **sequence meshing**, define their own internal problem space.

$$D_T = \langle D_O(S_{I,1},S_{I,2}),\ D_O(S_{F,1},S_{F,2}),\ D_P(PC_1,PC_2),\ D_A(SOL_1,SOL_2)\rangle$$

- ○ D_O is the difference function between states in the original space.
- ○ D_P computes differences between path constraints (PC's).
- ○ D_A measures the applicability of the old solution in the new scenario by determining the fraction of operators in the initial solution sequence (SOL_1) whose preconditions are not satisfied under the new problem specification.
- ○ S_I denotes an initial state.
- ○ S_F denotes a final (goal) state.
- ○ The subscript 1 indexes the retrieved solution.
- ○ The subscript 2 indexes the specifications on the desired solution to the new problem.

D_T is reduced when any of its four components is independently reduced. The problem-solving process in T-space succeeds when D_T = <NIL, NIL, NIL, NIL>. Interesting search problems occur when, in order to reduce one component in the difference vector, one or more of the other components must be increased. For example, the insertion of new operators into the solution sequence may have the unfortunate side-effect of violating an established precondition of an operator in the original sequence. In this case, reducing $D_O(I)$ or $D_O(F)$ results in increasing D_A. Our first-pass solution is to define a (linear) combination of the four components and choose the operator that maximally reduces this value, backtracking when necessary. Fortunately, it is often the case that differences in the 4-vector can be reduced in a componentwise-independent manner. Moreover, a modified version of the $\triangle$-MIN method [Carbonell, 1980] may apply, focusing the backtracking process when backtracking proves necessary.

- A difference table for indexing the T-operators is needed. Entries in the difference table take the form "To reduce <DIFFERENCE>, apply a member of <T-OPERATOR-SET>". The operators in the applicable set are usually ordered as a function of the heuristic measure of their utility in reducing the given difference. A sample difference table entry would be:
  - ○ If the preconditions to an operator in SOL_1 are not satisfied (that is, D_A is non-null), try **subgoal-preserving substitution** on the inapplicable operator, or try **solution-sequence splicing** to satisfy the violated preconditions.
- There are no path constraints in the transform space. Since we are mapping from one solution sequence to another, the intermediate states and T-

operators do not necessarily correspond to actual operations performed on an external world, and therefore are not subject to its restrictions. This simplification is offset by the more complex difference metric in T-space.

5.2.2 Some Examples

Consider a simple problem where analogical problem-solving may prove quite appropriate:

> John is located in Pittsburgh and must travel to New York City. However, when he called the airlines, he discovered that all the flights were booked. John never took the intercity train (Amtrak) before, but knows it is a possible means of long-distance travel.

John's plan might be the following: Call Amtrak to make a reservation. Make sure he has sufficient money for the ticket. Find out where to buy the ticket; buy it; and later go to the station and board the train. Why is this a reasonable plan? How could John have synthesized his plan? We cannot really say that John had a "script"[7] for taking trains, as he had not previously traveled by train, nor had he acquired the requisite, detailed information enabling him to do so.

A reasonable way of formulating the plan is by analogy with taking an airplane (or perhaps an intercity bus). The first step is for John to be reminded of taking an airplane (thus recalling: making reservations, tickets being costly, often purchasing the tickets in advance, later traveling to the airport, and so on). Note that it is crucial for John to be reminded of an experience (or a general procedure) where he was fulfilling a similar goal (intercity travel) and *not* one where superficial similarities abound (such as taking a subway, where both means of conveyance are called "trains", they travel on tracks, have many stops, and so on). Subway travel would not suggest the potential necessity of making a reservation, nor would it suggest the requirement for a reasonable sum of money to purchase the ticket. Hence, a comparison of goal states, as suggested in our general method, is indeed a crucial component in the similarity judgments necessary for modeling a reasonable reminding process.

The solution transformation process proceeds by applying the **subgoal-preserving substitution** T-operator, substituting TRAIN-TRAVEL for AIR-TRAVEL, as both operators reduce the same difference. Then, the parameter-substitution T-operator replaces "airport" by "train station", "airline ticket" by "train ticket", and so on. John must rely on his knowledge of how to satisfy the preconditions of AIR-TRAVEL, and hope that the same methods apply to TRAIN-TRAVEL. If this were not the case, further problem-solving would be necessary.

---

[7]By "script" I mean a slight variation of Schank and Abelson's terminology [Schank & Abelson, 1977; Cullingford, 1977], that is, a frozen plan: one or more normative sequences of planned actions whose purpose is to satisfy the preconditions of (and carry out) a high-level operator.

Now, let us reconsider the monkey-and-bananas and experimenter-and-bananas problems, in light of the analogical problem-solving model.

> A monkey watches a behavioral psychologist (that is, the experimenter) pick up a wooden box and place it under a hook in the ceiling. Next, the experimenter climbs on the box, places some bananas on the hook, climbs off the box, and returns it to its original location. Then, the experimenter releases the (hungry) monkey and leaves the room. How does the monkey plan to reach the bananas? Can he benefit from having observed the experimenter?

As we mentioned earlier, a "smart monkey" ought to learn from his observations of the experimenter. Let us see how analogical problem-solving applies here. For simplicity, assume the monkey does not have prior experience solving similar problems beyond his recent observation of the experimenter. The monkey's problem is: **initial state** = monkey on the floor, bananas on the ceiling, box in the room; **final state** = monkey in possession of the bananas; **path constraints** = physical abilities of the monkey. However, the solution to the experimenter's problem cannot be applied directly. (His problem was **initial state** = possession of the bananas, box in the room, experimenter on the floor; **final state** = Bananas on the ceiling, box *not* under the bananas; **path** constraints = physical abilities of the experimenter.)

Assuming the path constraints match, the differences between the initial states (and the differences between the final states) are so large as to preclude any reasonable attempt at direct analogical transformation. Therefore, the monkey must resort to standard MEA (in the original problem space). He selects the operator GET-OBJECT (applied to bananas). This operator suffers an unsatisfied precondition: The monkey cannot reach the bananas. Therefore, the active subgoal becomes: Reach the ceiling where the bananas are located. How may the monkey proceed at this juncture?

The entire problem can, of course, be solved by recursively applying standard MEA. However, there is a more direct solution method. If the monkey recalls his observation of the experimenter, he may realize that the problem of reaching the ceiling has already been solved (by the experimenter, as a subgoal to placing the bananas there—although the monkey need not understand the experimenter's higher-level goals). The monkey can apply the parameter-substitution T-operator (substituting "monkey" for "experimenter"), and optionally the **solution-sequence truncation** T-operator (eliminating the need to return the box to its original location after having used it). This problem-solving process in T-space results in a plan that the monkey can apply directly to reach the bananas, and thus achieve his original goal of having them.

The significant aspect of the experimenter-monkey-and-bananas example is that standard MEA and T-space MEA were combined into a uniform problem-solving process where standard MEA calls on analogical problem-solving to solve a subproblem more directly. The converse process is also possible, and potentially significant. For instance, in the Amtrak example, if John could not have satisfied one of the preconditions for taking the train by analogy with the corresponding AIR-TRAVEL precondition, he could have resorted to standard MEA to solve this subproblem. Hence, *analogical reasoning adds a powerful dimension to standard problem-solving when prior experience can be brought to bear, but remains largely unobstrusive when no relevant prior knowledge suggests itself.*

It would be useful for the problem solver to remember his new problem-solving experiences to use as a basis for future analogical reasoning. These could be remembered directly or abstracted into episodic traces, much like Schank and Abelson's scripts [Schank & Abelson, 1977; Cullingford, 1977], and hierarchically organized as a function of the goals they fulfill.

An interesting observation concerns the recursive closure of analogical MEA.[8] If the T-operator sequence of an analogical problem-solving transformation is remembered, the analogical MEA process can be applied to these transformations themselves. That is, one can construct an analogical mapping between two solution sequences by recycling a past analogical mapping among similar solutions, or by transforming a past, almost usable mapping by recursive application of analogical MEA to the analogical mapping itself. A significant point is that no infinite regress requiring new "hyper-analogical" methods occurs. The same analogical transformation process that applies to object-level solution sequences applies directly to transforming analogical mappings.

5.3 EVALUATING THE ANALOGICAL REASONING PROCESS

In an informal experiment, not meant to withstand statistical significance tests, I gave the following problem to five undergraduate history and art students:

Prove that the product of two even numbers is even.

Somewhat to my surprise and dismay, none of the five was able to solve this simple algebraic problem, although all five made serious attempts. I had intended to give the subjects similar but more difficult problems in subsequent stages of the experiment, measuring whether they improved in speed or accuracy from their recently-acquired experience solving analogically-related problems. Nevertheless, the experiment proved useful in demonstrating the reliance of human problem solvers on analogical mechanisms, as discussed below. Continuing with the experiment, I explained the proof process carefully enough to insure that all five subjects understood it:

1. Recall the definition of an even number: a number that is divisible by 2.
2. Write down an expression that represents an even number: You may write "2N" where N is any integer, to represent a number divisible by 2.

[8]This observation is due in part to Mitchell, personal communication.

3. Multiply two even numbers, writing: $2N \times 2M$, where M is also any integer. Multiplying we get 4NM.
4. Recall the representation of an even number: $2 \times$ any integer. Therefore you can write $4NM = 2 \times 2NM$, which by closure of integers under multiplication matches the representation of an even number. Hence, the product of two even numbers is even.

At this point, all five subjects claimed they understood the proof, and moreover expressed some feeling of embarrassment for not having derived such an "obvious" proof themselves. Then, I suggested they try the following problem:

Prove that the product of two odd numbers is odd.

With grim determination to redeem their previous poor performance all five attempted the problem and three of them succeeded. Briefly:

5. Odd numbers can be represented as "even + 1" $= 2N+1$ for any integer N.
6. The product is: $(2N+1) \times (2M+1) = 4NM + 2N + 2M + 1 = 2(2NM + N + M) + 1$, which is the representation of an odd number.[9]

This informal experiment strongly indicates that the second problem was solved by analogy from the solution to the first problem. The scratch papers collected from the subjects suggest direct attempts at transferring and modifying steps of the first solution. The insertion of an extra algebraic step[10] illustrates an application of the **subsequence splicing** T-operator. The global substitution of a representation for odd numbers in place of a representation for even numbers strongly suggests **parameter substitution**. Moreover, the mere fact that three of five subjects were able to solve a problem more complex than the one where all five failed previously, argues very convincingly for an analogical process exploiting the previous solution (or some abstraction thereof). However, it should be noted that this type of experiment does not, in itself, demonstrate dominance of analogical reasoning in human problem-solving, but rather it provides strong evidence for the existence of analogical processes in cognitive activities. Demonstrating the conjecture that analogy is the central inference mechanism for

[9]Interestingly, one subject chose to represent odd numbers as $2N+3$, which is correct but requires a bit of additional algebraic manipulation. When asked why she chose such a representation, her reply was "4 is a nice even number, and 7 is a nice odd number. The difference between them is 3. The next even number is 6; the next odd is 9; and the difference is *always* 3. So, I took 2N and added 3." What a graphic illustration of means-ends analysis to solve the subproblem of mapping from a representation of even numbers to a representation of odd numbers! Of the two subjects who did not present an adequate proof, one erred in an algebraic manipulation step, the other erroneously chose 3N as his representation for odd numbers.

[10]That is, distributing the product of the two odd numbers is required to fulfill a precondition for factoring the constant "2" from three of the four terms in: $4NM + 2N + 2M + 1$.

human problem-solving would require a much more thorough (and perhaps more controlled) set of psychological observations.

As a test of the computational feasibility of the analogical problem-solving process, a simple version of MEA was programmed to operate on the transform space, and given a subset of the T-operators with a corresponding difference table. It solved the product-of-two-odds problem starting from the solution for two even numbers.[11] The initial computer implementation of analogical MEA is not of particular interest—it demonstrates that the analogical problem-solving process actually works, but does little else. The truly interesting issues will arise when:

- a much fuller implementation is available allowing comparisons among different problem-solving methods over a representative corpus of problems,
- the learning from experience process discussed in the following section is fully integrated with the analogical transform process,
- and the analogical problem solver is integrated with a dynamically-changing long-term memory model.

5.4 LEARNING GENERALIZED PLANS

The analogical transformation process provides a method of exploiting prior experience in a flexible manner. That is, it requires only that the new problem be structurally similar, rather than identical, to one or more previously-solved problems.[12] Hence, simply storing solutions to new problems constitutes a form of learning—as these can serve as a basis from which solutions to yet newer problems may be analogized. However, there are other aspects to learning that present more interesting challenges. To wit, if a type of problem recurs with sufficient frequency, a human planner is apt to formulate a generalized plan for dealing with future instances of that problem, rather than reasoning analogi-

---

[11]The program used $2N-1$ to represent an odd number, since the SUB1 operator was inadvertently listed before ADD1 in the object-space difference table, and therefore the program had to splice in an additional algebraic step in the solution: $(2N-1)(2M-1) = 2(2NM - N - M) + 1$, which does not correspond to the $2N-1$ representation for odd numbers, and therefore had to apply **subsequence splicing** to add two algebraic operators that transformed the expression into $2(2NM - N - M + 1) - 1$. In fact, most of the computational effort was spent finding those two operators (adding and subtracting the same quantity, and refactoring the expression). This allocation of effort roughly corresponds to the substantial time spent by the subject who chose $2N+3$ as a representation with the resultant product being $2(2NM + 3N + 3M) + 9$, which did not exactly match the original representation, and was eventually refactored into $2(2NM + 3N + 3M + 3) + 3$.

[12]The MACROPS facility in STRIPS required corresponding initial states and goal states to be identical modulo parameterization of operators in order to reuse portions of past solution sequences [Fikes & Nilsson, 1971].

cally from a particular member of that cluster of similar experiences. A generalized plan is, in essence, similar to Schank's notion of a script [Schank & Abelson, 1977; Schank, 1980; Cullingford, 1977], that is, a parameterized branching sequence of events with expected goals and default actions.

5.4.1 Acquiring Generalized Solution Procedures

How is a generalized plan acquired from past problem-solving experience? Consider an inductive engine, such as those developed to formulate generalized concepts from sequences of positive and negative exemplars of the target concept, as discussed in Chapters 3 and 4 of this book and in [Hayes-Roth & McDermott, 1977; Waterman & Hayes-Roth, 1978; Winston, 1970; Dietterich & Michalski, 1981; Mitchell, 1978]. Instead of acquiring disembodied concepts from an external teacher providing training sequences of exemplars labeled "positive" or "negative", in experiential learning the exemplars consist of past problems and their respective solutions. These solutions are grouped together as exemplars of a generalized plan by virtue of being derived from a common ancestor in the analogical transform process. Thus, as in learning from observation, the concepts to be acquired are not known *a priori* by an external teacher, but correspond to clusters of experientially-related solutions to a common type of problem. The "type" is not artificially defined, but depends on the actual experience of the individual problem solver. More specifically, generalized plans are acquired by the following process:

- Whenever the analogical problem solver generates a solution to a new problem, that solution is tested in the external world. If it works, it becomes a member of the positive exemplar set, together with the prior solution from which it was analogized and other successful solutions to problems from the same analogical root.
- If the analogized solution fails to work when applied in the external world, the cause of the failure is stored and this solution becomes a member of the corresponding negative exemplar set.
- The positive and negative exemplar sets are given to an induction engine that generates a plan encompassing all the successful solutions and none of the unsuccessful ones. Thus, the training sequence is provided by past experience solving similar problems, rather than by an external teacher. And, the concept acquired is a generalized solution procedure rather than the description of a static object, as is typically the case in the concept acquisition literature. If the description language for the object-space operators is extended, additional generalization can occur (for example, in selecting more general operators that cover disjunctive subsequences in the generalized solution plan).

- Moreover, negative exemplars are near-misses,[13] since the analogical process generated them by making a small number of changes to known positive instances (that is, transformations to past solutions of the same general problem type, retaining the bulk of the solution structure invariant). Hence, near-miss analysis can point out the relevant discriminant features between positive and negative exemplars of the general planning structure under construction. In other words, the problem solver serves as an automated example generator, producing near-misses as a side effect when failing to generate an effective plan.
- Finally, in cases where the analogical problem solver fails to generate a solution for the new problem (as opposed to generating an erroneous solution that becomes a negative exemplar for the generalized plan formation process), different information can be acquired. The situations where a solution was recalled and a plan was formed analogically (independent of whether the plan worked) serve as positive exemplars to reinforce and perhaps generalize the similarity metric used to search memory. The cases where a recalled solution could not be analogized into a candidate plan for the new problem suggest that the old and new problems differed in some crucial aspect not adequately taken into account in the similarity metric, and thus serve as negative reinforcement to refine and constrain the similarity criterion.

Graphically, the information flow in the learning process is illustrated in Figure 5-2. The formula

Analogy: $P_i/C_i \rightarrow P_j/C_j$

should be interpreted as "The analogical transform process maps plan P_i applicable under conditions C_i into plan P_j applicable under conditions C_j." And, the formula

Environment: $P_j/C_j \rightarrow +$ (or $-$)

should read as "Plan P_j succeeded (or failed) when executed in the external environment under conditions C_j."

Figure 5-2 summarizes the process of acquiring generalized plans and updating the similarity criterion from experience. The analogized plans along with their conditions of applicability, form the input to a learning-from-examples engine. Successful solutions are classified as positive exemplars; unsuccessful ones are classified as near-miss negative exemplars. Moreover, the cases where the analogy transform process failed to yield a candidate plan become negative reinforcement instances to a parameter-tuning process, which is positively reinforced

[13]Winston [1970] defines a *near-miss* as a negative exemplar that differs from positive exemplars in a small number of significant features. Near misses are crucial in isolating defining characteristics of a concept in the learning-from-examples paradigm.

The analogical problem-solving process

Analogy: $P_1/C_1 \rightarrow P_2/C_2$	Environment: $P_2/C_2 \rightarrow +$
Analogy: $P_2/C_2 \rightarrow P_3/C_3$	Environment: $P_3/C_3 \rightarrow +$
Analogy: $P_1/C_1 \rightarrow P_4/C_4$	Environment: $P_4/C_4 \rightarrow -$
Analogy: $P_3/C_3 \rightarrow P_5/C_5$	Environment: $P_5/C_5 \rightarrow -$

Analogy: $P_3/C_3 \rightarrow$ <no-plan>$/C_6$
Analogy: $P_1/C_1 \rightarrow$ <no-plan>$/C_7$

Acquiring generalized plans from solutions attempts to similar problems

Input to a learning-from-examples process
Positive exemplars: P_1/C_1, P_2/C_2, P_3/C_3
Negative exemplars: P_4/C_4, P_5/C_5 (near misses)

Output from the learning-from-examples process
Generalized plan: P_G/C_G

Updating the similarity criterion used to recall relevant prior experience

Input to a parameter-tuning process
Present similarity metric
Positive reinforcement trials: C_1, C_2, C_3, C_4, C_5
Negative reinforcement trials: C_6, C_7

Output from the parameter-tuning process
Updated similarity metric

Figure 5-2: Acquiring generalized plans and updating the similarity metric.

by those cases where a (successful or unsuccessful) plan was formulated. Updating the similarity criterion should make future memory searches for solutions to similar problems more responsive to the features that enable the analogical transform system to map a recalled solution into a potential solution for the new problem. Thus, we see that analogical problem-solving interfaces naturally with a learning-from-examples method in that it provides an internal example generator requiring no external teacher.

Presently, I am extending the problem-solving engine to extract and use information from the planning process itself (not just problem descriptions and corresponding solutions), such as viable alternatives not chosen, causes of failure to be wary of in similar situations, and so on. The objective of this endeavor is to enable the learning-from-examples component to learn, or at least refine, the problem-solving strategies themselves, in addition to forming generalized plans.

Thus, general patterns of inference may be acquired from experience [Carbonell, 1982b].

Parts of the plan generalization process are currently being implemented to test the viability of the proposed knowledge-acquisition method, and preliminary results are encouraging. Although much of the theoretical and experimental work in acquiring problem-solving skills is still ahead of us, there is sufficient evidence to support the two original hypotheses: the integration of learning and problem-solving methods into a unified cognitive mechanism, and the utility of the learning-from-examples technique for acquiring planning skills as well as acquiring more static concepts.

As our discussion has demonstrated, learning can occur in both phases of analogical problem-solving: *(i)* the reminding process that organizes and searches past experience, and *(ii)* the analogical transformation process itself. Additional issues in the experiential adaptation of the reminding process are discussed below.[14]

5.4.2 Episodic Memory Organization

Memory of solutions to previous problems, whether observed or directly experienced, must be organized by similarities in goal states, initial states, means available, and path constraints present. Otherwise, there can be no reasonable reminding process when solving future problems of a similar nature. Hence, a hierarchical indexing structure on an episodic memory must be constructed dynamically and extended as the system gradually accumulates new experience. Given an effective memory model, the process of continuously expanding and structuring past experience becomes a relatively simple, but absolutely essential, aspect of learning that proceeds concurrently with analogical reasoning. Moreover, the memory model should retrieve general plans when these have proven reliable to the exclusion of the original episodic memory traces, which then effectively "fade" from memory. "Fading" means that the memory indexing structure is altered so they are no longer easily recalled in the reminding process. (This notion is akin to Schank's "mushing" process [Schank, 1979] and Anderson's masking by declining relative activation [Anderson & Greeno, 1981].)

5.4.3 Episodic Memory Restructuring

It is conceivable that in the lifetime of an adaptive problem solver, the nature of the problems it is called upon to solve may change gradually. The change

[14]The reader is referred to Schank [Schank & Carbonell, 1979; Schank, 1980], Lebowitz [1980] and Kolodner [1980] for various discussions on the type of basic episodic memory model implicit in this chapter. The memory organization scheme must be structured according to similarity criteria instrumental to the task of indexing and recalling past problem-solving experience [Carbonell, 1982a].

may manifest itself as decreased reliability of the difference function comparing new and old problem specifications, causing the reminding process to retrieve inappropriate solutions, or to miss relevant past experiences. Hence, a means of tuning the difference metric in a failure-driven manner is a requisite process for long-term adaptive behavior.

More specifically, the heuristic combining the four values in the D_T 4-vector may be tuned to yield appropriate values for certain classes of problems most commonly encountered. For instance, differences in path constraints are less meaningful to a problem-solver who has ample resources than to a more spartanly-endowed problem solver. If a graduate student later becomes a millionaire, the fact that he then commands more substantial resources should lessen the impact of resource-based path constraints in his problem-solving. Consequently, the similarity metric will cease to consider past solutions of otherwise similar problems that were solved when operating under more severe resource constraints. This is not a particularly desirable state of affairs, as resource-limited solutions are certainly viable, if not always desirable, to a problem solver commanding more resources. Therefore, the reminding heuristic should no longer weigh path-constraint differences as heavily. (Note that reminding is a constrained search process, whereas analogical mapping or instantiating a general solution pattern are generative processes. Hence, the reminding process need only retrieve approximate, *plausible* solutions.) Returning to our example, if that same millionaire later files for bankruptcy, the relevance of resource-based path constraints assumes significant proportions once again. A pauper will not be able to solve most problems by emulating a millionaire. Thus, the path-constraint component of the similarity/difference metric should reestablish its central role in the reminding heuristic. In this manner, the relevance of each component in the similarity measure is subject to long-term fluctuation.[15]

How can the relative weights in the similarity heuristic be tuned? When the reminding process fails to retrieve a viable initial state to the T-space problem solver, but the problem is later solved in the original problem space, the solution can be compared to episodic memory. If a solution to a previous problem is found to be very similar, then the problem descriptions should also have been found similar by the reminding heuristic. The component contributing the largest difference is then reduced in importance. The converse process also applies. If a solution retrieved as similar does not lead to a solution in T-space, the difference(s) that could not be reduced by the T-space problem solver are assigned more importance in the difference heuristic. These complementary

[15]This process is analogous to Berliner's application coefficients in SNAC [Berliner, 1979], whose values change gradually over the course of a game. Here change occurs more gradually over the lifetime of the problem solver, but I am proposing an adaptive rather than a pre-programmed contextual-weighting process. Note that whereas individual path constraints differ from problem to problem, I am discussing gradual changes in the relative significance of path constraints *vis a vis* other criteria in the similarity metric on average over many individual problem-solving episodes.

processes regulating the difference metric are designed to make all changes very gradually to insure against potentially unstable behavior. This form of experiential parameter tuning is a new application of a credit assignment technique dating back to Samuel [1963] .

5.4.4 T-Operator Refinement

If episodic memory is extended to contain T-space problem-solving traces, in addition to experienced events and solutions to past problems, then learning can occur in the T-operator domain. For instance, consider a T-operator present with high frequency in unsuccessful T-space solution attempts. It is conceivable that the entry (or entries) in the difference table indexing that T-operator are insufficiently constrained, suggesting the need for a discrimination process such as the following:

1. Compare T-space solution attempts where the T-operator in question was present only in failure paths, with solution attempts where it was present in successful solution paths.
2. If there are multiple entries in the difference table for that T-operator, and some entries correspond only to failure instances of the operator, delete these entries, as the operator is being applied to reduce a difference it proved incapable of reducing.
3. If a single entry corresponds to many more failures than successes, the description of the difference being reduced may be too general and ought to be factored into a disjunctive set of more specific differences. Later experience can help isolate which of these sub-differences the T-operator is actually capable of reducing. Then, the more specific differences (those that the T-operator in question proved capable of reducing) replace the previous more general entry in the difference table. Other differences in the factored disjunctive set that (as experience shows) cannot be reduced by the T-operator are discarded. It should be noted that the operation of factoring an arbitrary concept into a disjunctive set of sub-concepts is, in general, not a tractable process. However, given a hierarchical memory model and a non-monotonic inference capability,[16] approximately correct factorings can be achieved.

5.4.5 The Acquisition of New T-Operators

If the reminding process retrieved one or more solutions, but the analogy transform process failed to map these into a solution satisfying the specifications

---

[16]Non-monotonic inference is a plausible inference technique based on tentative deductions and assumptions that may prove invalid as additional knowledge is acquired [McDermott & Doyle, 1980].

of the new problem, and the original-problem-space problem solver found a solution, then we have a clear indication that the T-space problem solver is missing some essential T-operators. One approach to remedy this situation is the following process:

1. Compare the solution computed by the problem solver in the untransformed space with the various attempted transformations in T-space.
2. Find the intermediate state in the failed T-space solution attempt that minimizes the difference metric (D_T) to the solution computed by standard MEA.
3. Hypothesize a T-operator instance to be the transformation from the closest state (reached in the T-space solution attempts) to the actual solution. Save this T-operator instance.
4. If later problem-solving impasses cause failure-driven creation of more T-operator instances, then the application of a learning-from-observations technique, such as the *conceptual clustering* method presented in Chapter 11, may prove fruitful. If the exemplars are sufficiently similar, or form clusters of closely similar exemplars, new T-operators can be hypothesized according to the characteristic description of each conceptual cluster. "Sufficiently similar" in this context means that the common structure shared by the cluster of T-operator instances is not present in other active T-operators. Hence, the new operator will perform transformations different from those of any previously existing T-operator—that is, the new operator may prove generatively useful.
5. The newly-created T-operator may then be added to the set of active T-operators (subject to the refinement process above if the new operator proves unreliable).
6. The entry in the difference table indexing the new T-operator is a bounded generalization of the differences that each T-operator instance reduced at the time it was created. If these differences do not share a common component not present in other entries, more than one (disjunctive) entry must be made in the difference table.

Thus, new T-operators can be acquired if the problem solver is given a set of problems for which the same (previously unknown), general T-space transformation was required. Moreover, the operator acquisition and discrimination processes are equally applicable to refining and extending sets of operators in the original untransformed problem space (if the problem solver can tap an external source of knowledge upon failure, or relax processing constraints upon resource-limited failure). Acquiring T-operators, however, requires learning from observation, rather than the better understood and generally simpler process of learning from examples used to acquire generalized plans.

The learning mechanisms discussed in this section can prove effective if, and only if, the reasoning system is capable of remembering, indexing and retrieving past experience, including aspects of its internal processing in previous problem-solving attempts (such as hypothesized T-operator instances). Therefore, the necessity for *both* dynamic memory organization processes and a problem-solving mechanism capable of exploiting episodic memory is clearly manifest.

5.5 CONCLUDING REMARK

The primary objective of this paper has been to lay a uniform framework for analogical problem-solving capable of integrating skill refinement and plan-acquisition processes. Most work in machine learning has not addressed the issue of integrating learning and problem-solving into a unified process. (However, Chapter 6 of this book and Lenat [1977] are partial counter-examples.) Past and present investigations of analogical reasoning have focused on disjoint aspects of the problem. For instance, Winston [1980] investigated analogy as a powerful mechanism for classifying and structuring episodic descriptions. Kling [1971] studied analogy as a means of reducing the set of axioms and formulae that a theorem prover must consider when deriving new proofs to theorems similar to those encountered previously. In his own words, his system "...derives the analogical relationship between two [given] problems and outputs the *kind of information* that can be usefully employed by a problem-solving system to expedite its search." However, analogy takes no direct part in the problem-solving process itself. Hence, the extension of means-ends analysis to an analogy transform space is, in itself, a new, potentially-significant problem-solving method, in addition to supporting various learning mechanisms in an integrated manner.

ACKNOWLEDGMENTS

I wish to thank Allen Newell, David Klahr, and Derek Sleeman for useful comments and discussion on earlier drafts of this work, and Monica Lam for suggesting problems used to test the analogical process. This research was sponsored in part by the Office of Naval Research (ONR) under grant number N0014-79-C-0661, and in part by the Defense Advanced Research Projects Agency (DOD), ARPA order number 3597, monitored by the Air Force Avionics Laboratory under contract number F-33615-81-K-1539. The views and conclusions in this document are those of the author and should not be interpreted as representing the official policies, either expressed or implied, of the Defense Advanced Research Agency or the U.S. Government.

REFERENCES

Anderson, J. R. and Greeno, J. G., "Acquisition of Problem-Solving Skill," *Cognitive Skills and Their Acquisition*, J. R. Anderson (Ed.), Hillsdale, NJ: Erlbaum Assoc., 1981.

Anzai, Y. and Simon, H. A., "The Theory of Learning by Doing," *Psychological Review*, Vol. 86, pp. 124-140, 1979.

Berliner, H., "On the Construction of Evaluation Functions for Large Domains," *Proceedings of the Sixth International Joint Conference on Artificial Intelligence*, IJCAI-79, pp. 53-55, 1979.

Carbonell, J. G., "Δ-MIN: A Search-Control Method for Information-Gathering Problems," *Proceedings of the First AAAI Conference*, AAAI-80, August 1980.

Carbonell, J. G., "Metaphor: An Inescapable Phenomenon in Natural Language Comprehension," *Knowledge Representation for Language Processing Systems*, W. Lehnert and M. Ringle (Eds.), New Jersey: Erlbaum, 1982a.

Carbonell, J. G., "Towards a Computational Model of Metaphor in Common Sense Reasoning," *Proceedings of the Fourth Annual Meeting of the Cognitive Science Society*, 1982b, (Ann Arbor, MI).

Cullingford, R., *Script Application: Computer Understanding of Newspaper Stories,* Ph.D. dissertation, Yale University, Sept. 1977.

Dietterich, T. and Michalski, R., "Inductive Learning of Structural Descriptions," *Artificial* Intelligence, Vol. 16, 1981.

Fikes, R. E. and Nilsson, N. J., "STRIPS: A New Approach to the Application of Theorem Proving to Problem Solving," *Artificial Intelligence*, Vol. 2, pp. 189-208, 1971.

Hayes-Roth, F. and McDermott, J., "Knowledge Acquisition from Structural Descriptions," *Proceedings of the Fifth International Joint Conference on Artificial Intelligence*, IJCAI-77, pp. 356-362, 1977.

Kling, R. E., "A Paradigm for Reasoning by Analogy," *Artificial Intelligence*, Vol. 2, pp. 147-178, 1971.

Kolodner, J. L., *Retrieval and Organizational Strategies in Conceptual Memory: A Computer Model,* Ph.D. dissertation, Yale University, Nov. 1980.

Korf, R. E., "Toward a Model of Representation Changes," *Artificial Intelligence*, Vol. 14, No. 1, pp. 41-78, 1980.

Lebowitz, M., *Generalization and Memory in an Integrated Understanding System,* Ph.D. dissertation, Yale University, Oct. 1980.

Lenat, D., *AM: Discovery in Mathematics as Heuristic Search,* Ph.D. dissertation, Stanford University, 1977.

McDermott, D. V. and Doyle J., "Non-Monotonic Logic I," *Artificial Intelligence*, Vol. 13, pp. 41-72, 1980.

Mitchell, T. M., *Version Spaces: An Approach to Concept Learning,* Ph.D. dissertation, Stanford University, December 1978.

Moore, J. and Newell, A., "How can MERLIN Understand?," *Knowledge and Cognition*, L. Gregg (Ed.), Hillsdale, NJ: Erlbaum Assoc., pp. 253-285, 1974.

Newell, A. and Rosenbloom, P., "Mechanisms of Skill Acquisition and the Law of Practice," *Cognitive Skills and Their Acquisition*, J. R. Anderson (Ed.), Hillsdale, NJ: Erlbaum Assoc., 1981.

Newell, A. and Simon, H. A., *Human Problem Solving*, New Jersey: Prentice-Hall, 1972.

Nilsson, N. *Priciples of Artificial Intelligence*, Tioga Publishing Co., 1980.

Sacerdoti, E. D., *A Structure for Plans and Behavior*, Amsterdam: North-Holland, 1977.

Samuel, A. L., "Some Studies in Machine Learning Using the Game of Checkers," *Computers and Thought*, E. A. Feigenbaum and J. Feldman (Eds.), McGraw Hill, New York, pp. 71-105, 1963.

Schank, R. C., "Reminding and Memory Organization: An Introduction to MOPS", Technical Report 170, Yale University Comp. Sci. Dept., 1979.

Schank, R. C., "Language and Memory," *Cognitive Science*, Vol. 4, No. 3, pp. 243-284, 1980.

Schank, R. C. and Abelson, R. P., *Scripts, Goals, Plans and Understanding*, Hillside, NJ: Lawrence Erlbaum, 1977.

Schank R. C. and Carbonell, J. G., "Re: The Gettysburgh Address, Representing Social and Political Acts," *Associative Networks*, Findler, N. (Ed.), Academic Press, 1979, (Also Yale U. Comp. Sci. Report #127, 1978).

Waterman, D. A. and Hayes-Roth, F., "Inductive Learning of Relational Productions," *Pattern-Directed Inference Systems*, Waterman and Hayes-Roth, 1978 (Eds.), New York: Academic Press, 1978.

Winston, P., *Learning Structural Descriptions from Examples,* Ph.D. dissertation, MIT, September 1970.

Winston, P. H., *Artificial Intelligence*, Addison-Wesley, 1977.

Winston, P. H., "Learning and Reasoning by Analogy," *CACM*, Vol. 23, No. 12, pp. 689-703, 1979.

6

LEARNING BY EXPERIMENTATION: ACQUIRING AND REFINING PROBLEM-SOLVING HEURISTICS

Tom M. Mitchell
Paul E. Utgoff
Rutgers University

Ranan Banerji
St. Joseph's University

ABSTRACT

This chapter concerns learning heuristic problem-solving strategies through experience. In particular, we focus on the issue of learning heuristics to guide a forward-search problem solver, and describe a computer program called LEX, which acquires problem-solving heuristics in the domain of symbolic integration. LEX acquires and modifies heuristics by iteratively applying the following process: *(i)* generate a practice problem; *(ii)* use available heuristics to solve this problem; *(iii)* analyze the search steps performed in obtaining the solution; and *(iv)* propose and refine new domain-specific heuristics to improve performance on subsequent problems. We describe the methods currently used by LEX, analyze strengths and weaknesses of these methods, and discuss our current research toward more powerful approaches to learning heuristics.

6.1 INTRODUCTION

Efforts to build powerful, specialized, heuristic problem solvers have met with increasing success over the past decade. However, identifying and encoding the domain-specific heuristics necessary for high performance of these systems is a painstaking, difficult process. As the complexity of a heuristic program grows, it becomes increasingly difficult for the system builder to predict how the addition of a particular new heuristic or operator will affect overall system performance. In response to this problem, there has been increased interest over the past several years in developing semi-automated and fully-automated methods to help construct expert heuristic problem solvers [Waterman, 1970; Davis, 1981; Buchanan, 1978; Politakis, 1979] (See also Chapter 7 of this book). At the same time, in the Cognitive Psychology literature there have been several attempts to model acquisition of problem-solving skills in humans [Anzai, 1979; Neves, 1978] (See also Chapter 7 of this book).

The research presented here is directed toward devising methods by which heuristic problem-solving programs improve their problem-solving expertise through experience, by generating selected problems in the domain, solving them, and learning by analyzing their solutions. As part of this research we have designed and constructed a computer program, called LEX, that incorporates general methods for discovering domain-dependent problem-solving heuristics.

The organization of this chapter is as follows. The learning problem considered by LEX is described, followed by a discussion of the methods employed by the current system. This includes methods for *(i)* solving practice problems, *(ii)* performing the *credit assignment* task of isolating appropriate and inappropriate search steps, *(iii)* proposing and generalizing heuristics, and *(iv)* generating new practice problems with which to experiment. The final sections of the chapter discuss augmenting the system by giving it knowledge to conduct detailed analyses of problem solutions. This knowledge can be used to provide strong guidance for the generalization process, and to generate new terms in the language with which heuristics are described. Some of the material from this chapter is drawn from a collection of previously published articles, including [Mitchell, 1981; Mitchell, 1982a; Mitchell, 1982b; Utgoff, 1982].

6.2 THE PROBLEM

LEX begins with a heuristic search problem solver without the heuristics. It is given a set of operators for solving problems in symbolic integration, and it learns a set of heuristics that recommend in which situations the various operators should be applied. Whereas each operator given to LEX contains a set of preconditions that characterize a class of problem states to which that operator *can* validly be applied, learned heuristics characterize the more restrictive subclass of problem states to which the operator *should* be applied; that is, the subclass of problem states for which application of the operator leads to an acceptable solution. Heuristics are learned by *generalizing from examples* of problem states to which the operator is applied in solving practice problems. These training examples are generated by the program, by proposing, solving, and analyzing practice problems.

LEX operates in the domain of symbolic integration. It solves integration problems by searching through a space of mathematical expressions containing indefinite integrals. The operators for traversing the search space are the standard rules of integration (for instance, integration by parts) as well as transformations that characterize algebraic equivalence of expressions (such as the associative and distributive laws). The problem-solving goal is to derive a problem state that contains no integrals.

```
OP1   ∫ r·f(x) dx      ⇒   r ∫ f(x) dx

OP2   Integration by parts:
         ∫ u dv  ⇒  uv - ∫ v du
      (the precondition is internally represented
      as ∫ f1(x) f2(x) dx, where f1(x) corresponds
      to u and f2(x)dx corresponds to dv)

OP3   1·f(x)·  ⇒  f(x)

OP4   ∫ f1(x)+f2(x) dx  ⇒ ∫ f1(x) dx + ∫ f2(x) dx

OP5   ∫ sin(x) dx  ⇒  -cos(x) + C

OP6   ∫ cos(x) dx  ⇒  sin(x) + C

OP7   ∫ x^r dx   ⇒  [x^(r+1)]/(r+1)  + C
```

Figure 6-1: Some of the operators for symbolic integration.

Over 40 problem-solving operators are currently provided to LEX, some of which are shown in Figure 6-1. Each operator is interpreted as follows: If the general pattern on the left hand side of the operator is found within the problem state, then that pattern may be replaced by the pattern specified on the right hand side of the operator. For example, op1 indicates that if the problem state contains a subexpression of the form "∫ r·f(x) dx" (here "r" stands for any real number, and "f(x)" for any function of x), then that subexpression may be rewritten with the real number outside the integral.

In addition to its problem solver, representation for problem states, and problem-solving operators, LEX also begins with a language for describing heuristics. Each heuristic learned by LEX is of the form:

IF the current problem state matches the applicability condition P,
THEN apply operator O, with variable binding B.

Thus, the generalization task that LEX faces is that of determining the appropriate applicability condition, P, for each heuristic. Learning this applicability condition corresponds to learning the concept "situations in which operator O should be applied, with variable binding B."

The language for describing generalizations, or applicability conditions, of heuristics is based on a grammar for algebraic expressions containing indefinite integrals. The sentences derivable by this grammar are the expressions that form legal problem states. The sentential forms derivable by the grammar constitute legal generalizations. Briefly, the grammar contains non-terminal symbols that correspond to classes of functions (for example, trigonometric, polynomial) and classes of operators (such as function composition, multiplication, integration). These can be combined to form generalized algebraic expressions. Figure 6-2 shows this grammar in the form of a hierarchy. Each node in the hierarchy represents some substring of a sentential form, and each edge corresponds to a rule in the grammar.

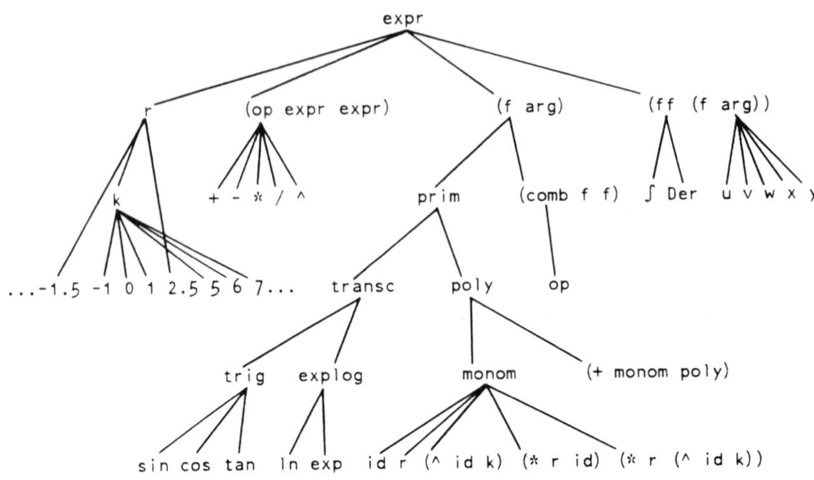

Figure 6-2: A grammar for a concept description language for symbolic integration.

Below is an example of the kind of heuristics that LEX can describe and learn. This heuristic may be interpreted as "*If* the current problem state contains an integrand which is the product of x and any transcendental function of x, *Then* try integration by parts, with u and dv bound to the indicated subexpressions."

$\int$ x transc(x) dx ⇒ op2 (Integration by parts),
with u = x
and dv = transc(x) dx

The language used to describe applicability conditions of heuristics determines, to a great extent, the range of heuristics that can be learned by the system. In the current system, this language is fixed. Section 6.4 discusses an approach to dynamically altering the language when necessary.

6.3 DESIGN OF LEX

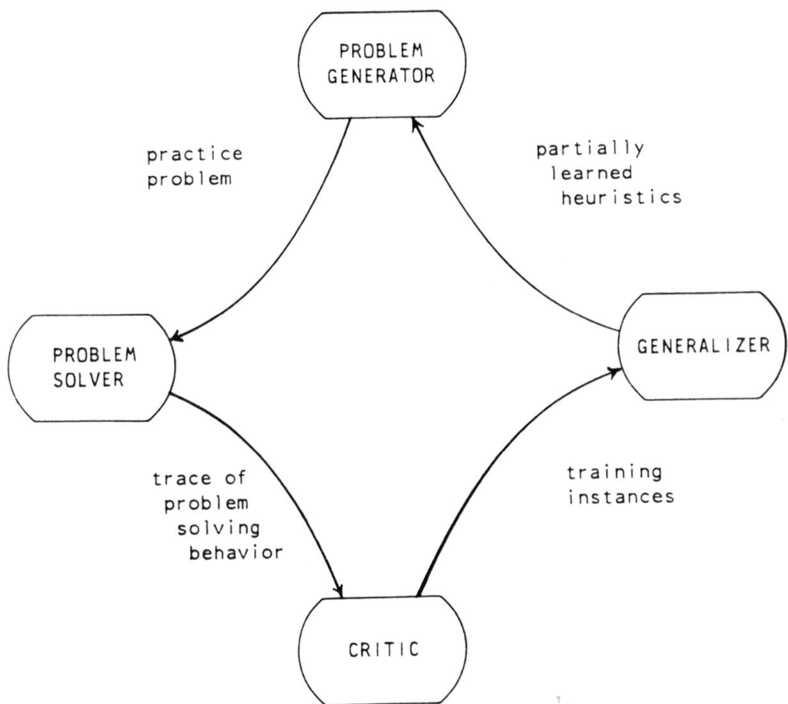

Figure 6-3: The major components of LEX.

LEX is based on four program modules, as shown in Figure 6-3. These modules are summarized below, and described in more detail in the following subsections.

1. **Problem Solver**— This module utilizes whatever operators and heuristics are currently available, to solve a given practice problem. The output of this module is a solution to the given problem, along with a detailed trace of the search performed in attempting to solve the problem.
2. **Critic**—This module analyzes the search performed by the Problem Solver. The output of this module is a set of positive and negative training instances from which heuristics will be inferred. Positive instances correspond to desirable search steps executed in solving the problem, whereas negative instances correspond to undesirable steps.

3. **Generalizer**—This module proposes and refines general heuristics intended to produce more effective problem-solving behavior on subsequent problems. It formulates heuristics by generalizing from the training instances provided by the Critic.
4. **Problem Generator**—This module generates practice problems to be considered by the other modules. It attempts to generate practice problems that will be informative (that is, problems that will lead to training data useful for proposing and refining heuristics), yet easy enough to be solved using existing heuristics.

6.3.1 Representing Incompletely-learned Heuristics

LEX learns heuristics incrementally, requiring many positive and negative training instances before converging to a final definition of any given heuristic. Therefore, at any given stage in the system's development, there are typically many partially-learned heuristics whose exact description is underdetermined by the data, knowledge, and assumptions currently held by the system. It is essential that the system have a way of describing what the system *does* and *does not* know about each such partially-learned heuristic. This information is important *(i)* to the Problem Solver, which must use the partially-learned heuristics in trying to solve problems, *(ii)* to the Generalizer, which must revise partially-learned heuristics as new training data become available, and *(iii)* to the Problem Generator, which must choose practice problems that will lead to refinements of partially-learned heuristics.

LEX represents each partially-learned heuristic by representing the range of *all alternative plausible descriptions of the heuristic*. A description is considered plausible if it applies to all the known positive instances associated with the heuristic, but to none of the negative instances. Thus, for each partially-learned heuristic, we refer to the set of all plausible descriptions of the heuristic as the *version space* of the partially-learned heuristic, relative to the observed instances and the language in which heuristics are described.

While, in principle, the version space of a partially-learned heuristic could be represented by listing all of its members, there are typically far too many plausible descriptions of a heuristic for this to be feasible. Fortunately, a much more compact method for representing version spaces is possible. Any version space can be represented compactly by storing only its maximally-specific and maximally-general elements, according to the following definition of "more specific".

Heuristic H1 is **more specific than or equal to** heuristic H2 if and only if both of the following conditions hold:

1. The applicability condition of H2 matches every instance matched by the applicability condition of H1 (that is, the applicability condition of H1 is more specific than or equal to the applicability condition of H1).
2. In each case where both H1 and H2 apply, their recommendations are identical (that is, they recommend the same operator and the same binding of operator arguments).

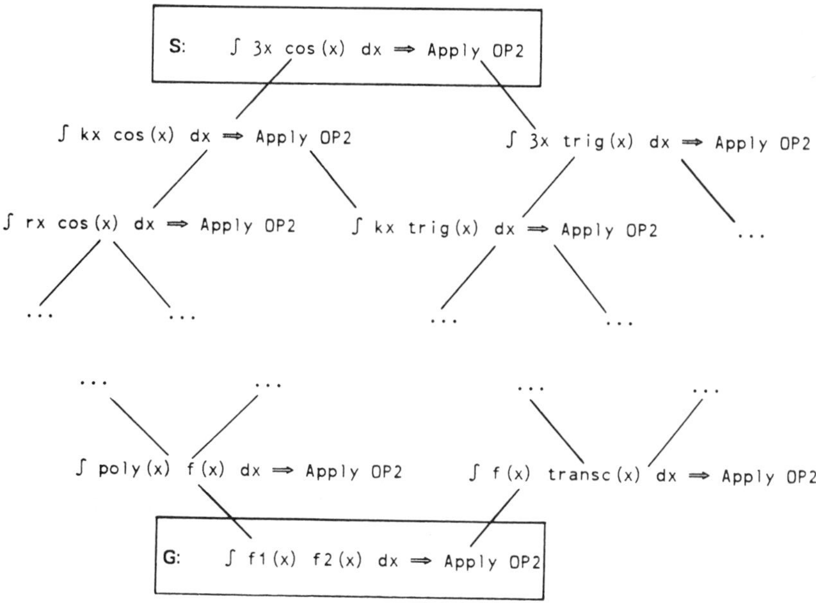

Figure 6-4: Representing a version space.

We will refer to the maximally-specific members of a version space as the subset S of the version space, and to the maximally-general (minimally-specific) members of the version space as the subset G. LEX represents the version space of each partially-learned heuristic by storing the subsets S and G of that version space, as illustrated in Figure 6-4. In this figure, some of the members of a particular version space are shown, with the more-specific-than relationship among them indicated. While there are very many plausible heuristic descriptions in this version space, the (singleton) sets S and G completely determine the version space by the following rule: a heuristic description is contained in the version space if and only if it is both *(i)* more specific than or equal to some member of G, and *(ii)* more general than or equal to some member of S.

This representation and use of version spaces for generalizing from examples has been used previously in the META-DENDRAL program for inferring rules of mass spectroscopy, and is described more fully in [Mitchell, 1978] and [Mitchell, 1982a]. In [Mitchell, 1978] a more formal definition of version spaces is given, along with proofs that the algorithm for incrementally updating the sets S and G is correct.

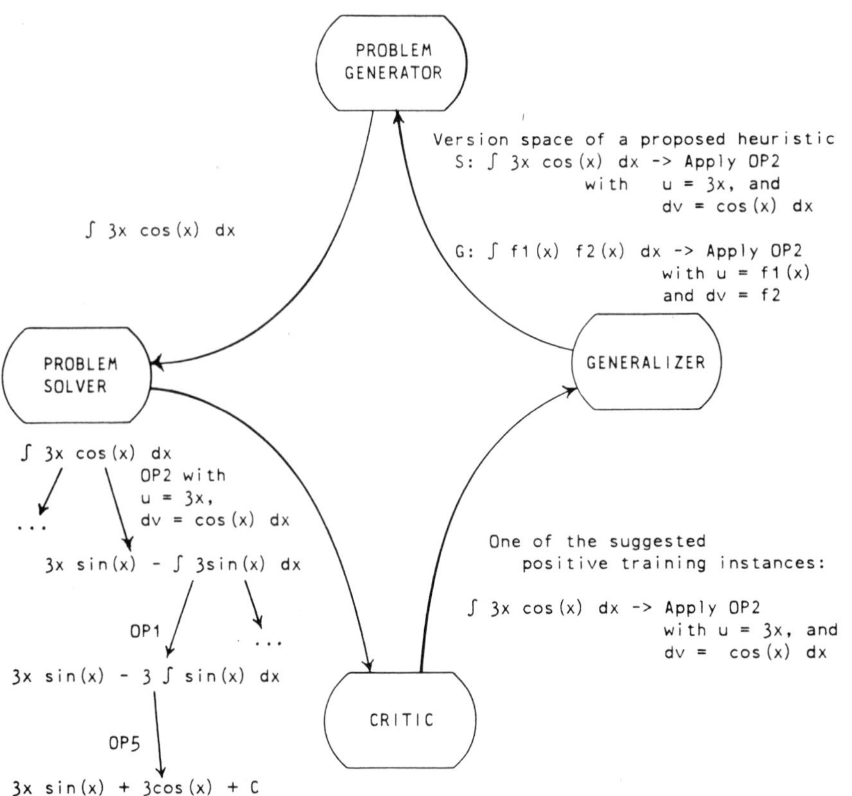

Figure 6-5: The learning cycle in LEX.

The remainder of this section presents the methods used by the four modules of LEX, in formulating and refining heuristics. The discussion centers around the example shown in Figure 6-5, which illustrates one particular practice problem considered by LEX, and the resulting version space of one heuristic. This figure shows the search tree generated by the Problem Solver, one of the training instances produced by the Critic, and the sets S and G computed by the Generalizer to describe the resulting proposed heuristic.

6.3.2 The Problem Solver

The Problem Solver uses a forward-search strategy guided by whatever heuristics are available during the current propose-solve-criticize-generalize cycle. The Problem Solver accepts as input a problem to be solved, along with a resource limit on the CPU time and memory space that it may expend in attempting to solve that problem. If the problem is not solved within the allocated resources, the Problem Solver stops and waits for a new problem.[1]Unsolved problems do not lead to any learning, because the credit assignment strategy of the Critic depends upon knowing the problem solution.

The Problem Solver generates a search tree, repeatedly choosing a node to expand and an operator with which to expand it, as shown below.

```
DO UNTIL problem is solved OR resource allocation is expended

BEGIN

IF no heuristics are applicable to any open node

 THEN expand the lowest cost open node, using any applicable operator

 ELSE IF exactly one heuristic applies to exactly one open node,

     THEN execute the step recommended by that heuristic,

     ELSE follow the recommendation of one of the applicable heuristics,
     choosing that heuristic which applies with the highest estimated
     degree of match (see explanation below).

END.
```

Here, the "cost" of a node refers to the sum of CPU time expended for each step leading from the root of the tree to that node. An open node refers to any node in the search tree with at least one applicable operator that has not yet been applied. The notion of "estimated degree of match" of a heuristic to a node is introduced to allow using partially-learned heuristics in a reasonable fashion. Notice that for a given partially-learned heuristic and search node, it is possible that some of the alternative plausible descriptions of the heuristic will match the node while others will not. Because of this we define the *degree of match* of a partially-learned heuristic to a given node as the proportion of the members of its version space that match the node. Because the degree of match is difficult to compute exactly, it is estimated by the proportion of members in the union of S and G that match the given problem state.

The ability of the Problem Solver to use partially-learned heuristics to con-

---

[1]LEX makes no distinction between problems that are unsolvable in principle, and those that are solvable in principle but unsolvable within the given resource limits.

trol search is important in allowing it to solve problems that will provide additional training data. In experiments with LEX, it has typically been the case that the majority of available heuristics are only partially learned. Even so, it is quite common that a partially-learned heuristic will apply to a particular node with a degree of match of 1. In such cases, even though the exact identity of the heuristic is not yet determined, the applicability of the heuristic to this particular node is fully determined (that is, it does not matter which of the alternative heuristic descriptions is correct, since they all apply to the node in question). The ability to distinguish such cases from those in which there is ambiguity regarding the heuristic recommendation is an important capability in the Problem Solver's use of partially-learned heuristics.

6.3.3 The Critic

After a solution has been determined, the Critic faces the task of assigning credit (or blame) to individual search steps for their role in leading to (or away from) a solution. The Critic examines the detailed search trace recorded by the Problem Solver, and selects certain search steps to be classified as positive or negative training instances for forming general heuristics. Each training instance corresponds to a single search step; that is, the application of a single operator to a given problem state, with a particular binding of operator arguments.

Figure 6-5 illustrates part of the search tree generated by the Problem Solver for a given practice problem, and one of the associated positive training instances produced by the Critic. The positive instance shown there corresponds to the first step along the path to the solution.

The criterion used by the Critic to produce training instances may be summarized as follows:

1. The Critic labels as a *positive instance* every search step along the lowest cost solution path found. Here, the cost of a solution is taken to be the sum of the execution times of all operators applied along the solution path.
2. The Critic labels as a *negative instance* every search step that *(i)* leads away from a node on the lowest cost solution path found, to a node not on this path, and *(ii)* when its resulting problem state is given anew to the Problem Solver, leads either to no solution or to a higher cost solution. Here a solution is considered higher cost if its cost is more than a certain factor times the cost of the lowest cost known solution (currently this factor is set to 1.15). The resource allocation given to the Problem Solver in this case is equal to the resources spent in obtaining the known solution.

Notice that the Critic is not infallible. It is possible for the Critic to produce positive training instances that are not on the minimum cost solution path, but are rather on the lowest cost solution path found by the Problem Solver. Also, it is possible for the Critic to label as negative a search step that is in fact part of the true (but never discovered) minimum cost solution path. Both kinds of errors can arise because the heuristic Problem Solver is not assured of finding the minimum cost solution. Criterion *2(ii)* above is included in order to reduce the likelihood that such errors will occur. Here, the Critic reinvokes the Problem Solver, giving it a problem state associated with a potential negative instance, in order to explore a portion of the problem space that may not have been sufficiently considered during the solution of the original problem. If the Problem Solver is unable to find an appropriate solution from the given state within the specified resource limits, the confidence that this is a negative instance is increased. If the Problem Solver finds a lower cost solution when it is reinvoked, this new solution is used in determining positive training instances. Of course, the only completely error-free strategy for labeling training instances requires a full breadth-first or uniform-cost search, which is usually prohibitively time consuming.

The Critic typically produces between two and twenty training instances from each solved problem, depending upon the length of the problem solution and the branching factor of the search (the search trees produced by the Problem Solver typically contain from a few to a few hundred search nodes). We have found empirically that even though the Critic cannot guarantee correct classifications, it rarely produces incorrect training instances. We have also found that in a significant number of cases, when the Critic calls the Problem Solver to consider a possible negative instance (see criterion *2(ii)* above) an improved solution is found. For example, in one run of LEX for a sequence of 12 training problems, this occurred 4 times. In those cases in which the Problem Solver does not find the best solution during its first attempt, the cause is usually a misleading recommendation by an incompletely-learned heuristic.

6.3.4 The Generalizer

The Generalizer considers the positive and negative training instances supplied by the Critic within the current learning cycle, in order to propose and refine heuristics to improve problem-solving performance. The generalization problem faced by this module is one of learning from examples. Given a sequence of training instances corresponding to search steps involving a given operator, the generalization problem here is to infer the general class of problem states for which this operator will be useful, along with the range of appropriate bindings for operator variables.

The Generalizer describes the version space for each proposed heuristic, by computing the sets S and G that delimit the plausible versions of that heuristic. For example, Figure 6-5 shows a positive training instance associated with op2 as input to the Generalizer. The output of the Generalizer in this case is a version space corresponding to a partially-learned heuristic, and represented by the (singleton) sets S and G shown in Figure 6-5. This partially-learned heuristic is proposed on the basis of the single training instance shown, and will be refined as subsequent instances become available. Below, we describe the procedures for proposing and refining problem-solving heuristics in LEX.

Proposing a new heuristic—When the Generalizer is given a new positive instance, it determines whether any member of the version space of any current heuristic applies to this instance. If not, a new heuristic is formed to cover the positive instance. This is the case in the example of Figure 6-5. In forming a new heuristic, the set S is initialized to the very specific version of the heuristic, that applies *only* to the current positive training instance (this is the most specific possible version consistent with the single observed training instance). G is initialized to the version of the heuristic that suggests the operator will prove useful in *every* situation where it can validly be applied; that is, it is initialized to the given precondition of the operator being recommended. Thus, in the example of Figure 6-5, G is initialized to the version whose precondition is the precondition for op2. Here, ∫ f1(x) f2(x) dx represents the integral of the product of any two real functions of x, and corresponds to the precondition ∫ u dv as it is stated in the system's generalization language.

At this point, S and G delimit a broad range of alternative versions of the proposed heuristic, corresponding to *all* the generalizations expressible in the given language that are consistent with this single training instance. As subsequent positive instances are considered, S becomes more general to include newly-observed instances in which op2 is found to be useful. Likewise, as subsequent negative instances are considered, G becomes more specific in order to exclude negative instances in which op2 may validly be applied, but in which it does not lead to an acceptable solution path. Thus, the range of alternative plausible versions of the heuristic delimited by S and G will narrow as new information is acquired through subsequent practice problems, and the uncertainty regarding the correct description of the heuristic is thereby reduced.

Refining incompletely-learned heuristics—If the Generalizer finds that an existing heuristic applies to a newly-presented positive or negative instance (that is, if its degree of match to the instance is nonzero), then that heuristic is revised by eliminating from its version space any version that is inconsistent with this training instance. In the current example, the next practice problem that is considered is ∫ 3x sin(x) dx (the following section explains why). The solution to this problem leads to both a positive and a negative training instance for the heuristic from Figure 6-5. Figure 6-6 shows these two new training instances, and the way in which they lead to a refinement of the version space of this heuristic. In the revised version space shown there, the most specific version, S, of the heuristic has been generalized just enough to allow it to apply to the new positive training instance. Here trig(x) replaces cos(x) so that the heuristic will apply to integrals containing *any* trigonometric function of x. The program determines this revision by first noting that the term cos(x) in the old S prevents that generalization from applying to the new instance. It then consults the grammar for expressing heuristics (shown in Figure 6-2) to determine the next more

```
Version Space of Heuristic

            S:  ∫  3x cos(x) dx -> Apply OP2 with
                                    u = 3x, and
                                    dv = cos(x) dx

            G:  ∫  f1(x) f2(x) dx -> Apply OP2 with
                                    u = f1(x), and
                                    dv = f2(x)dx
-----------------------------------------------------------
New Training Instances:

        Positive training instance:

                     ∫  3x sin(x) dx -> Apply OP2 with
                                        u = 3x, and
                                        dv = sin(x) dx

        Negative training instance:

                     ∫  3x sin(x) dx -> Apply OP2 with
                                        u = sin(x), and
                                        dv = 3x dx
-----------------------------------------------------------
Revised Version Space:

            S:   ∫ 3x trig(x) dx -> Apply OP2 with
                                    u = 3x, and
                                    dv = trig(x) dx

            G:
              g1:  ∫ poly(x) f2(x) dx -> Apply OP2 with
                                        u = poly(x), and
                                        dv = f2(x) dx

              g2:  ∫ f1(x) transc(x) dx -> Apply OP2
                                     with u = f1(x), and
                                     dv = transc(x) dx
```

Figure 6-6: Revising the version space of a heuristic.

general term that can be substituted in order to include this new instance.[2]

The general boundary of the revised version space of Figure 6-6 has also been altered so that it does not apply to the new negative training instance. In this case, there are two maximally-general versions (g1 and g2) of the heuristic consistent with the three observed training instances. Here, "poly(x)" refers to any polynomial function of x, and "transc(x)" denotes any transcendental function of x. As with revising the set S, revisions to G depend upon the generalization language being used. For instance, g1 is computed by replacing f1(x) (which represents "any real-valued function") by the next more specific acceptable expression. Notice in the hierarchy of Figure 6-2, this expression is "poly".

As subsequent training instances are considered, this partially-learned heuristic is further refined, and S and G converge to the heuristic description shown below. Notice that this description is contained in the version space represented in Figure 6-6, since it is more general than the S boundary set and more specific than the G boundary set of the version space.

$\int$ rx transc(x) dx $\Rightarrow$ apply op2 with u = rx, and dv = transc(x) dx

Although the Generalizer attempts to form a single conjunctive heuristic for each operator known to the system, sometimes it is not possible to cover all the positive instances and exclude all the negative instances with a single conjunctive generalization. The Generalizer deals with learning disjunctions in the following straightforward manner: if a positive instance associated with operator O is not consistent with any current heuristic that recommends operator O, then it proposes a new heuristic (that is, disjunct) for operator O that covers this instance. This new heuristic will be updated by all subsequent negative instances associated with operator O, and by any subsequent positive instances associated with operator O and to which at least some member of its version space applies. This technique for learning disjunctive concepts is similar to several described previously (for example, [Mitchell, 1978; Iba, 1979; Vere, 1978]).

How effective is the Generalizer at producing useful heuristics? One way to answer this question is to measure the improvement in problem-solving performance due to learned heuristics. In one experiment that illustrates typical behavior of LEX, a sequence of twelve hand-selected[3] training problems was presented to the Problem Solver, Critic, and Generalizer, and performance of the Problem Solver was measured at various stages in the training sequence. Perfor-

---

[2]Although the disjunction "cos(x) OR sin(x)" would be a more specific generalization than "trig", this disjunction is not currently in the generalization language, and therefore cannot be stated by the program. Of course if this disjunction were defined *a priori* as a separate term in the language, then it would be considered by the Generalizer.

[3]At the time that this experiment was conducted, we had not implemented the Problem Generator module.

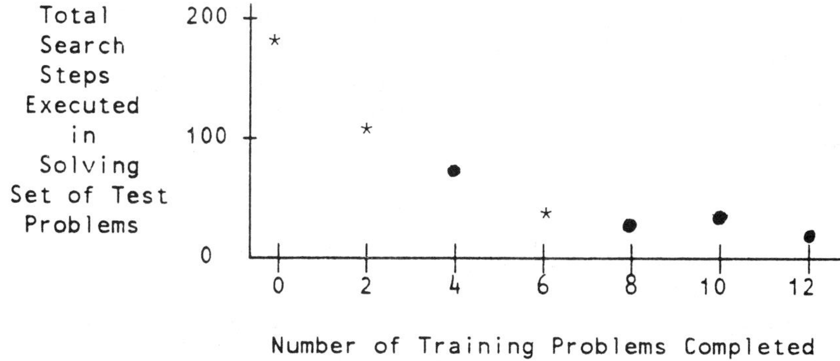

Figure 6-7: Performance Results

mance was measured by testing the Problem Solver on a set of five test problems before any training had occurred, and again after every second training problem. The five test problems were different from the set of twelve training problems, though the two sets were chosen to be similar enough that learned heuristics would be relevant to the test problems. This experiment is reported in greater detail in [Mitchell, 1981], and is summarized in Figure 6-7.

Fourteen heuristics were formed by LEX during this training session, covering thirteen of the 32 operators available to the system at that time. Twelve of these fourteen heuristics remained incompletely learned at the end of the training sequence (that is, their version space still contained multiple plausible descriptions of the heuristic).

Figure 6-7 shows the improvement in problem-solving performance (roughly two orders of magnitude) for this experiment, as measured by the total number of search steps required in attempting to solve the five test problems. At certain points during the training, the Problem Solver could not solve all five test problems within the given resource allocation.[4] Such points are shown as a "*" in Figure 6-7, and the number of search steps recorded in those cases is the number of steps executed before the solution attempt was aborted. While the exact values of the points on this curve would be different for different sets of training and test problems, the general form of the curve is quite repeatable, given reasonable test problems and a well-chosen sequence of training problems.

In addition to observing that problem-solving performance improved significantly using the learned heuristics, it is interesting to note that problem-solving performance did not improve monotonically as a function of training. In particular, while all five test problems could be solved following the fourth train-

[4]The Problem Solver was allowed four CPU minutes and 800,000 cons cells per test problem, running in RUCILISP on a DEC2060.

ing problem, only four of the test problems could be solved after the sixth training problem. This phenomenon was due to the proposal of new, partially-learned heuristics that led the Problem Solver to consider new (and not very useful) branches of the search in one of the test problems. Subsequent training refined these heuristics and the Problem Solver became able again to solve (this time more efficiently) all five test problems by the completion of the eighth training problem.

6.3.5 The Problem Generator

After a practice problem has been solved and analyzed, and the resulting training data has been used to propose and refine heuristics, the Problem Generator must propose a new practice problem. This module is responsible for focusing the system's efforts on useful activity, by choosing useful experiments. Its task is very different from that of a teacher of symbolic integration, or an outside trainer in most work on learning from examples. In contrast to an expert teacher, the Problem Generator must choose appropriate practice problems *without knowing* the heuristics that it is trying to teach. While the Problem Generator lacks this important information, it has other information that an expert teacher may not have: very detailed knowledge about the learner's current state (including knowledge of alternative versions of heuristics under consideration). As a result of these characteristics, the experimentation strategy of the Problem Generator is based primarily on generating problems designed to eliminate known ambiguities in LEX's heuristic knowledge.

The major criteria for generating problems are *(i)* to generate training problems whose solutions will provide informative new training data, and *(ii)* to generate training problems that can be solved using the available operators and current set of heuristics. The current implementation of the Problem Generator is based mainly on the first of these considerations, and consists of two different problem generation tactics.

The first problem generation tactic is to produce problems that will allow refinement of existing, partially-learned heuristics. This is done by selecting a partially-learned heuristic, then generating a problem state that matches some, but not all, of the members of the version space of that heuristic. For example, consider the partially-learned heuristic described by the version space at the top of Figure 6-6. The problem state $\int 3x \sin(x)\, dx$ matches some, but not all, of the alternative generalizations in this version space, and is therefore a useful problem to attempt to solve. By solving the problem, LEX will find out whether or not the heuristic should cover this problem state. If the answer is yes, a positive instance will be produced for this heuristic, and the S boundary of the version space will be generalized. If the answer is no, a negative instance will be produced, and the G boundary of the version space will be specialized. As it turns out, this problem leads to both a positive and a negative instance (corresponding to different bindings of operator arguments), and both version space boundaries are refined as shown in Figure 6-6.

How does the Problem Generator create a problem that matches part of a given version space? It begins by selecting a single member, s1, of the S boundary, and a more general member, g1, of the G boundary. (In the version space at the top of Figure 6-6 both boundary sets happen to be singleton sets.) It then creates, as follows, a problem state that matches g1, but does not match s1. One term in the generalization s1 is selected (in this case cos(x)), and the corresponding term in g1 is found (in this case f2(x)). The generalization hierarchy (see Figure 6-2) is then examined to determine a sibling of the term from s1, that is more specific than the corresponding term from g1. In this case, sin(x) is a sibling of cos(x) that is more specific than f2(x). This sibling is then substituted into s1, and the resulting generalization is fully instantiated to produce a problem state that matches g1, but not the original s1. In the current example, this leads to the problem state $\int$ 3x sin(x) dx. Notice that if the term 3x were chosen, rather than cos(x), as the basis for forming a new problem state, the new problem might instead be $\int$ 7x cos(x) dx. Furthermore, both of these terms could be replaced to produce the problem state $\int$ 7x sin(x) dx. Because of the need to create a problem that can be solved, the Problem Generator attempts to create a problem that is very similar to the most recently encountered positive instance for the heuristic. Therefore, only a single term from s1 is altered, and the resulting generalization is instantiated to correspond as closely as possible to the most recently encountered positive instance (a known solvable problem).

The second tactic for problem generation is to create a problem that will lead to proposing a new heuristic. This is accomplished by looking for pairs of operators whose preconditions intersect, but for which there is no current heuristic. Should a problem be encountered for which both operators apply, a heuristic will be needed to choose which of the two to apply. For example, consider op1 and op3 from Figure 6-1. The intersection of the preconditions of these operators is $\int$ 1·f(x) dx; that is, both op1 and op3 will apply to any problem that matches this applicability condition. This applicability condition is therefore instantiated to produce a specific problem state (such as $\int$ 1·cos(x) dx) which is then output by the Problem Generator. When the Problem Solver, Critic, and Generalizer consider this problem, a new heuristic will be proposed which will be useful in selecting between op1 and op3 in cases where they are both applicable.

The current Problem Generator incorporates the above two tactics for creating practice problems, and can employ any of several strategies for determining which tactic to apply at any given step. One such experimentation strategy is to apply the first tactic (refine an existing heuristic) whenever possible, and to apply the second tactic only when the first cannot be applied (for example, when the system begins operation and has no heuristics at all). While we have not yet done extensive testing of this module, it has been used to generate sequences of practice problems that lead to useful heuristics. The main observations that have come out of our preliminary experiments with this module are given below.

- It will be useful to extend the other system modules so that they can take into account the reason why the current problem has been suggested, and focus their activity accordingly. For example, if a problem is suggested in order to refine a particular heuristic, then the Problem Solver and Critic should be sure to consider the search steps that become training instances for that heuristic, and the Critic might allocate greater resources to obtain a reliable classification of that training instance.

- While the tactics described above are generally successful at creating informative problems to consider, they are not always successful at creating *solvable* problems. Some problems that are generated are simply not solvable with the set of operators known to the system. Other generated problems are solvable in principle, but cannot be solved within the allocated CPU time and space resources, using existing heuristics. In our initial experiments, more than half the generated problems turned out to be solved by the Problem Solver. Both of the current tactics produce a generalization which can be instantiated in any fashion to produce an informative problem. The instantiation is then controlled by a single heuristic: try to create a problem state that is as similar as possible to a previously-solved problem. More reliable methods for creating solvable instances of problems may require that the system have (or acquire) more appropriate knowledge about the characteristics of solvable problems.
- It may be useful to introduce a new tactic that produces problems that are guaranteed to be solvable, by beginning with a goal state, then applying inverses of the known operators to produce a problem state with a known solution. While the solution produced along with the problem will not necessarily be the optimal solution, it will provide an upper bound on the cost of the optimal solution. For this tactic to be useful, there must be a way of selecting sequences of operators that produce informative as well as solvable problems.
- There are also interesting questions to be considered regarding global strategies for exploring the problem domain. For example, should the Problem Generator focus first on refining existing heuristics, and then suggest problems that lead to new heuristics? Or is it better to build up a more broad set of heuristics, focusing at each step on problem types for which no heuristics yet exist, leaving refinement of these heuristics until a broad set of incompletely-determined heuristics are proposed?

6.4 NEW DIRECTIONS: ADDING KNOWLEDGE TO AUGMENT LEARNING

The current LEX system, as described in the previous section, is able to learn useful problem-solving heuristics in the domain of symbolic integration, by generalizing from self-generated examples. There are several features of the design of LEX that have an important impact on its capabilities. The ability to represent incompletely-learned heuristics is crucial; to the Problem Solver that must use these partially-learned heuristics in order to solve additional practice problems to obtain additional training data; to the Generalizer that must refine these heuristics; and to the Problem Generator that must be able to consider alternative plausible descriptions of a heuristic in order to suggest an informative practice problem. The ability of the Critic to produce reliable training instances is also crucial to system performance. In spite of the heuristic nature of the Critic's credit assignment method (following from the fact that only part of the search space is explored by the Problem Solver), the Critic in fact performs quite well in producing reliable classifications of training instances. Its ability to call the Problem Solver in a controlled manner to explore selected portions of the search space is important to increasing the reliability of its classifications of training instances. The Generalizer's use of the version space method for generalizing from examples is also a major feature of LEX, which gives it the capability to incrementally converge on heuristics consistent with a sequence of training instances observed over the course of many practice problems.

While LEX is able to learn useful heuristics, it also has significant limitations. One of the most fundamental difficulties is that learning is strongly tied to the language used to describe heuristics—the system can only learn heuristics that it can represent in the provided language. It is difficult to manually select an appropriate language before learning occurs, and LEX often fails to converge on an acceptable heuristic for a given set of training instances, simply because it does not have the appropriate vocabulary for stating the heuristic. For example, we have found that the addition of terms such as "odd integer" and "twice integrable function" to the language shown in Figure 6-2, would allow LEX to describe (and therefore learn) heuristics that it cannot currently represent. This constraint imposed by a fixed representation language is one of the most fundamental difficulties associated with this and some other approaches to learning from examples.

A second deficiency of LEX is its failure to take advantage of an important source of information for chosing an appropriate generalization: analysis of *why* a particular search step was useful in the context of the overall problem solution. By analyzing the role of a particular search step in leading to a problem solution, it is sometimes possible for humans to determine a very good general heuristic after observing only a single training instance. If LEX were to conduct such an analysis, it would converge much more quickly on appropriate heuristics, possibly with less sensitivity to classification errors by the Critic.

In this section, we describe our current research toward giving LEX new knowledge and reasoning capabilities to overcome the above limitations. In particular, we consider how knowledge about heuristic search and about the intended purpose of learned heuristics could allow LEX to *(i)* derive justifiable generalizations of heuristics via analysis of individual training instances, and *(ii)* respond to situations in which the vocabulary for describing heuristics is insufficient to characterize a given set of training instances. More detailed discussions of this material can be found in [Mitchell, 1982b] and [Utgoff, 1982]. The kind of knowledge considered here, regarding the intended purpose of learned heuristics, is one kind of meta-knowledge that can be useful in acquiring problem-solving strategies. The importance of meta-knowledge in acquiring problem-solving strategies is also discussed in other chapters of this book, such as Chapters 9 and 12.

6.4.1 Describing the Learner's Goal

In order to reason about *why* a given training instance is positive, and to determine which features of the training instance are relevant, it is necessary that the system have a definition of the criterion by which the instance is labeled as positive (that is, the criterion that determines the goal of its learning activity). LEX is intended to learn heuristics that lead the Problem Solver to minimum cost solutions of symbolic integration problems. This goal is implicit in the credit assignment procedure used by the Critic, which attempts to classify individual search steps as positive or negative according to this criterion. While this criterion is currently defined procedurally within the Critic, it is not defined declaratively, and the system therefore cannot reason symbolically about its learning goal. Here we present a declarative representation of this credit assignment criterion, then discuss in subsequent subsections how this knowledge provides the starting point for analyzing training instances, and extending the vocabulary of the language for describing heuristics.

To simplify the examples and discussion here, we assume a slightly modified credit assignment criterion, for which the goal of LEX is to learn heuristics that recommend problem-solving steps that lead to *any* solution (rather than the minimum cost solution). In this case, any search step that applies some operator, *op*, to some problem state, *state*, is a positive instance, provided it satisfies the predicate PosInst defined as follows:

PosInst(op, state) $\Leftrightarrow$
  $\sim$Goal(state) $\wedge$ [Goal(Apply(op, state)) $\vee$ Solvable(Apply(op, state))].

Here, Goal is the predicate for recognizing solution states, Apply is the function for applying operators to states, and Solvable is the predicate that tests whether a state can be transformed to a Goal state with the available operators.

Solvable is defined as follows:

Solvable(state) $\Leftrightarrow$
  ($\exists$ op) [Goal(Apply(op, state)) $\vee$ Solvable(Apply(op,state))]

6.4.2 Analyzing Training Instances to Guide Generalization

This section suggests how the declarative representation of the credit assignment criterion, PosInst, could be used by LEX to produce a justifiable generalization of a heuristic based on analysis of a single training instance. The key idea here is that by analyzing *why* the observed positive instance is classified as positive, in the context of the overall problem solution, it is possible to determine a logically sufficient condition for satisfying PosInst. Such an analysis leads to a *justifiable* generalization of the heuristic, that follows from the credit assignment criterion, together with knowledge about search and the representation of operators and problem states. This process is related to the process of operationalizing advice, as discussed by Mostow in Chapter 12 of this book and by [Hayes-Roth, 1980]. The particular method for analyzing solution traces is a generalization of the method of solution analysis presented in [Fikes *et al.*, 1972].

As an example, suppose that the system has just produced the problem solution tree shown in Figure 6-8, and the generalizer is now considering the first step along the solution path as a positive training instance for a heuristic that is to recommend op1. Assuming no heuristic yet exists for op1, the empirical generalization method described earlier will produce the following version space for the new heuristic:

S: $\int 7\ (x^2)\ dx \Rightarrow$ use op1

G: $\int r\ f(x)\ dx \Rightarrow$ use op1

In this example, analysis of how this training instance satisfies the credit assignment criterion will lead to additional information for refining the above version space of alternative hypotheses. The trace of this analysis is broken into four main stages, which attempt to determine some property of the integrand in the training instance which is *sufficient* to assure that the credit assignment criteria will be met. This sufficient condition for satisfying PosInst can then be used to further generalize the S boundary of the version space for this heuristic. The four main stages are *(i)* Generate an explanation that shows how the current positive instance satisfies PosInst, *(ii)* Extract from this explanation a sufficient condition for satisfying PosInst, *(iii)* Restate the sufficient condition in terms of the generalization language (that is, the language of applicability conditions for heuristics), as restrictions on various problem states in the solution tree, and *(iv)* Propagate the restrictions on various problem states through the solution tree, and combine them into a generalization that corresponds to a sufficient condition for assuring PosInst will be satisfied.

Stage 1: Produce an explanation of how the current training instance satisfies PosInst. This explanation is produced by instantiating the definition of PosInst for the positive instance in question. By determining which disjunctive clauses in the definition of PosInst are satisfied by the current training instance, and then by further expanding those clauses by instantiating predicates to which they refer, a proof is produced that PosInst(op1, State1). The result of this stage is an And/Or proof tree, which we shall call the *explanation tree* for the training instance. The tip nodes in the explanation tree are known to be satisfied because of the observed solution tree to which the training instance belongs. This explanation tree indicates how the training instance satisfies PosInst, and forms the basis for generalization by inferring sufficient conditions for satisfying PosInst.

The explanation tree for the positive training instance <op1, State1> is

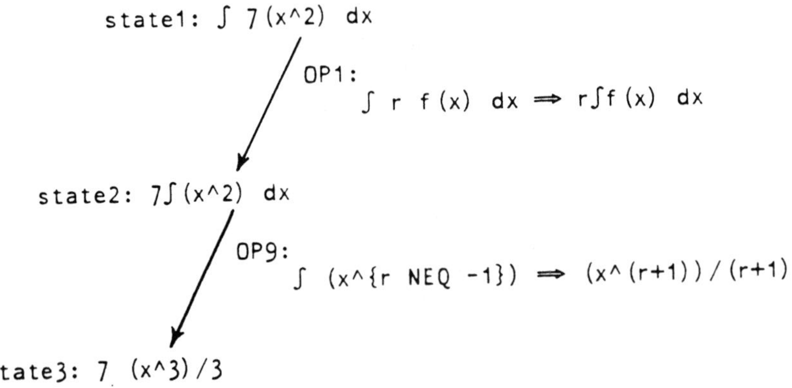

Figure 6-8: The solution tree for example 1.

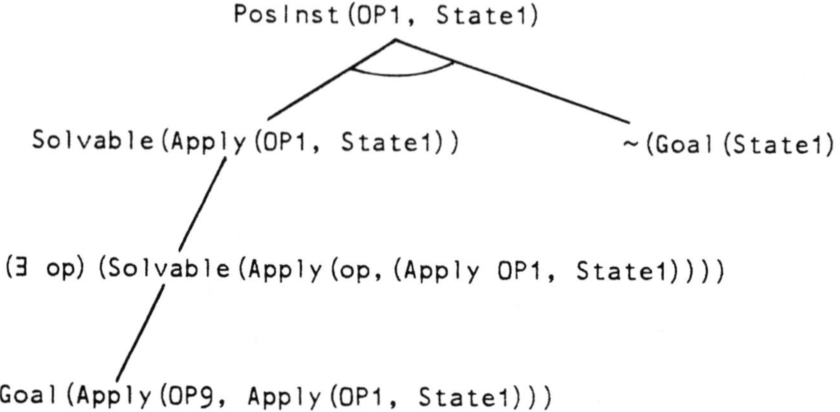

Figure 6-9: The explanation tree for PosInst(op1, State1).

shown in Figure 6-9. Nodes in the *explanation tree* correspond to statements about various problem states and operators in the associated *solution tree*. The explanation tree for the current example indicates that <op1, State1> is a Positive instance because *(i)* State1 is not a Goal state, and *(ii)* by applying op9 to the state resulting from the positive instance step, it is possible to reach a goal state. Subsequent stages of analysis of this explanation tree, shown below, extract this explanation (at an appropriate level of generality), and to restate it in the generalization language in which heuristics are expressed.

Stage 2: Extract a sufficient condition for satisfying PosInst. If the explanation tree is viewed as a proof that PosInst is satisfied by the current training instance, then it is clear that any set of nodes that satisfy this And/Or tree correspond to a sufficient condition for satisfying PosInst. In the current example, for instance, if all the tip nodes of the explanation tree are satisfied by a given state, s, then PosInst will be satisfied by the training instance <op1, s>. In this stage, a set of nodes that satisfy the And/Or tree is selected, and the corresponding sufficient condition for PosInst is formulated by replacing the problem state from the training instance by a universally-quantified variable. In the current example, if the tip nodes of the explanation tree are selected, then the resulting sufficient condition for PosInst may be stated as follows:

$$(\forall s)\ \text{PosInst}(\text{op1}, s) \Leftarrow (\sim\text{Goal}(s) \wedge \text{Goal}(\text{Apply}(\text{op9}, \text{Apply}(\text{op1}, s))))$$

Notice that there are many possible choices of sets of nodes to satisfy the And/Or tree, and correspondingly many sufficient conditions. This choice of nodes is one of the major control issues in the analysis of the training instance. Generally, nodes close to the root of the explanation tree lead to more general sufficient conditions. However, since the sufficient conditions formulated in this stage must be transformed by subsequent stages to statements in the generalization language for heuristics, the choice of covering nodes from the explanation tree must trade off *(i)* the generality of the corresponding sufficient condition, with *(ii)* the loss in generality that is likely when this sufficient condition is transformed into the generalization language for heuristics. As an example, consider the alternative choice of the two nodes at the second level of the explanation tree. This set of nodes leads to the following sufficient condition for PosInst:

$$(\forall s)\ \text{PosInst}(\text{op1}, s) \Leftarrow (\sim\text{Goal}(s) \wedge \text{Solvable}(\text{Apply}(\text{op1}, s)))$$

While this sufficient condition on satisfying PosInst is more general than the earlier sufficient condition, it turns out that this added generality will be lost when attempting to redescribe the sufficient condition in terms of the generalization language. The difficulty in this case stems from the fact that there is no straightforward translation from the predicate "Solvable" to a statement in the generalization language of LEX. In contrast, the sufficient condition corresponding to the tip nodes of the explanation tree involves only the predicate "Goal", which is easily characterized in terms of the generalization language.

Stage 3: Restate the sufficient condition in terms of the generalization language, as restrictions on various problem states involved in the solution tree. In the current example, the sufficient condition corresponding to the tip nodes of the explanation tree can be restated as follows:

$$(\forall s)\ \text{PosInst}(\text{op1}, s) \Leftarrow$$
$$(\text{Match}(\textstyle\int f(x)dx, s) \wedge \text{Match}(f(x), \text{Apply}(\text{op9}, \text{Apply}(\text{op1}, s))))$$

The predicate "Match" corresponds to the matching procedure used to compare applicability conditions, or generalizations, with problem states (that is, it tests whether the applicability conditions are satisfied in the problem state). The first conjunct above expresses the fact that "s" is *not* a Goal state ("s" contains an integral), and the second conjunct expresses the fact that Apply(op9, Apply(op1, s)) *is* a goal state (it is some expression that does not contain an integral sign). This second conjunct corresponds to a restriction on the state labeled State3 in Figure 6-8.

In general, the goal of this stage is to translate the sufficient condition into a conjunctive set of statements of the form Match(<generalization>, <problem-state>), where <generalization> can be any statement in the generalization language used by the system, and <problem-state> can be any expression that corresponds to a particular problem state in the solution tree for the current example.

The translation of sufficient conditions into the generalization language requires knowledge about the correspondence between the representation language in which the analysis is being done, and the generalization language used to describe heuristics. For instance, in the current example the following knowledge is used in the translation:

$(\forall s) \sim Goal(s) \Leftrightarrow Match(\int f(x)dx, s)$
and
$(\forall s)\ Goal(s) \Leftrightarrow Match(f(x)dx, s)$

Unfortunately, some expressions generated by analyzing the explanation tree may have no corresponding expression in the generalization language. For example, in the current LEX generalization language, there is no way of characterizing all "Solvable" functions. In this case, translating the sufficient condition corresponding to the second level nodes in the explanation tree may require further specializing the sufficient condition, by replacing Solvable(x) by sufficient conditions for Solvable. An example of such knowledge is the knowledge that all polynomial integrands are solvable. It is important to note that even if no such knowledge is available, it will always be possible to translate the sufficient condition into some weaker condition describable in the generalization language. This can always be accomplished by using the fact that the solution tree provides at least one problem state which satisfies the predicate, and the problem state is itself describable in the generalization language. Thus, for example, the condition Solvable(Apply(op1, s)) may, if no other relevant knowledge is available, be weakened and replaced by Match($7\int(x^2)dx$, Apply(op1, s)).

Stage 4: Propagate the restrictions on various problem states through the solution tree to determine equivalent conditions on the problem state involved in the current training instance. By examining the definitions of the operators involved in reaching a given state, x, it is possible to propagate restrictions on x through the solution tree to deduce the corresponding constraints on an earlier problem state. This back propagation of restrictions is necessary in order to restate the sufficient condition on PosInst in terms of a generalization that applies to the training instance. This propagation requires using the operators in a way different from the way in which they are used during forward search problem-solving, and is similar to the process of goal regression discussed in the literature on means-ends problem-solving and planning [Nilsson, 1980].

As an example, consider the second expression in the sufficient condition from stage 3: Match(f(x), Apply(op9, Apply(op1, s))). This condition, when back propagated through op9 becomes Match(f(x)$\int$(x $\uparrow$ (r$\neq$ -1)dx), Apply(op1, s)). The new generalization corresponds to the class of problem states which can be transformed using op9 into an expression that satisfies the original condition. Similarly, this new expression can be propagated back through op1 to yield an equivalent condition on State1: Match($\int$ r(x $\uparrow$ {r$\neq$ -1})dx, s). Thus, the sufficient condition from stage 3 can be restated as:

(∀s) PosInst(op1, s) ⇐
 (Match($\int$f(x)dx, s) ∧ Match($\int$ r(x $\uparrow$ {r $\neq$ -1})dx, s))

Since the second conjunct is more specific than the first, the above expression can be simplified to:

(∀s) [PosInst(op1, s) ⇐ Match($\int$ r(x $\uparrow$ {r $\neq$ -1})dx, s)]

Finally, we have found sufficient conditions for PosInst(op1, s) which are stated as a generalization that must match State1. While the sufficient condition determined by the above analysis is not the most general sufficient condition possible, it is satisfied by the current training instance and follows naturally from analyzing that instance. If this training instance were the first instance encountered for this particular heuristic, the resulting version space would reflect the extra information extracted from analyzing this instance, as shown below.

S: $\int$ r [x $\uparrow$ (r $\neq$ -1)] dx ⇒ Apply op1

G: $\int$ r f(x) dx ⇒ Apply op1

6.4.3 Automatically Extending the Vocabulary for Describing Heuristics

One of the most fundamental difficulties associated with current approaches to machine learning is the problem of acquiring an appropriate vocabulary with which to describe learned concepts. Nearly all existing systems assume some fixed vocabulary of terms with which to represent learned concepts (for instance, the LEX terms trigonometric, polynomial, exponential, and so on, as shown in Figure 6-2). In cases where this vocabulary is inappropriate, it will be impossible to describe (and hence to learn) the desired concept. In the LEX system, we have found that there are many cases where the current language for describing heuristics is insufficient to correctly characterize sets of training instances produced by the Critic.

As an example, consider the solution path shown in Figure 6-10, and the positive training instance corresponding to the first step of this solution path. If this positive training instance is observed, together with the positive training instance $\int \cos^7(x)dx$, and the negative training instance $\int \cos^6(x)dx$, then LEX will be unable to produce a heuristic that matches these two positive instances, and excludes the negative instance. The problem here is that the language in Figure 6-2 for describing heuristics has no term that includes both 5 and 7 while excluding 6.

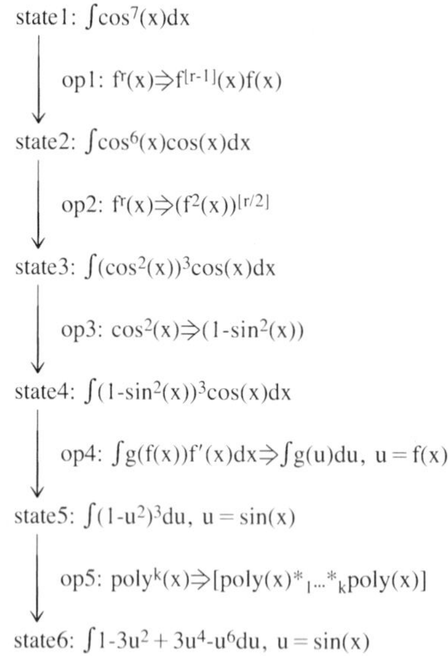

state1: $\int \cos^7(x)dx$
op1: $f^r(x) \Rightarrow f^{[r-1]}(x)f(x)$
state2: $\int \cos^6(x)\cos(x)dx$
op2: $f^r(x) \Rightarrow (f^2(x))^{[r/2]}$
state3: $\int (\cos^2(x))^3\cos(x)dx$
op3: $\cos^2(x) \Rightarrow (1-\sin^2(x))$
state4: $\int (1-\sin^2(x))^3\cos(x)dx$
op4: $\int g(f(x))f'(x)dx \Rightarrow \int g(u)du,\ u = f(x)$
state5: $\int (1-u^2)^3du,\ u = \sin(x)$
op5: $poly^k(x) \Rightarrow [poly(x)*_1...*_k poly(x)]$
state6: $\int 1-3u^2+3u^4-u^6du,\ u = \sin(x)$

Figure 6-10: Solution path for $\int \cos^7(x)dx$.

In this case, a solution analysis similar to that described in the previous section can lead to the generation of a new term to be added to the language of Figure 6-2. As in the previous case, the solution trace analysis first produces a set of statements about various nodes in the search tree, which characterize why the training instance is positive. These statements are then propagated through the problem-solving operators in the search tree to determine which features of the training instance were necessary to satisfy these statements. *It is during this propagation and combination of constraints that new descriptive terms may be suggested.*

For example, in the case of the solution path shown in Figure 6-10, suppose that the analysis first determines that the solution path leads to a solution because State6 is of the following form, which we assume satisfies the system's definition of a solvable state.

$$\int poly(x)*_1...*_k poly(x)dx$$

Then the set of states, X_1, for which application of op5 leads to such a solvable state can be computed as:

$$X_1 \Leftarrow op5^{-1}(\int poly(x)*_1...*_k poly(x)dx)$$

giving

$$X_1 = \int poly^k(x)dx$$

In turn, we can compute the set of states, X_2, for which application of op4 leads to such a solvable state, as shown below. Here, "range(op4)" indicates the set of all problem states that can be reached by applying op4 to some other problem state.

$X_2 \Leftarrow op4^{-1}(intersection(range(op4),X_1))$.

By this repeated backward propagation of constraints through the solution tree, it can be determined that application of the solution method of Figure 6-10 leads to a solvable state when the initial state (in this case State1) is of the form $\int cos^c(x)dx$ where c is constrained to satisfy the predicate "real(c) $\wedge$ integer((c-1)/2)", better known as "odd integer". Thus, detailed analysis of the solution path can suggest the need for new predicate terms in the language for describing heuristics. These terms (such as "odd integer") arise from combinations of existing terms, composed in a way that is determined by the particular operator sequence in the solution path being analyzed.

6.5 SUMMARY

The LEX system is an experiment in learning by experimentation. The current system, based on a generator of practice problems, problem solver, critic, and generalizer, indicates that useful problem-solving heuristics can be learned by employing empirical methods for generalizing from examples. It also indicates that more powerful and more general approaches to learning will be needed before practical systems can be built that improve their strategies in significant ways. One way of augmenting empirical learning methods by analytical methods has been discussed, which is based on giving the system the ability to reason about its goals, heuristic search, and the task domain. This research and the research of others (for example, that described in Chapters 8, 9, and 12 of this book) suggests that the addition of such meta-knowledge about the goals, the learner, and the problem-solving methods in the domain, is a promising area for further research.

ACKNOWLEDGMENTS

The LEX system has been developed over the past three years with the aid of several researchers in addition to the authors. We gratefully acknowledge the aid of William Bogdan, who helped implement the Critic; Bernard Nudel, who helped implement the Critic and Problem Solver; and Adam Irgon, who implemented the Problem Generator. Richard Keller has contributed to the newer work on using the intended purpose of heuristics for analyzing training instances. This research is supported by the National Science Foundation under Grant No. MCS80-08889, and by the National Institutes of Health under Grant No. RR-64309.

REFERENCES

Anzai, Y. and Simon, H., "The theory of learning by doing," *Psychological Review*, Vol. 36, No. 2, pp. 124-140, 1979.

Buchanan, B. G. and Mitchell, T. M., "Model-Directed Learning of Production Rules," *Pattern-Directed Inference Systems*, Waterman, D. A. and Hayes-Roth, F. (Eds.), Academic Press, New York, 1978.

Davis, R., "Applications of meta level knowledge to the construction and use of large knowledge bases," *Knowledge-based Systems in Artificial Intelligence*, Davis, R. and Lenat, D. (Eds.), McGraw-Hill, New York, 1981.

Fikes, R. E., Hart, P. E. and Nilsson, N. J., "Learning and executing generalized robot plans," *Artificial Intelligence*, Vol. 3, pp. 251-288, 1972.

Hayes-Roth, F., Klahr, P. and Mostow, D. J., "Knowledge acquisition, knowledge programming, and knowledge refinement", Technical Report R-2540-NSF, The Rand Corporation, Santa Monica, CA., May 1980.

Iba, G. A., "Learning disjunctive concepts from examples," Master's thesis, M.I.T., Cambridge, Mass., 1979, (also AI memo 548).

Mitchell, T. M., *Version Spaces: An approach to concept learning,* Ph.D. dissertation, Stanford University, December 1978, (also Stanford CS report STAN-CS-78-711, HPP-79-2).

Mitchell, T. M., Utgoff, P. E., Nudel, B. and Banerji, R., "Learning problem-solving heuristics through practice," *Proceedings of the Seventh International Joint Conference on Artificial Intelligence*, Vancouver, pp. 127-134, August 1981.

Mitchell, T. M., "Generalization as Search," *Artificial Intelligence*, Vol. 18, No. 2, pp. 203-226, March 1982.

Mitchell, T. M., "Toward Combining Empirical and Analytic Methods for Learning Heuristics," *Human and Artificial Intelligence*, Elithorn, A. and Banerji, R. (Eds.), Erlbaum, 1982.

Neves, D. M., "A computer program that learns algebraic procedures," *Proceedings of the 2nd Conference on Computational Studies of Intelligence*, Toronto, 1978.

Nilsson, N. *Principles of Artificial Intelligence*, Tioga, Palo Alto, 1980.

Politakis, P., Weiss, S. and Kulikowski, C., "Designing consistent knowledge bases for expert consultation systems", Technical Report DCS-TR-100, Department of Computer Science, Rutgers University, 1979, (also 13th Annual Hawaii International Conference on System Sciences).

Utgoff, P. E. and Mitchell, T. M., "Acquisition of Appropriate Bias for Inductive Concept Learning," *Proceedings of the 1982 National Conference on Artificial Intelligence*, Pittsburgh, August 1982.

Vere, S. A., "Inductive learning of relational productions," *Pattern-Directed Inference Systems*, Waterman, D. A. and Hayes-Roth, F. (Eds.), Academic Press, New York, 1978.

Waterman, D. A., "Generalization learning techniques for automating the learning of heuristics," *Artificial Intelligence*, Vol. 1, No. 1/2, pp. 121-170, 1970.

7

ACQUISITION OF PROOF SKILLS IN GEOMETRY

John R. Anderson
Carnegie-Mellon University

ABSTRACT

The ACT theory of learning is applied to the domain of high school geometry. The concern is with how students become skilled at planning a proof of a geometry problem. A general control structure is proposed for integrating backward and forward search in proof planning. This is embodied in a production system framework. Two types of learning are described. *Knowledge* compilation is concerned with how students transit from a declarative characterization of the domain to a set of operators for performing a specific task in that domain. *Tuning* is concerned with how students learn which problem features are predictive of the success of which operators.

7.1 INTRODUCTION

Much of my research has been concerned with the refinement of skills from general methods. I have developed a theory of learning called ACT which involves a set of mechanisms by which skills can be refined. These include knowledge compilation mechanisms for converting from declarative representation of a skill to a procedural representation. They also include a set of mechanisms for learning which problem features are predictive of the success of problem-solving operators. Much of the later discussion in this chapter is concerned with describing these mechanisms and their application to acquisition of proof skills in geometry. First, however, I will discuss the nature of the empirical phenomena that we are trying to simulate with our learning system and how our performance theory goes about organizing search for geometry proofs.

We have been studying how high school students learn to generate proofs in geometry and how they get better at generating proofs through practice. A major empirical base for this work comes from protocols of thirty 45-minute sessions that we had with one of our students (Subject R). In these sessions the student read textbook instructions and worked out textbook problems. We tried to confine our interruptions to clearing up serious misconceptions. R did all of his work in these sessions; his textbook and notes were taken away from him, and he was encouraged not to think about geometry between sessions. Thus, we have a more or less complete record of the learning that occurs in the first part of geometry. In the thirty sessions he worked through two column proofs, a section about angles, to where he was generating non-trivial proofs about triangle congruence. A substantial amount of learning occurs after this initial period. Therefore, we have supplemented our data base with spot protocols from more advanced high school students and from various adults who are relatively expert at generating geometry proofs.

Our goal has been to generate a computer simulation of the learning processes in geometry. The ultimate test of this program is that it be given textbook instruction and have a learning history like that of our high school student. The dimensions of this ultimate test are, of course, a little overwhelming. For the time being we have contented ourselves with simulating learning on fragments of the geometry text. A major concern in this research has been the so-called "sufficiency condition" for a psychological theory—that is proposing mechanisms powerful enough to produce the observed learning of the necessary skills.

The constraint that the behavior of the system be such that it corresponds to human behavior is a severe one but not one that is orthogonal to the frequent AI goal of getting a system capable of intelligent behavior. We have argued elsewhere [Anderson & Kline, 1977] that the psychological constraint may facilitate ultimately achieving a robust intelligent system, particularly if the goal is machine learning. Therefore, I would commend to the reader the learning proposal contained in here as a viable scheme for skill acquisition by a machine.

The simulation has been worked out in the context of the ACT system [Anderson, 1976] which is a simulation system based on hypotheses about the basic mechanisms of human cognition. The procedural knowledge of the ACT system is based on a production system architecture and the declarative component in ACT is based on a semantic network. The productions use the information in the semantic network as a working memory to match against. The learning investigations discussed in this chapter are principally focused on how new productions are developed in acquiring a skill. The ACT theory has been tested out on a wide variety of empirical domains including memory and inferential processes [Anderson, 1976], language acquisition and processing [Anderson *et al.*, 1977], [Anderson, 1981], and schema abstraction and prototype formation [Anderson *et al.*, 1979].

7.2 A MODEL OF THE SKILL UNDERLYING PROOF GENERATION

Most successful attempts at proof generation can be divided into two major episodes—an episode in which a student attempts to find a plan for the proof and an episode in which the student translates that plan into an actual proof. The first stage we call *planning* and the second *execution*. It is true that actual proof generation behavior often involves alternation back and forth between the two modes—with the student doing a little planning, writing portions of the proof, running into trouble, planning some more, writing some more, and so on. However, we believe that planning exists as a logically and empirically separable component of proof generation. Moreover, we believe that planning is the more significant aspect where the interesting learning occurs. Execution, while not necessarily trivial, is more "mechanical".

A plan, in the sense we are using it here, is an outline for action—the action in this case being proof execution. We believe that the plan students emerge with is a specification of a set of geometric rules that allows one to get from the givens of the problem, through intermediate levels of statements, to the to-be-proven statement. We call such a plan a *proof tree*.

Figure 7-1 illustrates (a) an example geometry problem and (b) a proof tree. In the tree, the goal to prove two angles congruent leads to the subgoal of proving the triangles $\triangle XVZ$ and $\triangle WVY$ congruent. This goal is achieved by the side-angle-side (SAS) postulate. The first side $\overline{VX} = \overline{VW}$ is gotten directly from the givens. Since these sides form an isosceles triangle, they also imply $\angle VXZ = \angle VWY$, the second part of the SAS congruence pattern. The third part $\overline{XZ} \cong \overline{WY}$ can be gotten from the other given that $\overline{XY} \cong \overline{WZ}$. A proof can be obtained from Figure 7-1 by unpacking various links in the proof tree. Such a proof is given below. The reader should be noted that some of these links map into multiple lines of proof. The link connecting $\overline{XY} \cong \overline{WZ}$ to $\overline{XZ} \cong \overline{WY}$, for instance, maps into the 9 lines 4−12 in the proof. This is one of the important reasons why we characterize the proof tree as an *abstract* specification of a proof.

The proof tree is, of course, not something that students typically draw out for themselves. Rather it is a knowledge structure in the head. Various remarks of students suggest to us that it is a real knowledge structure, not just a product of our theoretical fantasies. For instance, one student described a proof as "an upside down pyramid".

Statement	Reason
1. $\overline{VX} \cong \overline{VW}$	given
2. $\overline{XY} \cong \overline{WZ}$	given
3. $\triangle XYZ$ is isosceles	definition
4. $\angle VXZ = \angle VWY$	base $\angle$'s of isosceles
5. $XY = WZ$	def. of $\cong$
6. $YZ = YZ$	symmetric property of equality

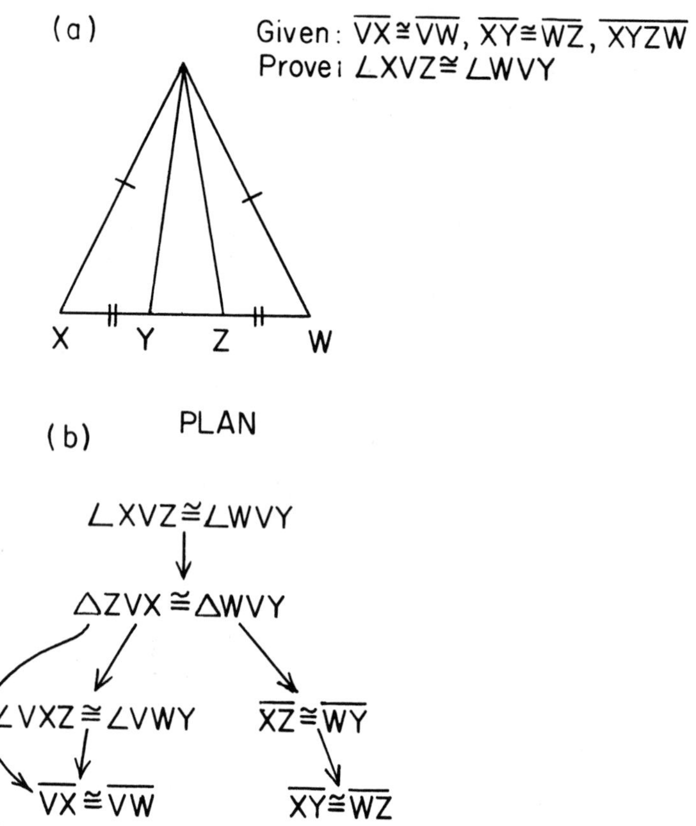

Figure 7-1: A problem with its proof tree and detailed proof.

7. XY + YZ = YZ + WZ	addition property of equality
8. XY = ZW	given
9. XZ = XY + YZ	segment addition
10. WY = YZ + WZ	segment addition
11. XZ = WY	substitution
12. $\overline{XZ} \cong \overline{WY}$	def. of $\cong$
13. $\triangle XVZ \cong \triangle WVY$	SAS
14. $\angle XVZ \cong \angle WVY$	corresponding parts of congruent $\triangle$'s

Creating a proof tree is not a trivial problem. The student must either try to search forward from the givens trying to find some set of paths that converge satisfactorily on the statement to be proven, or he must try to search backward from the statement to be proven, trying to find some set of dependencies that lead back to the givens. Using unguided forward or backward search, it is easy to become lost in the combinatorial possibilities. We will argue that students use a mixture of forward and backward search. This mixture, along with various search heuristics they acquire, enables students to deal with the search demands of proof problems found in high school geometry texts.

7.2.1 An Example of Planning

Before discussing the learning processes, I would like to discuss how our simulation organizes its search for a proof tree. I will discuss an example problem derived from Chapter 4 of Jurgensen, Donnelly, Maier and Rising [1975]. This problem is illustrated in Figure 7-2. It is among the most difficult problems found in that chapter. We would first like to discuss how our ACT simulation performed on this problem.

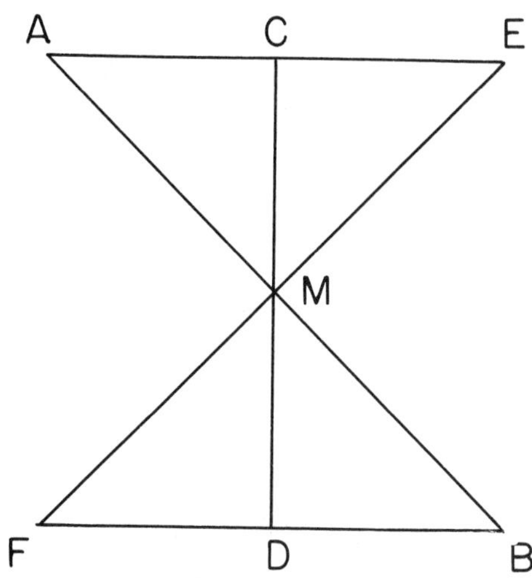

Given: M is the midpoint of $\overline{AB}$ and $\overline{CD}$
Prove: M is the midpoint of $\overline{EF}$

Figure 7-2: Problem for simulation of planning.

ACT's search for a proof tree involves simultaneously searching backward from the to-be-proven statement and searching forward from the givens. We see our students combine forward and backward search. An attempt is made to try to bring these two searches together. This search process creates a network of logical dependencies. When successful ACT will eventually find in its search some set of logical dependencies that defines a satisfactory proof tree. This proof tree will be embedded within the search network. This larger network we call the *problem net*.

Figure 7-3 illustrates the problem net at an early state of its development for the problem in Figure 7-2. The first two reasoning forward productions[1] to apply are

P1: IF X, Y, and Z are on a line
and U, Y, and V are on a line
THEN ∠XYU ≅ ∠ZYU because they are vertical angles

P2: IF Y is the midpoint of $\overline{XZ}$
THEN $\overline{XY} \cong \overline{YZ}$ by definition

The first production, for vertical angles, generates from the diagram in Figure 7-2 that ∠AMC ≅ ∠BMD and that ∠CME ≅ ∠DMF. This is indicated in Figure 7-3 by arrows leading from the vertical angles reason to the angle congruences. The second production translates the two givens about midpoints into inferences about line congruence.

With this information in hand the following working forward production can apply:

P3: IF $\overline{XY} \cong \overline{UV}$
and $\overline{ZY} \cong \overline{WV}$
and ∠XYZ ≅ ∠UVW
THEN △XYZ ≅ △UVW because of SAS

This production embodies the side-angle-side rule (SAS). Applied to the first level of forward inferences in Figure 7-3 it adds the inference that △AMC ≅ △BMD. It has been our experience that almost everyone presented with this problem works forward to this particular inference as the first step to solving the problem.

Meanwhile ACT has begun to unwind a plan of backward inferences to achieve the goal. It has translated the midpoint goal to a goal of proving the congruence $\overline{EM} \cong \overline{FM}$. This is accomplished by the following production rule:

P4: IF the goal is to prove that Y is the midpoint of $\overline{XZ}$
THEN set as the subgoal to prove $\overline{XY} \cong \overline{YZ}$

This in turn is translated by the following production:

[1]Both of these productions and the others in this paper are given in a considerably more informal syntax than what is implemented in the ACT production system. However, it is our judgment that the renditions above are considerably more intelligible and do not omit much that is essential.

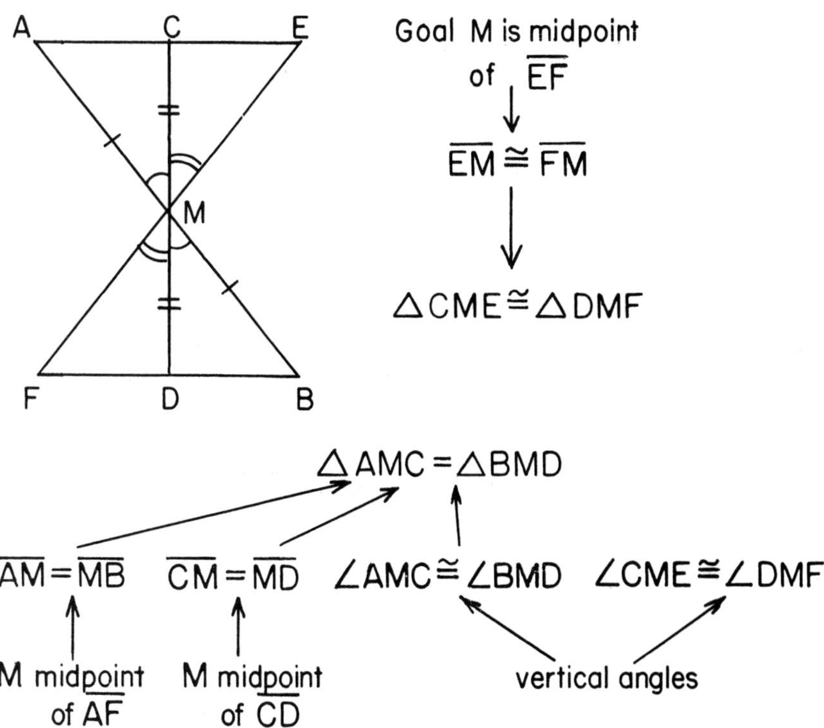

Figure 7-3: Problem network early in planning.

P5: IF the goal is to prove $\overline{XY} \cong \overline{UV}$
and $\overline{XY}$ is part of triangle 1
and $\overline{UV}$ is part of triangle 2
THEN set as the subgoal to prove that triangle 1 is congruent to triangle 2

Matching this production to the diagram, ACT determines that △CME contains $\overline{EM}$ and that △DMF contains $\overline{FM}$. This leads to the subgoal of proving △CME ≅ △DMF.

Note that the forward inferences have progressed much more rapidly than the backward inferences. This is because backward inferences, manipulating a single goal, are inherently serial, whereas the forward inferences can apply in the ACT simulation in parallel. With respect to the serial-parallel issue it should be noted that the backward and forward search progress in parallel.

Figure 7-3 illustrates the limit to the forward inferences that ACT generates. While there are, of course, more forward inferences that could be made, this is the limit to the inferences for which ACT has productions available.

Figure 7-4 illustrates the history of ACT's reasoning backward efforts to establish that $\triangle CME \cong \triangle DMF$. ACT first attempts to achieve this by the side-side-side (SSS) postulate. This subgoal is set by the following production:

P6: IF the goal is to prove that $\triangle XYZ \cong \triangle UVW$
THEN try to use SSS by proving $\overline{XY} \cong \overline{UV}$, $\overline{YZ} \cong \overline{VW}$, and $\overline{ZX} \cong \overline{WU}$

This effort is doomed to failure because the triangle congruence has been set as a subgoal of proving one of the sides congruent. When ACT gets to the goal of establishing $\overline{EM} \cong \overline{FM}$ it recognizes the problem and backs away. Our subject, like ACT, had a certain propensity to plunge into hopeless paths. Presumably one component of learning is to stop setting such hopeless subgoals.

I will skip over ACT's unsuccessful attempt to achieve the triangle congruence by side-angle-side (SAS) and look in detail at its efforts with the angle-side-angle (ASA) postulate. Two of the three pieces required for this, $\angle CME \cong \angle DMF$ and $\overline{CM} \cong \overline{MD}$, have already been established by forward inferences. This leaves the third piece to be established—that $\angle ECM \cong \angle FDM$. This can be inferred by supplementary angles from something that is already known—that $\triangle AMC \cong \triangle BMD$. However, ACT does not have available the postulate for making this inference. This corresponds to a blindness of our subject with respect to using the supplementary rule. Although the opportunity did not arise in this problem because he was following a different path to solution, many times he overlooked opportunities to achieve his goals by the supplementary angle rule.

Having failed the three available methods for proving triangle congruence, ACT backed up and found a different pair of triangles, $\triangle AME$ and $\triangle BMF$, whose triangle congruence would establish the higher goal that $\overline{EM} \cong \overline{FM}$. (It turns out that, by failing on the supplementary angle needed to establish $\triangle CME \cong \triangle DMF$ and trying $\triangle AME \cong \triangle BMF$, ACT finds the shorter proof.)

Fortuitously, ACT chooses ASA as its first method. The attempt to apply this method is illustrated in Figure 7-5. One of the angle congruences is obtained by the following working backward rule:

P7: IF the goal is to prove that $\angle XYZ \cong \angle UYW$
and X, Y, and W are on a line
and Z, Y, and W are on a line
THEN the goal can be inferred because of vertical angles

Note that this inference was not made by the forward-reasoning, vertical-angle production. This turns out to be due to a difficulty that the ACT pattern matcher has in seeing lines define multiple angles. The segments $\overline{AM}$ and $\overline{ME}$ that

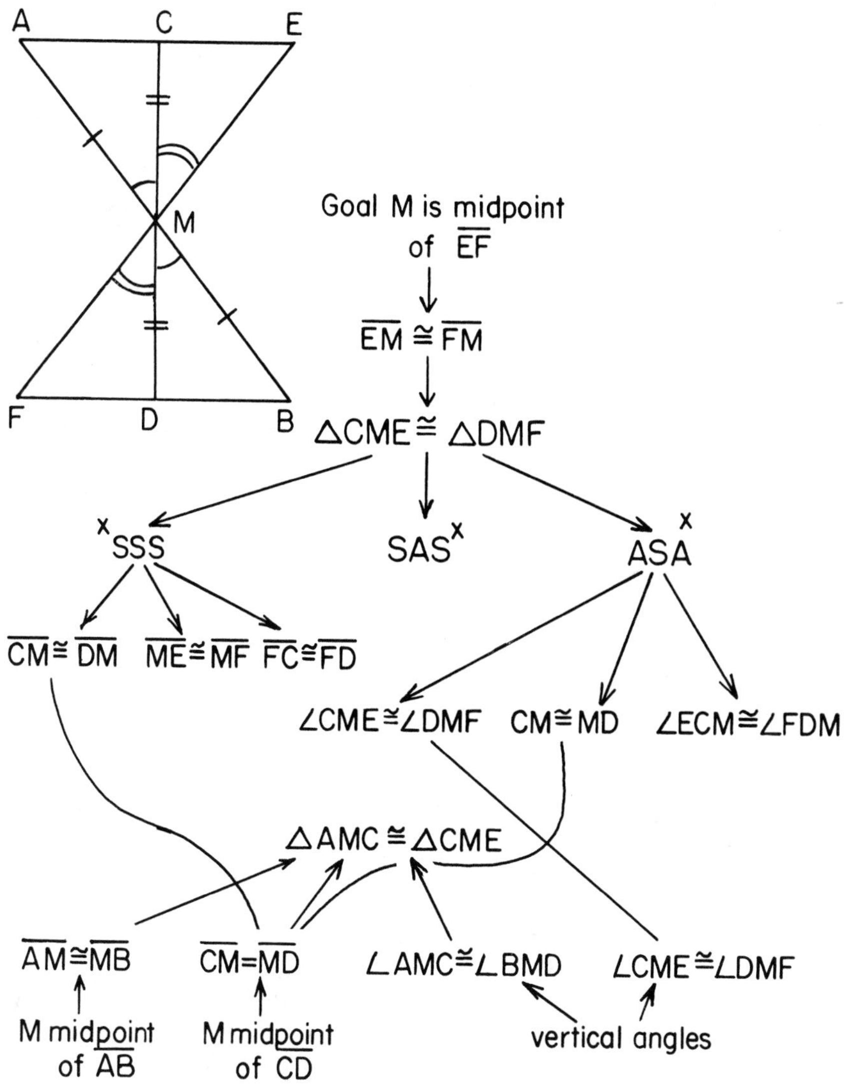

Figure 7-4: Trace of backward-chaining efforts by ACT.

define ∠AME were already used in extracting the angles ∠AMC and ∠CME for use by the forward-reasoning vertical angle postulate.

ACT is also able to get the other parts of the ASA pattern. The side $\overline{AM} \cong \overline{BM}$ has already been gotten by forward inference. The fact that ∠EAM ≅ ∠FBM can be inferred from the fact that △AMC ≅ △BMD sincelte angles are

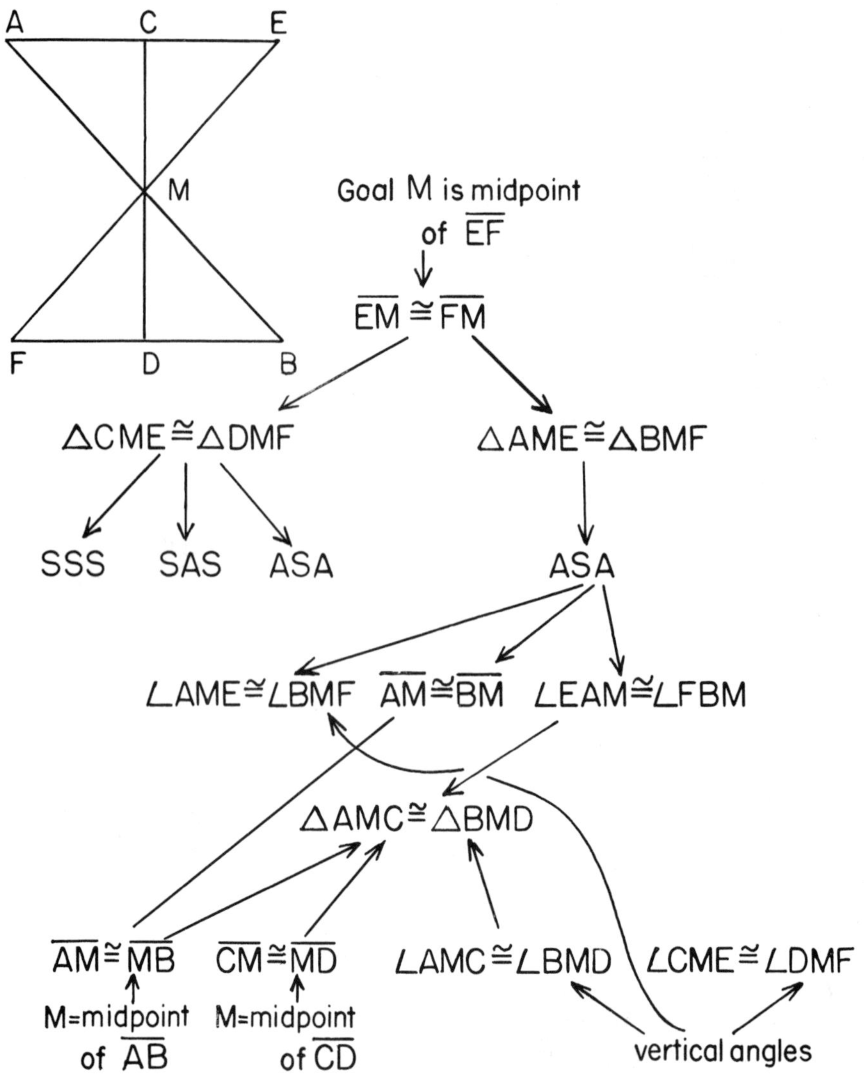

Figure 7-5: Application of ASA method by ACT.

corresponding parts of congruent triangles. With this ACT has found its proof tree embedded within the search net. That proof tree is highlighted in Figure 7-5.

7.2.2 Comparison of ACT to Subject R

It is of interest to see how ACT's behavior compares to that of a typical student. We have gathered extensive protocols from one subject, R. R took geometry from us in grade 7 as a special enrichment opportunity one year before he would normally take geometry in school. We have a more or less complete record of all his learning and work at geometry through Chapter 4 of Jurgensen, Donnelly, Maier, and Rising [1975]. In particular, we have a record of his performance on the critical problem in Figure 7-2.

Subject R's performance did not correspond to that of ACT in all details. This is to be expected because ACT's choices about what productions to apply have an important probabilistic component to them. However, one can still ask whether ACT and subject R have the same character to their inferences. One way of defining this is whether ACT could have produced R's protocol if the probabilities came out correct. By this criterion ACT is compatible with much of R's protocol.

Like ACT, R began by making the forward inferences necessary to conclude $\triangle AMC \cong \triangle BMD$ and then making this conclusion. Like ACT these inferences were made with little idea for how they would be used. Then like ACT, R began to reason backward from his goal to prove that M was the midpoint of $\overline{EF}$ to the goal of proving triangle congruence. However, unlike ACT he was lucky and chose the triangle $\triangle AME \cong \triangle BMF$ first. Unlike ACT again, but this time unlucky, he first chose SAS as his method for establishing the triangle congruence. He got $\overline{AM} \cong \overline{MB}$ from previous forward inference and the $\angle EAM \cong \angle FBM$ from the fact that $\triangle AMC \cong \triangle BMD$—just as ACT obtained this in trying to use ASA. However, he then had to struggle with the goal of proving $\overline{AE} \cong \overline{BF}$. Unlike ACT, subject R is reluctant to back up and he tenaciously tried to find some way of achieving his goal. He was finally told by the instructor to try some other method. Then he turned to ASA. He already had two pieces of the rule by his efforts with SAS and quickly got the third component $\angle AME \cong \angle BMF$ from the fact that they were vertical angles. Note that subject R also failed to make this vertical angle inference in forward mode and only made it in backward mode.

In conclusion, R's behavior is very similar in character to that of ACT. The only major exception is R's reluctance to back up when a particular method is not working out.

7.3 LEARNING

What has been described so far is a general framework in which a student can plan proofs. I believe that much of the basic architecture is a reflection of general reasoning methods the student brings to geometry for solving problems. However, the basic architecture is not enough to enable the student to be successful and facile at planning proofs in geometry. The student obviously must learn things specific to geometry. I will now discuss two stages of learning that are important to geometry. The first stage involves creating production embodiments of the basic search operators that make forward and backward inferences. Once the student has these operators he must tune them so that they will be selected in the appropriate situations and not selected in situations where they will not achieve the goals.

7.4 KNOWLEDGE COMPILATION

Knowledge compilation [Neves & Anderson, 1981] is the process by which subjects go from a declarative representation of a skill to a procedural representation. The declarative representation is applied to the task by means of general interpretive productions. After achieving a procedural form, in contrast, the knowledge applies directly because it is encoded in production form. In recognition of the obvious analogy, we call this process knowledge compilation. However, unlike computer compilation, this process in ACT is *gradual* and occurs through *practice*.

When students read a definition, postulate, or theorem, it seems unreasonable to suppose that they immediately convert it into a procedural form such as the productions presented in the discussion of Figures 7-3 through 7-5. One reason that it is unreasonable is that the same fact of geometry can give rise to a great many possible productions reflecting various ways that the information can be used. For instance, consider the textbook definition of supplementary angles:

"Supplementary angles are two angles whose measures have sum 180."

Below are productions that embody just some of the ways in which this knowledge can be used. These productions differ in terms of whether one is reasoning forward or backward, what the current goal is, and what is known.

P8: IF $m\angle A + m\angle B = 180^o$
THEN $\angle A$ and $\angle B$ are supplementary

P9: IF the goal is to prove $\angle A$ and $\angle B$ are supplementary
THEN set as a subgoal to prove $\angle A + \angle B = 180^o$

P10: IF $\angle A$ and $\angle B$ are supplementary
THEN $m\angle A + m\angle B = 180^o$

P11: IF $\angle A$ and $\angle B$ are supplementary
and $m\angle A = X$
THEN $m\angle B = 180^o - X$

P12: IF $\angle A$ and $\angle B$ are supplementary
and the goal is to find $m\angle A$
THEN set as a subgoal to find $m\angle B$

P13: IF the goal is to prove $\angle A \cong \angle B$
and $\angle A$ is supplementary to $\angle C$
and $\angle B$ is supplementary to $\angle D$
THEN set as a subgoal to prove $\angle C \cong \angle D$

A basic point is that the definition of supplementary angles is fundamentally declarative in the sense that it can be used in multiple ways and does not contain a commitment to how it will be used. It is unreasonable to suppose that, in encoding the definition, the system anticipates all the uses to which it might be put and creates a procedural structure for each.

Rather than assuming students directly encode this textbook information into procedures, I assume that they first encode this information declaratively. In the ACT system encoding information declaratively amounts to growing new semantic network structure. General *interpretive* procedures then use this information according to the features of the particular circumstance. When declarative knowledge is used multiple times in a particular way, automatic learning processes in the ACT theory will begin to create new procedures that directly apply the knowledge without the interpretive step. This kind of learning is called *procedural compilation*.

In individual subjects we see a gradual shift in performance which we would like to put into correspondence with this compilation from the interpretive application of declarative knowledge to direct application of procedures. After reading, say, a particular postulate, students' applications of that postulate is both slow and halting. Students will often recite to themselves the postulate before trying to apply it—or even go back and reread it. It seems that they need to activate the declarative representation in their working memory so that interpretive procedures can apply to the data of this representation. They typically match separately fragments of the postulate to the problem. We will see that such fragmentary application is typical of a general knowledge interpreter applying to a declarative representation. With repeated use, however, application of the postulate smoothes out. It is no longer explicitly recalled and it is no longer possible as observer or subject to discriminate separate steps in the application of the procedure. It certainly has the appearance of the postulate being embodied in separate pattern recognition productions such as those described with respect to Figures 7-3 through 7-5.

7.4.1 Knowledge Schemas

We have found a schema-like representation to be very useful for structuring the initial declarative encoding of a geometry fact. Table 7-1 illustrates a schema encoding for the SAS postulate which is stated in the text as:

> "If two sides and the included angle of one triangle are congruent to the corresponding parts of another triangle, the triangles are congruent."

The diagram in Figure 7-6 accompanied this statement. The postulate schema in Table 7-1 is divided into background, hypothesis, conclusion, and comment.

The hypothesis and conclusion reflect the if/then structure of the condition, which our subject was fairly facile at extracting. The background information amounts to a description of the diagram and contains the constraints which allow the variables (sides and angles) to be properly bound. The comment contains additional information relevant to its use. Here we have the name of the postulate which prescribes what the student should write as a reason.

Table 7-1: SAS Schema

Background
- s1 is a side of △XYZ
- s2 is a side of △XYZ
- A1 is an angle of △XYZ
- A1 is included by s1 and s2
- s3 is a side of △UVW
- s4 is a side of △UVW
- A2 is an angle of △UVW
- A2 is included by s3 and s4

Hypothesis
- s1 is congruent to s3
- s2 is congruent to s4
- A1 is congruent to A2

Conclusion
- △XYZ is congruent to △UVW

Comment
- This is the side-angle-side postulate

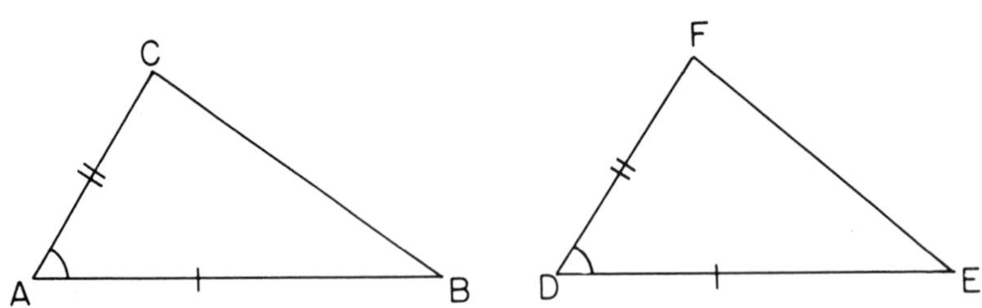

Figure 7-6: Diagram accompanying the SAS postulate.

I regard the knowledge structure in Table 7-1 to be schema-like; it is a unit organized into parts according to "slots" such as background, hypothesis, conclusion, and comment. The knowledge structure is declarative in that it can be used in multiple ways by interpretive procedures. For instance, the following production would be evoked to apply that knowledge in a working backwards manner:

P14: IF the goal is to prove a statement
and there is a schema that has this statement as conclusion
THEN set as subgoals to match the background of the schema
and after that to prove the hypothesis of the schema

If the schema is in working memory and its conclusion matches the current goal, this production will start up the application of the schema to the current problem. First the background is matched to bind the variables and then the hypotheses are checked.

To appreciate how learning switches the student from the initial piecemeal interpretive application to direct, unitary procedures, it would be useful to sketch out a few more of the productions that are used in the initial interpretive application. Let us consider some of the productions involved in working backwards. After production P14, which starts things, the next production to apply would be

P16: IF the goal is to match a set of statements
THEN match the first statement in the set

Production P14 had set the subgoal of matching the statements in the background. This production above starts that process going by focusing on the first statement in the background. This production is followed by a production which iterates through the statements of the background.

P17: IF the goal is to match a statement in a set
and the problem contains a match to the statement
THEN go on to match the next statement in the set

(Actually, there is a call to a subroutine of productions which execute the matches to each statement. See [Neves & Anderson, 1981].) After all statements in the background have been matched, the following production sets the goal to prove the hypotheses:

P18: IF the goal is to match a set of statements
and the last statement in that set has been matched
THEN go on to the goal that follows

Note productions P14, P16, P17, and P18 are sufficiently general that it is reasonable to propose that even a novice in geometry has them from prior skills.

7.4.2 Composition

There are two major processes in knowledge compilation—*composition* and *proceduralization*. When a series of productions apply in a fixed order, composition will create a new production that accomplishes the effect of the sequence in a single step (see [Neves & Anderson, 1981]). Composition, operating on the sequence of P14, P16, and P17, applied to the SAS schema, would put forth the production

P19: IF the goal is to prove a statement
and there is a schema that has this statement as conclusion
and the schema has a statement as the first member of its background
and the problem contains a match to the statement
THEN set as subgoals to match the background
and within this subgoal to match the next statement of the background
and after that to prove the hypotheses of the schema

This production only applies in the circumstance that the sequence P14, P16, and P17 applied and has the same effect in terms of changes to the data base. The details underlying composition are discussed in [Neves & Anderson, 1981], but the gist of the process is easy to describe. The composed production collects in its condition all those clauses from the individual productions' conditions except those that are the product of the actions of earlier productions in the sequence. As an example of this exception, P16 has in its condition that the goal is to match the set of statements. Since this goal was set by P14 earlier in the sequence, it is not mentioned in the condition of the composed production P19. Thus, the condition is a test of whether the circumstances are right for the full sequence of productions to execute. The action of the composed production collects all actions of the individual productions except those involved in setting transitory goals that are finished with by the end of the sequence. As an example of this exception, P16 sets the subgoal of matching the first statement of the background but P17 meets this subgoal. Therefore, the subgoal is not mentioned in the action of the composed production P19.

This composition process can apply to the product of earlier compositions. Although there is nothing special about compositions of three, consider what the resulting production would be like if P19 were composed with two successive iterative applications of P17:

P20: IF the goal is to prove a statement
and there is a schema that has this statement as conclusion
and the schema has a statement as the first member of the background
and the problem contains a match to this statement
and the schema has another statement as the next member of its background
and the problem contains a match to this statement
and the schema has another statement as the next member of its background
and the problem contains a match to this statement
THEN set as subgoals to match the background
and within this the next statement of the background
and after that to prove the hypotheses of the schema

It should be noted that such productions are not really specific to the SAS schema. Indeed, productions such as P19 and P20 might have been formed from compositions derived from the productions applying to other, earlier schemata. If so, these composed productions would be ready to apply to the current schema. Thus, there can be some general transfer of practice through composition. However, there is a limit on how large such composed productions can become. As they get larger they require more information in the schema be retrieved from long-term memory and held active in working memory. Limits on the capacity of working memory imply limits on the size of the general, interpretive conditions that can successfully match.

7.4.3 Proceduralization

Proceduralization is a process that builds specialized versions of productions by eliminating retrieval of information from long-term memory. Rather the information that would have been retrieved from long-term memory is encoded directly into the specialized version of the production. To illustrate the process of proceduralization, consider its application to the production P20. This statement contains in its condition four clauses that require retrieval of information from long-term memory:

1. There is a schema that has this statement as conclusion.
2. The schema has a statement as the first member of its background.
3. The schema has another statement as the next member of its background.
4. The schema has another statement as the next member of its background.

Applied to the SAS schema these statements match the following information:

1. The SAS schema has as its conclusion "$\triangle XYZ \cong \triangle UVW$".
2. The first statement of its background is "S1 is a side of $\triangle XYZ$".
3. The next statement of its background is "S2 is a side of $\triangle XYZ$".
4. The next statement of its background is "A1 is an angle of $\triangle XYZ$".

What is accomplished by matching these statements in P20 is to identify the SAS schema, its conclusion, and the first three statements of its background. A specialized production can be built which contains this information and does not require the long-term memory retrievals:

```
P21:   IF  the goal is to prove that △XYZ ≅ △UVW
           and S1 is a side of △XYZ
           and S2 is a side of △XYZ
           and A1 is an angle of △XYZ
     THEN  set as subgoals to match the background of the SAS schema
           and within this to match the next statement in the schema
           and after that to prove the hypothesis of the schema
```

This production is now specialized to the SAS schema and does not require any long-term memory retrieval. Rather, built into its condition are the patterns retrieved from long-term memory.

The effect of this proceduralization process is to enable larger composed productions to apply because the proceduralized productions are not limited by the need to retrieve information into working memory. This in turn allows still larger compositions to be formed. The eventual product of the composition process applied to the top-down evocation of the SAS schema, initially via productions P14, P16, P17, and P18 would be:

```
P22:  IF   the goal is to prove that △XYZ is congruent to △UVW
           and S1 is a side of △XYZ
           and S2 is a side of △XYZ
           and A1 is an angle of △XYZ
           and A1 is included by S1 and S2
           and S3 is a side of △UVW
           and S4 is a side of △UVW
           and A2 is an angle of △UVW
           and A2 is included by S3 and S4
    THEN   set as subgoals to prove:
             S1 is congruent to S3
             S2 is congruent to S4
             A1 is congruent to A2
```

This production serves to apply the SAS postulate in working backward mode. When the knowledge reaches this state the complete SAS postulate has been put into a single production.

As will be discussed in later portions of the paper, composition need not stop when the postulate has been completely incorporated into a single production. It can continue to merge productions to compress even longer sequences of actions into a single production.

In the ACT implementation, composition works on pairs of productions that fire in succession. It operates every opportunity it gets. There are two factors that limit the size of the eventual productions. First, too large productions will not match to working memory. Second, the composition is specific to the particular production sequence. The larger the production sequence the less likely that the opportunity for that exact sequence will be repeated on another problem. If the opportunity for the sequence is not repeated, the composed production will not fire and so cannot enter into further compositions. It should be noted in this regard that composed productions do not replace the components from which they were composed. So, if a problem appears that requires a novel combination of the components inconsistent with the higher compositions, the individual component productions are available.

The proceduralization step occurs in ACT at the first opportunity. This means that proceduralized versions of productions are quickly built. In this feature ACT is probably too fast a learner for a human simulation. In applying proceduralization to account for a number of phenomena from the psychological literature, Neves and Anderson [1981] had to assume that proceduralization progressed relatively slowly. This could be achieved in the current program by making proceduralization probabilistic or by requiring a production fire a number of times in the same way before it can be proceduralized.

7.4.4 Tuning the Search for a Proof

Having operators proceduralized is not enough to guarantee successful proof generation. There is still a potentially very large search space of forward and backward inferences. Finding the proof tree in this net would often be infeasible without some search heuristics that cause the system to try the right inferences first.

A heuristic in this discussion amounts to adding some discriminative conditions to a production to restrict its applicability. While satisfying these conditions does not guarantee success of the operator, it does make it more likely. This is the nature of a heuristic—to select operators on the basis of tests that suggest higher than average probability of success.

It is interesting to note that novices do not deal with proofs by plunging into endless search. They are very restrictive in what paths they attempt and are quite unwilling to consider all the paths that are legally possible. The problem is, of course, that the paths they select are often non-optimal or just plain dead-ends. Thus, at a general level, expertise does not develop by becoming more restrictive in search, rather it develops by becoming more appropriately restrictive.

I have been able to discover four ways by which subjects can learn to make better choices in searching for a proof tree. One is by *analogy* to prior problems—using with the current problem methods that succeeded in similar past problems. The second, related technique is to *generalize* from specific problems operators that capture what the solutions to these specific problems have in common. The third is a *discrimination* process by which restrictions are added to the applicability of more general operators. These restrictions are derived from a comparison of where the general operators succeeded and failed. The fourth process is a *composition* process by which sequences of operators become collapsed into single operators that apply in more restrictive situations. I will discuss each of these methods of learning search heuristics in turn.

7.4.4.1 Learning by Analogy

The process of using analogy to past problems can, in some ways, be characterized as a degenerate learning process. Figure 7-7 illustrates an early opportunity for analogy in the chapter on triangles. The student has just seen a solution to the problem in part (a) and then is presented with the problem in part (b). Our subject R noticed the similarity between the two problems, went back to the first, and almost copied over the solution.

Analogy of this sort is an interesting kind of learning in that it amounts to learning very specific operators. (See Chapter 5 of this book for a more general method of learning by analogy.) For example, for the problem in part (a) we would have a schema that described the specific problem and its solution:

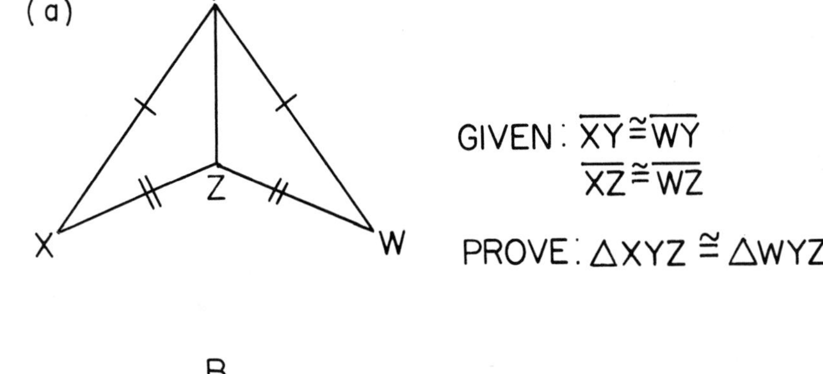

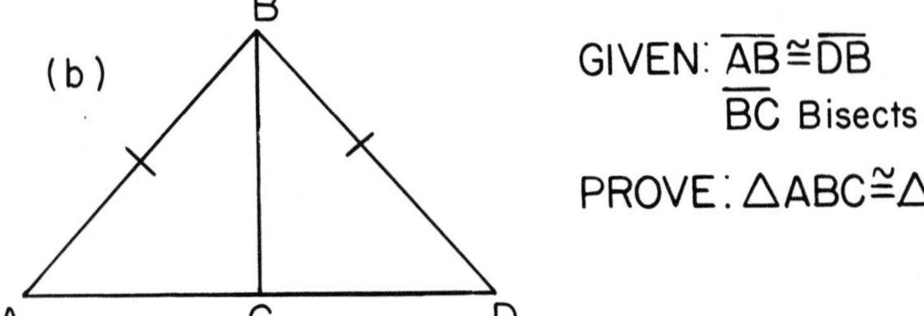

Figure 7-7: Two problems with obvious similarity.

PROBLEM SCHEMA
Background
There is a triangle $\triangle XYZ$
There is a triangle $\triangle WYZ$
Givens
$\overline{XY} \cong \overline{WY}$
$\overline{XZ} \cong \overline{WZ}$
Goal
$\triangle XYZ \cong \triangle WYZ$
Method
$\overline{YZ} \cong \overline{YZ}$ by reflexivity
$\triangle XYZ \cong \triangle WYZ$ by SSS

To account for the effectiveness of analogy we must assume that the student has a facility to partially match the background and givens of one problem to the background and given of another problem. This is because there is not a perfect match between the two problems. We have recently developed such partial matching facilities for the ACT theory [Kline, 1981].

One problem with analogy to specific problems is that it appears to be effective only in the short run because students' memory for specific problems tends to be short-lived. All examples of analogy in R's protocols come within the same section of a chapter. There are no examples of problems in one section reminding R of problems in an early section. Therefore, it seems that pure analogy tends to produce no permanent benefits.

A second problem with pure analogy is that it is superficial. Any point of similarity between two problems increases the partial match. It is no accident that the two pairs of triangles in Figure 7-7 are oriented in the same direction, although this is completely irrelevant for the success of the analogy.

In ACT analogy depends on partial matching processes which are quite "syntactic" in character. That is, the partial match process just counts up the degree of overlap in the problem description without really evaluating whether the overlaps are essential to the appropriateness of the solution or not. In myself I note a tendency to respond to overlap between problems in this same superficial way. Consider the three problems in Figure 7-8. At a deep level the first two problems are really quite similar. Larger triangles contain smaller triangles. To prove the containing triangles congruent it is first necessary to prove the contained triangles congruent. The contained triangles in the two problems are congruent in basically the same way and they overlap with the containing triangles in basically the same way. However, on first glance the two problems seem quite different. In contrast, on first glance, the two problems in parts (a) and (c) of Figure 7-8 appear to have much in common. Now it is true that upon careful inspection one can determine that the first pair provides a more useful analogy than the second pair. However, it seems that analogy in problem-solving of this sort is to serve a *noticing* function. Similar problems spontaneously come to mind as possible models for solutions. If the superficial similarity between problems (a) and (b) is not sufficient for the analogy to be noticed there will never be the opportunity for careful inspection to realize how good the deep correspondence is.

There is one very nice illustration of the problem with the superficiality of analogy in the protocol of R. This concerns a pair of problems that come in the first chapter. Figure 7-9 illustrates the two problems. Part (a) illustrates the initial problem R studied along with an outline of the proof. Later in the section R came across problem (b) and immediately noticed the analogy. He tried to use the first proof as a model for how the second should be structured. Analogous to the line RO = NY he wrote down the line AB > CD. Then analogous to the second line ON = ON he wrote down BC > BC! His semantic sensitivities caught this before he went on and he abandoned the attempt to use the analogy.

7.4.4.2 Generalization

I have characterized solving problems by analogy as superficial. Part of what is superficial about the approach is that the analogy is based only on the statement of the problems, not on the structures of their solution. Analogy, in the sense discussed, cannot use the structure of the solution, because the proof for the second problem is not available yet. Analogy is being used in service of finding the second proof.

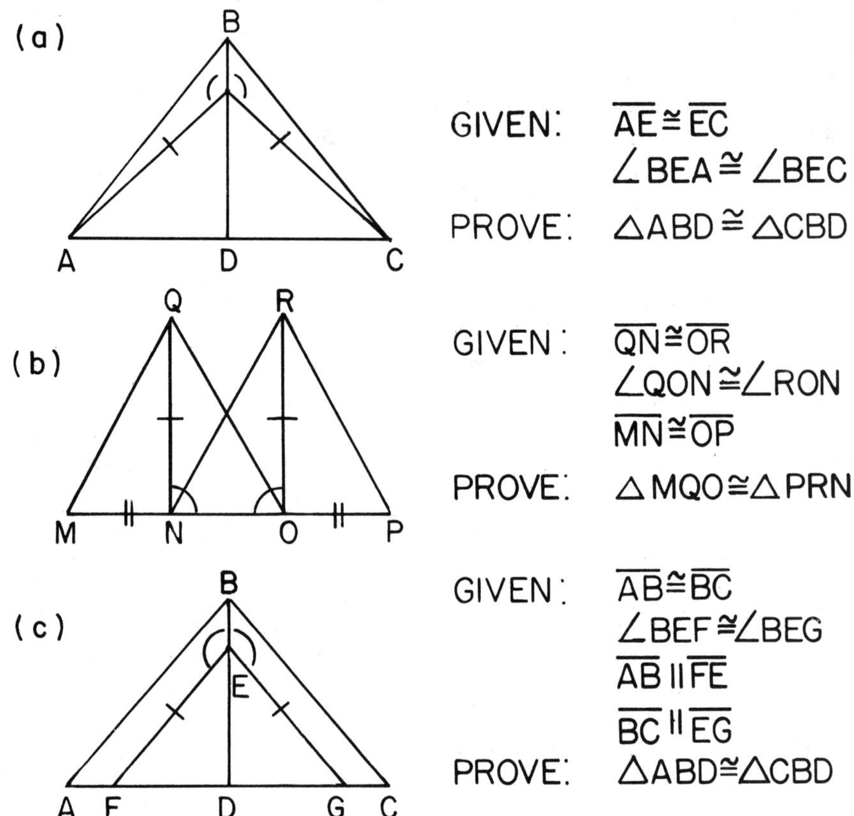

Figure 7-8: Problems illustrating the limited validity of superficial analogy.

Generalization, on the other hand, is based on a comparison between two problems and their solutions. By using the structure of the solution, it is possible to select the relevant aspects of the problem statement. A rule is formulated by the generalization process which tries to formulate what the two problems and their solutions have in common. That rule can then be used should similar problems appear. For instance, consider the first two problems in Figure 7-8. The generalization process applied to these two examples would encode what they have in common by the following schema:

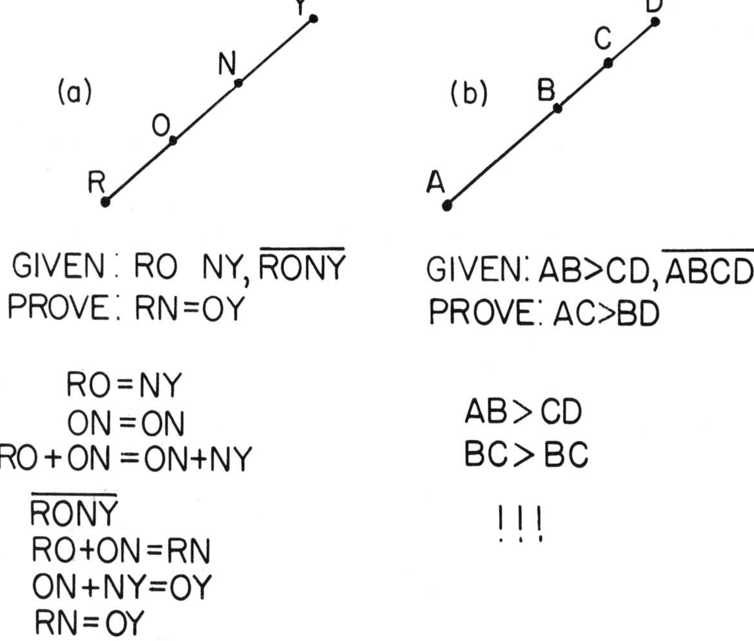

Figure 7-9: A problem where superficial analogy goes wrong.

GENERALIZED SCHEMA:

Background

$\triangle XYZ$ contains $\triangle SYZ$

$\triangle UVW$ contains $\triangle TVW$

Givens

$\overline{SY} \cong \overline{TV}$

$\angle YSZ \cong \angle VTW$

Goal

$\triangle XYZ = \triangle UVW$

Method

$\triangle SYZ = \triangle TVW$ by SAS

$\overline{YZ} \cong \overline{VW}$ by corresponding parts

$\angle XYZ \cong \angle UVW$ by corresponding parts

$\triangle XYZ \cong \triangle UVW$ by SAS

These generalizations are based on the same partial matching process that underlies analogy. However, the partial matching occurs between solved problems not just between problem statements. Because the product of the partial match is a fairly general problem description, it is likely to apply to many problems. Thus it is likely to be strengthened and become a permanent part of the student's repertoire for searching for proofs. This contrasts to the specific examples that serve as the basis for analogy. These specific examples are likely to be forgotten.

7.4.4.3 Discrimination

Discrimination provides a complementary process to generalization. It takes operators that are too general and thus are applied in incorrect situations and places restrictions on their range of applicability. If the operator to be discriminated is embodied as a production, discrimination adds an additional clause to restrict the range of situations where the production condition will match. ACT determines what additional clauses to add by comparing the difference between successful and unsuccessful applications of the rule.

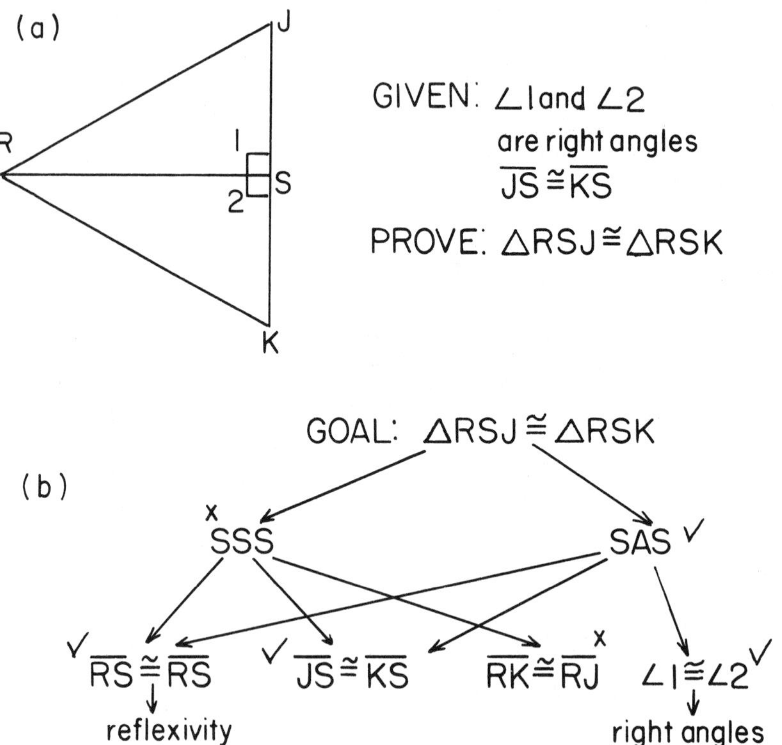

Figure 7-10: Problem leading to a discrimination.

Figure 7-10 illustrates an analysis of a problem which led subject R to form a discrimination. In part (a) I have a representation of the problem and in-part (b) I have indicated in search net form R's attempt to solve the problem. First he tried to use SSS, a method which had worked on a previous problem that had a great deal of superficial similarity to this problem. However, he was not able to get the sides $\overline{RK}$ and $\overline{RS}$ congruent. Then he switched to SAS, the other method he had at the time for proving triangles congruent. Interestingly, it was only in the context of this goal that he recognized the right angles were congruent. After he had finished with this problem, he verbally announced the rules to use SSS only if there was no angle mentioned. This can be seen to be the product of discrimination. The "don't use SSS if angle" comes from a comparison of the previous problem in which no angle was mentioned with the current problem that did mention angles.

Discrimination requires that the system determine when a production has made an error. This is not easy in all domains, but fortunately it is fairly easy in the proof planning domain. After ACT has completed a proof plan it has a structure like that in Figure 7-5 illustrating the logical connections among the inferences required to derive the proof. This is the proof tree embedded in the search net. Any planning production that contributed to the creation of the proof tree is regarded as successful. Productions that led to the creation of irrelevant portions of the search net are regarded as misfirings. These are the ones that are subject to discrimination. These are not all of the unsuccessful productions. To see that this is so, consider an example: Suppose that a goal is set to prove two angles congruent by showing they are corresponding parts of congruent triangles. Suppose all methods tried for proving congruent triangles fail and the angle congruence is eventually proven by resorting to the supplementary angle postulate. The mistake is not in the productions that proposed methods for proving the triangles congruent. These would receive a neutral evaluation. The mistake was in the production that set the subgoal of triangle congruence.

As in the composition case, generalization and discrimination are invoked whenever possible in the ACT simulation. Whenever the program solves a new problem it compares its solution to past solutions to check for generalization. Similarly, whenever an error is made in the use of a production a comparison is made to the last successful operation of that production and a discrimination is formed. This undoubtedly implies a better memory for past instances than is realistic psychologically.

7.4.4.4 Composition

I feel that composition has an important role to play in forming multiple operator sequences just as it played an important role in the initial proceduralization of operators. Figure 7-11 illustrates an example where composition can apply. The first production to apply in solving this problem would be:

P24: IF the goal is to prove $\angle X \cong \angle U$
and $\angle X$ is part of $\triangle XYZ$
and $\angle U$ is part of $\triangle UVW$
THEN the subgoal is to prove $\triangle XYZ \cong \triangle UVW$

This production would set as a subgoal to prove $\triangle ABC \cong \triangle DBC$. At this point the following production might apply:

P25: IF the goal is to prove $\triangle XYZ \cong \triangle UVW$
and $\overline{XY} \cong \overline{UV}$
and $\overline{ZX} \cong \overline{WU}$
THEN the subgoal is to prove $\overline{YZ} \cong \overline{VW}$

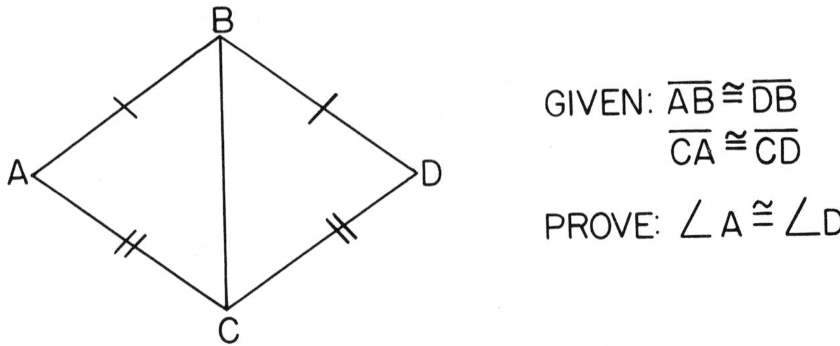

Figure 7-11: Problem leading to a composition.

This production, applied to the situation in Figure 7-11, would set as the subgoal to prove $\overline{BC} \cong \overline{BC}$ as a step on the way to using SSS. At this point, the following production would apply:

P26: IF the goal is to prove $\overline{XY} \cong \overline{XY}$
THEN this may be concluded by reflexivity

This production would add $\overline{BC} \cong \overline{BC}$ and allow the following production to apply:

P27: IF the goal is to prove $\triangle XYZ \cong \triangle UVW$
and $\overline{XY} \cong \overline{UV}$
and $\overline{YZ} \cong \overline{VW}$
and $\overline{ZX} \cong \overline{WU}$
THEN the goal may be concluded by SSS

where XY = AB, UV = DB, YZ = BC, VW = BC, ZX = CA, and WU = CD. This adds the information that △ABC ≅ △DBC. Finally, the following production will apply which recognizes that the desired conclusion is now established:

P28: IF the goal to prove ∠X ≅ ∠U
and △XYZ ≅ △UVW
THEN the goal may be concluded because of congruent parts of congruent triangles

The composition process, operating on this sequence of productions, would eventually produce a production of the form:

P29: IF the goal is to prove ∠A ≅ ∠D
and ∠A is part of △ABC
and ∠D is part of △DBC
and $\overline{AB} \cong \overline{DB}$
and $\overline{CA} \cong \overline{DC}$
THEN conclude $\overline{AB} \cong \overline{AB}$ by reflexivity
and conclude △ABC ≅ △DBC by SSS
and conclude the goal because of congruent parts of congruent triangles

The variables in this production have been named to correspond to the terms in Figure 7-11 for purposes of readability. This production would immediately recognize the solution to a problem like that in Figure 7-11.

7.5 SUMMARY OF GEOMETRY LEARNING

It would be useful to summarize the student's progress as he gathers more experience and becomes more expert at generating proofs in geometry. There are two initial sources of information. There are the postulates, theorems, and definitions that he reads in the textbook instructions. The second source is the *examples* of worked out problems (either solved in the text or by the student himself). The rules are declaratively encoded into a schema-like form to which general problem-solving productions can apply. As discussed, the rules in this form are applied in a piecemeal way. The twin processes of knowledge compilation, composition and proceduralization, eventually transform each rule into a procedural form in which each rule is embodied by a production.

The examples can be used through analogy to guide the solution of problems. Solution by analogy involves interpretive processing of the examples much as the initial use of the general rules. However, as noted, specific examples are very limited in their range of applicability. The processes of compilation and generalization applied to these examples can lead the student to the same kind of general, proceduralized, unitary operators as can compilation applied to the rules. To the extent that generalization leaves in features of the original problems, the operators from this source might not be as general as the operators derived directly from the rules, but rather will remain tuned to specific problem characteristics.

Finally, the processes of discrimination and composition create larger multiple-inference operators which are much more discriminant in their range of applicability. In the extreme, special rules could evolve that outline full proof trees for certain kinds of problems. To the extent that new problems fit the specifications of these advanced operators, solution will be quick and efficient. However, to the extent that new problems pose novel configurations of features not covered by the advanced operators, the student will have to fall back to the slower and more general operators for working backwards. The view of expertise developed here, then, is very much the one that was developed for chess [Chase & Simon, 1973; Simon & Gilmartin, 1973]; that is, experts in geometry proof generation have simply encoded many special case rules.

ACKNOWLEDGMENTS

This research is supported by grant IST-80-15357 from the National Science Foundation.

REFERENCES

Anderson, J. R., *Language, Memory, and Thought*, Lawrence Erlbaum Associates, Hillsdale, NJ, 1976.

Anderson, J. R., "A theory of language acquisition based on general learning mechanisms," *Proceedings of the Seventh International Joint Conference on Artificial Intelligence*, IJCAI, Vancouver, British Columbia, August 1981.

Anderson, J. R. and Kline, P., "Design of a production system," *SIGART Newsletter*, June 1977.

Anderson, J. R., Kline, P. and Lewis, C., "A production system model for language processing," *Cognitive Processes in Comprehension*, Carpenter, P. and Just, M. (Eds.), Lawrence Erlbaum Associates, Hillsdale, NJ, 1977.

Anderson, J. R., Kline, P. J. and Beasley, C. M., "A general learning theory and its application to schema abstraction," *The Psychology of Learning and Motivation*, Bower, G. H. (Ed.), Academic Press, 1979.

Chase, W. G. and Simon, H. A., "The mind's eye in chess," *Visual Information Processing*, Chase, W. G. (Ed.), Academic Press, New York, NY, 1973.

Jurgenson, R. C., Donnelly, A. J., Maier, J. E. and Rising, G. R., *Geometry*, Houghton Mifflin Company, Boston, MA, 1975.

Kline, P. J., "The superiority of relative criteria in partial matching and generalization," *Proceedings of the Seventh International Joint Conference on Artificial Intelligence*, IJCAI, Vancouver, British Columbia, August 1981.

Neves, D. and Anderson, J. R., "Knowledge compilation: Mechanisms for the automatization of cognitive skills," *Cognitive Skills and Their Acquisition*, Anderson, J. R. (Ed.), Lawrence Erlbaum Associates, Hillsdale, NJ, 1981.

Simon, H. A. and Gilmartin, K., "A simulation of memory for chess positions," *Cognitive* Psychology, Vol. 5, pp. 29-46, 1973.

8

USING PROOFS AND REFUTATIONS TO LEARN FROM EXPERIENCE

Frederick Hayes-Roth
Teknowledge Inc.

ABSTRACT

To learn, a learner needs to formulate plans, monitor the plan execution to detect violated expectations, and then diagnose and rectify errors which the disconfirming data reveal. In this paper, five heuristic methods are presented for repairing flawed beliefs. These beliefs are considered as theories that predict effects of actions. Theories presuppose particular structural characteristics. When data disconfirm a theory, the heuristics proposed suggest specific ways to remedy the theory, including restricting the conditions for invoking the theory and weakening the theory's predictions. The five methods accomplish retraction, exclusion, avoidance, assurance and inclusion of outcomes that disconfirm a theory's predictions. Each proposed theory fix produces as a by-product new domain concepts that capture environmental characteristics of instrumental value to the learner. The techniques proposed here provide the first analytical methods for constructing new knowledge. They extend and make practical the ideas of proofs and refutations originally introduced by Lakatos.

8.1 INTRODUCTION

Much of what we call "intelligence" has evolved so that creatures who possess it can plan successfully to achieve goals. Goal attainment requires an ability to deduce a plan of action that should achieve the goal and an ability to carry out planned actions. Ordinary creatures must acquire at least some of these abilities during their lifetimes because they do not possess them at birth. This acquisition process is what we call "learning". Intelligent creatures learn to plan effectively.

Learning to plan effectively is difficult, because the learner possesses incomplete knowledge. The learner's knowledge of the world evolves gradually in response to its experiences. At any stage in its cognitive development, the learner possesses a limited set of beliefs about the world; an accurate and comprehensive characterization of the world would require vastly more. Unless the learner's environment adheres to a small number of simple laws, the learner can only develop an approximate understanding of environmental behavior. Since no natural habitat satisfies this constraint, natural learning systems always produce incomplete and error-ridden knowledge. The learner cannot avoid occasional mistakes.

In this paper, I describe learning methods that can rectify error-ridden knowledge and extend the range of its applicability by generating new concepts. In response to a failed plan, these methods suggest ways to diagnose and correct problematic beliefs. These corrections generally improve the learner's knowledge by eliminating sources of error. Each proposed modification changes some aspect of the learner's erroneous knowledge so that similar plan failures do not recur. Five different ways to repair knowledge will be described.

Henceforth, we will focus on machine learning and refer to a learning program, rather than a natural organism. The learning entity we will consider is called TL (the learner). TL plans to achieve its goals and employs heuristic methods to rectify its erroneous knowledge. This paper focuses on TL's learning heuristics. The proposed heuristics extend and operationalize earlier, related ideas developed by Lakatos [1976]. Lakatos describes how mathematicians iteratively formulate concepts, prove theorems about these concepts, and confront refutations that force them to revise their concepts and theorems. His narrative account illuminates only the most superficial features of this learning cycle. By contrast, the heuristic methods discussed in this paper provide mechanizable procedures to reformulate concepts as needed in order to rectify and salvage disconfirmed theories.

8.2 THE LEARNING CYCLE

The learning cycle consists of several phases (see Figure 8-1). First, TL formulates a plan to achieve some goal. In this phase, TL uses its knowledge to develop causal chains from starting conditions to goal attainment. I will call the plan justified if, according to TL's assumptions and theories, TL's planned actions logically entail attainment of the goal. If TL can "prove" that the planned actions will achieve the plan's goals conditional only upon TL's assumptions and theories, I will say TL has "justified" its plan.[1]

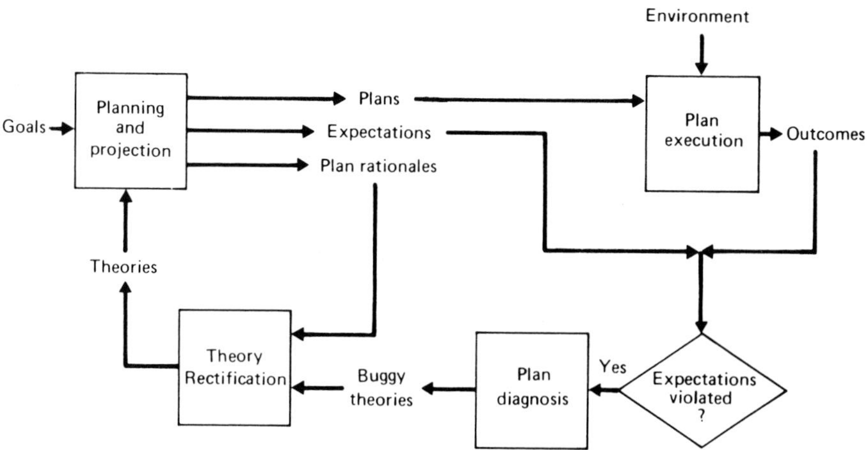

Figure 8-1: The Learning Cycle

The failure of a justified plan to achieve its goal reveals an error in TL's knowledge. In particular, a disconfirmed plan reveals a localized fault in the

[1]One reviewer felt that this definition, although informal, nonetheless was too strong. It seemed to preclude his informal approach, which often justifies a plan by noting it "worked once or twice" before. However, even such a "weak" justification fits the scheme employed in this paper. The reviewer's theory and its proof are shown below:

```
Theory:  If I execute plan P, I will achieve goal G.

Proof:
   1. Plan P has achieved goal G once or twice before (given,
      assumption).
   2. Any plan which has achieved a goal once or twice before will
      work successfully again (given, theory).
   3. If I execute plan P, I will achieve goal G (follows from 1 and
      2).
```

plan's "proof", that is, a bug in the plan's rationale (or justification). The methods proposed in this paper localize the fault within the rationale and debug the plan by fixing the unit of knowledge responsible for the fault.

Theory T

Has Parts:

Assumed Conditions (Prerequisites)	C_T
Planned Actions	A_T
Predicted Effects (Consequents)	E_T

Relations:

For all situations s, there exists a subsequent situation s′, where $C_T(s) \wedge \text{Perform}(A_T, s) \Rightarrow E_T(s')$

Figure 8-2: A unit of knowledge, called a "theory".

Each unit of TL's knowledge is modeled in a uniform and simple way, as indicated in Figure 8-2. Each knowledge unit contains three parts: assumed conditions which the unit prerequires, planned actions for TL, and predicted effects of the plan. When the theory includes no planned actions, its predicted effects correspond to theoretical consequents of the theory's antecedents. In essence, a knowledge unit predicts the effects of actions which are conditional on some prerequisites. Because of their predictiveness, I refer to all such units of knowledge as theories.[2] By definition, TL acts in accordance with its theories. TL plans to make desired outcomes predictable. TL justifies its plans by developing rationales that support the expectation of goal attainment. As long as the environment satisfies the prerequisites of TL's plans, TL rationally expects to achieve its goals by following its plans.

Inevitably, plans fail. Failures derive from several different sources: *(i)* a plan may actually be unjustifiable with respect to TL's current theories; *(ii)* a previously justified plan may not have adapted to subsequent changes in theories on which it depends; or *(iii)* the plan's current rationale is faulty. In the first case, to repair the faulty plan, TL should develop a plan rationale that shows how the goals of the plan derive from the plan's assumed conditions and actions. Thus, learning in this case requires only ordinary methods of problem-solving and deduction. In the second case, TL should revise the plan's rationale to conform to TL's current theories. In case *(iii)*, however, TL must recognize that the

[2]I realize that this terminology conflicts with conventional usage of the word theory. However, none of the alternatives seems more desirable. These include belief, conjecture, hypothesis, supposition, assumption, heuristic, conditional, and unit. The proposed term theory captures the central feature of this type of belief: it is part of a systematic body of knowledge supporting a wide class of inferences.

plan's failure refutes one or more of TL's theories. TL must identify the implicated theory, analyze the possible theoretical flaws, and formulate and adopt one or more theory repairs that circumvent the flaws. How this may be done is the subject of the next section.

8.3 FIVE HEURISTICS FOR RECTIFYING REFUTED THEORIES

In this section, I describe five heuristics for rectifying refuted theories. The five learning methods will be described first in general terms, and later in more detail. Each technique prescribes one way to modify a theory which has proved faulty; the theory's faultiness is manifested by the fact that although its assumed conditions were satisfied and TL successfully executed its prescribed actions, if any, the theory predicted some effects that failed to materialize. Any situation which exhibits these features refutes the theory and is called a counterexample. The proposed learning methods presuppose that every theory's conditions are accurately observable, which is a strong assumption. Learning in situations that violate this assumption lies beyond the scope of this paper. A brief description of each learning method follows.

1. **Retraction Method:** Restricting the theory's predictions to be consistent with observations. This method revises the theory so it no longer predicts those effects that were empirically disconfirmed. One specific, operational implementation of this method replaces the current theory's predicted effects by predictions which generalize both the original predicted effects and the empirically observed, disconfirming effects. Thus, this method rectifies a theory by retracting those predictions which do not conform with observations.
2. **Exclusion Method:** Barring the theory from applying to the current situation. This method revises a faulty theory so its prerequisites exclude the theory from applying in situations like the current one. This is the "Monster-barring" method of Lakatos. TL chooses a feature that characterizes the disconfirming situation and disallows the theory's application in future situations with that feature. The simplest operational implementation of this method revises the theory by conjoining to its prerequisites the negated description of the disconfirming situation. This method rectifies a theory by preventing it from making the same error in similar future situations.
3. **Avoidance Method:** Ruling out situations that predictably deny the theory's predictions. This method modifies a refuted theory by incorporating prerequisites that preclude theory disconfirmations like the current one. When faced with a refuted theory, TL deduces from its other current theories sufficient antecedents of the situational events that empirically disconfirmed the theory's expectations. These sufficient antecedents define situation predicates which TL believes can guarantee the theory will make

faulty predictions. TL then revises the refuted theory by excluding from the theory's domain of applicability all situations that exhibit these sufficient conditions. The simplest operational implementation of this method revises the theory by conjoining to its prerequisites the negation of one of these predicates. In doing so, TL rectifies the faulty theory by restricting it from applying to situations that TL's unrefuted theories imply would surely disconfirm it.

4. **Assurance Method:** Ruling in situations that predictably assure the theory's entailments. This method is analogous to the previous one. In this case, the method modifies a refuted theory by incorporating prerequisites that insure the realizations of the theory's predicted effects. When faced with a refuted theory, TL deduces from its other current theories antecedents which seem to guarantee attainment of the predicted but disconfirmed effect. These sufficient antecedents define situational predicates that assure confirmation of the theory's predictions. TL then revises the refuted theory by excluding from the theory's domain of application all situations which do not exhibit these sufficient conditions. The simplest operationalization of this method revises the theory by conjoining to its prerequisites one of these predicates. By doing so, TL rectifies the faulty theory by restricting its applications to those situations that TL's unrefuted theories imply will guarantee successful outcomes.

5. **Inclusion Method:** Restricting the theory by ruling in confirming cases. This method rectifies a faulty theory by specializing it to those few special cases where it seems to make valid predictions. When faced with particular situations that refute a theory, TL may modify the theory to rule in the numerous alternative situations in which the theory's predictions are confirmed. In this manner, TL attempts to enumerate empirically the situations in which the theory works. In the simplest operationalization of this method, TL conjoins to the theory's planned actions a new set of alternative prerequisites or actions that TL believes correlate reliably with successful outcomes. Based on empirical experience or simulated trials, TL identifies those situations in which the theory's predictions do hold and restricts the theory to apply to just these cases.

The remainder of the paper is organized as follows. In the next section, I re-express the key definitions and learning methods symbolically. Subsequently, the learning methods are illustrated by means of examples drawn from a simple card game. In addition to exemplifying each of the five learning heuristics, I show how rectifying theories produces new domain concepts. Problems of computational approaches and implementation are discussed in the penultimate section. In the last section, I attempt to explain the significance of this approach to machine learning.

8.3.1 Symbolic Formulation of the Learning Problem and the Heuristics

I will attempt to formulate the learning heuristics as precisely as possible. Both predicate calculus and lambda calculus help. However, the focus on actions and instrumental behaviors necessitates some underlying framework for modeling time, causality, and the succession of states and situations. To avoid a lengthy and complicated digression, I have chosen to adopt the simplest possible framework as a foundation for defining the learning heuristics. These heuristics, not the formalism for representing them, constitute the meat of this paper.

As a basis for the learning methods, I presuppose a real, observable, dynamic world in which conditions vary continually. A time variable could be used to index instantaneous world states if useful. A situation is a world state spanning an interval of time during which observable events occur. A natural ordering of situations arises from the temporal relationships among their constituent events. In the ordinary way, I speak of one situation S′ succeeding another if its denoted world state immediately follows that denoted by S. The prime symbol designates this successor relation.

Situations are abstractions conceived by an observer for pragmatic purposes. Thus, I introduce distinguished situations as required. Typically, I speak of a sequence of situations S, S′, S″, ... which represents a progression of world states arising from events beyond TL's control. When TL actively affects changes in world state, I will show TL's role by claiming that TL's performance of some actions A brings about conditions E in the succeeding state S′:

$$\text{PERFORM}(A,S) \Rightarrow E(S')$$

By assumption, predecessors and successors exist for all situations.

A theory T consists of *(i)* assumed conditions or prerequisites, denoted C_T, *(ii)* possibly some actions that TL is supposed to execute, which are denoted A_T and *(iii)* some predicted effects or consequents, which are denoted E_T. The reader should interpret C_T and E_T as situational predicates and A_T as a procedure parameterized for a situation argument. If the theory specifies no actions, the meaning of T is that, for all situations S, $C_T(S) \Rightarrow E_T(S')$. This type of theory describes environmental events that do not depend on TL's own actions. When A_T is non-null, however, the theory represents the belief that successful execution of these actions in situations where $C_T(S)$ is true will guarantee the theory's predicted effects, $E_T(S')$. We can denote this as, for all situations S:

$$C_T(S) \wedge \text{PERFORM}\ (A_T,\ S) \Rightarrow E_T(S') \qquad (1)$$

To justify a plan T, TL must prove the conditional expression in (1). TL does this by assuming the validity of other theories and constructing a conventional proof. Assumptions which are taken to be true without proof are degenerate theories in which C and A are null. Every theory which is used to justify a theory T is called a justification of T. Whenever a situation S satisfies the left-hand side of (1), the theory's predicted effects are warranted expectations.[3] If a theory is justified and all of its justifications are satisfied by the current situation, the theory's expectations are justified by that situation. In such a case, if the situation denies the theory's expectations, the theory itself and at least one of its justifications are refuted. That is, the theory and the corresponding justification are faulty. The faulty justification can be identified by retracing the steps in the proof to find one whose antecedents are satisfied but whose consequent is falsified by the situation.[4]

To describe the learning heuristics, let's suppose the faulty theory is T, such that (1) holds. Where no confusion arises, I will omit the subscript T from the presentation. In particular, suppose that some situation S occurred that satisfied the theory's left-hand side but where E(S) was false. I will denote by D(S) a complete description of the situation S in which TL applied T, and denote by D′(S′) a complete description of the subsequent situation. Like C and E, D and D′ denote situational predicates. The five learning methods are operationalized as follows.

1. **Retraction Method:** Restricting the theory's predictions. To rectify T, replace E_T = (λ (S) (E S)) by (λ (S) (E′ S)) where E′ = a common generalization of E_T and D′. One specific way to compute E′ is by forming the lambda abstraction over constant S′ of the maximal abstraction of $E_T(S')$ and D′(S′) [Hayes-Roth & McDermott, 1978; Vere, 1975]. (λ (S) (E S)) is the LISP form for the predicate E with situation variable S.
2. **Exclusion Method:** Barring the theory from applying to the current situation. To rectify T, replace C_T = (λ (S) (C S)) by (λ (S) (C′ S)) where $C' = C \wedge (\sim D)$. This technique completely bars the current counterexample. One could be less specific and bar any class of situations analogous to that described by D. Any predicate d implied by D would work as well. Specifically, an alternative rectification employs such a weaker restriction to produce a more general theory. This is done by making $C' = C \wedge (\sim d)$ where $D(S) \Rightarrow d(S)$.
3. **Avoidance Method:** Ruling out situations that predictably deny the theory's predictions. To rectify T, replace C_T = (λ (S) (C S)) by (λ (S) (C′ S)) where $C' = C \wedge P$ for some situation predicates P and Q,where $D(S) \Rightarrow Q(S) \Rightarrow \sim E(S')$ and $P(S) \Rightarrow \sim Q(S)$. In words, TL must prevent the theory from being applied when Q is satisfied, and prerequiring P is a

[3]Unwarranted expectations are predictions which lack this type of theory-based justification.

[4]This is the general problem of assigning "blame" in AI systems. The framework developed here establishes sufficient conditions to insure that the problem is solvable. "Solving" the blame assignment problem means making steady progress on improving faulty knowledge. The proposed methods diagnose faulty theories effectively and generate refined theories that avoid making the same error twice.

way to do that. To identify such a preventive predicate P, work backwards from knowledge about Q(S), the feature known to deny $E_T(S')$. If there is a theory whose consequents include ~Q, let its antecedent or left-hand side (assumed conditions and actions) define P. Conversely, if some theory's left-hand side is Q, let the negation of its right-hand side (R, its predicted effects) define P. Because $Q \Rightarrow R$, $\sim R \Rightarrow \sim Q$, $P = \sim R \Rightarrow \sim Q$ as required.

4. **Assurance Method:** Ruling in situations that predictably assure the theory's predictions. To rectify T, replace $C_T = (\lambda(S)\ (C\ S))$ by $(\lambda(S)\ (C'\ S))$ where $C' = C \wedge P$ for some P where $D(S) \Rightarrow \sim E_T(S') \Rightarrow \sim P(S)$ and where $C_T(S) \wedge \text{PERFORM}\ (A_T, S) \wedge P(S) \Rightarrow E_T(S')$, that is, conditional on C_T and A_T, P should be sufficient for E_T. As a simple variant of this idea, TL can rectify T by adding actions to A_T instead of, or in addition to, adding to the assumed conditions. The performance of these additional actions should be equivalent to guaranteeing P.
5. **Inclusion Method:** Restricting the theory by ruling in confirming cases. To rectify T, replace $C_T = (\lambda\ (S)\ (C\ S))$ by $(\lambda\ (S)\ (C'\ S))$ where C′ is a predicate that is satisfied by the descriptions of situations that confirmed T. If these previous confirming situations are denoted $S_1, S_2, \ldots, S_n$, the simplest technique is to make $C' = C \wedge (D_1 \vee D_2 \vee \ldots \vee D_n)$ where each D_i is the situation description (predicate) of the corresponding S_i. Subsequently, if the revised theory is refuted by S, a less general predicate C″ can be formed using either the version space method of Mitchell [1978] or the counterfactual method of Vere [1980] to rule out the disconfirming S while ruling in the confirming situations $S_1, \ldots, S_n$.

8.3.2 Illustrating the Learning Heuristics

In this section, I illustrate the learning heuristics in a simple domain by showing how TL rectifies an erroneous plan in a card game.

This example is drawn from the simple card game hearts. It illustrates a bug which many players manifest in early stages of skill development. To understand the bug, the reader needs to understand a few rules of the game. The game is played with three or four players who play clockwise around the table. Initially, all the cards in the deck are divided among the players. The player having the two of clubs plays first. The play consists of a sequence of tricks in which each player plays one card in turn. Each player must play a card in the same suit as the suit of the first card played in the trick, unless the player is void in that suit. The player who plays the highest card in the suit led wins the trick and leads the next trick. The player is charged for any points of the cards won by that player. The queen of spades has 13 points and each heart has one. The goal of the game is to take as few points as possible or to win all 26 possible points (that is, "go low" or "shoot-the-moon").

The initial buggy plan TL developed is sketched below. Readers who would like to see how this buggy plan can be operationalized automatically should consult [Mostow, 1981].

```
Plan 1:                 Flush the queen of spades.
Effects:            (1) I will force the player who has the
                          queen of spades to play that card.
                    (2) I will avoid taking 13 points.
Conditions:         (1) I do not hold the queen of spades.
                    (2) The queen of spades has not been played.
Actions:                First I win a trick to take the lead, and
                          whenever I lead a trick I play a spade.
```

8.3.3 Faults Revealed by the Violated Expectations of Plan 1

In the first plan, TL expects to force a player to play the queen of spades and, thereby, avoid taking the queen. However, the following events occur:

```
TL plays the king of spades (KS).
Mary plays the queen of spades (QS).
John plays the three of spades (3S).

TL wins the trick.
TL takes 13 points.
```

The last event violates its expectation and reveals a faulty theory. The plan, as a theory, is faulty. Its conditions and actions are satisfied, but one of its goal assertions is denied. Each heuristic will now be illustrated as a method to improve one of the theories originally used in deriving the unsuccessful plan.

1. **Retraction Method:** Restricting the theory's predictions. This method prescribes amending the predicted effects of the plan. One simple way this fix can be performed is by modifying the theory simply to exclude the denied expectation. The amended theory is shown below. Underlines indicate modified components of the plans.

```
Plan 2:                 Flush the queen of spades.
Effects:            (1) I will force the player who has the
                          queen of spades to play it.
                    (2) ... retracted ...
Conditions:         (1) I do not hold the queen of spades.
                    (2) The queen of spades has not been played.
Actions:                First I win a trick to take the lead, and
                          whenever I lead a trick I play a spade.
```

   This particular plan plays a useful role in other strategic ways than those for which the original plan was intended. For example, it would be useful whenever TL wished to flush the queen, regardless of who takes the points. Such a tactic is often used by a player who is willing to risk shooting-the-moon if, and only if, he or she can win the queen of spades.

2. **Exclusion Method:** Barring the theory from applying to the current situation. This heuristic prescribes amending the conditions of the plan to exclude the situation that revealed the bug. Perhaps, in this way the theory

can be incrementally refined to apply only when appropriate. In this case, for example, TL can modify the previous plan to rule out the action it performed. The revised plan in this case would be as follows:

```
Plan 3:                  Flush the queen of spades.
Effects:             (1) I will force the player who has
                           the queen of spades to play it.
                     (2) I will avoid taking 13 points.
Conditions:          (1) I do not hold the queen of spades.
                     (2) The queen of spades has not been played.
                     (3) I do not play the king of spades.
Actions:                 First I win a trick to take the lead, and
                           whenever I lead a trick I play a spade.
```

Notice in this case the added condition (3) which bars TL from playing the king of spades. This revised plan illustrates both the strengths and weaknesses of this type of fix. This fix eliminates the particular problem which motivated it, but the new plan is still faulty. Of course, if the same type of disconfirmation arises later because TL plays an ace of spades, an additional fix of the same type will lead to a bug-free plan. However, TL is "lucky" to fix the plan in this way, because the fix has not been shown to be causally connected to the denied assertion. For this reason, Lakatos eschewed "monster-barring". Nevertheless, it can be quite constructive and appropriate, as this example reveals.

3. **Avoidance Method:** Ruling out situations that predictably deny the theory's predictions. This heuristic requires TL to reason about the probable cause of the theory's failure. Why did the plan fail in this case? The faulty assertion contended TL would avoid taking points. In the actual situation, TL took 13 points because it won the trick and the queen of spades was played in the trick. These events contributed to the denial of the faulty assertion. From this, TL can infer at least two ways to preclude this type of denial. One way prerequires that the queen is not played. The other prerequires that TL does not win the trick. Given the overall objective of the plan, to flush the queen of spades, the first fix seems unproductive. So TL adopts the second fix, as shown below:

```
Plan 4:                  Flush the queen of spades.
Effects:             (1) I will force the player who has
                           the queen of spades to play it.
                     (2) I will avoid taking 13 points.
Conditions:          (1) I do not hold the queen of spades.
                     (2) The queen of spades has not been played.
                     (3) I do not win the trick in which
                           the queen of spades is played.
Actions:                 First I win a trick to take the lead, and
                           whenever I lead a trick I play a spade.
```

In this case, TL has added another condition to exclude the misapplication of the earlier theory. TL can go farther however. Given the rules of the game, which TL supposedly knows and represents as theories, it can deduce sufficient conditions to achieve the new condition and posit these as part of the theory.

This discussion presupposes non-trivial capabilities, including inferring ways to preclude a denial and avoiding choices of fixes that interfere with the plan objectives. I will defer these computational issues until Section 8.4.

To deduce a sufficient condition of some proposition, deny that proposition, deduce its consequents, and choose one of these. The negation of that consequent is a sufficient condition. That is, p is sufficient for q means not q implies not p, hence not (not p) identifies a sufficient condition. In this case, TL negates the new condition (3) to yield "I win the trick in which the queen of spades is played". From this premise and the rules of the game, it can infer that it must play the highest card in the suit led. It negates this to produce the alternative plan shown below.

```
Plan 5:                  Flush the queen of spades.
Effects:             (1) I will force the player who has
                           the queen of spades to play it.
                     (2) I will avoid taking 13 points.
Conditions:          (1) I do not hold the queen of spades.
                     (2) The queen of spades has not been played.
Actions:                 First I win a trick to take the lead, and
                           whenever I lead a trick I play a spade
                           which is not the highest spade.
```

The careful reader may have noticed that both illustrative fixes introduced by method 3 have produced predicates that cannot be evaluated in all situations. This helps motivate several observations. First, such incompletely determinable predicates occur commonly in human knowledge. Second, the knowledge produced by applying the method of avoidance is both useful and vulnerable to refutation. The importance and frequent occurrence of this type of uncertain knowledge motivates other types of intelligent planning, namely planning aimed at predicting the likely value of uncertain predicates. For more on this subject, see [Mostow, 1981].

4. **Assurance Method:** Ruling in situations that predictably assure the theory's predicted effects. This heuristic prescribes changing the erroneous theory to insure that the disconfirmed expectation follows logically from the assumptions. In this case, the disconfirmed expectation predicted that TL would not take 13 points. However, TL did. Here, again, TL uses the method of deducing sufficient conditions. It wants to find a sufficient condition to guarantee "I will avoid taking 13 points". To do this, it negates the assertions, infers consequents, and chooses one of these to negate and prerequire. This leads to a chain of inferences as that shown below:

```
Premise:                 I do take 13 points.
Rule:                    The winner of the trick takes the
                         points in the trick.
Infer:                   I win the trick.
```

```
Rule:             The person who plays the highest card
                    in the suit led wins the trick.
Infer:            I play highest card in the suit led.

Given:            Mary plays the queen of spades.
Infer:            I play a spade higher than the queen of
                    spades.

Negate:           I play a spade lower than the queen of
                    spades.
```

As a consequence, TL can revise its theory as follows:

```
Plan 6:               Flush the queen of spades.
Effects:          (1) I will force the player who has
                        the queen of spades to play it.
                  (2) I will avoid taking 13 points.
Conditions:       (1) I do not hold the queen of spades.
                  (2) The queen of spades has not been played.
Actions:              First I win a trick to take the lead, and
                        whenever I lead a trick I play a spade
                        below the queen.
```

5. **Inclusion Method:** Restricting the theory by ruling in confirming cases. This heuristic employs an empirical approach to plan debugging. It is motivated by the possibility that an unfulfilled expectation may be caused by one's own actions. In many cases, TL can experimentally or hypothetically evaluate the likely consequences of alternative actions to the ones it actually performed when the counterexample arose. For example, it can iteratively enumerate all possible actions it might have performed consistent with its plan during the trick in which it took 13 points. Then, if any of these alternatives avoids violating the expectation, it can modify its plan to incorporate these alternatives as part of the plan.

   For example, in this case, TL can enumerate all possible actions consistent with its plan to lead spades. Suppose it had led the two of spades; in this case, because Mary played the queen, TL would not have won the trick or taken any points. Thus, the two of spades is an alternative that insures the plan's assertions against denials arising from TL's own actions. TL similarly evaluates all of the alternative spades, from two through ace, consistent with its plan. Of these, ten alternatives avoid the refutation. So the following plan is proposed.

```
Plan 7:               Flush the queen of spades.
Effects:          (1) I will force the player who has
                        the queen of spades to play it.
                  (2) I will avoid taking 13 points.
Conditions:       (1) I do not hold the queen of spades.
                  (2) The queen of spades has not been played.
Actions:              First I win a trick to take the lead, and
                        whenever I lead a trick I play a spade
                        in {2S, ..., 10S, jack of spades}.
```

8.3.4 Rectified Theories Identify New Concepts

Concepts correspond to descriptive predicates, and many concepts arise because new predicates are needed to correctly specify theories. Much of our knowledge corresponds to concepts identified in the process of rectifying faulty theories. I point out two concepts among others that have emerged from the rectifications of Plan 1 illustrated in the previous section. In Plans 6 and 7 these concepts arose:

Concept 1: A spade below the queen.
Concept 2: A spade in the set {2S, 3S, ..., 10S, jack of spades}.

These two concepts were constructed because the faulty Plan 1 inadequately constrained its domain of applicability. These new concepts were synthesized by different operational methods applied to existing knowledge. In fixing the plan two different ways, TL characterized conditions under which the plan would presumably work better than before. The two fixes both correspond to Lakatos' notion of "lemma incorporation", because they make implicit assumptions explicit. What is interesting about these two fixes is that they are semantically equivalent. The first corresponds to an intensional, non-enumerative definition of the set which the second defines extensionally. The important thing is that both concepts arose because of their instrumental value to the learner. The coincidence in meaning between these two discoveries helps illuminate the tendency of these different learning methods to converge on correct, useful characterizations of the domain.

The coincidence between these two new domain concepts helps convey another aspect of discovery. Many coincidental relationships arise among concepts in interesting domains. Lenat's AM program [Lenat, 1976] searches for and exploits just such coincidences. The heuristics of AM provide additional weak discovery methods that could be applied profitably to the concepts TL has discovered. For example, generalizations of the concept "a spade below the queen" will prove useful in the game of hearts. Among these I note "a card below the highest point card in the current trick" and "a card below the highest card in the current trick". Both of these concepts also happen to have instrumental value in this domain, and so will many others formed analogically from concepts derived exclusively as a by-product of theory rectification.

8.4 COMPUTATIONAL PROBLEMS AND IMPLEMENTATION TECHNIQUES

A fully automated version of The Learner (TL) would require solutions to several difficult computing problems. The perspective I have taken identifies these five primary problems: *(i)* Operationalizing advice—TL must accept expert advice and translate it into an initial working program; *(ii)* Justifying plans—TL must record rationales for its initial operational plans along with expectations that can trigger learning when violated; *(iii)* Diagnosing faulty theories—TL must attribute blame to specific theories and label those "faulty"; *(iv)* Rectifying theories—TL must apply specific variants of the five learning heuristics to rectify the faulty theories; *(v)* Assimilating new knowledge—TL must incorporate the new theories into its knowledge base and reiterate the planning-performing-learning cycle.

Full, effective solutions to all of these problems will require much additional progress. My colleagues and I have attacked all of these tasks with limited resources and have achieved limited results over the past few years. In this section, I summarize our approaches and results. Where appropriate, I indicate the most promising paths for additional research.

1. **Operationalization.** Most learning of interest to me begins when an informed, experienced teacher (professional) advises a student (trainee). The expert's knowledge is usually conveyed verbally. The learner receives a string of verbal symbols that must be transformed into an executable program. This can require many kinds of interpretive, heuristic, and analytic techniques [Hayes-Roth, 1980, 1981; Mostow, 1981]. We have called this transformation task operationalization. Operationalization is a large, interesting problem that has barely been touched upon by previous research.

   In general, I suppose TL plans to achieve goals by performing specific actions in particular circumstances. Each plan corresponds to one of TL's theories and usually depends on subplans, which also correspond to theories. During the process of operationalizing the initial advice, TL generates these theory plans by reasoning about its current knowledge. By reassembling existing theories, TL constructs plans that it expects to achieve goals. Only faulty reasoning or faulty theories will cause plan failures, that is, failures to achieve goals of the plan.

   Our previous approaches to operationalization still seem promising, although the number and breadth of related tasks seems somewhat forbidding. Because most expert knowledge consists of facts and heuristic rules, operationalizing advice generally means understanding domain descriptions and reasoning with these to fit heuristic rules into general problem-solving methods. This requires an ability to analyze domain definitions and synthesize heuristic computer programs consistent with these definitions. During each analysis step, the operationalization process produces an intermediate result that it can justify by citing the corresponding transformation rule and the sources on which it operated. These justifications form the rationale for the final, operational plans TL produces.

2. **Justifying Plans and Generating Expectations.** Operationalization and ordinary planning methods both can produce goal-seeking plans of the sort TL uses. A plan rationale is a proof of the plan's apparent validity. Plan proofs are typical by-products of planning efforts, but TL considers these

by-products as centrally important. While at Rand Corporation, I initiated a project called the "Planners' Workbench" intended to develop a general purpose system for recording plan rationales generated either by machine or human planners.

Our approach to justifying plans involved a few basic insights. First, recording plan rationales requires a language for plan elements, including syntax, terms, expressions, and sentential operators. Through experimentation, we found a variety of types of justifications arising in real planning situations. The extensive variety raises doubts about the degree to which human planning (or sophisticated machine planning) reduces to syntactic, deductive reasoning. In general, human plans employ subjective justifications, frequently of the sort that several supporting reasons outweigh a set of countervening arguments. Nevertheless, even these "mushy" arguments could be formalized as assumptions which enter the plan rationale as premises. While the extent of inductive and subjective reasoning surprised everyone on our project, the learning methods proposed here could always work effectively. However, the technical difficulty of recording plan rationales emerged as a key problem.

Triggering plan diagnosis requires TL to recognize that outcomes violate expectations and goal attainment, in particular. Thus, expected outcomes must be articulated, and specific outcomes must be compared with general expectations. Ordinarily, a plan addresses a particular goal which TL can actively monitor. Often, too, plans participate in a hierarchical plan structure. Each subplan's goal corresponds to an action or assumed condition of its superior plan. Failing to achieve a subplan's goal causes a breakdown during the plan's execution. A learning system needs to monitor plan executions for such failures.

Expectations can be arbitrarily general, and the related task of monitoring outcomes can be arbitrarily difficult. This highlights the importance of expectation-driven learning. The preceding paragraph cited one example of a general sort of expectation monitoring, namely that failures in plan execution implicate subplans for actions or prerequisites. The next section discusses another type of useful, general expectation. That one concerns a converse or dual of plan execution failures: goals should be attained only when associated plans execute successfully.

3. **Diagnosing Faulty Theories.** TL needs to attribute blame to specific faulty theories. This need motivates the whole approach of proofs, refutations, and rectifications. TL uses a counterexample to an expected effect as a basis for refuting the plan's rationale. Assuming *(i)* the rationale is organized as a syntactically valid proof and *(ii)* the predicates occurring in the plan and its rationale can be evaluated, every counterexample implicates one specific theory. This requires a systematic backchaining from the faulty plan to the first inference in the proof with a disconfirmed consequent in the presence of valid antecedent premises.

Computationally, this may be done in a variety of ways. The major choice one faces is whether to precompute and store dependencies of predicted effects upon antecedents or whether these dependencies should be evaluated dynamically while monitoring plan outcomes.

The second assumption, that predicates permit accurate evaluation, places a strong constraint on TL's capabilities. The earlier hearts examples in this paper illustrate a variety of predicates that range from easily evaluated to impossible to evaluate (at particular times). A predicate like "the highest card in the suit led occurring in the current trick" generally permits accurate evaluations only after all players play their cards in the trick. Given the outcome of the trick, that predicate does permit evaluation. Generally, we cannot know when the trick starts whether a particular card will satisfy the predicate. Thus, TL must reason with uncertainty while executing its plan. This in no way reduces the value of the proposed learning methods. Uncertainty in action is a consequence of living with incomplete knowledge in a dynamic world.

Of course, several means exist for reducing uncertainty and these play major roles in intelligent behavior. A learner ought to recognize the value of improving estimates of uncertain predicates and develop plans toward that end. The steps of the learning cycle would apply to this type of task, too.

4. **Rectifying Theories.** This paper has aimed at developing practical procedures for fixing faulty theories. These heuristic methods presuppose some computational capabilities which are not yet widely available in component forms. As a result, it will take some effort to assemble a powerful TL system. The primary capabilities required are symbolic deduction and heuristic search. Many times, this paper has presupposed that TL embodies these capabilities. That seems reasonable, because no new techniques are required. On the other hand, experience in large AI applications shows repeatedly that considerable effort may be required to engineer a practical solution using existing techniques. A practical application of the five proposed learning heuristics will depend upon selection of a specific problem domain and procedures tailored to the knowledge representations and complexities of that domain.

A knowledge engineer who wants to build a version of TL for some specific domain can choose from a variety of existing methods for the deduction and heuristic search skills TL requires. As an example, consider the third learning method discussed, avoidance. A TL program needs to deduce sufficient conditions for plan failure and negate these by presupposition. This deduction uses typical operators of predicate calculus, general purpose program transformation rules, and possible domain-specific transformations to reason from the description of the undesirable event to its antecedents. The steps in this reasoning process reflect inferences of both syntactic and semantic types, depending on whether domain-independent or domain-dependent relationships are employed. When one of TL's existing theories supports a reasoning step, the resulting rectification depends on the supporting theory for its justification. Thus, the task of producing a sufficient antecedent for a desired goal is best formulated as a heuristic search with deductive and program transformational operators. One path in this search tree eventually connects an antecedent clause to the negated goal clause. Each link in this path reflects the application of a transformation. Some of these transformations will introduce domain-specific theories as a basis for relating adjacent clauses.

Rectification, because it is a heuristic search process, can produce alternative fixes. Each alternative fix represents a plausible new theory. Each new theory rests on other theories for its justification. Such a system will require means for storing and applying alternatives and experimentally evaluating them.

5. **Assimilating New Knowledge.** The proposed learning methods can produce numerous fixes to each faulty theory. This will lead to a large number of coexisting alternatives. This increases the complexity of all of the five tasks in the learning cycle. Does this nullify the value of the proposed methods? I don't think so, because this conclusion seems inevitable. No way exists which can reason with certainty about the best fix to any faulty theory. Knowledge refinement is intrinsically a heuristic problem.

   Several familiar techniques could apply fruitfully to help control the complexity which arises in this type of non-deterministic learning. These techniques would reduce complexity by intelligently controlling the heuristic search underlying knowledge refinement. A few pertinent examples include: *(i)* Preferring general theories to specific ones, because these have greater utility; *(ii)* Seeking canonical representations of theories to reduce duplication; *(iii)* Testing new proposed theories by simulation prior to incorporating them into the knowledge base; *(iv)* Experimentally evaluating alternative fixes in controlled situations to determine the most fruitful fix to adopt; and *(v)* Preferring fixes with minimal intrinsic uncertainty, to minimize uncontrollable errors in application. I assume each of these heuristics, as well as many others, can improve the performance of a TL system. Without these types of restrictions, a TL system will almost certainly face an uncontrollable combinatorial explosion.

8.5 CONCLUSIONS

The complexity of the real world precludes us from developing complete, error-free, and consistent knowledge of any substantial domain. As a consequence, we must always be learning. More specifically, we must always be alert for opportunities to learn improved ways to predict the future and attain goals. Opportunities arise whenever our current theories make refuted claims.

I have shown five heuristic methods for rectifying erroneous theories. Each of these methods is an effective generator of new theories. Each refutation leads to multiple new theories, and each method of fixing theories may be operationalized in more than one way. The proposed techniques constitute the first practical operationalization of the method of proofs and refutations originally suggested by Lakatos. In addition, I have shown how rectified theories manifest new domain concepts, which can support other kinds of learning.

This framework suggests a potentially very important and practical approach to machine learning tasks. For machine learning, the proposed methods provide a generator for improved theories and new concepts of instrumental utility. As in other areas of AI, real success at a hard problem requires both a generator and a good evaluator. This paper has provided an initial generator without really contributing much to the problem of defining a good evaluator. However, evaluation in this type of problem is inherently difficult, because one can never know the value of a potential idea without employing it. This necessitates either empirical or subjective approaches to evaluation. Because no generally valid subjective scheme seems possible, an empirical approach to evaluation seems unavoidable. Thus, learning and performance are of necessity interwoven activities.

I have focused in this paper exclusively on things to be learned from refutations of overly general theories with observable theoretical constructs. The same methods, however, can be fruitfully applied to other types of learning problems. In particular, I will describe briefly how these methods can rectify overly specific theories.

An overly specific theory, by definition, fails to predict an event because the theory's conditions bar the theory from applying to the current situation. In short, the situation confirms the theory's predicted effects but not its conditions. The learner can use the methods of proofs and rectifications here too. In this case, a general expectation is violated that contends all events will accord with some theory's expectations. That is, a theory's predicted outcomes should occur only if the theory's conditions are satisfied. But this is equivalent to saying that the theory's predicted effects (viewed as conditions) predict the theory's conditions (viewed as expectations). Thus, each original theory is associated with a second one, namely its converse.

When the five proposed heuristics are applied to refuted converses, they rectify them and narrow their sufficient conditions. This has the dual effect of narrowing the specification of the necessary conditions for the original theory. Taken together, a theory and its converse define the necessary and sufficient conditions for the theory's predicted effects.

In conclusion, it seems obvious that skill in learning, as is the case for so many other types of expertise, depends heavily on the knowledge the learner already possesses. The methods discussed in this paper provide techniques for using existing theories to construct better ones.

ACKNOWLEDGMENTS

The author gratefully acknowledges the support of the National Science Foundation and Rand's Project Air Force for the research upon which this paper is based. Additional support has been provided by Teknowledge. I have profited from collaborations with Jack Mostow and Phil Klahr and from constructive reviews by Barbara Hayes-Roth and the editors of this volume.

REFERENCES

Hayes-Roth, F. and McDermott, J., "An interference matching technique for inducing abstractions," *CACM*, Vol. 21, pp. 401-410, 1978.

Hayes-Roth, F., Klahr, P. and Mostow, D. J., "Knowledge acquisition, knowledge programming, and knowledge refinement", Technical Report R-2540-NSF, The Rand Corporation, May 1980.

Hayes-Roth, F., Klahr, P., and Mostow, D. J., "Advice-taking and knowledge refinement: an iterative view of skill acquisition," *Skill Acquisition and Development*, J. A. Anderson (Ed.), Erlbaum, 1981.

Lakatos, I., *Proofs and Refutations: The Logic of Mathematical Discovery*, Cambridge University Press, 1976.

Lenat, D. B., "AM: An artificial intelligence approach to discovery in mathematics as heuristic search", Technical Report SAIL AIM-286, AI Lab, Stanford University, 1976.

Mitchell, T. M., *Version spaces: an approach to concept learning,* Ph.D. dissertation, Stanford University, 1978.

Mostow, D. J., *Mechanical transformation of task heuristics into operational procedures,* Ph.D. dissertation, Carnegie-Mellon University, Dept. of Computer Science, April 1981, (Available as CMU-CS-81-113.).

Vere, S. A., "Induction of concepts in the predicate calculus," *Proceedings of the Fourth International Joint Conference on Artificial Intelligence*, IJCAI, Tbilisi, USSR, 1975.

Vere, S. A., "Multilevel counterfactuals for generalizations of relational concepts and productions," *Artificial Intelligence*, Vol. 14, pp. 139-164, 1980.

PART FOUR

LEARNING FROM OBSERVATION AND DISCOVERY

9

THE ROLE OF HEURISTICS IN LEARNING BY DISCOVERY: THREE CASE STUDIES

Douglas B. Lenat
Stanford University

ABSTRACT

As artificial intelligence (AI) programs are called upon to exhibit increasingly complex behaviors, their builders are faced with the growing task of inserting more and more knowledge into the machine. One long-range solution is for the program, by itself, to learn via discovery. The first case study presented, AM, demonstrates that new domains of knowledge can be developed mechanically by using heuristics. Yet as new domain concepts, facts, and conjectures emerge, specific new *heuristics*, or informal judgmental rules, are needed. They in turn can be discovered by using a body of heuristics for guidance. The second case study, EURISKO, has already achieved some promising results in this endeavor. If this process—using heuristics to guide "learning by discovery"—is so powerful and simple, one wonders why, for instance, nature has not adopted an analogous mechanism to guide evolution. Indeed, the final part of the article is a speculation that evolution *does* function in that manner. In place of the conventional Darwinian process of *random* mutation, we hypothesize a more powerful *plausible* generation scheme.

9.1 MOTIVATION

The overall motivation of this paper comprises *(i)* a general interest in the phenomena of learning and discovery, *(ii)* a specific concern that, as expert systems continue to increase in size and complexity, they must shoulder more of the burden of their own organization, management, and content, and *(iii)* a recognition of the analogy between a machine learning and a species evolving. This third point, the resemblance to biological evolution, is developed in Section 9.7.

Several recent programs in artificial intelligence (AI) perform complex tasks demanding a large corpus of expert knowledge [Feigenbaum, 1977]. These include, for example, the PROSPECTOR program for evaluating the mineral potential of a site, the MYCIN program for medical diagnosis, and the MOLGEN program for planning experiments in molecular genetics. To construct such a system, a knowledge engineer talks to a human expert, extracts domain-specific knowledge, and adds it to a growing knowledge base usable by a computer program (see Figure 9-1). The critical stage of this process, the limiting step, is the transfer of expertise. From the program's point of view, the limitation is the slow rate at which it acquires knowledge. This is the central problem facing knowledge engineering today, the bottleneck of knowledge acquisition.

HUMAN EXPERT — KNOWLEDGE ENGINEER — KNOWLEDGE-BASED PROGRAM

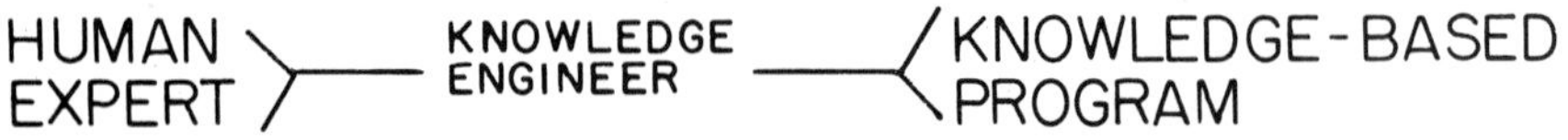

Figure 9-1: The bottleneck of knowledge acquisition is *transfer of expertise*. This comprises *(i)* the expert's difficulty in articulating what he knows, and *(ii)* the impedance mismatch between the concepts and vocabulary of the expert and the knowledge engineer.

Two possible solutions to this problem suggest themselves, although they are not mutually exclusive. First, one might try somehow to widen the channel joining expert to program, for example by building a sophisticated natural language interface.

The difficulty with this is that the expert must communicate not merely the "facts" of his field, but also the heuristics: the informal judgmental rules which guide him. These are rarely thought about concretely, and almost never appear in journal articles, textbooks or university courses. Thus, even with a wider channel, the expert would have difficulty in verbalizing his heuristics.

The second possible solution is to sever the umbilicus entirely: eliminate the knowledge engineer and the human expert, expose the program to the environment, and let it discover new knowledge on its own. Can this be done? Since knowledge comprises both facts and heuristics, the question divides into two parts: can new domain concepts and relationships be discovered, and can new domain heuristics be discovered? This paper is addressed to these questions, and it presents evidence that the answers are affirmative.

Along the way, an elementary "theory of heuristics" accrues. Our initial definition of a heuristic is: a piece of knowledge capable of suggesting plausible actions to follow or implausible ones to avoid. In Section 9.3, it becomes apparent that this is insufficient; for a body of heuristics to be effective (useful for guiding rather than merely for rationalizing in hindsight), each heuristic must specify a situation or context in which its actions are especially appropriate or inappropriate. The theory developed in Section 9.4 is based on this definition.

9.2 OVERVIEW

9.2.1 The Central Line of the Argument

1. **New domains of knowledge δ can be developed by using heuristics.** Radically new concepts and relations connecting them can be discovered by employing a large corpus of heuristics both to suggest plausible actions and to prune implausible ones. To accomplish this requires heuristics of varying levels of generality and power, an adequate representation for knowledge, some initial hypotheses about the nature of domain δ, and the ability to gather data and test conjectures about that domain.
2. **As new domains of knowledge emerge and evolve, new heuristics are needed.** A field may change by the introduction of some new device, theory, technique, paradigm, or observable phenomenon; each time it does so, the corpus of heuristics useful for dealing with that field may also change. Consider the body of heuristics useful in planning a trip from San Francisco to London. Over the last century, many new ones have been added, and many old ones have undergone revision.
3. **New heuristics can be developed by using heuristics.** The first two points imply that new heuristics must be discovered. How is this done? Since "heuristics" is a domain of knowledge, like electronics, or mathematics, or travel planning, perhaps all that is necessary is to set δ = heuristics in point 1. That is, let the field of heuristics itself grow via heuristic guidance. To do this would require many types of heuristics (some quite general, some specific to dealing with other heuristics, etc.), an adequate representation for heuristics, and some hypotheses about the nature of heuristics.
4. **As new domains of knowledge emerge and evolve, new representations are needed.** Just as the potency of a fixed body of heuristics decreases as we move into new fields, so, too, does the potency of whatever scheme is being used to represent knowledge. Representations must evolve as domain knowledge accrues.
5. **New representations can be developed by using heuristics.** Points 1 and 4 imply that new representations for knowledge must be devised from time to time, and that existing schemes must change. How can this happen? Since "representation of knowledge" is a field, just as is mathematics, or electronics, or heuristics, or travel planning, perhaps we can somehow set δ = representation in point 1. That is, allow heuristics to manage the development of new representations.

The final point is that there is no sixth point to make. The preceding five statements comprise a research program to follow, one plan of attack upon the central problem, the bottleneck of automatic knowledge acquisition.

Other directions of attack are promising, and are being pursued vigorously by several AI researchers. For most fields, some necessary component required by point 1 above is missing (for example, the automatic acquisition of data is awkward or impossible). In such cases, the human expert must be preserved "in the loop" of Figure 9-1. Any aids for interviewing the expert are then quite important, tools which facilitate the *manual* knowledge acquisition process depicted in Figure 9-1. Indeed, much recent AI activity focuses on developing such tools: AGE, EMYCIN, EXPERT, HEARSAYIII, RLL, ROGET, ROSIE, and the various knowledge representation languages.

This chapter presents work to date, by the author, along the research program outlined in Table 9-1 Although the development parallels the ordering given therein, the amount of space devoted to each point is not uniform. Much of the paper is concerned with recounting the experience of building AM, a computer program which searches for interesting new concepts and conjectures in elementary mathematics (point 1; see Table 9-1). The analysis of AM's eventual demise provides an illustration of 2. Much of the remainder is used to develop the rudiments of a theory of heuristics, which theory is required for 3. The second case study, EURISKO, is a program illustrating 3, 4, and 5.

The resemblance between a computer program attempting to learn about and master its environment, and a species attempting to evolve viably, is quite strong. DNA can be considered a program for producing and maintaining an organism, in which case evolution is mapped into the process we call *automatic programming*. Early experiences with automatic programming have shown just how weak a method random mutation is for modifying large, complex programs. Significant success was achieved only by incorporating a large amount of knowledge, including much heuristic knowledge, to guide the mutation process. The final case study of this paper enlarges this analogy, proposing that nature may already have happened upon a heuristically-guided mechanism for guiding evolution. By now, evolution may be a "plausible generate and test" process, rather than the strict Darwinian "random generate and test". Drawing upon experiences with EURISKO, we extend this to include the speculation that even the mutation and development of new heuristics for evolution are by now under heuristic control.

Table 9-1: Automatic knowledge acquisition via discovery: The Research Program.

1. New domains of knowledge can be developed by using heuristics.
2. As new domains of knowledge emerge and evolve, new heuristics are needed.
3. New heuristics can be developed by using heuristics.
4. As new domains of knowledge emerge and evolve, new representations are needed.
5. New representations can be developed by using heuristics.

9.2.2 Controlling the Use of Heuristic Knowledge

There is an implied "control structure" for the processes of using and acquiring knowledge (solving and proposing problems, using and discovering heuristics, choosing and changing representations, and so on). In fact, it is a nontrivial assumption that a *single* control loop is powerful enough to manage both types of processes. Why assume this? Our experiences with expert systems in the past [Feigenbaum, 1977] have taught us that the power lies in the knowledge, *not* in the inference engine.

What is that topmost control loop? It assumes that there is a large corpus of heuristics for choosing (and shifting between) representations. From time to time, some of these heuristics evaluate how well the current representations are performing; for example, is there now some operation which is performed very frequently, but which is notoriously slow in the current representation? At any moment, if the representations used seem to be performing suboptimally, some attention will be focused on the problem of shifting to other ones, maintaining the same knowledge simultaneously in multiple representations, devising whole new systems of representation, etc. Similarly, we assume there are several heuristics which monitor the adequacy of the existing stock of heuristics, and, as need arises, formulate (and eventually work on and solve) tasks of the form, "Diagonalization is used heavily, but has no heuristics associated with it; try to find some new specific heuristics for dealing with diagonalization." A typical rule for working on such a task might say, "To find heuristics specific to C, try to analogize heuristics specific to concepts which were discovered the same way that C was discovered."

It is assumed that these representation heuristics and heuristic heuristics have run for a while, and the system is in a kind of equilibrium. The representations employed are well suited to the tasks being performed, and the heuristics being followed serve as quite effective guides for "plausible move generation" and "implausible move elimination". The system now proceeds for a while along its object-level pursuits, whatever they may be—proving theorems in plane geometry, discovering new concepts in programming, and so on. Gradually, the object level may evolve; new concepts will be uncovered and focused upon, new laboratory techniques will be discovered, long-standing open questions will be answered, and so on. As this occurs, the old representations for knowledge, and the old set of guiding heuristics, may become less ideal, less effective. This in turn would be detected by some of the "meta"-heuristics discussed in the last paragraph, and they would cause the system to recover its equilibrium, to search for new representations and new heuristics to deal effectively once again with the objects and operations at the object level (see Figure 9-2).

In other words, new concepts, conjectures, theorems, and so on, emerge all the time; as they are investigated, some turn out to be useful and some turn out to be dead ends. Using a fixed set of guiding heuristics, the rate at which useful new discoveries are made will decline gradually over time; eventually it is

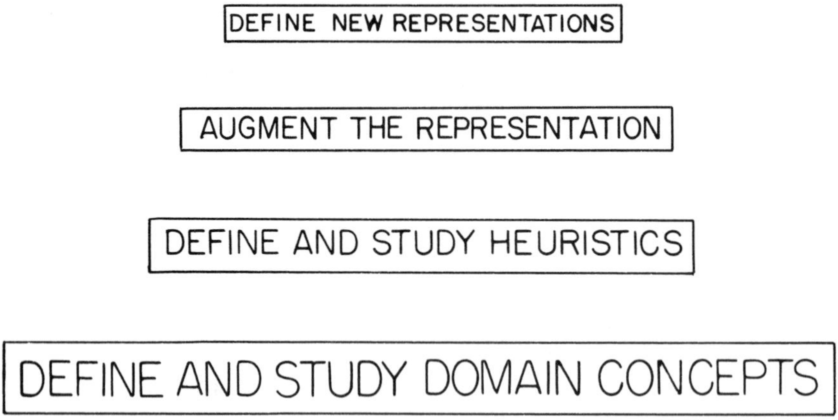

DEFINE NEW REPRESENTATIONS

AUGMENT THE REPRESENTATION

DEFINE AND STUDY HEURISTICS

DEFINE AND STUDY DOMAIN CONCEPTS

Figure 9-2: Implied control structure of discovery systems. As activities at one level decline in efficacy, the system is forced to spend a little time at the next higher level before proceeding.

worth pausing in the search for domain-specific knowledge, and turning instead to the problem of finding new heuristics, perhaps by articulating and generalizing from experiences in the task domain. The discoverer later returns to his original task, armed with new and, he hopes, more powerful heuristics. This cycle of looking for domain concepts, occasionally punctuated by an effort to find new heuristics, continues until, gradually, it becomes harder and harder to find new heuristics. At that point it becomes worthwhile to look for new kinds of slots, attached procedures, assertions—in short, augmenting whatever the current representation of knowledge is in the system. If even this begins to be inadequate, it may be worthwhile to explore for entirely new and different representations for knowledge, though this is an activity with which humans have had very few successes to date.

The top level control structure is thus homeostatic, detecting and correcting for any inappropriateness of representations employed or heuristics employed. For these purposes, we believe it suffices to have (and use) a corpus of heuristics for guidance. Of course that top level loop could itself be implicitly defined by a set of heuristic rules, and we would expect such rules to change from time to time, albeit very slowly. If, for example, no new concepts or operations were defined at the object level for a long period of time, then the need for close monitoring of the adequacy of the representations being employed would evaporate. One important point is that it is not necessary to distinguish meta-heuristics from object-level heuristics; they can be represented the same way, they can be managed by the same interpreter, etc. For example, the very general recursive rule, "To specialize a complex construct, find the component using the most resources, and replace it by several alternate specializations", applies to specializing laboratory procedures, mathematical functions, heuristics (including itself!), and representational schemes.

9.3 CASE STUDY 1: THE AM PROGRAM; HEURISTICS USED TO DEVELOP NEW KNOWLEDGE

9.3.1 How Discoveries Are Made

"How was X discovered?" When confronted with such a question, the philosopher or scientist will often retreat behind the mystique of the all-seeing I's: illumination, intuition and incubation. A different approach would be to provide a rationalization, a scenario in which a researcher proceeds reasonably from one step to the next, and ultimately synthesizes the discovery X. In order for the scenario to be convincing, each step the researcher takes must be justified as a plausible one. Such justifications are provided by citing heuristics, more or less general rules of thumb, judgmental guides to what is and is not an appropriate action in some situation.

For example, consider the heuristic in Table 9-2. It says that if a function f takes a pair of A's as arguments, then it is often worth the time and energy to define $g(x)=f(x,x)$, that is, to see what happens when f's arguments coincide. If f is multiplication, this new function turns out to be squaring; if f is addition, g is doubling. If f is union or intersection, g is the identity function; if f is subtraction or exclusive-or, g is identically zero. Thus we see how two useful concepts (squaring, doubling) and four important conjectures might be discovered by a researcher employing this simple heuristic.

Table 9-2: A heuristic which leads to useful concepts and conjectures.

IF $f{:}A\times A\rightarrow B$,
THEN define $g{:}A\rightarrow B$ as $g(x)=f(x,x)$

Can we apply this methodology to construct a computer program that attempts to learn via discovery? To answer this, we present our first case study, AM, a program which models one aspect of elementary mathematics research, developing new concepts under the guidance of a large body of heuristic rules. While finished, polished mathematics may look static and dry, mathematics "in the making" is an empirical endeavor, fraught with search, uncertainty, massive quantities of data, and the need for good judgment to guide the overall process.

The local heuristics communicate via an agenda mechanism, a global list of tasks for the system to perform and reasons why each task is plausible. A single task can direct AM to define a new concept, to explore some facet (property, slot, attribute) of an existing concept, to examine some empirical data for regularities, and so on. Repeatedly, the program selects from the agenda the task having the best supporting reasons, and then executes it.

Each concept is represented internally as a data structure with a couple dozen slots or facets, such as "Definition", "Examples" and "Worth"; see Tables 9-3 and 9-4 The notation "S: v" is used to indicate that the slot or property S has value v. Thus "Extreme-ex: 2,3" in Table 9-3 means that 2 and 3 are extreme examples of prime numbers. "Worth: 800" means that, on a scale of 0 to 1000, the concept of prime numbers rates a value of 800. "Defined-using: Divisors-of" means that the concept "Primes" was originally defined by using the pre-existing concept "Divisors-of".

Initially, most facets of most concepts are blank. There are 115 of these structured modules provided initially, each one corresponding to an elementary set-theoretic concept (for example, union). This provides a definite but immense "space" which AM begins to explore, guided by a corpus of 250 heuristic rules.

Table 9-3: Frame-like representation for a static mathematical concept from AM. Note that of the numbers examined for primeness so far, 840 satisfy the definition and 5000 do not. Ten conjectures have been made about primes so far, and only three still appear to be valid.

NAME: Primes
STATEMENT
    English: Numbers with two divisors
SPECIALIZATIONS: Odd-primes, Small-primes, Pair-primes
GENERALIZATIONS: Positive-natural-numbers
IS-A: Set
EXAMPLES:
    Extreme-exs: 2,3
    Extreme-non-exs: 0,1
    Typical-exs: 5,7,11,13,17,19
    Typical-non-exs: 34, 100
CONJECTURES:
    Good-Conjecs: Unique-factorization, Formula-for-d(n)
    Good-Conjec-Units: Times, Divisors-of, Exponentiate, Nos-with-3-divis, Squaring
ANALOGIES: Simple Groups
WORTH: 800
ORIGIN: Divisors-of-1 (Doubletons)
    Defined-using: Divisors-of
    Creation-date: 3/19/76 18:45
HISTORY:
    N-Good-Examples: 840   N-Bad-Examples: 5000
    N-Good-Conjectures: 3   N-Bad-Conjectures: 7

Some of the slots were filled in at the time the concept was created (for example "Name", "Statement", "Is-a", "Worth" and "Origin"). Some of these values changed with time ("Worth"). Other slots were incrementally updated to reflect statistical records ("History"). Other slots were filled in only as the results of AM executing a specific task ("Examples"), perhaps noticing a fortuitous regularity during that process ("Conjectures"). Some slots are *virtual*—that is, they are not initially filled in; rather, they are defined in terms

Table 9-4: Frame-like representation for a mathematical function from AM.

NAME: Compose
ABBREVIATION: - o -
STATEMENT
    English: Compose two functions F and G into a new one FoG
    DOMAIN: F, G are functions
    IF-potentially-relevant: F, G are functions with known domain and range
    IF-truly-relevant: Domain of F and Range of G have some intersection
    IF-resources-available: at least 2 CPU seconds, at least 200 cells
    THEN-add-task-to-agenda: Fill in entries for some slots of FoG
    THEN-conjecture: Properties of F hold for FoG, Properties of G hold for FoG
    THEN-modify-slots: Record FoG as an example of Compose
    THEN-print-to-user: English(Compose)
    THEN-define-new-concepts: Name FoG;
        ORIGIN Compose F,G;
        WORTH: Average(Worth(F),Worth(G))
        DEFN: Append(Defn(G),Defn(F))
        Avg-cpu-time: Plus(Avg-cpu(F),Avg-cpu(G))
        IF-Potentially-Rele: If-Potentially-Rele(G)
        IF-Truly-Rele: If-Truly-Rele(G)
CODED-IF-PART: λ(F,G) ... <LISP code which carries out the 3 IF- tests>
CODED-THEN-PART: λ(F,G) ... <LISP code which carries out the 5 THEN- actions>
CODED-IF-THEN-PARTS: λ(F,G) ... <LISP code uniting previous 2 slots>
COMPILED-CODED-IF-THEN-PARTS: #30876 <compiled version of previous slot>
SPECIALIZATIONS: Composition-of-bijections
GENERALIZATIONS: Combine-concepts
    Immediate-Generalizations: Combine-functions
IS-A: Function
EXAMPLES:
    Good-Examples: Compose Count and Divisors
    Bad-Examples: Compose Count and Count
CONJECTURES: Composing F and F is sometimes very good and usually bad
ANALOGIES: Sequence
WORTH: 700
VIEW: Append
ORIGIN: Specialization of Append-concepts with slot = Defn
    Defined-Using: Specialize
    Creation-date: 11/4/75 03:18
HISTORY:
    N-Good-Examples: 14   N-Bad-Examples: 19
    N-Good-Conjectures:2   N-Bad-Conjectures: 1
    N-Good-Tasks-Added: 57   N-Bad-Tasks-Added: 34
    Avg-Cpu-Time: 1.4 seconds   Avg-List-Cells: 160

of other, more primitive slots, and their values will be filled in the first time they are asked for. (For example, consider "Compiled-coded-if-then-parts". The first time an interpreter calls for its value, it gets shunted to the definition of that slot, which says to find the value for "Coded-if-then-parts" and run the compiler on it. That in turns spawns requests for both "Coded-if-part" and "Coded-then-part", which in turn spawn requests for the various "If-" and "Then-" slots, which (finally!) do indeed exist on the "Compose" concept.)

AM extends its knowledge base, ultimately rediscovering hundreds of common concepts (such as, numbers) and theorems (such as, unique factorization). Some heuristics are used to select which specific facet of which specific concept to explore next, while others are used to actually find some appropriate information about the chosen facet. Other rules prompt AM to notice simple relationships between known concepts, to define promising new concepts to investigate, and to estimate how interesting each concept is. The AM program is more fully described in [Davis & Lenat, 1981], from which some of this section's material has been excerpted.

Before discussing how to synthesize a new theory, consider briefly how to analyze one, how to construct a plausible chain of reasoning which terminates in a given discovery. One can do this by working backwards, by reducing the creative act to simpler and simpler creative acts.

Consider, as our first example of a math heuristic, the following plausible strategy:

> "If f is a function which transforms elements of A into elements of B, then consider just those members of A which are transformed into extremal elements of B. This set is an interesting subset of A."

If f is "Intersection", this heuristic says it is worth considering pairs of sets which map into extremal kinds of sets. Well, what's an extremal kind of set? Perhaps we already know about extremely small sets, such as the empty set. Then the heuristic would cause us to define the relationship of two sets having empty intersection—that is, disjointness. The heuristic also causes us to investigate the other extreme, where sets overlap as *much* as possible—namely, the relation subset.

If f is "Employed-as", then the above heuristic says it is worth defining, naming, and studying the group of people with no jobs (zero is an extremely small number of jobs to hold), and the group of people who hold down more than one job (two is an extremely large number of jobs to hold). So this heuristic leads to the defining of the concepts of unemployment and moonlighting.

If f is "Divisors-of", then the heuristic would suggest defining the set of numbers with no divisors, the set of numbers with one divisor, with two divisors, and with three divisors. The third of these four sets is the concept of prime numbers. Other heuristics cause us to gather data, to do that by dumping each number from 1 to 1000 into the appropriate set(s), to reject the first two sets as too small, to notice that every number in the fourth set is a perfect square, to take their square roots, and, finally, to notice that they then coincide precisely with the third set of numbers. Now that we have the *definition* of primes, and we have found a surprising *conjecture* involving them, we shall say that we have *discovered* them. (Note that we are nowhere near a proof of that conjecture.)

So, applying the above heuristic rule actually *reduces* the task of "how in the world might someone have invented the concept of prime numbers" to the more elementary problem of "how in the world might someone have invented divisors-of".

But suppose we know this general rule: "If f is an interesting function, consider its inverse." It reduces the task of discovering divisors-of to the simpler task of discovering multiplication. Eventually, this task reduces to the discovery of very basic notions, like substitution, set-union, and equality. To explain how a given researcher might have made a given discovery, such an analysis can be continued until that inductive task is reduced to "discovering" notions which the researcher already knew, which were his conceptual primitives. (See Figure 9-3.)

Suppose a large collection of these heuristic strategies has been assembled (for example, by analyzing a great many discoveries and writing down new heuristic rules whenever necessary). Instead of using them to explain how a given idea might have evolved, one can imagine starting from a basic core of knowledge and "running" the heuristics to generate new concepts. We're talking about reversing the process described in the last few paragraphs; not how to rationalize discoveries in hindsight, but how to *make* them.

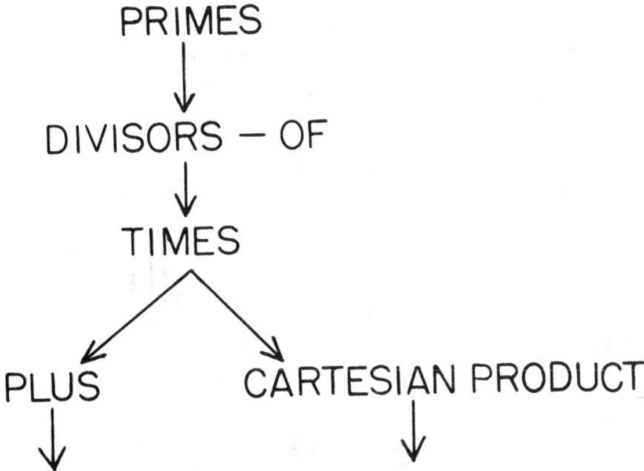

Figure 9-3: Reducing each concept's discovery to that of a simpler one. Note that multiplication can be discovered if the researcher knows either addition of numbers or Cartesian products of sets.

Why, then, is the act of creation so cherished? If some significant discoveries are merely one or two "heuristic applications" away from known concepts, why are even one-step discoveries worth communicating and getting excited about? The answer is that the discoverer is moving upward in the tree, not downward. He is not rationalizing, in hindsight, how a given discovery might have been made; rather, he is groping outward into the unknown for some new concept which seems to be useful or interesting. The downward, analytic search is much more constrained than the upward, synthetic one. Discoverers move upward; colonizers (axiomatizers and pedagogues) move downward. (See Figure 9-4.) Even in this limited situation, the researcher might apply the "Repeat" heuristic to multiplication, and go off along the vector containing exponentiation, hyper-exponentiation, and so on. Or he might apply "look at inverse of extrema" to Divisors-of in several ways, for example looking at numbers with very many divisors.

Once a discovery has been made, it is much easier to rationalize it in hindsight, to find some path downward from it to known concepts, than it was to make that discovery initially. Analysis (Figure 9-3) is less branchy than synthesis (Figure 9-4). That is the explanation of the phenomenon we have all experienced after working for a long time on a problem, the feeling, "Why didn't I solve that sooner!" When the reporter is other than ourselves, the feeling is more like "I could have done that, that wasn't so difficult!" It is the phenomenon of wondering how a magic trick ever fooled us, after we're told how it was performed. It enables us to follow mathematical proofs with a false sense of confidence, being quite unable to prove similar theorems. It is the reason why we can use Polya's heuristics [Polya, 1945] to parse a discovery, to explain a plausible route to it, yet feel very little guidance from them when faced with a problem and a blank piece of paper.

There is still that profusion of upward arrows to contend with. One of the triumphs of AI has been finding the means to muffle a combinatorial explosion of arrows. One must add some heuristic guidance criteria; that is, some additional knowledge indicating which directions are expected to be the most promising ones to follow, in any situation. So by a *heuristic*, from now on, we shall mean a contingent piece of knowledge, such as the top entry in Table 9-5, rather than an unconstrained Polya-esque maxim (Table 9-5b). The former is a heuristic, the latter is an explosive.

There is a partial theory of intelligence here, which claims that discovery can be adequately guided by a large collection of such heuristic rules. It was to test this hypothesis that we built and experimented with the AM program.

9.3.2 Constructing and Running the AM Program

AM consists of a large corpus of primitive mathematical concepts, each with a few associated heuristics—situation/action rules which function as local "plausible move generators". Some suggest tasks for the system to carry out,

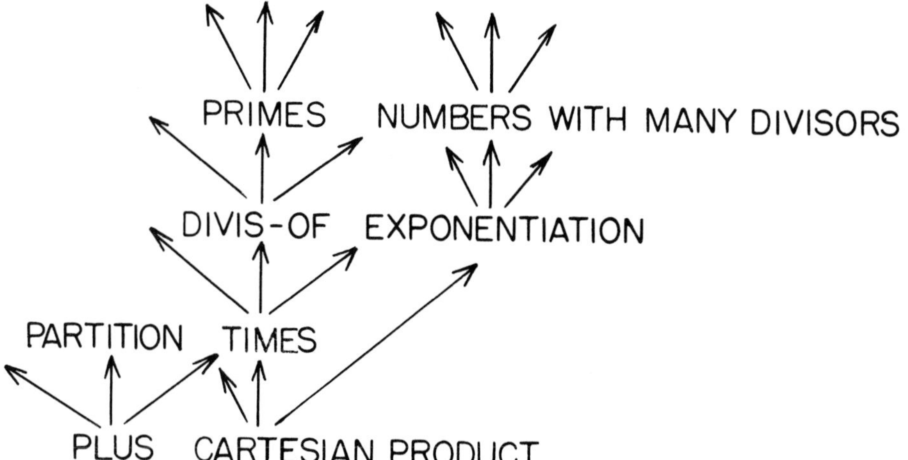

Figure 9-4: The more explosive upward search for new concepts.

Table 9-5: A contingent heuristic rule and an explosive one.

(a) IF the range of one operation has a large intersection with the domain of a second,
  and they both have high worth,
  and either there is a conjecture connecting them
   or the range of the second operation has a large intersection
    with the domain of the first,
 THEN compose them and study the result.

(b) Compose two operations and study the result.

some suggest ways of satisfying a given task, and so on. AM's activities all serve to expand AM itself, to enlarge upon a given body of mathematical knowledge. To cope with the large size of the potential "search space" involved, AM uses its heuristics as judgmental criteria to guide development in the most promising direction. It appears that the process of inventing worthwhile, new (to AM) concepts can be guided successfully using a collection of a few hundred such heuristics.

Modular representation of concepts provides a convenient scheme for organizing the heuristics; for example, the following strategy fits into the "Examples" facet of the "Predicate" concept:

> "If, empirically, 10 times as many elements fail some predicate P, as satisfy it, then some generalization (weakened version) of P might be more interesting than P."

AM considers this suggestion after trying to fill in examples of each predicate (function that always returns True or False). In fact, after AM attempts to find examples of "Set-Equality", so few are found that AM decides to generalize that predicate. The result is the creation of a new predicate which means "Has-the-same-length-as"—that is, a rudimentary precursor to natural numbers.

AM is initially given a collection of 115 core concepts, with only a few facets filled in for each concept. Its sole activity is to choose some facet of some concept, and fill in that particular slot. In so doing, new notions will often emerge. Uninteresting ones are forgotten, mildly interesting ones are kept as parts of one facet of one concept, and very interesting ones are granted full concept-module status. Each of these new modules has dozens of blank slots; hence, the space of possible actions (blank facets to fill in) grows rapidly. The same heuristics are used both to suggest new directions for investigation and to limit attention, both to sprout and to prune.

The particular mathematical domains in which AM operates depend upon the choice of initial concepts. Currently, AM begins with nothing but a scant knowledge of concepts which Piaget might describe as *prenumerical*: the set of initially supplied concepts includes static structures (sets, bags, lists) and many active operations (union, composition, canonize). Note that AM is not told anything about proof, single-valued functions, or numbers. For each concept, we supplied very little information besides its definition. In addition, AM contained 243 heuristic rules for proposing plausible new concepts, for filling in data about concepts, and for evaluating concepts for "interestingness". Among them are the two heuristics we saw earlier, for looking at the inverse of extrema and for looking at the new function $g(x) =_{df} f(x,x)$.

From this primitive basis, AM quickly discovered elementary numerical concepts (corresponding to those we refer to as natural numbers, multiplication, factors, and primes) and wandered around in the domain of elementary number theory. "Discovering" a concept means that *(i)* AM recognized it as a distinguished entity (for example, by formulating its definition), and also *(ii)* AM decided it was worth investigating, either because of the interesting way it was formed, or because of surprising preliminary empirical results. AM was not designed to *prove* anything, but it did *conjecture* many well-known relationships, including de Morgan's laws and the unique factorization theorem.

AM was not able to discover any "new-to-mankind" mathematics purely on its own, but has discovered several interesting notions hitherto unknown to the author. A couple bits of new mathematics have been inspired by AM—relationships involving highly composite numbers, which were noticed in an unusual way by AM, which in turn led to dramatically shorter proofs of them. AM also defined some well-known concepts in novel ways—for example, prime pairs were defined by restricting addition to primes; that is, for which primes p, q, r is it possible that $p+q=r$?

Everything that AM does can be viewed as testing its underlying body of heuristic rules. Gradually, this knowledge becomes better organized, its implications clearer. One benefit of actually constructing AM is that of using it as an experimental vehicle upon which to test theories about learning and discovery; one can vary the concepts AM starts with, vary the heuristics available, and so on, and study the effects on AM's behavior. Several such experiments were performed. One involved adding a couple dozen new concepts from an entirely new domain, plane geometry. AM busied itself exploring elementary geometric concepts, and was almost as productive there as in its original domain. New geometric concepts were defined, and new conjectures formulated.

Perhaps the greatest difference between AM and typical heuristic search procedures is that AM has no well-defined target concepts or target relationships. Rather, its "goal criterion"—its sole aim—is to maximize the quality of the activities it performs, the priority ratings of the top tasks on the agenda. It does not matter precisely which definitions or conjectures AM discovers or misses, so long as it spends its time on plausible tasks. For example, no stigma is attached to the fact that AM never discovered real numbers; it was rather surprising that AM managed to discover natural numbers! Even if it had not done that, it would have been fine if AM had simply gone off and developed ideas in set theory. The most similar phenomenon one can liken this "freedom from targets" to is biological evolution. The latter parts of this chapter argue that this similarity is neither coincidental nor merely metaphorical.

Let's take a moment to discuss the totality of the mathematics which AM carried out. All of the discoveries mentioned below were made by AM working by itself, with a human being observing its behavior. Most of the obvious set-theory relations (for example, de Morgan's laws) were eventually uncovered. AM never derived a formal notion of infinity, but it naively established conjectures like "a set can never be a member of itself", and procedures for making indefinitely large chains of new sets ("insert a set into itself"). After this initial period of exploration, AM decided that "equality" was worth generalizing, and thereby discovered the relation "same-size-as". "Natural numbers" were based on this, and soon most simple arithmetic operations were defined. Since addition arose as an analog to union, and multiplication as a repeated substitution followed by a generalized kind of unioning, it came as quite a surprise when AM noticed that they were related (namely, $n+n=2xn$). AM later rediscovered multiplication in three other ways: as repeated addition, as the numeric analog of the Cartesian product of sets, and by studying the cardinality of power sets. These operations were defined in different ways, so it was an unexpected (to AM) discovery when they all turned out to be equivalent. These surprises caused AM to give the concept "Times" quite a high "Worth" rating. Exponentiation was defined as repeated multiplication. AM never found any obvious properties of exponentiation, hence lost all interest in it.

Soon after defining multiplication, AM investigated the process of multiplying a number by itself: squaring. The inverse of this turned out to be interesting, and led to the definition of square-root. Perfect squares and perfect fourth-powers were isolated. Many other numeric operations and kinds of numbers were isolated: odds, evens, doubling, halving, and so on. The associativity and commutativity of multiplication indicated that it could accept a "Bag" of numbers as its argument. When AM defined the inverse operation corresponding to "Times", this property allowed the definition to be, "any bag of numbers whose product is *n*". This was just the notion of factoring a number *n*. Minimally-factorable numbers turned out to be what we call primes. Maximally-factorable numbers were also thought to be interesting, and some astonishing properties about them were conjectured, and ultimately proved by hand (by Knuth's hand).

AM conjectured the fundamental theorem of arithmetic (unique factorization into primes) and Goldbach's conjecture (every even number greater than 2 is the sum of two primes) in a surprisingly symmetric way. The unary representation of numbers gave way to a representation as a bag of primes (based on unique factorization), but AM never thought of exponential notation. Since the key concepts of remainder, greater-than, greatest common divisor, and exponentiation were never mastered, progress in number theory was arrested.

When a new base of geometric concepts was added, AM began finding some additional general associations. In place of the strict definitions for the equality of lines, angles, and triangles, came new definitions of concepts we refer to as parallel, equal-measure, similar, congruent, translation, rotation, plus many which have no common name (for example, the relationship of two triangles sharing a common angle). An unexpected geometric interpretation of Goldbach's conjecture was found: Given all angles of a prime number of degrees, 0,1,2,3,5,7,11,...,179°, any angle between 0 and 180° can be approximated (to within 1°) as the sum of two of those angles.

During the course of its longest run (a couple hours), AM defined several hundred concepts, about half of which were reasonable, and noticed hundreds of simple relationships involving them, most of which were trivial. Each "discovery" involved relying on over 30 heuristics, and almost all heuristics participated in dozens of different discoveries; thus, the set of heuristics is not merely "unwound" to produce the discoveries. Since the heuristics did lead to the discoveries, they must in some sense be an encoding for them, but they are not a conscious or (even in hindsight) obvious encoding. Skepticism of a program's generality is necessary and healthy. Is AM's knowledge base "just right"—that is, finely tuned to elicit this one chain of behaviors? The answer is "No!" The whole point of this project is to show that a relatively small set of general heuristics can guide a nontrivial discovery process. Each activity, each task, was proposed by some heuristic rule, like "look for extreme cases of X," which was used time and time again, in many situations. It was not considered fair to insert heuristic guidance which could "guide" only in a single situation. Moreover, the set of heuristics, and the initial set of concepts, was decided upon in advance, and there were very few additions or modifications to that knowledge once we began to run the program.

To convey a bit of AM's flavor, we present an excerpt of the system running. It has been retouched, but less so than one might suppose (for example,

AM actually printed out the font changing commands). It illustrates that AM is not a theorem prover, nor is AM randomly manipulating entries in a knowledge base, nor is it exhaustively searching any space. AM is carefully growing a network of data structures representing mathematical concepts, by repeatedly using heuristics both *(i)* for guidance in choosing a task to work on next, and *(ii)* for providing methods to satisfy the chosen task. Although AM appears to have reasonable natural language abilities, this is a typical AI illusion: most of the phrases AM types are mere tokens, and the syntax which the user must obey is unnaturally constrained. As a gauge of AM's abilities, the reader may be interested to know that Task 2 was to fill in examples of "Sets", AM defined "Natural Numbers" during Task 32, and "Times" was defined during Task 122.

AM prints out phrases indicating what it is doing at each moment, and a human being, referred to as the user, watches AM's activities. All the user's comments are prefaced by "USER". Most of the concepts mentioned below are self-explanatory. Potential jargon includes:

Bag: a multiset; a set which can have repeated elements.
Divisors-of: includes primes and nonprimes. Divisors-of(18) = {1 2 3 6 9 18}.

```
***Task 65***: Filling in examples of the following concept:
       ⌜Divisors-of⌝
3 Reasons:
(1) No known examples for Divisors-of so far.
(2) Times, which is related to Divisors-of, is now very interesting.
(3) Focus of attention: AM recently defined Divisors-of.

26 examples found, in 9.2 seconds.
  For instance: Divisors-of(6)={1 2 3 6}.

***Task 66***: Considering numbers which have very small sets of
       Divisors-of
2 Reasons:
(1) Worthwhile to look for extreme cases.
(2) Focus of attention: AM recently worked on Divisors-of.

  Filling in examples of numbers with 0 divisors.
  0 examples found, in 4.0 seconds.
  Conjecture: no numbers have 0 divisors.

  Filling in examples of numbers with 1 divisors.
  1 examples found, in 4.0 seconds. e.g.: Divisors-of(1)={1}.
  Conjecture: 1 is the only number with 1 divisor.

  Filling in examples of numbers with 2 divisors.
  24 examples found, in 4.0 seconds. e.g.: Divisors-of(13)={1 13}.
  No obvious conjecture.  This kind of number merits more study.
  Creating a new concept: ⌜Numbers-with-2-divisors.⌝

  Filling in examples of numbers with 3 divisors.
  11 examples found, in 4.0 seconds. e.g.: Divisors-of(49)={1 7 49}.
  49 is Odd and Perfect Square.  Checking if either always holds.
```

```
  All numbers with 3 divisors are also Squares.!!!
  This kind of number merits more study.
  Creating a new concept: ´Numbers-with-3-divisors.ı


***Task 67***: Considering the square-roots of
        Numbers-with-3-divisors.
2 Reasons:
(1) Numbers-with-3-divisors are unexpectedly also perfect Squares.
(2) Focus of attention: AM recently worked on
        Numbers-with-3-divisors.

  All square-roots of Numbers-with-3-divisors seem to be
  Numbers-with-2-divisors.  For example,
  Divisors-of(Square-root(169))=Divisors-of(13)={1 13}.

  Formulating the converse to this statement.
  Empirically, it seems to be true.
  The square of each Number-with-2-divisors seems to be a
  Number-with-3-divisors.
  This is very unusual. (Chance of coincidence is < .001)
  Boosting interestingness factor of the concepts involved:
  Interestingness of ´Divisors-ofı raised from 300 to 400.
  Interestingness of ´Numbers-with-2-divisorsı
    raised from 100 to 600.
  Interestingness of ´Numbers-with-3-divisorsı
    raised from 200 to 700.
```

USER: Call the set of numbers with 2 divisors "Primes."

```
***Task 68***:  Considering the squares of Numbers-with-3-divisors.
        2 Reasons:
(1) Squares of Numbers-with-2-divisors were interesting.
(2) Focus of attention: AM recently worked on
    Numbers-with-3-divisors.
                        .
                        .
                        .
```

The first task illustrated (Task 65) involves exploring the concept of "divisors of a number". After tiring of finding examples of this relation, AM investigates extreme cases. That is, it wonders which numbers have very few or very many divisors. Numbers with 0 or 1 divisor are essentially nonexistent, so they're not found to be interesting. AM notices that numbers with 3 divisors always seem to be squares of numbers with 2 divisors (primes). This raises the interestingness of several concepts, including primes. Soon (Task 79), another conjecture involving primes is noticed: many numbers seem to factor into primes. This causes a new relation to be defined which associates, to a number x, all prime factorizations of x. The first question AM asks about this relation is, "Is it a function?" This question is the full statement of the unique factorization conjecture: the fundamental theorem of arithmetic; namely, that each number has one, and only one, factorization into primes. AM recognized the value of this relationship, and assigned it a high interestingness rating.

In a similar manner, though with lower hopes, it noticed some more relationships involving primes, including Goldbach's conjecture. AM soon went off examining cute but useless concepts such as "numbers which can be written as the sum of a pair of primes, in only one way", "numbers which can be written as the sum of a prime number of primes, in precisely a prime number of ways", and "prime triples" (three consecutive odd numbers which are all prime).

As AM forayed into number theory, it had only heuristics from set theory to guide it. For instance, when dealing with prime pairs (twin primes), there were no specific heuristics relevant to them; they were defined in terms of primes, which were defined in terms of divisors-of, which was defined in terms of multiplication, which was defined in terms of addition, which was defined in terms of set-union, which (finally!) had a few attached heuristics. Because it lacked number theory heuristics embodying what we would call common sense about arithmetic, AM's fraction of useless definitions went way up (numbers which are both odd and even, prime triples, the conjecture that there is only one prime triple (3,5,7) but without understanding why, and so on). Only the addition of specific number theory heuristics would forestall this type of collapse, and even then merely temporarily.

There are two relevant conclusions from the AM research: *(i)* it is possible for a body of heuristics to effectively guide a program in searching for new concepts and conjectures involving them, and *(ii)* as new domains of knowledge emerge, the old corpus of heuristics may not be adequate to serve as a guide in those new domains; rather, new specific heuristics are necessary. Notice that these are also the first two points in the argument of this paper (see Table 9-1).

9.3.3 As New Task Domains Emerge, So Too Do New Heuristics

Let's continue to explore the notion of a heuristic having a domain of relevance. Consider the following very special situation: you are asked to guess whether a conjecture is true or false. What heuristics are useful in guiding you to a decision rapidly? If the conjecture is in the field of plane geometry, one very powerful technique is to draw a diagram and see whether it holds in that analogic model. But if the conjecture is in the field of point-set topology, or real analysis, this is a terrible heuristic which will often lead you into error. For instance, if the conjecture mentions a function, then any diagram you draw will probably picture a function which is everywhere infinitely differentiable, even if such is never stated in the conjecture's premises. As a result, many properties will hold in your diagram that can never be proven from the conjecture's premises. The appropriate technique in topology or analysis is to pull out your book of 101 favorite counterexamples, and see whether any of them violate the conjecture. If it passes all of them, then you may guess it is probably true.

This example dramatizes the idea that the power or utility of a heuristic changes from domain to domain. Thus, as we move from one domain to another, the set of heuristics which we should use for guidance changes. Many of them have higher or lower utility, some entirely new heuristics may exist, and some of the old ones may be actually detrimental if followed in the new domain. For instance, the "If falling object, Then catch it" rule is useful for most situations, but each year people are burned when they try to catch falling clothes irons and soldering irons.

Heuristics are compiled hindsight; they are nuggets of wisdom which, if only we'd had them sooner, would have led us to our present state much faster. Even the synthesis of a new discovery via analogy, aesthetic criteria (symmetry), or random combination, can be considered to be the result of employing guidance heuristics—for example, "Analogies are useful in formulating biological and sociological theories," "Symmetry is useful in postulating the existence of fundamental particles in physics," "Randomly looking for regularities in elementary number theory and plane geometry may be profitable." Those guidance heuristics were, in turn, based on several past episodes, and hence are themselves compiled hindsight. Nilsson and others have argued for the primacy of search; we are simply stating a special case: the primacy of compiled experiential knowledge. Instead of having the power to examine a search tree wherever we please, we must sit and wait for time to present "event nodes" to us one after another. We observe them, record them, digest them, abstract them. The abstractions of past events provide us with very efficient judgmental knowledge for governing our future actions—heuristics.

As new empirical evidence accumulates, it may be useful to recompile the heuristics. Certainly by the time you have opened up a whole new field, you *must* recompile them. Working in point-set topology with geometry heuristics is not very efficient, nor was AM's working in number theory using only heuristics from set theory. The set of heuristics must evolve as well; some old ones are no longer useful, some must be refined to suit the new domain, and some entirely new heuristics may be useful. As the task varies, or as time varies and one gains new experiences, one's set of guiding heuristics is no longer optimal. The utility of a heuristic will vary, then, both across tasks and across time, and this variance is not necessarily continuous.

Exactly what kinds of changes can occur in a domain of knowledge that might require you to alter your set of heuristics? In other words, what are the sources of granularity in the space of "fields of knowledge"? First, there might be the invention of a new piece of apparatus, yielding heuristics which tell you how to use such a thing, when it is relevant, how to fix one, what kind to buy, and so on. Second, there might be a new technique devised, one which does not actually depend upon any new apparatus. Third, a new phenomenon may be observed. Fourth, and most unusually, there may be a newly explicated or newly isolated concept or field, one which was always around but never spoken about explicitly. The notion of paradigms is such a concept, and the whole field of heuristics itself is such a field. For example, there exist heuristics for when to apply heuristics, for whom to invite to talk about heuristics, for how to evaluate a heuristic's worth, and so on.

In other words, "heuristics" itself is a field of study. It has some objects of study (heuristics), a set of questions about phenomena involving those objects (Where do heuristics come from? What is their source of power?), and some methods for experimentally answering those questions (build large AI programs guided by heuristics, and experiment with those programs).

As an analogy to "heuristics", consider the field of "grammars". It may be discussed theoretically, independent of any particular language, yet to *develop* that theory the researcher no doubt was always grounded in a context of some language or other. Similarly, to develop a general theory of heuristics one must constantly deal with heuristics for some specific field or task. Eventually the theory of grammars advanced to the stage of formalization where it no longer needed such grounding, but heuristics is far from there yet.

In brief, the sources of granularity in the space of "domains of knowledge" are precisely those components which, if varied, lead to a new domain of knowledge. In other words, they define what we mean by a domain of knowledge or a paradigm: a set of phenomena to study, a body of specific problems about those phenomena which are considered worth working on, and a set of methods (both theoretical and experimental, mental and material) for attacking such questions.

9.4 A THEORY OF HEURISTICS

9.4.1 Why Heuristics Work

Our remarks so far about heuristics actually sound more like 2nd-order correction terms to some as yet unstated more fundamental theory. What is that basic 0th-order theory? What is the central assumption underlying heuristics? It appears to be the following: "Appropriateness(action,situation) is continuous." That is, Appropriateness, viewed as a function of actions and of situations, is a *continuous* function of both variables.

Table 9-6: The central assumption underlying heuristics and two special cases.

0th : **Appropriateness(action,situation) is a continuous function.**

Corrolary 1: If action A is appropriate in situation S,
Then A is appropriate in most situations which are very similar to S.

Corrolary 2: If action A is appropriate in situation S,
Then so are most actions which are very similar to A.

Corollary 1: For a given action, its appropriateness is a continuous function of situation. Heuristics specify which actions are appropriate (or inappropriate) in a given situation. One corollary of the central assumption is that if the situation changes only slightly, then the judgment of which actions are appropriate also changes only slightly. Thus, compiled hindsight is useful, because even though the world changes, what was useful in situation X will be useful again sometime in situations similar to X. There are two special cases of Corollary 1 worth mentioning.

The first of these, call it Corollary 1a, says that if the task appears to be similar to one you have seen elsewhere, then many of the features of the task environment will probably be very similar as well—for example, the kinds of conjectures which might be found, the solvability and difficulty anticipated with a task, the kinds of blind alleys which one might be trapped in, and so on, may all be the same as they were in that earlier case. For instance, suppose that a certain theorem, UFT, was useful in proving a result in number theory. Now another task appears, again proving some number theory result. Because the tasks are similar, Corollary 1a suggests that UFT be used to try to prove this new result. This is the basic justification for using analogy as a reasoning mechanism. A sentiment similar to this was voiced by Poincare' during the last century: *The whole idea of analogy is that 'Effects', viewed as a function of situation, is a continuous function.* The second special case of Corollary 1 says that the world does not change much over time, and is the foundation for the utility of memory. In a world changing radically and rapidly enough, memory would be a useless frill; consider the plight of an individual atom in a gas.

Corollary 2: For a given situation, appropriateness is a continuous function of actions. This means that if a particular action was very useful (or harmful) in some situation, it is likely that any very similar action would have had similar consequences. Corollary 2 justifies the use of inexact reasoning, of allocating resources toward finding an approximate answer, of satisficing. It is the basis for employing "generalization" as a mechanism for coping with the world; if the appropriateness function were not (usually) continuous as a function of actions, then most generalizations would be false. The world changes slowly, continuously, as a function of situation. McCarthy and Hayes' frame problem [McCarthy & Hayes, 1969] may be viewed as the temptation to exploit this regularity: Even though one cannot logically prove that action A (for example, the reader sneezing now) has no effect on the truth or falsity of proposition P (for example, that Reagan is still President after the sneeze), it is overwhelmingly likely to be still true, and we wish to have some way of exploiting this near-constancy.

If the central assumption holds, then the ideal interpreter for heuristics is the one shown in Figure 9-5. Note that this is very similar to a pure production system interpreter. In any given situation, some rules will be expected to be relevant, because they were truly relevant in situations very similar to the present one. One or more of them are chosen and applied (obeyed, evaluated, executed, fired, and so on). This action will change the situation, and the cycle begins anew. Of course one can replace the "locate relevant heuristics" subtask by a copy of this whole diagram; that is, it can be performed under the guidance of a body of heuristics specially suited to the task of finding heuristics. Similarly, the task of selecting which rule(s) to fire, and in what order, and with how much of each resource available, can also be implemented as an entire heuristic rule system procedure.

By examining the loop in Figure 9-5 we can quickly "read off" the possible bugs in heuristics, the list of ways in which a heuristic can be "bad":

- It might not be interpretable at all.
- It might be interpretable but it might never even be potentially relevant.
- It might be potentially relevant but its "If" part might never be satisfied.
- It might trigger, but never be the rule actually selected for execution (firing).
- It might fire, but its "Then" part might not produce any effect on the situation.
- It might produce a bad effect on the situation.
- It might produce a good effect, but take so long that it is not cost-effective.

This is reminiscent of John Seely Brown's work on a generative theory of bugs [Brown & VanLehn, 1980], and is meant to be. Perhaps by viewing heuristics as performers, this approach can lead to an effective method for diagnosing buggy heuristics, hence improving or eliminating them.

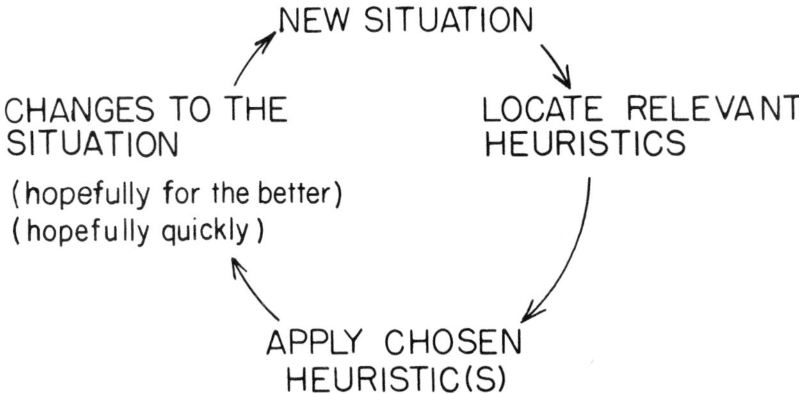

Figure 9-5: The 0th-order interpreter for a body of heuristic rules.

There are several things wrong with the 0th order theory. The reader may have noticed that the first of the two corollaries in Table 9-6 is almost precisely the negation of an empirically-derived statement we made earlier, namely that the space of task domains is inherently and profoundly quantized. Corollary 1, on the other hand, claims that it is continuous. As we mentioned earlier, the empirical observations appear to be 2nd-order correction terms to a theory of heuristics, and Table 9-6 is a very simplified 0th-order theory. Intermediate between them lies a 1st-order theory which interfaces to each.

That 1st-order theory says that the 0th-order theory is often a very useful fiction. It is cost-effective to behave as if it were true, if you are in a situation where your state of knowledge is very incomplete, where there is nevertheless a great quantity of knowledge already known, where the task is very complex, and so on. At a much earlier stage, there may have been too little known to express very many heuristics; much later, the environment may be well enough understood to be algorithmized; in between, heuristic search is a useful paradigm. Predicting eclipses has passed into this final stage of algorithmization; medical diagnosis is in the middle stage where heuristics are useful; building programs to search for new representations of knowledge is still pre-heuristic.

Table 9-7: The 1st-order theory of heuristics: The 0th-order theory is a useful fiction.

1st :	IF you are in a complex, knowledge-rich, incompletely-understood world, THEN it is frequently useful to behave as though it were true that appropriateness(action,situation) is continuous in both variables.

By making this 1st-order theory explicit, some new 2nd-order corrections become apparent. For instance, the adjective "frequently", used in Table 9-7, can be replaced by a body of rules which govern when it is and is not useful to behave so.

9.4.2 The Power of Each Individual Heuristic

We have discussed the nature of using a corpus of heuristics, but what is the nature of a single one? We have already said that it has some domain of relevance. What does that mean? We have already spoken of "Appropriateness" as a function of situation; perhaps we can extend this metaphor by imagining graphs of "Appropriateness" of a heuristic. If we could somehow graph the utility or power of the heuristic, as a function of task domain, we might expect to see a curve resembling that of Figure 9-6. Namely, there is some range of tasks for which the heuristic has positive value. Outside of this, it is often counterproductive to use the heuristic, although the utility may drop to zero rather than falling below zero as pictured. For tasks sufficiently far away, the utility approaches zero, because the heuristic is never even considered potentially relevant, and hence never fires. As one example, consider the heuristic that says "If you want to test a conjecture, Then draw a diagram." As we have seen, this has high utility within Euclidean plane geometry, but as the axioms of the theory are changed, its worth declines. By the time you reach point-set topology or real analysis, its value is negative. Eventually, domains like philosophy are reached, where drawing diagrams can rarely be done meaningfully. (As Figures 9-6 through 9-8 indicate, we hope that "draw a diagram" is a good heuristic for the domain of "Heuristics".) As another example, consider the heuristic "If a predicate rarely returns True, Then define new generalizations of it." This is useful in set theory, worse than useless in number theory, and useless in domains where "predicate" is undefined.

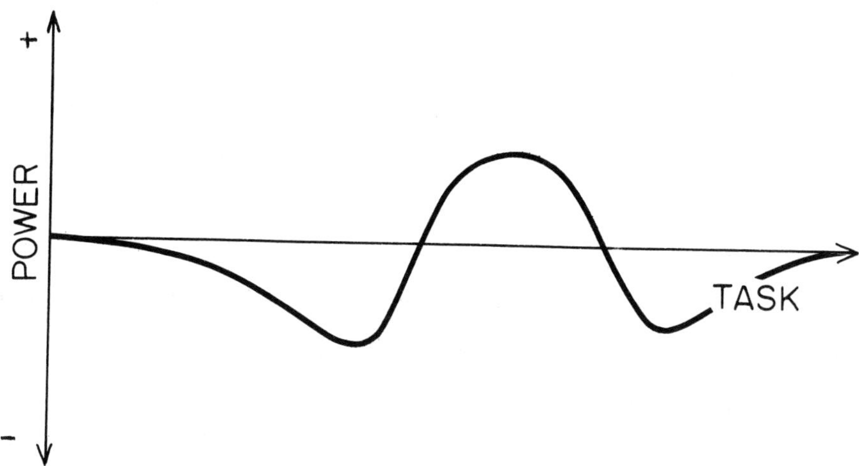

Figure 9-6: The graph of a heuristic's power as a function of the task it is applied to.

If we specialize the "Then-" part of a heuristic (see Figure 9-7), it will typically have higher utility but only be relevant over a narrower domain. Consider, for example, the case where "generalize a predicate" is specialized into "generalize a predicate by eliminating one conjunct from its definition". The latter is more powerful, but only applies to predicates defined conjunctively (see "dropping condition generalization" in Chapter 4 of this book). Notice the area under the curve appears to remain roughly constant; this is a geometric interpretation of the trade-off between generality and power of heuristic rules. It is also worth noticing that the new specialized heuristic may have negative utility in regions where the old general one was still positive, and it will be meaningless over a larger region as well.

By examining Figure 9-7 it is possible to generate a list of possible bugs that may occur when the actions ("Then-" part) of a heuristic are specialized. First, the domain of the new one may be so narrow that it is merely a spike, a

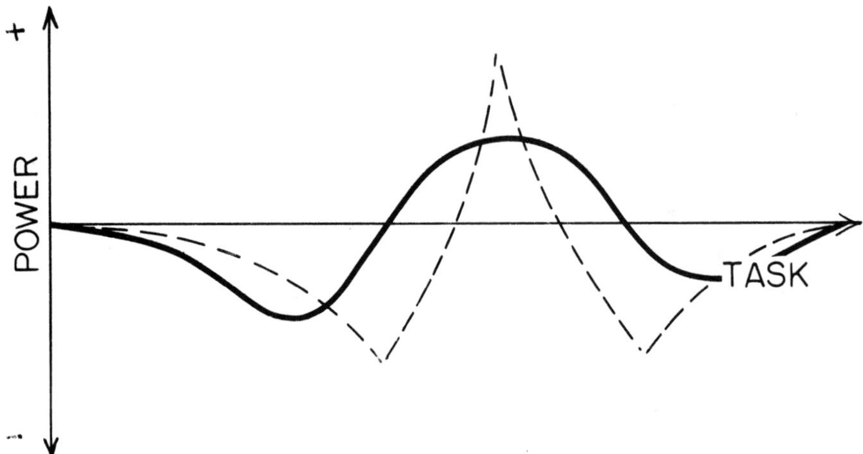

Figure 9-7: The change in power when a heuristic (*) has its "Then-" part specialized (+).

delta function. This is what happens when a general heuristic is replaced by a table of specific values. Another bug is if the domain is not narrowed at all; in such a case, one of the heuristics is probably completely dominated by the other. A third type of bug appears when the new heuristic has no greater power than the old one did. For example, "Smack a vu-graph projector if it makes noise" has much narrower domain, but no higher utility, than the more general heuristic, "Smack a device if it's acting up." Thus, the area under the curve is greatly diminished. Being able to perform this kind of systematic analysis, just because we visualized graphing "Appropriateness" as a mathematical function, justifies our use of that metaphor.

While the last paragraph warned of some extreme bad cases of specializing the "Then-" part of a heuristic, there are some extreme good cases which frequently occur. The utility (power) axis may have some absolute desirable point along it (for example, some guarantee of correctness or efficiency), and by specializing the heuristic it may exceed that threshold, albeit over a narrow range of tasks. In such a case, the way we *qualitatively* value that heuristic may alter, and indeed we may term it "algorithmic" or "real-time". One way to rephrase this is to say that algorithms are merely heuristics which are so powerful that guarantees can be made about their use. Conversely, one can try to apply an algorithm outside its region of applicability, in which case the result may be useful and that algorithm is then being used as a heuristic. The latter is frequently done in mathematics (for example, pretending one can differentiate power series expansions to guess at the value of the series). Finally, note that the specialization of the heuristic to one which applies only on a set of measure zero is not necessarily a bad thing; tables of values *do* have their uses.

Specializing the "If-" part of a heuristic rule results in its having a smaller region of non-zero utility. That is, it triggers less frequently. As Figure 9-8 shows, this is like placing a filter or window along the x-axis, outside of which the power curve will be absolutely zero. In the best of cases, this removes the negative-utility regions of the curve, and leaves the positive regions untouched. For example, we might preface the "Draw a diagram" heuristic with a new premise clause, "If you are asked to test a geometry conjecture". This will cause us to use the rule only in geometry situations, a domain where it has already been demonstrated to possess a high utility.

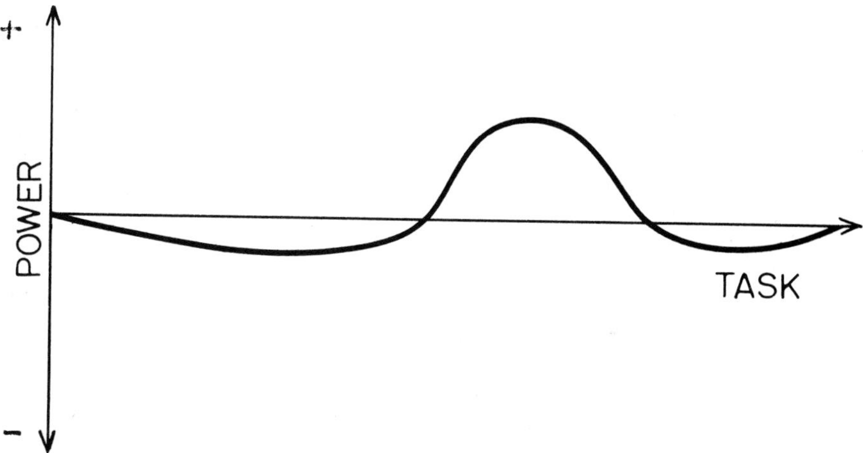

Figure 9-8: The graph of a heuristic's power after its "If-" part has been optimally specialized.

By examining Figure 9-8 we can generate a list of possible bugs arising from specializing the conditions ("If-" part) of a heuristic rule. The new window may be narrowed to a spike, thus preventing the rule from almost ever firing ("... and if you are working on problem 652 ..."). There may be no narrowing whatsoever; in that case, it would typically add a little to the time required to test the "If-" part of the rule, while not raising the power at all ("... and if 37 is prime ..."). Of course the most serious error is if it clips away some—or all!—of the positive region. Thus, we would not want to replace a general diagram-drawing recommendation with one which advised us to do so only for real analysis conjectures.

The space of domains is granular, quantized; hence these power curves are step-functions (or histograms) rather than smooth curves as we have drawn them. One implication of this is that there is a very precise point along the task axis where the utility drops from positive to negative (or zero). Often, this is a very large, very sudden drop across a single discontinuity in the axis (for example, when a new product is marketed, an expert dies, or a theorem is proved).

What are implications of this simple "theory of heuristics"? One effect is to determine in what order heuristics should be chosen for execution; this is discussed in the next paragraph. A second effect is to indicate some very useful slots that each heuristic can and should have, attributes of a heuristic that can be of crucial importance: the peak power of the rule, its average power, the sizes of the positive and negative regions (both projections along the task axis (x-axis) and the areas under the curves), the steepness with which the power curve approaches the x-axis, and so on. To illustrate, let us consider the latter attribute. Why is it useful to know how steeply the power curve approaches Utility = 0 (the x-axis)? If this is *very* steep, then it is worth investing a great amount of resources determining whether the rule is truly relevant in any situation, for if it is slightly irrelevant, then it may have a huge negative effect if used. Conversely, if the slope is very gentle, then very little harm will result from slightly inappropriate applications of the rule. Hence, not much time need ever be spent worrying about whether or not it is truly relevant to the situation at hand.

The whole process of drawing the power curves for heuristics is still conjectural. While a few such graphs have been sketched, there is no algorithm for plotting them, no library of thousands of catalogued and plotted heuristics, not even any agreement on what the various power and task axes should be. Nevertheless, it has already proven to be a useful metaphor, and has suggested some important properties of heuristics which should be estimated (such as the just-mentioned downside risk of applying a heuristic in a slightly inappropriate situation). It is a qualitative, empirical theory [Newell & Simon, 1976], and predicts the form that a quantitative theory might assume.

How should heuristics be chosen for execution? In any given situation, we will be at a point along the x-axis, and can draw a vertical line (in case of multidimensional task axes, we can imagine a hyperplane). Any heuristics which have positive power (utility) along that line are then useful ones to apply (according to our theory of heuristics), and the ones with high power should be applied before the ones with low power. Of course, it is unlikely we would know the power of a heuristic precisely in each possible situation; although diagrams such as Figures 9-6 through 9-8 may be suggestive, the data are almost never available to draw them quantitatively for a given heuristic. It is more likely that we would have some measure of the average power of each heuristic, and would use that as a guess of how useful each one would be in the current situation. Since there is a trade-off between generality and power, a gross simplification of the preceding strategy is just to apply the most specific heuristic first, and so on. This is the scheme AM used, with very few serious problems. If all heuristics had precisely the same multiple integral of their power curves, this would coincide with the previous scheme. Of course, there are always some heuristics which, while being very general, are really the most important ones to listen to if they ever trigger, for example, "If a conflagration breaks out, Then escape it."

Notice that the "generality versus power" trade-off has turned into a statement about the conservation of volumes in n×m-dimensional space, when one takes the multiple integral of all the power curves of a heuristic. In particular, there are trade-offs among all the dimensions: a gain along some utility dimension (say, convincingness) can be paid for by a decrease along another (say, efficiency) or by a decrease along a task dimension (a reduction of breadth of applicability of the heuristic). One historically common bug has been over-reliance upon, and glorification of, heuristics which are pathologically extreme along some dimension (tables, algorithms, weak methods, and so on).

Heuristics are often spoken of as if they were incomplete, uncertain knowledge, much like mathematical conjectures or scientific hypotheses. This is not necessarily so. The epistemological status of a heuristic, its justification, can be arbitrarily sound. For example, by analyzing the optimal play of Blackjack, a rather complex table of appropriate actions (as a function of situation) is built up. One can reduce this into a simplified "basic strategy" of just a few rules, and know quite precisely just how well those rules should perform. That is, heuristics may be built up from systematic, exhaustive search, from "complete" hindsight. Another example of the formal, complete analysis of heuristic methods is well known from physics, where Newtonian mechanics is known to be only an approximation to the world we inhabit. Relativistic theories quantify that deviation precisely. But rather than supplanting Newtonian physics, they bolster its use in everyday situations, where its inadequacies can be quantitatively shown to be too small to make worthwhile the additional computation required to do relativistic calculations.

Many, nay most, heuristics *are* merely conjectural, empirical, aesthetic, or in other ways epistemologically less secure than the basic strategy in Blackjack and Newtonian physics. The standard use of heuristics is to pretend they are true and let them guide your behavior; the standard use of a conjecture is to guide you while you search for a proof of that conjecture. If a conjecture turns out to be false, it may yet stand as a useful heuristic.

9.4.3 The Space of Heuristics

The utility of an entire set of heuristics could be graphed as a function of the tasks that it is being applied to, and we would expect such a "mega-heuristic" to produce a curve similar to the one in Figure 9-6. Hopefully, the set of heuristics is more useful than any member, thus it is probably much broader and taller (or less negative) than any single heuristic inside it. One cannot simply "add" the curves of its members; the interactions among heuristics are often quite strong, and independence is the exception rather than the rule. Often, two heuristics will be different methods for getting to the same place, or one will be a generalization or isomorph of the other, and so on. As a result the set will really not benefit very much from having both of them present. On the other hand, sometimes heuristics interact synergistically, and the effects can be much greater than simple superposition would have predicted. The opposite of this sometimes happens: two experts have given you heuristics which separately work, yet which contradict each other. Using either half-corpus would solve your problem, but mixing them causes chaos. (For example, one mathematician gives you heuristics for finding empirical examples and generalizing, while a second gives you heuristics for formally axiomatizing the situation; either may suffice, but trying to heed both causes their advice to cancel each other out, and a third, much less desirable course of action is chosen instead.)

Just as a set of heuristics can be conceptually grouped into a large "mega-heuristic", an individual heuristic may be atomized into a cloud of much smaller heuristics. Much of the expertise we tap from human experts, when building expert systems, is their feel for the proper level at which to state and use heuristic knowledge. If the heuristics are too small, they stop being meaningful chunks of wisdom to the human expert, and risk having many stray interactions. Often, languages which enforce a small grain size for rules have facilities to "chain" them together to prevent such crosstalk. If the heuristic rules are too large, we begin to lose the benefits of taking a heuristic rule-guided approach: additivity, synergy, ease of entry and explanation, and modifiability. Ultimately, we are left with one heuristic which is an opaque lump of LISP code performing the entire task.

No treatment of heuristics can be complete without some consideration of the space of all the world's heuristics. By examining and generalizing heuristics from a dozen disparate fields (including set theory, number theory, biological evolution, evolution of naval fleets, LISP programming, game playing, and oil spill cleanups), we have built up some data and conjectures involving heuristic-space. Consider arranging all the world's heuristics in a generalization/specialization hierarchy, with the most general ones at the top. At that top level lie the so-called weak methods (generate and test, hill-climbing, matching, means-ends analysis, and so on). At the bottom are millions of very specific heuristics, involving domain-specific terms like "king-side" and "Pittsburgh". One may picture a Christmas tree, with a pure angel at the top, and the worthwhile gifts at the bottom.

In between are heuristics such as "Look for fixed points," "Examine extreme cases," "See what happens when a process is repeated" and "Given f(x,y), examine what happens when x = y." These are more specific than the weak methods at the top of the tree, yet are far from domain-dependent heuristics below them. Progressing downward, more and more conditions appear on the left-hand sides of the heuristics ("If-" parts), and more specialized advice appears on the right-hand sides ("Then-" parts).

A purely "legal-move" estimate of the size of this tree gives a huge final number, based on the lengths and vocabularies of heuristic rules in AM; one may suppose that in a typical heuristic there are about 20 blanks to be filled in and about 100 possible entries for each blank (predicate, argument, action, and so on) related to AM's math world. So there are 10^{40} syntactically well-formed heuristics just in the elementary mathematics corner of the tree. Of course, most of these are (thankfully!) never going to fire, and almost all the rest will perform irrelevant actions when they do fire. From now on, let's restrict our attention to the tree of only those heuristics which have positive utility at least in some domains.

What does that tree actually look like? One can take a specific heuristic and generalize it gradually, in all possible ways, until all the generalizations collapse into weak methods. Such a preliminary analysis led us to expect the tree to be of depth about 50, and in the case of an expert system with a corpus of a thousand rules, we might expect a picture of them arranged so to form an equilateral triangle. But if one draws the power curves for the heuristics, it quickly becomes apparent that most generalizations are no less powerful than the rule(s) beneath them! Thus the specific rule can be eliminated from the tree. The resulting tree has depth of roughly 3 or 4, and is thus incredibly shallow and bushy. Professors Herbert Simon, Woody Bledsoe, and the author analyzed the 243 heuristics from AM, and were able to transform their deep tree (depth 12) into an equivalent one containing less than fifty rules and having depth of only four.

Looking at many heuristics arranged in a generalization/specialization hierarchy, we observed that all but the top and bottom levels could usually be eliminated. Consider this non-mathematical heuristic: "Smack a vu-graph projector in case it acts up." It and several levels of its generalizations can be eliminated, since they are no more powerful than the general "Smack a malfunctioning device" heuristic. Some *very* specific rule, such as "Smack a Omigawd 807 vu-graph projector on its right side if it hums," might embody some new, powerful, specific knowledge (such as the location of the motor mount and this brand's tendency to misalign), and thus need to stay around.

This "shallow tree" result should make advocates of weak methods happy, because it means that there really is something special about that top level of the hierarchy. Going even one level down (to more specific rules) means paying attention not to an additional ten or twenty heuristics, but to hundreds. It should also please the knowledge engineering advocates, since most of the very specific domain-dependent rules also had to remain. It appears, however, to be a severe blow to those of us who wish to automatically synthesize new heuristics via specialization, since the result says that that process is usually going to produce something no more useful than the rule you start with. Henceforth, we shall term this the "shallow tree problem".

There are two ways out of this dilemma, however. Notice that "utility of a heuristic" really has several distinct dimensions: efficiency, flexibility, power for pedagogical purposes, usefulness in future specializations and generalizations, and so on. Also, "task features" has several dimensions: subject matter, resources allotted (for example, user's time, CPU time, and space), degree of complexity (consider Knuth's numeric rating of his problems' difficulty), time (that is, date in history), paradigm, and so on. If there are n utility dimensions and m task dimensions, then there are actually $n \times m$ different power curves to be drawn for each heuristic. Each of them may resemble the canonical one pictured in Figure 9-6. If by specializing a heuristic we create one which has the appearance of Figure 9-7 in any one of these n×m graphs, then it is a useful specialization.

Consider the "Focus of Attention" heuristic, that is, one which recommends pursuing a course of action simply because it has been worked on recently. Using this as one reason to support tasks on its agenda made AM appear more intelligent to human observers, yet actually take longer to make any given discovery. Thus, it is useful in the "convincingness" dimension of utility, but may be harmful vis-a-vis "efficiency".

As another example, consider the heuristics "Smack a vu-graph projector that's acting up," "Smack a child who's acting up," and "Smack a vu-graph projector or child that's acting up." There may be some utility dimensions in which the third of those is best (for example, scope or humor). However, the rationale or justification for the first two heuristics is quite different; random perturbation toward stable state versus reinforcement learning. Therefore, the third heuristic is probably going to be deficient along other utility dimensions (clarity, usefulness for analogizing).

But there is an even more basic way in which the "shallow tree problem" goes away. There are really a hundred different useful relationships R that two heuristics can have connecting them: "Possibly-triggers", "More-restrictive-IF-part", "Faster", "My-average-power-higher-than-your-peak-power", "Asks-fewer-questions-of-the-user", and so on. For each such relation, an entire graph—note that even the generalization/specialization relation generated a graph, not a tree (see Figure 9-9)—can be drawn of al the world's heuristics (or all those in some given program). In some of these trees or graphs, we will find the broad, shallow grouping that was found for the AM heuristics under generalization/specialization. For others, such as "Possibly-Triggers", we may find each rule pointing to a small collection of other rules, and hence the depth would be quite large. There are still many difficult questions to study, even with the theory in this primitive state; for example, how does the shape of the tree (the graph of heuristics related by some attribute R) relate to the the ways in which R ultimately proves itself to be useful or not useful? Already, one powerful correlation seems to be recognized: In cases where the depth of the tree (of heuristics related by R) is great, that relation R is a good one to generalize and specialize along; in cases where the resulting tree is very broad and shallow, other methods (notably analogy) may be more productive ways of getting new heuristics. For example, since the tree is broad under R=Generalization, analogy may be useful; since the tree is narrow under R="Possibly-triggers", generalization and specialization may be more useful there.

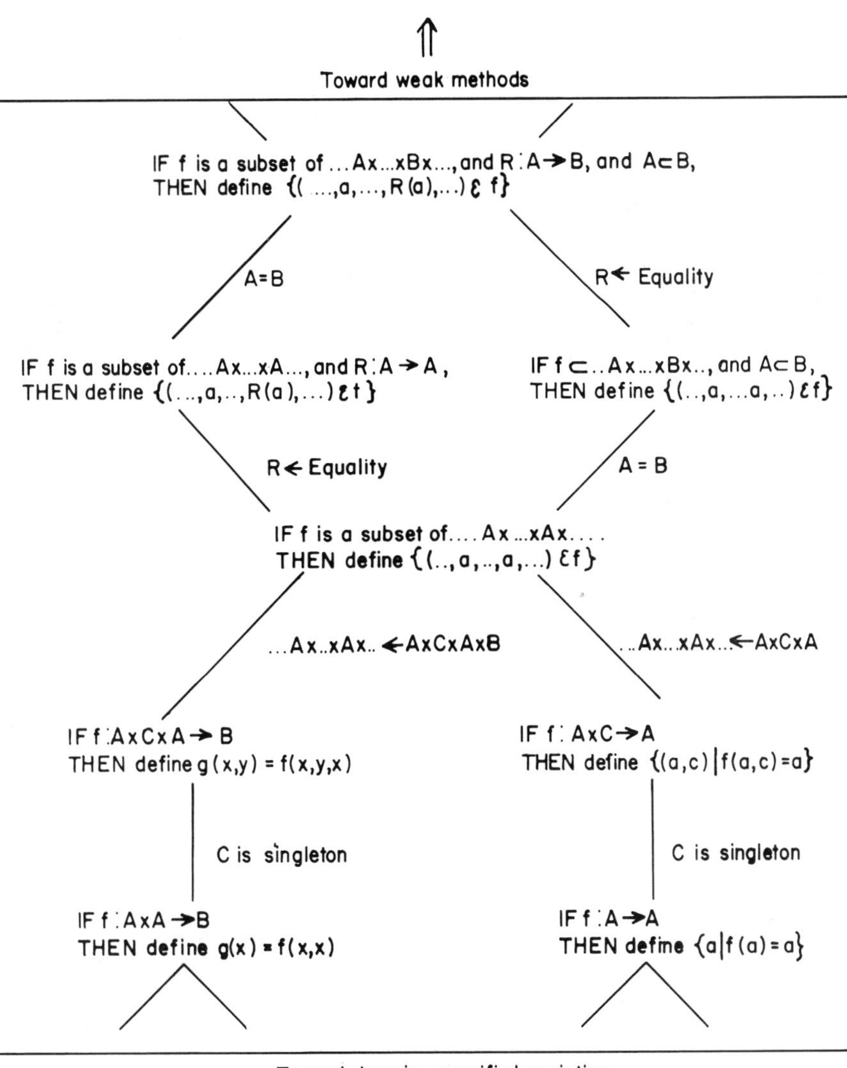

Figure 9-9: A tiny fragment of the graph of heuristics, related by generalization/specialization. Note the similar derivation of Coalescing and Fixed-point heuristics.

9.5 CASE STUDY 2: THE EURISKO PROGRAM; HEURISTICS USED TO DEVELOP NEW HEURISTICS

9.5.1 Meta-Heuristics are Just Heuristics

Assuming that "heuristics" is another field of knowledge, just like electronics or mathematics, it should be possible to discover new ones and to modify existing ones by employing a large corpus of heuristics. Is there something special about the heuristics which inspect, gather data about, modify, and synthesize other heuristics? That is, should we distinguish "meta-heuristics" from "domain heuristics"? According to our general theory, as presented in the last section, domains of knowledge are granular but nearly continuous along every significant axis (complexity of task, amount of quantification in the task, degree of formalization, and so on). Thus, our first hypothesis should be that it is not necessary to differentiate meta-level heuristics from object-level heuristics—nay, that it may be artificial and counterproductive to do so.

Table 9-8 illustrates two heuristics which can deal with both heuristics and mathematical functions. The first one says that if some concept f has always led to bad results, then f should be marked as less valuable. If a mathematical operation, like "Compose", has never led to any good new math concepts, then this heuristic would lower the number stored on the "Worth" slot of the "Compose" concept. Similarly, if a heuristic, like the one for drawing diagrams, has never paid off, then *its* "Worth" slot would be decremented.

The second heuristic says that if some concept has been frequently worthless, yet occasionally useful, then it is cost-effective to seek new, specialized versions of that concept, because some of them might be much more frequently utile (albeit, in narrower domains of relevance). Composition of functions is such a math concept—it has led AM to some of its biggest successes and most explosive failures; this heuristic would add a task to AM's agenda, which said "Find new specializations of 'Compose'." When it was eventually worked on, it could result in the creation of new functions, such as "Composition of a function with itself", "Composition resulting in a function whose domain and range are equal", "Composition of two functions which were derived in the same way", and so on. Incidentally, AM *has* produced these.

The same heuristic (Table 9-8, H20b) also applies to heuristics. In fact it applies to *itself*. It is itself sometimes useful and sometimes not, and so frequently it truly does pay to seek new, specialized variations of that heuristic. Four possible specializations are heuristics which demand, for example, that f has proven itself useful at least three times, that f be specialized in an extreme way, that f has proven itself extraordinarily useful at least once, and that the specializations still be capable of producing any of the successful past creations of f.

Table 9-8: Two heuristics that are capable of working on heuristics, as well as on math concepts.

H20a:	IF the results of performing f have always been numerous and worthless, THEN lower the expected worth of f
H20b:	IF the results of performing f are only occasionally useful, THEN consider creating new specializations of f

9.5.2 Attributes of a Heuristic

In AM, heuristics examine existing frame-like concepts, and lead to new and different concepts. To have heuristics operate on and produce heuristics, it suffices to represent each heuristic as a full-fledged, frame-like concept. Let's see an example of this. In order to "work", to be able to do something, heuristic H20a needs to reset the value of the "Worth" slot of the concept f it operates on. If each math concept has a "Worth" slot, then the rule can work on math concepts. If each heuristic is represented as a unit, and has a "Worth" slot, then H20a can also work on heuristics.

Similarly, a heuristic which referred to such slots as "Average-running-time", "Date-created", "Is-a-kind-of", "Number-of-instances", and so on, could only operate upon units (be they mathematical functions or heuristics) having such slots. Table 9-9 illustrates (some of the slots from) a heuristic represented in that way. Notice its similarity to the representation of a mathematical operation (Table 9-4). The heuristic resembles the function (compare Tables 9-9 and 9-4) much more than the math function resembles the static math concept (compare Tables 9-3 and 9-4).

Earlier, we defined a heuristic to be a contingent piece of guidance knowledge: in some situation, here are some actions that may be especially fruitful, and here are some that may be extremely inappropriate. While some heuristics have pathological formats (for example, algorithms which lack contingency, or delta function spikes which can be succinctly represented as tables), most heuristics seem to be naturally stated as rules having the format "If conditions, Then *actions*". As the body of heuristics grows, the conditions fall into a few common categories (testing whether the rule is potentially relevant, testing whether there are enough available resources to expect the rule to work successfully to completion, and so on). The right hand sides (actions) of rules also seem to fall into a few categories: add new tasks to the agenda, print explanatory messages, define new concepts. Each of these categories is worth making into a separate named attribute (slot) which heuristic rules can possess; Sections 9.5.3 and 9.6 will show the power which can arise from drawing such distinctions. So instead of a heuristic having an "If" slot and a "Then" slot, it will have a bundle of slots which together comprise the conditions of applicability of the heuristic, and another bundle of slots which comprise the actions (see Table 9-9). It is also worth defining compound slots in terms of these: a composite

"If" part, a composite "Then" part, a combined "If/Then" lump of LISP code, a compiled version of the same, and so on. These are what were earlier termed virtual slots.

All the attributes mentioned in the previous paragraph are effective, executable conditions and actions. These are paramount, since they serve to define the heuristic—they are the *criterial* slots. Many non-effective, non-criterial slots are important as well, for describing the heuristic. Some of these relate the heuristic to other heuristics, such as generalizations, specializations, classes of heuristics ("Is-a"), and non-heuristic concepts ("View"). Several slots record its origins ("Defined-using", "Creation-date") and the case studies of its uses so far ("Examples").

Once a rich stock of slots (types of attributes) is present for heuristics, several new ones can be derived from them in two ways. First, one can take a slot and ask some questions about it: how does it evolve over time in length, what relationships exist among entries that fill it, how useful are those values, and so on. Each such question spawns a new kind of slot. For instance, after considering the "Extreme-Examples" slot, EURISKO created several new kinds of slots which looked at the values stored in "Extreme-Examples" and performed some computations on them; three of them were "Avg-Number-Of-Extreme-Examples", "Relns-Among-My-Extreme-Examples", "Avg-Worth-Of-Extreme-Examples".

The second way to create new slots from old ones is to take a pair of slots (say, "Then-Conjecture" and "If-Truly-Relevant") and a relation (such as, "Implies") and define a new unary function F on heuristics—a new kind of slot that any heuristic can have. $F(h_1)$ contains h_2 (that is, h_2 is a legal entry on the F slot of h_1) only if (in the present case) the "Then-Conjecture" slot of h_1 implies the "If-Truly-Relevant" slot of h_2. A good name for this new slot F might be "Can-Trigger", because it lists some heuristics which might trigger when h_1 is fired. Of course not all of the n^2 "cross-term" type slots are going to be useful—especially since every time you conceptualize them all, you have reset the number of slots in the system from n to n^2 and now you would have to consider *their* cross-terms, and so on. Nevertheless, this provides a *generator* for a large space of potentially worthwhile new slots. Some heuristics can guide the system in selecting plausible ones to define, monitoring the utility of each selection, and obliterating any which empirically appear to rarely lead to any significant future solutions or discoveries. An example of such a process is given in Section 9.7.

9.5.3 Discovering a New Heuristic

The AM heuristics create new concepts via specializing existing ones, generalizing (either from existing ones or from newly gathered data), and analogizing. These are the three directions new heuristics will come from. We have exemplified specialization already. One point about generalization is worth

Table 9-9: Frame-like representation for a heuristic rule from AM. The rule is composed of nothing but attribute:value pairs. After each attribute or slot (often heavily hyphenated) is a colon, and then a list of the entries or values for that attribute of the Generalize-rare-predicate heuristic.

NAME: Generalize-rare-predicate
ABBREVIATION: GRP
STATEMENT
    English: If a predicate is rarely true, Then create generalizations of it
    IF-potentially-relevant
    IF-just-finished-a-task-dealing-with: a predicate P
    IF-about-to-work-on-task-dealing-with: an agenda A
    IF-in-the-middle-of-a-task-dealing-with: *never*
    IF-truly-relevant: P returns True less than 5% of Average Predicate
    IF-resources-available: at least 10 CPU seconds, at least 300 cells
    THEN-add-task-to-agenda: Fill in entries for Generalizations slot of P
    THEN-conjecture: P is less interesting than expected
        Generalizations of P may be better than P
        Specializations of P may be very bad
    THEN-modify-slots: Reduce Worth of P by 10%
        Reduce Worth of Specializations(P) by 50%
        Increase Worth of Generalizations(P) by 20%
    THEN-print-to-user: English(GRP) with "a predicate" replaced by P
    THEN-define-new-concepts:
CODED-IF-PART: λ(P) ... <LISP function conjoining all the IF- parts>
CODED-THEN-PART:λ(P) ... <LISP function appending all the THEN- parts>
CODED-IF-THEN-PARTS:λ(P) ... <LISP function combining the previous 2 slots>
COMPILED-CODED-IF-THEN-PARTS: #30875
SPECIALIZATIONS: Generalize-rare-set-predicate
    Boundary-Specializations: Enlarge-domain-of-predicate
GENERALIZATIONS: Modify-predicate, Generalize-concept
    Immediate-Generalizations: Generalize-rare-contingent-piece-of-knowledge
    Siblings: Generalize-rare-heuristic
IS-A: Heuristic
EXAMPLES:
    Good-Examples: Generalize Set-Equality into Same-Length
    Bad-Examples: Generalize Set-Equality into Same-First-Element
CONJECTURES: Special cases of this are more powerful than Generalizations
    Good-Conjec-Units: Specialize, Generalize
ANALOGIES: Weaken-overconstrained-problem
WORTH: 600
VIEW: Enlarge-structure
ORIGIN: Specialization of Modify-predicate via empirical induction
    Defined-using: Specialize
    Creation-date: 6/1/78 11:30
HISTORY:

N-Good-Examples: 1	N-Bad-Examples: 1
N-Good-Conjectures: 3	N-Bad-Conjectures: 1
N-Good-Tasks-Added: 2	N-Bad-Tasks-Added: 0
Avg-Cpu-Time: 9.4 seconds	Avg-List-Cells: 200

making: heuristics which serve as plausible move generators originated by generalizing from past successes; those heuristics which prune away implausible moves originate by generalizing from past failures. Since successes are much less common than failures, it is not surprising that most heuristics in most heuristic search programs are of the pruning variety. In fact, many authors define heuristic to mean nothing more than a pruning aid.

One of the typical "common sense number theory" heuristics which AM lacked was the one which decides that the unique factorization theorem is probably more significant than Goldbach's conjecture, because the first has to do with multiplication and division, while the latter deals with addition and subtraction, and "Primes" is inherently tied up with the former operations. How could such a heuristic be discovered automatically? This is the starting point for the example we will now begin, an example which concludes in the following section, "Heuristics Used to Develop New Representations". Why should this be so? What exactly does discovering heuristics have to do with representing knowledge?

The connection between heuristics and representation is profound. Consider even the special case where we restrict our representations to frame-like ones. The larger the number of different kinds of slots that are known about, the fewer keystrokes are required to type a given frame (concept, unit) into the system. Thus, if "N-Good-Conjecs" were not known, it might take forty keystrokes rather than one to assert that there were three good conjectures known involving prime numbers. Moreover, no special-purpose machinery to process such an assertion would be known to the system. The larger your vocabulary, the shorter your messages can be.

This is akin to the power INTERLISP derives from the thickness of its manual, from the huge number of useful predefined functions. A broad vocabulary streamlines communication. Not only does a profusion of slot types facilitate entering (typing in) a concept, it makes it easier to modify it once it is entered. This is because *(i)* fewer keystrokes are needed in toto, and *(ii)* the possible kinds of things you might need to type in are explicitly presented to you (in a menu). Finally, the profusion of slots makes it easier to discover new heuristics, because *(i)* it is a process of combining terms in a more powerful, higher level language, and *(ii)* specialized knowledge may exist, rules which refer to particular slots of heuristics, telling when and how the combination process should be done.

So we see that the task of discovering heuristics can be profoundly accelerated, or retarded, by the choice of slots we make for our representation. In the case of an excellent choice of slots, a new heuristic is often simply a new entry on one slot of some concept. Let's see how that can be. Recall that primes were originally discovered by the system as extrema of the function "Divisors-of". This was recorded by placing the entry "Divisors-of" in the slot called "Defined-using" on the concept called "Primes" (see Table 9-3). Later, conjectures involving "Primes" were found, empirically-observed patterns connecting "Primes" with several other concepts, such as "Times", "Divisors-of", "Exponentiation", and "Numbers-with-3-divisors". This is recorded on the "Good-Conjec-Units" slot of the "Primes" concept. Notice that all the entries on the "Defined-Using" slot of "Primes" are also entries on its "Good-Conjec-Units" slot. This recurred several times, that is for several concepts besides "Primes", and ultimately the heuristic H9 (below) became relevant (its "If-" part became satisfied):

H9: IF (for many units u) all of the entries on the r slot are also present on the s slot,
THEN-ASSERT that (with justification H9) r is always going to be a subslot of s.

This heuristic said that it would probably be productive to pretend that "Defined-Using" was always a subslot of "Good-Conjec-Units". One slot is a subslot of another if any legal entry for the former is presumed to be a legal entry for the latter as well. Thus, "Extreme-Examples" is a subslot of "Examples", since any extreme example of a concept u is certainly an example of u as well. So H9 applies in the current situation, with r = "Defined-Using" and s = "Good-Conjec-Units". H9 created a new heuristic, whose effect was the following: "As soon as EURISKO defines any new concept X in terms of Y, it should expect there to be some interesting conjectures between X and Y." In our usual "If/Then" format we might express this rule by saying:

H100: "IF a concept is created with a value in its "Defined-Using" slot,
THEN place that value in its "Good-Conjec-Units" slot, with justification H9."

There is already a very general rule in the system, which says to verify suspected members of any slot (members whose justification is questionable). When H100 appears in the system, and is used to add suspected entries to the "Good-Conjec-Units" slots of units, this general rule will cause tasks to appear on the agenda, tasks which try to confirm or deny whether they deserve to be there.

The main point here is that H100 was not synthesized as a long, complicated expression such as shown above. Rather, all EURISKO did was to go to the concept called "Defined-Using" (the data structure which holds all the information the program knows about that kind of slot in general), and record that one of its superslots is "Good-Conjec-Units". In other words, it added one atom to one list. We should also give this an explicit justification, namely H9, since it is a heuristic, not a fact. That required a second trivial action at the LISP level. Table 9-10 shows what this record looks like in our current program. The new heuristic is simply the words which are emboldened there; all the non-bold text was present in the program already (though most of it was written by the program itself at earlier times, not filled in by human hands).

Thanks to the large number of useful specialized slots, large "If/Then" rules can be compactly, conveniently and efficiently represented as simple links. Some of these useful slots are very general, but many are domain dependent.

Thus, as new domains of knowledge emerge and evolve, new kinds of slots must be devised if this powerful property is to be preserved. The next natural question is, therefore, "How can useful new slots be found?" The last two sentences are the final two points of our original five-point program (Table 9-1), and the next section answers them by way of continuing the example we have begun in this section.

Table 9-10: Part of the concept containing centralizing knowledge about all "Defined-Using" slots.

NAME: Archetypical-"Defined-Using"-slot
SPECIALIZATIONS:
    SubSlots: Really-Defined-Using, Could-Have-Defined-Using
GENERALIZATIONS:
    SuperSlots: Origin, Good-Conjec-Units (Justif: H9)
IS-A: Kind of slot
WORTH: 300
ORIGIN: Specialization of Origin
    Defined-using: Specialize
    Creation-date: 9/18/79 15:43
AVERAGE-SIZE: 1
FORMAT: Set
FILLED-WITH: Concepts
CACHE? Always-Cache
MAKES-SENSE-FOR: Concepts

9.6 HEURISTICS USED TO DEVELOP NEW REPRESENTATIONS

The example here shows how new kinds of slots can be discovered and used to advantage. This is just an extension of a given representation, rather than true exploration in "the space of all representations of knowledge". I believe the latter will someday be possible, using nothing more than a body of heuristics for guidance, but we do not yet have enough experience to formulate the necessary rules.

Each kind of representation makes some set of operations efficient, often at the expense of other operations. Thus, an exploded-view diagram of a bicycle makes it easy to see which parts touch each other, sequential verbal instructions make it easy to assemble the bicycle, an axiomatic formulation makes it easy to prove properties about it, and so on.

As a field matures, its goals vary, its paradigm shifts, the questions to investigate change, the heuristics and algorithms to bring to bear on those questions evolve. Therefore, the utility of a given representation is bound to vary both from domain to domain and within a domain from time to time, much as did that of a given corpus of heuristics. The representation of today must adapt or give way to a new one—or the field itself is likely to stagnate and be supplanted.

Where do these new representations come from? The most painless route is to merely select a new one from the stock of existing representational schemes. Choosing an appropriate representation means picking one which lets you quickly carry out the operations you're now going to carry out most frequently.

In case there is no adequate existing representation, you may try to extend one, or devise a whole new one (good luck!), or (most frequently) simply employ *a set* of known ones, whose union makes all the common operations fast. Thus, when I buy a bicycle, I expect both diagrams and printed instructions to be provided. The carrying along of multiple representations simultaneously, and the concomitant need to shift from one to another, has not been much studied, or attempted, in AI to date, except in very tiny worlds (for example, the missionaries and cannibals puzzle).

There are several levels at which "new representations" can be found. At the lowest level, one may say that AM changed its representation every time it defined a new domain concept or predicate, thereby changing its vocabulary out of which new ones could be built.

Much more significant would be the definition of new kinds of slots, typically ones specific to, and very useful for, some newly discovered field of knowledge. For instance, when AM found the unique factorization conjecture, it would have been good if it had defined a new kind of slot, Prime-Factors, that every number could have had. A rule capable of this second-level representation augmentation is the following one:

IF most units in the system have very large *s* slots (many entries therein),
THEN propose a new task: replace *s* by new specializations of *s*.

The vague terms in the rule would have specific computational interpretations, of course; for instance, "very large" might mean "more than ten", "more than three times the average size of all slots", "larger than any other slot", or (most useful from a computational efficiency viewpoint) "larger than the average number of slots a unit has". It might cause the "Examples" slot to be broken into several subslots, such as "Extreme-Examples", "Typical-Examples", "Boundary-Examples", and so on. It might cause "Factors" to be split up into "Prime-Factors", "Large-Factors", and so on. Note that the subslots will not, in general, be disjoint.

The third and final level at which "new representations" can be interpreted is as an actual shift from one entire scheme to another, perhaps novel, one. The following two rules indicate when a certain type of shift is appropriate:

IF the problem is a geometric one,
THEN draw a diagram.

IF most units have most of their possible slots filled in,
THEN shift from property lists to record structures.

All the heuristics of this type are specializations of the general one which says:

IF some operation is performed frequently,
THEN shift to a representation in which it is very inexpensive to perform.

Let us continue our example. Here is a heuristic which is capable of reacting to a situation by defining an entirely new slot, built up from old ones, which it expects will be useful:

H10: IF a slot s is very important, and all its values are units,
THEN-CREATE-NEW-KIND-OF-SLOT containing "all relations among the values of my s slot"

When the number stored in the "Worth" slot of the "Good-Conjec-Units" concept is large enough, the system attends to the task of explicitly studying "Good-Conjec-Units". Several heuristics are relevant and fire; among them is H10, the rule shown above. It then synthesizes a whole new unit, calling it "Relations-Among-Entries-On-My-'Good-Conjec-Units'Slot". Every known way in which entries on the "Good-Conjec-Units" slot of a concept C relate to each other will be recorded on this new slot of C.

For instance, take a look at the "Primes" concept (Table 9-3). Its "Good-Conjec-Units" slot contains the following entries: "Times", "Divisors-of", "Exponentiation", "Squaring" and "Numbers-with-three-divisors". The first two of these entries are inverses of each other; that is, if you look over the Times unit, you will see a slot called Inverse which is filled with names of concepts, including Divisors-of. Similarly, still looking over the Times unit, one can see a slot called Repeat which is filled with the entry Exponentiation, and one can see a slot called Compose filled with Squaring. So Inverse and Repeat and Compose are some of the relations connecting entries on the Good-Conjec-Units slot of Primes, hence the program will record Inverse and Repeat and Compose as three entries on the "Relations-Among-Entries-On-My-'Good-Conjec-Units'Slot" slot of the Primes concept. Note that by a "unit" we mean a concept represented as a full-fledged frame inside the program.

Now it so happens that several concepts wind up with "Compose" and "Inverse" as entries on their "Relations-Among-Entries-On-My-'Good-Conjec-Units'Slot" slot. The alert reader may suspect that this is no accident, and an alert program should suspect that, too. Indeed, the following heuristic says that it might be useful to behave as if "Compose" and "Inverse" were always going to eventually appear there:

H11: IF (for many units u) the s slot of u contains the same values v_i,
THEN-ADD-VALUE v_i to the "Expected-Entries" slot of the "Typical-s-slot" unit.

This causes the program to add "Compose" and "Inverse" to the slot called "Expected-Entries" of the concept called "Relations-Among-Entries-On-My-'Good-Conjec-Units'Slot". This one small act, the creation of a pair of links, is in effect creating a new heuristic which says:

IF a concept gets entries X and Y on its "Good-Conjec-Units" slot,
THEN predict that it will get "Inverse(X)","Inverse(Y)", and "Compose(X,Y)" there as well.

How is this actually used? Consider what occurs when the program defines a new concept C, which is defined using "Divisors-of". As soon as that concept is formed, the heuristic link from "Defined-Using" to "Good-Conjec-Units" automatically fills in "Divisors-of" as an entry on the "Good-Conjec-Units" slot of C. Next, the links just illustrated above come into action, and place "Inverse" and "Compose" on the "Relations-Among-Entries-On-My-'Good-Conjec-Units'Slot" slot of C. That in turn causes the inverse of "Divisors-of", namely "Times", to be placed on the "Good-Conjec-Units" slot as well as the already-present entry, "Divisors-of". Finally, that causes the program to go off looking for conjectures between C and either multiplication or division. When a conjecture comes in connecting C to one of them, it will get a higher initial estimated worth than one which does not connect to them.

If only we'd had the new heuristics back when Primes was first defined, they would have therefore embodied enough "common sense" to prefer the Unique Factorization Theorem to Goldbach's conjecture. If we'd had them earlier, these heuristics would have led us to our present state much sooner. Because of our assumptions about the continuity of the world, such heuristics should still be useful from time to time in the future.

There's nothing special about mathematics; the newly synthesized heuristics have to do with very general slots, like "Defined-Using" and "Good-Conjec-Units". As soon as a new concept (say, "Middle-Class") is defined using "Income", the program immediately fills in this underlined information:

NAME: Middle-Class
Defined-using: Income
Relations-Among-Entries-On-My-"Good-Conjec-Units"Slot: <u>Inverse, Compose</u>
Good-Conjec-Units: <u>Income, Spending, Earned-Interest</u>

Thus, it goes off looking for (and will expect more from) conjectures between "Middle-Class" and any of "Income", "Spending" and "Earned-Interest". Thus, the new slot *is* useful, though it has a terrible name, and the new little heuristics (which looked like little links or facts but were actually permission to make "daring guesses") were powerful after all.

We have relied heavily on our representation being very structured; in a very uniform one (say, a calculus of linear propositions, with the only operations being assert and match) it would be difficult to obtain enough empirical data to easily modify that representation. This is akin to the nature of discovering domain facts and heuristics: if the domain is too simple, it is *harder* to find new knowledge and, in particular, new heuristics. Heuristics for propositional calculus are much fewer and weaker than those available for guiding work in predicate calculus; they in turn pale before the rich variety available for guiding theorem proving "the way mathematicians really do it". This is an argument for attacking seemingly difficult problems which turn out to be lush with structure, rather than working in worlds so constrained that their simplicity has sterilized them of heuristic structure.

9.7 CASE STUDY 3: BIOLOGICAL EVOLUTION; HEURISTICS USED TO GENERATE PLAUSIBLE MUTATIONS

9.7.1 The Overall Hypothesis

This section presents a speculative theory, based upon the metaphor of DNA viewed as a "program" for constructing and maintaining an organism. The field of Automatic Programming studies computer programs, such as AM and EURISKO, which synthesize new and different programs, or which modify and improve themselves. When DNA molecules do this, we call it evolution. Biological research has to date identified several mechanisms which change DNA (substitution, insertion, deletion, translocation, inversion, recombination, segregation, transposition, and so on). Current theories assume the basic process of evolution to be random mutation (using these mechanisms) followed by natural selection, a paradigm of a weak generator and a rigorous test. Early automatic programming systems were also built to work via this same "random generate and test" process. But that mechanism failed, and we now recognize the reasons for that failure and the prescription for success. To whit, the early automatic programming programs lacked expert knowledge, knowledge about programming in general and knowledge about the particular task domain their target programs were to work in. Recent automatic programming programs embodying such knowledge have begun to achieve reasonable performance.

These results lead us to hypothesize, by analogy, that the generation of mutations may be highly non-random, that the dominant process of evolution in higher organisms is by now "plausible generate and test". Long before our three billion line genetic "program" evolved randomly, nature may have happened upon a more powerful method of "automatic programming", such as heuristic search: the accretion and use of knowledge to guide the mutation process.

The early (1958-70) researchers in automatic programming were confident that they could succeed by having programs randomly mutate into desired new ones. This hypothesis was simple, elegant, aesthetic, and incorrect. The amount of time necessary to synthesize or modify a program was seen to increase exponentially with its length. Switching to a higher-level language (the analogue of recombination and gene duplication) merely chipped away somewhat at the exponent, without muffling the combinatorial nature of the process. All the attempts to get programs to "evolve" failed miserably, casualties of the combinatorial explosion.

During the last decade, significant progress has been made in automatic programming, by providing such systems with great quantities of knowledge about programming in general and knowledge about the specific field in which the synthesized programs are supposed to operate. By employing this knowledge to constrain and guide them in their search, programs have finally begun to synthesize large new programs and modify themselves successfully. (See, for example, [Green *et al.*, 1974; Barstow, 1979; Lenat, 1975; Davis & Lenat, 1981].)

A study of the earlier "random mutation" automatic programming work reveals that only after some such knowledge was added were the systems capable of successfully producing new programs or changes of more than a very few lines in length.

The key to the solution (using knowledge to guide the code synthesizer) appears quite simple in hindsight. How is such knowledge to be acquired? In the case of most automatic programming systems, it is provided by human experts. In the case of some programs, including AM, EURISKO, and others described elsewhere in this volume, it is discovered automatically. The necessary machinery for learning from experience is not very complex: accumulate a corpus of empirical data and make simple inductive generalizations from it. The first requires some kind of memory, the second requires some kind of pattern-matching ability. Processes similar to memory and matching are well known to exist already at the molecular level (reliable information storage in nucleic acids, reliable matching of tRNA to mRNA at ribosomes) and at higher levels as well (memory in the brain, pattern matching by the immune system). Certainly the complexity of the two processes required for empirical induction (memory and pattern matching) are orders of magnitude more elementary than, say, the functioning of our immune system or central nervous system.

From this we are led to hypothesize that the generation of mutations may be highly non-random. Instead of "random generate and test", the dominant mechanism of evolution in higher organisms today may be "plausible generate and test".

Suppose one were given five years to build a large computer program to forecast weather, and one knew little about programming *or* meteorology. Then it is clearly cost effective to take a couple years to develop some expertise in both fields. Similarly, while it is *possible* that nature evolved a three billion line program using only recombination, gene duplication, and so on, it might be much more efficient to record and use knowledge: general knowledge about evolving and specific knowledge about the particular species itself and its genetic ancestry. In the past billion years, nature may have happened upon this more powerful method of "automatic programming": building up a body of knowledge to guide the mutation process.

How might this work? Some of the organism's DNA records past states of the genome (the DNA molecule) from earlier generations, and patterns in that record may be noticed and exploited. For example, consider cephalo-pelvic proportion (the relation between an infant's biparietal diameter and its mother's pelvic diameter). If skull size of some species were to increase significantly, the females would have great difficulty giving birth, and the members of the population having such an increase would be selected against. The only exception is when the species' mean pelvic diameter simultaneously and fortuitously increases. Thus, if we could somehow look back over the genetic history of a successful species such as *homo sapiens*, it would appear that increases in skull size are almost always accompanied (or immediately preceded) by increases in pelvic diameter. Once such a pattern is noticed, it can be used to guide future mutation, to encourage specific related groupings of mutations. When an increase in skull size is going to happen (a mutation occurs in the appropriate genes of the DNA in a germ line cell), a simultaneous increase in pelvic diameter should be made. A species would be better off if it could recognize and use such patterns—such heuristics. In this case, the heuristic said "If biparietal diameter is increasing, Then increase the chance of pelvic diameter increasing."

Consider a species capable of storing its genetic history, noticing empirical regularities in it, and using them to guide constellations of interrelated mutations in the future. Its rate of evolution might dwarf that of species which had to rely on fortuitous co-occurrences of random genetic events. Notice there is no inherent "direction" that such plausibility constraints are defining; rather, it is simply a mechanism for avoiding what seems, empirically and historically, to be deleterious, and for seeking what seems empirically to be advantageous. Certainly there is nothing surprising in this; many creatures compile their experiences, in hindsight, into heuristic rules which guide their future behavior. Herein we are suggesting that it may also be true of the DNA molecule itself.

Species whose evolution was guided by heuristics (compiled from the species' genetic history) would be better adapted at evolving. Their rate of evolution would be higher, but, more significantly, the fraction of offspring having a favorable co-occurrence of mutations would be elevated. Their DNA would be longer and largely unexpressed, containing much information which is historical and useful for inferring regularities in evolution but not needed for the maintenance of an adult organism. By also using this historical record for developmental functions, its integrity would be assured over many generations; ontogeny of such creatures would resemble a recapitulation of their phylogeny. The obvious hypothesis that this is leading to is that while evolution *began* as random generation, by now the evolution of most higher animals and plants may be under the guidance of a large corpus of heuristics, judgmental rules abstracting a billion years of experience into prescriptions and (much more rarely) proscriptions regulating and coordinating clusters of simultaneous mutations. Random mutation would still be present, but in higher organisms its effect might be mere background noise.

9.7.2 Lessons from Automatic Programming

We begin by sketching the "DNA as program" analogy. Information in the DNA molecule[1] is essentially in secondary storage analogous to magnetic tapes

[1]Each nucleotide contains two bits of information, since there are four possible bases it could contain. Three nucleotides in a row form an instruction or codon. A codon contains six bits of information, so there are at most 64 possible instructions. The task of the program is to assemble a sequence of amino-acids (a protein), and each codon specifies what the next amino-acid should be, or else says STOP.

or disks; it must be swapped into core, that is, copied from secondary storage into main memory (by mRNA), and brought to a processor (ribosome) to be run. The ribosome translating an mRNA into an amino-acid sequence resembles a Turing machine reading along its input tape and writing out a new one. Feedback closes this loop (for example, via production of repressor proteins) and raises the power of the mechanism to that of a universal Turing machine. The sophistication of the system is best displayed during the development of the fetus, when many delicate changes in gene expression must be coordinated. Only about a tenth of the four million genes in human DNA code for known proteins; the function of the other gene "subroutines" may include regulating pathways: developmental, metabolic, and perhaps (we hypothesize) evolutionary ones.

Early AI researchers quite naively but reasonably assumed that if you wanted to tell a program *what* to do, without telling it precisely *how*, then you would have to employ some kind of random program generator, and follow it up with a test to see if the program was the desired one. As R. M. Friedberg [1958] (then at IBM) said:

> "Environment dictates *what* problems must be dealt with, but not *how* to deal with them... It is difficult to see a way of telling it *what* without telling it *how*, except by allowing it to try out procedures at random or according to some unintelligent system and informing it constantly whether or not it is doing what we wish."

That is, computer scientists' intuitions then were precisely in agreement with biologists' today: the adequacy of random generate and test. Over the last twenty years, several painful research experiences have changed those computer science intuitions; we now sketch a few of them.

The first effort along these lines was Friedberg's [1959]. His program searches through the space of all machine language programs containing 64 instructions. It replaces each instruction in turn, looking for a local maximum of performance, and then repeats this procedure over and over again, a hundred times a second on an IBM704. When the target program was a couple instructions long (for example, adding two 1-bit numbers), it took hundreds of thousands of generations to evolve such a program. When the target program was longer, say five or six lines long, it rarely had appeared even after millions of generations.

But the immense number of generations required was not the biggest surprise. To his shock, Friedberg found no stable islands in the search. Gradual hill-climbing was no better than generating an entire program from scratch each time. He built a system which tried completely new computer programs every "generation", which simply put together a new, random sequence of machine language instructions, ignoring the design of its "parents" completely no matter how close their behavior was to that of the desired target program. This random program generator out-performed his gradual hill-climbing program-evolver every time.

The frequent local maxima upon which a hill-climber gets trapped proved devastating. The only way that Friedberg was ever able to get any successes out of the program-evolver was by building in some heuristic rules to guide its search for new programs:

- Do local optimization of each instruction in turn.
- Partition a problem and deal with its parts in order of difficulty.
- Prime the system by telling it which data bits are the input, and which are the output.
- If a program succeeds, reward all its component instructions; that is, increase the chance of selecting a program with many of the same instructions in the same locations.

One trouble with machine language programs is that they are doubly unstable; a small change in their flowchart may engender an enormous number of changes in which locations in memory contain which instructions; conversely, a small change in the contents of some core locations may dramatically change the function computed by the program. Maybe the right level to work at, then, is that of flowcharts.

Fogel, Walsh and Owens decided in 1966 [Fogel *et al.*, 1966] to attempt something very much like this: their program roamed about in the space of finite state automata, using operations close to those that we would have for mutating flow charts—redirecting arrows, adding nodes, relabeling arcs, and so on. Each generation, his program would select a mechanism of mutation and alter the then-best finite state automaton.

As before, hill-climbing via random mutation seemed too slow, stagnating at local maxima. Incremental approaches to competence didn't seem to be working, yet if Fogel allowed large simultaneous variations, he would have had even worse behavior. He says:

> "The efficiency of pure trial-and-error exploration is sharply reduced with an increase in the dimensionality of the domain being explored. As long as the investigator is interested only in a single aspect of his environment, random exploration may prove worthwhile, but as soon as he attempts to map a domain of more practical interest he encounters so many possibilities that only *carefully-guided* trial-and-error exploration is likely to prove profitable... In man's initial exploration of the unknown, the scientific method would have been a luxury; however, with the increased scope and depth of his inquiry, use of the scientific method becomes an absolute necessity."

What, then, is the solution being proposed? Flowchart modifying should be guided by knowledge: knowledge about how to design and carry out telling experiments rather than random modifications, and knowledge about whatever task domain the synthesized program is supposed to perform in.

Consider the case of writing a program to test a number for primality.

One general piece of programming knowledge is that a program should begin with some initializations, enter a computational loop, and ultimately return some value. Any flowchart not having that structure can be immediately eliminated from consideration. A general piece of knowledge looks at the definition of prime numbers, sees that it specifies "... whose only divisors are 1 and n", and recognizes this as a constraint on the flowchart: the central loop should terminate early with a "not-prime" answer sometimes, and if the loop runs to completion then the answer should be "is-prime". A specific domain-dependent piece of knowledge is that there are many primes and many non-primes, so any flowchart which always returns 'Yes' (or always returns 'No', as one of Fogel's automata did) is bound to be wrong. Without such knowledge, it is hard to get off the local maximum that says "Always return 'No' to the question of n being prime". By employing a collection of such pieces of knowledge, the space of allowable flowcharts shrinks dramatically in size. The chances of finding a successful flowchart are raised dramatically.

Arthur Samuel, working at about the same time as Fogel, wrote his famous checker-playing program [Samuel, 1967]. It was designed to get better and better over time, by gradually improving its scoring polynomial (a function that evaluated the overall worth of a checkerboard position from, say, Red's point of view). Samuel found it important to add several heuristics to guide the mutation of his scoring polynomial, including: recall your earlier predictions, and rate them in hindsight; artificially lower the coefficients of new terms to forestall wild initial fluctuations; count a recent fluctuation more heavily than an old one; and it is worth risking introducing a *few* of the 38x38 cross-terms at any one time.

My own research in automatic programming recapitulated much the same error. I began in 1972 with a program called PW1 [Green *et al.*, 1974], which had a few templates or schemata for recursive LISP functions, and which had a set of 10-20 functions it could plug in for each function mentioned in the schema. One of the templates was:

```
F(x) =df [ λ (x)  IF f1(x)=b1
                  THEN f2(x)
                  ELSE f5( f3(First-element-of(x)), f4(All-but-1st-element-of(x)) ) ]
```

The program picked a random instantiation and mutated it until its input/output behavior agreed with the example input/output pairs which comprised the specification of the desired program. For instance, suppose the desired target program was one which found the smallest element of a list of numbers x. The user would type in a few input/output pairs as examples, such as:

```
Input  (1 3 5 0 8),          Output  0
Input  (9 8 7 6),            Output  6
Input  (1 3 5 7),            Output  1
```

PW1 randomly chose functions to substitute for f1, f2, and so on, until it found an F whose input/output behavior agreed with all the examples.

The simple function schema above can be instantiated in many ways, to yield definitions of "Largest-element-of", "Smallest-element-of", "Length",

"Has-odd-length", "Reverse", "Contains-repeated-elements", "Sort", and (unfortunately) millions of others. The first attempts had to be halted after hours of computer time had been extended fruitlessly seeking a valid definition of "Smallest-element".

My first intuition was to fix this by having the definition gradually evolve. To this end, several mutated versions were created simultaneously by the system, and the one which had input/output results most closely matching the user-provided examples was chosen as the survivor in the next generation. To my surprise at the time, this was not noticeably better than the original, completely random generation scheme.

PW1 did eventually synthesize several short target programs, but only after I adopted the method of supplying it with some frequency hints (for example, "first-element" is the most likely function to try for f1 in the schema), some applicability constraints, and a few simple ways in which to look directly at the input/output pairs in constraining which functions to try (for example, if the outputs are always members of the input lists, then f5 must be a function whose output is always one of its inputs).

Recently, impressive synthesized programs have been produced from the PSI system [Barstow, 1979] of Cordell Green *et al.* Their automatic programming system is guided by hundreds of rules about programming in general and about the task domain of the target program (the one being synthesized) in particular. PSI draws much of its power from a high-level abstract model of what environment it is in (including what the user wants), what it has done in the past, and so on.

All our experiences in AI research have led us to believe that for automatic programming, the answer lies in *knowledge*, in adding a collection of expert rules which will guide code synthesis and transformation. Each rule is a kind of compiled search, a bit of condensed hindsight. While far from complete or foolproof, they are far superior to blind changes in program instructions (Friedberg) or flowcharts (Fogel) or even mutation of duplicated program chunks (Lenat).

9.7.3 Idea #1: Add Heuristics to DNA

Finally, we are ready to turn to the biological analogue of this idea. Just as automatic programming taught us to guide program synthesis and transformation by heuristic rules, so it might be cost-effective for evolution of higher organisms to be guided by heuristic rules.

Consider extending the "DNA as program" analogy by somehow adding knowledge to the DNA, knowledge about which kinds of mutations are plausible, which kinds have been tried unsuccessfully, what combinations have and have not performed well in the past, and so on. If there is a way to encode such knowledge, such heuristic guidance rules, then we might expect that an organism with that kind of compiled hindsight would evolve in a much more regular, rapid fashion. The "test" would still be natural selection, but instead of blind generation, the DNA would be conducting (and recording) plausible experiments.

What would such heuristics look like? That is, how might they be "implemented" in the DNA program? Almost surely they would be written in the alphabet of bases, but their interpretation might not be as codons for proteins (in which case their expression would have to be suppressed). At times of reproduction, however, they would specify allowable (and prevent other) changes to be made in the new copy of the DNA molecule. That is, heuristics would sanction certain complex copying "errors" (for example, statically by inserting noncoding sequences, or dynamically by interfering with the repair polymerases) and prevent others (for example, via site-specific repair enzymes).

The "If-" parts of such heuristics could be almost completely specified by position (proximity to genes to which the heuristic wishes to refer), and the start of such a heuristic would have to be signalled by some special sequence of bases (much like parentheses in LISP). Each heuristic could have some demarcated domain or scope. Thus, "use a repressor/anti-repressor mechanism rather than an induction mechanism" might hold true for a patch of DNA which synthesized the organism's most important enzymes, and it would be easy to specify the scope by placement along the genome. So-called mutation "hot-spots" are a unary example of this kind of heuristic; heuristics taking more than one "argument" would of course be much more powerful, just as the site-specific mutators are more powerful than a global increase in the overall mutation rate could ever be.

The "Then-" part of a heuristic could direct gene rearrangement, duplication, placement of mutators and intervening sequences, and so on.

Perhaps more likely would be for each heuristic to code for a very rarely expressed protein. The heuristic could code for (or regulate) an enzyme which reentered the nucleus, "matched" against some number of patterns in the DNA, bound itself to those regions (the "If-" part), and thereby increased the chance of a certain type of mutation occurring at those regions (the "Then-" part). Such an enzyme might be produced in such small quantities, and with such small frequency, that it would be unlikely to be noticed in most cases. Its effects would be felt only if it affected germ line cells, and it might only be expressed in them, and rarely at that. A final possibility is that it would be expressed only during embryogenesis, that each neonate's germ cells' DNA has already been altered, thus determining (to within sexual recombination and random mutation) the spectrum of changes which it might potentially pass along to its offspring.

9.7.4 Idea #2: They May Already Be There

Nature might already have become as good at programming in the last billion years as we have in the last forty. DNA might have *already* evolved from random generate and test into an expert program (expert at mutating itself in plausible coordinated ways, expert at designing improved progeny). Since the heuristics deal with DNA subsequences, and they themselves are also DNA subsequences, they (or at least some of them) might be able to modify, enlarge, improve themselves and each other. That is, by now the heuristics themselves may be developing under the guidance of heuristic rules, which encapsulate a billion years of experience at devising and changing and using heuristics. This is how EURISKO uses a set of heuristics to improve and extend itself.

What I conjecture is that nature (that is, natural selection) began with primitive organisms and a random-mutation scheme for improving them. By this weak method (random generation, followed by stringent testing), the first primitive heuristics accidentally came into being. They immediately overshadowed the less efficient random-mutation mechanism, much as oxidation dominated fermentation once it evolved.

Each heuristic proposes a plausible change (call it D) in the DNA. The progeny which incorporate D (call them P^D) also get a new heuristic indicating that that kind of change has been made and is good. This might be as simple as adding one new noncoding sequence inside that mutated gene. It might be as complex as producing a whole new mutated gene and keeping the old one around as a pseudogene. The progeny P which do not incorporate D get no such heuristic. If P^D is viable, then the new heuristic it contains will have proven to be correct. Incorrect heuristics die out with the organisms that contain them.

Consider a very simple example. Here is a mechanism which embodies the heuristic "If a gene has mutated successfully several times in the recent past, then increase its chance of mutating in the next generation, and conversely." All we need to posit is that somehow a short, noncoding sequence—we'll call it an asterisk—is added to a gene each time it mutates. To see how this would operate, consider human DNA: any genes which have several such asterisks testify that they have been mutated successfully, advantageously, many times in the past; genes with few or no asterisks suggest that modifying them has always led to detrimental changes in the offspring. All we need now do is propose some mechanism (for example, stereochemical) whereby genes with many asterisks are more likely to be mutated, duplicated, and so on, than genes with few or none. Since the asterisks provide no specific benefits to the individual, they will gradually be lost over time, so that when a gene no longer *should* be mutated, its asterisk count will slowly decline over several generations. Whether or not it was ever actually adopted, the power of this simple mechanism is clear.

As the species evolves, so do the heuristics. One big lesson from the AM program was the need for new heuristics to evolve continuously. Otherwise, as animals got more and more sophisticated, they would begin to evolve more and more slowly. Random mutations, or those guided by a fixed set of heuristics, would become less and less frequently beneficial to the complex organism, less frequently able even to form part of a new stable subassembly, as Simon suggests [Simon, 1969].

Using a higher level language like gene duplication, rearrangement, and recombination, instead of sequence mutation, would give only a constant factor of improvement (that is, as if we did automatic programming by random changes in LISP programs instead of in assembly language programs), and this constant must fight against the rapidly decreasing number of organisms born each year as one ascends the evolutionary ladder. Thus we expect a phylogenetic increase in the number of heuristics, the sophistication of those heuristics, and the relative proportion of DNA devoted to heuristics.

Heuristics condense past history into judgmental rules. They are kernels of knowledge which, if only they had been present earlier, would have gotten us to our present state much faster. A heuristic prescribes some action which is appropriate in a given kind of situation, or proscribes one which is dangerously inappropriate. They are useful because the world is continuous: if several features of the current situation are similar to some earlier one, then the set of actions which are, and are not, appropriate will probably also be similar. Thus it is cost-effective to compile experiences into heuristics, and to then use the heuristics for guidance. Even if the environment is rapidly changing, some useful heuristics may be extractable, so long as there are some regularities to those environmental changes. Physics equations are no less useful just because the world is constantly changing; if anything, they are *more* useful than they would be in a static world where abstraction would be a luxury. So it is with bioheuristics for evolution: by embodying a deep enough model of the past, the heuristics can cope with a diversity of future problems.

Until the EURISKO program was conceived, this would have been the end of the story. We would guess that new heuristics evolve randomly, and in the rare cases that they are improvements, they get perpetuated by the progeny which have them. Thanks to EURISKO, we see that since the heuristics are represented just like any other DNA, they can work on themselves as well: they can suggest plausible (and/or warn of classes of implausible) changes to make in both *(i)* the DNA which synthesizes proteins, and *(ii)* the DNA which serves as heuristics.

There is a rapidly growing body of evidence of the ways in which DNA sequences are found to guide the evolution of DNA sequences. For instance, recombination among introns modulates the evolution of a gene. Let's look at an example of this: it is extremely important to keep the a, b, and d globin genes separate, but their internal structure is very similar. To inhibit recombination, the spacers between them can be made very different, and the introns within them can diverge dramatically (since mutations in introns are not as deleterious to the functioning of the gene as mutations to the coding regions). In fact, there is evidence that both of these kinds of divergence do occur for the globins.

Heuristics might be present at several levels. At the molecular level, rules such as the following ones might be useful, and presently implemented:

1. If similar genes must be kept distinct,
   THEN use very distinct spacers between them to inhibit recombination.

2. If similar genes must be kept distinct,
   THEN insert many introns in them and let the introns mutate greatly.

3. If the amount of a gene is to be variable,
   THEN tandemly repeat it, thereby enabling unequal sister chromatic exchange.

4. If a gene is to be tandemly repeated, for the very first time,
   THEN duplicate a larger region via looping out, and then insert the loop (*a la* Schimke).

5. If the overall rate of mutation is to be raised (or lowered) significantly,
   THEN slightly increase the rate of (anti)mutator mutations, e.g. as m in T4.

6. If two genes are related functionally in development, i.e., expressed cotemporally,
   THEN locate them near each other on the genome.

7. If two genes should be located near each other but for some reason can not be moved,
   THEN produce a repressor or activator gene to effect them both.

8. If a gene should be made (non)constitutive,
   THEN move a transposable element in and then out, leaving a promoter (repressor) behind.

Some comments are in order: Heuristic 4 is a rephrasing of one of Schimke's ideas [Schimke, 1980]. Heuristic 6 would override the natural tendency for genes which arose evolutionarily at the same time to be near each other on the genome. Heuristic 8 refers to the residue of 200-500 b.p. LTR which were at the end of a transposable element, but were left behind when it moved. Each residue functions as a promoter or a repressor (depending upon the polarity of the transposable element when it was adjacent to the gene). The sequence of such residues provides another kind of "history" data upon which simple patterns may be induced.

Higher level heuristics may also be present. In fact, a quite sophisticated model of the world might be built up by now, purely by the DNA making guesses, designing progeny consonant with those guesses, and letting natural selection rule out those based on false assumptions. Let's take an example. There may be a body of heuristics related to an abstract entity S, which you and I know as snow, perhaps more precisely as glaciation, and a concept H, which we might take to mean heat, or perhaps body heat.

9. If there is more S in the world, then improve mechanisms to conserve H.

10. If H is to be dissipated, then evaporation is a good way to do it.

11. If a quantity must be conserved, then cut down on mechanisms which squander it.

12. If it is desired to cut down on a mechanism, then reduce features which facilitate it.

13. If it is desired to facilitate evaporation, then increase body parts having large surface areas.

14. If you want to conserve H, then increase sleep and dormancy.

15. If you increase sleep and dormancy, then you also increase passive vulnerability.

16. If you want to decrease passive vulnerability, then increase body armor.

17. If you want to decrease passive vulnerability, then increase perception skills.

18. If you want to conserve H, then increase subcutaneous fatty layer.

19. If there is more S in the world, then whitening of body parts is good.

20. If there is more S in the world, then glucose level is threatened.

21. If locomotive muscles are increased, then glucose level may rise.

22. If teeth and claws are sharpened and increased, then glucose level may rise.

23. If neck is lengthened, then glucose level may rise.

24. If neck is lengthened, then passive vulnerability may decrease.

25. If predators are declining, then increase passive vulnerability.

... and so on.

Even though most of the terms used in the heuristics are incomprehensible to the DNA itself, it might nevertheless use these rules, carry out inference upon them, and come up with a better-designed animal. The EURISKO-simulated animal became (in a single generation) smaller, whiter, lighter-boned, had bigger and sharper teeth, larger jaw muscles, larger leg muscles, increased brain size, slept more, sought safer burrows, had thicker and stiffer fur, an added layer of subcutaneous fat, smaller ears, and one of a set of possible mechanisms to metabolize lactic acid more effectively. The changes along any one parameter might be tiny, but *(i)* they would all complement each other, some even compensating for imbalances introduced by others, and *(ii)* the total of all these changes might be a significant change in the ability of the organism to withstand colder environments.

If the rules were sophisticated enough, the modifications might not be "hard-wired" in, but rather *canalized* to let the actual environment tune the degree to which they took effect.

The offspring differs in perhaps thousands of small ways—a constellation of related changes that mesh with each other, that accomplish some goals. These are not the teleological goals of creationists—goals which were somehow placed in DNA long ago; rather, they are short-term goals proposed by the DNA itself, on the basis of its knowledge about evolution, the structure of the environment, and possibly some feedback on the changes occurring in that environment.

We are not supposing that there is any *direct* sensing of temperature, snow, humidity, predators, and so on, by the DNA. Rather, the heuristics guide the production of, say, two types of progeny: the first are slightly more cold adapted, and the second more heat adapted. The first has an assertion that the climate is getting snowier, the second that the climate is getting more tropical. Initially, they are produced in equal numbers. If one group dominates, then its assertion about the climate is probably the correct one. After a few generations, if the deme is indeed entering a glacial age, the offspring will become skewed (in almost every single litter) toward more and more cold-adaptedness. Each of these offspring will in turn add an extra "very" to the genetic hypothesis that it is growing very, very, ..., very cold out.

A sophisticated model of the physical environment may have been accreted over many generations, many individuals, and many variables. By now a large knowledge base may exist about ecology, geology, glaciation, seasons, gravity, predation, symbiosis, causality, conservation, behavior, evolution and knowledge itself. In a small number of generations, man has managed to invalidate many of these bits of knowledge, this model of the world. If the heuristics can trace this breakdown to the increasing size of our brains, they might take quick corrective action, preserving homeostasis and the validity of their knowledge base by drastically decreasing human brain size over just a few generations. While this is of course a fanciful tongue-in-cheek extreme case, it (and the longer example above) demonstrates the power, the coordination, that a body of heuristics could evince if it were guiding the process of evolution.

The nouns in the above rules (for example, "fatty layer") would point to gene complexes responsible for morphological structure (such as, enzymes that determine the thickness of the fatty layer) without comprehending *why* they had such an effect. Of course the DNA molecule would not "understand" what a predator was, or what fat was, or what snow was, but it would have a large corpus of facts about each of those mysterious (to it) concepts, related changes to make, frequency of their occurring, and so on. But then again, what more do we as AI researchers mean when we say that one of our programs "understands" a concept?

9.7.5 Idea #3: Heuristics Drive—And Are Preserved By—Embryogenesis

Joshua Lederberg raised the following difficulty with our ideas as presented so far: even if heuristics *would* be induced, why aren't they lost rather quickly? After all, in a few generations, some small error is bound to creep in, and would probably garble the heuristic. Yet the individual would not be any less fit, only the rate of evolution of the progeny would suffer, hence he would pass this defect along. By now, for example, we might expect that most of the traces of how *homo sapiens* evolved would have been obliterated from our DNA, even if they had been originally stored there.

The solution to this dilemma may be to overlay *(i)* the DNA corresponding to the heuristics with *(ii)* some parts of the genome that are required for the survival of the individual organism. For example, the parts of a gene currently separated by introns may each be meaningful "fossils" of older, smaller genes (see point 4 in the next section).

An alternate way of overlaying heuristics with something indispensable would be for the heuristics to form (part of) the developmental program of the individual; if an important heuristic is lost, then the embryo may not develop viably. This accounts for the old saw "Ontogeny recapitulates Phylogeny".

Thirteen years ago Herbert Simon said that DNA was a recipe for producing an organism, not a blueprint; that human embryogenesis was the following of a program, not a diagram of a finished product. We are adding that this program is a production system and that it is built out of heuristic rules, such as, "If an organism's body shape is *X*, then a tail should be added for stability." Another rule firing later triggers the elimination of the tail, when it is no longer needed. This is a symbiotic relationship: the heuristics enable embryogenesis to take place without some horrendously complicated central control, and in return they become indispensable.

In general, the rules will be ordered by the time they evolved, earliest ones first. Sometimes, as we who work with production systems know, a later rule will fire a bit early, and may change the world in such a way that some of the intermediate rules will never be relevant; that is, several intermediate steps may get skipped from time to time. The discrepancies between ontogeny and phylogeny include this type, and other, more subtle ones [Gould, 1977].

The linkage between development genes and evolution heuristics need not be so crude. It may be the sequence of gene expressions, the control pathways, that are the ancient records, rather than the genes themselves. These pathways may remain more stable than the gene sequences themselves, which more rapidly evolve to suit their new environment. If this were true, the genes controlling the expression of other genes would also in effect control the evolution of those other genes.

9.7.6 Biological Phenomena Accounted For

The central hypothesis of Section 9.7 of this chapter has been that heuristics may somehow already be guiding evolution of higher organisms. Specific mechanisms for effecting this process have intentionally been omitted; a few vague possibilities have been hinted at. Nevertheless, several biological phenomena can be accounted for using this hypothesis; they are briefly listed here. Certainly one can hypothesize some alternate explanations of every one of them; definitive experiments must be designed and carried out to test the theory.

1. The rapid evolution of very complex organisms, organs, behavior patterns, and so on. Controversy over the adequacy of the current stock of mutation mechanisms is still raging [Duncan & Weston-Smith, 1977].

2. The rate of evolution is not slower for complex organisms than for simpler ones. Not only is the absolute amount of time it took to evolve, say, the human eye surprisingly brief, but the rate at which complex creatures evolve seems to be, if anything, *higher* than the rate at which simple ones do. Random generation processes are usually characterized by local maxima, by slowing down of the rate of improvement as the complexity of the product increases. By contrast, heuristic search procedures speed up as more and more heuristics are added.
3. The nonuniformities in the rate of evolution. Consistency, constancy, regularity are attributes of stochastic processes. Uniformity is demanded by unguided randomness, not by intelligent heuristic search. For example, some proteins evolve at rates ten times as slow as others, yet the rate of evolution is almost constant for proteins within certain classes. As Wilson *et al.* say: "It has been hard to understand why the rate is steady within a given class. As explanations involving natural selection did not seem satisfactory, some workers proposed a non-Darwinian explanation... of the evolutionary clock..." [Wilson *et al.*, 1977] Heuristic learning programs like AM and EURISKO generally do *not* exhibit smooth, gradual progress, but rather more the nonuniform kinds of behaviors cited above.
4. The biological function of much of the unexpressed DNA in higher organisms. Some of this may be used to store the records of the species' genetic evolution; some may be used to store condensations or abstractions of that history, for example, in the form of very rarely expressed sequences which produce enzymes that selectively mutate the genome.
5. The fraction of non-coding DNA increases phylogenetically. We expect that the percentage of DNA which codes for heuristics rather than for proteins would increase with the complexity and sophistication of the organism. Man should have more heuristics than chickens, which should have more than *E. coli*. This is not because we're "better", but just because our DNA program is longer and more involved. If our ability to adapt is to be anywhere near as good as bacteria's, we must compensate for our unwieldy program size and long generation time by employing powerful judgmental rules, heuristics which put each generation to maximum use.
6. The C-value problem (some very close species differ by a factor of 20 in their amounts of DNA). This phenomenon has already been evinced by EURISKO. What happens is that one of the new heuristics is bad, and it generates large quantities of new genetic material (in EURISKO's case, bad new concepts and heuristics) before it is recognized as bad (by other heuristics) and turned off. In EURISKO, one such heuristic was, "It is worth composing every pair of operations now known, to form new operations, some of which might be very powerful." This initiated an exponential explosion in the number of operations defined in each successive

generation. In nature, this would mean that the length of the genome might increase very rapidly over a small number of generations, with no apparent benefit to the individuals or the species. When the bad heuristic is deactivated, the increase halts, but it may not be easy to track down all the useless by-products produced by that heuristic. Slowly, over much, much longer time scales, the extraneous material may be excised in the usual garbage-collection manner, through accidental deletions which turn out to be viable.

7. The large morphological advances of some species (like man) compared with others (like chimps, frogs, and cockroaches), even though at the DNA sequence level they both advanced an equal number of base mutations. As Wilson, Carlson and White [1977] note, the speed at which an organism morphologically evolves seems totally unrelated to the rate at which his individual proteins evolve: "In spite of having evolved at an unusually high organismal rate, the human lineage does not appear to have undergone accelerated sequence evolution... This result raises doubts about the relevance of sequence evolution to the evolution of organisms." Our theory accounts for this by simply noting that heuristic search is powerful, and its efficacy is directly related to the number and quality of the heuristics available. Programs with more heuristics can (often) get more done in N CPU cycles (witness the recent successes of expert systems; see [Feigenbaum, 1977]). The rate of evolution should depend more upon the number and quality of heuristics than upon the raw number of changes in the DNA molecule which occur. That is, a huge program can be improved more by adding a few good heuristics than by allotting a few more CPU cycles.
8. The molecular basis for ontogeny recapitulating phylogeny. Insect larvae resemble adult forms of lower articulate animals more than they resemble their own parents; embryonic jellyfish look more like polyps than like adult jellyfish; as they develop, human embryos resemble microorganisms, fish, reptiles, and finally earlier mammals [Gould, 1977]. Our explanation is that during embryogenesis, the fetus develops not via an algorithm (an explicit, fixed procedure), but via an extremely efficient set of heuristics for guidance, heuristics which implicitly encode the blueprint for the final neonate. One of them might say, "If you see the organism in state x, then gills are a good improvement." Another might fire much later, after several other developments have been made: "If the organism is in state y, then gills are no longer needed." We are therefore postulating that the DNA contains not a blueprint for the finished product, but rather a description (compiled into heuristics) of the changes that were made over the eons in the DNA, changes which led to the evolution of our species. Hence evolution and development are related processes (being guided by heuristic rules) operating over very different time scales. As the organism develops, the heuristics get relatively weaker and weaker, the rate of morphological change declines to a point where it is called something else (development

into adulthood), then to a point where it is not even noticed (adulthood), and finally perhaps is interpreted as senescence. Note we predict that an individual's DNA will change slowly but continuously over its lifetime, and that the mean rate of such changes should increase phylogenetically.

9. So-called parallel evolution. Before speciation, a body of more or less general heuristics has evolved. After the species divide, they may differ physiologically yet share the same heuristics. Thus their future morphological evolution may seem surprisingly parallel. Parallel evolution is no doubt due to several species being forced to cope with the same gross environmental change; having some common heuristics increases the likelihood of their finding the same solution.
10. The ABC result (mutation rate per gram of DNA is not constant, but rather is proportional to the lengths of the DNA molecules making up the sample) [Abrahamson *et al.*, 1973]. Our explanation here is simply that mutations are mediated by the heuristics, whose relative number increases (roughly) in proportion to DNA length. One random change in a part of the DNA which is a heuristic can be expected to have a more dramatic influence than a random mutation somewhere in a coding region.

The foremost problem, of course, is cracking the "heuristic code". What is the mechanism of the heuristics' functioning? Faith in unity and simplicity can both guide our investigations and buoy our spirits with the hope that the answer is not a convoluted one. Perhaps one can look at the changes when a heuristic is transferred to various organisms, and induce what it says. How close are the analogues between programming and genetics? If the heuristics truly are "If/Then" type rules, what is the interpreter?

Even if it turns out that nature has not yet hit upon the mechanism of heuristic search, there is still idea #1: design heuristics for plausible and implausible mutations, for record-keeping, for dealing with other heuristics: synthesizing, modifying and evaluating them. They will have to be non-coding sequences; there will have to be an interpretation mechanism for obeying them at reproduction time. Using extant techniques (for example, plasmids), one could synthesize such sequences and insert them into DNA and study the results, thereby improving the entire process of evolution.

9.8 CONCLUSIONS

We began by noting that the limiting step in the construction of expert systems was building the knowledge base, and that one solution would be for the program itself to automatically acquire new knowledge, to learn via discovery.

The heuristic search paradigm seems adequate to guide a program in formulating useful new concepts, gathering data about them, and noticing relationships connecting them. However, as the body of domain-specific facts grows, the old set of heuristics becomes less and less relevant, less and less capable of guiding the discovery process effectively. New heuristics must also be discovered.

Since heuristics is a domain of knowledge much like any other, one can imagine an expert system that works in *that* field. That is, a corpus of heuristics can grow and improve and gather data about itself. This process is very slow and explosive, yet it can be greatly facilitated by having "the right representation". In the case of a schematized representation, this means having the right set of slots or attributes, the right set of attached procedures, and so on. We saw how heuristics can lead to the development of useful new kinds of slots, to improved representations of knowledge. It was hypothesized that the same representation we use for attributes and values of object-level concepts could also be used to represent heuristics and even to represent representation. To draw some examples from the RLL system [Lenat & Greiner, 1980]: "Primes" (a set of numbers), "Generalize-Rare-Predicate" (a heuristic), "Generalize-Rare-Heuristic" (a meta-heuristic), and "Is-a" (a representation concept) are all represented adequately as units with slots having values. A single interpreter runs both meta-heuristics and heuristics, and is itself represented as a collection of units. While meta-heuristics *could* be tagged to distinguish them from heuristics, the *utility* of doing so rests on the existence of rules which genuinely treat them differently somehow, and to date such rules have not been encountered.

One of the necessary steps in this research was the explication of at least a rudimentary theory of heuristics, an analysis of their innate source of power, their nature. This turned out to rest upon the continuity of our world; if the situation is very similar, so is the set of (in)appropriate actions to take. Corollaries of this provide the justification for the use of analogy and even for the utility of memory. The central assumption was seen to be just that—an assumption which is often false in small ways, but which is nevertheless a useful fiction to be guided by.

By graphing (in our mind's eye) the power curves of a heuristic (the utility of that heuristic as a function of task being worked on), we were able to see the gains, and dangers, of specializing and generalizing them to get new heuristics. Such curves determine a preferred order for obeying relevant heuristics, and suggest several specific new attributes worth measuring and recording for each heuristic (for example, the sharpness with which it flips from useful to harmful, as one leaves its domain of relevance).

By arranging all the world's heuristics (well, at least all of AM's, and later several more from chess, biological evolution, naval fleet design, device physics, plumbing, game-playing and oil spills) into a hierarchy using the relation "More-General-Than", we were surprised to find that hierarchy very shallow, thereby implying that analogy would be more useful a method of generating new heuristics than would specialization or generalization. By noting that both "Utility" and "Task" have several dimensions, most of this problem went away. By noting that two heuristics can have *many* important relations connecting them, of which "More-General-Than" is just one example, the shallowness "problem" turns into a powerful heuristic: if a new heuristic h is to differ from an old one along some dimension (relation) r, then use analogy to get h if r's graph is shallow, and use generalization/specialization if r's graph is deep. We also discussed some useful slots which heuristics can have, and a method for generating new kinds of slots.

We then examined an application of this methodology to biology; namely, the speculation that DNA has evolved into an expert program, that is, one with heuristics for suggesting which (families of) mutations are plausible and implausible. This process began as neo-Darwinistic "random generate and test", but that process is not a fixed point: evolution itself has evolved by now into a better process, one guided by past experiences, a "plausible generate and test". Since the individual is viable today, his lineage is largely a series of successes; occasionally, often indirectly, knowledge of failures can be present as well. Plausible move suggesters, the bulwark of AM's successful behaviors, are thus more frequent than implausible move pruners. Such bioheuristics depend upon—nay, they *embody*—knowledge of the evolutionary history of the genome. As a species evolves viably, its body of heuristics is gradually altered (by adding new ones and modifying old ones) to capture the additional history, to compile the new hindsight. Most of the "library of heuristics" are kept as unexpressed DNA, though it may be that expression does occur briefly, during development. This both ensures the preservation of the heuristics intact, and causes development to resemble a reenactment of the evolution of the species.

But the analogy extends not merely from AM, but from EURISKO as well. Since bioheuristics are necessarily encoded into the DNA sequence, they can refer to (and operate on) themselves, in addition to referring to the other parts of the DNA (the structural, protein-encoding DNA). While the first heuristics originated fortuitously, the learning of new heuristics is itself by now probably under strict heuristic control. Thus the heuristics gradually grow in such a way as to better and better reflect the structure of the outer environment: the pressures, the common modes of flux, the interrelations between components. The species becomes better and better adapted to evolving in a complex, changing environment. The "plausibility" with which mutations are skewed increases, and this precisely counterbalances the natural deleterious effects of the combinatorial explosion, the exponential growth in the amount of time it takes to improve a program of a given length. In short, the growing "intelligence" of the mutation process is just strong enough to match the *need* for such sophistication. These are radical biological hypotheses, and Section 9.7 has justified them primarily by analogy to the need for heuristics to guide automatic program synthesis. Of course analogy is not proof nor foolproof. The purpose of that section has been to suggest a potentially significant hypothesis for future investigation by biologists.

Before the overall research program outlined in Table 9-1 can be completed, much more must be known about analogy, and more complete theories of heuristics and of representation must exist. Toward that goal we must obtain more empirical results from programs trying to find useful new domain-specific heuristics and representations.

ACKNOWLEDGMENTS

Productive discussions with John Seely Brown, Bruce Buchanan, Bill Clancey, Johan deKleer, Jon Doyle, Russ Greiner, Mark Stefik and Mike Williams have heavily influenced this work. Section 9.3 summarizes the lessons learned from AM, for which I thank Bruce Buchanan, Ed Feigenbaum, Cordell Green, Don Knuth and Allen Newell. The data for Section 9.4's "shallowness" conclusion about the tree of heuristics was gathered while I was at CMU, with the aid of Herb Simon and Woody Bledsoe. Much of Sections 9.5 and 9.6 rely upon RLL, a self-describing and self-modifying representation language constructed by Russ Greiner, Greg Harris, and the author. The biological speculation presented in Section 9.7 has been honed during discussions with Danny Bobrow, John Seely-Brown, Doug Brutlag, L. Cavalli-Sforza, Lindley Darden, Randy Davis, Ed Feigenbaum, Peter Friedland, Rick Hayes-Roth, Horace Judson, Larry Kedes, Joshua Lederberg, Mark Stefik, Doug Wallace, Mike Williams and David Zipser. This does not, however, imply their approval or acceptance of the hypothesis. Encouragement to integrate these various themes was provided by Jaime Carbonell, Richard Michalski and Tom Mitchell. Finally, I wish to thank Xerox PARC's CIS and Stanford's HPP for providing superb environments (intellectual, physical and computational) in which to work. Financial support was provided by ONR (N00014-80-C-0609) and Xerox.

REFERENCES

Abrahamson, S., Bender, M. A., Conger, A. D. and Wolff, S., "Uniformity of radiation-induced mutation rates among different species," *Nature*, pp. 460-462, October 1973.

Barstow, D., *Knowledge Based Program Construction*, Elsevier, 1979.

Brown, J. S. and VanLehn, K., "Repair theory: A generative theory of bugs in procedural skills," *Journal of Cognitive Science*, Vol. 4, No. 4, 1980.

Davis, R., "Applications of meta level knowledge to the construction and use of large knowledge bases," *Knowledge-Based Systems in Artificial Intelligence*, Davis, R. and Lenat, D. (Eds.), McGraw-Hill Book Company, New York, NY, 1981.

Davis, R. and Lenat, D. B., *Knowledge Based Systems in Artificial Intelligence*, McGraw Hill, New York, 1981.

Duncan, R. and Weston-Smith, M. (eds.), *The Encyclopedia of Ignorance: Everything you ever wanted to know about the unknown*, Pergamon Press, New York, 1977, (pages 205-411).

Feigenbaum, E. A., "The Art of Artificial Intelligence," *IJCAI5*, MIT, IJCAI, Cambridge, 1977.

Fogel, L., Owens, A., and Walsh, M., *Artificial Intelligence Through Simulated Evolution*, John Wiley and Sons, Inc., New York, 1966.

Friedberg, R. M., "A Learning Machine: Part I," *IBM Journal of Research and Development*, Vol. 2, No. 1, January 1958.

Friedberg, R. M., "A Learning Machine: Part II," *IBM Journal of Research and Development*, Vol. 3, No. 3, July 1959.

Gould, S. J., *Ontogeny and Phylogeny*, Belknap Press, Harvard University, Cambridge, 1977.

Green, C., Waldinger R., Barstow, D., Elschlager, R., Lenat, D., McCune, B., Shaw, D., and Steinberg, L., "Progress Report on Program-Understanding Systems", Technical Report AIM-240, STAN-CS-74-444, Stanford, 1974.

Lenat, D. B., "BEINGS: Knowledge as Interacting Experts," *IJCAI4*, IJCAI, Tbilisi, USSR, 1975.

Lenat, D. B., and Greiner, R. D., "RLL: A Representation Language Language," *Proceedings of the First Annual Meeting of the American Association for Artificial Intelligence*, Stanford, August 1980.

McCarthy, J. and Hayes, P. J., "Some Philosophical Problems from Artificial Intelligence," *Machine Intelligence 6*, B. Meltzer and D. Michie (Eds.), Edinburgh University Press, 1969.

Newell, A., and Simon, H. A., "Computer Science as Empirical Inquiry: Symbols and Search," *CACM*, Vol. 19, No. 3, March 1976.

Polya, G., *How to Solve It*, Princeton University Press, 1945.

Samuel, A., "Some Studies in Machine Learning in the Game of Checkers II," *IBM Journal of Research and Development*, Vol. 11, No. 6, November 1967.

Schimke, R. T., "Gene Amplification and Drug Resistance," *Scientific American*, Vol. 243, No. 5, November 1980.

Simon, H. A., *The Science of the Artificial*, MIT Press, 1969.

Wilson, A. C., Carlson, S. S., and White, T. J., "Biochemical Evolution," *Am. Rev. Biochem.*, No. 46, pp. 573-639, 1977.

10

REDISCOVERING CHEMISTRY WITH THE BACON SYSTEM

Pat Langley
Gary L. Bradshaw
Herbert A. Simon
Carnegie-Mellon University

ABSTRACT

BACON.4 is a production system that discovers empirical laws. The program represents information at varying levels of description, with higher levels summarizing the levels below them. BACON.4 employs a small set of data-driven heuristics to detect regularities in numeric and nominal data. These heuristics note constancies and trends, causing BACON.4 to formulate hypotheses, to define theoretical terms, and to postulate intrinsic properties. The introduction of intrinsic properties plays an important role in BACON.4's rediscovery of Ohm's law for electric circuits and Archimedes' law of displacement. When augmented with a heuristic for noting common divisors, the system is able to replicate a number of early chemical discoveries, arriving at Proust's law of definite proportions, Gay-Lussac's law of combining volumes, Cannizzaro's determination of the relative atomic weights, and Prout's hypothesis. The BACON.4 heuristics, including the new technique for finding common divisors, appear to be general mechanisms applicable to discovery in diverse domains.

10.1 INTRODUCTION

The years between 1800 and 1860 were active ones for chemistry. They saw the first quantitative measures of chemical reactions, the revival of the atomic theory, the painstaking determination of atomic weights, and the crowning success of the periodic table. The evolution of chemical thought has many parallels to the development of early physics in the previous century, but many differences may be found as well. These similarities and differences have led us to apply our ideas about the discovery process, initially drawn from early physics, to the domain of chemistry. In this paper we report the results of that effort.

BACON.4 is the fourth in a line of discovery systems developed by the authors. The earlier programs in this series merit some discussion, since their successes and failures have led directly to the current system. The prototype system, BACON.1 [Langley, 1978], can be viewed as an implementation of the General Rule Inducer proposed by Simon and Lea [1974]. The program showed considerable generality by solving sequence extrapolation tasks, learning conjunctive and disjunctive concepts, and discovering simple physical laws. BACON.2 [Langley, 1979] included additional heuristics for dealing with sequential information; these let the program note recurring sequences of symbols and discover complex polynomial functions (including Bode's law) by examining differences. BACON.3 [Langley, 1981] represented information at increasing levels of description, with higher levels describing more complex laws and accounting for more of the original data. This extended representation enabled the system to treat its hypotheses as new data, to which its heuristics could be applied recursively. BACON.3 successfully rediscovered versions of the ideal gas law, Coulomb's law, Kepler's third law, Ohm's law, and Galileo's laws for the pendulum and constant acceleration.

Although successive versions of BACON have differed considerably, all have incorporated similar data-driven heuristics to direct their search for interesting laws. This places the BACON systems in sharp contrast with previous discovery systems such as AM [Lenat, 1977] and meta-DENDRAL [Buchanan *et al.*, 1972], which incorporated theory-driven discovery techniques. A major goal of our research has been the identification of general discovery mechanisms, and we have focused on data-driven approaches because they seem more likely to provide insight into general mechanisms than theory-driven ones.[1] Below we present the details of BACON.4, as well as some of its accomplishments. After this, we summarize some early chemical discoveries, and then trace the path traversed by the system in its rediscovery of these laws.

BACON.4 focuses on the process of descriptive discovery, in which one attempts to describe a set of data in some succinct form. Of course, there are many other aspects to the discovery process, such as determining what data to gather, formulating explanatory theories, and making experimental predictions. Thus, the current system addresses one important part of the scientific process, while leaving other components for future research. In addition, we should note

[1]BACON.5 is a more recent version of the system [Langley *et al.*, 1981; Langley *et al.*, 1982] that incorporates expectation-driven heuristics in addition to the data-driven ones used in BACON.4. However, these rules base their expectations on discoveries the system has made previously, so they can be stated in a very general fashion. BACON.5 also includes a generalized version of the BACON.2 differencing heuristic.

that BACON.4 was not designed to replicate the historical details of the discovery process, but is intended as a sufficient model of how discovery might occur. The series of BACON programs are named after Sir Francis Bacon (1561-1626), the early philosopher of science, because we think he would have found the data-driven nature of the program's heuristics congenial.

10.2 AN OVERVIEW OF BACON.4

BACON.4 is a production system that discovers descriptive laws that summarize data. The program incorporates a small set of heuristics for finding constancies and trends in data, and for formulating hypotheses and defining theoretical terms based on these regularities. These heuristics are stated as condition-action rules called *productions*, using Forgy's OPS4 programming language [Forgy, 1979]. BACON.4 is intended to be a general discovery system; the data-driven, Baconian nature of its heuristics were designed with this goal in mind.

In this section we discuss the details of BACON.4 and its organization. First we describe the system's representation of hypotheses, and the conditions under which they are proposed. Next we discuss the program's trend detectors, and their responsibility for defining theoretical terms. Finally, we examine BACON.4's ability to postulate new intrinsic properties which may be associated with independent terms taking on nominal values.

10.2.1 Formulating Hypotheses

Standard analyses of the scientific method partition the world into data or observations, and hypotheses or laws that explain or summarize those data. In fact, an earlier version of our system, BACON.1 [Langley, 1978], made just such a distinction. BACON.4 replaces this dichotomy with a continuum along which information is represented at varying levels of description. The lowest of these levels may appropriately be called data, whereas the highest may be labeled hypotheses. But the intermediate levels are actually hybrids of these two concepts. A description at one level acts as an hypothesis with respect to the descriptions below it, and as a datum for the description above it.

Consider some data obeying the ideal gas law. This law may be stated as $pV/nT = 8.32$, where p is the pressure on a gas, n is the number of moles, T is the temperature, and V is the volume of the gas. Suppose BACON.4 is given data showing that when p is 1, n is 1, and T is 300, the value of V is 2496.0. If the first three terms are under the system's control (independent variables), one can think of their values as conditions on the value of V (the dependent variable). Now suppose that after gathering additional data by varying p but holding n and T constant, BACON.4 finds that pV is 2496.0 whenever n is 1 and T is 300. This second level description summarizes all first level observations with similar conditions, but it can be treated as data in turn. Upon varying T, the program generates other second level summaries; taken together, these lead to the third level summary that pV/T is 8.32 whenever n is 1. Continuing in this way, the system arrives at the ideal gas law when the fourth level of description is reached.

In determining when to generate a new description to summarize a set of lower level descriptions, BACON.4 draws on a generalized version of the traditional inductive inference rule. This heuristic looks for recurring values of a dependent variable. It may be stated as:

If you see a number of descriptions at level L
in which the dependent variable (D) has the same value (V),
then create a new description at level L + 1
in which the value of D is also V,
and which has all conditions common to the observed descriptions.

This production may detect constant dependent terms that take either numerical or nominal (symbolic) values. BACON.4 has primitive facilities for ignoring small amounts of noise in numerical data. However, it cannot deal with significant deviations from regularity, nor can it recover from overgeneralizations once they have been made. The conservative strategy of including all common conditions serves to offset this latter limitation.

10.2.2 Defining Theoretical Terms

In the ideal gas example given above, the dependent terms (V, pV, pV/T, etc.) about which generalizations were made became progressively more complex. Values of V were used at the first level of description, while values of pV were used for the second. In stating the final law, BACON.4 used the complex arithmetic combination pV/nT. Such a combination of directly observable variables may be viewed as a type of theoretical term, a term that is not directly observable but whose values are computable from observables [Tuomela, 1973]. Although a term like pV/nT may be replaced by its definition at any time,[2] its use can simplify the statement of a complex law considerably. How does the program arrive at useful theoretical terms such as pV/nT?

BACON.4 uses a heuristic search method to explore the space of theoretical terms, much as Lenat's AM program [Lenat, 1977] did for the space of mathematical concepts. We will call the heuristics for directing this search trend detectors. These detectors note increasing and decreasing monotonic relations between pairs of variables that take on numeric values. Consider the heuristic for noting decreasing relations, which may be stated as:

---

[2]The definition of pV/nT would be stored simply as the ratio of pV/T and n; in turn, pV/T would be defined as the ratio of pV and T, while pV would be stored as the product of its components. BACON.4 cannot actually replace a term with its definition, but since there are no conceptual difficulties, we expect there would be no complications in implementation.

If the values of dependent variable a_1 increase as the corresponding values of variable a_2 decrease in a number of descriptions at level L,
then note a monotonic decreasing relation between a_1 and a_2, and calculate the slope of a_1 with respect to a_2.

As this rule states, once a trend has been found, the system computes the slope of the curve relating the two terms. If the slope is constant, then the system creates two new theoretical terms defined as linear combinations of the related variables.[3] If the slope varies (the relation is not linear), then BACON.4 computes the product or ratio of the related terms, depending on the direction of the relation and the signs of the numbers involved, and treats this product or ratio also as a new theoretical term.

Once a theoretical term has been defined, no distinction is made between it and directly observed dependent variables. Thus, the constancy detector may produce generalizations about the values of theoretical terms like pV, leading to descriptions such as those in the ideal gas example. In turn, numerical relations may be found between the values of these newly derived theoretical terms, leading to complex combinations of directly observable variables, such as pV/nT. This recursive ability to apply the same heuristics to progressively more complex terms at higher levels of description gives BACON.4 considerable power in searching for empirical laws.

10.2.3 Postulating Intrinsic Properties

Although BACON.4's trend detectors are useful for relating numeric variables, they prove ineffective when an independent nominal or symbolic variable influences the values of a numeric dependent term—for example, when inserting the different wires A, B, and C, into a circuit alters the current. In such cases, the program calls on a heuristic for postulating an intrinsic property of the nominal variable (such as conductance):

If a_1 is an independent nominal variable,
and a_2 is a numeric dependent variable,
and the values of a_1 change when the values of a_2 change in a number of descriptions at level L,
then propose an intrinsic property whose values are taken from the values of a_2,
and associate these values with the conditions on the descriptions.

As the rule states, the values of this intrinsic property (which is a new theoretical term) are set equal to the observed values of the numeric dependent term, and

[3]These terms represent the slope and intercept of the line. If y is found to be a linear function of x with slope m and intercept i, BACON.4 creates a slope term defined as $(y - i)/x$ and an intercept term defined as $y - mx$. If the intercept is very close to zero, BACON.4 instead defines the ratio term y/x.

each value is associated with the conditions under which the observation was made. The intrinsic values are retrieved whenever these conditions are met.

Upon defining an intrinsic property and specifying its values, BACON.4 also defines a new variable which is the ratio of the values of the dependent variable and the intrinsic property. Since this ratio, which we call a conjectured property, is guaranteed to be 1.0 for the observations that led to its postulation, it does not provide any new knowledge or have any immediate effect, beneficial or harmful. However, if BACON generalizes the conditions under which the intrinsic values are retrieved, then the conjectured property can take on values other than unity, and the system may discover new empirical laws.

The generalization process operates in the following manner.[4] When BACON.4 varies a new independent variable (for example, the battery), the resulting values of the dependent variable (current) are compared to the original values of the intrinsic property (conductance). If a linear relation is found between these two sets of values, BACON.4 infers that the independent term just varied is not associated with the intrinsic property (that is, that the conductance is independent of which battery is in the circuit). Henceforth, the program will retrieve the value of the intrinsic property regardless of the value of the irrelevant term. This creates the possibility of discovering new empirical laws in which the conjectured property (current divided by conductance) takes on new values. This in turn leads the system to postulate new intrinsic properties at higher levels of description (in this case, associating a voltage with each battery). In contrast, if no linear relation is found, BACON.4 infers that the value of the varied term is a relevant condition on the retrieval of the intrinsic values. In the following section, we discuss examples of each situation.

10.3 THE DISCOVERIES OF BACON.4

In this section, we present some of BACON.4's discoveries, focusing in particular upon its heuristic for postulating intrinsic properties and conjectured properties. First, we show how the system arrives at the concepts of conductance and voltage along the path to rediscovering Ohm's law. This example demonstrates in more detail the generalization technique that we outlined in the previous section. Next, we trace the program's rediscovery of Archimedes' law of displacement, along with the development of the notions of volume and density. Finally, we discuss briefly some other laws BACON.4 has rediscovered.

---

[4]An earlier version of the program [Bradshaw *et al.*, 1980] generalized at the outset, assuming the intrinsic term was associated only with the most recently varied independent variable. Although this strategy worked well when a property was associated with a single variable, it led to disaster when this was not the case. The more conservative approach avoids this difficulty.

10.3.1 Ohm, Voltage, and Resistance

Ohm's law relates the current I of an electric circuit to its voltage V and its resistance R. The law may be stated as I = V/R. In physical terms, the voltage is associated with the battery used in the circuit, while resistance is associated with the wire. An earlier version of BACON, described by Langley [1981], discovered a version of Ohm's law when given numeric information about the wire, such as its length and diameter. However, BACON.4 can discover a similar[5] version of the law when it is provided with only nominal information about the batteries and wires used.

In doing this, BACON.4 is given experimental control over two variables—the battery and the wire—from which it can construct simple circuits. These variables take on nominal values such as A, B, and C, and X, Y, and Z, respectively. The program can tell when two of these symbols are the same or different, but nothing more. The single dependent variable is the current I observed in the circuit, which takes on numeric values. Table 10-1 presents some data that might be observed for various combinations of batteries and wires.[6] The values of I were calculated assuming voltages of 4.613 for battery A, 5.279 for B, and 7.382 for C, while the resistances were 1.327 for wire X, 0.946 for Y, and 1.508 for Z. (Of course, BACON.4 was not provided with this information, but only with the values of I for each battery-wire combination.)

Table 10-1: Postulating the property of conductance.

BATTERY	WIRE	I (CURRENT)	C (CONDUCTANCE)	I/C (VOLTAGE)
A	X	3.4763	3.4763	1.0000
A	Y	4.8763	4.8763	1.0000
A	Z	3.0590	3.0590	1.0000
B	X	3.9781	3.4763	1.1444
B	Y	5.5803	4.8763	1.1444
B	Z	3.5007	3.0590	1.1444
C	X	5.5629	3.4763	1.6003
C	Y	7.8034	4.8763	1.6003
C	Z	4.8952	3.0590	1.6003

[5]A more general version of the law distinguishes between the external resistance R_e associated with the wire and the internal resistance R_i associated with the battery. This version may be stated as $I = V/(R_i + R_e)$. In this example, we assume the internal resistance of the battery is negligible. Given numeric information about the wire, BACON can discover this more general version, but not when it is given only nominal information.

[6]BACON.4 asks the user for the independent terms it should vary, the values it should use for them, and the dependent variables it should examine. Once it has been given this information, the system runs a complete factorial design experiment, examining the dependent values for every possible combination of independent values. In other words, BACON.4 runs its own experiments, though it does not design them.

Consider the first three rows of the table, which show the currents associated with various wires when the battery is held constant. Since the wire is a nominal term that influences the values of I, BACON.4 postulates an intrinsic property whose values are equal to the values of the current. We would interpret this theoretical term as the conductance C of the wire, or the inverse of the resistance. Initially, these values are associated with both the wire and the battery with which they occurred. The program also calculates the values of the ratio I/C, a conjectured property which must be 1.0 for these rows by definition. Since I/C will subsequently be interpreted as an intrinsic property, that is, voltage, associated with the battery, we are by this procedure implicitly selecting the voltage of the first battery tested, A, as the unit of measurement.

More interesting discoveries are made when the second three rows are observed. Since the wires are the same as before but the battery differs, BACON.4 compares the newly observed values of I with the previously established values of C. Because a linear relation is found, the system infers that the conductance is associated only[7] with the wire being used. The values of C associated with each of the three wires are retrieved, and the values of the conjectured property, I/C, are calculated; for these rows the values of I/C are 1.1444 rather than 1.0. When the battery is varied again, BACON.4 retrieves the values of C immediately and discovers that I/C is now 1.6003. Table 10-2 summarizes the values of I/C and the conditions under which they occur.

Table 10-2: Postulating the property of voltage.

BATTERY	I/C	VOLTAGE V	I/CV
A	1.0000	1.0000	1.0000
B	1.1444	1.1444	1.0000
C	1.6003	1.6003	1.0000

At this point, BACON.4 is again forced to postulate an intrinsic term. The values of the new term are associated only with the battery, since this is the only condition on the value of I/C. We would call this property the voltage V of the circuit. As before, the program also defines a new conjectured property, I/CV, which is guaranteed to be 1.0 in the given situation by definition. BACON.4 stops here, having found the relative conductance of each wire and the relative voltage of each battery. Note that these values are not the ones used in generating the data that were given initially to BACON.4, but are multiples of them, the multiplier being 1.327 for the conductances and 0.2168 for the voltages. BACON.4 has simply defined new units of conductance and voltage.

---

[7]If the internal resistance of the battery had been significant, a linear relation would not occur and BACON.4 would take a more conservative path.

Table 10-3: First level data for the displacement law.

COMPOSITION	OBJECT	V	C	$S_{C,V}$	$I_{C,V}$
SILVER	A	100.0	105.326	1.0	5.326
SILVER	A	200.0	205.326	1.0	5.326
SILVER	A	300.0	305.326	1.0	5.326
SILVER	B	100.0	107.115	1.0	7.115
SILVER	B	200.0	207.115	1.0	7.115
SILVER	B	300.0	307.115	1.0	7.115
SILVER	C	100.0	109.482	1.0	9.482
SILVER	C	200.0	209.482	1.0	9.482
SILVER	C	300.0	309.482	1.0	9.482

10.3.2 Archimedes, Volume, and Density

The legend behind Archimedes' discovery of the law of displacement is an interesting one. As the story goes, the king of Syracuse had given a contractor an exact amount of gold for the purpose of making a crown. After receiving the crown, he heard a rumor that some of the gold had been replaced by an equal weight of silver. The ruler was angry but unable to prove the contractor's guilt without destroying the crown, so he gave the problem to Archimedes. The mathematician went to take a bath while thinking about the matter, and as he was entering the tub, he realized that the volume by which the water raised was equal to the volume of his body which had submerged. Understanding that this would provide a solution, he leaped from the tub and ran naked through the streets, shouting, "Eureka, eureka!"

While Archimedes' insight is quite different in style from the systematic summaries of BACON.4, the law of displacement provides another instance where intrinsic properties prove useful. Suppose BACON.4 has experimental control over two nominal variables—the object being examined and the composition of that object—and one numeric variable—the volume v of liquid in an easily measured container. As with Archimedes, BACON.4 does not initially know the volumes of the objects because of their irregular shapes. However, the only observable dependent variable—the combined volume, C, of the object and the liquid—will let the program devise a new measure.

The program begins by varying the volume of liquid into which a given object is inserted. The results of a number of such observations are presented in Table 10-3. Each row in this table corresponds to an observation, while each column represents the observed values for a single variable. Two theoretical terms, $s_{c,v}$ and $i_{c,v}$, are defined when the program notes a linear relation between the values of v and c. These correspond to the slope and intercept of the line, respectively.

Table 10-4 summarizes the results of the first table along with additional observations made when the composition is varied. Note that the slope of the line $s_{c,v}$ is invariant, while different values of $i_{c,v}$ are associated with each composition/object pair. Since BACON.4 has no numeric independent terms to relate to its dependent ones, it defines an intrinsic property whose values are as-

Table 10-4: Postulating the property of irregular volume.

COMPOSITION	OBJECT	$s_{C,V}$	$i_{C,V}$	O	$i_{C,V}/O$
SILVER	A	1.0	5.326	5.326	1.0
SILVER	B	1.0	7.115	7.117	1.0
SILVER	C	1.0	9.482	9.482	1.0
GOLD	D	1.0	6.313	6.313	1.0
GOLD	E	1.0	4.722	4.722	1.0
GOLD	F	1.0	8.817	8.817	1.0
LEAD	G	1.0	5.016	5.016	1.0
LEAD	H	1.0	3.493	3.493	1.0
LEAD	I	1.0	6.827	6.827	1.0

sociated with each of these pairs. This term corresponds to the volume of the object that was placed in the water, which we represent by the symbol o. The system defines the ratio term $i_{c,v}/o$, a conjectured property, which has the constant value 1.0 for all objects, but from this tautological relation nothing new is learned. BACON.4 halts after assigning intrinsic values to each of the object/composition pairs, having specified a new technique for measuring the volumes of irregular objects.

Table 10-5: Relating weights to irregular volumes.

COMPOSITION	OBJECT	W	O	W/O
SILVER	A	55.923	5.326	10.5
SILVER	B	74.708	7.115	10.5
SILVER	C	99.561	9.482	10.5
GOLD	D	121.841	6.313	19.3
GOLD	E	91.135	4.722	19.3
GOLD	F	170.168	8.817	19.3
LEAD	G	57.182	5.016	11.4
LEAD	H	39.820	3.493	11.4
LEAD	I	77.828	6.827	11.4

Now suppose that later the program runs a different experiment in which the independent variables are the object and the composition of the object, and the dependent term is the weight w of the object. Table 10-5 gives some data that might be observed in such an experiment. If the same objects are used as before, the intrinsic value (volume o) associated with each will be retrieved and BACON.4's trend detectors will note a linear relation between the values of w and o. Since the intercept is zero, the ratio w/o is defined; this has recurring values which lead to a number of higher-level descriptions. Table 10-6 summarizes these results; note that a different value of w/o is associated with each value of the composition. Again an intrinsic property, d, is proposed, this time based on the values of w/o. BACON.4 formulates a final conjectured property, w/od, and then quits, having discovered the relative densities for each of the elements it has examined. (Of course, BACON.4 does not call the density d by this name, nor does it attach the semantics to this term that the reader would.)

Table 10-6: Postulating the property of density.

COMPOSITION	W/O	DENSITY D	W/OD
SILVER	10.5	10.5	1.0
GOLD	19.3	19.3	1.0
LEAD	11.4	11.4	1.0

10.3.3 Additional BACON.4 Discoveries

We have just seen how BACON.4 has rediscovered Ohm's law and Archimedes' law of displacement. In addition, the system[8] has discovered four other laws in which intrinsic properties play a role. These are:

Snell's law of refraction: This law relates the angle of incidence i and the angle of refraction r of a ray of light as it passes from one medium to another. The intrinsic properties are the indices of refraction of each medium, n_1 and n_2, and the law may be stated sine i/sine r $= n_1/n_2$. Here the input data consist of the sines of the two angles along with the media through which the light passes.

The law of conservation of momentum: This law relates the velocities v_1 and v_2 of two objects o_1 and o_2 to each other, independently of the time they are observed. The intrinsic properties are the inertial masses of the objects, m_1 and m_2, while the law may be stated as $m_1v_1 = m_2v_2$. Here the input data consist of the names of objects, along with their velocities at various points in time.

The law of gravitation: BACON.4 discovered an experimentally based version of this law, which relates the attractive force F between two objects o_1 and o_2 to the distance d between them. The intrinsic properties are the gravitational masses of the objects m_1 and m_2. The law may be stated as $F = Gm_1m_2/d^2$, where G is a constant. In this case, the data consist of the object names, the distance between them, and the resulting force.

Black's specific heat law: This law[9] relates the temperatures t_1 and t_2 of two liquids along with their masses m_1 and m_2, to the final temperature t_f of the mixture. The intrinsic properties are the

---

[8]In fact, these discoveries were made by the earlier version of BACON.4, using its less conservative strategy for retrieving intrinsic values. Although we have not actually run the current version on these tasks, we anticipate no major difficulties.

[9]Because of the complexity of this law, BACON.4 was never run on the complete set of data. The system used some two hours of CPU time in dealing with 1/12 of the 972 observations that it would need to arrive at the final version of the law. This allowed it to discover the simplified relationship that holds between c_2, m_2, t_2, and t_f when the other terms are held constant.

specific heats c_1 and c_2 of the two liquids, and the law may be stated as $c_1 m_1 t_1 + c_2 m_2 t_2 = (c_1 m_1 + c_2 m_2) t_f$. Here the data consist of the names of the two liquids, their respective masses, their initial temperatures, and the resulting final temperature.

These results provide further evidence of the general applicability of BACON.4's heuristics to the discovery of physical laws and the ubiquity of intrinsic properties in these laws.

The above four laws also point to a different means by which postulating intrinsic terms can aid the discovery process. The reader may have noted that each of these laws expresses a symmetric relation between two sets of variables. For example, conservation of momentum relates the mass and velocity of one object to the mass and velocity of another object. The law is equally applicable whether A is the first object and B the second, or vice versa. In such cases, BACON.4 is told that the nominal variables (in this instance the two objects) are analogous, and that a value found for one is also a reasonable value for the other. The system[10] uses this information about analogous variables in assigning intrinsic properties.

Suppose that BACON.4 has postulated an intrinsic property (such as m_1) that is associated with a set of nominal independent variables (such as o_1). If an analogous set of independent terms is present (such as o_2), then an analogous intrinsic property (such as m_2) is created and associated with this set. The values of the new property are stored in such a way that they may be retrieved either for this property or its analog if the appropriate conditions are met. The effects of this strategy are best visualized in terms of the tables we have been using for our examples. We have seen how the generalization process lets the system retrieve intrinsic values and place them in new rows so they can lead to new empirical laws. Similarly, reasoning by analogy lets the system retrieve these same values and place them in new columns. If existing intrinsic properties were not retrieved in these situations, BACON.4 would be forced to postulate new terms, and these would lead to tautological laws that were much less interesting than the symmetrical discoveries outlined above.

[10]Again, we should state what has actually been implemented. The earlier version of BACON.4 used this technique to discover laws in which analogous terms were used. However, we have not yet worked out the details of this method with respect to the more conservative retrieval strategies the system now employs. We do not feel this is a major problem; it simply has not been the current thrust of our research effort.

10.4 REDISCOVERING NINETEENTH CENTURY CHEMISTRY

One is convinced of a theory's generality not only by the number of phenomena it explains, but by the diversity of those phenomena. As we showed in the last section, BACON.4 has enjoyed considerable success in rediscovering laws from physics, but since the program was designed with physical discovery in mind this was not too surprising. We felt that early chemistry would provide a challenging test for our theory of the discovery process, and in this section we describe the results of that test.

We begin by summarizing the discoveries of chemists in the first half of the nineteenth century. Although we have not attempted to replicate these discoveries in detail, this should give the reader some idea of the task at hand. After this, we describe an additional mechanism that the chemistry domain forced us to introduce into BACON.4. We follow this with a summary of the system's chemical discoveries, with special emphasis on the role of the new technique. Finally, we show how BACON.4 can arrive at different representations of the same chemical laws.

10.4.1 Chemistry from Proust to Cannizzaro

Quantitative chemistry had its origins in the 1790's, when experimenters decided to focus their attention on the weight of objects instead of other attributes, such as color, texture, or hardness.[11] In 1797, J. L. Proust proposed the law of definite proportions, which stated that a given element always contributed the same percentage to the weight of a given compound. Berthollet challenged this claim, pointing to counterexamples in which variable proportions occurred, such as mixtures of sugar and water. However, chemists soon came to distinguish between chemical and physical combinations (compounds and mixtures), and Proust's law was generally accepted by 1807.

In 1808, John Dalton set forth the law of simple proportions. This law related to situations in which a pair of elements A and B could combine to form different compounds. Now the law of definite proportions predicted that for a given compound, the elements A and B would combine with a constant weight ratio, but it predicted nothing about the relation between these ratios for the various compounds of A and B. Dalton discovered that although these ratios differed for the various compounds, they always occurred in small integer multiples of the smallest ratio. For example, while 1.3 grams of oxygen combines with 1.0 gram of carbon to form carbon monoxide, some 2.6 grams of oxygen combines with the same amount of carbon to form carbon dioxide. The second amount of oxygen is twice the first amount.

In explaining the law of simple proportions, Dalton invoked the notion of atoms of elements combining to form particles of the resulting compound. Only

[11] An excellent account of this history may be found in Chapters 28 and 29 of [Arons, 1965].

certain combinations of atoms could occur, leading to the integer relations that had been observed. To determine the formula of the compound, Dalton used his rule of greatest simplicity: if two elements combine in only a single way, assume a binary compound (such as NO); if two combinations are known, assume a binary and a ternary compound (for example, NO_2 or N_2O). Based on this assumption, Dalton calculated the relative atomic weights of the elements. In fact, the rule of greatest simplicity was wrong in a number of instances. Dalton was aware of inconsistencies in his results (since in some cases different reactions implied different atomic weights), but no better approach presented itself at the time.

Meanwhile, Joseph Gay-Lussac was experimenting with chemical reactions between gases. In 1809, he announced that he had found a law of definite proportions for the volumes of gases. Moreover, he found that the volumes of the materials contributing to and resulting from the combination always occurred in small integer ratios with respect to each other. For example, 200 ml of hydrogen and 100 ml of oxygen combined to form 200 ml of water vapor. Gay-Lussac presented this as evidence for Dalton's atomic theory, as well as for the hypothesis that equal volumes of a gas contain equal numbers of particles regardless of composition. However, Dalton rejected this proposal because it implied that some compounds (such as water) were less dense than their components. Since Dalton believed that elementary gases were monatomic, Gay-Lussac's hypothesis implied for him that compounds must be denser than their components, a contradiction with the evidence.

Only two years later, in 1811, Amadeo Avogadro suggested that some elements might be diatomic, that is, that in their isolated state they occurred as pairs of atoms. This required a distinction between molecules, which satisfied the equal-volumes/equal-numbers hypothesis, and atoms, which did not. Thus, Avogadro postulated that hydrogen and oxygen were diatomic elements and that water was the ternary compound H_2O. This interpretation also countered Dalton's objection to Gay-Lussac, since a molecule of water could now, without contradiction, be less dense than a molecule of oxygen. Unfortunately, Avogadro's contemporaries paid little attention to his suggestion, and nearly fifty years passed before its power was recognized.

In 1860, Stanislao Cannizzaro buttressed Avogadro's theory with a straightforward method for determining molecular formulae and relative atomic weights. Cannizzaro examined the percentage of the weight that an element (e.g., hydrogen) contributed to a number of compounds (e.g., water, hydrogen chloride). Upon multiplying these fractions by the density of the element at a standard temperature and pressure, he found all of the resulting products to be small integer multiples of the smallest of the set. These divisors corresponded to the relative atomic weights of the elements, and Cannizzaro could derive the correct molecular formulae (for example, H_2O for water) from his table.

Earlier, another possibly lawful regularity had been noted by William Prout in 1815. Most of the computed atomic weights and combining ratios were very nearly multiples of those for hydrogen. Prout hypothesized that the higher elements might consist of clusters of hydrogen atoms. But the relations were not exact, and as better determinations of the atomic weights became available, it was apparent that there were important exceptions (e.g., chlorine). Consequently, Prout's hypothesis was rejected by most chemists, and was not revived until, in the present century, the largest anomalies were explained by the discovery of isotopes.

10.4.2 Finding Common Divisors

Dalton's, Guy-Lussac's, and Cannizzaro's discoveries involved more than postulating intrinsic properties and noting recurring values. In addition, they found in a number of cases that a set of values could be expressed as small integer multiples of one another. As we have described it, BACON.4 has no heuristics for discovering such relations. In order to replicate these discoveries,[12] we added a new heuristic that searched for common divisors in proposed intrinsic values.

A common divisor for a set of values is a number that, when divided into those values, generates a set of integers. The greatest common divisor of a set of values is simply the largest common divisor. Note that the common divisor itself need not be an integer, and will not be in the cases we examine. The greatest common divisor of a numerical set may be found using an extension of Euclid's algorithm.

First, select the smallest member in the set and divide it into all values in the set, producing a revised set. If all members of the revised set are integers, then stop since the smallest value in the set is the greatest common divisor. Otherwise, find the smallest remainder in the revised set (for example, .0523 for the set {12.0, 18.0523, 15.479}) and multiply the smallest value by this remainder. Divide the original set by this product, producing still another set. If all members of the new set are integral, then this product is the greatest common divisor. Otherwise, find the smallest remainder of the new set, multiply this by the current product, and iterate. This method will eventually generate the greatest common divisor of the original set; that is, when the set is divided by this value, a set of integers will result.

However, scientists do not always postulate integer proportions for intrinsic properties. For example, no one suggested that the specific heats of all liquids were evenly divisible by some common divisor. Clearly, there must be some criterion for determining when a "reasonable" common divisor has been found. For instance, one might insist that the divisor be a member of the original set.

---

[12]We have added new mechanisms to BACON cautiously, with the goal of keeping our theory of discovery as simple as possible. Before introducing a new heuristic, we attempt to ensure its generality by finding a number of cases in which it can be used. We discuss the generality of the new mechanism in a later section.

We rejected this heuristic, since one can imagine a chemist arriving at Prout's hypothesis without a familiarity with hydrogen.

A second approach would require that certain characteristics hold for the resulting integers. Thus, one might accept a common divisor only if it led to small integers, such as those less than 100. As soon as the method described above generated a non-integral value greater than 100, the search would stop. A less restrictive criterion,[13] which includes smallness as a special case, requires that the interval between the smallest and the largest integers fall below a threshold. Thus, one would be as satisfied with integer values between 100 and 200 as with a set falling between 0 and 100. The search would then stop when the method generated a non-integer set with too large an interval.

In addition, the system must have some means for distinguishing integers from non-integers. This is required even in the absence of noise, since the calculations will introduce roundoff errors. To deal with such situations, BACON.4 includes a user-modifiable parameter that determines the degree of acceptable deviation from integer values. This parameter was set to 0.03 in the runs described below. Thus, if the remainder of a number is less than 0.03 or greater than 0.97, that number is considered to be an integer. If all numbers are determined to be integers, then the divisor has been found. If not, then some remainder greater than 0.03 is selected as the new multiplier.

BACON.4 calls on this method for finding common divisors whenever a new set of dependent values is about to be assigned to an intrinsic property.[14] If a reasonable divisor is found, then the values are divided by this number and the resulting integers are associated with the nominal values instead. When the ratio of the dependent term and the intrinsic property is computed (a conjectured property), this will equal the divisor rather than 1.0. In cases where different divisors are found under different circumstances, BACON.4 is able to relate the values of the conjectured property to other terms even though the intrinsic values themselves may never be retrieved. Thus, the discovery of a common divisor may let the system break out of the tautological path that postulating conjectured properties can produce. In the following section, we show the importance of this technique in making a number of chemical discoveries.

10.4.3 BACON.4 on the Chemical Data

BACON.4 bases its understanding of chemistry on the results of various chemical reactions. In examining the data derived from these reactions, the

[13]This is the criterion currently implemented in BACON.4. We owe thanks to Marshall Atlas for suggesting this idea.

[14]This property may have just been defined, or it may have been proposed many cycles before. In the latter case, new values would be specified only if the old values could not be retrieved because their relevant conditions were not met.

program treats three variables as independent—the element contributing to the reaction, the resulting compound, and the weight of the element used, or w_e. For each combination of independent values, BACON.4 examines the associated values of three dependent terms—the weight of the compound resulting from the reaction (w_c), the volume of the element (v_e), and the volume of the compound (v_c).[15] Thus, one can imagine an early chemist measuring out a quantity of an element by weight and combining it with others under conditions he knows will lead to a certain compound. Having done this, he measures the weight of the resulting compound, along with the volumes of both the compound and the element.

Table 10-7 shows those data the program collects when the element is hydrogen. (The system is also presented with similar data for the elements oxygen and nitrogen.) Since the weight of the element is varied first, BACON.4 notes linear relations between w_e and each of w_c, v_e, and v_c. Since the intercepts of these lines are zero, only the ratio terms w_e/w_c, w_e/v_e, and w_e/v_c are defined. Each of these ratios has a constant value for a given element/compound combination, leading to the second-level summaries presented in Tables 10-8 and 10-9.

Table 10-7: First level chemical data.

ELEMENT	COMPOUND	W_E	W_C	V_E	V_C	W_E/W_C	W_E/V_E	W_E/V_C
hydrogen	water	10.0	90.00	112.08	112.08	0.1111	0.0892	0.0892
hydrogen	water	20.0	180.00	224.16	224.16	0.1111	0.0892	0.0892
hydrogen	water	30.0	270.01	336.25	336.25	0.1111	0.0892	0.0892
hydrogen	ammonia	10.0	56.79	112.08	74.72	0.1761	0.0892	0.1338
hydrogen	ammonia	20.0	113.58	224.16	149.44	0.1761	0.0892	0.1338
hydrogen	ammonia	30.0	170.37	336.25	224.16	0.1761	0.0892	0.1338
hydrogen	ethylene	10.0	140.10	112.08	112.08	0.0714	0.0892	0.0892
hydrogen	ethylene	20.0	280.21	224.16	224.16	0.0714	0.0892	0.0892
hydrogen	ethylene	30.0	420.31	336.25	336.25	0.0714	0.0892	0.0892

Table 10-8 summarizes the values of w_e/w_c for hydrogen, as well as the results from later experiments in which the elements are oxygen and nitrogen. Upon arriving at these second level descriptions, BACON.4 notes that it has only nominal independent terms. This leads it to postulate the intrinsic property $I_1 = w_e/w_c$. These values have no reasonable common divisor,[16] so the values of w_e/w_c are used directly. Each intrinsic value is associated with a particular element/compound pair; these numbers correspond to the constant weight ratios first discovered by Proust. The program also defines the conjectured property w_e/w_cI_1. This is guaranteed to be 1.0 for the cases used in assigning values to I_1, but other values could occur in future experiments, leading the system to propose a new intrinsic property at a higher level of description.

[15] All volumes are for the substances in gaseous form under standard conditions.

[16] In fact, the values for nitrogen in Table 10-8 are evenly divisible by 0.032. However, this is not a general trend and its occurrence does not significantly affect the program's behavior.

Table 10-8: Second level summary for weight proportions.

ELEMENT	COMPOUND	W_E/W_C	I_1	$W_E/W_C I_1$
hydrogen	water	0.1111	0.1111	1.0
hydrogen	ammonia	0.1761	0.1761	1.0
hydrogen	ethylene	0.0714	0.0714	1.0
oxygen	nitrous oxide	0.3648	0.3648	1.0
oxygen	sulfur dioxide	0.5000	0.5000	1.0
oxygen	carbon dioxide	0.7396	0.7396	1.0
nitrogen	nitrous oxide	0.6378	0.6378	1.0
nitrogen	ammonia	0.8224	0.8224	1.0
nitrogen	nitric oxide	0.4664	0.4664	1.0

The values of w_e/v_c for hydrogen, oxygen, and nitrogen are shown in Table 10-9. Here BACON.4 has defined the second intrinsic property I_2, based on the values of this ratio. However, this time useful common divisors are found; these are 0.0446 for hydrogen, 0.715 for oxygen, and 0.625 for nitrogen. The values of I_2 shown in the table are simply the values of w_e/v_c divided by these numbers. Again, the values of the intrinsic property are associated with pairs of elements and compounds.

One may interpret these numbers as the coefficients of the element in the balanced equation for the chemical reaction determined by the pair. Thus, the value of I_2 for hydrogen and water would be 2, while that for oxygen and water would be 1. These are identical with the numbers Cannizzaro found (by following the same route) when he divided his products of densities and weight proportions by their common divisors. The program also defines the ratio[17] w_e/v_cI_2, which has a constant value for each element; in fact, these values are precisely the greatest common divisors found for these elements.

Table 10-9: Second level summary for Cannizzaro products.

ELEMENT	COMPOUND	W_E/V_C	I_2	$W_E/V_C I_2$
hydrogen	water	0.0892	2.0	0.0446
hydrogen	ammonia	0.1338	3.0	0.0446
hydrogen	ethylene	0.0892	2.0	0.0446
oxygen	nitrous oxide	0.715	1.0	0.715
oxygen	sulfur dioxide	1.430	2.0	0.715
oxygen	carbon dioxide	1.430	2.0	0.715
nitrogen	nitrous oxide	1.250	2.0	0.625
nitrogen	ammonia	0.625	1.0	0.625
nitrogen	nitric oxide	0.625	1.0	0.625

At this point, BACON.4 has discovered three invariants dependent only on

[17]In fact, BACON.4 examines the ratio v_c/w_e. In searching for common divisors, it considers both this term and its inverse. In this case, common divisors are found for the inverse, so the product v_cI_2/w_e is defined instead of the ratio shown. We have presented the simpler picture in the interests of clarity.

the element; Table 10-10 summarizes these findings, to which we have also added the corresponding values for sodium.[18] The first of these invariants states that the conjectured property, w_e/w_cI_1, is always 1.0; however, this rule introduces no new information, since it is tautological. The second specifies the values of w_e/v_cI_2 associated with ea ch element; since these are different BACON.4 proposes the higher level intrinsic term I_3. The values of w_e/v_cI_2 are divisible by 0.0446, leading the program to assign values for I_3 of 1.0 for hydrogen, 16.0 for oxygen, 14.0 for nitrogen, and 23.0 for sodium. These are precisely the relative atomic weights that Cannizzaro derived from his table of densities and proportions. BACON.4 also defines the ratio $w_e/v_cI_2I_3$ (a conjectured property with the value 0.0446), but this generates no new knowledge.

Table 10-10: Relative atomic weights and densities of the elements.

ELEMENT	W_E/W_CI_1	W_E/V_CI_2	I_3	$W_E/V_CI_2I_3$	W_E/V_E	I_4	W_E/V_EI_4
hydrogen	1.0	0.0446	1.0	0.0446	0.0892	2.0	0.0446
oxygen	1.0	0.715	16.0	0.0446	1.430	32.0	0.0446
nitrogen	1.0	0.625	14.0	0.0446	1.25	28.0	0.0446
sodium	1.0	1.027	23.0	0.0446	1.027	23.0	0.0446

The third regularity relates to the values of w_e/v_e. Earlier, BACON.4 had found these values to be independent of the compound being considered, but dependent on the element. Moreover, the recurring values are all divisible by 0.0446, so BACON.4 introduces yet another intrinsic property; this is called I_4 and its values are simply those of w_e/v_e divided by 0.0446. This gives values of 2.0 for hydrogen, 32.0 for oxygen, 28.0 for nitrogen, but 23.0 again for sodium which, unlike the others, is a monatomic gas. These ratios may be interpreted as the relative densities of the elements in their gaseous form, which, according to Gay-Lussac's principle, are proportional to the corresponding molecular weights.

10.4.4 Finding Alternate Frameworks

In the last section, we described BACON.4's chemical discoveries when it exerted experimental control over the weight of an element, or w_e. However, one can imagine scenarios in which a scientist varies the values of w_c, v_e, or v_c instead. For example, whether one controls the weight or the volume of an element or compound is purely a matter of choice. And the characteristics of the compound are easily viewed as the independent variables if the method of electrolysis is used to break that compound into its components.

Replacing one independent term with another has an interesting effect on BACON.4. In all cases, the system still finds linear relations between the inde-

[18] BACON.4 was not actually run with the sodium data. We add it here because the inclusion of a monatomic gas makes clear the distinction that BACON.4 subsequently discovers between atomic and molecular weight.

pendent variable and the three dependent ones. However, recall that the program always relates dependent terms to independent or intrinsic ones rather than to one another. As a result, BACON.4 defines different theoretical terms and finds different associated constancies in each of the four situations. That is, the system arrives at different conceptual frameworks depending on the manner in which experiments are run.

Table 10-11: Alternate chemical frameworks generated by BACON.4.

INDEPENDENT TERM	W_E	V_E	W_C	V_C
theoretical	w_e/w_c	v_e/v_c	w_e/w_c	v_e/v_c
terms	w_c/v_e	w_e/v_e	w_c/v_c	w_c/v_c
generated	w_c/v_c	w_c/v_e	w_c/v_e	w_e/v_c

Table 10-11 presents the theoretical terms resulting from the use of each term as an independent variable. In each case, BACON.4 defines three ratio terms and states the conditions under which these are constant. Each set of three laws is equivalent to the others in the sense that any triple can be derived from any other triple, though the program cannot actually carry out this derivation. Note that six ratios exist,[19] each occurring in two of the four possible combinations.

Three of these terms are especially interesting, since they did not occur in the run described above. One of these is w_c/v_c, or the density of the compound. Another is v_e/v_c, or the ratio of volumes for the element and the compound. Stating that this term is constant is equivalent to Gay-Lussac's law of definite proportions for volumes. Finally, the term w_c/v_e is simply the ratio of the two previously mentioned ratios. These theoretical terms were not generated in the above run for a simple reason; each of their components were treated as dependent variables, and BACON.4 attempts to relate dependent terms to independent terms, rather than to each other.

10.5 CONCLUSIONS

In this chapter, we described the BACON.4 system and summarized its rediscovery of a number of empirical laws. Clearly, we have simplified BACON's discovery task along a number of dimensions, and these simplifications suggest some important directions for future research. The first issue relates to noise in the observed data. We know that both Dalton's and Gay-Lussac's data were inexact, yet this did not prevent them from noting the relevant regularities. Although BACON.4's heuristics can be generalized to allow for some variation, the introduction of noise raises a more subtle problem. In its current form, BACON.4

[19]In fact, the inverses of these terms are sometimes defined. We have ignored this distinction for the sake of comparison between the different situations.

can entertain only one hypothesis at a time. So far, this has been sufficient, since in the absence of noise the system's heuristics have always been powerful enough to direct search down useful paths. But before future versions of BACON can deal with the increased search required to discover approximate laws, they should be able to consider competing hypotheses, as well as design critical experiments to distinguish between them.

A second issue relates to the presence of irrelevant variables. We know that chemists made little progress until they decided to turn their attention to the weights and volumes of elements and compounds. One can easily imagine a BACON-like system methodically considering and rejecting variables in a noise-free environment. However, the dual presence of irrelevant terms and noise makes the task much more difficult, since one can never be entirely sure that an independent variable is irrelevant. Future versions of BACON may simply have to endure much more search than their predecessors, and this should not be overly surprising, since the history of science tells us that discovery is often a slow and tedious process.

A final issue concerns the relation between data-driven and theory-driven discovery. The careful reader may have noted that although BACON.4's heuristics are data-driven in spirit, they produce some theory-driven effects. For example, once a theoretical term has been defined, it need not be redefined in other contexts; instead, the system immediately computes the values of the term, hoping to find them constant. Similarly, after the conditions on an intrinsic property have been sufficiently generalized, BACON.4 retrieves its values in new cases so they may contribute to new laws. Future versions of BACON should explore other possibilities for generating theory-driven behavior from data-driven heuristics. Incorporating notions of symmetry would be one such possibility. Suppose the system discovered a partial law (stated as a constant theoretical term) relating variables associated with one object, but had not yet incorporated an analogous set of terms associated with another object. If BACON hypothesized that the form of the final law was symmetrical, it would immediately consider an analogous theoretical term based on the original one; upon combining the two, it would arrive at the final law.

Having considered the limitations of BACON.4, we should also say a few words about the system's generality. As we stated earlier, the program was designed with examples from early physics in mind, such as Snell's law and the law of conservation of momentum. In our concern for generality, we gave the program data from the new domain of chemistry. To our pleasure, we found that we needed to introduce only a single new heuristic which (working in conjunction with the existing heuristics) was able to replicate many of the early chemical discoveries. However, the generality of a theory is a function of the generality of its components. If a program contains *ad hoc* heuristics which are used only once, one would not think that program very general.

For instance, how general is the heuristic for noting common divisors? Within the chemistry domain, this heuristic was used in three instances; common divisors were found for the values of w_e/v_c, w_e/v_e, and for w_e/v_cI_2, with the last of these leading to the relative atomic weights. Although BACON.4 arrives only at summaries of data, one can imagine how the discovery of common divisors might suggest explanations of those data as well. Upon finding that the relative atomic weights were all nearly divisible by the weight of hydrogen, Prout suggested that all atoms were composed of varying numbers of hydrogen atoms. Using similar forms of reasoning, future versions of the program may move beyond descriptive laws into the realm of explanation.

The notion of common divisors or integer ratios also occurs in some of the more recent areas of physics. Millikan's oil drop experiment was an explicit search for a common divisor, in that case interpreted as the charge on an electron. Physicists searched the characteristic spectra of the elements for integer proportions, discovering instead Balmer's formula for the lines of the hydrogen spectrum and its generalizations. And the very basis of modern physics and chemistry, the concept of the quantum, assumes that only integer values of certain properties can occur. Although we have not let BACON.4 attempt to deal with these problems, they suggest that the heuristic for noting common divisors is a general one which will continue to play an important role in our future research on the discovery process.

ACKNOWLEDGMENTS

This research was supported by Grant MH-07722 from the National Institutes of Mental Health, Grant F33615-78-C-1551 from the Advanced Research Projects Agency of the Department of Defense, and a grant from the Alfred P. Sloan Foundation.

The views and conclusions contained in this document are those of the authors and should not be interpreted as representing the official policies, either expressed or implied, of the Defense Advanced Research Projects Agency or the US Government.

REFERENCES

Arons, A. B., *Development of Concepts of Physics: The Rationalization of Mechanics to the First Theory of Atomic Structure*, Addison-Wesley, Reading, MA, 1965.

Bradshaw, G. L., Langley, P. and Simon, H. A., "BACON.4: The discovery of intrinsic properties," *Proceedings of the Third National Conference of the Canadian Society for Computational Studies of Intelligence*, Victoria, pp. 19-25, May 1980.

Buchanan, B. G., Feigenbaum, E. A., and Sridharan, N. S., "Heuristic theory formation," *Machine Intelligence 7*, D. Michie (Ed.), American Elsevier Publishing Co., New York, pp. 267-290, 1972.

Forgy, C. L., "OPS4 User's Manual", Technical Report CMU-CS-79-132, Carnegie-Mellon University, Dept. of Computer Science, July 1979.

Langley, P., "BACON.1: A general discovery system," *Proceedings of the Second National Conference of the Canadian Society for Computational Studies in Intelligence*, Toronto, pp. 173-180, July 1978.

Langley, P. W., *Descriptive Discovery Processes: Experiments in Baconian Science,* Ph.D. dissertation, Carnegie-Mellon University, Dept. of Psychology, December 1979.

Langley, P., "Data-driven discovery of physical laws," *Cognitive Science*, No. 5, pp. 31-54, 1981.

Langley, P., Bradshaw, G., and Simon, H. A., "BACON.5: The discovery of conservation laws," *Proceedings of the Seventh International Joint Conference on Artificial Intelligence*, Vancouver, pp. 121-126, August 1981.

Langley, P., Bradshaw, G., and Simon, H. A., "Data-driven and expectation-driven discovery of empirical laws," *Proceedings of the Fourth National Conference of the Canadian Society for Computational Studies of Intelligence*, Saskatoon, pp. 137-143, May 1982.

Lenat, D. B., "Automated theory formation in mathematics," *Proceedings of the Fifth International Joint Conference on Artificial Intelligence*, IJCAI, Cambridge, MA, pp. 833-842, August 1977.

Simon, H. A. and Lea, G., "Problem solving and rule induction: A unified view," *Knowledge and Cognition*, L. Gregg (Ed.), Lawrence Erlbaum Associates, Hillsdale, N.J., 1974.

Tuomela, R., *Theoretical Concepts*, Springer-Verlag, New York, 1973.

11

LEARNING FROM OBSERVATION: CONCEPTUAL CLUSTERING

Ryszard S. Michalski
Robert E. Stepp
University of Illinois at Urbana-Champaign

ABSTRACT

An important form of learning from observation is constructing a classification of given objects or situations. Traditional techniques for this purpose, developed in cluster analysis and numerical taxonomy, are often inadequate because they arrange objects into classes solely on the basis of a numerical measure of object similarity. Such a measure is a function only of compared objects and does not take into consideration any global properties or concepts characterizing object classes. Consequently, the obtained classes may have no simple conceptual description and may be difficult to interpret.

The above limitation is overcome by an approach called *conceptual* clustering, in which a configuration of objects forms a class only if it is describable by a concept from a predefined concept class. This chapter gives a tutorial overview of *conjunctive* conceptual clustering, in which the predefined concept class consists of conjunctive statements involving relations on selected object attributes. The presented method arranges objects into a hierarchy of classes closely circumscribed by such conjunctive descriptions. Descriptions stemming from each node are logically disjoint, satisfy given background knowledge, and optimize a certain global criterion.

The method is illustrated by an example in which the conjunctive conceptual clustering program CLUSTER/2 constructed a classification hierarchy of a large collection of Spanish folk songs. The conclusion suggests some extensions of the method and topics for further research.

11.1 INTRODUCTION

An omnipresent problem in science is to construct meaningful classifications of observed objects or situations. Such classifications facilitate human comprehension of the observations and the subsequent development of a scientific theory. This problem is a form of the very general, well-known principle of "divide and conquer" used in a variety of problem-solving situations. It is also related to the problem of decomposing any large-scale engineering system (for example, an AI system) into smaller components, in order to simplify its design and implementation.

The nature of processes leading to useful classifications remains little understood, despite considerable effort in this direction. From the viewpoint of machine learning, the process of constructing classifications is a form of "learning from observation" ("learning without a teacher"). This form of machine learning has been systematically studied in such areas as cluster analysis and numerical taxonomy. The central notion used there for creating classes of objects is a numerical measure of *similarity* of objects. Classes (clusters) are collections of objects whose intra-class similarity is high and inter-class similarity is low.

A measure of similarity is usually defined as a proximity measure in a multi-dimensional space spanned by selected object attributes. Such a measure is, therefore, meaningful only if the selected attributes are relevant for describing perceived object similarity. The presence of irrelevant attributes will distort this measure. Moreover, all attributes defining the description space are given equal weight in the process of determining classes. The problem, then, becomes one of structuring attributes into classes, in order to determine the most relevant attributes. Factor analysis and multi-dimensional scaling have been used for this purpose, but these methods were designed primarily for numerical variables. They cannot adequately handle the many-valued, nominal (categorical) variables which occur often in human classifications.

The use of numerical measures of similarity for constructing classifications has other disadvantages. Such measures take into consideration only the properties of compared objects without regard to any context or concepts useful for characterizing object configurations. Consequently, the resulting classes do not necessarily have any simple conceptual description and may be difficult to interpret. The problem of determining the *meaning* of the obtained classes is simply left to the researcher. This is a significant disadvantage of traditional methods because a researcher analyzing data typically wants to create classes that are not only mathematically well defined, but that also have a meaningful conceptual interpretation.

This chapter describes an approach to the problem of automatic construction of classifications, in which a configuration of objects forms a class only if it can be closely circumscribed by a conjunctive concept involving relations on selected object attributes. The problem undertaken can be defined as follows:

Given:

- A set of objects (physical or abstract),
- A set of attributes to be used to characterize the objects,
- A body of background knowledge, which includes the problem constraints, properties of attributes, and a criterion for evaluating the quality of constructed classifications.

Find:

- A hierarchy of object classes, in which each class is described by a single conjunctive concept. Subclasses that are descendants of any parent class should have logically disjoint descriptions and optimize an assumed criterion (a *clustering quality criterion*).

Structuring objects into such *conjunctive hierarchies* is called *conjunctive conceptual clustering*. It is a special case of *conceptual clustering* in general, which we define as a process of constructing a *concept network* characterizing a collection of objects, with nodes marked by *concepts* describing object classes, and links marked by the relationships between the classes.

The idea of conceptual clustering and a general method for determining conjunctive hierarchies was introduced by Michalski [1980a]. This chapter is a tutorial overview of conjunctive conceptual clustering and the algorithm implemented in the program CLUSTER/2 (a successor to the earlier program CLUSTER/PAF [Michalski & Stepp, 1981]). The algorithm is illustrated by its application to a practical problem in the area of musicology. The conclusion discusses some possible extensions of the method and suggests topics for future research. To improve the readability of this chapter, Table 11-1 provides a list of basic symbols and operators together with a short explanation.

11.2 CONCEPTUAL COHESIVENESS

In conventional data analysis, the similarity between any two objects is characterized by a single number: the value of a similarity function applied to symbolic descriptions of objects. These symbolic descriptions are vectors, whose components are scores on selected object attributes.

Such measures of similarity are *context-free,* that is, the similarity between any two objects A and B depends solely on the properties of the objects, and is not influenced by any context (the "environment" surrounding the objects). Some authors have introduced *context-sensitive* measures of similarity, where the similarity between objects A and B depends not only on A and B, but also on other objects in the collection to be clustered. One such similarity measure is the reciprocal of *mutual distance* [Gowda & Krishna, 1978]. To determine the mutual distance from object A to object B, objects in the collection are ranked according to the Euclidean distance to A (the closest object gets rank 1) and then

Table 11-1: A Table of Basic Symbols and Operators

&	conjunction (logical product)
$\vee$	disjunction (logical sum)
e_i	an event (a description of an object)
LEF	a lexicographical evaluation functional
DOM(p)	the domain of variable p
$\delta(e_1,e_2)$	the syntactic distance between events e_1 and e_2
α	a complex
ℓ-complex	a logical complex
s-complex	a set complex
E	the event space
$s(\alpha)$	number of unobserved events in complex α
$p(\alpha)$	number of observed events in complex α
$t(\alpha)$	total number of events in complex α
E	an event set
k	the number of clusters
$RU(e_1...,\alpha_1...)$	the refunion operator
$GEN(\alpha)$	a generalization of complex α
$COV(E_1 \mid E_2)$	a cover of event set E_1 against E_2
$G(e \mid E_o)$	a star of event e against event set E_o
$RG(e \mid E_o)$	a reduced star of event e against event set E_o
$RG(e \mid E_o,m)$	a bounded reduced star with the bound m

according to the Euclidean distance to B. The mutual distance from object A to object B is the sum of the rank of A with respect to B, and the rank of B with respect to A. Thus the similarity between compared objects depends on their relation to other objects.

Taking neighboring objects into consideration solves some clustering problems, but in general is not sufficient. The difficulty lies in the fact that both of the above types of similarity measures are *concept-free,* that is, depend only on the properties of individual objects and not on any external concepts which might be useful to characterize object configurations. Consequently, methods that use such measures are fundamentally unable to capture the "Gestalt properties" of object clusters, that is, properties that characterize a cluster as a whole and are not derivable from properties of individual entities. In order to detect such properties, the system must be equipped with the ability to recognize configurations of objects that correspond to certain "concepts." To illustrate this point, let us consider the problem of clustering the points in Figure 11-1.

A person considering Figure 11-1 would typically describe the observed points as "arranged in two diamonds". Thus, the points A and B, although closer to each other than to other points, are placed in separate clusters. Here, human solution involves partitioning the points into groups not on the basis of pairwise distance, but on the basis of *concept membership*. Points are placed in the same cluster if collectively they represent the same concept. In our example, the concept is "diamond".

This idea is the basis of conceptual clustering. From the viewpoint of conceptual clustering, the "similarity" between two points A and B, which we shall

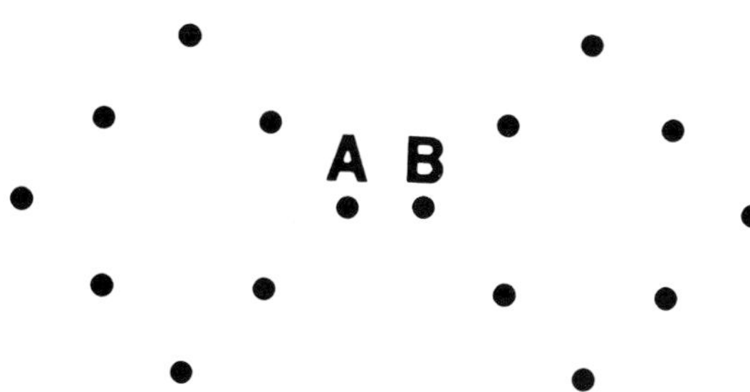

Figure 11-1: An illustration of conceptual clustering.

call the *conceptual cohesiveness* of A and B, depends not only on those points and surrounding points E, but also on a set of concepts C which are available for describing A and B together:

Conceptual cohesiveness(A,B) = f(A,B,E,C)

To illustrate this measure, let us assume that the set of concepts C consists of geometrical figures, such as sequences of straight lines, circles, rectangles, triangles, etc. A measure of conceptual cohesiveness could be defined, for example,[1] as:

$$f(A,B,E,C) = \max_i \{\frac{\#e(i)-1}{area(i)}\}$$

where,

i indexes all geometrical figures that are specified in C and that cover points A and B,

#e(i) is the total number of data points from E covered by figure i,

and

area(i) is the area of figure i.

Note that the constant "-1" in the numerator assures that the conceptual cohesiveness reduces to a conventional similarity measure (a reciprocal of distance) when no context points in E are taken into consideration and C is a straight line of unit thickness linking the data points.

---

[1]This measure is mentioned solely to illustrate the difference between traditional similarity and conceptual cohesiveness. It is not used in the method of conceptual clustering described here.

11.3 TERMINOLOGY AND BASIC OPERATIONS OF THE ALGORITHM

This section gives a brief overview of the terminology needed to describe the conjunctive conceptual clustering method. This terminology was introduced by Michalski [1980a].

11.3.1 Variables and Their Types

Let x_1, x_2,..., x_n denote discrete variables that are selected to describe objects in the population to be analyzed. For each variable a domain is defined, containing all possible values the variable can take. We shall assume that the domains of variables x_i, $i=1,2,...,n$ are finite, and therefore can be represented as:

$$DOM(x_i) = \{0,1,...,d_i\text{-}1\}, \quad i = 1,2,...,n$$

In general, the domains may differ not only with respect to their size, but also with respect to the structure relating their elements. In the case of numerical variables, this structure is defined by the scale of measurement. We distinguish among *nominal* (*categorical*), *linear* (*quantitative*), and *structured* variables, whose domains are unordered, totally-ordered, and graph-ordered sets, respectively. Structured variables represent generalization hierarchies of related values. We distinguish between two types of generalization hierarchies for structured variables:

1. Unordered—when the leaf values in the hierarchy constitute an unordered set.
2. Ordered—when the leaf values in the hierarchy constitute an ordered set.

Figures 11-2 and 11-3 present an example of an unordered and an ordered generalization hierarchy, respectively. In Figure 11-2, the leaves represent specific shapes, and the internal nodes ("polygon", "oval", "4-sided") represent generalizations or linguistic equivalents of these shapes. In Figure 11-3, the leaves represent specific quantities, and the internal nodes represent ordered generalizations or linguistic equivalents of these quantities.

11.3.2 Event Space

An *event* is an object description in the form of a vector of values of the assumed variables x_1, x_2,...,x_n. The *event space* is the space of all possible such events.

11.3.3 Syntactic Distance

The *syntactic distance* $\delta(e_1, e_2)$ between two events e_1 and e_2 is defined as the sum of the syntactic distances between the values of each variable in the events e_1 and e_2. As described by Michalski and Larson [1978], the syntactic distance between two variable values is a number from 0 to 1, determined by a

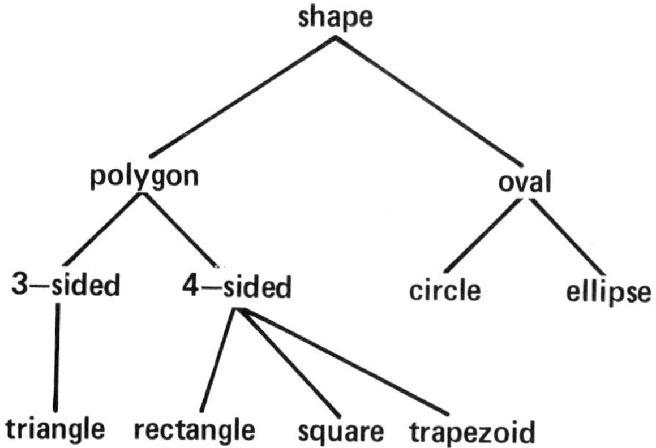

Figure 11-2: An example of an unordered generalization structure.

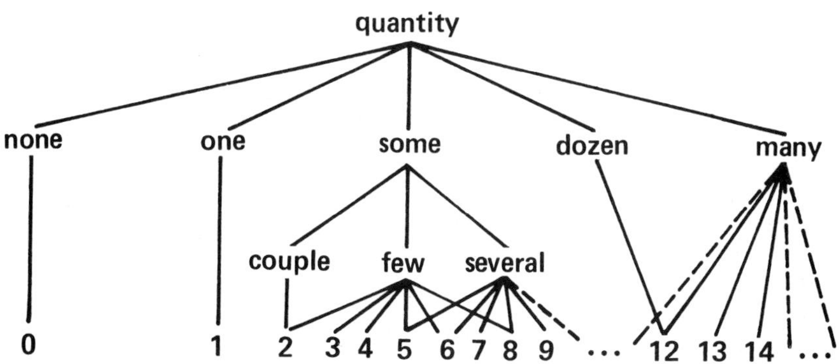

Figure 11-3: An example of an ordered generalization structure.

measure which reflects the domain type of the variable. For a nominal variable, the syntactic distance is either 0, if the values taken by the variable in each event are identical, or 1, if the values are not identical. For a linear variable, the syntactic distance is the ratio of the absolute difference between the values to the total span of the domain of the variable. For a structured variable, the evaluation of syntactic distance depends on the type of generalization hierarchy. Since structured variable values in events are leaves of a generalization hierarchy, the syntactic distance between such values for unordered and ordered hierarchies is evaluated the same way as for nominal and linear variables, respectively.

11.3.4 Relational Statements

A *relational statement*[2] (or a *selector*) is a form:

$[x_i \# R_i]$

where,

R_i, the *reference*, is a list of elements from the domain of variable x_i, linked by the *internal disjunction*, denoted by " $\vee$ ".

\# stands for the relational operator "$=$" or "$\neq$".

The selector $[x_i = R_i]$ ($[x_i \neq R_i]$) is interpreted as "value of x_i is one of the elements of R_i" ("value of x_i is not an element of R_i"). In the case of linear variables, the notation of a selector can be simplified by using relational operators $\geq$, $>$, $<$, $\leq$, and a range operator "..", as illustrated below. Here are a few examples of a selector, in which variables and their values are represented by linguistic terms:

[length > 2]	(length is greater than 2)
[color = blue $\vee$ red]	(color is blue or red)
[size $\neq$ medium]	(size is not medium)
[weight = 2..5]	(weight is between 2 and 5, inclusively)

11.3.5 Complexes

A logical product of selectors is called a *logical complex* (ℓ-complex) $\&_{i \in I}[x_i \# R_i]$, where $I \subseteq \{1,2,...,n\}$. An event e is said to satisfy an ℓ-complex if values of variables in e satisfy all the selectors in the complex.

For example, event e = (2, 7, 0, 1, 5, 4, 6) satisfies ℓ-complex $[x_1 = 2 \vee 3][x_3 \leq 3][x_5 = 3..8]$ (concatenation of selectors denotes conjunction). An ℓ-complex can be viewed as an exact symbolic representation of the events which satisfy it. For example, the above ℓ-complex is the symbolic representation of all events for which x_1 is 2 or 3, x_3 is smaller than or equal to 3, and x_5 is between 3 and 8.

A collection of events for which there exists an ℓ-complex satisfied by these events and only by these events is called a *set complex* (s-complex). If the distinction between ℓ- and s- complexes is not important, then we shall use simply the term *complex*.

---

[2]This form is a special case of a referential selector defined in the annotated predicate calculus (Chapter 4 of this book). This form was first introduced in the variable valued logic system one (VL_1), described by Michalski [1975a].

11.3.6 Sparseness

Let $\mathbf{E}$ be an event space, and $E \subseteq \mathbf{E}$ be a set of events representing objects to be clustered. The events in E are called observed events, and events in $\mathbf{E} \setminus E$ are called unobserved events. Let α be a complex which covers (includes) some observed events and some unobserved events. The number of observed events (points) in α is denoted by $p(\alpha)$. The number of unobserved events in α is called the *absolute sparseness* of α *in* $\mathbf{E}$ and denoted by $s(\alpha)$. The total number of events contained in α is thus $t(\alpha) = p(\alpha) + s(\alpha)$. The *relative* sparseness *of a complex* is denoted by $r(\alpha)$ and is defined as the ratio of the absolute sparseness of the complex to the total number of events covered by the complex, in other words:

$$r(\alpha) = 1 - \frac{p(\alpha)}{t(\alpha)}$$

An ℓ-complex is a generalized description of the observed events contained in the corresponding s-complex. The relative sparseness of a complex can be used as a very simple measure of the degree to which the ℓ-complex generalizes over (or *fits*) the observed events. If the sparseness is zero, then the description covers only observed events (has zero degree of generalization). As the relative sparseness of the complex increases, so does the degree to which it generalizes over the observed events. The maximum relative sparseness value of 1 is achieved when the complex covers only unobserved events.

The clustering algorithm presented in Section 11.5.1 generates a collection of complexes that are pairwise disjoint. Such a collection, called a *disjoint clustering*, describes a partition of all observed events into disjoint classes. The fit between a disjoint clustering and the observed events can be measured by the *relative sparseness* of the clustering, defined as the average of the relative sparsenesses of the complexes in the clustering. Since the complexes in a clustering are disjoint and the total number of observed events is constant, the ranking of clusterings will not change if the relative sparseness measure is replaced by the *absolute* sparseness measure (the sum of absolute sparsenesses of complexes). The latter measure is much simpler computationally and, therefore, is used in the presented clustering algorithm. Henceforth, we shall simply use the term sparseness to denote this measure of fit.

An advantage of sparseness as a measure of fit is its simplicity. A disadvantage, however, is that it takes into consideration the whole event space, no matter which variables spanning the space are actually present in the ℓ-complexes. Therefore, another measure is introduced, called *projected* sparseness, which evaluates a clustering in a subspace of the original event space, defined by specially selected "relevant" variables. To define this measure, let us observe that complexes of a disjoint clustering may involve different subsets of variables. Because complexes are pairwise disjoint, any pair of complexes must contain at least one common variable with disjoint references in both complexes. A variable with this property for any pair of complexes in a clustering is called a *discriminant variable* of the clustering. For example, x_1, x_3, and x_4 are discriminant variables of the clustering:

$$\{[x_1 \geq 3]\ [x_2 = 1 \vee 2]\ [x_3 = 1],\ \ [x_1 < 3]\ [x_3 = 2 \vee 3]\ [x_4 = 3],\ \ [x_2 = 1]\ [x_4 \leq 2]\}.$$

The event space spanned over only the discriminant variables is called the *projected event space* of the clustering. The projected sparseness of a clustering is the sum of the absolute sparsenesses of complexes in the projected event space.

11.3.7 Refunion Operator

The *refunion* operator RU transforms a set of events and/or complexes into a single complex covering the events and/or complexes. For each variable, the set of all values the variable takes, in all given events and complexes, is determined. These sets are used as the reference of the variable in the generated complex. For example, given:

$e_1 = (2,3,0,1)$

$e_2 = (0,2,1,1)$ and

$\alpha = [x_1 = 2..3]\ [x_2 = 4]\ [x_3 = 0]\ [x_4 = 2]$

the refunion complex, $RU(e_1,e_2,\alpha)$, denoted α', is:

$\alpha' = [x_1 = 0 \vee 2 \vee 3]\ [x_2 = 2 \vee 3 \vee 4]\ [x_3 = 0 \vee 1]\ [x_4 = 1 \vee 2]$

It can be shown that the refunion complex has the minimum sparseness (absolute or relative) among all complexes covering the given events and/or complexes [Michalski, 1980c].

11.3.8 GEN Operator

The generalizing operator GEN simplifies and generalizes any given complex by applying an appropriate generalization rule (see Section 4.5 in Chapter 4 of this book) to each selector in the complex:

1. To linear selectors, the "closing the interval" rule is applied: The reference is clustered into one or a few disjoint intervals, such that the ratio of the number of unobserved values to the width of the enclosing interval is at or below a certain *sparseness threshold*. For example, the reference $1 \vee 2 \vee 3 \vee 7 \vee 8$ is turned into one interval 1..8, if the assumed threshold is 3/8 or more. If the threshold is less than 3/8, the reference is turned into two intervals $1..3 \vee 7..8$.
2. To structured selectors, the "climbing the generalization hierarchy" rule is applied: A reference with more than one value is replaced by the most specific node in the generalization hierarchy which "covers" the reference.
3. After steps (1) and (2) are completed, the "dropping the condition" rule is applied to all selectors: A selector is removed if the ratio of the number of

missing reference values to the number of values in the domain of the variable is below a certain sparseness threshold.

To illustrate the GEN operator, consider the complex α', given above, and assume that variables x_1 and x_2 are linear, variable x_3 is structured, and variable x_4 is nominal, that the domain of x_3 is a generalization hierarchy in which the value "small" is the parent node of values 0 and 1, and that the domain of x_4 contains values 0, 1, 2. Assume also that the sparseness threshold for all variables is 0.5. Then we have:

$$\text{GEN}(\alpha'): \; [x_1 \leq 3][x_2 = 2..4][x_3 = \text{small}]$$

where the references for x_1 and x_2 are generalized by closing the interval, the reference for x_3 is generalized by climbing the generalization tree, and the selector for variable x_4 is removed by dropping the condition.

11.3.9 Cover

Let E_1 and E_2 be two disjoint event sets, that is, $E_1 \cap E_2 = \emptyset$. A cover $\text{COV}(E_1|E_2)$ of E_1 against E_2 is any set of s-complexes $\{\alpha_j\}_{j \in J}$ such that for each event $e \in E_1$ there is an s-complex α_j, $j \in J$, covering it, and none of the complexes α_j cover any event in E_2:

$$E_1 \subseteq \cup_{j \in J} \alpha_j \subseteq \mathbf{E} \setminus E_2$$

By representing complexes of the cover as ℓ-complexes, a cover can be expressed as a logical disjunction of these complexes.

A cover in which all s-complexes are pairwise disjoint is called a *disjoint cover*. If E_1 is a collection to be clustered and $E_2 = \emptyset$, then a disjoint cover $\text{COV}(E_1|\emptyset)$, or simply $\text{COV}(E_1)$, represents a disjoint clustering of events. The algorithm described in Section 11.5 generates a disjoint clustering of events by repetitively constructing a special type of cover, called a *star*.

11.3.10 Star

The *star* $G(e|E_o)$ of event e against event set E_o ($e \notin E_o$) is the set of all maximally general[3] complexes covering the event e and not covering any event in E_o. Informally, it is the set of all maximally general descriptions of event e which do not intersect with set E_o. Figure 11-4 presents a star of event e against events denoted by "•" in the two dimensional space spanned over linear variables. The star consists of complexes α_1, α_2, and α_3. Complex α'_3 is a "reduced" complex α_3, as explained below.

In the algorithm described in the next section, the "theoretical" stars (defined above) are subjected to two major modifications. The first is to min-

[3]A complex α is maximally general with respect to a property P if there does not exist a complex α^* with property P such that $\alpha \subset \alpha^*$.

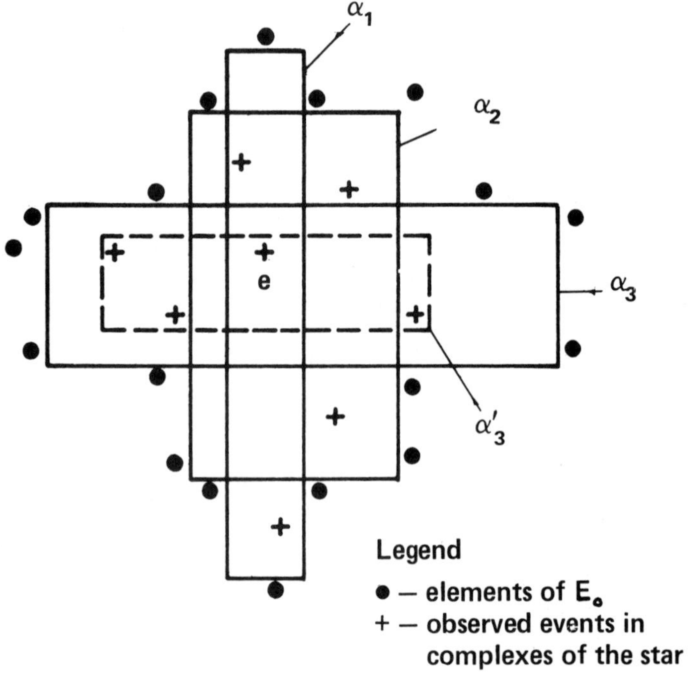

Figure 11-4: An illustration of the star $G(e|E_0)$.

imize the sparseness of complexes in the stars, and the second is to "bound" the stars, that is, to select from them a certain number of "best" complexes, according to a context-dependent criterion. The first modification is performed by procedure Redustar, described below, and the second by procedure Boundstar described in Section 11.5.1.2.

11.3.11 Redustar Procedure

Complexes in stars $G(e|E_0)$ are maximally general, and therefore may describe objects in an overgeneralized way. The Redustar procedure generates a star, and then maximally reduces the sparseness of each complex in it, while preserving the coverage of observed events. For example, complex α'_3 in Figure 11-4 is such a reduced complex obtained from complex α_3. The steps of the procedure are:

1. Elementary stars, $G(e|e_i)$, $e_i \in E_0$, are determined.

   To generate an elementary star $G(e|e_i)$ of an event e against another event e_i, all variables that have different values in e than in e_i are identified. Suppose, with no loss of generality, that these variables are

$x_1,x_2,...,x_g$, and that $e_i = (r_1,r_2,..., r_g,...,r_n)$. The complexes of the star $G(e|e_i)$ are then $[x_j \neq r_j]$, $j=1,2,...,g$, because these are the maximally general complexes which cover e and do not cover e_i. The number of complexes in an elementary star is at most n, and, because $e_i \neq e$, at least 1.

2. The complete star $G(e|E_o)$ is determined.

The star $G(e|E_o)$ is generated by first setting up the logical product & $G'(e|e_i)$, $e_i \in E_o$, where $G'(e|e_i)$ is the disjunction of complexes from the elementary star $G(e|e_i)$. Next, the multiplication of complexes is performed, using absorption laws, until a disjunction of nonredundant complexes is obtained. This multiplication is carried out in steps, each step being a multiplication of a disjunction of complexes by a disjunction of selectors (the elements of consecutive elementary stars). The set of the complexes in the resulting disjunction is $G(e|E_o)$.

3. Complexes in $G(e|E_o)$ are reduced and simplified.

The sparseness of each complex in the star is reduced as much as possible without "uncovering" any of the observed events. This is done by performing the refunion of all the observed events contained in each complex. The complexes are then generalized and simplified by applying the GEN operator. The resulting set of complexes is a reduced star $RG(e|E_o)$.

The theoretical basis for the above algorithm generating the star $G(e|E_o)$ is described in Michalski [1975b].

11.3.12 NID Procedure

This procedure transforms a set of Nondisjoint complexes Into a set of Disjoint complexes (that is, a disjoint clustering). If input complexes to NID are already disjoint, the procedure leaves them unchanged. The steps of the procedure are:

1. "Core" complexes are determined.

Observed events covered by more than one complex from the given set are placed on the *multiply-covered event list* (m-list). If the m-list is empty, then the complexes are only weakly intersecting, that is, the intersection area contains only unobserved events. In this case, the procedure terminates with an indication that the combination of complexes is a *weakly intersecting clustering*. Otherwise, each complex is replaced by the Refunion of the observed events contained in the complex that are not on the m-list (i.e., that are singly covered). The obtained Refunions are called "core" complexes.

2. A best "host" complex is determined for each event on the m-list.

An event is selected from the m-list and is "added" to each of the k core complexes by generalizing each complex to the extent necessary to cover the event. Such a generalization is performed by applying the Refunion operator to the event and the complex. As a result, k modified complexes are obtained. By replacing one of the core complexes in the initial set with the corresponding modified complex, in k different ways, a collection of clusterings is obtained. These clusterings are evaluated according to the assumed clustering quality criterion (see the next section). The best clustering is determined, and the complex in it that covers the given event from the m-list is considered to be the best "host" for this event. The best clustering is retained and the remaining ones are eliminated. By repeating the above operation for every event on the m-list, a set of k disjoint complexes is obtained whose union covers the same observed events as the original set of nondisjoint complexes.

If an event cannot be "added" to any complex without causing the result to intersect other complexes, then the event is placed on the *exceptions list*.

11.4 A CRITERION OF CLUSTERING QUALITY

The problem of how to judge the quality of a clustering is difficult, and there seems to be no universal answer to it. One can, however, indicate two major criteria. The first is that descriptions formulated for clusters (classes) should be "simple", so that it is easy to assign objects to classes and to differentiate between the classes. This criterion alone, however, could lead to trivial and arbitrary classifications. The second criterion is that class descriptions should "fit well" the actual data. To achieve a very precise "fit", however, a description may have to be complex. Consequently, the demands for simplicity and good fit are conflicting, and the solution is to find a balance between the two.

A number of other measures can be introduced for evaluating clustering quality. CLUSTER/2 uses a combined measure which can include any of the following elementary criteria:

- the fit between the clustering and the events
- the simplicity of cluster descriptions
- the inter-cluster difference
- the discrimination index
- the dimensionality reduction

The fit between a clustering and the data is computed in two different ways, denoted as T and P. The T measure is the negative of the total sparseness of the clustering, and the P measure is the negative of the sum of the projected sparsenesses of the complexes. The reason for using the negative values is to increase the degree of match as the sparseness decreases.

Simplicity of cluster descriptions is defined as the negative of the complexity, which is the total number of selectors in all descriptions.

Inter-cluster difference is measured by the sum of the degrees of disjointness between every pair of complexes in the clustering. The degree of disjointness of a pair of complexes is the number of selectors in both complexes after removing selectors that intersect. For example, the pair of complexes:

- [color = red] [*size = small or medium*] [shape = circle]
- [color = blue] [*size = medium or large*]

has the degree of disjointness 3, because 2 of the 5 selectors intersect (intersecting selectors are italicized). This criterion promotes clusterings with classes having many differing properties, and is analogous to the criterion of requiring maximal distance between clusters, used in conventional methods of clustering.

The *discrimination index* is the number of variables that singly discriminate among all the clusters, that is, variables having different values in every cluster description.

Dimensionality reduction is measured by the negative of the essential dimensionality, defined as the minimum number of variables required to distinguish among all complexes in a clustering. It can be computed by applying to the clustering the variable-valued logic minimization algorithm A^q [Michalski, 1975b]. When the discrimination index is greater than zero, the essential dimensionality is exactly one.

The definitions of the above criteria are such that the increase of any criterion value improves the quality of the clustering. The relative influence of each criterion is specified using the "Lexicographical Evaluation Functional with tolerances" (LEF) [Michalski, 1980b]. The LEF is defined by a sequence of *criterion-tolerance* pairs (c_1,τ_1), (c_2,τ_2), ..., where c_i is an elementary criterion selected from the above list, and τ_i is a *tolerance threshold* ($\tau \in [0..100\%]$). In the first step, all clusterings are evaluated on the first criterion, c_1, and those that score best or within the range defined by the threshold τ_1 are retained. Next, the retained clusterings are evaluated on criterion c_2 with threshold τ_2, similarly to the above. This process continues until either the set of retained clusterings is reduced to a singleton (the "best" clustering) or the sequence of criterion-tolerance pairs is exhausted. In the latter case, the retained clusterings have equivalent quality with respect to the given LEF, and any one may be chosen arbitrarily. The selection of elementary criteria, their ordering, and the specification of tolerances is made by a data analyst.

11.5 METHOD AND IMPLEMENTATION

This section describes the algorithm for conjunctive conceptual clustering implemented in the program CLUSTER/2 (the successor to the program CLUSTER/PAF [Michalski & Stepp, 1981]). The algorithm consists of a *clustering module* and a *hierarchy-building module*, which are described in Sections

11.5.1 and 11.5.2, respectively. Section 11.5.1.4 gives an example illustrating the details of the clustering module.

11.5.1 The Clustering Module

11.5.1.1 The Full-search Version of the Algorithm

The basic algorithm underlying the implementation of the clustering module was introduced in [Michalski, 1980a]. Its goal can be described as follows:

Given:

- A collection of events to be clustered, E
- The number of clusters desired, k, and
- The criterion of clustering quality, LEF

Find:

- A disjoint clustering of the collection of events that optimizes the given criterion of clustering quality LEF.

We shall first describe a straightforward, exhaustive-search version of the algorithm, and then show how this version is modified to increase efficiency. The steps are:

1. Initial seeds are determined.

   From the given collection of events E, k events (the initial seeds) are selected. The seeds may be chosen randomly or according to some criterion. (After this first step, seeds are always selected according to certain rules; see step 5).

2. Stars are constructed for seeds.

   For each seed e_i, a reduced star $RG(e_i|E_0)$ is constructed by procedure Redustar, where E_0 is the set of remaining seeds.

3. An optimized clustering (a disjoint cover of E) is built by selecting and modifying complexes from stars.

   Every combination of complexes, created by selecting one complex from each star, is tested to see whether it contains intersecting complexes. If so, the complexes are made disjoint by procedure NID.

4. A termination criterion is evaluated.

   If this is the first iteration, the obtained clustering is stored. In subsequent iterations the clustering is stored only if it scores better than previously-stored clusterings according to the LEF (see Section 11.4). The algorithm terminates when a specified number of iterations does not produce a better clustering (this number is defined by a termination criterion, described below).

5. New seeds are selected.

New seeds are selected from sets of observed events contained in complexes of the generated clustering, one seed per complex. Two seed-selection techniques are used. One technique selects "central" events, defined as events nearest the geometrical centers of the complexes (as determined by the syntactic distance). The other technique, stemming from the "adversity principle[4]", selects "border" events, defined as events farthest from the centers. Ties for central or border events are broken in favor of events which have not been used recently as seeds. The technique of selecting central events is used repetitively in consecutive iterations as long as the clusterings improve. When the improvement ceases, border events are selected.

After selecting seeds, a new iteration of the algorithm begins from step 2.

The algorithm is summarized by the flow chart in Figure 11-5.

Along with a clustering, the algorithm generates k ℓ-complexes describing individual clusters, and determines how these complexes score on the evaluation criteria in the LEF. The algorithm stops when the *termination criterion* is satisfied. The termination criterion is a pair of parameters (b,p), where b (the *base*) is a standard number of iterations the algorithm always performs, and p (the *probe*) is the number of additional iterations beyond b performed after each iteration which produced an improved cover. The general structure of the algorithm is based on the so-called dynamic clustering method [Diday & Simon, 1976].

The most computationally costly part of this algorithm is the construction of an optimized clustering, given k seed events (step 3). For an illustration, let us assume that $k=2$ and that k "seeds", e_1 and e_2, have been selected from the collection E. In the first step, stars $G_1 = G(e_1|\text{remaining seeds})$ and $G_2 = G(e_2|\text{remaining seeds})$ are generated. Figure 11-6 presents complexes of these stars as branches of a search tree. Branches from the root represent complexes of star G_1 that are α_{11}, α_{12}, ...,α_{1m_1}, and branches at the second level (repeated m_1 times) represent complexes of star G_2 that are α_{21},α_{22},...,α_{2m_2}. Each combination of complexes, containing one complex from each star, corresponds to one path in the tree. Because any such combination may contain intersecting complexes, procedure NID is applied to each, and the result is a disjoint clustering. These clusterings are ordered according to the quality criterion LEF, and the best one is selected.

---

[4]This principle states that if a border, "near hit" event truly belongs to the given cluster, then when selected as the seed it should produce the same clustering as when a central event is used as a seed.

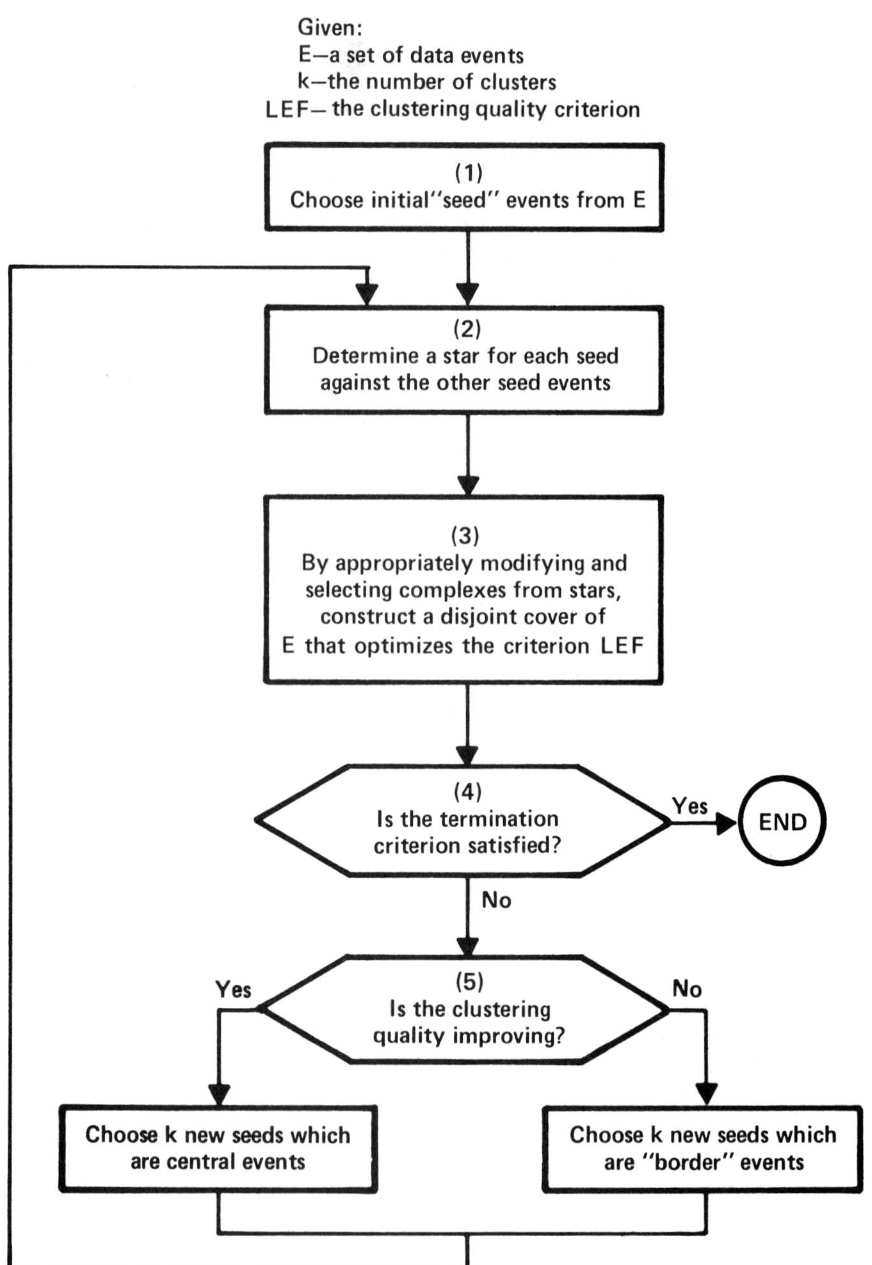

Figure 11-5: The flow chart of the clustering module.

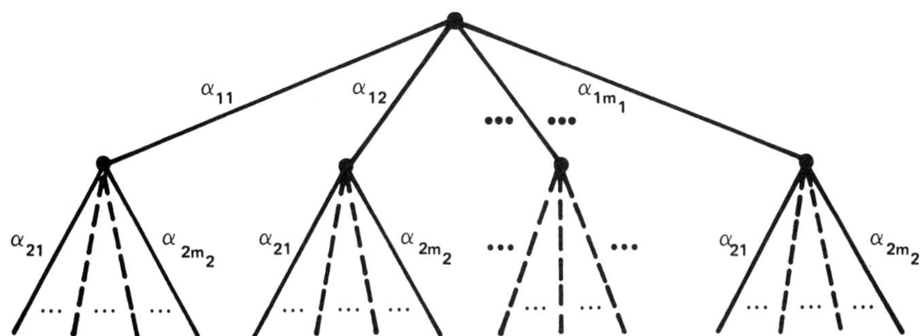

Figure 11-6: The exhaustive-search search tree for k = 2.

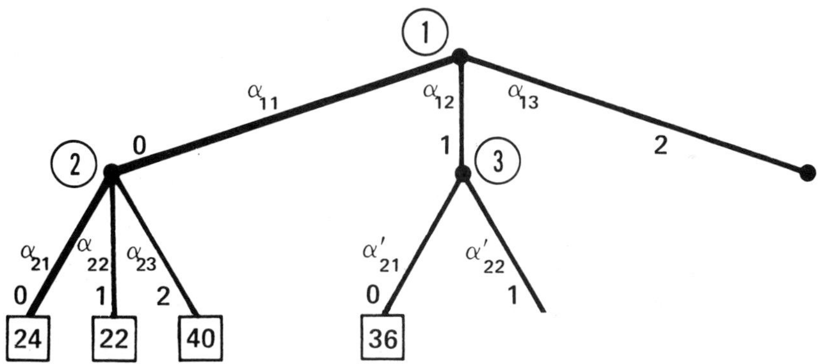

Figure 11-7: The Path-Rank-Ordered search tree for k = 2 used in CLUSTER/2.

11.5.1.2 Path-Rank-Ordered (PRO) Search Procedure Used in CLUSTER/2

The above strategy for determining a clustering from seeds is very simple, but unfortunately too inefficient for solving any interesting practical problems. This is due to the fact that the stars may contain very many complexes. When there are n variables and k seeds, a star may contain up to n^{k-1} complexes (there are at most n complexes in any of the k-1 elementary stars needed to compute the complete star). Thus, when n = 30 and k = 3, there could be up to $n^{k-1} = 900$

complexes, and the search tree could have up to 900-way branching at each node, and up to $900^3 = 729$ million leaves. Absorption laws (as defined in Boolean algebra) will usually eliminate many redundant complexes, but the star may still be too large. Artificial intelligence research on various heuristic search procedures offers various possibilities for reducing the search (for example, Nilsson [1980] or Winston [1977]). To solve this problem, we have adopted some of the known ideas and also developed some new ones. The result is a search procedure called Path-Rank-Ordered (PRO) search that incorporates the following four techniques:

1. Bounding the stars (procedure Boundstar).

   The number of complexes in a star is bounded by a fixed integer m, which assures that the search tree has at most m-way branching. A bounded star contains not just m arbitrary complexes from the initial star, but the m "best" ones.

   At each step of star generation (a multiplication of a set of complexes by the next elementary star; see the Redustar procedure in Section 11.3.11), complexes are first reduced and then arranged in descending order according to the assumed clustering quality criterion LEF. Only the first m complexes are retained for the next multiplication step. This operation is also performed at the end of star generation, so that the final star has at most m complexes. The stars so obtained are called *bounded reduced stars* and denoted RG(e|E_0,m).

   Some elementary criteria measure global properties of a clustering rather than properties of just a single complex (such as the inter-cluster differences). Consequently, when evaluating a complex descending from a node in the search tree that is not the root, the complex is evaluated in the context of complexes associated with the path from the root to this node.

   By bounding the star we gain significantly in efficiency, but give up the assurance that the obtained clustering will be optimal. This is not a significant loss, however, because the clustering obtained at the end of each iteration contributes only the seeds to the next iteration, and thus its optimality is not very important.

2. Generating stars dynamically.

   Because it is necessary to evaluate complexes in the context of previously selected complexes, bounding a star has to be done differently at each node of the search tree. CLUSTER/2 uses a "lazy" strategy, in which a star is generated only when it is needed to expand a node on the path being explored.

3. Searching in order of path rank.

   As we mentioned above, complexes in a bounded star are arranged in descending order according to the LEF. In the search tree, the branch to the best complex is assigned the *branch index* 0, the branch to the next best complex is assigned the branch index 1, and so on, up to the index m-1. The *path index* of a path from the root to a leaf is the sum of the branch indices along the path.

The paths from the root to a leaf represent potential clusterings and are investigated in the ascending order of their path index. Thus, the first path investigated is the one with path index 0, that is, the path containing only the "best" complexes from each star. The next paths considered are those with a path index of one. There are k such paths.

As paths of increasing path index are generated and evaluated, a search termination criterion is applied. This criterion consists of two parameters, *search-base* and *search-probe*. A search-base number of paths is always expanded and evaluated. Then, a search-probe number of additional paths is considered. Each path is processed by NID, and if some complexes are transformed to make them disjoint, the clustering-quality criterion is evaluated again. Whenever a new clustering is better than any previous clustering, it is saved and another search-probe number of additional paths is explored. If the above probing fails to find a better clustering, the search terminates.

4. Tapering the search tree.

The bound of the stars, m, is decreased with the increase of the path index. The search tree is, therefore, more fully developed on the side containing the "higher quality" complexes.

Figure 11-7 shows an example of a search tree generated by CLUSTER/2. The tree is a modification of the tree in Figure 11-6, resulting from the application of the above efficiency-increasing techniques. In Figure 11-7, the maximum value of bound m is set to 3. The root is expanded by constructing the star G(seed$_1$|other seeds,3), whose complexes are α_{11}, α_{12}, and α_{13} (listed in decreasing order of their "quality", as determined by the LEF). The branches representing these complexes are assigned branch indices 0, 1, and 2, respectively. The node attached to branch 0 is expanded next. The star G(seed$_2$|other seeds,3) is generated, creating complexes α_{21}, α_{22}, and α_{23}. Branches corresponding to these complexes are assigned branch indices 0, 1, and 2, respectively. The path 0-0 (having the lowest path index of 0, denoted by heavy lines in Figure 11-7) is considered first. The associated clustering $\{\alpha_{11}, \alpha_{21}\}$ is processed by NID, and the result is saved as the best clustering so far. Next, path 0-1 is considered. The associated clustering $\{\alpha_{11}, \alpha_{22}\}$ is processed by NID and evaluated. If it is better than the previous clustering, it is saved. In order to explore the path 1-0 (the second path with path index 1), the star G(seed$_2$|other seeds,2) is generated. The star contains complexes α'_{21} and α'_{22}. The clustering $\{\alpha_{12}, \alpha'_{21}\}$ associated with the currently investigated path is evaluated. Assuming that the termination criterion has the parameters search-base = 2 and search-probe = 2, and that the evaluation scores are as shown in Figure 11-7, the tree search terminates after investigating the fourth path 0-2 (since this path exhausts the probing without finding a better clustering). Path 0-1, with the evaluation score of 22, is the best clustering found.

11.5.1.3 Dynamic Modification of Classifications

The obtained clustering partitions all the observed events into disjoint classes. The set-theoretic union of complexes in the clustering does not, however, necessarily cover the whole event space. Consequently, when a given classification is applied to a new event that is "outside" this union, it is not possible to assign this event to any class. In such a case, the classification (clustering) is automatically adjusted to accommodate the new event. This is done by applying the NID procedure (Section 11.3.12), modified as follows. The complexes of the current clustering play the role of "core" complexes, and the new event is treated as an element of the m-list. The event is incorporated into the complex that is the best "host" for it, as determined by NID. As a result, the original complex becomes the Refunion of itself and the event. This way, the initial classification is modified to incorporate the new, unforeseen event. Such a process has a psychological justification, as it is common for people to modify their classifications when some object fails to fit them, by appropriately perturbing the boundaries of the classes.

11.5.1.4 An Example Illustrating the Clustering Module

The following simple example illustrates some further details of the clustering module algorithm. There are ten objects, each described by four variables: x_1, x_2, x_3, and x_4, with three-valued domains, $DOM(x_i) = \{0,1,2\}$, $i=1,2,3,4$. Variables x_1 and x_3 are linear, variable x_2 is structured, and variable x_4 is nominal. The generalization hierarchy of the domain of x_2 is shown in Figure 11-8. Object descriptions (events in the population E) are presented in Figure 11-9. For simplicity, let us assume that the goal is to partition objects into only two classes ($k=2$) using a LEF in which the primary criterion (with tolerance of 0%) is to minimize the total sparseness, and the secondary criterion is to maximize the simplicity of the clustering, (that is, the negative of the number of selectors). Figure 11-10 shows a geometrical representation of the events using a generalized logic diagram [Michalski, 1978]. Each cell in the diagram is labeled by the event it represents. Empty cells represent unobserved events.

The steps of the algorithm follow the diagram in Figure 11-5.

Iteration 1

Step 1 (Figure 11-5, block 1): A subset of $k=2$ observed events (seeds) is selected from the population $E = \{e_i\}$, $i=1,2,...,10$. The seeds can be selected randomly, or they can be chosen as events which are most syntactically distant from each other. In the latter case, as experiments show, the algorithm will usually converge faster. For selecting such "outstanding" events, program ESEL [Michalski & Larson, 1978] is used. For the sample problem, let us make a "bad" choice and select two events close to each other, such as e_1 and e_2.

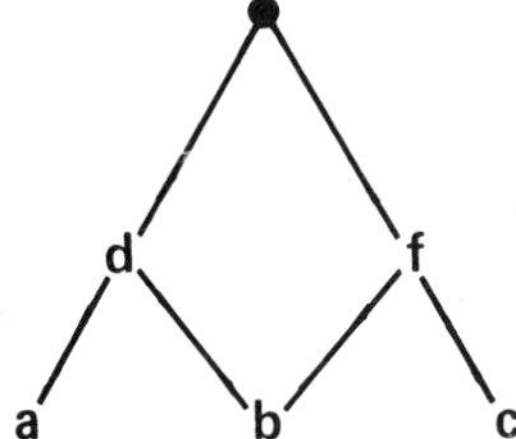

Figure 11-8: The generalization hierarchy of the domain of variable x_2.

Event	x_1	x_2	x_3	x_4
e_1	0	a	0	1
e_2	0	b	0	0
e_3	0	c	1	2
e_4	1	a	0	2
e_5	1	c	1	1
e_6	2	a	1	0
e_7	2	b	0	1
e_8	2	b	1	2
e_9	2	c	0	0
e_{10}	2	c	2	2
Variable Type:	L	S	L	N

(L: linear; N: nominal; S: structured)

Figure 11-9: A data set describing ten objects, using four variables.

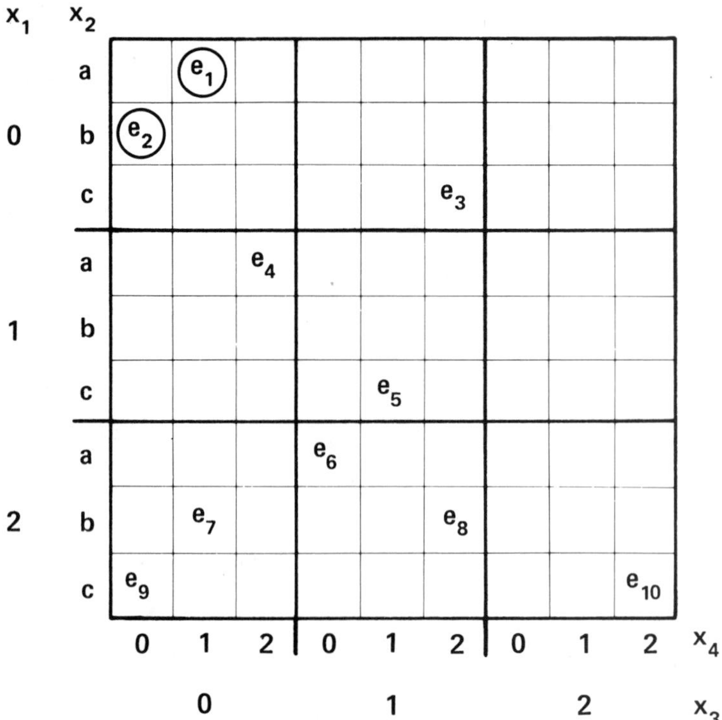

Figure 11-10: A geometrical representation of events e_1 to e_{10}. Encircled events are initial seeds.

Step 2 (Figure 11-5, block 2): Bounded reduced stars $RG(e_1|e_2,m)$ and $RG(e_2|e_1,m)$, with $m=5$, are generated by procedure Boundstar (described in Section 11.5.1.2):

$$RG(e_1|e_2,m) = \{[x_2 = a][x_3 = 0 \vee 1],\ [x_4 = 1 \vee 2]\}$$

$$RG(e_2|e_1,m) = \{[x_2 = b \vee c],\ [x_4 = 0 \vee 2]\}$$

These stars contain all possible complexes, because $m>2$. After applying the *closing the interval* and *climbing the hierarchy* generalization rules, the stars become:

$$RG(e_1|e_2,m) = \{[x_2 = a][x_3 = \leq 1],\ [x_4 = 1 \vee 2]\}$$

$$RG(e_2|e_1,m) = \{[x_2 = f],\ [x_4 = 0 \vee 2]\}$$

The reference "b $\vee$ c" in the selector for the structured variable x_2 has been replaced by a more general value, f (Figure 11-8).

Step 3 (Figure 11-5, block 3): From each star a complex is selected and appropriately modified, such that the resulting set of k=2 complexes is a disjoint cover of E, and is an optimal or suboptimal cover among all possible such covers, according to the clustering quality criterion. There are four combinations of complexes to consider:

			Sparseness	Complexity
(a)	complex 1:	$[x_2 = a][x_3 \leq 1]$	15	2
	complex 2:	$[x_2 = f]$	47	1
			62	3

(b)	complex 1:	$[x_4 = 1 \vee 2]$	These covers are not disjoint. Procedure NID (Section 11.3.12) is applied to each cover, but the sparseness of resulting clusterings in each case is ≥ 62 and their complexity is 3.
	complex 2:	$[x_2 = f]$	
(c)	complex 1:	$[x_2 = a][x_3 \leq 1]$	
	complex 2:	$[x_4 = 0 \vee 2]$	
(d)	complex 1:	$[x_4 = 1 \vee 2]$	
	complex 2:	$[x_4 = 0 \vee 2]$	

Cover (a) is selected since it has the minimum total sparseness.

Step 4 (Figure 11-5, block 4): The termination criterion is tested. In our example, the parameters of the termination criterion are: base=2 and probe=2 (Section 11.4). The current iteration is the first of the two base iterations.

Step 5 (Figure 11-5, block 5): A new set of seeds is determined. These new seeds are central events, among the observed events covered by (a). Complex $[x_2 = a][x_3 \leq 1]$ covers the set $\{e_1,e_4,e_6\}$, and complex $[x_2 = f]$ covers the set $\{e_2,e_3,e_5,e_7,e_8,e_9,e_{10}\}$ (notice that value f of x_2 is a generalization of b and c according to Figure 11-8). The central events (as determined by syntactic distance) in these sets are e_4 and e_8, respectively, so they become new seeds.

Iteration 2

Step 2:

New stars $RG(e_4|e_8,m)$ and $RG(e_8|e_4,m)$ are generated:

$$RG(e_4|e_8,m) = \{[x_2 = a][x_3 \leq 1], [x_1 \leq 1][x_3 \leq 1], [x_3 = 0]\}$$

$$RG(e_8|e_4,m) = \{[x_1 = 2], [x_2 = f], [x_3 = \geq 1]\}$$

Step 3:

All combinations of complexes (obtained by selecting one complex from each star) are subjected to procedure NID and then evaluated. The best clustering is:

		Sparseness	Complexity
complex 1:	$[x_1 \leq 1][x_3 \leq 1]$	31	2
complex 2:	$[x_1 = 2]$	22	1
		53	3

Step 4:
This is the last of the base iterations.

Step 5:
Complex $[x_1 \leq 1][x_3 \leq 1]$ covers events $\{e_1,e_2,e_3,e_4,e_5\}$ and $[x_1 = 2]$ covers $\{e_6,e_7,e_8,e_9,e_{10}\}$. Since this clustering is an improvement over the previous one (since it has a lower sparseness), the new seeds selected are central events: e_1 and e_8.

Iteration 3

This iteration produces the same clustering as iteration 1.

Step 4: This is the first of the two "probe" iterations.

Step 5: Since the clustering obtained is not better than the previous one, border events are selected as the new seeds: e_2 and e_6.

Iteration 4

This iteration produces a new clustering:

		Sparseness	Complexity
complex 1:	$[x_3 \geq 1]$	49	1
complex 2:	$[x_3 = 0]$	22	1
		71	2

It is the second "probe" iteration. If the obtained clustering was better than the previous best clustering, another probe=2 iterations would be scheduled. Since the sparseness of the clustering obtained in this iteration (71) is not an improvement over the previous best sparseness (53), the termination criterion is satisfied. The best resulting clustering is the one produced in iteration 2:

$[x_1 \leq 1][x_3 \leq 1]$

$[x_1 = 2]$

Figure 11-11 shows the diagrammatic representation of this solution.

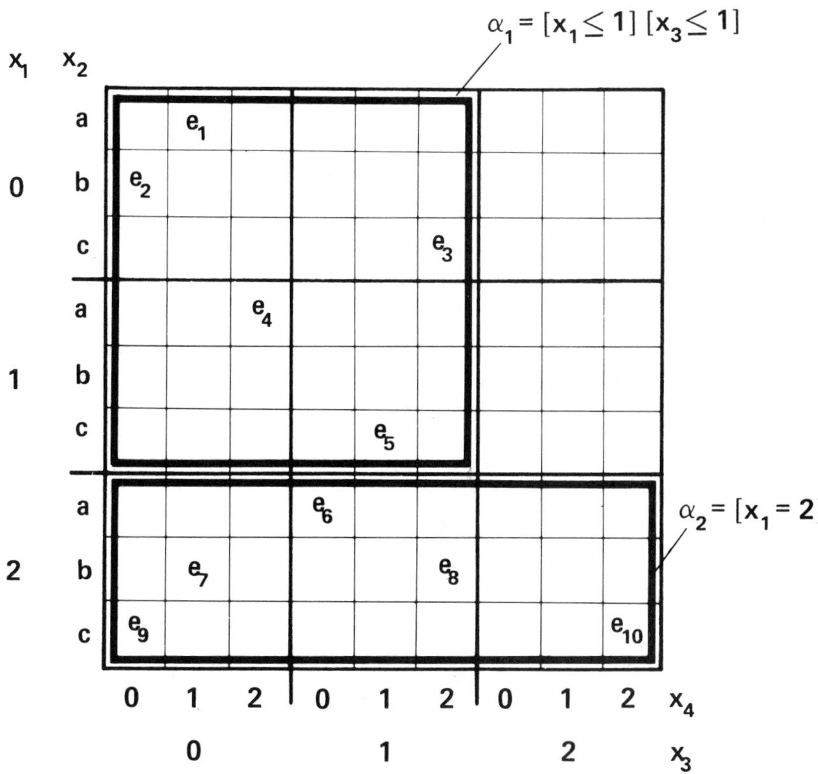

Figure 11-11: A diagrammatic representation of the clustering $\{\alpha_1, \alpha_2\}$.

11.5.2 The Hierarchy-building Module

The hierarchy-building module uses the clustering module to determine a hierarchy of clusters. It performs two loops, one iterative and one recursive. The iterative loop repeats the clustering module for a sequence of values of k in order to determine the value for which the most desirable clustering is obtained. Such an approach is computationally acceptable because, in practical applications, most interesting hierarchies will have a relatively small number of branches (that is, a small value of k) at each level.

The recursive loop applies the above iterative process at each node of the hierarchy. In the first step, the process is executed for the root, representing the initial event set E. Clusters of E and their conjunctive descriptions are determined. Consecutive steps repeat the same operation for the nodes representing clusters obtained during the previous step. The hierarchy continues to grow from the top down until the "continue-growth" criterion fails to be met. This criterion requires that the fit between the clusters and their descriptions at every level of the hierarchy must be better than at the previous level.

In order to determine the optimal value of k, we must modify the clustering quality criterion so that it can be used to compare clusterings with different numbers of complexes. Such a criterion must reflect the dependency of the fit between the clustering and data on the value of k. As the number of clusters k increases, the fit (measured by the negative of sparseness) will likely increase, since smaller complexes will have smaller sparseness. On the other hand, increasing k increases the complexity of the clustering and therefore is undesirable. A simple criterion that takes into consideration the above trade-off is to require the product

$$\text{Total sparseness} \times (k + \beta)$$

to achieve a minimum value, where β is an experimentally determined parameter balancing the relative effect of the sparseness and the number of clusters k on the solution.

11.6 AN EXAMPLE OF A PRACTICAL PROBLEM: CONSTRUCTING A CLASSIFICATION HIERARCHY OF SPANISH FOLK SONGS

This example presents an application of the above method to the development of a classification hierarchy of 100 Spanish folk songs. The folk songs were characterized by 22 musicological attributes, listed in Figure 11-12. These attributes, as well as other relevant data, were provided by musicologist Pablo Poveda, who studied this problem using traditional methods of numerical taxonomy [Poveda, 1980]. The results obtained by using the traditional methods were not very satisfying, because the generated clusters lacked descriptions, and therefore were difficult to interpret.

The top five levels of the conjunctive hierarchy produced by CLUSTER/2 are presented in Figure 11-13. The criterion of clustering quality was to "minimize the total sparseness". The number of clusters (k) at each level was 2, to meet the requirement of the musicologist.

The top node of the hierarchy corresponds to the whole collection of songs. All the other nodes represent various classes (categories) of songs. The description of each class is a conjunctive statement involving selected folk song attributes. In Figure 11-13, instead of providing the whole cluster description associated with each branch, we show, for simplicity, only the discriminant variables occurring in the given cluster. As it turned out, all nodes in the hierarchy have only one discriminant variable. For example, at the first level, the discriminant variable is the harmonic structure, which takes the value "monophonic" in one cluster and "polyphonic" in the other cluster.

One interesting aspect of the generated hierarchy is that the value sets of some variables have been split into ranges. These ranges can be considered as new (generalized) values of variables. For example, while producing the second

	Variable	Domain
x_1:	Tonal Range	{1..11}
x_2:	Number of Tones	{1..10}
x_3:	Degree of Rubato	{0..5}
x_4:	Degree of Embellishment	{0..5}
x_5:	Degree of Melisma	{0..5}
x_6:	Number of Musical Phrases	{0..5}
x_7:	Degree of Musical Tension	{0..5}
x_8:	Degree of Melodic Line Blending	{0..5}
x_9:	Harmonic Structure	{Monophonic, Polyphonic}
x_{10}:	Religious Setting	{Religious, Secular}
x_{11}:	Sex of Singers	{Same Sex, Mixed Sexes}
x_{12}:	Rhythm	{Weak, Strong, Triple-beat}
x_{13}:	Harmony	{None, Non-Phrygian, Phrygian}
x_{14}:	Homophonic	{Yes, No}
x_{15}:	Instrumental Accompaniment	{Yes, No}
x_{16}:	Female singer	{Yes, No}
x_{17}:	Accompanied by Dancing	{Yes, No}
x_{18}:	A Serenade	{Yes, No}
x_{19}:	A Love song	{Yes, No}
x_{20}:	A Solo	{Yes, No}
x_{21}:	Uses Phrygian Scale	{Yes, No}
x_{22}:	Panegyric	{Yes, No}

Figure 11-12: Variables used to describe 100 Spanish folk songs.

level clustering of the monophonic folk songs (the left branch), the range of the degree of "rubato" was split into two ranges 0..3 and 4..5, which can be characterized as "low" and "high", respectively. Similar partitioning of value sets was performed on the degree of embellishment, the degree of melisma, the tonal range, and the number of tones in a song.

The leaf nodes in the hierarchy shown in Figure 11-13, marked by $\alpha_1,\alpha_2,...,\alpha_{11}$ represent groups of songs, whose complete description consists of discriminant variables indicated along the path from the root to the leaf and some additional properties generated by CLUSTER/2, but not shown in Figure 11-13. For example, the group of songs represented by α_1 (8 songs) has the following complete description:

α_1 = [harmonic structure = monophonic] [rubato = low][tonal range = low] [type = secular][instruments used = no]	(discriminant variables along the path from the root to leaf α_1)
&	
[no. of distinct tones = 5..8][dance = no] [panegyric = no][no. of phrases = 1..2] [melisma = 0..2][tension = 1..3]	(additional properties generated by the program at the leaf node)

The hierarchy in Figure 11-13 is a simple and meaningful classification of the folk songs. The classes are easy to interpret due to the provided descriptions. If the clustering quality criterion LEF is changed (by selecting different elementary criteria, a different order of the criteria, and/or different tolerances for

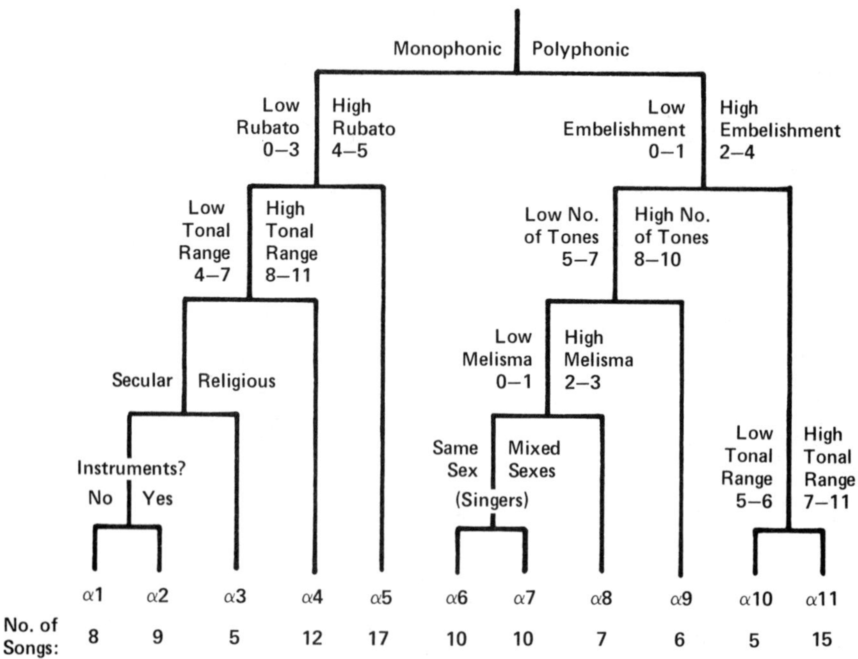

Figure 11-13: A classification hierarchy of Spanish folk songs produced by CLUSTER/2.

them) the generated hierarchy may be different. This way the algorithm can generate several alternative hierarchies. The ultimate judgment of which one is the most appropriate for the given application is made by the data analyst.

CLUSTER/2 has also been applied to problems in other domains. One experiment, in the field of agriculture, was to structure a collection of 47 cases of soybean diseases. Each case was described by a vector of 35 components, representing symptoms and characterizations of the diseased plants. CLUSTER/2 "re-discovered" disease classes known to plant pathologists, and provided a description of each class which closely matched the known symptoms of the corresponding diseases [Michalski & Stepp, 1981].

11.7 SUMMARY AND SOME SUGGESTED EXTENSIONS OF THE METHOD

The described method for conjunctive conceptual clustering determines a hierarchy of classes characterizing a collection of objects. Each class has a description in the form of a single conjunctive statement, logically disjoint from descriptions of other classes with the same parent node in the hierarchy, and optimized according to a certain clustering quality criterion. The major difference between this method and methods of numerical taxonomy lies in its extension of the concept of the measure of similarity into a more general notion of "conceptual cohesiveness". Such a measure takes into consideration not only the properties of individual objects, but also their relationship to other objects and, most importantly, their relationship to some predetermined concepts characterizing object collections.

This work represents our early results on the subject of conceptual clustering, and, naturally, many problems remain to be solved. Here are some interesting topics for further research:

- In this method, the variables for describing objects are assumed to be determined *a priori*, and may not be the most appropriate ones for clustering the given objects. A desirable extension of the method would be to implement constructive induction mechanisms able to determine new, more relevant variables during clustering. The use of such variables could lead to simpler and/or more interesting clusterings. A closely related problem of deriving new variables for learning generalized descriptions of concepts from their examples is discussed in Chapter 4.
- The presented method describes object classes solely by conjunctive statements. Although a conjunctive statement is one of the most common descriptive forms used by humans, it is nevertheless a quite limited form. An interesting extension of the work would be to use descriptions which involve additional operators, such as logical implication or equivalence.
- The purpose of building classifications is often to simplify decision making by collecting into one class those situations, observations, or objects that require a similar decision or action. To do this well, the criterion of clustering quality should include knowledge of the goals, purposes, and intentions associated with the problem under investigation.
- In the method described, the classes are organized into a hierarchy. The links of the hierarchy represent just the generalization (set inclusion) relationship between the parent and child nodes. The method could be extended to generate a graph structure (a "classification network") in which links might also represent other relationships between classes. For example, within such a graph, some links might denote properties that are inherited from parent nodes, and other links might denote properties that differentiate between sibling classes.
- For applications involving clustering visual information, an interesting extension would be to use as conceptual building blocks various standard geometrical shapes, such as circles, ellipses, triangles, rectangles, and so on, and to allow nondisjoint clusterings.
- The problems which are suitable to the CLUSTER/2 algorithm involve objects which can be sufficiently described by variable-value pairs, which are

those objects whose internal structure is irrelevant to the problem at hand. When the internal structure of objects is to be considered (when relevant variables include relationships between features of object subparts), the techniques presented here are not adequate (although still applicable, by transforming the structural properties into propositional attributes). An adequate method for clustering such objects requires a richer descriptive language, such as first-order predicate logic or its extension—for example, the annotated predicate calculus described in Chapter 4 of this book.

ACKNOWLEDGMENTS

The authors thank Mr. Pablo Poveda for providing data used in the musicological experiment, and Professor Richard Selander for providing the numerical taxonomy program NUMTAX. Partial support of this research was provided by the National Science Foundation under Grants Nos. MCS-79-06614 and MCS-82-05166.

REFERENCES

Diday, E. and Simon, J. C., "Clustering Analysis," *Communication and Cybernetics 10*, K. S. Fu (Ed.), Springer Verlag, Heidelberg, New York, 1976.

Gowda, K. C., and Krishna, G., "Disaggregative clustering using the concept of mutual nearest neighborhood," *Man and Cybernetics*, IEEE Transactions on Systems, pp. 888-894, December 1978, (Vol. SMC-8, No. 12).

Michalski, R. S., "A Planar Geometrical Model for Representing Multi-Dimensional Discrete Spaces and Multiple-Valued Logic Function", Technical Report 897, Department of Computer Science, University of Illinois, January 1978.

Michalski, R. S., "Variable-Valued Logic and Its Applications to Pattern Recognition and Machine Learning," *Multiple-Valued Logic and Computer Science*, David Rine (Ed.), North-Holland, 1975a.

Michalski, R. S., "Synthesis of optimal and quasi-optimal variable-valued logic formulas," *Proceedings of the 1975 International Symposium on Multiple-Valued Logic*, Bloomington, Indiana, May 1975b.

Michalski, R. S., "Pattern Recognition as Rule-Guided Inductive Inference," *IEEE Transactions on Pattern Analysis and Machine Intelligence*, Vol. PAMI-2, No. 4, July 1980a.

Michalski, R. S., "Knowledge Acquisition Through Conceptual Clustering: A Theoretical Framework and an Algorithm for Partitioning Data into Conjunctive Concepts," *Policy Analysis and Information Systems*, Vol. 4, No. 3, pp. 219-244, 1980c, (A Special Issue on Knowledge Acquisition and Induction).

Michalski, R. S. and Larson, J. B., "Selection of most representative training examples and incremental generation of VL_1 hypotheses: the underlying methodology and the description of programs ESEL and AQ11", Technical Report 867, Computer Science Department, University of Illinois, 1978.

Michalski, R. S., and Stepp, R. E., "Concept-based Clustering versus Numerical Taxonomy", Technical Report 1073, Department of Computer Science, University of Illinois, 1981.

Nilsson, N. *Priciples of Artificial Intelligence*, Tioga Publishing Co., 1980.

Poveda, P., "Classification of Folksongs According to the Principles of Numerical Taxonomy", (Unpublished Report, School of Music, University of Illinois at Urbana-Champaign).

Winston, P. H., *Artificial Intelligence*, Addison-Wesley, 1977.

PART FIVE

LEARNING FROM INSTRUCTION

12

MACHINE TRANSFORMATION OF ADVICE INTO A HEURISTIC SEARCH PROCEDURE

David Jack Mostow
USC Information Sciences Institute

ABSTRACT

A key problem in learning by being told is *operationalization*: the development of procedures to implement advice that is not directly executable by the learner, such as the advice "avoid taking points" in the card game hearts. One way to operationalize such advice is to reformulate it in terms of a general "weak method", such as heuristic search. This chapter is a case study in the mechanical mapping of domain-specific problems onto general methods, using as a detailed example the derivation of a heuristic search procedure for the advice "avoid taking points." The derivation consists of a series of problem transformations leading from the advice statement to an executable procedure. The operators used to perform these transformations are implemented in a program called FOO as domain-independent transformation rules that access a knowledge base of task domain concepts. Some of the rules construct a crude generate-and-test procedure; others improve it by deriving new heuristics based on domain knowledge and problem analysis. To test its generality, FOO was also used to operationalize a music composition task; many of the same rules proved applicable.

12.1 INTRODUCTION

There are many kinds of *learning by being told*, spanning a broad spectrum of sophistication. A trivial way for a machine to "learn" a task is by reading in a program to perform it. A potentially much more useful way is by accepting high-level advice. For example, one might learn the card game hearts by being told the rules of the game and some advice on how to win, such as "avoid taking points." A central problem with this mode of learning arises when, owing to the structure of the task and the environment in which it is performed, the advice is non-operational—not directly executable by the learner. For example, the rules of hearts make it illegal to avoid taking points by simply refusing to take tricks with points; thus the advice must be incorporated into the choice of what card to play. In order to be operational, advice must be executable using available data, but taking points depends on the outcome of the trick, which is unknown at card-choosing time. The process of making advice operational is called *operationalization*, and is the topic of this chapter, which is based on a more detailed discussion available in [Mostow, 1981].

The "advice" to be operationalized need not come solely from an external tutor. It might be gleaned from experience and observation, as in the *knowledge refinement* learning paradigm described in Chapter 8 of this book. To illustrate this paradigm, consider how a hearts-playing program might be developed. The heuristic "avoid taking points" is initially provided by an advisor, or perhaps discovered by analyzing lost games and attributing the losses to having taken points. The heuristic is converted into an operational plan, like "play a low card", so it can be incorporated into the program. Experience with the revised program reveals weaknesses in this plan, such as being forced to take lots of points after playing all one's low cards in the first part of the game. Analysis of cases where the plan failed to satisfy the advice suggests additional heuristics to remedy bugs in the plan, such as "get rid of your high cards when it is safe to do so." These heuristics are then operationalized, the iterative learning process continues, and the program's performance improves.

Note that the task domain in this example has multiple agents, incomplete information, and probabilistic processes; thus operationalization involves issues not addressed in planners for domains with a single agent who has complete information about the state of the world. Moreover, it may be impossible to produce a procedure that always satisfies the advice—there is no infallible way to avoid taking points. Thus operationalization differs from conventional notions of automatic programming by its heuristic nature: the procedures it produces may not always work.

In general, operationalization converts knowledge about a task domain into procedures useful in performing the task. In this sense, AI researchers are engaged in operationalization when they convert domain knowledge into intelligent programs. Typically this involves taking a problem expressed in the language of a particular task domain, together with knowledge about the domain, and reformulating them to fit a general computational method like heuristic search. This process can be viewed as mapping the problem into a call on a general procedure for the method, by finding suitable values for the arguments (which may include generators, tests, and search orderings).

Previous research has made some progress toward getting computers to do this automatically. Newell [1969] formalized the "weak methods" of generate-and-test, *hill-climbing*, *heuristic search*, *matching*, and *means-end analysis* as data-flow graphs composed of generators and tests. Moore [1971] encoded the data-flow graph for heuristic search as a MERLIN schema and represented the Logic Theorist program [Newell *et al.*, 1957] as an operational "further specification" of it (MERLIN could prove theorems by executing it), but the generators and tests were derived from the LT specifications by hand. Tappel [1980] used transformations on data-flow graphs to derive efficient algorithms for generating prime numbers and finding shortest paths through a graph. Perhaps the most advanced effort so far toward automatic application of AI techniques is the UNDERSTAND program [Simon, 1977], which reads an English description of the Tower of Hanoi problem and operationalizes it as a means-end analysis problem by building an appropriate state space representation and operators.

The central motivation of this chapter is the mechanization of AI: how can the "knowledge engineering" process of mapping a domain-specific problem onto a general AI method be automated? This theme is illustrated by means of a detailed example in which the hearts advice "avoid taking points in the current trick" is operationalized as a heuristic search problem. This process is modeled as a sequence of transformations leading from an initial representation of the advice to a heuristic search procedure that examines different scenarios for a trick to see whether playing a given card might lead to taking points. The transformations are performed by some of over 200 rules implemented in a program named FOO.[1] (Note that "heuristic search" refers throughout the chapter to the kind of procedure constructed using FOO, not to the process of finding the transformation sequence!) A briefly-described second example tests the generality of these rules by using them to operationalize a music composition task as a heuristic search problem. (The dissertation on which this chapter is based [Mostow, 1981] contains details omitted here and treats several other operationalization methods.) The emphasis is not on the heuristic search method itself (hereafter abbreviated HSM), but on the process whereby advice is mapped onto the method. In short, although learning is typically thought of as knowledge acquisition, the learning problem treated in this chapter is *knowledge* transformation: the conversion of advice into an executable procedure.

The rest of the chapter is organized as follows. Section 12.2 discusses the kinds of knowledge required to operationalize "avoid taking points" as a heuristic search problem. Section 12.3 defines a generic heuristic search procedure and its schematic representation in FOO. Slots in the schema correspond to problem-specific components of this procedure, such as the tests used to prune paths. Section 12.4 describes the instantiation of this schema for the "avoid taking points" example, and the exhaustive search procedure it specifies. Section 12.5 shows how this procedure is refined by FOO using domain knowledge and analysis. Section 12.5.7 presents highlights of the music example. Section 12.6 evaluates the generality of the approach. Section 12.7 summarizes the sig-

[1]For "First Operational Operationalizer".

nificance of the results and suggests areas for further research. The Appendix to this chapter lists the rules mentioned in the example.

12.2 KINDS OF KNOWLEDGE USED

Reformulating "avoid taking points" as a heuristic search problem requires several things. First, some *problem representation* is needed to represent the initial and transformed versions of the advice. In FOO, "avoid taking points in the current trick" is represented as

```
(AVOID (TAKE-POINTS ME) (TRICK))
```

This can be paraphrased as: "Avoid letting player ME (the recipient of the advice) take points during the trick." Some constructs of this LISP-like language are defined below:

- (achieve P) denotes the goal of satisfying the predicate P.
- (during s e) is true if event e occurs during scenario s.
- (⇒ P Q) is true if P implies Q.
- (exists x S Px) is true if S contains an element that satisfies P.
- (forall x S Px) is true if every element of S satisfies P.
- (set-of x S Px) denotes the set of elements of S that satisfy P.
- (the x S Px) denotes the unique element of S that satisfies P.
- (for-some x S Ex) denotes any event Ex such that x is in S.
- (each x S Ex) denotes the event sequence Ex_1, ..., Ex_n, where S = $\{x_1, ..., x_n\}$.
- (choose x S Ex) denotes choosing an element x from S and doing Ex.
- (scenario e_1 ... e_n) denotes the sequence of events e_1, ..., e_n.
- (project f S) denotes the sequence $f(x_1)$, ..., $f(x_n)$, where S = x_1, ..., x_n.
- (first S) denotes x_1, where S = x_1, ..., x_n.
- (# S) denotes the size of the set S.
- (prefix S x_k) denotes the sequence x_1, ..., x_k, where S = x_1, ..., x_n.
- (prefixes-of S) denotes the set {(prefix S x_1), ..., (prefix S x_n)}, where S = x_1, ..., x_n.

Reasoning about the problem requires *domain knowledge*. To understand hearts advice, one must understand the terms used to express it, the actions available for implementing it, and the rules of the game. Most of FOO's knowledge about hearts is encoded as definitions of concepts used in the game. The concepts are represented as functions. Concepts used in the advice "avoid taking points" and later in the chapter are defined below:

- "Avoid an event throughout a scenario means try not to let it occur during the scenario."[2]

```
AVOID = (LAMBDA (E S) (ACHIEVE (NOT (DURING S E))))
```

- "Take points means take a point card."

```
TAKE-POINTS = (LAMBDA (P)
                 (FOR-SOME C (POINT-CARDS) (TAKE P C)))

POINT-CARDS = (LAMBDA ()
                 (SET-OF C (CARDS) (HAS-POINTS C)))
```

- "A trick is a scenario in which each player plays a card and then the winner takes the trick."

```
TRICK = (LAMBDA ()
           (SCENARIO (EACH P (PLAYERS) (PLAY-CARD P))
                     (TAKE-TRICK (TRICK-WINNER))))
```

The PLAYERS function is defined as the sequence of players in the current trick.

- "To play a card, a player chooses from his legal cards."

```
PLAY-CARD = (LAMBDA (P)
               (CHOOSE (CARD-OF P) (LEGALCARDS P)
                   (PLAY P (CARD-OF P))))
```

The choice variable is named (CARD-OF P) to distinguish between cards played by different players; this name is used in defining other concepts, *e.g.*, the cards played in the trick:

```
CARDS-PLAYED = (LAMBDA () (PROJECT CARD-OF (PLAYERS)))
```

- "The player leading a trick can play any non-heart in his hand, and can lead a heart if hearts are broken or he has only hearts. The other players must follow suit if they can."

```
LEGALCARDS = (LAMBDA (P) (SET-OF C (CARDS) (LEGAL P C)))
```

---

[2]This particular concept is of course not specific to hearts, but one might define it differently in another domain.

```
LEGAL = (LAMBDA (P C)
          (AND [HAS P C]
               [⇒ (LEADING P)
                  (OR [CAN-LEAD-HEARTS P]
                      [NOT (IN-SUIT C (HEARTS))])]
               [⇒ (FOLLOWING P)
                  (OR [VOID P (SUIT-LED)]
                      [IN-SUIT C (SUIT-LED)])]))
```

- "The suit led is the suit of the first card played in the trick."

```
SUIT-LED = (LAMBDA () (SUIT-OF (FIRST (CARDS-PLAYED))))
```

- "Taking a trick means taking all the cards played in it."

```
TAKE-TRICK = (LAMBDA (P)
               (EACH C (CARDS-PLAYED) (TAKE P C)))
```

- "The player of the highest card in the suit led takes the trick."

```
TRICK-WINNER =
 (LAMBDA ()
    (THE P (PLAYERS)
      (= (CARD-OF P)
         (HIGHEST-IN-SUIT-LED (CARDS-PLAYED)))))
```

```
HIGHEST-IN-SUIT-LED =
    (LAMBDA (S)
      (THE C S
         (AND [IN-SUIT C (SUIT-LED)]
              [NOT (EXISTS X S (HIGHER-IN-SUIT X C))])))
```

```
HIGHER-IN-SUIT = (LAMBDA (C1 C2)
                   (AND [HIGHER C1 C2]
                        [= (SUIT-OF C1) (SUIT-OF C2)]))
```

- "A sequence of cards has points if it includes one or more point cards."

```
HAVE-POINTS = (LAMBDA (S) (EXISTS C S (HAS-POINTS C)))
```

- "A card is out if an opponent has it."

```
OUT = (LAMBDA (C)
        (EXISTS P (OPPONENTS-OF ME) (HAS P C)))
```

```
OPPONENTS-OF = (LAMBDA (P1)
                   (SET-OF P2 (PLAYERS) (NOT (= P2 P1))))
```

• "A player with no cards in a suit is void in that suit."

```
VOID = (LAMBDA (P SUIT)
          (NOT (EXISTS C (CARDS-IN-HAND P)
                    (IN-SUIT C SUIT))))
```

```
CARDS-IN-HAND = (LAMBDA (P)
                    (SET-OF C (CARDS) (HAS P C)))
```

Inference methods are used to reason about the problem on the basis of such domain knowledge. In FOO, these methods are represented as *problem transformation rules*. Each rule has a left-hand pattern, a right-hand pattern, and a condition. An expression that matches the left-hand pattern and satisfies the condition can be rewritten by filling in the right-hand pattern. Some rule conditions are tested by simple procedures; others generate subproblems which are themselves solved by a sequence of rules. (The details of FOO's rule representation are given in [Mostow, 1981]; for readability, this chapter presents rules informally.)

FOO's rules are general, but some of them access its domain knowledge, for example:

RULE124: (f e_1 ... e_n) → e′, where f is defined as (lambda (x_1 ... x_n) e) and e′ is the result of substituting e_1 ... e_n for x_1 ... x_n throughout e

Unfold the definition of a concept in the problem. [Darlington & Burstall, 1976]

The notation (f e_1 ... e_n) → e′ denotes rewriting an expression of the form (f e_1 ... e_n) as e′, where (f e_1 ... e_n) denotes the function f applied to the arguments e_1 ... e_n. RULE124 is used to unfold the definition of AVOID in the first step of the "avoid taking points" example:

```
(AVOID (TAKE-POINTS ME) (TRICK))
--- [UNFOLD by RULE124] --->
(ACHIEVE (NOT (DURING (TRICK) (TAKE-POINTS ME))))
```

The resulting expression means "try not to let player ME take points during the trick." Other rules are introduced later in the context of their use, and are listed in the Appendix for reference.

I provided the *control knowledge* required for operationalization by hand-guiding the process. Thus the example was generated interactively: I encoded the initial advice and chose the sequence of rules that successively transformed it into an operational procedure. At each point in the derivation, I selected a subexpression of the problem and a rule to apply to it, and FOO applied the rule. In short, FOO provides a representation for operationalization problems, and a set of problem transformation rules, but lacks a problem solver for solving operationalization problems on its own. Given the complexity of such problems—the "avoid taking points" example is over 100 steps long, and many different rules could have been applied at each step—automating the control of the operationalization process is a challenging problem. An approach to it is proposed in [Mostow, 1981].

To map "avoid taking points" onto a general method like heuristic search, we need (at least implicitly) some *representation of the method.* The heuristic search method can be represented as a data-flow graph [Newell, 1969], in which the boxes represent generators and tests to be filled in for the particular problem. FOO's representation of HSM is described in more detail in the next section.

Finally, operationalizing a problem in terms of a method requires knowledge about *how to map the problem to the method.* This kind of knowledge is represented in FOO as transformation rules. Some of these rules construct a crude generate-and-test search for a given problem by instantiating components of the general data-flow graph. For example, the search space for "avoid taking points in the current trick" is taken to be the set of possible card sequences for the trick. The initial search procedure tests each of these sequences to see if it will cause player ME to take points. Other rules refine this procedure into a more efficient one based on properties of the problem and the task domain. For instance, sequences in which player ME's card is lower than an opponent's need not be tested, since they cannot cause player ME to win the trick. Applying FOO's instantiation and refinement rules requires both domain knowledge and reasoning methods.

12.3 A SLIGHTLY NON-STANDARD DEFINITION OF HEURISTIC SEARCH

In order to formulate "avoid taking points" as a heuristic search problem, FOO needs some representation of HSM. Newell [1969] described the general problem statement for HSM as follows:

Given: a set $\{x\}$, the problem space;
a set of operators $\{q\}$ with range and domain in $\{x\}$;
an initial element, x_0;
a desired element, x_d;

Find: a sequence of operators, q_1, q_2, ..., q_n, such that they transform x_0 into x_d:

$$q_n[q_{n-1}[\ldots q_1(x_0)\ldots]] = x_d$$

He described the heuristic search procedure as follows:

> The initial element x_0 is the initial current position; operators are selected and applied to it; each new element is compared with x_d to see whether the problem is solved; if not, it is added to a list of obtained posi-

tions (also called the "try list" or the "subproblem list"); and one of these positions is selected from which to continue the search... The search is guided (the tree is pruned) by appropriate selection and rejection of operators and elements.

In FOO's representation of HSM, everything is expressed in terms of (operator) sequences, called *paths*; the search procedure extends a path by explicitly appending an operator to it. The fact that operators map one state to another is implicit in the tests applied to paths. In other words, the search procedure does not apply operators to states; this eliminates the need to maintain an explicit state description. This procedure can be described by modifying Newell's description (differences are underlined):

> The *null path* is the initial current position; *choice elements* are selected and *appended* to it; each new *path* is *tested* to see whether the problem is solved; if not, it is added to a list of *paths*; and one of these *paths* is selected from which to continue the search. The search is guided by appropriate selection and rejection of *choice elements* and *paths*.

The choice elements need not be operators; this procedure applies to any problem of the form:

Find a sequence of choices satisfying a given criterion.

As an example, consider how this procedure applies to the "eight queens" problem: place eight queens on a chess board in such a way that none of them is attacking any of the others, that is, no two are on the same rank, file, or diagonal.[3] Here the choice elements are squares on a chess board. The null path corresponds to a bare board. A path is a sequence of n squares corresponding to the positions of the first n queens placed. A simple algorithm is as follows:

1. Initially the path set contains only the null path (empty board).
2. Choose a path from the path set.
3. Extend it by one square (that is, place another queen).
4. Test the path to see if the problem is solved (that is, if the path consists of eight distinct squares, none of which are on the same rank, file, or diagonal).
5. If not, add the path to the path set and go to step 2.

This crude generate-and-test algorithm has no heuristics: it just generates sequences of squares and tests each sequence to see if it is a solution. The algorithm can be made more efficient by incorporating various heuristics. Paths that cannot lead to a solution can be *pruned* from the search. For example, a path with two queens on the same rank, file, or diagonal can be pruned from the path set, since it cannot possibly be extended into a solution. The search can be or-

[3]A program to solve this problem is derived by transformational implementation in [Balzer, 1981].

dered so as to find a solution faster. For example, one might try squares close to the edge of the board before squares in the center, since the diagonals through them contain fewer squares; this strategy leaves more squares legal for subsequent queens. Finally, some of the solution constraints can be *compiled out* of the search. For example, placing the nth queen on the nth rank guarantees that no two queens will be placed on the same rank, and prevents generating the same board configuration via more than one path, without eliminating any potential solution from the set of generated configurations.

In general, the first step in operationalizing a heuristic search problem is to identify the sequence of choice points involved and the set of admissible alternatives at each one, and to express the solution criterion as a function of the choice sequence. This provides enough information to specify an executable but inefficient (combinatorially explosive) generate-and-test search procedure, whose data-flow graph has the form shown in Figure 12-1. This procedure is then refined into a genuine heuristic search, shown in Figure 12-2, by using constraints on the overall solution as early as possible in the search to order or reject paths, to order or filter the alternatives at each choice point, and even to reduce the depth or breadth of the search space itself.

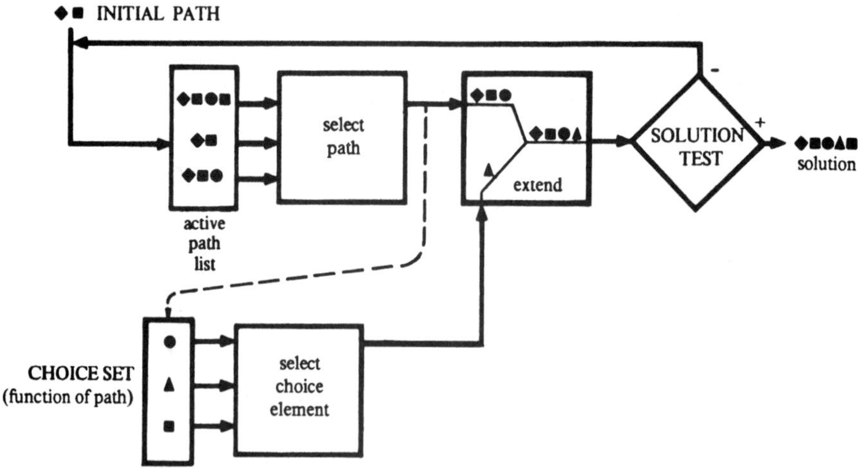

Figure 12-1: Generate-and-Test Procedure

The components of the generic heuristic search procedure that must be filled in to solve a particular problem make up FOO's HSM schema and are described below.

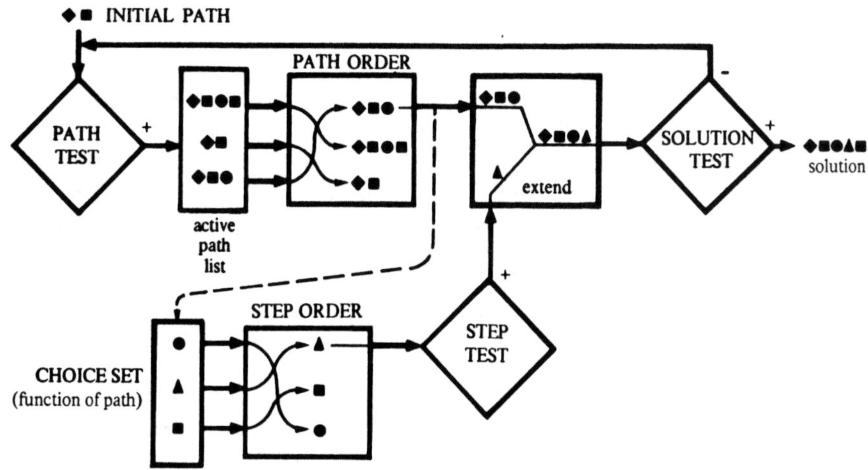

Figure 12-2: Generic Heuristic Search Procedure

- The search starts with a single path, the **initial-path**, typically the null sequence.
- The alternative extensions for a path are given by the **choice-set** function. Since the choice set may vary at different points in the search, the function takes a choice point as its argument.
- The order in which alternative choice elements are generated is controlled by a **step-order** predicate. Elements that satisfy this predicate are considered first. This order may vary at different choice points, so the predicate takes a choice point index as a second argument.
- The choice set is filtered by a **step-test** predicate; thus the extensions to a given path are enumerated by a generate-and-test process, with the choice-set function as generator and the step-test predicate as test. The step-test also takes a choice point index as a second argument.
- The order in which paths are selected for extension is controlled by a path-order predicate on paths; paths satisfying this predicate are considered first.
- A newly generated path must satisfy a **path-test** in order to be added to the active list.
- A solution path must satisfy both a **solution-test** based on the search criterion, and a **completion-test** that checks if the path covers the complete sequence of choice points.

12.4 INSTANTIATING THE HSM SCHEMA FOR A GIVEN PROBLEM

There are several steps involved in translating a particular problem like "avoid taking points" into the language of the general HSM problem statement:

1. The problem must be recognized as one of finding a sequence of choices satisfying some condition. If FOO's rule for recognizing such problems does not match the initial problem description, the problem must be reformulated to fit the rule.
2. To formulate the search space for the problem, it is necessary to recognize that taking points in a trick depends on the cards chosen by all the players; this choice sequence defines the search space.
3. The search criterion is then reformulated as a function of this sequence. The reformulated criterion tests whether player ME's card is the highest card in the suit led.
4. Given the choice sequence and search criterion for the problem, the HSM schema can be instantiated to specify a generate-and-test search procedure.
5. The procedure must be made executable on the data available to player ME.

12.4.1 Mapping a Problem onto the HSM Problem Statement

The first step in mapping "avoid taking points" onto the HSM problem statement is to reformulate it so the applicability of HSM can be recognized:

```
(AVOID (TAKE-POINTS ME) (TRICK))
--- [unfold definition of AVOID by RULE124] --->
(ACHIEVE (NOT (DURING (TRICK) (TAKE-POINTS ME))))
```

This reformulated version means "try not to let player ME take points during the trick." It fits FOO's rule for recognizing potential heuristic search problems:

RULE306: *Use heuristic search to evaluate predicate on a scenario where choices are made.*

FOO is able to identify the expression (DURING (TRICK) (TAKE-POINTS ME)) as such a predicate by examining the definition of the scenario TRICK, which contains a sequence of PLAY-CARD events in which each player chooses a legal card and plays it. FOO's actual rule for recognizing potential HSM problems looks more like

RULE306: (P ... e ...)
→ (HSM with (problem : (P ... e ...))—*predicate to be evaluated*
(object : e)—*scenario*
(choice-seq : (choice-seq-of e)))—*choices made in scenario*
if e contains an event sequence with choices in it

RULE306 suggests using HSM to evaluate (DURING (TRICK) (TAKE-POINTS ME)), that is, to try to find a sequence of choices satisfying it:

```
            (DURING (TRICK) (TAKE-POINTS ME))
            --- [by RULE306] --->
            HSM1
(HSM1 ← PROBLEM : (DURING (TRICK) (TAKE-POINTS ME)))
(HSM1 ← OBJECT : (TRICK))
(HSM1 ← CHOICE-SEQ : (CHOICE-SEQ-OF (TRICK)))
```

This notation means that the expression (DURING (TRICK) (TAKE-POINTS ME)) is to be evaluated by HSM1, an instance of HSM; RULE306 fills in three of HSM1's components. The notation (X ← Y : Z) means "the value for the Y component of schema X is filled in as Z."

12.4.2 Finding the Sequence of Choices that Affect the Predicate

To formulate a search procedure for the problem, we must identify the search space: the points where choices are made, the alternatives at each point, and the tests a solution path (sequence of choices) must satisfy. The sequence of choice points is extracted from the definition of TRICK:

```
(CHOICE-SEQ-OF (TRICK)))
--- [by RULE124, analysis] --->
(EACH P1 (PLAYERS)
      (CHOOSE (CARD-OF P1)
           (LEGALCARDS P1)
           (PLAY P1 (CARD-OF P1))))
```

That is, the choices made in a trick consist of each player choosing a legal card to play. Some other information about the search space can now be extracted from the choice sequence description:

```
(HSM1 ← CHOICES : (CARDS-PLAYED))
(HSM1 ← INDICES : (PLAYERS))
(HSM1 ← INDEX : P1)
(HSM1 ← CHOICE-SETS : (LAMBDA (P1) (LEGALCARDS P1)))
(HSM1 ← INITIAL-PATH : NIL)
(HSM1 ← COMPLETION-TEST :
             (LAMBDA (PATH) (= (# PATH) (# (PLAYERS)))))
```

Some of the HSM components filled in here (CHOICES, INDICES, and INDEX) are not used in the search procedure itself—they provide intermediate information used by rules that instantiate other schema components. The value (CARDS-PLAYED) of the CHOICES component defines the search space in terms of a non-deterministic sequence of chosen objects, namely the sequence of cards played. The choice points are indexed by player, and each player's CHOICE-SET consists of his or her legal cards. The COMPLETION-TEST specifies that a solution sequence must include a card for each player.

It remains to identify the test that a solution path must satisfy. That is, which card sequences will cause player ME to take points? The next section shows how this SOLUTION-TEST is found.

12.4.3 Reformulating the Search Criterion in Terms of the Choice Sequence

The search space has now been identified as the possible card sequences for the trick. The problem of reformulating the search criterion as a test on such sequences is represented as:

```
(REFORMULATE (DURING (TRICK) (TAKE-POINTS ME))
             (CARDS-PLAYED))
```

It means answering the question, "How does my taking points depend on the cards played in the trick?" Reformulating the search criterion as a function of (CARDS-PLAYED) takes over 40 steps. This process, summarized below, illustrates some of the reasoning methods encoded as rules in FOO.

First the search criterion is elaborated by unfolding the definition of TRICK:

```
(DURING (TRICK) (TAKE-POINTS ME))
--- [UNFOLD by RULE124] --->
(DURING (SCENARIO
           (EACH P1 (PLAYERS) (PLAY-CARD P1))
           (TAKE-TRICK (TRICK-WINNER)))
        (TAKE-POINTS ME))
```

This expression is analyzed to determine when player ME will take points. Case analysis shows that if player ME takes points, it occurs either while cards are being played or when the winner takes the trick. The first case—taking points when cards are played—is eliminated by determining that a TAKE-POINTS event cannot occur during a sequence of PLAY-CARD events. This is accomplished by performing an intersection search through FOO's knowledge base of concept definitions and finding that TAKE-POINTS and PLAY-CARD have no sub-events in common. (The sub-events of an event are the action concepts used to define it.) To simplify the second case—taking points when the winner takes the trick—the definitions of TAKE-TRICK and TAKE-POINTS are unfolded so as to express both arguments to DURING in terms of the same function TAKE:

```
(DURING [TAKE-TRICK (TRICK-WINNER)] [TAKE-POINTS ME])
--- [by RULE124, analysis] --->
(EXISTS C1 (CARDS-PLAYED)
   (EXISTS C2 (POINT-CARDS)
      (DURING [TAKE (TRICK-WINNER) C1] [TAKE ME C2])))
```

FOO can then *partial-match* (TAKE (TRICK-WINNER) C1) against (TAKE ME C2) by equating (TRICK-WINNER) = ME and C1 = C2. The latter equality permits C2 to be eliminated, producing:

```
(AND [HAVE-POINTS (CARDS-PLAYED)]
     [= (TRICK-WINNER) ME])
```

That is, player ME can take points only by taking a trick in which a point card is played. The requirement that player ME take the trick is reformulated as a predicate on (CARDS-PLAYED) by analyzing the definition of TRICK-WINNER:

```
(= (TRICK-WINNER) ME)
--- [by RULE124, analysis] --->
(= (CARD-OF ME) (HIGHEST-IN-SUIT-LED (CARDS-PLAYED)))
```

That is, one wins a trick by playing the highest card in the suit led. At this point, the original search criterion (DURING (TRICK) (TAKE-POINTS ME)) has been re-expressed in terms of (CARDS-PLAYED):

```
(AND [HAVE-POINTS (CARDS-PLAYED)]
     [= (CARD-OF ME) (HIGHEST-IN-SUIT-LED (CARDS-PLAYED))])
```

The desired solution-test can now be filled in:

```
(HSM1 ← SOLUTION-TEST :
      (LAMBDA (CARDS-PLAYED1)
         (AND [HAVE-POINTS CARDS-PLAYED1]
              [= (CARDS-PLAYED1 ME)
                 (HIGHEST-IN-SUIT-LED CARDS-PLAYED1)])))
```

This test is a predicate on a card sequence, denoted by the lambda variable CARDS-PLAYED1. A sequence is treated as a function from an index to a value; thus (CARDS-PLAYED1 ME) denotes the card played by player ME. The test is satisfied if CARDS-PLAYED1 includes one or more point cards and player ME's card is the highest in the suit led in the sequence.

Default values for the step and path constraints are filled in at the same time:

```
(HSM1 ← PATH-TEST : (LAMBDA (CARDS-PLAYED1) T))
(HSM1 ← PATH-ORDER : (LAMBDA (CARDS-PLAYED1) NIL))
(HSM1 ← STEP-TEST : (LAMBDA (P1 C1) T))
(HSM1 ← STEP-ORDER : (LAMBDA (P1 C1) NIL))
(HSM1 ← PATH : CARDS-PLAYED1)
```

These defaults provide conservative values that may be refined later based on additional knowledge. Thus the path list and the choice sets are initially unpruned and unordered.

12.4.4 Making the Choice Set Evaluable

The HSM schema has so far been instantiated as follows (omitting components used only during the instantiation process itself):

```
(HSM1 WITH
      (INITIAL-PATH : NIL)
      (CHOICE-SETS : (LAMBDA (P1) (LEGALCARDS P1)))
      (STEP-ORDER : (LAMBDA (P1 C1) NIL))
      (STEP-TEST : (LAMBDA (P1 C1) T))
      (PATH-ORDER : (LAMBDA (CARDS-PLAYED1) NIL))
      (PATH-TEST : (LAMBDA (CARDS-PLAYED1) T))
      (SOLUTION-TEST :
         (LAMBDA (CARDS-PLAYED1)
              (AND [HAVE-POINTS CARDS-PLAYED1]
                   [= (CARDS-PLAYED1 ME)
                      (HIGHEST-IN-SUIT-LED CARDS-PLAYED1)]))))
      (COMPLETION-TEST :
         (LAMBDA (PATH) (= (# PATH) (# (PLAYERS))))))
```

This defines a generate-and-test search. Repeatedly, a card sequence (starting with the null INITIAL-PATH) is selected from the active path list and extended by a card chosen from the legal cards of the next player in the sequence. A sequence that passes the COMPLETION-TEST and SOLUTION-TEST satisfies the search criterion, since it will cause player ME to take points.

This generate-and-test search is not quite operational, because the generator function (LAMBDA (P1) (LEGALCARDS P1))) is generally unevaluable: player ME cannot enumerate an opponent's legal cards by direct observation. (Detecting this problem automatically would require a model that predicts what information will be available to player ME at a given point in the game.) The problem is solved by expanding the choice set to the set of *possibly* legal cards, where a card is "possibly legal" for P1 unless player ME specifically knows otherwise:

```
(LEGALCARDS P1)
--- [by RULE124, RULE318] --->
(SET-OF C1 (CARDS) (POSSIBLE (LEGAL P1 C1)))
```

This transformation is made by

RULE318: P → (possible P), where (possible P) is true unless P is known to be false.

The revised generator function is evaluable but too unconstrained: the entire deck of cards will be considered as possible choices for each player unless effective tests can be found that reject impossible choices. The more tests used, the fewer impossible scenarios considered. Omitting a test may result in considering as "possible" a scenario that could be ruled out based on available data. This could lead to the erroneous conclusion that playing a card could cause player ME to take points when in fact it could not.[4]

To find such tests, FOO first unfolds the definition of (LEGAL P1 C1), the first conjunct of which is (HAS P1 C1): P1 must have C1 to be able to play it. Since player ME cannot inspect opponents' hands, this conjunct is not directly evaluable, so the following rule applies:

RULE319: P → (P ; (⇒ Q when R)),
where Q is a necessary condition for P when R holds

This rule is useful when the condition P cannot be evaluated directly. Here (P ; (⇒ Q when R)) indicates an annotation (⇒ Q when R) attached to the expression P, meaning that Q is a necessary condition on P whenever R holds. Such Q and R are found by the following strategy:

To find a necessary condition for $P(e_1 \dots e_n)$,
Find a predicate Q defined (directly or indirectly) in terms of P, and
Find $x_1 \dots x_k$ *that reduce the expression* $P(e_1 \dots e_n) \Rightarrow Q(x_1 \dots x_k)$ *to a simple condition R.*

To find necessary conditions on (HAS P1 C1), FOO searches its knowledge base for predicates defined in terms of HAS. One such predicate is OUT. The expression (⇒ (HAS P1 C1) (OUT X)) reduces to (IN P1 (OPPONENTS-OF ME)) for X = C1. That is, card C1 must be out in order for an opponent P1 to have it. Even if one cannot tell whether a *specific* opponent has a given card, one can tell that the card is out if one does not have it oneself and it has not been played. (This fact is derived in FOO using a generalization of the pigeon-hole principle [Mostow, 1981].) Thus player ME can evaluate (OUT C1) and use it as a necessary condition for (HAS P1 C1) whenever (IN P1 (OPPONENTS-OF ME)) holds. This fact is attached to (HAS P1 C1) as an annotation:

```
--- [by RULE319, analysis] --->
(HAS P1 C1) ←
; ⇒ (OUT C1) WHEN (IN P1 (OPPONENTS-OF ME))
```

I assume a run-time evaluation mechanism that uses such annotations. To evaluate (HAS P1 C1) when P1 ≠ ME, player ME would check (OUT C1). If (OUT C1) is false, P1 does not have C1 and cannot play it. This prevents consideration of scenarios in which an opponent plays a card held by player ME or played earlier.

Another predicate defined (indirectly) in terms of HAS is VOID. This leads to the observation that player P1 cannot follow suit when void:

[4]The search could be constrained even further by considering only *plausible* scenarios rather than all *possible* scenarios. This would require knowledge of other players' goals so as to predict their likely behavior, but FOO lacks an explicit goal model.

```
--- [by RULE319, analysis] --->
(HAS P1 C1) ←
; ⇒ (NOT (VOID P1 (SUIT-LED))) WHEN (IN-SUIT C1 (SUIT-LED))
```

If C1 is in the suit led and P1 is known to be void in that suit (for example when P1 has previously failed to follow suit), (HAS P1 C1) must be false. Checking this condition prevents consideration of scenarios where a player known to be void follows suit.[5]

At this point, the previously non-operational LEGALCARDS generator has been corrected to generate possibly legal cards, where "possible" means "violates no known necessary conditions". The resulting executable generate-and-test procedure is shown as a data-flow graph in Figure 12-3.

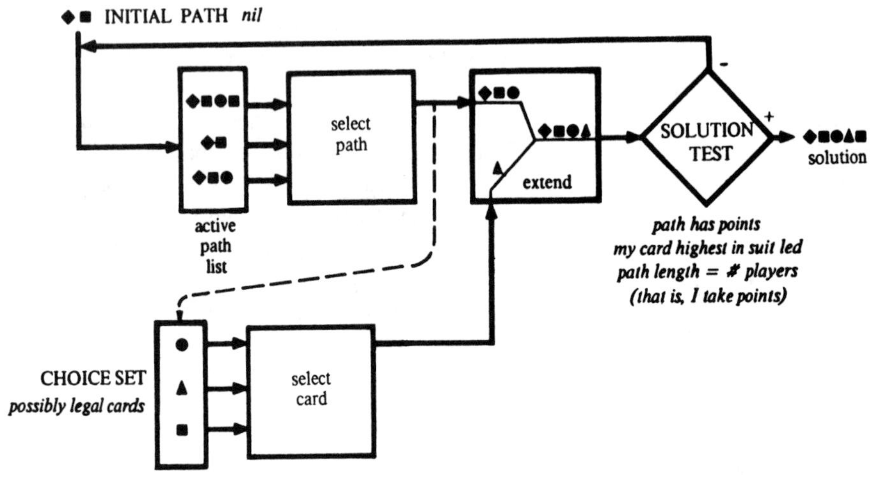

Figure 12-3: Initial Search for "Avoid Taking Points".

12.5 REFINING HSM BY MOVING CONSTRAINTS BETWEEN CONTROL COMPONENTS

A good way to design an efficient heuristic search procedure for a problem like "avoid taking points" is to construct a simple procedure and then refine it

[5]Actually, this reasoning applies to any suit, not just the suit led; a slightly modified RULE319 would derive this fact.

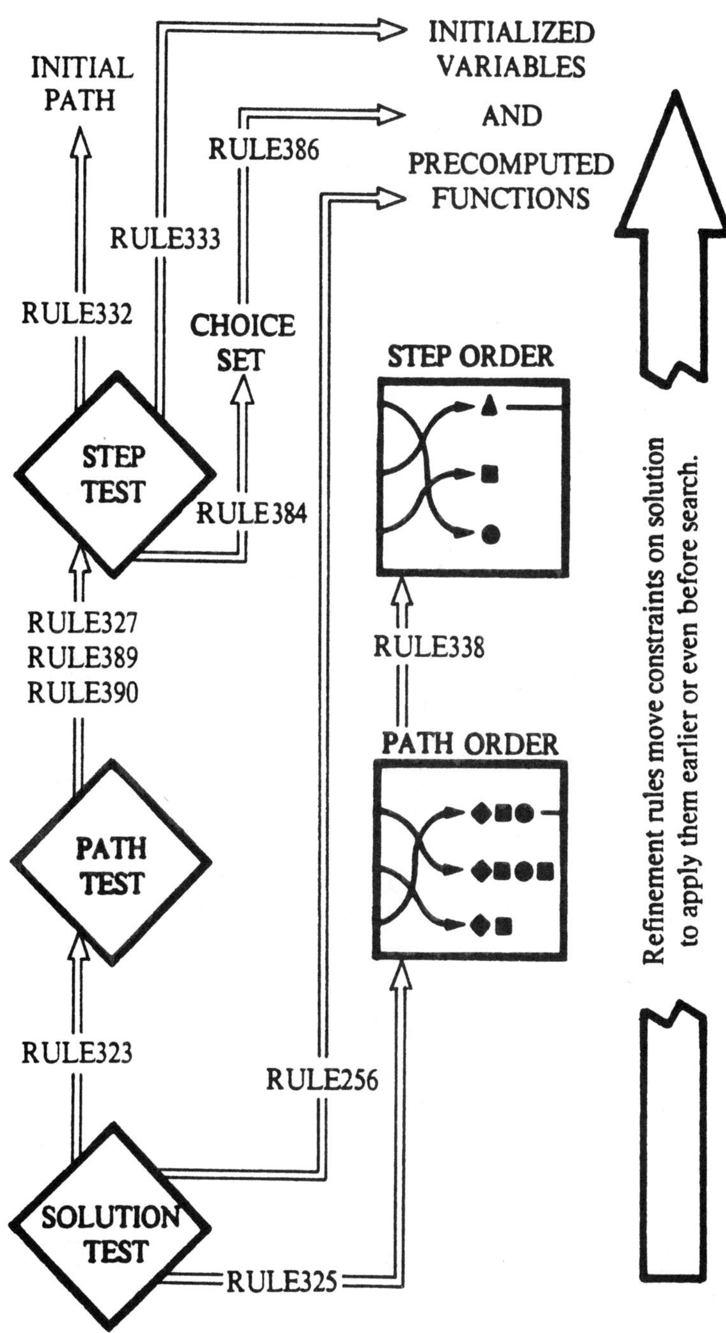

Figure 12-4: HSM Refinement Rules

step by step into a more efficient one. The generate-and-test procedure derived in the previous section exhaustively tests each possible complete card sequence for the trick to see if it would cause player ME to take points. Such a procedure can be refined into an efficient heuristic search by moving problem constraints between components of the HSM data-flow graph so as to apply them earlier in the search, as suggested in Figure 12-4. This can improve the search in various ways:

- *Pruning* search paths that cannot lead to a solution reduces the branching factor. (Section 12.5.1)
- *Ordering* the search to consider promising paths first finds a solution faster. (Section 12.5.2)
- *Compiling* constraints out of the search reduces the depth of the search space. (Section 12.5.3)
- *Modifying* the data-flow graph by splitting or adding components can improve it. (Section 12.5.4)
- *Collapsing* equivalent choices into abstracted elements reduces the search space. (Section 12.5.5)

Section 12.5.6 describes the procedure derived by applying FOO's rules for some of these refinements.

12.5.1 Pruning the Search by Applying Tests Earlier

A general strategy for refining a search is to

> *Reduce the branching factor of the search by pruning partial paths that cannot lead to a solution.*

Clearly, the key to applying this strategy is to efficiently identify partial paths that cannot lead to a solution, that is, cannot be extended into a complete sequence of choices that satisfies the solution-test. Identifying such dead ends by enumerating and testing all their extensions would defeat the purpose. Such exhaustive search can be avoided by analysis of the solution-test P(s) to determine whether partial paths that do not satisfy P can be pruned without discarding any potential solutions. Ideally, P is a monotonically necessary condition, that is, if P(s) holds, then so does P(s′) for every initial subsequence s′ of s. If this is the case, any partial path that does *not* satisfy P can be pruned safely from the search, since it cannot possibly be extended into a solution path. This pruning is accomplished by adding P to the path-test. In fact, this reasoning applies not only to P itself but to any necessary condition on P, that is, to any predicate Q such that P(s) implies Q(s′) for every initial subsequence s′ of s. For example, if P is a conjunction, it is worth analyzing each of its conjuncts to see if it is monotonically necessary.

Moreover, if a path-test can be reformulated as a property required of every path element, it can be used to prune the choice elements for extending paths. That is, if a path-test P(s′) implies (∀ c ∈ s′) Q(c), then Q can be incorporated into the step-test.

For example, consider the initial HSM formulation of "avoid taking points," where the path-test is `(LAMBDA (CARDS-PLAYED1) T)` and the solution-test is:

```
(LAMBDA (CARDS-PLAYED1)
   (AND [HAVE-POINTS CARDS-PLAYED1]
        [= (CARDS-PLAYED1 ME)
           (HIGHEST-IN-SUIT-LED CARDS-PLAYED1)]))
```

The first conjunct in this expression is not monotonically necessary, since a card sequence that does not have points can be extended into one that does simply by appending a point card to it. However, the second conjunct *is* monotonically necessary, since in order to be the highest card for the whole trick, player ME's card must be the highest at each point in the trick. Actually, a slight qualification is required: this conjunct only makes sense for paths in which player ME has already played a card. If P is the condition that player ME's card be highest, and the predicate M characterizes those paths in which player ME has already played, then (⇒ M P) is monotonically necessary and can be added to the path-test:

```
--- [by RULE323, analysis] --->
(HSM1 ← PATH-TEST :
       (LAMBDA (CARDS-PLAYED1)
          (⇒ [IN ME (INDICES-OF CARDS-PLAYED1)]
              [= (CARDS-PLAYED1 ME)
                 (HIGHEST-IN-SUIT-LED CARDS-PLAYED1)])))
```

The general rule used to make this refinement is

RULE323:	(HSM with	(solution-test : (lambda (s) (and ... Ps ...))
		(path-test : (lambda (s) R))
→	(HSM with	(path-test : (lambda (s) (and R (⇒ M Ps)))))

where the monotonicity condition (forall s′ (prefixes-of s) (⇒ Ps Ps′)) reduces to M
If the solution-test includes an (almost) monotonically necessary constraint P,
Then determine the condition M under which P is monotonically necessary,
And add (⇒ M P) to the path-test.[6]

In the above example, M is `(IN ME (INDICES-OF CARDS-PLAYED1))`. Note that RULE323 automatically catches (in M) the sort of exception a programmer might forget.

At this point, the highest-card constraint has been moved from the solution-test, where it was only used to test complete card sequences, to the

[6]Since P will be used to prune only paths satisfying M, it is not safe to remove P from the solution-test.

path-test, where it is used to test incomplete sequences, thereby pruning all paths in which player ME plays a card lower than an opponent's or fails to follow suit. However, further improvement is possible by moving the highest-card constraint from the path-test to the step-test. While paths violating the highest-card constraint were previously pruned away, this refinement prevents their being generated at all. That is, it restricts the generation of scenarios to those in which player ME takes the trick. In general, this kind of refinement reformulates a path constraint as a choice element constraint, presumably cheaper to test, since it depends on a single element rather than a sequence. If choice elements that violate this constraint are rejected as path extensions, fewer paths will be generated. In effect, such a refinement reduces the branching factor of the search, that is, the number of alternatives considered at each choice point.

The general rule for moving a constraint from path-test to step-test is

```
RULE327:     (HSM with     (path-test : (lambda (s) (and ... Ps...)) ...))
                           (step-test : (lambda (i c) R))
     →       (HSM with     (step-test : (lambda (i c) (and R Qc))))
```

if Ps can be reformulated as (forall i (indices-of s) Qs_i)

If the path-test includes a constraint Ps,
And Ps is equivalent to (forall i (indices-of s) Qs_i) for some predicate Q,
Then add the constraint Qc to the step-test.

RULE327 applies when a path-test predicate P on a path s = $c_1 \dots c_n$ can be recast as a conjunction of the form (and $Qc_1 \dots Qc_n$) for some predicate Q. Here, s is CARDS-PLAYED1 and P is

```
(LAMBDA (CARDS-PLAYED1)
  (⇒ [IN ME (INDICES-OF CARDS-PLAYED1)]
      [= (CARDS-PLAYED1 ME)
         (HIGHEST-IN-SUIT-LED CARDS-PLAYED1)]))
```

This condition means "if player ME's card has been played, it is the highest so far in the suit led." Transformed into a universally quantified form by unfolding HIGHEST-IN-SUIT-LED, it matches the rule:

```
--- [by RULE124, RULE327, analysis] --->
(HSM1 ← STEP-TEST :
  (LAMBDA (P1 C1)
    (⇒ (NOT (AFTER ME P1))
        (AND [= (SUIT-OF (CARDS-PLAYED1 ME)) (SUIT-LED)]
             [NOT (HIGHER-IN-SUIT C1 (CARDS-PLAYED1 ME))]))))
```

The effect of this step-test when considering possible cards player P1 might play (assuming player ME has followed suit) is to ignore any card in the suit led higher than player ME's card, since it cannot cause player ME to take points. In short, the highest-card constraint has been moved from the solution-test via the path-test to the step-test, where it reduces the search space to scenarios in which player ME takes the trick.

12.5.2 Ordering the Search by Predicting Success

The refinements just described prune branches of the search or eliminate their generation in the first place. In contrast, the refinements described in this section *re-order* the search to find a solution faster when one exists. The general strategy is to

Order the search to consider first those paths most likely to lead to a solution.

The key to applying this strategy is the efficient identification of promising partial paths. Of course, trial and error is as inappropriate for identifying promising paths as it was for identifying hopeless ones. As before, the remedy is analysis of the solution-test, which in this example is

```
(LAMBDA (CARDS-PLAYED1)
   (AND [HAVE-POINTS CARDS-PLAYED1]
        [= (CARDS-PLAYED1 ME)
           (HIGHEST-IN-SUIT-LED CARDS-PLAYED1)]))
```

Unlike the second conjunct, the first conjunct is not monotonically necessary: although no point cards may have been played so far in a trick, a subsequent player might play one. How then can this constraint be exploited earlier in the search?

The answer lies in the fact that if a path has points, so do all its possible extensions. Thus, other things being equal, a path with points is more likely to lead to a solution than one without points, and a solution should be found faster by considering such paths first. (Recall that a "solution" is a card sequence that will cause player ME to take points.) In short, (HAVE-POINTS CARDS-PLAYED1) is *monotonically sufficient* and can therefore be used as a search-ordering heuristic:

```
--- [by RULE335, analysis] --->
(HSM1 ← PATH-ORDER :
      (LAMBDA (CARDS-PLAYED1) (HAVE-POINTS CARDS-PLAYED1)))
```

The general idea behind this refinement is expressed by

RULE335: (HSM with (solution-test : (lambda (s) (and ... Ps ...))))
→ (HSM with (path-order : (lambda (s) Ps)))
if P satisfies the monotonicity condition (forall s′ (prefixes-of s) (⇒ Ps′ Ps)).
If the solution-test includes a monotonically sufficient constraint P,
Then move P to the path-order.

The points constraint can be further exploited by using it to control not only the order in which existing paths are considered, but also the order in which paths are generated to begin with. For example, paths with points can be generated first by using point cards before non-point cards when extending paths in which no points have yet been played:

```
--- [by RULE338, analysis] --->
(HSM1 ← STEP-ORDER :
      (LAMBDA (P1 C1)
          (OR [HAVE-POINTS CARDS-PLAYED1]
              [HAS-POINTS C1])))
```

The general rule for this refinement is

RULE338: (HSM with (path-order : (lambda (s) Ps)))
→ (HSM with (step-order : (lambda (i c) Qc)))
where Qc is the result of simplifying P(s&c)
If the path-order contains a constraint P on paths $c_1 \dots c_k$,
And $P(c_1 \dots c_k)$ *is equivalent to* $Q(c_k)$,
Then add Q to the step-order.

Here s&c denotes the result of appending element c onto sequence s.

An extension to this approach would enhance the data structure representation of a path, s, to include an extra bit B(s), indicating whether s has points. The value of B(s&c) would be computed solely as a function of B(s) and c without re-examining the elements of s. Since FOO lacks an explicit representation for describing data structures, this refinement was not implemented.

12.5.3 Reducing the Depth of the Search

Further improvements in the search procedure formulated thus far can be made by exploiting assumptions about when and why the search will be performed. For example, the purpose of the search is to help player ME choose a card, not just to predict whether there exists some possible scenario in which ME takes points. Thus player ME's card can be treated as an input parameter to the search procedure; the procedure will be called for each of player ME's legal cards to decide whether playing it can possibly cause player ME to take points. Similarly, it is logical to assume that the search will be performed when it is time for player ME to choose a card. This means the search can make use of any data that will be known at that time, such as the cards played by player ME's predecessors.

These refinements are effected by making player ME's card an input parameter, named MY-CARD1, and changing the INITIAL-PATH from NIL to the sequence of cards played in the current trick up to and including MY-CARD1. These changes reduce the depth of the search space. Also, the expression (SUIT-LED) is replaced by the parameter SUIT-LED1, since the suit led will be known at search time.

The details of how these refinements were made using FOO are given in [Mostow, 1981]; they are less interesting than the refinements based on monotonically necessary and sufficient conditions because they were made in a somewhat *ad hoc* manner, due partly to difficulties in representing knowledge about choice and time. The general ideas underlying the refinements can be stated as follows. First,

Reduce the depth of the search by eliminating one or more choice points.

The key here is to use additional problem constraints to compile choices out of the search, for example:

Start the search at the point following any choices already determined before search time.

This idea can be stated more precisely as:

RULE332: *To analyze a property of a choice $f(c_i)$ in a choice sequence $f(c_1)$, ..., $f(c_n)$,*
Use the search space formed by the choice sequence $f(c_{i+1})$ ... $f(c_n)$,
Since at the time $f(c_i)$ is chosen, $f(c_1)$ ... $f(c_{i-1})$ will already be known.

Another way to speed up a search is *caching*, discussed in [Lenat *et al.*, 1979]:

Cache a choice-sequence-dependent expression whose value will not change during the search.

This strategy is used to speed up the step-test by replacing `(SUIT-LED)` with a temporary variable `SUIT-LED1` whose value is computed once at the start of the search:

RULE333: *If a sub-expression $P_{f(s)}$ of the step-test refers to the choice sequence, s,*
[But the value of f(s) will have been determined by the time the search begins,]
Then rewrite $P_{f(s)}$ as P_v,
And cache the value of f(s) in v at the beginning of the search.

As RULE333 is currently implemented, the bracketed clause is not tested, since FOO lacks a model of what data will be available when.

12.5.4 Transforming the Data-Flow Graph Itself

Of course, the search procedure derived above could be improved in many ways. For example, the revised step-test includes the condition `(= (SUIT-OF MY-CARD1) SUIT-LED1)`. Since this condition is totally determined by the search parameters `MY-CARD1` and `SUIT-LED1`, it could be tested just once at the beginning of the search, but doing so would require adding an INITIAL-TEST (applied only to the `INITIAL-PATH`) to the generic heuristic search procedure in Figure 12-2. This illustrates a limitation of using a fixed set of HSM components: one can always invent refinements that involve adding new components. A more powerful approach allows refinement rules expressed as transformations on data-flow graphs [Tappel, 1980].

To illustrate the potential usefulness of transformations on the data-flow graph itself, consider the step-test, which restricts the generation of paths to those where `MY-CARD1` is the highest card played in `SUIT-LED1`:

```
(LAMBDA (P1 C1)
   (⇒ [= (SUIT-OF C1) SUIT-LED1]
       [NOT (HIGHER C1 MY-CARD1)]))
```

If player ME leads the trick, SUIT-LED1 must be bound to (SUIT-OF MY-CARD1) before the search begins; otherwise it can be bound to the actual suit led in the trick. A natural way to deal with this detail is to split the whole search procedure into two copies, one for each case, and refine each one by exploiting the assumption on which it is based. However, this *clone-and-specialize* transformation violates the fixed-graph limitation.

12.5.5 Moving to a Smaller Search Space

One way to reduce the branching factor of a search is to use a step-test to filter the generation of alternatives at each choice point (Section 12.5.1). A more sophisticated (but unimplemented) way is to move the search to an abstracted version of the original search space:

> To reduce a search space, suppress operator details irrelevant to the search criterion, and use the resulting abstractions in place of the original operators [Mostow & Hayes-Roth, 1979].

Operator abstraction has been used to reduce search in planning systems, but the abstraction process has been limited: operators have been abstracted by deleting some of their preconditions [Newell *et al.*, 1960; Sacerdoti, 1977] or by ignoring variable bindings [Sacerdoti, 1974; Klahr, 1978]. In contrast, the abstractions proposed below would be synthesized based on analysis of the search criterion and knowledge about the task domain.

For instance, from the point of view of avoiding taking points, certain properties of the card played by an opponent are irrelevant. If the card has no points and is not in the suit led, its suit and rank are unimportant. If it is in the suit led, all that matters is whether it is higher or lower than player ME's card; its exact rank is unimportant. This suggests reducing the choice set from a set of cards to a set of abstract alternatives like {LOSING-CARD, HIGH-CARD-IN-SUIT, POINT-CARD}. These alternatives represent equivalence classes of cards, where the equivalence relation is strongly situation-dependent. For instance, in some cases playing any heart will have the same impact on the outcome of the trick, while in others the particular heart played might determine who wins the trick. One might look dynamically for easily derived equivalences and use them to reduce the search space for the particular situation at hand, according to the heuristic:

> *Do not consider more than one alternative from a set of equivalent ones.*

Suppose an abstract alternative is defined as the set of all choices x satisfying some predicate P(x); for LOSING-CARD, P(x) means "card x will not take the trick." Then:

1. Look for sufficient conditions S(x, x′) under which P(x) and P(x′) are equivalent. For example, if x and x′ are in the same suit and held by the same player, and nobody else holds any of the intervening cards, then x can take the trick if and only if x′ could.
2. Partition the choice set into equivalence classes $C_x = \{x' \mid S(x, x')\}$. If player ME holds the four, six, and seven of hearts, and the five has already been played, these three cards are in the same equivalence class.
3. Replace the old choice set with a new one containing a single representative of each class. Since the revised choice set generates cards (rather than some kind of abstracted element), the other HSM components still work.
4. Perform the search as usual. For example, test whether player ME can take points by playing the four of hearts; the same answer will hold for the six and seven.

A similar approach is to:

Consider an alternative only if it is optimal and no equivalent one has been considered.

This approach is based on the concept of *extreme cases* [Lenat & Harris, 1978]:

1. Find a condition $\geq(s, s')$ guaranteeing that s can be extended into a solution if s′ can.
2. Define Dominates(s,s′) as $s \geq s' \wedge \sim s' \geq s$. This predicate can be used to order paths by considering s before s′ if s dominates s′.
3. Add a path-test Optimal(s) $= \sim\exists s' \mid$ Dominates(s′, s): if a maximally promising path s peters out, so will every less promising path s′.
4. Add a path-test $\sim\exists s' \mid s' \geq s \wedge s' \neq s \wedge$ Tried(s′): do not consider s if you have already tried an equally promising path s′.
5. If either test can be reformulated as a function of the last choice alone, make it a step-test.

This approach looks for sufficient conditions in each situation, rather than doing a single analysis once and for all. This might capture an aspect of human play—figuring out what will happen if player p plays card x, and then jumping to the conclusion that the same thing will happen if p plays any other card in the class C_x. The major obstacle in implementing this approach, of course, is to automate the discovery of useful equivalence and domination conditions.

12.5.6 Heuristic Search Procedure for "Avoid Taking Points"

After the refinements performed by FOO, the HSM schema has been instantiated as follows:

```
(HSM1 WITH
    (VARIABLES : (SUIT-LED1 MY-CARD1))
    (BINDINGS : ((SUIT-LED) (CARD-OF ME)))
    (INITIAL-PATH : (PROJECT CARD-OF (PREFIX (PLAYERS) ME)))

    (CHOICE-SETS :
       (LAMBDA (P1)
          (SET-OF C1 (CARDS)
             (POSSIBLE
                (AND [HAS P1 C1]
               ; ⇒ (OUT C1) WHEN (IN P1 (OPPONENTS-OF ME))
               ; ⇒ (NON-VOID P1) WHEN (IN-SUIT C1 (SUIT-LED))
                     [⇒ (LEADING P1)
                         (OR [CAN-LEAD-HEARTS P1]
                             [NEQ (SUIT-OF C1) H])]
                     [⇒ (FOLLOWING P1)
                         (OR [VOID P1 (SUIT-LED)]
                             [IN-SUIT C1 (SUIT-LED)])]))))))

    (STEP-ORDER :
       (LAMBDA (P1 C1)
          (OR [HAVE-POINTS CARDS-PLAYED1] [HAS-POINTS C1])))

    (STEP-TEST :
       (LAMBDA (P1 C1)
          (⇒ [NOT (AFTER ME P1)]
              [AND [= (SUIT-OF MY-CARD1) SUIT-LED1]
                   [⇒ [= (SUIT-OF C1) SUIT-LED1]
                       [NOT (HIGHER C1 MY-CARD1)]]]])))

    (PATH-ORDER :
       (LAMBDA (CARDS-PLAYED1) (HAVE-POINTS CARDS-PLAYED1)))

    (PATH-TEST :
       (LAMBDA (CARDS-PLAYED1)
           (⇒ [IN ME (INDICES-OF CARDS-PLAYED1)]
               [= (CARDS-PLAYED1 ME)
                  (HIGHEST-IN-SUIT-LED CARDS-PLAYED1)])))

    (SOLUTION-TEST :
       (LAMBDA (CARDS-PLAYED1)
          (AND [HAVE-POINTS CARDS-PLAYED1]
               [= (CARDS-PLAYED1 ME)
                  (HIGHEST-IN-SUIT-LED CARDS-PLAYED1)])))

    (COMPLETION-TEST :
       (LAMBDA (PATH) (= (# PATH) (# (PLAYERS))))))
```

The procedure thereby specified, shown as a data-flow graph in Figure 12-5, operates as follows:

The object of the search is to find a sequence of cards satisfying the

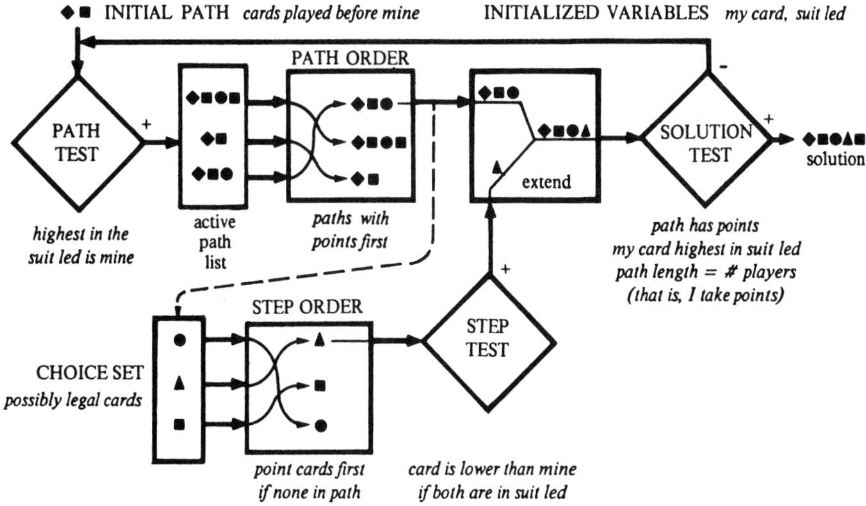

Figure 12-5: Refined search for "Avoid Taking Points".

solution-test and completion-test. The solution-test requires the sequence to contain one or more point cards, with player ME's card the highest in the suit led. The completion-test requires the sequence to contain a card for each player. Together, they specify a sequence of cards that will cause player ME to take points.

The choice set for player P1 consists of those cards that might possibly be legal for P1 to play, according to the information available to player ME. For example, in order to play a card C1, P1 must have C1. Player ME may be unable to test this directly, but can still check a couple of necessary conditions. First, if P1 $\neq$ ME, C1 must be out, and in particular, cannot already have been played. This prevents consideration of scenarios in which the same card is played more than once, or in which a card taken in an earlier trick miraculously reappears. Second, C1 cannot be in the suit led if P1 is known to be void in that suit.

The search conservatively takes as the choice set all cards satisfying the known necessary conditions; the branching factor of the search could be reduced by checking additional necessary conditions, or by considering only *plausible* scenarios for the trick. The latter refinement would require a model of other players' goals in order to predict their likely behavior.

The variables SUIT-LED1 and MY-CARD1, bound to values computed or selected before the search, represent the suit led and a card player ME is considering playing.

The search proceeds by selecting a card sequence from the active path list, appending a card, testing the new sequence to see if it is a solution, and deciding whether to add it to the list. The INITIAL-PATH contains MY-CARD1 and the cards already played in the trick.

The path-order gives priority to paths in which points have been played.

The step-test filters the generation of paths to those in which player ME wins the trick.

The step-order gives priority to point cards when extending a sequence with none.

The path-test prunes paths in which player ME cannot take the trick. Since the step-test prevents the generation of such paths, the path-test need not really be applied to any paths other than the initial-path. This could be accomplished by adding an initial-test component to the HSM schema, and would terminate the search immediately in cases where player ME does not follow suit.

The search procedure requires a run-time environment with several features:

- 3-valued logic: unevaluable expressions return UNKNOWN without causing run-time errors.
- Annotations: evaluation methods can be tried that do not always succeed.
- Simulation: the effects of an action can be predicted by modeling state changes.
- Historical reference: expressions can be evaluated relative to past states or events [Balzer & Goldman, 1979].

These features seem reasonably straightforward to build into an evaluator, but implementing them was beyond the scope of the research. Consequently the search procedure was not implemented.

12.5.7 Another Example: Compose a Cantus Firmus

So far, FOO's HSM schema and its rules for instantiating and refining this schema have been illustrated solely in terms of the "avoid taking points" example. As a test of generality, I applied the same rules to a task from the domain of music: "Compose a *cantus firmus*." A *cantus firmus* is a sequence of musical tones of equal length satisfying certain aesthetic constraints. A program to generate such sequences [Meehan, 1971] was based on aesthetic constraints given in a textbook on counterpoint [Salzer & Schacter, 1969]. The goal of my experiment was to use the rules from the hearts example, or similar ones, to derive a heuristic search procedure for generating tone sequences satisfying four constraints arbitrarily chosen from the textbook:

- C1. "As a rule, the *cantus* will not contain fewer than eight or more than sixteen tones."
- C2. "The *cantus firmus* should not contain intervals larger than an octave, dissonant leaps, or chromatic half steps."

- C3. "A tenth between the lowest and the highest tone is the maximum range."
- C4. "Each *cantus firmus* must contain a climax or high point... The climax tone should not be repeated."

The derivation of a heuristic search procedure for this problem has much in common with the hearts example. The initial generate-and-test procedure simply generates tone sequences and tests each one to see if it satisfies constraints C1-C4. The refined HSM procedure incorporates these constraints earlier in the search. The same HSM rules were used to construct a generate-and-test search from the problem description, and to move monotonically necessary constraints from the solution-test to the path-test and step-test. Some highlights:

1. Constraint C4 was simplified by choosing a climax tone before generating the *cantus*. The idea of restricting a problem by determining one of its features *a priori* is expressed by

   RULE256: (P ... (f s) ...) → (and [= (f s) v] [P ... v ...])
   where v is to be selected from (range f) before s is constructed
   To construct an object s so as to satisfy a constraint P(s, f(s)),
   Choose a value v for f(s),
   And solve the two subproblems P(s, v) and f(s)=v.

   Before the search begins, a value CLIMAX1 is chosen to be the climax tone of the *cantus*. This value could be generated randomly or, as in [Meehan, 1971], supplied as an input; the point is that the decision to select it before the search simplifies the operationalization of constraint C4.

2. A constraint that is not monotonically necessary or sufficient can sometimes be split into a conjunction of monotonic constraints, which can then be moved earlier in the search. For example,

   ```
   (LAMBDA (TONE-SEQUENCE1)
      (= (CLIMAX TONE-SEQUENCE1) CLIMAX1))
   ```

   is split into the monotonically sufficient

   ```
   (IN CLIMAX1 TONE-SEQUENCE1)
   ```

   and the monotonically necessary

   ```
   (FORALL X1 TONE-SEQUENCE1 (NOT (HIGHER X1 CLIMAX1)))
   ```

3. The ideal refinement rule compiles a constraint out of the search altogether. One such rule is:

```
RULE386:      (HSM with      (path : s)
                             (choice-sets : (... (set-of x S (P ... (g s) ...)) ...)))
       →      (HSM with (choice-sets : (f (g s))))
f ← (lambda (y) (set-of x S (P ... y ...)))
if (P ...) is otherwise independent of s
```

If the choice set has the form {x in S | P(x, g(s))}
Where S and range(g) are small
And P does not otherwise depend on the path variable s,
Then define a new function f(y) = {x in S | P(x,y)}
And change the choice set to f(g(s)),
Where f is precomputed and stored in a table before the search begins.

RULE386 applies after the choice set for the next note has been restricted to those tones separated from the previous note by an acceptable melodic interval (constraint C2), computed by generating every tone and testing the interval between it and the last note. RULE386 replaces this generate-and-test loop with a precomputable table that lists all acceptable successors for each tone. Instead of enumerating the entire set of (TONES) when extending a tone sequence, the search will consider only acceptable successor tones. This refinement effectively compiles C2 out of the search.

12.6 EVALUATION OF GENERALITY

The purpose of the *cantus firmus* example was to test the generality of FOO's knowledge about heuristic search problems— its general schema representation of HSM, its instantiation rules for filling in this schema so as to constitute a generate-and-test procedure, and its refinement rules for transforming this procedure into a genuine heuristic search.

The same HSM schema was general enough to cover both the hearts and the music examples.

The process of formulating the initial generate-and-test procedure was very similar in the two examples: the same HSM rules were applied in the same order, even though the analysis rules used were quite different. This striking parallelism supports the generality of the instantiation rules.

The refinement rules used in the hearts example were checked to see if they could be applied to the music example. Some were directly applicable, such as RULE323, which moves a constraint from the solution-test to the path-test, and RULE327, which moves a constraint from the path-test to the step-test. (Both these rules were used more than once in each example.) Other rules added to cover the music example closely resembled rules used in the hearts example; this suggests that it may be worthwhile to look for common generalizations or a more fundamental rule-generating process.

In short, there was a great deal of overlap between the HSM rules used in the two examples, even though different rules were required to solve the analysis problems engendered by different uses of the same HSM rule. This suggests that FOO does indeed have some general knowledge about operationalizing a problem in terms of HSM.

One would expect other examples to use additional rules. Some of these rules might require changes to the schema or not fit any fixed schema, *e.g.*:

- Generalize the initial state to be a set of paths rather than a single path.
- Add a test applied only to the initial-path.
- Distinguish cheaply evaluated or highly constraining tests and put them first in the data-flow graph.
- Split the data-flow graph into several copies and refine each one to fit a different case.

12.7 CONCLUSION

The ultimate goal of this research is to automate the process of applying general AI techniques to problems expressed in domain-specific terms. This chapter has modeled this process as a series of problem transformations and has described some general rules used to reformulate two dissimilar tasks as heuristic search problems. Some of these rules recognize a potential HSM problem in a task description and construct a generate-and-test procedure for it. Others refine such a procedure into a true heuristic search by (unlike conventional optimizing compilers) exploiting domain knowledge and analyzing problem constraints.

Much work remains to be done:

- FOO's rules should be tested on other domains, generalized, and extended.
- The same strategy should be used to apply other AI methods: construct a simple procedure, then successively refine it based on domain knowledge and analysis.
- FOO's fixed set of HSM components enables rules to refer to them by name, at the cost of being unable to modify the basic heuristic search data-flow graph to fit different problems. Graph-transforming refinement rules [Tappel, 1980] should be developed to eliminate this inflexibility, but referring to components of the changing graph will require a more complex naming scheme.
- An automatic operationalizer would need a problem-solver to guide the operationalization process and a model to predict which expressions will be executable at run-time. The dissertation on which this chapter is based [Mostow, 1981] outlines a means-end analysis approach to the problem-solving issue.
- The lack of a built-in representation for opponents' goals was motivated by the desire for generality but prevented refining the "avoid taking points" search based on the relative plausibility of different scenarios for the trick. A practical operationalizer would need to reason about the mental behavior of agents in the task environment, including itself [Konolige & Nilsson, 1980].

- The purely *analytic* approach presented here attempts to design a search procedure independent of any specific task situation. It should be combined with *empirical* techniques for exploiting properties of particular task situations (see Chapter 6 of this book) and improving a search procedure as it executes [Lenat *et al.*, 1979].

The central theme in current AI research is the exploitation of domain knowledge to achieve high performance. Future research on the mechanical application of AI techniques to real tasks must address this theme. The fundamental challenge in this work is to develop *domain-independent techniques for exploiting domain-specific knowledge*. Such techniques can be expected to play an important role in future advice-taking systems that devise procedures to do what they are told.

ACKNOWLEDGMENTS

I owe many ideas about operationalization to my dissertation committee: Rick Hayes-Roth, Allen Newell, Jaime Carbonell, and Bob Balzer. I am grateful to Jim Meehan for unearthing and documenting the *cantus*-generating program he wrote as an undergraduate. This chapter benefitted considerably from helpful suggestions by the editors, insightful comments by Jim Bennett and Steve Tappel, careful readings by Tom Dietterich, and useful criticisms by Bill Swartout and Lee Erman. Of course, I alone am responsible for any errors.

This research was supported in part by a National Science Foundation Graduate Fellowship, in part by the National Science Foundation under Grant No. MCS77-03273 to the Rand Corporation, in part by the Defense Advanced Research Projects Agency (DOD), ARPA Order No. 3597, monitored by the Air Force Avionics Laboratory under Contract F33615-78-C-1511, in part by the Heuristic Programming Project at Stanford University, and in part by DARPA Contract MDA-903-81-C-0335 to USC Information Sciences Institute.

The views and conclusions contained in this document are those of the author and should not be interpreted as representing the official policies, either expressed or implied, of the National Science Foundation, the Rand Corporation, the Defense Advanced Research Projects Agency, or the U.S. Government.

This chapter is a revised, condensed version of Chapter 3 of [Mostow, 1981], and describes dissertation research performed at Carnegie-Mellon University.

REFERENCES

Balzer, R., "Transformational implementation: an example," *IEEE Transactions on Software* Engineering, Vol. SE-7, No. 1, pp. 3-14, Jan. 1981.

Balzer, R., and Goldman, N., "Principles of good software specification and their implications for specification languages," *Proc. Conf. Specifications Reliable Software*, Boston, MA, pp. 58-67, 1979.

Darlington, J., and Burstall, R. M., "A system which automatically improves programs," *Acta Informatica*, Vol. 6, pp. 41-60, 1976.

Klahr, P., "Partial proofs and partial answers", Technical Report P-6239, The Rand Corporation, Santa Monica, CA, 1978, (Presented at 4th Workshop on Automated Deduction, University of Texas, Austin, 1979).

Konolige, K., and Nilsson, N. J., "Multiple-agent planning systems," *AAAI80*, American Association for Artificial Intelligence, Stanford University, pp. 138-142, 1980.

Lenat, D., and Harris, G., "Designing a rule system that searches for scientific discoveries," *Pattern-Directed Inference Systems*, D. A. Waterman and F. Hayes-Roth (Eds.), Academic Press, New York, pp. 25-51, 1978.

Lenat, D. B., Hayes-Roth, F., and Klahr, P., "Cognitive economy in artificial intelligence systems," *IJCAI-6*, Tokyo, Japan, pp. 531-536, 1979.

Meehan, J., "CANTUS", (Computer program to generate *cantus firmus*. Senior undergraduate honors project, Yale University).

Moore, J., *The design and evaluation of a knowledge net for Merlin,* Ph.D. dissertation, Carnegie-Mellon University, 1971.

Mostow, D. J., *Mechanical Transformation of Task Heuristics into Operational Procedures,* Ph.D. dissertation, Carnegie-Mellon University, 1981, (Available as CMU-CS-81-113).

Mostow, D. J. and F. Hayes-Roth, "Operationalizing heuristics: some AI methods for assisting AI programming," *IJCAI-5*, Tokyo, Japan, pp. 601-609, 1979.

Newell, A., "Heuristic programming: Ill-structured problems," *Progress in Operations Research*, J. Aronofsky (Ed.), Wiley, New York, pp. 363-414, 1969.

Newell, A., Shaw, J., and Simon. H. A., "Empirical explorations of the logic theory machine: A case study in heuristics," *Proceedings of the 1957 Western Joint Computer Conference*, Western Joint Computer Conference, pp. 218-230, 1957, (Reprinted in E. Feigenbaum and J. Feldman (editors), *Computers and Thought*, McGraw-Hill, 1963).

Newell, A., Shaw, J., and Simon, H. A., "Report on a general problem-solving program for a computer," *Proceedings of the International Conference on Information Processing*, UNESCO, Paris, pp. 256-264, 1960.

Sacerdoti, E. D., "Planning in a hierarchy of abstraction spaces," *Artificial Intelligence*, Vol. 5, pp. 115-135, 1974.

Sacerdoti, E. D., *A Structure for Plans and Behavior*, Amsterdam: North-Holland, 1977.

Salzer, F., and Schacter, C., *Counterpoint in Composition: the Study of Voice Leading*, McGraw-Hill, New York, 1969.

Simon, H. A., "Artificial intelligence systems that understand," *IJCAI-5*, Cambridge, MA, pp. 1059-1073, 1977.

Tappel, S., "Some algorithm design methods," *AAAI80*, Stanford University, pp. 64-67, 1980.

APPENDIX: INDEX OF RULES

RULE124 (page 373): Unfold definition

RULE256 (page 397): To achieve P(f(s)), choose f(s) = v and achieve P(v)

RULE306 (page 378): Use HSM to evaluate predicate on scenario with choices

RULE318 (page 382): P → (possible P)

RULE319 (page 383): Find necessary condition

RULE323 (page 387): Move monotonically necessary constraint from solution-test to path-test

RULE327 (page 388): Move constraint from path-test to step-test

RULE332 (page 391): Start the search at the point following any predetermined choices

RULE333 (page 391): Cache expressions whose values stay constant during the search

RULE335 (page 389): Move monotonically sufficient constraint from solution-test to path-order

RULE338 (page 390): Move constraint from path-order to step-order

RULE386 (page 398): Compile a constraint into a precomputable table

13

LEARNING BY BEING TOLD: ACQUIRING KNOWLEDGE FOR INFORMATION MANAGEMENT

Norman Haas
Gary G. Hendrix
SRI International

ABSTRACT

This chapter discusses machine-learning aspects of a project whose broad goal is to create computer systems that can aid users in managing information. The specific learning problem discussed is how to enable computer systems to acquire information about domains with which they are unfamiliar from people who are experts in those domains, but have little or no training in computer science. The information to be acquired is that needed to support question-answering or fact-retrieval tasks, and the type of learning to be employed is learning by being told.

13.1 OVERVIEW

13.1.1 The KLAUS Concept

Our interest in knowledge acquisition is motivated by the desire to create computer systems that can aid users in managing information. The core idea of what we call a KLAUS[1] system is that of a machine that can hold a conversation with a user in English about his specific domain of interest, subsequently retrieve and display information conveyed by the user, and apply various types of external software systems to solve user problems. Such software would include data base management systems, report generators, planners, simulators, and statistical packages.

---

[1] "KLAUS" stands for Knowledge Learning And Using Systems.

Interactive dialogues in natural language appear to be a convenient means for obtaining most of the application-specific knowledge needed by intelligent systems for information management. But systems that acquire knowledge about new domains through natural-language dialogues must possess some very special capabilities.

KLAUS systems must support interactive, mixed-initiative dialogues. Because a user may provide new knowledge in an incremental and incomplete manner, the system must keep track of what it has already been told, so that it can deduce the existence of missing information and explicitly ask the user to supply it. Moreover, it must carefully distinguish what it does not know from what it knows to be false.

A primary requirement of a KLAUS system is that it be capable of simultaneously learning both new concepts and the linguistic constructions used to express them. KLAUS systems must acquire domain-specific language expertise, not only to understand natural language statements formulated by the user about his domain, but also for generating natural language responses to user requests.

The intimate connection between language and reasoning is reflected in the need to acquire concepts and language simultaneously. This poses a great challenge in the task of creating KLAUS systems. Thus, this chapter is largely concerned with the problems of learning concepts and language simultaneously.

13.1.2 Research Problems for KLAUS Systems

Before systems can be created that are capable of learning about new domains through interactive dialogues in English, several fundamental research problems must be resolved:

- A powerful natural language processing capability is required. Although much progress has been made in recent years, previous work has presupposed a complete knowledge base. Knowledge acquisition dialogues require numerous adaptations and extensions to the technology.
- A structure for lexical entries must be specified so that the system can acquire new lexical information. Because such information constitutes a key link between surface linguistic form and underlying meaning, structural specification is a challenging task for certain categories of words, particularly verbs.
- The linguistic constructions that people use in introducing new concepts must be identified and analyzed, so they can be interpreted correctly by the natural language processing system. Such constructions range from simple syntactic patterns to complex analogies.
- Seed concepts and seed vocabulary must be identified for inclusion in a core system. It is not obvious which words and concepts would be most useful in helping users describe new domains.
- A flexible scheme of knowledge representation is necessary. Such a

representation must have general expressive power, since it may be applied to diverse domains and must support the addition of new information. It should include inherent features that can aid in organizing knowledge and supporting incremental acquisition.

- An efficient problem-solving capability is needed to answer questions and draw inferences for integrating newly-acquired information. This capability must be based on general principles, because no application-specific problem-solving procedures will be included in the system. (How to learn application-specific problem-solving procedures is a separate and interesting research question.)
- A methodology is needed for integrating new concepts into the system's knowledge base. Because users will often provide only partial descriptions of new concepts, methods must be devised for ascertaining what additional facts should be sought from the user to ensure proper linkage between the new concepts and those previously acquired.
- A set of readily understandable questions is needed for eliciting information from the user. The length and number of questions should be kept to a minimum, so as not to impose an excessive burden on users.
- Facilities must be provided for allowing a user to change his mind about what he has told the system. That is, users should be able to instruct the system to modify, revise or refute information it has been told previously.
- Means are required for detecting and dealing with inconsistent data.

These problems must be dealt with in an integrated manner, balancing the requirements of one facet of the system against those of other facets. Our initial attempts to cope with this complex web of issues are described below.

13.1.3 Other Learning Systems

Our learning-by-being-told approach to learning is quite different from other approaches studied in knowledge acquisition research. In particular, our aim is to collect and organize aggregations of individual facts for use in question-answering tasks. The collecting of individual facts contrasts with work on the acquisition of rules for judgmental reasoning, as exemplified by the work of Davis [1977]. In rule acquisition, knowledge is viewed not so much as a collection of facts, but as a set of rules that in their aggregate comprise an algorithm for making some type of decision. Learning by being told is also quite different from approaches based on learning from examples [Dietterich & Michalski, 1979] or learning by analogy (see Carbonell, Chapter 5, and Winston [1975]).

13.2 TECHNICAL APPROACH: EXPERIMENTS WITH THE KLAUS CONCEPT

We have recently developed and tested a pilot KLAUS, called NANOKLAUS. A sample transcript of interactions with this system is contained in the appendix to this chapter. Readers are encouraged to glance through this transcript before proceeding with the reading of this text.

The principal components of NANOKLAUS are a natural language processing module, a formal deduction module that operates on a data base of well-formed formulas (wffs) in first-order logic, and a number of support procedures that aid in assimilating knowledge about new subject domains and in maintaining the data base.

13.2.1 Seed Concepts

NANOKLAUS comes preprogrammed with a fixed set of syntactic and semantic rules covering a small subset of English. It also comes with seed concepts and a seed vocabulary, which are to be extended as the the system learns about a new domain. For example, the system comes with a preliminary taxonomy of concepts already encoded. This basic set includes such things as PHYSICAL OBJECTS, PERSONS, MEASURES, and the like. NANOKLAUS also has preset lexical entries for the basic function words of English, as well as of such words as "unit", "kind", and "plural" that are used frequently in articulating definitions of new words and concepts. These seed concepts allow the untrained NANOKLAUS to "understand" inputs such as those of Interactions 3 and 4 of the transcript.

The choice of seed concepts for a system that must bootstrap its entry into new domains is problematical. Most of the concepts we selected for NANOKLAUS are classes of THINGs and RELATIONs. They have been included in the system either simply to avoid forcing users to relate everything to the most general concept (THING), or because they have a special status in English. For example, because use of pronouns depends partially on gender, the class MALE is included and associated with the pronoun "he".

It is important *not* to think of the seed concepts as a set of primitives, in terms of which all other concepts must be defined. Concept acquisition in NANOKLAUS is not based on definitions. Rather, new concepts are introduced by the user and progressively refined by adding more and more facts connecting the new concept to other concepts. English sentences introducing a new concept simply place it in a relationship with old concepts. Each new fact acts as a constraint that the concepts it mentions must satisfy. Thus, concept acquisition is a process of pruning away possibilities, rather than building up from primitives. For arguments as to the general unworkability of the latter approach, see [Fodor, 1975].

To illustrate the notion of progressive refinement as opposed to definitions, consider the simple statement "The JFK is a ship." This statement serves to introduce the notion of the JFK, and to place it in a relationship to the concept of

SHIP. But it does not define the notion of being the JFK, in that it does not supply the necessary and sufficient conditions for being the JFK. Subsequent facts learned about the JFK serve to further restrict, but not necessarily to define, the concept.

NANOKLAUS uses seven principles of knowledge organization to integrate new knowledge:

1. There are things.
2. There are subclasses of things. (Things can be classified taxonomically.)
3. There are relations among things.
4. There are subclasses of relations.
5. Some relations are functions (that is, n to 1 maps).
6. Sometimes a given set of constraints is sufficient to distinguish a unique individual.
7. Equals are interchangeable.

NANOKLAUS is not programmed to hold explicit conversations about these principles, but rather to *utilize* them in its internal operations.

13.2.2 NANOKLAUS's Natural Language Component

The natural language component of NANOKLAUS is based on LIFER [Hendrix, 1977] and uses a pragmatic grammar in the style of LADDER [Hendrix *et al.*, 1978]. In particular, its grammar consists of a number of highly specific, special-purpose rules for processing various types of sentences.[2] For example, the grammar may be thought of as including a rule of the form:

```
<SENTENCE> ⇒ <PRESENT>  THE  <KNOWN-COUNT-NOUN>
             | (DISPLAY <KNOWN-COUNT-NOUN>)
```

which is used to match such inputs as:

What are the ships?
Show me the officers.
List the carriers.

The metasymbol <PRESENT> matches the italicized portion of these inputs, THE matches "the", and <KNOWN-COUNT-NOUN> matches the last word in each of the examples. (Count nouns refer to discrete objects that can be counted, such as ships and ports. NANOKLAUS does not deal with mass nouns, for example, "steel" and "water".)

Whenever a sentence is found that matches this pattern, the function DISPLAY is called with the value of <KNOWN-COUNT-NOUN>. This function

---

[2]The rules used by NANOKLAUS are much more linguistically motivated than those used in LADDER. In our discussion, we have suppressed the complexity of the rules and response functions actually used, so as to characterize the essence of the methodology more succinctly.

thereupon retrieves from the data base and displays to the user all currently known instances of objects that might be referred to by the <KNOWN-COUNT-NOUN>.

Although most of the linguistic processing performed by the system follows fairly standard practice, the pragmatic grammar is distinguished by its explicit identification of a number of syntactic structures used principally to introduce new concepts. As an oversimplified example, NANOKLAUS might be thought of as looking for the syntactic pattern:

```
<SENTENCE> ⇒ <A> <NEW-WORD> <BE> <A> <KNOWN-COUNT-NOUN>
```

to account for such inputs as:

```
A CARRIER IS A SHIP.
```

The system's definition of the category `<NEW-WORD>` allows `<NEW-WORD>` to match any LISP atom (or atom sequence). The syntactic category <KNOWN-COUNT-NOUN> originally contains only count nouns associated with seed concepts, such as "thing", "person", "physical object" and the like.

When one of NANOKLAUS's concept-defining patterns is recognized, an assimilation procedure associated with the pattern is called. This procedure usually adds new facts to the system's set of wffs and generates new entries in its lexicon. The various assimilation procedures also have provisions for interacting with the user/teacher. Response generation is accomplished by means of preprogrammed phrases and templates.

For example, when the routine associated with the last pattern shown above is called, it first makes a new lexical entry in category <KNOWN-COUNT-NOUN> for the atom matched by the `<NEW-WORD>`. In this case, "CARRIER" becomes a new `<KNOWN-COUNT-NOUN>`. Then the routine creates a new sort predicate[3] for `CARRIER` in the system's knowledge base and enters the assertion that "for every x, if x is a `CARRIER` then x is a `SHIP`". Finally the routine asks questions of the user to determine relationships between the sorts of objects that are `CARRIER`s and other sorts of objects that are `SHIP`s. Interactions 7 and 23 of the transcript illustrate this interaction.

13.2.3 NANOKLAUS's Knowledge Base and Deduction Component

First-order logic was chosen as the basis for NANOKLAUS's knowledge representation scheme because of its generality and because of the computational soundness and power of problem-solving systems that use it.

---

[3]A *sort predicate* is a one-argument predicate that indicates what kind, class, or *sort* of thing an object is. For example, `CARRIER` and `SHIP` are sort predicates in the formula `(ALL X) (CARRIER(X) ⇒ SHIP(X))`. We use the word "sort" rather than "class" to avoid the connotation that a sort predicate is associated with a set of objects, which could be extensionally defined.

13.2.3.1 Typical Wffs Used by NANOKLAUS

The introduction of sort predicates mentioned above provides an example of how NANOKLAUS makes use of constructs from first-order logic. Whenever NANOKLAUS learns a new count noun, it creates a new single-place predicate to characterize objects of the associated sort. For example, we have seen that, upon learning the concept of a carrier, NANOKLAUS creates a predicate called "CARRIER" and asserts the fact:

```
(ALL X) (CARRIER(X)  ⇒  SHIP(X)).
```

As another example of NANOKLAUS's use of formulas in logic, when NANOKLAUS learns that carriers and submarines are distinct sorts of objects, it effectively asserts the fact:

```
(ALL X) (NOT (CARRIER(X) AND SUBMARINE(X)).
```

When NANOKLAUS learns of a new individual, such as the JFK (see Interaction 26), it creates a new constant term in the logic system and relates it to one of the sorts, namely:

```
KITTYHAWK(JFK).
```

Upon learning a new verb, such as "command" (see Interaction 18), NANOKLAUS creates a new predicate with the proper number of argument positions and constrains the domains of those arguments by assertions such as:

```
(ALL X Y) (COMMAND(X Y) ⇒ (OFFICER(X) AND SHIP(Y))).
```

Most of the assertions made by a user are translated into propositions in a straightforward manner. For example, "Brown commands the Saratoga" (see Interaction 43) produces:

```
COMMAND(BROWN SARATOGA).
```

13.2.3.2 Consistency

NANOKLAUS checks each new fact as it is asserted to determine whether it is consistent with its previous knowledge. This gives rise to the behavior shown in Interactions 27, 44 and 45 of the transcript. NANOKLAUS currently has no provision for unlearning. Therefore, if a new assertion causes an inconsistency because a previous assertion was not correct, there is no provision for withdrawing the incorrect assertion.

13.2.3.3 More Reasons for Using First-Order Logic

The notion of using first-order logic in combination with automatic deduction as the basis of an intelligent system dates back to the very beginning of AI research. Newell and Simon [1956] published a paper on "The Logical Theorist" in 1956, and McCarthy, in his 1959 "Advice Taker" proposal (republished as [McCarthy, 1968]), suggested using such a combination as the basis of a system capable of commonsense reasoning.

Following a vigorous start, work on the use of logic as a basis for AI systems fell on hard times during the 1960's and early 70's after experimentation by

Green [1969] and by others showed that the computational effort required to solve problems in first-order logic using Robinson's [1965] resolution principle grows exponentially with the number of wffs used in the axiomatization of a domain. However, more recent work, such as [Hayes, 1973; Kowalski, 1974; Moore, 1975] and [Weyhrauch, 1980], has suggested how control information may be used to increase the efficiency of the deduction process.

But our main motivation for using first-order logic is that KLAUS systems are incremental learning systems and therefore must be capable of dealing with *incomplete* knowledge. As pointed out by Moore [1982]:

> Any knowledge representation formalism that is capable of handling the kinds of incomplete information people can understand must at least be able to:
>
> - Say that something has a certain property without saying which thing has that property: `(SOME X) P(X)`
> - Say that everything in a certain class has a certain property without saying what everything in that class is: `(ALL X) (P(X) ⇒ Q(X))`
> - Say that at least one of two statements is true without saying which statement is true: `P OR Q`
> - Explicitly say that a statement is false, as distinguished from simply not saying that it is true: `NOT(P)`
>
> Any representation formalism that has these capabilities will be, at the very least, an extension of classical first-order logic, and any inference system that can deal adequately with these kinds of generalizations will have to have at least the capabilities of an automatic deduction system.

13.2.4 Acquisition Procedures: Using Dialogue to Aid Assimilation

By and large, it is unreasonable to expect users to volunteer all the information NANOKLAUS needs to assimilate a new concept. In particular, users cannot be expected to know what conclusions NANOKLAUS will draw about a newly taught concept from its previous knowledge, since they know neither the details of its current state of knowledge nor the details of its assimilation procedures. NANOKLAUS must ask the user explicitly for the information it needs. Therefore, whenever a new concept (or word) is presented to NANOKLAUS, a special procedure is called that temporarily assumes control of the dialogue, prompting the user for whatever additional information it may require to assimilate the new concept.

NANOKLAUS must phrase its questions so as to make them readily understandable by people unfamiliar with computers or linguistics. This introduces a number of human engineering considerations. The acquisition of new verbs offers a cogent illustration of the problem.

English verbs are highly idiosyncratic. Consequently, making proper entries for them in a lexicon is a formidable task. Among other criteria, one must ascertain whether a verb is transitive, whether it can be used in the passive voice, whether its indirect object can become the object of a FOR or TO prepositional phrase, whether it is reflexive or nonreflexive, and how the syntactic cases of its arguments may be "normalized" when the verb appears in different syntactic constructions. NANOKLAUS's users cannot be expected to describe verbs in linguistic terms; therefore, to elicit the same information, the system must ask a series of questions that users *can* understand. Interactions 18 and 19 in the transcript are typical verb acquisition exchanges. While the dialogue is moderately natural and can be used by a nonlinguist, there is obviously considerable room for improvement in its design.

13.2.5 Some Major Limitations of NANOKLAUS Technology

Many of the major limitations of NANOKLAUS can be seen simply by reading through the transcript and noting that, although English is being used, the conversation is nevertheless highly stylized and artificial. For the most part, NANOKLAUS is limited to learning about very concrete types of objects and their interrelations. It has no capacity to deal with time, process, causality, intent, want, belief or judgment. This, of course, severely limits its range of application.

Even when considering concrete objects and their interrelations, NANOKLAUS can deal with only highly specific statements. For example, NANOKLAUS has no capacity do deal with analogy, as in:

```
A SOFTBALL IS LIKE A BASEBALL, BUT BIGGER AND SOFTER.
```

In general, the interpretation of information volunteered by people about new domains may necessitate deep reasoning and require information from other domains. Much of the volunteered information may contain inconsistencies that the user himself has no way (or particular reason) to resolve. The NANOKLAUS system represents a starting point for work on learning by being told; still, it barely scratches the surface of a vast body of difficult problems.

13.3 MORE TECHNICAL DETAILS

In this section we present additional details about some of the more interesting aspects of the NANOKLAUS system.

13.3.1 NANOKLAUS's Sort Hierarchy

NANOKLAUS's knowledge representation system uses a many-sorted, first-order logic that combines features from [Moore, 1975] and [Hendrix, 1979]. The backbone of the system is a treelike data structure reflecting the hierarchy of sorts used by the system (see Figure 13-1). The data structure maintains information about the immediate ancestors and descendants of each sort, including whether an ancestor is exhausted (spanned) by some or all of its descendants, and whether two or more sibling sorts are mutually exclusive. The sort hierarchy is a "tangled" tree, where any given sort may have multiple ancestors. It is no accident that a sort hierarchy should serve as the primary data structure for an English-based acquisition system. "Is-a" hierarchies are used by many natural language processing systems; it appears that something very similar to a sort hierarchy plays a central role in the way humans organize their knowledge [Lindsay & Norman, 1972].

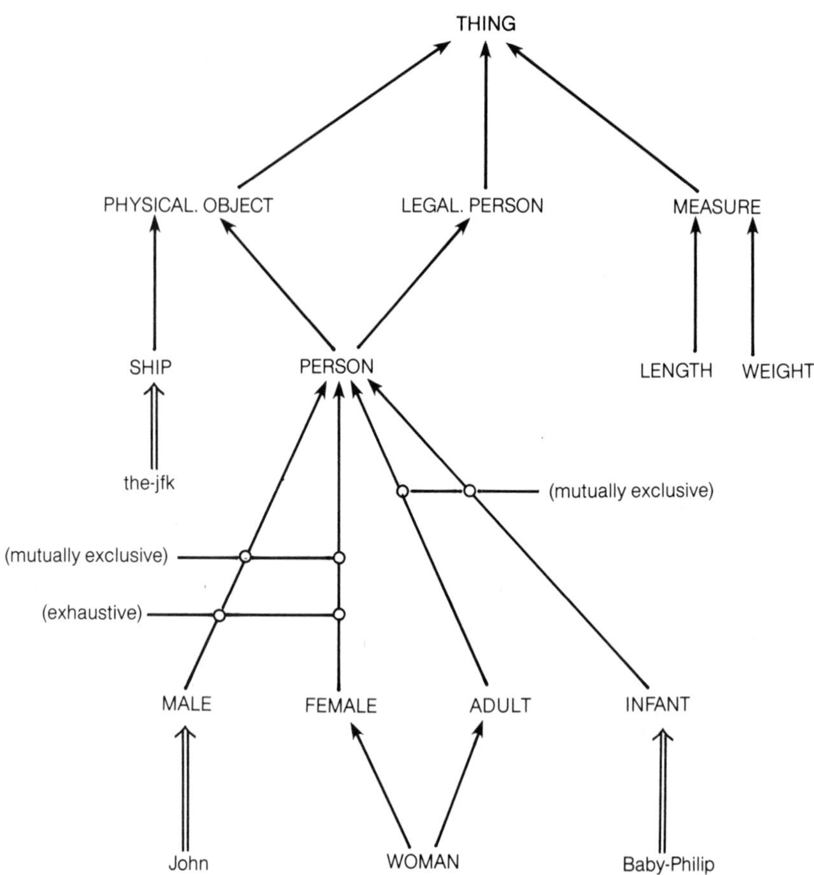

Figure 13-1: Typical Sort Hierarchy

Straightforward utilization of sort information is illustrated throughout the transcript in the appendix, but especially in Interactions 7 to 14 and 25 to 29.

The sort hierarchy is implemented by means of a special-purpose network representation indicating entailments of systems of unary predicates. Facts stored in this representation can be used exactly like the other facts in the fact store, but are organized to support rapid access to sort information—which is used in the language subsystem as well as in the deduction subsystem. Whenever syntactic combinations are proposed, the parser uses sort information to determine if noun phrases are valid arguments of verbs, adjectives, and relational nouns—thus reducing ambiguity. The response generator consults the sort hierarchy when selecting pronouns for anaphoric reference. If a referent is described as a MALE or a FEMALE, the nominative singular pronoun chosen will be "he" or "she", respectively; if not described as either, but known to be a member of the set of PERSONs, the phrase "he or she" will be used, otherwise "it" will be selected. This can be seen in Interactions 71 and 72 in the transcript.

Sort information is also used to assign default sorts to omitted arguments of verbs. For instance, if an assertion is made that a particular officer commands, NANOKLAUS knows from the acquisition dialogue it had with its teacher that the officer commands *something*, and that that thing must be of sort SHIP (see Interaction 45).

Measures, or dimensioned quantities, occupy a distinguished place in NANOKLAUS's sort hierarchy; MEASUREs are a distinct sort of THINGs, comprised of LENGTHs, WEIGHTs, PRICEs, etc. The user can introduce additional sorts of measures. He can also tell the system about new UNITs in which MEASUREs are measured, as well as the conversion factors between different units of the same measure (see Interaction 5). NANOKLAUS can perform conversion when answering questions (compare Assertion 47 and Questions 58 and 59), although its arithmetic capabilities are quite limited.

13.3.2 NANOKLAUS's Verb System

One of NANOKLAUS's strengths is its ability to deal with a large number of syntactic variations in verb usage. For example, facts asserted in active voice may be queried in both active and passive voice. In general, NANOKLAUS translates clauses into internal structures of the form:

```
(VERB-PREDICATE Arg1 Arg2 Arg3)
```

using information about permissible syntactic patterns in which the clause's verb can occur.

The basic verb patterns handled by NANOKLAUS are summarized in Table 13-1. [NANOKLAUS does not handle modal verbs (for example, "want" and "know"), or verbs with adverbial particles (for example, "pick up" and "preside over"), or sentential objects (for example, "The captain requested *that the ship change course*").] The objective of NANOKLAUS's verb acquisition dialogues (Interactions 18 and 19) is primarily to determine which patterns may be used with a new verb. The system does not need to ask about each pattern. For example, if pattern A3 is not used with a given verb, patterns A3D, A3W, P3, P3′, and P3D are automatically ruled out.

Table 13-1: Verb Usage Patterns

Pattern	Arg1 (A)	Arg2 (B)	Arg3 (C)	Sample Sentence of this Pattern
A3	Subj	NP1	NP2	A = Joe gave B = Sue C = a-ball.
A3D	Subj	NPd	NP	A = Joe gave C = a-ball to B = Sue.
A3W	Subj	NP	NPw	A = Joe supplied B = Sue with C = a-ball.
P3	(NPb)	NP	Subj	C = a-ball was given B = Sue (by A = Joe).
P3′	(NPb)	Subj	NP	B = Sue was given C = a-ball (by A = Joe).
P3D	(NPb)	NPd	Subj	C = a-ball was given to B = Sue (by A = Joe).
A2	Subj	-	NP	A = Joe wrote C = a-letter.
A2′	Subj	NP	-	A = Joe wrote B = Sue.
A2D	Subj	NPd	-	A = Joe wrote to B = Sue.
P2	(NPb)	-	Subj	C = a-letter was written (by A = Joe).
P2′	(NPb)	Subj	-	B = Sue was written (by A = Joe).
A1	Subj	-	-	A = Joe wrote.
A1′	-	-	Subj	C = a-vase broke. (from A2 of A = Joe broke C = a-vase.)

Pattern names indicate active (A) or passive (P) voice, the number of top-level noun phrases occurring in the sentence, and (in some cases) an indication of a dative noun phrase (D) moved into a "to" or "for" prepositional phrase, or an indication of a "with" (W) prepositional phrase.

Notation:

Subj = the surface subject of the sentence.
NP1 = the first unmarked <NP> in the verb phrase.
NP2 = the second unmarked <NP> in the verb phrase.
NP = the only unmarked <NP> in the verb phrase.
NPb = <NP> marked by the preposition "by." May be omitted.
NPw = <NP> marked by the preposition "with". (not instrumental)
NPd = <NP> marked by either "to" or "for". (dative)

To appreciate the range of variation in English verbs, consider the following sentences, each of which describes a situation using a ditransitive verb construction (the A3 pattern of Table 13-1). The symbol '*' marks ungrammatical sentences; '?' marks sentences whose grammaticality is questionable.

A3

John cooked Mary the fish.
?John supplied the school the books.
*John ran Mary the machine. (John ran it for Mary.)
John served Mary the fish.
John caught Mary the fish.

The following sentence sets are variations of the above, using the same verbs but in different syntactic patterns. In each set the same pattern is used throughout. Notice that not all verbs can be used grammatically in each pattern and that, moreover, some patterns (those marked by '—') act to describe a different situation from the ones described above.

A3w	—John cooked Mary with the fish. John supplied the school with the books. —John ran Mary with the machine. —John served Mary with the fish. —John caught Mary with the fish.
A3d (for)	John cooked the fish for Mary. ?John supplied the books for the school. John ran the machine for Mary. —John served the fish for Mary. John caught the fish for Mary.
A3d (to)	*John cooked the fish to Mary. John supplied the books to the school. *John ran the machine to Mary. John served the fish to Mary. *John caught the fish to Mary.
A2′	—John cooked Mary. John supplied the school. —John ran Mary. John served Mary. —John caught Mary.
A1	John cooked. ?John supplied. —John ran. John served. ?John caught.
A1′	The fish cooked. *The books supplied. The machine ran. *The fish served. *The fish caught.

There are two principal steps in the translation of a clause expressed in English into a proposition in first-order logic. First, syntactic analysis recognizes which of the various verb patterns is being used. Then syntactic cases (such as SUBJ and NP1) are mapped into argument positions for the predicate associated with the verb sense. For example:

```
JOHN GAVE SAM FIDO
```

is in the A3 pattern. According to Table 13-1, its subject JOHN is therefore mapped to Arg1, its indirect object (or NP1) to Arg2, and its direct object (or NP2) to Arg3. The end result is the proposition:

```
(GAVE JOHN SAM FIDO)
```

The related sentence:

```
FIDO WAS GIVEN TO SAM
```

is in the P3D pattern, so the subject is mapped to Arg3 and the dative SAM to Arg2, resulting in (GAVE _ SAM FIDO), which in turn is converted into (EXIST X)(GAVE X SAM FIDO).

13.3.3 Relating KLAUS Systems to Conventional DBMSs

In several ways, basic KLAUS systems such as NANOKLAUS are similar to conventional DBMSs (database management systems) in that they are intended to file, sort, selectively recall, and display data in various formats. However, DBMSs are systems for dealing with data structures through a formal command/query language, whereas a KLAUS is a system for learning and manipulating *concepts* through interactions in English. Furthermore, conventional DBMSs store only single-fact sentences, such as:

THE KENNEDY IS OWNED BY THE U.S.

Facts involving logical connectives, such as "OR" in:

THE KENNEDY IS EITHER IN PORT OR AT SEA,

or involving quantification, such as:

ALL CARRIERS CARRY DOCTORS,

are not ground literals and cannot be represented explicitly in a conventional DBMS. They can, however, be represented, discussed and reasoned about in the first-order logic supporting a KLAUS.

13.4 CONCLUSIONS AND DIRECTIONS FOR FUTURE WORK

NANOKLAUS is best described as a fragile, proof-of-concept system that was built to establish the feasibility of achieving the broader KLAUS goals. The natural language research group at SRI International is now implementing a more sophisticated KLAUS, called MICROKLAUS. MICROKLAUS will cover a broader range of English constructions by replacing NANOKLAUS's LIFER-based pragmatic grammar with Jane Robinson's [Robinson, 1980] DIAGRAM grammar. MICROKLAUS will also feature a more efficient deduction system than the one used by its predecessor.

Our work on the subject of knowledge acquisition has only recently begun and there are many capabilities that we have yet to address. For example, NANOKLAUS has no provision for learning by analogy, acquiring or reasoning about the internal structures of processes, dealing with causality, handling mass terms, allowing users to change their minds about previously asserted "facts", or dealing with multiple senses of words.

The KLAUS project is not limited to the study of knowledge acquisition, but is intended to provide technology for a system that combines a knowledge of how to use various software packages with an ability to learn facts about new domains. It is intended that an advanced KLAUS system act as a kind of broker between multiple external agents, one of whom happens to be the user.

The following deceptively simple hypothetical dialogue illustrates the value and the basic characteristics of such an advanced KLAUS:

```
1. User:     > DO I HAVE NEW MAIL?

2. KLAUS:      You have one message
                  FROM: HENDRIX
                  SUBJECT:  NSF funds have been cut by Congress
               Do you want to read it now?

3. User:     > YES

4. KLAUS:      (Presents message about funding cuts at NSF.)

5. User:     > WHO ARE THE PROJECT LEADERS ON OUR NSF GRANTS?

6. KLAUS:      The following table presents the PIs of
                  NSF projects in the AI Center.

               PI           Project

               Fischler     1202
               Grosz        6194
               Robinson     7483
               Waldinger    7409
               Witkin       8682

7. User:     > FORWARD THE MESSAGE TO THEM.
```

In this dialogue, the user first asks about his mail (Utterance 1).[4] Then the user says he wants to read his message, whereupon KLAUS displays it. It is about funding cuts at NSF. The user decides to find out who the project leaders of the relevant projects are, so he asks Question 5. Subsequently, in Request 7, he asks that the message be forwarded to these leaders.

Most of the capabilities required for this dialogue can be found in existing systems. However, no system yet built is able to support the entire interaction as shown, because all systems to date lack a controlling and coordinating top level that would enable a single system to

- Interact with the user in natural language.
- Decide which of several subsystems should be invoked to meet the user's needs.

---

[4]This dialogue does not require KLAUS to understand the title or body of the message; however, KLAUS must understand that there was a message and that it was from Hendrix.

- Automatically create and execute the calling sequences to invoke those subsystems.
- Maintain a dialogue context with the user that reflects and integrates the various local contexts that have been established by and for the use of subsystems.

In other words, present systems lack a crucial level of awareness of the interrelationships and potential interactions of the various software packages, the user, and the domain of application. In short, processing the sample dialogue requires knowledge of the domain of application and of available programs, as well as knowledge of the way these pieces fit together in a larger framework. How to acquire, represent, and apply such knowledge in a computer-based system are major problems for future research.

ACKNOWLEDGMENTS

The deduction system supporting NANOKLAUS was developed in large part by Mabry Tyson with Robert Moore, Nils Nilsson and Richard Waldinger as advisors. Beth Levin made major contributions to NANOKLAUS's verb acquisition algorithm. Barbara Grosz, Earl Sacerdoti, and Daniel Sagalowicz provided very useful critiques of early drafts of this chapter. This research was supported by the Defense Advanced Research Projects Agency with the Naval Electronic Systems Command under contracts N00039-79-C-0118 and N00039-80-C-0575.

REFERENCES

Davis, R., "Interactive transfer of Expertise: Acquisition of new inference rules," *Proceedings of the Fifth International Joint Conference on Artificial Intelligence*, IJCAI, Cambridge, MA, pp. 321-328, August 1977.

Dietterich, T. G. and Michalski, R. S., "Learning and generalization of characteristic descriptions: Evaluation criteria and comparative review of selected methods," *Proceedings of the Sixth International Joint Conference on Artificial Intelligence*, IJCAI, Toyko, Japan, pp. 223-231, August 1979, (see also chapter 3 of this book).

Fodor, J. A., *The Language of Thought*, Thomas Y. Crowell Company, New York, NY, 1975.

Green, C., "Theorem-proving by resolution as a basis for questioning-answering systems," *Machine Intelligence*, Meltzer, B. and Michie, D. (Eds.), American Elsevier Publishing Company, New York, NY, pp. 183-205, 1969.

Hayes, P. J., "Computation and deduction," *Proc. 2nd Sym. on Mathematical Foundations of Computer Science*, Czechoslovak Academy of Sciences, pp. 105-116, 1973.

Hendrix, G. G., "The LIFER manual: A guide to building practical natural language interfaces", Technical Report Technical Note 138, AI Center, Stanford Research Institute, February 1977.

Hendrix, G. G., "Encoding knowledge in partitioned networks," *Associative Networks: The Representation and Use of Knowledge in Computers*, Findler, N. V. (Ed.), Academic Press, New York, NY, 1979.

Hendrix, G. G., Sacerdoti, E. D., Sagalowicz, D. S. and Slocum, J., "Developing a natural language interface to complex data," *ACM Transactions on Database Systems*, Vol. 3, No. 2, pp. 105-147, June 1978.

Kowalski, R., "Predicate Logic as a Programming Language," *Information Processing 74*, North-Holland Publishing Company, Amsterdam, pp. 569-574, 1974.

Lindsay, P. H. and Norman, D. A., *Human Information Processing*, Academic Press, New York, NY, 1972.

McCarthy, J., "Programs with common sense," *Semantic Information Processing*, Minsky, M. (Ed.), MIT Press, Cambridge, MA, pp. 403-417, 1968.

Moore, R., "Reasoning from incomplete knowledge in a procedural deduction system", Technical Report AI-TR-347, AI Lab, Massachusetts Institute of Technology, 1975.

Moore, R., "Automatic Deduction for Commonsense Reasoning: An Overview," *The Handbook of Artificial Intelligence*, A. Barr and E. A. Feigenbaum (Ed.), William Kaufman, Inc., Los Altos, California, 1982.

Newell, A. and Simon, H. A., "The logic theory machine," *IRE Transactions on Information Theory*, Vol. IT-2, No. 3, pp. 61-79, September 1956.

Robinson, J. A., "A machine-oriented logic based on the resolution principle," *Journal of the Association for Computing Machinery*, Vol. 12, No. 1, pp. 23-41, January 1965.

Robinson, J. J., "DIAGRAM: An extendable grammar for natural language dialogue", Technical Report Technical Note 205, AI Center, Stanford Research Institute, February 1980.

Weyhrauch, R. W., "Prolegomena to a Theory of Mechanized Formal Reasoning," *Artificial* Intelligence, Vol. 13, No. 1/2, pp. 133-170, April 1980.

Winston, P. H., "Learning structural descriptions from examples," *The Psychology of Computer Vision*, Winston, P. H. (Ed.), McGraw-Hill Book Company, New York, NY, ch. 5, 1975, (Original version published as a Ph.D. dissertation, MIT AI Lab, September, 1970).

APPENDIX: TRAINING NANOKLAUS ABOUT AIRCRAFT CARRIERS

What follows is a transcript of a dialogue with the NANOKLAUS system. The consecutive numbers at the left of some lines are NANOKLAUS prompts. Inputs typed by the user are italicized. Sentences in braces are descriptive annotations. Some of the interaction has been deleted to shorten the transcript. A graphical representation of the sort hierarchy produced by the dialogue is presented in Figure 13-2.

@NANOKLAUS

Welcome to NANOKLAUS !
Just say ıHelpı if you need help.

1_ *What do you know about?* {The user asks NANOKLAUS what classes of things have been described to it.}

I know about PHYSICAL OBJECTS, PEOPLE, MEN, WOMEN, MEASURES, and THINGS (of course).

2_ *A length is a measure* {The user introduces LENGTH.}

You're saying that anything that is a LENGTH is also a MEASURE.
Ok, now I understand LENGTH.

3_ *A foot is a unit of length* {The user introduces FOOT.}

FOOTS are the first units of LENGTH you've defined.
Now I understand FOOT.

4_ *The plural of foot is feet*

FEET - got it. Thanks.

5_ *A meter is a unit of length*

How is it related to FOOT? *There are 3.3 feet in a meter.* {Whenever an additional unit of a measure is declared, NANOKLAUS requests the factor for conversion to one of the previously declared units.}

Now I understand METER.

6_ *A physical object has a length* {The user gives the domain over which an attribute named LENGTH may range, and implicitly indicates that the value of this attribute must be an element of the set of lengths, declared in (2).}

So PHYSICAL OBJECTS have LENGTHS.
Must a PHYSICAL OBJECT have exactly one LENGTH? *yes* {NANOKLAUS determines that the relationship between physical objects and lengths is functional.}

7_ *A ship is a physical object*

You're saying that anything that is a SHIP is also a PHYSICAL OBJECT.
Is PERSON a proper subclass of SHIP? *no* {When a new subset of an existing set is created, NANOKLAUS queries the user to determine how it relates to that set, as well as to other previously introduced subsets of that set.}

Is PERSON necessarily composed of entirely different members from SHIP? *yes*
Do PERSON and SHIP span the set of all PHYSICAL OBJECTS? *no*
Ok, now I understand SHIP.

8_ *A ship is a unit* {Sets may be subsets of more than one set.}

You're saying that anything that is a SHIP is also an UNIT.
What is an UNIT? *a thing*

{NANOKLAUS always wants to know how the set and superset relate to the existing taxonomy (the taxonomy is always a connected graph). Note that it generated the incorrect indefinite article in the question, but see Interaction 9 below.}

You're saying that anything that is an UNIT is also a THING.
Which of the following, if any, are proper subclasses of UNIT:
PHYSICAL OBJECT or MEASURE? *neither of them*
Which of the following classes, if any, could never have any members
in common with UNIT:
PHYSICAL OBJECT or MEASURE ? *neither of them*
Ok, now I understand UNIT.
Ok, now I understand SHIP.
9_ *A unit*

{The user corrects NANOKLAUS's English.}

OK, A UNIT
10_ *A submarine is a ship*
11_ *A destroyer is a ship*
12_ *A carrier is a ship*
13_ *A Kittyhawk is a carrier*
14_ *A Forrestal is a carrier*

{Feedback from NANOKLAUS, such as seen in Interaction 8, is omitted for the sake of brevity.}

You're saying that anything that is a KITTYHAWK is also a CARRIER.
Is KITTYHAWK a proper subclass of FORRESTAL? *no*
Is KITTYHAWK necessarily composed of entirely different
members from FORRESTAL? *yes*
Do KITTYHAWK and FORRESTAL span the set of all CARRIERS? *no*
Ok, now I understand KITTYHAWK.
15_ *A Hermes is a carrier*
16_ *A task group is a unit*
17_ *An officer is a person*
18_ *An officer can command a ship*
Give the -ed and -en forms of COMMAND
(for example, for GO: WENT GONE):
commanded commanded

{Here the verb COMMAND is introduced as mapping into a predicate over (officer, ship) pairs.}

If an OFFICER can COMMAND a SHIP something , type in the most general
description of that thing, otherwise type <carriage return>

{NANOKLAUS tried to determine if COMMAND doesn't in fact take a third argument.}

If an OFFICER can COMMAND something a SHIP, then please type in
the most general description of that thing,
otherwise type <carriage return>
If an OFFICER can COMMAND something to a SHIP, then please type in
the most general description of that thing, otherwise <carriage return>

{In this context, 'to' marks an indirect object, not the destination of a verb of motion.}

If an OFFICER can COMMAND a SHIP to something, then please type in
the most general description of that thing, otherwise <carriage return>
Can a SHIP be COMMANDED by an OFFICER ? *yes*

{NANOKLAUS acquires information enabling it to map into a canonical predicate calculus form from passive occurrences of the verb and occurrences in which some of the noun phrases are omitted.}

Can a SHIP COMMAND ? *no*
Can an OFFICER COMMAND ? *yes*
19_ *An officer can assign a task group a unit*

{Another example, this time a ditransitive verb.}

Give the -ed and -en forms of ASSIGN
(for example, for GO: WENT GONE):

assigned assigned
Can an OFFICER ASSIGN a UNIT TO a TASK GROUP ? *yes*
Could a UNIT be ASSIGNED a TASK GROUP by an OFFICER ? *yes*
Can an OFFICER ASSIGN a UNIT with a TASK GROUP ? *no*
Can an OFFICER ASSIGN a TASK GROUP ? *no*
Can an OFFICER ASSIGN ? *yes*
20_ *Some ships can be nuclear*

{NANOKLAUS is taught an adjective, which it maps into a unary predicate whose domain is ships.}

You're saying that at least one SHIP could be nuclear.
21_ *A nationality is a thing*
22_ *A ship has a nationality*
So SHIPS have NATIONALITIES.
Must a SHIP have exactly one NATIONALITY? *yes*
23_ *A rank is a thing*
You're saying that anything that is a RANK is also a THING.
Which of the following, if any, are proper subclasses of RANK:
PHYSICAL OBJECT, LEGAL PERSON, MEASURE, UNIT, or NATIONALITY? *none of them*
Which of the following classes, if any, could never have any members in common with RANK:
PHYSICAL OBJECT, LEGAL PERSON, MEASURE, UNIT, or NATIONALITY ? *all of them*
Ok, now I understand RANK.
24_ *An officer has a rank*
25_ *A carrier has a doctor who is a person*
So CARRIERS have PEOPLE for DOCTORS.
Must a CARRIER have exactly one DOCTOR? *no*

{Here the attribute named DOCTOR takes values that must be members of the set of persons.}

26_ *The JFK is a Kittyhawk*
You're saying that JFK is one instance of a KITTYHAWK.
Ok, now I know about JFK.

{First introduction of an individual.}

27_ *The JFK is a Forrestal*
You're saying that JFK is one instance of a FORRESTAL.
Sorry, but JFK is an individual of the following types: KITTYHAWK, and one of them conflicts with FORRESTAL.

{NANOKLAUS used its knowledge of subset relationships to discover and then report an inconsistency in its user's assertions.}

28_ *The Saratoga is a Forrestal*
29_ *The Enterprise is a carrier*
30_ *The Bulwark is a Hermes*
31_ *US is a nationality*
32_ *UK is a nationality*
33_ *US is the nationality of the JFK*
Proving (US is the nationality of JFK)
Asserting that (US is the nationality of JFK)

{Asserts the value of an attribute. Note that, instead of blindly entering the fact in the fact store, NANOKLAUS first checks as to whether it already knows the fact.}

34_ *The nationality of the Saratoga is US*
35_ *The nationality of the Enterprise is US*
36_ *The nationality of the Bulwark is UK*
37_ *Moffet is an officer*
38_ *Brown is an officer*
39_ *Captain is a rank*
40_ *The rank of Brown is captain*
41_ *Captain is the rank of Moffet*
42_ *The JFK is commanded by Moffet*
Proving (MOFFET commanded JFK)
Asserting that (MOFFET commanded JFK)

{Uses verbs to describe an event or situation. Note transformation from passive to active voice by NANOKLAUS.}

43_ *Brown commands the Saratoga*
Proving (BROWN commanded SARATOGA)
Asserting that (BROWN commanded SARATOGA)

{NANOKLAUS employs an untensed logic; its canonical expression of its knowledge is always past tense.}

44_ *Moffet commands the JFK.*
Proving (MOFFET commanded JFK)
I already knew that. {NANOKLAUS detected that it had previously been told this, although in a different voice.}

45_ *Brown commands.*
Proving (BROWN commanded Some ship) {NANOKLAUS filled in the omitted argument and then determined that it had been told of an event or situation that could conceivably have been a description of the same event or situation.}
Is any one of the following statements true concerning this event:
the SHIP is SARATOGA ? *Yes*
46_ *Brown commands a Forrestal.*
Proving (BROWN commanded Some forrestal)
Is any one of the following statements true concerning this event:
the FORRESTAL is SARATOGA ? *Yes.*
47_ *1072 feet is the length of the JFK*
Asserting that (1072 FEET is [equal to] the LENGTH of JFK)
48_ *The length of the Bulwark is 650 feet*
49_ *ctg18 is a task group*
50_ *ctg36 is a task group.*
51_ *Moffet assigned the Saratoga to ctg36*
Proving (MOFFET assigned CTG36 SARATOGA)
Asserting that (MOFFET assigned CTG36 SARATOGA)
52_ *The Saratoga was assigned to ctg18 by Brown*
Proving (BROWN assigned CTG18 SARATOGA)
Asserting that (BROWN assigned CTG18 SARATOGA)
53_ *The Enterprise is a nuclear ship* {Uses a predicate adjective.}
54_ *What are the ships?* {The user interrogates NANOKLAUS to verify that it has assimilated what it has been told. Note that the user has not explicitly described any of the answers as ships.}
ENTERPRISE, JFK, SARATOGA, AND BULWARK.
55_ *Who commands the Kittyhawks?*
(MOFFET JFK).
56_ *Who commands the JFK?*
MOFFET.
57_ *Brown commands what?*
SARATOGA.
58_ *What is the length of the JFK?*
1072 FEET.
59_ *How many meters is the length of the JFK?*
Proving (Some length is [equal to] the LENGTH of JFK)
324.8485. {Using the unit conversion factor.}
60_ *What is the nationality of the Saratoga?*
US.
62_ *Brown assigned what ships?*
Proving (BROWN assigned Some task group Some ship)
(CTG18 SARATOGA). {I.e., Brown assigned CTG18 Saratoga.}
63_ *Who assigned ships to ctg36?*
Proving (Some officer assigned CTG36 Some ship)
(MOFFET SARATOGA).
64_ *Who assigned ctg18 the Saratoga?*
Proving (Some officer assigned CTG18 SARATOGA)
BROWN.
65_ *Who assigned the Saratoga?*
Proving (Some officer assigned Some task group SARATOGA)
(MOFFET CTG36) and (BROWN CTG18).
66_ *Which ships are nuclear?*
Proving (Some ship is a nuclear ship)
ENTERPRISE.
67_ *What do you know about carriers?*
US is the nationality of JFK. {NANOKLAUS has access to its

```
US is the nationality of SARATOGA.
US is the nationality of ENTERPRISE.
UK is the nationality of BULWARK.
MOFFET commanded JFK.
BROWN commanded SARATOGA.
1072 FEET is [equal to] the LENGTH of JFK.
the LENGTH of BULWARK is [equal to] 650 FEET.
MOFFET assigned CTG36 SARATOGA.
BROWN assigned CTG18 SARATOGA.
ENTERPRISE is a nuclear ship.
```

fact store indexed by sort, as well as by predicate. Here it reports all the atomic facts it has about carriers.}

69_ *Now describe ship*

```
SHIP:
A SHIP is a PHYSICAL OBJECT and UNIT.
Therefore it is also a THING.
SUBMARINES and CARRIERS are SHIPS.
SUBMARINES and CARRIERS cannot have any members in common.
SHIP has the following attributes and types:
NATIONALITY.
SHIPS can be NUCLEAR.
```

{Here it describes all the generic and sort information it has about a given sort.}

71_ *Please describe Moffet then describe Brown.*

{In response to this request, NANOKLAUS displays all the facts it knows about a particular individual.}

```
Moffet is an  officer.  His or her rank is CAPTAIN.  MOFFET
commanded JFK.  MOFFET assigned CTG36 SARATOGA.

Brown is an  officer.  His or her rank is CAPTAIN.  BROWN commanded
SARATOGA.  BROWN assigned CTG18 SARATOGA.
```

72_ *Now tell me about Saratoga.*

```
Saratoga is a  forrestal.  Its nationality is US.  BROWN
commanded SARATOGA.  MOFFET assigned CTG36 SARATOGA.  BROWN assigned
CTG18 SARATOGA.
```

76_ *Who commands what?*

```
Proving  (Some officer commanded Some ship)
(MOFFET JFK) and (BROWN SARATOGA).
```

77_ *good bye*

```
See you later
```

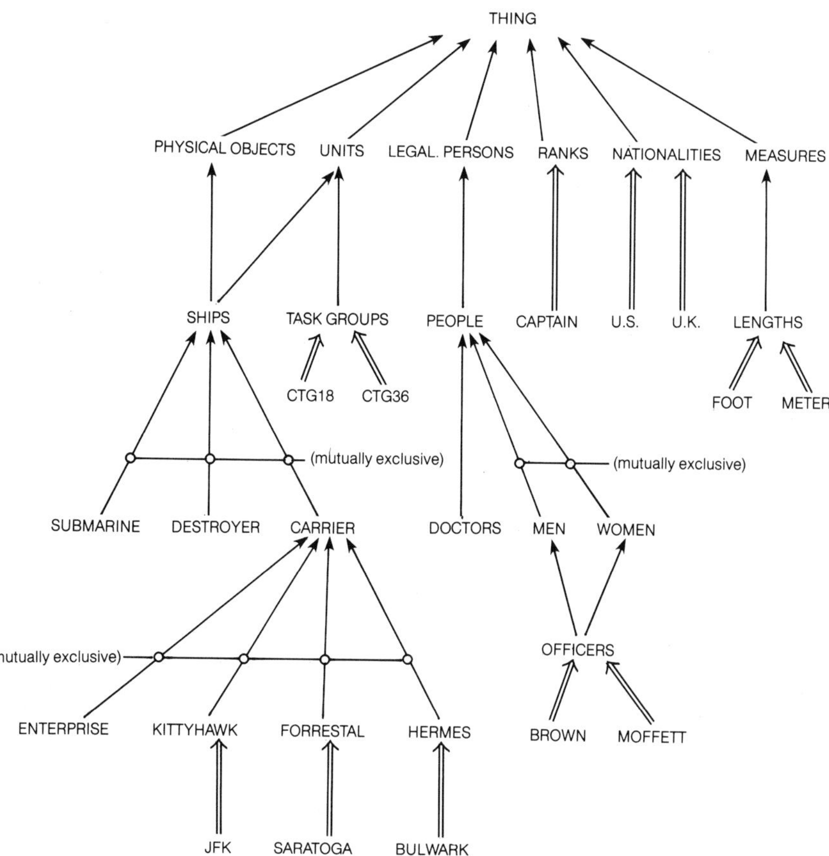

Figure 13-2: Sort Hierarchy Produced by Transcript Dialogue

14

THE INSTRUCTIBLE PRODUCTION SYSTEM: A RETROSPECTIVE ANALYSIS

Michael D. Rychener
Carnegie-Mellon University

ABSTRACT

In building systems that acquire knowledge from tutorial instruction, progress depends on determining certain functional requirements and ways for them to be met. The Instructible Production System (IPS) project has explored learning by building a series of experimental systems. These systems can be viewed as being designed to explore the satisfaction of some of the requirements, both by basic production system mechanisms and by features explicitly programmed as rules. The explorations have brought out the importance of considering in advance (as part of the kernel design) certain functional components rather than having them be filled in by instruction. The need for the following functional components has been recognized:

- interaction language
- organization of procedural elements
- explanation of system behavior
- accommodation to new knowledge
- connection of goals with system capabilities
- reformulation (mapping) of knowledge
- evaluation of behavior
- compilation to achieve efficiency and automaticity

Since the experimental systems have varied in their effectiveness, some general conclusions can be drawn about the relative merits of various approaches. Seven such approaches are discussed here, with particular attention to the three whose behavior can be most effectively compared, and which reflect the temporal development of the project.

14.1 THE INSTRUCTIBLE PRODUCTION SYSTEM PROJECT

The Instructible Production System (IPS) project [Rychener & Newell, 1978] was begun in the fall of 1975 to study the construction and behavior of large-scale systems of production rules. Our hypothesis, extrapolated from work in cognitive psychology [Newell & Simon, 1972], was that intelligence would result, as a system grew in size, from an ability to deal with more situations and to apply more knowledge to solve problems. The motivation to use production systems had the same source [Newell & Simon, 1972]. To increase the scientific interest of building such systems, and ultimately to improve the chances of continuing growth and viability, it was stipulated from the start that the system was to be built by gradual "instruction" rather than by deliberate programming.[1] The research evolved into a series of explorations of the design of a starting system (KERNEL), from which the much larger system would be grown. The explorations spanned a four-year time period, until mid-1979, and involved the efforts of over a half dozen people.[2]

The setting in which instructional experiments took place was chosen to be one of "learning by doing". In this paradigm, the instructor of the system watches and advises the system while it is solving problems in its chosen domain of expertise (see the work of Anzai and Simon [1979]). This is a good way to study learning because it combines attributes of both learning by being told and learning by independent exploration, while avoiding some of their drawbacks. That is, the instructor still instructs by telling, but the fact that the system is doing something at the same time allows the instructor to verify (partially) that the new knowledge is appropriate to the system's current knowledge. In addition, the system is in a sense exploring in an environment that has new situations for it, under the guidance of the instructor and in the framework of problems posed by the instructor. When new knowledge interacts in some way with the system's existing knowledge, that interaction has the greatest chance of being understood in the context of a situation where that knowledge is being applied. The system is forced to deal with new situations in its own way, using its own conceptual system, with the extra help of the instructor's advice. But advice to the system is often limited, in that the system's knowledge may not be stored so as to be brought to bear in all appropriate situations, and in that the

[1]Actually, production systems are quite difficult to program, so an instruction mode has the potential of bringing a large system into the realm of feasibility. What is desired is that the production system itself be able to manage its knowledge, find interactions of new knowledge with old [Rychener, 1975], check consistency, formulate and select answers for questions that arise when new and old knowledge statements are compared, and do assorted other tasks that can't even be predicted at this time. To complete this knowledge management task would require a great deal of knowledge itself, and the IPS project has only begun to realize what might be required for this much larger research goal.

[2]See the Acknowledgments near the end of the paper.

instructor can often see only the effects of the knowledge, rather than the knowledge itself, depending on how well the system can describe itself.

More precisely, the dialogue between instructor and system is ruled by a number of constraints:

- The instructor of the system gains all information about IPS by observing its interactions with its environment (including the instructor).
- The dialogue takes place in (restricted) natural language.
- The dialogue is mixed initiative, with both participants free to try to influence the direction.
- Instruction may be about any topic or phenomenon in the system's external or internal environment (subject to the other restrictions).
- Knowledge accumulates over the lifetime of the system.

These constraints are intended to embody the essence of instruction as it occurs in a number of natural situations. At the same time, they tend to rule out explicit "programming" by the instructor, and thus place a larger burden on the system's learning abilities, and indeed on its general intelligence.

Throughout the IPS experiments, the underlying knowledge organization was *Production Systems* (PS's) [Forgy & McDermott, 1977; Young, 1979; Anderson, 1976; Rychener, 1976; Newell & Simon, 1972], a form of rule-based system in which learning is formulated as the addition to, and modification of, an unstructured collection of production rules. As mentioned above, this assumption of architecture has some support from psychological theory [Newell & Simon, 1972]. Behavior is obtained through a simple *recognize-act cycle* with a sophisticated set of principles for resolving conflicts among rules [McDermott & Forgy, 1978; Rychener, 1977]. The dynamic short-term memory of the system is the *Working Memory* (WM), whose contents are matched each cycle to the conditions of rules in the long-term memory, *Production Memory*. As will be explained in a later section, information transfer from the environment (including instructor) to the system takes place by depositing conventionalized symbol structures into the WM. Those structures then become subject to manipulation by the system's procedural methods expressed as rules (to be defined and illustrated after the next subsection). The IPS project developed several dialects of the OPS language [Forgy & McDermott, 1977; Forgy, 1979b; Rychener, 1980] to support its experiments.

14.1.1 Relation to Other Learning Research

In terms of a model recently proposed for learning systems by Buchanan, *et al.* [1979], the IPS work focused on certain aspects of the learning problem while neglecting others. Their model consists of:

- A performance module that actually performs tasks.
- A critic that evaluates performance, locates errors, and recommends corrective actions.

- A learning module that responds to the critic by modifying performance.
- An instance selector that poses training problems.
- A blackboard [Lesser & Erman, 1977] for globally modifiable data and intermodule communication.
- A world model for domain-specific knowledge and assumptions.

In all of the IPS explorations, both performance and learning modules were embodied in the production memory, and were thus intermixed. This paper is concerned principally with elaborating and refining the subcomponents of these two modules. This emphasis is inherent to the instructional situation, where the instructor plays the role of critic and instance selector. WM functioned as the blackboard, and world-model knowledge (usually minimal) was represented as rules whose actions placed facts into WM and otherwise maintained consistency with the domain's assumptions.

To further the comparison of the IPS project with other artificial intelligence and psychology research, it is useful to discuss briefly our position with respect to a number of current issues. The topic of instruction for an IPS can be characterized as:

- self-contained procedures for specific tasks
- problem-solving operations within such procedures
- domain-specific heuristics, in the same context

rather than such things as:

- rules or heuristics that work only within the computational context of a special-purpose control structure or mechanism different from the recognize-act paradigm of PS's (as in various "expert" systems, for example, those for medical diagnosis)
- causal models for explanation and prediction (as in attempts to model physical devices, Socratic tutoring approaches, and so on)
- concepts (as in various pattern classification and concept formation studies)
- language grammars
- numerical functions and relationships

Thus, the IPS work was not concerned primarily with such mechanisms as generalization, specialization, discrimination, property intersection, rule induction, and pattern induction. These mechanisms were considered to be second-order refinements[3] on what we gave an IPS by instruction; in fact, we expected them to become more relevant as the basic problems with IPS were solved and the system began to exhibit coherent and interesting task behavior. Also, they are mechanisms that are best applied when much larger quantities of empirical

---

[3]This is not to say that they are second order in all knowledge domains and studies, but just in our narrow focus. It is a matter of *relative* importance.

data or knowledge are involved. In other words, the emphasis was on the gradual transfer of knowledge from instructor to system, and our focus remained the structure and content of a body of knowledge, and its effective use to obtain behavior. This is in contrast to having the system develop the knowledge from general axioms, from knowledge primitives, or from large bodies of unstructured facts, which would involve abstract manipulations, inductions, and searches. These would reduce the amount of interaction, and would require more searching and intelligence on the part of the system. They would take place in large spaces that would be distant from instructional and interactive situations, and would thus be hard to formulate heuristics for. Similarly, because of our limited understanding, we neglected such issues as credit and blame assignment, convergence of learning over time, speed of convergence, and searching as an alternative to direct instruction. In fact, PS's as an architecture are amenable to a number of interesting operations with regard to the above-mentioned topics, leaving open many research avenues.[4]

To state the matter more positively, learning in an IPS was by accumulation of fairly specific rules and methods. In many cases, the rules acquired could be viewed within some well-known organization, such as means-ends analysis or schemas, but usually this organization was not obtained from an act of specializing or instantiating an existing general knowledge structure. Rather, as discussed in later sections of this paper, either the instructor or the system was oriented towards maintaining a particular organization on the specific knowledge that it received. The IPS work has a closer kinship to studies in intelligent computer-aided instruction, and perhaps in educational psychology (particularly programmed learning), than to other attempts at learning systems. (This kinship will be discussed further in Section 14.4.) There is also a strong relation to the construction of "expert" systems, involving accumulation of a body of specific domain knowledge. More relationships are discussed at the end of the next subsection.

14.1.2 Basic Definitions and Discussion

There are a few key concepts whose definitions will clarify some issues with respect to the IPS project's approach to encoding knowledge. These also reveal a position on planning and other control structure topics.

A *goal* is a data structure that represents an external command, an internal need to achieve some state, or a need to execute successfully some sequence of actions. An example, taken from a simulated manufacturing domain, is:

```
Make a car for a customer's order.
```

where the customer's order is another data structure describing details of the item to be made. In the OPS3 [Rychener, 1980] dialect of OPS, this might be represented as:

---

[4]Anderson addresses such topics in Chapter 7 in this volume.

```
ws011: (make car goal (order ws014))
ws014: (customer order data
                (type car) (body sedan) (color blue)
                (engine-size medium)
                (accessories (radio a/c)))
```

These structures consist of an internal name, a three-element header, and then a set of attribute-value pairs, where the value may be a set of items. Details of this and other representations used within various versions of IPS are beyond the scope of this paper. For the remainder of the introductory examples that follow, a liberal English translation is used for readability.

A *rule* (that is, a production) in OPS consists of a number of conditions and a number of actions. Each condition is a pattern that matches some element of WM, such as a goal (in various states of activation: active, suspended, succeeded, failed), a structure describing something perceived in the environment, or a data structure describing some internal state. The actions of a rule typically assert new data structures or goals, and can also modify or delete existing structures.

A *method* in IPS is a set of rules that work together to satisfy a goal. It is typically very specialized to a certain goal class, and usually consists of a number of steps, with various intermediate data generated to indicate the progress towards completion. The following is a method for satisfying the above sample goal. It is not meant to reflect accurately all of the details of actual IPS methods, but just the general flavor of the approach.

```
M1:   If there is a goal to make a car for a customer's order
        and the order specifies the car's body as some type,
      then have the goal to make a body of that type for the car.

M2:   If there is a goal to make a car for a customer's order
        and the order specifies an engine of some size for the car
        and the car's body has been made,
      then have the goal to install an engine of that size in the
      car.

M3:   If there is a goal to make a car for a customer's order
        and the order specifies accessories
        and the car's engine has been installed,
      then know that the car is ready for accessories.

M4:   If there is a goal to make a car for a customer's order
        and the order specifies a radio
        and it is known that the car is ready for accessories,
      then have the goal to install a radio in the car.

M5:   If there is a goal to make a car for a customer's order
        and the car has a body as specified in the order
        and the car has an engine as specified in the order
        and the car has all of its accessories installed,
      then know that the goal to make a car has been satisfied.
```

The first two rules, M1 and M2, generate subgoals for doing specific subtasks of the main goal. The completion of one subgoal, in this method, triggers the rule that generates the next. The rule M3 recognizes some conditions signifying a certain stage in the method's progress, and summarizes that in a new data structure, so that later rules in the method don't need to make tests that are overly specific or detailed or that would multiply the number of combinations of conditions needed. M4 is an example of a rule that takes advantage of M3's summarization, and M5 is a rule that recognizes the completion of the main goal by testing each of the required aspects of the finished product. (An alternative, but less reliable, test would involve simply knowing that each step in a process was performed successfully.)

The total set of rules to perform the making of the car would, of course, be much larger than is shown above, in order to specify the details of the various subgoals of the above method. (Subgoals ultimately reduce to primitives such as those described in a later section.) One rule from a method for one of the subgoals is the following:

```
S1:   If there is a goal to install a radio in a car,
      then have the goal to move the car to the accessory assembler
        and have the goal to get a radio to the accessory assembler
        and have the goal to put the radio in the car using the
          assembler.
```

As shown, rule S1 asserts a number of subgoals. Though they are given in a particular order, the first two apparently could be done without regard to their order, and the last would probably make use of the results of the first two in order to ensure that the "assembler" has been provided with all the necessary inputs. The actual, detailed representations may include goal-subgoal pointers (for example, expressed as attribute-value pairs). All of the sequencing implied by this discussion, though, would be readily implemented as the presence (or absence) of conditions that would be recognized by rules. The generality of the recognize-act computational paradigm, with its global WM holding goals and data, relieves the rule encoder of some of the burden of specifying control information. This facilitates both initial instruction and later elaboration of the knowledge. As will be brought out further below, this ability to represent procedural knowledge as collections of rules, such as the ones just given, is one of the principal reasons for using PS's as a medium for instructible systems that are to grow by gradually adding details.

It can now be pointed out that the work with IPS takes a peculiar position on the central artificial intelligence topic of *planning*, differing from a number of past approaches. The essence of the approach here is for the system to "muddle through"[5] tasks that are problematic, rather than doing a lot of planning, prepara-

---

[5]A system muddles through a problem when it engages in trial and error, without carefully the considering consequences of its actions, relying instead on taking corrective actions after mistakes occur.

tion, and anticipation of difficulties. A deliberate plan is never formulated and stored in a data structure for analysis, but behavior simply unfolds in response to changing conditions. Flaws or other interruptions in the flow of behavior are treated as new subproblems, and resolved by calling forth applicable methods or further instruction. It is not excluded that later on the system might be instructed to plan ahead in some fashion, or to add a reflective capability that would allow recognition of general classes of problems with known solutions and treat them accordingly [Anzai & Simon, 1979].[6] The main aim here is to understand the basic goal structures and knowledge in a domain where many specific facts, brought to bear appropriately, are sufficient to produce effective behavior. Current general methods are unable to cope with such problems due to inability to control the search in such a large space.

14.1.3 Overview

Through analysis of seven major attempts to build instructible PS's with various orientations, there were gradually formulated eight main functional components. Defining the eight components sharpened our understanding of the problems of the performance and learning modules, making them amenable to further research and design efforts. Beyond the narrow focus of the IPS project, this clarification can perhaps contribute to research on learning systems in general. After the eight components are listed in the next section, a broad overview of the IPS project is undertaken. The seven attempts, forming an evolutionary sequence, are cast into the functional component framework. In the process of doing this, lessons are extracted that apply to the whole enterprise as well as to individual explorations.

Members of the IPS project are no longer working together intensively to build an instructible PS, but individual studies that will add to our knowledge about one or more of these components are continuing. Progress in developing efficient PS's has been important to the IPS project [Forgy, 1979a], but will not be discussed further here.

14.2 ESSENTIAL FUNCTIONAL COMPONENTS OF INSTRUCTIBLE SYSTEMS

The components listed in this section are to be interpreted loosely as dimensions along which learning systems might vary.[7] In constructing a particular system, a point in a design space is located and developed. It is assumed that the mechanisms of a particular design embody approaches to several, or per-

---

[6] Carbonell, Chapter 5 in this volume, also bears on this topic.

[7] This approach owes a lot to Moore and Newell's [1973] dimensions for understanding systems.

haps all, of these dimensions.[8] Almost all of the systems discussed in the next section, in fact, do not represent complete designs with respect to all functional components, but rely to some extent on further instruction to fill them in (usually this optimism was not justified). Also, as is the case in many design areas, a single mechanism can serve to fulfill the demands of several components at once. Observation of a system's behavior allows the formulation of the kinds of modifications, with respect to the design space of components, that could lead to improvement in the overall ability to build IPSs. To the extent that the functions of these components are expressed by explicit goals in an IPS, there is opportunity to exercise the overall system in the improvement of particular components.

14.2.1 Interaction

The content and form of communications between an instructor and an IPS can have a lot to do with ease and effectiveness of instruction. In particular, it is important to know how closely communications correspond to internal IPS structures. Inputs from the instructor can be in the form of entire methods or individual rules, in the form of more elementary WM units (whose composition into rules is thus less prominent in the external interactions), or in some other fragments even further removed from actual construction of rules. For example, consider the following rule (which is taken from the example of the preceding section):

```
M2:    If there is a goal to make a car for a customer's order and
         the order specifies an engine of some size for the car
         and the car's body has been made,
       then have the goal to install an engine of that size in the
       car.
```

One approach might be to give the rule in its entirety. Alternatives that make the interaction more fine grained would have the instructor saying things like:

```
Note that the order specifies a medium-size engine for the car.
What size of engine does the order specify?
Test the previous result.
Try installing it.
```

With respect to the system-output direction of interaction, we must ask how well the manifest behavior of an IPS indicates its progress on a task. This issue is subject to considerations similar to those for input.

An IPS can have various orientations towards interactions, ranging from passive acceptance to active scrutiny. For instance, it can attempt, with varying

[8]It is thus not considered fruitful to design systems that do each of these functions separately, or to talk about the structure of one without considering the overall system structure and orientation.

degrees of effort, to maintain consistency and to assimilate new structures into existing ones. An IPS will be most effective when its orientation is expressed as goals, and thus subject to refinement by instruction.

14.2.2 Organization

Each version of IPS approaches the issue of obtaining correct and coherent behavior by attempting to organize its "procedural" knowledge. The need for such an attempt arises from two sources: one is to move the instructor away from having to specify control constructs, that is, away from programming (which is difficult and violates the idea of instruction); another is that some form of systematic approach to control is needed, due to the inherent weakness[9] of production systems in this area. This may involve such techniques as collecting sets of rules into methods and using signal conventions for sequencing within methods. Whether IPS can explain its static organization and whether the instructor can see the details of procedural control are important subissues.

To illustrate some alternative organization approaches, recall the following rule:

```
M2:   If there is a goal to make a car for a customer's order and
        the order specifies an engine of some size for the car
        and the car's body has been made,
      then have the goal to install an engine of that size in the
      car.
```

In this rule, control is maintained by the third condition, which ensures that the rule will not be activated until the preceding step of making the car's body is finished. One imaginable alternative is simply to remove that condition, and have the subgoal asserted potentially before it can be properly worked on. In this case, of course, the method for the subgoal would be likely to stop, blocked by the lack of a car body in which to install the engine. This shortened version of M2 is probably easier to modify and more modular, but it may make it more difficult for the instructor (for instance) to explain or coordinate the extra unfinished goals in WM. Another alternative makes the local sequencing of M2 more explicit by a step "counter" that is common to all rules in a method—knowing the current step is a way of knowing or summarizing the method's progress:

```
M2s:        If it is step 2 of a goal to make a car for a
            customer's order
              and the order specifies an engine of some size for
            the car
            then have the goal to install an engine of that size in
            the car.
```

[9]"Weakness" refers to lack of a definite theoretical position built into the language itself.

```
M2t:        If it is step 2 of a goal to make a car for a
            customer's order
              and the car's engine has been installed,
            then mark the step of the goal to be 3.
```

These examples bring out an important trade-off in control conventions: explicit steps reduce the number and complexity of contextual conditions that a rule must test, and thus simplify it, but they reduce the flexibility of control by locking the system into some particular order of execution.

A key question facing the builders of IPS, and even of PS's more generally, is whether a procedural organization can exploit the full flexibility that seems inherent in PS architectures. Flexibility derives from having the control be open, on each PS cycle, to global recognitions that can change the direction of processing by noting new facts, eliminate unnecessary steps by recognizing the satisfaction of the current goal or some higher one, and in general maintain the ability to switch to more efficient means for satisfying a goal. Flexibility enhances adaptability to changes in the situation, to new knowledge or techniques (acquired, perhaps, without regard for actual application situations), to recognizable errors, and to new orderings of sequences of actions that might be appropriate to different situations. Certainly PS's can be programmed like conventional algorithmic languages, but there is potential for much more flexible, "intelligent" procedures.

14.2.3 Explanation

A key operation in an instructible system is that of explaining how the system has arrived at some behavior, whether correct or not. In the case of wrong behavior, IPS must reveal enough of its processing to allow the more intelligent instructor to determine what knowledge is missing, incorrect, or improperly represented. In the case of correct behavior, the instructor may wish clarification or elaboration on how it resulted. Ideally the explanation can occur at a point where it is also possible to make necessary corrections and additions before IPS gets too far off the track.

For example, the state of WM in the middle of executing the "make a car" method might look like:

```
a goal to make a car for a customer's order,
the car's body has been made,
the car's engine has been installed,
a goal to make a radio,
the car's location is L24,
there is junk at location L25.
```

The explanation component would have to be able to detect unfinished goals, partially finished methods, unusual objects in the environment, and so on. This would be facilitated, for instance, if goals and subgoals had pointers to each other, if operators left some record of attempts, and so on—but too much of this sort of information can degrade the system's performance. Another problem is posed for the explanation component in selecting a small enough subset of critical items so that their communication is tolerable to the instructor.

14.2.4 Accommodation

When corrections to IPS's knowledge have been formulated by the instructor, the next step involves getting IPS to accommodate itself to new knowledge, that is, to augment or modify itself, in response to the usual form of interactions with the instructor. In the IPS framework, these modifications are taken to be changes to the rules of the system, rather than changes to the less permanent WM. As with interaction, IPS can assume a passive or active orientation toward this process. A key problem in the process of accommodation is to properly modify behavior in one situation while maintaining other correct behavior from past instruction. One aspect of this is to find the location in the knowledge structure of the system where the modification is to occur, so that related, interacting knowledge can be taken into account.

Suppose, in the preceding (explanation) example, that a problem is caused by a failure to satisfy the prerequisites for making a radio. Then a rule like the following might suffice to fix the problem:

```
If there is a goal to make a radio
   and there is a goal to start the radio machine
   and there is not a power supply at L14

Then have the goal to get a power supply at L14.
```

Note that this patch rule has to have enough conditions in it so that it can win the conflict resolution[10] over another (incomplete) rule, especially the rule that causes the starting of the radio machine without having all its requirements filled. Presumably there would be a rule in the system to set up subgoals to fulfill the prerequisites of making a radio, so that an alternative to the above patch rule might be to find and edit that rule by adding another subgoal. The deeper cause of why the rule was incorrect, for example, in analyzing the inputs to the radio machine, is more difficult to deal with, but might be worth the extra accommodation effort, as it might avoid future errors. One approach might be to set up a rule as a monitor to watch for similar errors (that is, those that omit some item of data) in the fulfilling of prerequisites.

14.2.5 Connection

This functional component and the ones that follow are considered "advanced" as opposed to the preceding "basic" components: they are much more difficult to formulate and implement.

---

[10]The relevant conflict resolution principle here is specificity: a rule that matches more data, or more specific (detailed) data, will be preferred; see [McDermott & Forgy, 1978; Rychener, 1977; Forgy & McDermott, 1977] for details.

Manifest errors are not the only way a system indicates a need for instruction: inability to connect a current problem with existing knowledge that might help in solving it is perhaps a more fundamental and frequent failing. An IPS needs ways both to assimilate problems into an existing knowledge framework and to recognize the applicability of, and discriminate among, existing methods. This concept of connection might also be termed "near contact", in that a close (but not exact) match to existing methods is involved, with differences resolvable by a few simple operations on the goal. An interesting issue revolves around how actively IPS processes new problems for both present and future connection. Connection abilities, particularly recognizing close or partial matches and transforming goals [Mostow, 1981], are important due to the desirability of having IPS know when it needs instruction versus when it can make use of existing knowledge. The other side of this coin is the problem of discriminating among several methods that appear to be appropriate to a given new problem.

As a simple example, suppose the familiar "make a car" goal had been stated,

```
Make a sedan for a customer's order.
```

This can be readily transformed into the known form, if the possibility of mapping it is recognized. It might require noticing that sedan is a value of the "body" attribute in "make car" goals. A definition of "sedan" might also provide sufficient clues.

14.2.6 Reformulation

Another way that IPS can substitute for instruction is for it to reformulate existing knowledge to apply in new circumstances. This can also be termed mapping, analogy, transfer, serendipity, or "far contact". There are two aspects to this function: finding knowledge that is potentially suitable for mapping, and performing the actual mapping.[11] In contrast to connection, this component involves permanent transformation of knowledge in rules, either directly or by altering rules' effects at each firing, dynamically.

For example, suppose the goal,

```
Make a truck for a customer's order.
```

were to come along and a method specifically for making trucks did not exist. Then some kind of analogical process might be appropriate, given the existing method for making a car. Namely, the goal might be transformed to "make a car", with the proviso that when "make a car" ran into problems, control would revert to an analogy method that would try to bridge the gap and fill in the missing step so that the "car" method could be resumed. This might be the case for making the truck's body, which would require special action, but we can sup-

---

[11]Carbonell, Chapter 5 in this volume, does this using means-ends analysis.

pose that adding an engine and accessories might be nearly identical in cases of truck and car.

14.2.7 Evaluation

Since the instructor has limited access to what IPS is doing, it is important for IPS to be able to evaluate its own progress, recognizing deficiencies and errors as they occur so that instruction can take place as closely as possible to the dynamic point of error. Defining what progress is and formulating relevant questions to ask in order to fill gaps in knowledge are two key issues. The assignment of blame for an error is the responsibility of the instructor in this IPS framework, with the explanation component assisting in diagnosis. It can also be helpful to include in evaluation some capabilities for having IPS produce additional external behavior, as in a "monitoring" or "careful execution" mode of operation.

The following rules illustrate the recognition of some possible error conditions:

```
E1:    If an object with type junk is produced by a machine,
       then have the goal of warning the instructor that
           the machine has produced that object.

E2:    If there is a goal to make a car for a customer's order
         and more than 20 minutes have elapsed since the order
           arrived
         and there is not the result that the car's body has
           been made,
       then have the goal of warning the instructor that
           progress is slow on the order.
```

14.2.8 Compilation

Rules initially formed as a result of the instructor's input may be amenable to refinements that improve IPS's efficiency. This follows from several factors: during instruction, IPS may be engaged in search or other "interpretive" execution (including a richer goal structure); instruction may provide IPS with fragments that can only be assembled into efficient form later; and IPS may form rules that are either too general or too specific. Improvement with practice is the psychological analog of this capability. Anderson *et al.* [1978] have formulated several approaches to compilation, such as condensing, into a single rule, rules that typically occur in a fixed sequence.

The improvement that can be obtained from compilation is illustrated by the following rule, whose actions consist of direct environmental commands rather than goals and subgoals:

```
C1:    If there is a goal to make a car for a customer's order
         and the order specifies a sedan body and a medium
           engine
       then start the sedan machine
```

```
and start the engine4 machine
and move an object from L22 to L23.
```

14.2.9 Discussion of Components

It is evident that realizing the components described in this section is made difficult by the myriad combinations of knowledge that can occur. Because an IPS is potentially working in various environments of different complexity, it is difficult to take advantage of stereotypes in procedural forms. Others have in fact made progress by assuming fixed-format rules (for example, transformational grammars) or simplified execution schemes (such as backward chaining). Our approach contrasts with those in avoiding any assumptions about the form of the environment and in leaving the system architecture open for general procedures.

14.3 SURVEY OF APPROACHES

Each attempt to build an IPS has started with a hand-coded *kernel* system, with enough structure in it to support all further growth by instruction. The kernels established the internal representations and the overall approach to instruction. At the very least, such kernels require the ability to interact with the instructor and to construct new rules. Three properties are desired in such a kernel system:

- It is to be hand coded, and as modular as possible.
- Everything in it is to be potentially modifiable by instruction. Usually it is constructed as if it were acquired by instruction, that is, with rules of similar form to those resulting from instruction.
- It is to be open to expansion in any of a number of directions, depending on which problems the instructor wishes to explore.

Seven kernels or kernel approaches were studied during the history of the IPS project, and they are presented below in roughly chronological order. KERNEL1, ANA, KERNEL2 and IPMSL were fully implemented. The remainder either were suspended at various early stages of development (with their best features incorporated into newer proposals) or are still being elaborated and developed in the context of other research. Table 14-1, near the end of this chapter, summarizes a number of attributes of the kernels.

14.3.1 The Abstract Job Shop Task Environment

The task domain for the IPS project was the manipulation of objects in a symbolic *task environment* (TE), a simulated, simplified "factory", in which an IPS system has a limited set of "sensory" and "motor" *operators*. A typical job shop is shown in Figure 14-1. Each *object* in this toy environment is represented as a LISP property list. The TE itself is an object with a particular set of components, termed *locations*, arranged in an array and represented as rectangles in Figure 14-1.

Moneyl Order4	Coupe	Manual	Red	Radio	A/C
Engin4 Engin6					
Scrap Clock	Sedan	Auto	Blue	Power	Asmblr

Figure 14-1: Abstract Job Shop

The entire ensemble, in the spirit of keeping it as an "external environment", is separate from the processes and memories of the PS architecture, except for the interface provided by the following operators:

- **View.** A representation of its argument, an object, is placed in WM (as if obtained through an "eye").
- **Scan.** An object is sought in the TE containing a given attribute-value pair. It is Viewed, if found.
- **Trans.** The top object at one location is transported to another location.
- **Start.** A machine (an object with a special set of properties) is started. It goes through one cycle of its operation, which is all within the action cycle of the rule containing the invocation.
- **Compare.** The values of a specified attribute of two objects are compared, producing a difference according to the values' type.

Note that the above operators are invoked as actions in rules, making modifications in the TE and reporting changes in the TE by asserting data into WM. All of this occurs within a single recognize-act cycle of the PS. The most important and complex operator is Start, which activates machines. A machine is a special-format object that takes some objects as inputs (in some cases consuming them) and produces other objects as outputs. Usually constraints on the machine's operation make problems in the domain more challenging.

Some sample problems, of varying difficulty, are the following:

- Examine the object at the top position of some location.

- Examine the object at the top position of some location.
- Compare two objects.
- Find an object with a given set of properties.
- Transport an object with a given set of properties to a given location.
- Manufacture an object with a given set of properties, within some budgetary and time limits.

The "find" class of task involves searching through the TE, Viewing objects and comparing them with the desired description. It is thus a prototypical task of interest in instructional situations. "Transport" problems are complicated by a feature of objects stored at a location: they are stacked on top of each other such that to move one, it has to be at the top of a stack. Getting an object to the top can involve moving objects elsewhere, with the potential for creating conflicts with other subgoals in a larger plan. While details of the pictured TE need not be given, it can be described as an assembly line layout for making automobiles. While this TE is straightforward, the language for defining TEs can express great complexity.

14.3.2 KERNEL Version 1

The starting point for IPS was the adoption of a pure means-ends strategy: given explicit goals, rules are the means to reducing or solving them. Four classes of rules are distinguished:

- means rules
- recognizers of success
- recognizers of failure
- evocation of goals from goal-free data

The KERNEL1 [Rychener & Newell, 1978] approach goes further than this in its organization component, which consists of ways for grouping rules into methods (as defined and illustrated in Section 14.1). The main mechanism of grouping is to have rules of the above types share a common goal pattern. The interaction component consists of a straightforward processor for language strings that correspond to methods and to system goals (among which are queries). Keywords in the language are used to signal that the kernel is to insert method sequencing tags. There are also keywords that delimit rule boundaries within methods. The explanation component is unspecified at the start, leaving it to the instructor to develop (and instruct) methods that could generate helpful information by piecing together various goals and data in WM. This reliance on instruction turned out to be a serious weakness, though a lot of the right kind of information was available in WM.

Although KERNEL1 was used as a basis for instruction, its effectiveness was severely hampered by its weak or nonexistent components for explanation, accommodation, connection and reformulation. Only small progress was made in the areas of evaluation[12] and compilation.[13] Much of the flavor of the means-ends approach was retained in later kernels.

KERNEL1 is illustrated in the protocol below; the objective is to instruct IPS to perform the simple task of examining the top object at some location in the TE. The method to be instructed can be summarized as follows: To examine the top object at some location, first View the location, then test if any objects are there; if so, find the first and use it as the result; otherwise, "nothing" is the result. Note that the "test if any objects" part of this method is a subgoal, to be instructed separately. The first clause of this method is given to KERNEL1 as follows:[14]

```
To examine the object at the top position                    (A)
       of some location,
  want view location that location in the TE               (⇒ B)
  then want test the status of the value                (C, (A1))
       of the composition of that location,

       . . .
```

The marginal notations in the above indicate that the instruction gives rise to a rule with a condition element 'A', the main goal of the method, and two action elements ('B' and 'C'), which are subgoals of the main goal. In addition, there is a modification (indicated by the subscript '1') to the goal element to achieve sequencing to the next step of the method (not shown). The complete input for this method involves four clauses of similar length and form to the one given, all given without a break for system responses. KERNEL1 adds some sequencing control to other rules in the method by inserting the main goal as a condition, suitably modified with step counters. These additions are one advantage of using KERNEL1 over programming directly in OPS rules, although the distance between the two forms of coding is not conceptually large—they are both forms of programming, as distinct from tutorial instruction.

While a large fraction of the rules of KERNEL1 are devoted to processing the (admittedly clumsy) input language illustrated above, the main design objective and achievement was to embed simple means-ends connections, as expressed by instruction text, in an organization that would ensure production of the desired behavior; that is, organization, rather than interaction, was the main focus. Unfortunately, two properties of the above style of interaction are very detrimental to effectiveness. First, KERNEL1 accepts the input passively, with no

[12]Described briefly in an unpublished appendix to this chapter, available from the author.

[13]This consisted of recognizing the applicability of techniques such as those in [Anderson *et al.*, 1978], to our means-ends rules.

[14]An unpublished appendix (available from the author) to this chapter contains the full instruction text, along with a more detailed explanation.

interaction (for example, questioning) involved. Second, the instructor receives no feedback on the correctness of the many parts until the entire method is tried. KERNEL1 failed to provide an adequate basis for interaction, explanation, and performance due to a number of practical considerations: difficulty in knowing the side conditions of rules (those other than the main goal); lack of a mechanism for constructing tests of proper goal satisfaction; lack of having goal-subgoal links created automatically; and goal representation deficiencies—particularly, failure to distinguish different occurrences of the same goal (as in recursion) and to allow goals to be augmented with new information as processing developed. The instructor was relied upon to provide too much programming detail, in a situation where a programming approach is considered harmful.

In spite of its shortcomings, KERNEL1 accomplished a few important tasks, as far as overall IPS project goals were concerned. It established the basic means-ends form for the organization component. It clarified the need for more PS efficiency, and for improvement in the explanation, accommodation, and other functional components. In short, it gave us a better appreciation of the difficulty of the instruction task.

14.3.3 Additive Successive Approximations (ASA)

Some of the drawbacks of KERNEL1, especially those surrounding interaction, can be remedied[15] by orienting instruction towards fragments of methods that can be more readily refined at later times. Interaction consists of having the instructor designate items in IPS's environment (especially WM) in four ways: condition (for data or configurations that are important context to be taken into account while working on a goal), action (for operators appropriate to solving a goal), entity (to create a symbol and some associated knowledge about the entity), and relevant (to associate one of the other three designated items with a particular goal). The system is to respond to a 'relevant' designation by building rules with the given conditions or actions, or by building rules that create or augment knowledge expressions. These designations result in methods that are very loose collections of rules, each of which contributes some small amount towards achieving the goal. Accommodation is done as *post-modification* of an existing method in its dynamic execution context, through ten method-modification methods. Some of these are: delay an action, advance an action, remove an action, conditionalize an action, and put two actions into a strict sequence.

Though the ASA ideas were never implemented, some aspects of the approach were used in the KERNEL2 system, described in detail below. Probably ASA would suffer from the same difficulties described in connection with KERNEL2.

---

[15]These ideas were introduced by A. Newell in October, 1977.

14.3.4 Analogy (ANA)

A concerted attempt to deal with issues of connection and reformulation is represented by McDermott's ANA program [McDermott, 1978]. Starting out with the ability to solve a few very specific problems, it attacked subsequent similar problems by analogizing from its known methods. Initial methods to solve TE problems were hand coded, a deviation from the kernel constraints given above. In ANA, connection is achieved by coding special *method* description rules, which recognize the class of goals that appear possible for a method to deal with by analogy. The possibility that an analogy may work is discovered by following taxonomic links originating at a given goal's actions and object arguments. When a link is traversed, revealing the object (class) or action (class) at the end of it, a method description rule may become satisfied, thus making a connection on which an analogy can be based. A preliminary analogy is set up using the discovered correspondence of objects or actions, the goal is modified by substitution, and the method is started. As it executes, rules recognize points where the analogy breaks down. General analogy methods are able either to patch the method directly with specific substitutions or to query the instructor for new means-ends rules.

In either case, reformulation occurs because rules record the patches for use in later similar problems. Compilation occurs, with visible improvement in performance, as fewer and fewer of the error recognition rules are brought into play. Thus, ANA combines connection, reformulation, evaluation and compilation components.[16]

14.3.5 KERNEL Version 2

With basic ideas similar to ASA and to Waterman's Exemplary Programming [Waterman, 1978], the KERNEL2 approach [Rychener, 1979] focused on the process of IPS interacting with the instructor to build rules in a dynamic execution context. The instructor essentially steps through the process of achieving a goal, with IPS noting what is done and marking elements for inclusion in the rules to be built when the goal is achieved. The organization of methods in KERNEL2 is less adventurous than proposed in ASA, keeping more to the traditional control and means-ends concepts of KERNEL1. Similarly, it provides few innovations with respect to accommodation, explanation, and the other IPS components. KERNEL2 includes a semantic network of information about its methods, for use as a "help" facility. It is the basis from which the IPMSL system, below, is built.

Based on the preceding description, KERNEL2 would seem to offer little advance over KERNEL1. However, the following protocol illustrates the large difference that occurs with the shift towards interaction that is more frequent and in

---

[16]For another approach to learning by analogy, see Carbonell, Chapter 5, in this volume.

a dynamic method-execution context. The protocol below is not an actual interaction between instructor and KERNEL, due to a shift in the domain of IPS away from the TE used for KERNEL1. KERNEL2 was actually implemented, though, and the following is representative of the style of instruction achieved. The actual interaction language has been smoothed out somewhat in this protocol. "I:" precedes inputs from the instructor, and "K:", the outputs of KERNEL2.

```
I: Examine the object at the top position of L23

K: Unable to do WS003:
     Examine object at top position of L23

I: Goal of rule: WS003                                      (A)

K: OK, working on new rule P39

I: Add: want view location L23 in the TE                   (⇒ B,)

K: View location result is L23 in the TE                   (Note 1)

K: L23 has member TE, composition (M1 M2 C5),
     type stack

I: Add: want test the status of the value of the           (C)
             composition of L23
K: Unable to do WS009: Test status of value of
     composition of L23

I: L23 is a variable in P39

K: OK

I: Build P39                                    (rule: A ⇒ B, C)

K: OK

I: Goal of rule: WS009

K: OK, working on new rule P40
```

Expressions are given at the right margin to mark places in the text where certain rule elements have been specified, in a way similar to the protocol for KERNEL1. The rule that is constructed as a result of this dialogue is, in fact, almost identical to the one built by KERNEL1. Of interest is what is happening at the point where "*Note 1*" occurs: here is an example of the utility of dynamic context. At this point, KERNEL2 actually executes an operator on the TE, and displays the result, so that the instructor can easily formulate what he wants done with that result in the succeeding steps of the method being instructed.

To summarize the key aspects of KERNEL2, interaction happens in the context of a concrete attempt at solving a goal. The effect of this immediate feedback is that the instructor can have a much better idea of how much the system knows about the present context. Interactions are far removed from the constructed rules, corresponding both to small pieces of those rules and to interactive commands that might be given to the system to have it do something. The dynamic context provides stimuli to the instructor, helping to avoid errors and omissions, and placing less burden on the instructor's memory. When a piece of a rule given by the instructor is a recognizable goal to the system, it automatically tries to achieve the goal, and the instructor can watch this activity and observe its results. KERNEL2 is much simpler in structure than KERNEL1 (fewer rules, and more easily coded), due to radical simplification of its input language. Instructions to KERNEL2 are much shorter, and feedback to the instructor is immediate.

14.3.6 Conclusions on Direct Approaches

The above approaches are all *direct* in the sense that the orientation is towards rules and pieces of rules rather than towards knowledge that is structured in some other more natural form. One conclusion from the direct approaches is that instruction must be organized in units other than rules—rules are too large and tend not to be a natural form for instruction, especially when various PS control and supporting structures are taken into account. Also, rules tend to require a belabored, repetitious style of instruction, where the natural tendency is to make assumptions about the capabilities of the receiver of instruction, and to use various forms of ellipsis. The instructor should not be allowed to perceive instruction as programming, as this is an unnatural mode of instruction.

In the *higher-level* approaches that follow, more is attempted in terms of functional components for explanation, accommodation, and the advanced components. Another common theme is the need for a more active, "agenda" orientation, including system goals that are pursued along with those of the instructor.

14.3.7 Problem Spaces

Problem spaces [Newell, 1980][17] were proposed as a higher-level organization for IPS, in which all behavior and interactions were to be embedded in search. A *problem space* consists of a collection of knowledge elements that compose *states*, plus a collection of *operators* that produce new states from known ones. A *problem* consists of an initial state, a goal state, and possibly path constraints. Control in a problem space organization is achieved through an executive routine that maintains and directs the global state of ongoing searches. Newell's problem space hypothesis claims that all goal-oriented cognitive activity occurs in problem spaces, not just activity that is problematical.

---

[17]This approach was formulated by A. Newell and J. Laird in October, 1978.

According to the proposal, interaction would consist of giving IPS problems (presumably WM structures) and search control knowledge (hints as to how to search specific spaces, presumably expressed as rules). Every kernel component would be a problem space too, and thus subject to the same modification processes. The concrete proposal as it now stands concentrates on interaction, explanation (which involves sources of knowledge about the present state of the search), and organization.

14.3.8 Semantic Network (IPMSL)

The IPMSL (Instructible PMS Language, where PMS is a computer description formalism) system [Rychener, 1979] viewed accumulation of knowledge as additions to a semantic network. In this view, interaction consists of definition and modification of nodes in a net, where such nodes are PS rules. The network stores four classes of attributes: taxonomic (classifying methods and objects), functional (input-output relations for methods), structural (component parts of methods and objects), and descriptive (various characteristics). Display and net search facilities are provided as aids to explanation and accommodation, though the instructor is responsible for storing the required information in the network in the first place. The availability of traditional semantic network inferences makes it possible for IPMSL to develop a more uniform approach to connection and reformulation, since they provide a set of tools for relating and mapping knowledge into more tractable expressions. Because IPMSL is a digression into a task domain different from the Abstract Job Shop, emphasis was placed on descriptive capabilities rather than on mechanisms for procedural organization. Thus the semantic network orientation was not integrated with KERNEL2 approaches to the acquisition and description of procedural knowledge. The remaining step towards integration would be to have KERNEL2 record information in the network, as methods are built up using its interaction primitives.

14.3.9 Schemas

The use of schemas as a basis for an IPS kernel[18] made slot filling the primary information-gathering operation. A slot would be implemented as a set of rules. The slots are: executable method; test of completion; assimilation (connects present WM with the schema for a goal); initialization (gathers operands for a method); model (records the instruction episode for later reference); accommodation (records patches to the method); status (records gaps in the knowledge); monitoring (allows careful execution); and organization (records method structure). Orientation towards instruction would be active, as in ASA. Explanation would consist of interpreting the model slot, and accommodation, of fitting additions into the model. Connection would use a dis-

---

[18]Schemas were first proposed for IPS by Rychener, May, 1978

crimination network composed of the aggregated assimilation slots of all schemas. Compilation would be needed here, to map model to method.

The following protocol illustrates the flavor of the proposed schema approach. A system based on this approach, but outside the IPS framework, is currently under development, but for expository reasons, the protocol here is a simulated one. There are notations similar to those for the KERNEL2 protocol above. Notes in the right margin in some cases give the names of slots being filled by the adjacent interactions. Other notes refer to explanations in the next paragraph.

```
I: Examine the object at the top position of L23

K: Unknown goal WS003:                                        (A)
    Examine object at top position of L23

K: What is the goal WS003 attempting to achieve?

I: The name of some object,                                (TEST)
    the position of that object is 1,
    the member of that object is L23

K: Does this result differ from a view object in the
    TE, because of ´at the top positionı?

I: Yes                                              (ASSIMILATION)

K: Part of the desired information of the goal can be
    obtained from a view operation

K: To view requires an object or location to               (INIT)
    work on, which L23 seems to satisfy
                                                            (⇒ B)
K: L23 has member TE, composition (M1 M2 C5),             (Note 1)
    type stack

K: Viewing L23 did not produce the desired attributes

I: You need to view the object at the top position
    of L23

K: I lack objects with position 1 with member L23

I: Test the status of the composition of L23                  (C)

K: Unknown goal WS009:                               (rule: A ⇒ B, C)
    test status of composition of L23                     (Note 2)

K: What is goal WS009 attempting to achieve?

I: Whether the composition of L23 is empty or nonempty     (TEST)
```

```
K: I have nothing that produces that result

I: The composition of L23 is (M1 something),
          so its status is nonempty
```

The most striking feature of this protocol is that IPS is taking much more initiative in determining the direction of the dialogue. It is questioning the relation of new information to what already exists, and is actively trying to fill in missing slots in its new schemas. At "Note 1" IPS tries an experiment with a TE operator, to get at least a partial result that might aid in solving the goal. At "Note 2", IPS is entering into the context of a new schema. Presumably, the former schema will be reactivated at a later time when the subgoal's schema is satisfactorily filled in.

The schemas approach as sketched here makes a few significant additions to KERNEL2. The orientation towards filling slots is the primary source of the improved, natural style of interaction. Schemas implemented as PS's are self-activating and procedural. The slots can contain more than just stereotyped values, namely arbitrary methods and structures of rules; and goals for filling slots will reside in the global WM, and thus can be filled flexibly, and in a data-dependent way (that is, as data become available that are recognized as relevant).

14.3.10 Conclusions on Higher-Level Approaches

The approaches discussed above illustrate the advantages of using higher-level organizations for the overall instructional process. The importance of carefully attending to the style of instruction should be evident. Adopting these approaches has the two-fold benefit of providing a more natural communication medium for the instructor of the system, and of providing goals and methods for the system itself to mold new knowledge into well-organized, flexible, complete, and reliable methods. The system can also be more free than before to experiment for itself, given its agendas and search mechanisms. Higher-level approaches aid in developing effective versions of the more advanced functional components, in that such components are natural consequences of adopting any of the above specific approaches. The accompanying tables summarize the seven approaches.

14.4 DISCUSSION

The IPS project has invented and explored the consequences of a number of plausible learning system components in the "learning by being told" paradigm. One contribution is the means-ends organization of KERNEL1, along with its approach to debugging using a dynamic goal tree context, and compiling by eliminating temporary goal structures. Means-ends also holds the promise of expanding a system's abilities in directions where explicit goals can be formulated.

Table 14-1:

Component \ IPS:	KERNEL1	ASA	ANA	KERNEL2
Interaction	whole method query goal	four desig. forms	patch goal	many desig. query goal
Organization	sequenced methods	loose means-ends links	hand-coded for analogy	sequenced methods help net of functional info
Explanation	(WM data)	?	?	(KERNEL1)
Accommodation	whole rules -blindly	method-modif. methods	(KERNEL1) (see Reform.)	(KERNEL1)
Connection	(*ad hoc* means-ends rules)	?	method descr. rules taxonomy search	(KERNEL1)
Reformulation	?	?	patch rules map actions & objects	?
Evaluation	monitor of goals	?	recog. of break-down of analogy	instructor, in dynamic context
Compilation	(compose out goal structures)	(needed even more than in KERNEL1)	patch rules analogize faster	(KERNEL1)
Implemented?	yes	no	yes	yes
Reference	[Rychener & Newell, 1978]	(see KERNEL2)	[McDermott, 1978]	[Rychener, 1979]
Failings	too much like programming poor goal repr. overemph. language instructions too long weak explanation no method-modif. methods orientation too passive	would control work?	no approach to instruction	too slow task was shifted
Starting size	325 rules, incl. 50 in monitor, added later		295 rules, incl. 55 in TE methods	45 rules
Instruction	9 elementary tasks = 160 rules	0	4 tasks = 140 rules	Kernel grew = 55 rules
Final size	485 rules		435 rules	100 rules (see IPMSL)

Key: Potential or theoretical capabilities ("left to instruction") are in ()s; numbers of rules are rounded.

Table 14-1, continued

IPS:	Problem Spaces	Semantic Net (IPMSL)	Schemas
Component Interaction	problems search control	KERNEL2 + net defining, updating	actively fill slots + KERNEL2
Organization	problem spaces for all compon. & methods	KERNEL2 + network: function, taxonomy, structure, description	schemas with 9 types of slots; esp. method, model, init, test
Explanation	knowledge about state of search	supported by network info	(model slot interp.)
Accommodation	(problem space)	supported by network info	(edit model) (status slt)
Connection	(problem space)	(net inferences & searching)	discrim. net
Reformulation	(problem space)	(network info)	?
Evaluation	executive	?	monitor slot
Compilation	specific, *ad hoc* search control	?	(transform model slot)
Implemented?	no	yes	no
Reference	[Newell, 1980]	[Rychener, 1979]	
Failings		too big & slow	
Instruction/ Testing		160 rules in net	
Start size		450 rules = 100 KERNEL2 + 120 basic net + 230 advanced net	
Final size		610 rules	

Key: Potential or theoretical capabilities ("left to instruction") are in ()s; numbers of rules are rounded. In unimplemented proposals, ()s are reserved for very vague possibilities.

The use of explicit tests and failure recognizers can add reliability and robustness to means-ends execution. A second contribution has been the study of knowledge acquisition in a dynamic execution context (illustrated by the KERNEL2 dialogue above). Other contributions include the development of the problem space idea, the orientation of a learning system towards active assimilation and accommodation (as in schemas), the ability to dynamically use analogies, the use of rules to implement semantic networks, and the organization of rules into schemas. This paper has tried to motivate the need for more study of approaches to instruction and of ways of achieving the functional components, by exhibiting an evolutionary sequence and by pointing out the deficiencies of various partial designs. Our studies to date into these issues have been greatly facilitated by the use of a flexible, expressive medium, the OPS PS architecture.

Two key problems remain unsolved and open for further research: achieving the kind of procedural flexibility and robustness that would seem to be inherent in the PS architecture; and devising ways for a system to effectively manage its knowledge (however organized), that is, techniques for accommodation as defined above. Procedural flexibility has been discussed above in association with the organization component. The ideal flexibility ought to derive from the global recognize-act cycle, where heuristics and optimizations could be applied at each step to guide and complete goal processing. For a system to manage its knowledge, much more needs to be known about the structure of methods and how they are modified and augmented. The IPS project has failed to get beyond the most basic of method manipulations, partly due to its emphasis on other aspects of the overall problem and partly due to the inherent difficulty of the problem area.

Explorations within our particular framework can profit from and stimulate research in information processing psychology. Of particular interest would be a protocol analysis of instructional dialogues in an environment similar to our TE, after the fashion of Newell and Simon [1972]. Additional information would be provided by querying the subject to determine what rules have been learned, after a session with an unknown problem environment. The structuring of the instructional session by a human tutor with a human subject is important, as it may give some indication of the underlying knowledge representations involved. The best attempts by psychologists at studying instructional learning at this level of detail seem to be found in work such as Klahr's collection [1976]. On the AI side, the work of Collins [1978] seems to be the closest in spirit. It may be in general that people do not require the painstaking explanations that seem to be needed by PS's. At least, this holds for PS's with very little knowledge, as discussed here. That is, humans are better learners because they know more and can fill in gaps in the instructional interaction. Thus it may be that our PS work must develop new techniques that haven't been necessary with human education. On the other hand, humans' learning might improve if we knew better how to organize instruction to suit their internal knowledge structures, or if we could train them to use a more efficient knowledge organization.[19]

ACKNOWLEDGMENTS

This research was sponsored by the Defense Advanced Research Projects Agency (DOD), ARPA Order No. 3597, monitored by the Air Force Avionics Laboratory Under Contract F33615-78-C-1551. The views and conclusions contained in this document are those of the author and should not be interpreted as representing the official policies, either expressed or implied, of the Defense Advanced Research Projects Agency or the U.S. Government.

Much of the work sketched in this chapter has been done jointly over the course of several years. Other project members are (in approximate order of duration of commitment to it): Allen Newell, John McDermott, Charles L. Forgy, Kamesh Ramakrishna, Pat Langley [1980] (see also Chapter 10 of this volume), Paul Rosenbloom and John Laird. The present author's perspective, emphasis, and statement of conclusions may differ considerably from those of other project members; the broad scope of the IPS project fostered and encouraged a diversity of approaches. But much credit goes to the group as a whole for the overall contributions of the research. Helpful comments on this paper were made by Allen Newell, Jaime Carbonell, David Neves, Robert Akscyn and Kamesh Ramakrishna. The editors and reviewers of this book have also been very helpful.

REFERENCES

Anderson, J. R., *Language, Memory, and Thought*, Lawrence Erlbaum Associates, Hillsdale, NJ, 1976.

Anderson, J. R., Kline, P. J., and Beasley, C. M. Jr., "A Theory of the Acquisition of Cognitive Skills", Technical Report 77-1, Yale University, Dept. of Psychology, January 1978.

Anzai, Y. and Simon, H. A., "The theory of learning by doing," *Psychological Review*, Vol. 86, No. 2, pp. 124-140, 1979.

Buchanan, B. G., Mitchell, T. M., Smith, R. G. and Johnson, C. R. Jr., "Models of Learning Systems", Technical Report STAN-CS-79-692, Stanford University, Computer Science Dept., January 1979.

Collins, A., "Explicating the Tacit Knowledge in Teaching and Learning", Technical Report 3889, Bolt, Beranek and Newman, Inc., March 1978.

Forgy, C. L., *On the Efficient Implementation of Production Systems*, Ph.D. dissertation, Carnegie-Mellon University, Dept. of Computer Science, February 1979.

---

[19]The author would appreciate references to current work along the lines discussed in this paragraph.

Forgy, C. L., "OPS4 User's Manual", Technical Report CMU-CS-79-132, Carnegie-Mellon University, Dept. of Computer Science, July 1979.

Forgy, C. and McDermott, J., "OPS, a domain-independent production system language," *Proceedings of the Fifth International Joint Conference on Artificial Intelligence*, IJCAI, Cambridge, MA, pp. 933-939, August 1977.

Klahr, D., *Cognition and Instruction*, Lawrence Erlbaum Associates, Hillsdale, NJ, 1976.

Langley, P. W., *Descriptive Discovery Processes: Experiments in Baconian Science,* Ph.D. dissertation, Carnegie-Mellon University, Dept. of Psychology, December 1979.

Lesser, V. R. and Erman, L. D., "A retrospective view of the HEARSAY-II architecture," *Proceedings of the Fifth International Joint Conference on Artificial Intelligence*, IJCAI, Cambridge, MA, pp. 790-800, August 1977.

McDermott, J., "ANA: An Assimilating and Accommodating Production System", Technical Report CMU-CS-78-156, Carnegie-Mellon University, Dept. of Computer Science, December 1978, (Also appeared in IJCAI-79, pp. 568-576).

McDermott, J. and Forgy, C., "Production system conflict resolution strategies," *Pattern-Directed Inference Systems*, Waterman, D. A. and Hayes-Roth, F. (Eds.), Academic Press, New York, NY, pp. 177-199, 1978.

Moore, J. and Newell, A., "How can MERLIN understand?," *Knowledge and Cognition*, Gregg, L. W. (Ed.), Lawrence Erlbaum Associates, Potomac, MD, pp. 201-252, 1973.

Mostow, D. J., *Mechanical transformation of task heuristics into operational procedures,* Ph.D. dissertation, Carnegie-Mellon University, Dept. of Computer Science, April 1981, (Available as CMU-CS-81-113.).

Newell, A., "Reasoning, problem solving and decision processes: the problem space as a fundamental category," *Attention and Performance VIII*, Nickerson, R. (Ed.), Lawrence Erlbaum Associates, Hillsdale, NJ, pp. 693-718, 1980.

Newell, A. and Simon, H. A., *Human Problem Solving*, Prentice-Hall, Englewood Cliffs, NJ, 1972.

Rychener, M. D., "The STUDNT production system: a study of encoding knowledge in production systems", Technical Report, Carnegie-Mellon University, Dept. of Computer Science, October 1975.

Rychener, M. D., *Production systems as a programming language for artificial intelligence applications,* Ph.D. dissertation, Carnegie-Mellon University, Dept. of Computer Science, December 1976.

Rychener, M. D., "Control requirements for the design of production system architectures," *SIGART Newsletter*, Vol. 64, pp. 37-44, August 1977, (ACM.).

Rychener, M. D., "A Semantic Network of Production Rules in a System for Describing Computer Structures", Technical Report CMU-CS-79-130, Carnegie-Mellon University, Dept. of Computer Science, June 1979, (Also appeared in IJCAI-79, pp. 738-743.).

Rychener, M. D., "OPS3 Production System Language Tutorial and Reference Manual", Technical Report, Carnegie-Mellon University, Dept. of Computer Science, March 1980, (Internal Working Paper.).

Rychener, M. D. and Newell, A., "An instructable production system: basic design issues," *Pattern-Directed Inference Systems*, Waterman, D. A. and Hayes-Roth, F. (Eds.), Academic Press, New York, NY, pp. 135-153, 1978.

Waterman, D. A., "Rule-Directed Interactive Transaction Agents: An Approach to Knowledge Acquisition", Technical Report R-2171-ARPA, The Rand Corporation, February 1978.

Young, R. M., "Production systems for modelling human cognition," *Expert Systems in the Micro Electronic Age*, Michie, D. (Ed.), Edinburgh University Press, Edinburgh, Scotland, pp. 35-45, 1979.

PART SIX

APPLIED LEARNING SYSTEMS

15

LEARNING EFFICIENT CLASSIFICATION PROCEDURES AND THEIR APPLICATION TO CHESS END GAMES

J. Ross Quinlan
The Rand Corporation[1]

ABSTRACT

A series of experiments dealing with the discovery of efficient classification procedures from large numbers of examples is described, with a case study from the chess end game king-rook versus king-knight. After an outline of the inductive inference machinery used, the paper reports on trials leading to correct and very fast attribute-based rules for the relations lost 2-ply and lost 3-ply. On another tack, a model of the performance of an idealized induction system is developed and its somewhat surprising predictions compared with observed results. The paper ends with a description of preliminary work on the automatic specification of relevant attributes.

15.1 INTRODUCTION

This paper reports on experiments that recover valuable information from large masses of low-grade data by a process of inductive inference. The data are relatively unstructured examples and counterexamples of a concept of considerable complexity. The information that is sought is a means of identifying examples of the concept or, in other words, a classification rule. The distinguishing characteristics of this work are the large numbers of examples employed in forming the concepts and the computational efficiency of the classification

---

[1]*Currently with The New South Wales Institute of Technology, Australia.*

rules discovered in this way as compared with other classification methods for the same task. (In one case, the classification rule is five times as fast as the best alternative method that I could devise.)

The concepts to be developed have been drawn from the chess end game king-rook versus king-knight, which can be difficult even for masters [Kopec & Niblett, 1980]. This end game has proved to be an excellent testing ground, providing classification tasks of a range of difficulties and a large underlying universe of more than a million possible configurations of pieces. However, it should be noted that the inductive inference machinery that has been developed is in no way tied to this application, and is currently being used by other workers for a different aspect of chess [Shapiro & Niblett, 1982] and in a medical domain [Bratko & Mulec, 1981].

The induction algorithm used for this project is called ID3. ID3 takes objects of a known class described in terms of a fixed collection of properties or attributes, and produces a decision tree over these attributes that correctly classifies all the given objects. Two qualities differentiate it from other general-purpose inference systems such as INDUCE [Michalski, 980a], SPROUTER [Hayes-Roth & McDermott, 1977] and THOTH-P [Vere, 1978]. The first concerns the way that the effort required to accomplish an induction task grows with the difficulty of that task. ID3 was specifically designed to handle masses of objects, and in fact its computation time increases only linearly with difficulty as modeled by the product of:

- the number of given exemplary objects,
- the number of attributes used to describe objects, and
- the complexity of the concept to be developed (measured by the number of nodes on the decision tree)

[Quinlan, 1979a]. On the negative side, this linearity is purchased at the cost of descriptive power. The concepts developed by ID3 can only take the form of decision trees based on the attributes given, and this "language" is much more restrictive than the first-order or multivalued logic in which the above systems express concepts. [Dietterich & Michalski, 1979] gives an analysis and survey of inductive inference methodologies.

The main body of this report contains four sections. The first, Section 15.2, introduces ID3 as a descendant of Hunt's Concept Learning System (CLS). Section 15.3 summarizes applications of ID3 to discovering decision trees for the relations "knight's side is lost n-ply" where n is 2 or 3; detailed accounts appear in [Quinlan, 1979b; Quinlan, 1980]. The last two sections deal with recent work along different dimensions. Section 15.4 considers the question of discovering approximate rather than exact rules. It develops a model of how an idealized induction system might behave when shown only a fraction of all possible objects, and compares the predictions of this model to observed results. Section 15.5 tackles the problem of defining features used to describe objects, and outlines techniques aimed at automating the discovery of the attributes themselves.

15.2 THE INDUCTIVE INFERENCE MACHINERY

ID3, a descendant of Hunt's CLS [Hunt *et al.*, 1966], is a comparatively simple mechanism for discovering a classification rule for a collection of objects belonging to two classes. As mentioned above, each object must be described in terms of a fixed set of attributes, each of which has its own (small) set of possible *attribute values*. As an illustration, "color" and "baud rate" might be attributes with sets of possible values {red,green,blue} and {110,300,1200,2400,4800} respectively.

A classification rule in the form of a decision tree can be constructed for any such collection C of objects. If C is empty then we associate it arbitrarily with either class. If all objects in C belong to the same class, then the decision tree is a leaf bearing that class name. Otherwise C contains representatives of both classes; we select an attribute and partition C into disjoint sets C_1, C_2, ... , C_n where C_i contains those members of C that have the ith value of the selected attribute. Each of these subcollections is then handled in turn by the same rule-forming strategy. The eventual outcome is a tree in which each leaf carries a class name, and each interior node specifies an attribute to be tested with a branch corresponding to each possible value of that attribute.

To illustrate this process, consider the collection C below. Each object is described in terms of three attributes: "height" with values {tall,short}, "hair" with values {dark,red,blond} and "eyes" with values {blue,brown}, and is followed by '+' or '−' to indicate the class to which it belongs.

C =	short,blond,blue: +	short,dark,blue: −	tall,dark,brown: −
	tall,blond,brown: −	tall,dark,blue: −	short,blond,brown: −
	tall,red,blue: +	tall,blond,blue: +	

If the second attribute is selected to form the root of the decision tree, this yields the tree shown in Figure 15-1. The subcollections corresponding to the values 'dark' and 'red' contain objects of only a single class, and so require no further work. If we select the third attribute to test for the 'blond' branch, this yields the tree in Figure 15-2. Now all subcollections contain objects of one class, so we can replace each subcollection by the class name to get the decision tree shown in Figure 15-3.

An object is classified by starting at the root of the decision tree, finding the value of the tested attribute in the given object, taking the branch appropriate to that value, and continuing in the same fashion until a leaf is reached. Notice that classifying a particular object may involve evaluating only a small number of the attributes depending on the length of the path from the root of the tree to the appropriate leaf. In the above case, the first step is always to inquire about the value of an object's "hair" attribute. If this value is "dark" or "red" the object can be classified immediately without looking at its other attributes. If the value is 'blond' then we must determine its value of "eyes" before classifying it. We never need to determine the value of the "height" attribute.

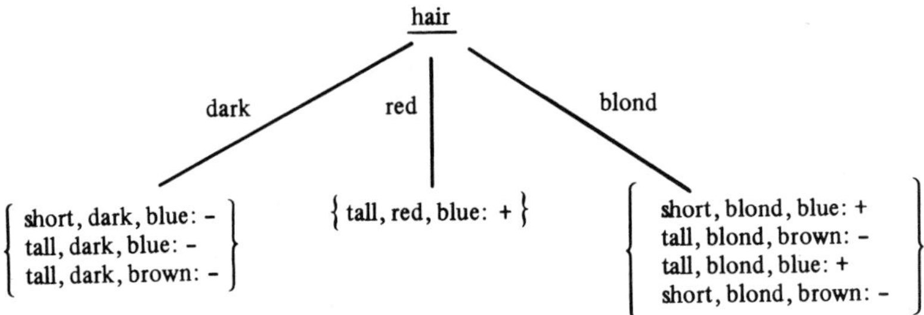

Figure 15-1: One-level decision tree.

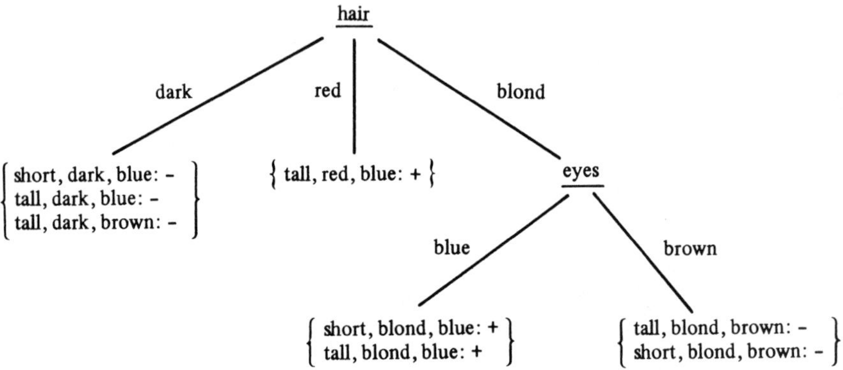

Figure 15-2: Two-level decision tree.

This rule-forming procedure will always work provided that there are not two objects belonging to different classes but having identical values for each attribute; in such cases the attributes are inadequate for the classification task. However, it is generally desirable that the tree be able to classify objects which were not used in its construction, and so the leaves corresponding to an empty set of examples (where a class is chosen randomly) should be kept to a minimum. If we adopted the simple-minded algorithm:

> "Select the first attribute for the root of the tree, the second attribute for the next level, and so on."

the result would tend towards the complete tree with a leaf for each point in the attribute space—clearly an unsatisfactory situation. The whole skill in this style of induction lies in selecting a useful attribute to test for a given collection of

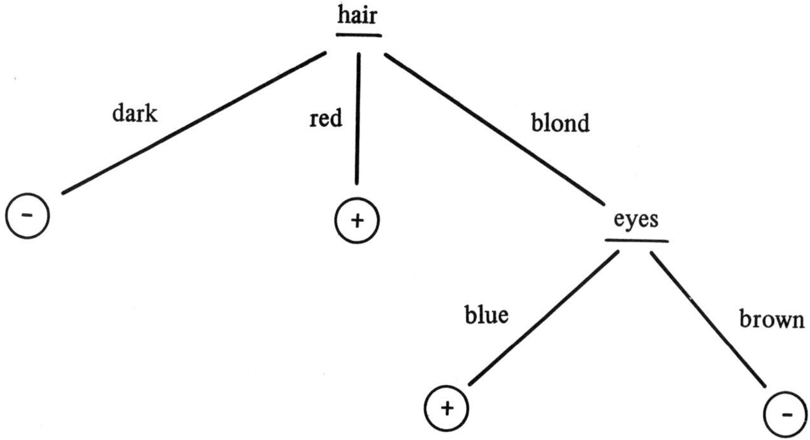

Figure 15-3: Decision tree with class names.

objects so that the final tree is in some sense minimal. Hunt's work used a lookahead scheme driven by a system of measurement and misclassification costs in an attempt to get minimal-cost trees. ID3 uses an information-theoretic approach aimed at minimizing the expected number of tests to classify an object

A decision tree may be regarded as an information source that, given an object, generates a message which is the class of that object ("plus" or "minus", say). The attribute selection part of ID3 is based on the plausible assumption that the complexity of the decision tree is strongly related to the amount of information conveyed by this message. If the probability of these messages is p^+ and p^- respectively, the expected information content of the message is

$$-p^+ \log_2 p^+ - p^- \log_2 p^-$$

With a known set C of objects we can approximate these probabilities by relative frequencies, so that p^+ becomes the proportion of objects in C with class "plus". So we will write M(C) to denote this calculation of the expected information content of a message from a decision tree for a set C of objects, and define $M(\{\}) = 0$. Now consider as before the possible choice of A as the attribute to test next. The partial decision tree is shown in Figure 15-4. The values A_i of attribute A are mutually exclusive (even though different attributes may not be), so the new expected information content will be:

$$B(C,A) = (\text{probability that value of A is } A_i) \times M(C_i)$$

where again we can replace the probabilities by relative frequencies. The suggested choice of attribute to test next is that which gains the most information, in other words, for which

$$M(C) - B(C,A)$$

is maximal.

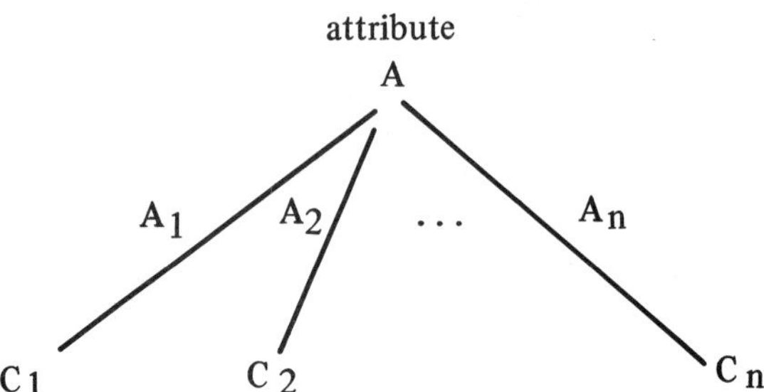

Figure 15-4: Partial decision tree.

To illustrate the idea, consider the choice of the first attribute to test from the example given earlier. The collection C of objects contains 3 in class '+' and 5 in '−', so

$$M(C) = -3/8 \log_2 3/8 - 5/8 \log_2 5/8$$
$$= 0.954 \text{ bits}$$

Testing the first attribute gives the results shown in Figure 15-5. The information still needed for a rule for the "tall" branch is:

$$-2/5 \log_2 2/5 - 3/5 \log_2 3/5 = 0.971 \text{ bits}$$

and for the "short" branch:

$$-1/3 \log_2 1/3 - 2/3 \log_2 2/3 = 0.918 \text{ bits}$$

Thus the expected information content:

$$B(C,\text{"height"}) = 5/8 * 0.971 + 3/8 * 0.918$$
$$= 0.951 \text{ bits}$$

The information gained by testing this attribute is:

$$0.954 - 0.951 = 0.003 \text{ bits}$$

which is negligible. The tree arising from testing the second attribute was given previously. The branches for "dark" (with 3 objects) and "red" (1 object) require no further information, while the branch for "blond" contained 2 "plus" and 2 "minus" objects and so requires 1 bit. We have:

$$B(C,\text{"hair"}) = 3/8 * 0 + 1/8 * 0 + 4/8 * 1$$
$$= 0.5 \text{ bits}$$

and the information gained by testing "hair" is 0.954 − 0.5 = 0.454 bits. In a similar way the information gained by testing "eyes" comes to 0.347 bits. Thus the principle of maximizing expected information gain would lead ID3 to select "hair" as the attribute to form the root of the decision tree.

The procedure described above for constructing decision trees assumes that

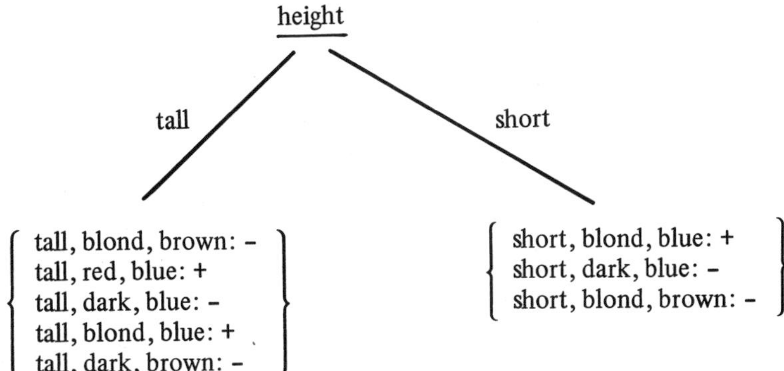

Figure 15-5: Binary attribute discrimination.

counting operations on the set of objects C (such as determining the number of "plus" objects with value A_i of attribute A) can be performed efficiently, which means in practice that C has to be kept in fast memory. What happens if the size of C precludes this? One way around the difficulty is given by the version space strategy [Mitchell, 1979] in which C is digested one object at a time. Such an approach depends on maintaining two sets S and G of maximally specific and maximally general rules that could account for all objects seen so far; these sets delimit all possible correct rules. However, when the rule is a decision tree over a large attribute space, the sizes of S and G will also become unmanageable. The line taken in ID3 is an iterative one which forms a succession of decision trees of (hopefully) increasing accuracy, until one is found that is entirely accurate. The method can be summarized as:

- select at random a subset of the given instances (called the *window*)
- *repeat*
    - ○ form a rule to explain the current window
    - ○ find the exceptions to this rule in the remaining instances
    - ○ form a new window from the current window and the exceptions to the rule generated from it

  until there are no exceptions to the rule

The process ends when a rule is formed that has no exceptions and so is correct for all of C. Two different ways of forming a new window have been tried. In the first, the current window is enlarged by the addition of up to some specified number of exceptions, and so the window grows. The second method attempts to identify "key" objects in the current window and replace the rest with exceptions, thus keeping the window size constant. Both methods were explored in trials with a non-trivial classification problem involving 14 attributes and nearly 2,000 objects for which a correct decision tree contained 48 nodes [Quinlan, 1979a]. The main findings were:

- The methods converge rapidly; typically only 4 iterations were required to find a correct decision tree.
- It was possible to develop a correct tree from a final window containing only a small fraction of the 2,000 objects.
- The process was not very sensitive to parameters such as the initial window size.
- The time to obtain a correct decision tree for a classification problem increases linearly with the difficulty of the problem as defined by the simple model given in the introduction.

These features, particularly the last, have enabled ID3 to discover correct decision trees for some very large classification problems.

15.3 THE LOST N-PLY EXPERIMENTS

One application of ID3 has been to discover classification rules for part of the end game (white) king-rook versus (black) king-knight. The relations completed are "knight's side is lost (in at most) n-ply" for n=2 and n=3; the 4-ply case is currently being tackled. The formal definition of "lost n-ply" is:

1. A black-to-move position is lost 0-ply if and only if
   a. the king is in checkmate, or
   b. the knight has been captured, the position is not stalemate, the white rook has not been captured and the black king cannot retaliate by capturing it.
2. A white-to-move position is lost n-ply (n odd) iff there is a white move giving a position that is lost n−1 ply.
3. A black-to-move position is lost n-ply (n even) iff all possible black moves give positions that are lost n−1 ply.

These definitions ignore the repetition and 50-move rules of chess, but are quite accurate for small values of n.

The obvious question is, why bother looking for classification rules when simple algorithms such as minimax will decide whether a position is lost n-ply? The answer is that a decision tree will classify a position in terms of its properties rather than by exploring the game tree. If attributes can be found that are adequate for this classification task and that are also relatively cheap to compute, then the classification of a position in terms of these attributes might well be faster than the minimax search of the game tree.

There are more than 11 million ways of placing the four pieces to form a legal black-to-move position; the corresponding figure for white-to-move is more than 9 million. (The difference arises because, for instance, the white king cannot be in check in a black-to-move position.) These counts include many symmetric variants of essentially the same position, and when these are removed the numbers become approximately 1.8 million and 1.4 million, respectively. About 69,000 of the 1.8 million black-to-move positions are lost 2-ply, while roughly 474,000 of the 1.4 million white-to-move positions are lost 3-ply.

The first attempt at the lost 2-ply relation was made with a set of 25 attributes. 18 of these were low-level geometric properties of a position, such as:

> the distance from the black king to the knight

with values "1", "2" and ">2" king-moves, and:

> the two kings are on opposite sides of and next to a row or column occupied by the rook

with values "true" and "false". The remaining 7 attributes were somewhat higher-level and involved more computation, for example:

> the only move the black king can make creates a mating square for the rook

The attribute space with $3^6 \times 2^{19}$ points was much larger than the number of black-to-move positions. However, many different positions led to the same vector of attribute values; and, in fact, the 1.8 million positions dwindled to just under 30,000 distinct vectors. An implementation of ID3 coded in Pascal for a DEC KL-10 found a correct decision tree of 334 nodes in 144 seconds.

A second attempt was made on this problem in order to try out a different style of attribute, and to remove a minor inadequacy of the first set of attributes affecting a handful of positions. Instead of being for the most part low-level and geometric, the new attributes were all high-level, truth-valued features signaling key patterns of pieces on the board. Each of the 23 attributes was meant to capture some important mechanism of the lost 2-ply classification task. For example, one of the attributes took the value "true" if the position was of one of the forms shown in Figure 15-6. This attribute was intended to detect some situations in which the black king cannot move safely. As expected, these new attributes were more directly pertinent to the classification problem than were their geometric predecessors. They had the effect of compressing all possible positions into a smaller set of 428 distinct vectors. The same implementation of ID3 found a decision tree containing 83 nodes in less than 3 seconds.

These trials resulted in two decision trees for classifying an arbitrary black-to-move position as lost 2-ply or not. Their performance was then compared to two other means of arriving at the same classification. The first of these was the minimax search mentioned previously, which simply mirrors the definition of lost n-ply. The second was a "smarter" classification method called *specialized search* which examines only part of the game tree. For instance, to determine whether a position is lost 1-ply we only have to consider white moves that capture the knight or white rook moves to the edge of the board (for a possible mate). Specialized search thus employs domain knowledge; it is harder to write and debug than minimax, but is much faster.

For the purposes of comparison, all methods were implemented in Pascal.

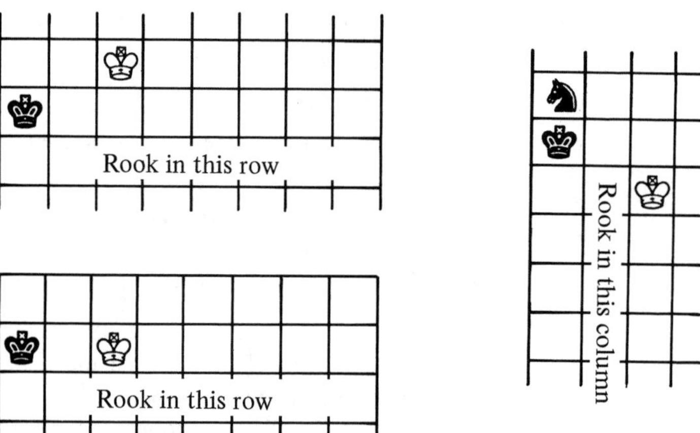

Figure 15-6: Chess board patterns used exemplifying classification attributes.

One thousand black-to-move positions were generated at random and each position classified by each method. Table 15-1 shows the average time required by each of them to classify a position on the DEC KL-10. Minimax was by far the slowest method, followed by specialized search. Both decision trees gave faster classifications, and the second significantly so—about 8 times faster than minimax. Given the relative sizes of the decision trees and the different styles of attribute, their performance was quite similar.

Table 15-1: Comparison of classification methods for lost 2-ply.

Classification Method	CPU Time (msec)
Minimax search	7.67
Specialized search	1.42
Using first decision tree	1.37
Using second decision tree	0.96

With these experiments complete, attention turned to the lost 3-ply relation. This was (as expected) harder than 2-ply because the patterns on the board that are used as attributes are further removed from the final outcome, and, whereas positions lost 2-ply make up less than 4% of all black-to-move positions, the 3-ply classes are more evenly balanced with 34% of all white-to-move positions lost.

The 49 attributes developed for 3-ply included both the types used for

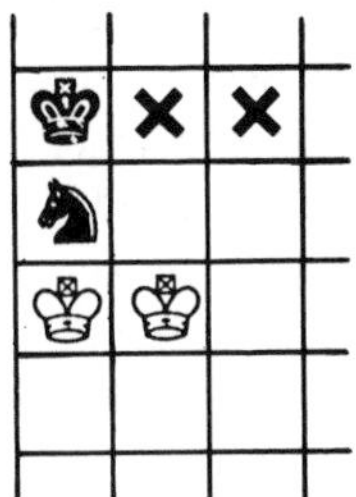

Figure 15-7: Instance of relevant classification pattern

2-ply. The majority of 35 were once more features signaling patterns on the board of special relevance to the classification task. An example is shown in Figure 15-7, where the white king could occupy either position shown, and the rook can move to some square in the same row as the black king, other than those marked X; this detects some cases in which the black king can be forced to move away from its knight. Four more attributes were geometric, such as flagging positions in which the white king is in check. The ten remaining attributes were predicates that, although complex, were based on simplified sequences of moves. For example, one of these predicates was:

> white rook is safe from reprisal 2-ply by the black king if white king takes the knight or threatens to do so

which was given by the approximation:

- the rook is more than two squares from the black king, or
- one blank square separates the rook from the black king, but the rook is either next to or threatens the knight, or
- the rook is next to the black king, but either the knight is also next to it or there is a square that is next to the white king, knight and rook.

The attributes were found to be adequate for the 3-ply classification task; in fact, it was subsequently noticed that a subset of 39 of them was adequate. They gave good compression, the 1.4 million white-to-move positions boiling down to 715 different vectors of attribute values. ID3 was run on a CDC Cyber 72 and found a correct decision tree of 177 nodes in 34 seconds.

Again, a variety of classification techniques for lost 3-ply was tried. The minimax search was similar to the previous one, and the specialized search was built on the 2-ply specialized search using additional rules such as:

- To decide whether a position is lost (not more than) 3-ply it is advisable to check first if it is lost 1-ply.
- In establishing whether a position is lost exactly 3-ply, white moves that capture the knight need not be considered.

One thousand white-to-move positions were generated randomly, and the average Cyber CPU time taken to classify them by the different methods appears in Table 15-2. Minimax search is now right out of contention, while the induction-generated tree is five times faster than specialized search.

For the lost n-ply task, it seems clear that, as n increases, the advantage of attribute-based classification over methods that search the game tree becomes more pronounced. When an adequate set of attributes has been found for the 4-ply case, this approach should give a classification method that is 15-20 times faster than specialized search.

Table 15-2: Comparison of classification methods for lost 3-ply.

Classification Method	CPU Time (msec)
Minimax search	285.0
Specialized search	17.5
Using decision tree	3.4

15.4 APPROXIMATE CLASSIFICATION RULES

The experiments reported in the previous section were aimed at producing decision trees covering the entire universe of possible positions. These decision trees were exact since they will classify correctly each object used in forming them, that is, each object in the universe. But what if size or the cost of examining it precludes the use of the entire universe in this way? This section looks at the accuracy of rules formed from partial information. It develops a model of the best performance that can be expected from any inductive inference scheme, and compares the predictions of this model to some experimental observations.

For a classification problem over some universe U of objects we will define "the" correct decision tree T to be one that classifies all objects in U without error and which contains fewest nodes of all such correct trees. Recall that an object x is classified by directing it to one of the leaves of the decision tree, where this leaf is labeled with the class to which x belongs. Any object will be directed to one and only one leaf, so we can denote by B_i the set of objects from U that will be mapped to the ith leaf of the correct tree T. The set of blocks B_i corresponding to the different leaves of T is then a partition of U.

Let us turn now to the problem of constructing an approximate decision tree by examining only some subset of U (commonly referred to as the *training set*). How much can we expect of whatever inductive inference system we use to form the approximate tree? Each block B_i can be thought of as delineating some subconcept in the classification. Clearly, no induction system can possibly identify this subconcept unless it sees at least one instance of it, or in other words, unless at least one element of B_i is included in the training set. We say, then, that an inductive inference system is *perfect* if, whenever the training set contains at least one object from B_i, the approximate decision tree that the induction system arrives at will classify correctly *all* objects from B_i. As defined in this way, perfection is indeed difficult to achieve.

Let a training set S containing N objects be selected at random (with replacement) from the universe U. When this training set is fed to such a perfect induction system, the output will be an approximate decision tree T^*. We now derive the probability P that an object x selected at random from U will be correctly classified by T^*. This will occur under either of the following conditions:

1. The training set S contains at least one object from the block B_i to which x belongs. By the perfection assumption T^* will be correct for all B_i and thus in particular for x.
2. The training set contains no such object. But each object will be assigned to some class, and it may happen that T^* fortuitously assigns x to its correct class, albeit for the wrong reason.

Let $p(B_i)$ denote the probability that a randomly-chosen object belongs to block B_i. The probability that S contains no object from the same block as x can be written as:

$$P_1 = \sum_i p(B_i) \times (1 - p(B_i))^N$$

where the summation is over all blocks. Again, let $p(c_j)$ denote the probability that an object chosen at random will be assigned by T^* to class c_j. We will assume that T^* is somehow representative of the universe U, in that the probability that an object chosen at random from U will belong to class c_j will also be $p(c_j)$. The probability that T^* will "guess" the correct classification for object x is then:

$$P_2 = \sum_j p(c_j)^2$$

Putting these together, the probability that an arbitrary object will be classified correctly by T^* is given by:

$$P = 1 - P_1 + P_1 \times P_2$$

Unfortunately this expression uses information which depends on knowing the correct decision tree T. The values of $p(c_j)$ can be estimated from the training set or by sampling, but the value of P_1 depends on the distribution of $p(B_i)$ over the leaves of T. However, if we examine a term of P_1:

$$p(B_i) \times (1 - p(B_i))^N$$

we see that its value is small no matter what the value of $p(B_i)$. In fact it reaches its maximum value when:

$$\frac{d}{d\,p(B_i)}\, p(B_i) \times (1 - p(B_i))^N = 0$$

which occurs when:

$$p(B_i) = 1 / (N+1)$$

So we can set an upper bound on P_1 by replacing each term in the summation with its maximum possible value of:

$$N^N / (N+1)^{N+1}$$

For all but small N the value of:

$$N^N / (N+1)^N$$

approaches $1/e$, and so each term is approximately:

$$1 / (2.72\ N)$$

The result is that

$$P_1 = |B| / (2.72\ N) - d$$

where $|B|$ is the number of blocks B_i and d is a positive error term. Substituting in the above expression for P gives:

$$P = 1 - (|B| / 2.72\ N) \times (1 - \sum_j p(c_j)^2) + d'$$

where again d' is positive. Ignoring d' we have a lower bound on the probability that an arbitrary object will be classified by the approximate tree T^*. This expression still involves the number of blocks $|B|$, but this is the number of leaves of T and can be estimated, for example, from the number of leaves on T^*.

The purpose of the preceding analysis is to establish a relationship between the size of the training set and the accuracy of the approximate tree derived from it, in a form that sidesteps the underlying structure of the universe—that is, the way objects are organized into blocks. For small values of N the results are unremarkable. The interest centers on cases where N is very large, even though it may be only a small fraction of the size of the universe. Consider an example of one million objects belonging to two equiprobable classes where the correct tree contains 100 leaves. If 10,000 objects (only 1% of the universe) is given as a training set to a perfect induction system, the analysis predicts that the resulting approximate tree will correctly classify more than 99% of all objects, no matter how awkward the distribution of objects among the blocks B_i. Moreover, the model predicts that the error rate of the approximate tree is independent of how many objects are in the universe!

A number of experiments was conducted to test the above results. These consisted of forming approximate decision trees for the knight's side lost 3-ply relation from training sets of various sizes. The universe was the set of canonical white-to-move positions numbering 1.4 million of which 474,000 belong to the class "lost". The earlier experiments had produced an exact decision tree for this problem which contained 88 leaves, so the number of leaves on "the" correct tree was known to be at most 88. The constants relevant to the analysis were thus:

$$|B| \leq 88$$

and

$$\sum_j p(c_j)^2 = 0.55$$

For each experiment, a training set of predetermined size was selected at random from all possible white-to-move positions. The set of attribute vectors corresponding to these positions was then passed to ID3 which formed a decision tree from them alone. This approximate tree was tested on a different set of 10,000 positions also selected at random. Each test position was classified by both the correct and approximate decision trees and differences noted. The number of such errors detected was compared with the expected maximum number of errors predicted by the model, i.e., $(1-P) * 10{,}000$. The figures appear in Table 15-3. For example, the middle line concerns the case in which the training set contained 5,000 positions or 0.36% of the universe. The approximate tree derived from these positions proved accurate for all but 8 of the 10,000 test positions. The model predicts that the probability of a correct classification in this case exceeds 0.9971 which would give an expected maximum of 29 errors over the 10,000 trials. In each case in Table 15-3, the observed number of errors was compatible with the predicted bound, although the bound is conservative for smaller values of N. (For very large values of N, all distributions of $p(B_i)$ give a value of P_1 which is near zero; the differences between the actual distribution and the maximally unhelpful one used for the model result in smaller variations of P, so the predicted bound might be expected to become tighter.)

As an aside, the fact that the observed error rates for approximate trees found by ID3 are close to the bounds of the hypothetical perfect induction system is indirect evidence that ID3 is not performing too badly!

Table 15-3: Comparison of observed and predicted error rates with different training set sizes.

Size of training set	Percentage of whole universe	Errors in 10,000 trials	Predicted maximum errors
200	0.01%	199	728
1,000	0.07%	33	146
5,000	0.36%	8	29
25,000	1.79%	7	6
125,000	8.93%	2	1

15.5 SOME THOUGHTS ON DISCOVERING ATTRIBUTES

The work on lost n-ply relations supports the view that almost all the effort (for a non chess-player, at least) must be devoted to finding attributes that are adequate for the classification problem being tackled. The second set for lost 2-ply required three weeks to define, while the 3-ply attributes consumed nearly 2 man-months. In either case, once the attributes had been specified and the description of the positions in terms of them had been computed, ID3 made short work of finding a correct decision tree.

An attempt is currently under way as part of the 4-ply work to find some attributes automatically. In particular, a search is being made for attributes based on patterns of pieces on the board, as two-thirds of the attributes used for lost 3-ply are of this type. The hypothesis is that such patterns can be discovered by generalizing on individual positions known to be lost 4-ply. The method has been to select a single such *seed* position that is lost exactly 4-ply and subject it to three forms of generalization.

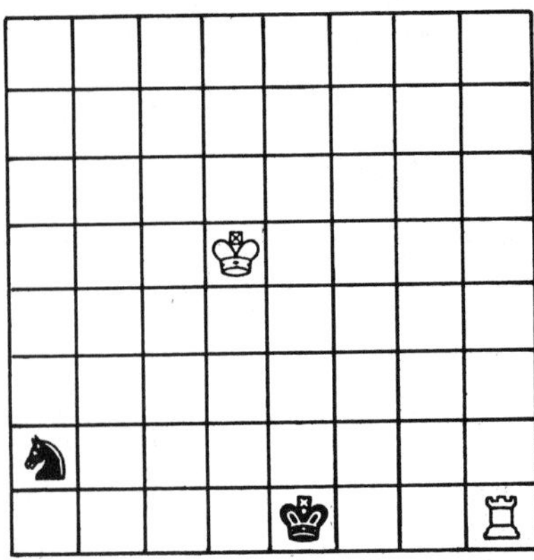

Figure 15-8: Exemplary winning position.

The first and most powerful form is to decide that one or more of the pieces in the seed position are probably irrelevant to what is going on in that position, and to discard them from the pattern. Consider, for example, the position shown in Figure 15-8. There, the black king must move out of check, and the rook can then skewer the king and knight, capturing the latter at its next move. The whereabouts of the white king has no bearing on this outcome and so that piece can be dropped from the pattern. The effect is to make this pattern match any position with the rook, black king and knight as shown, no matter where the white king happens to be. The method for deciding that this sort of generalization is appropriate starts by looking in a file of positions lost exactly 4-ply for those that have three of the four pieces in the same places as they occupy in the seed position. For each such position F that has all pieces except p occupying the same places, a set of places L(p) for p is augmented by adding the place occupied by p in F. After a complete scan of the file, L(knight) for example contains a set of places the knight can occupy such that, if the other pieces are unchanged the position will still be lost 4-ply. Now consider the hypothesis that piece p is truly irrelevant to the fact that the seed position is lost. From the piece p, the seed position, and the makeup of the file, it is possible to estimate the number of positions that should have been found in the file under this hypothesis. If the size of L(p) is sufficiently close to this number, then the hypothesis is judged to have been confirmed and piece p is discarded from the pattern. One very significant feature found in this way is shown in Figure 15-9, where the rook and black king have been deemed irrelevant. This does not mean that *all* such positions are lost 4-ply, but rather that the presence of this pattern is a relevant indicator when classifying a position. In fact, more than 10% of all positions lost exactly 4-ply are of this form, so it is a useful feature indeed!

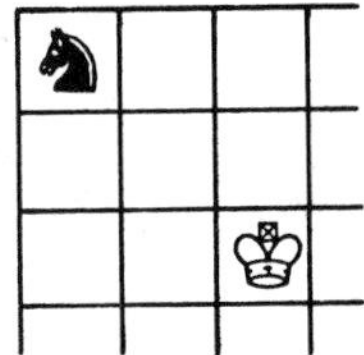

Figure 15-9: Highly useful partial pattern.

The second form of generalization is to allow pieces to occupy one of a number of places on the board. We know already that any one piece p can be at any of the places in L(p) without affecting the lost status of the seed position. The idea here is to check whether more than one piece can simultaneously be treated in the same way, and is again determined by counting. Suppose for example we find the number of positions in the file which have the two kings in the same places as in the seed, but where the knight is anywhere in L(knight) and the rook occupies any place in L(rook). If this number is close to the expected proportion of the product of the sizes of L(knight) and L(rook), the places occupied by these pieces may both be generalized. One pattern found this way is shown in Figure 15-10, where the white king has been dropped as before, and the rook and black king may occupy any of the indicated places. This feature accounts for nearly 4% of all positions lost exactly 4-ply.

The final generalization form is to allow patterns of pieces to be shifted over the board, preserving their interrelationship rather than their actual places. The shifting may or may not require that the pattern of pieces maintain some constant distance from one edge of the board. We start with the seed position from which the pieces thought to be irrelevant have been excluded, and see how

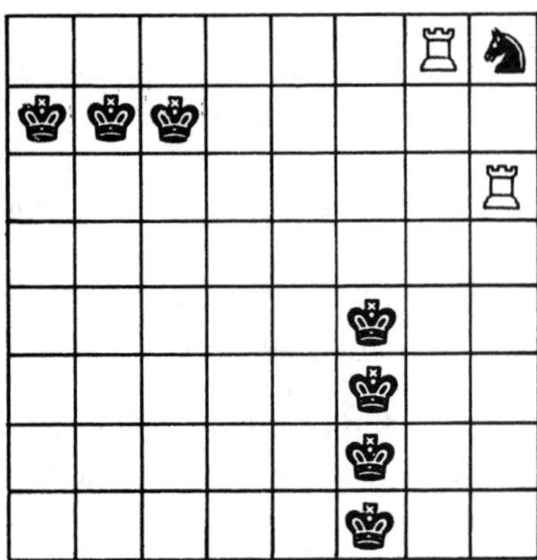

Figure 15-10: Feature indicating 4% of 4-ply losses by black.

often a similar configuration obtainable by a row or column shift occurs in the file of positions. If the number of row-shifted alternatives found is comparable with the number expected under the hypothesis that all such alternatives are also lost 4-ply, the hypothesis is accepted; the case for columns is handled in the same way. One attribute discovered by this means is the one shown in Figure 15-11, which can be slid along the edge, and accounts for about 1% of all lost 4-ply positions.

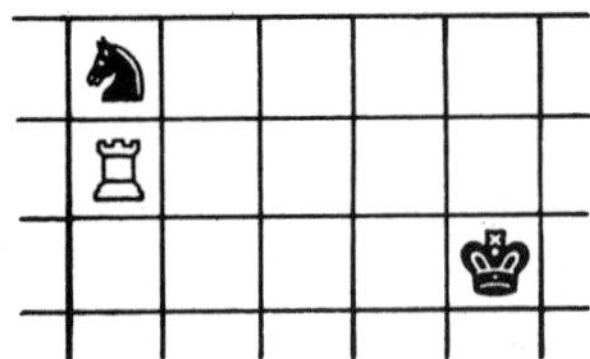

Figure 15-11: Attribute accounting for 1% of 4-ply losses by black.

The major weaknesses of this approach to attribute generation come from the way patterns are represented. There seems to be no easy method of combining the second and third forms of generalization, to allow for situations where one or more pieces may occupy more than one place and where the whole pattern can then be moved around the board. Nor is it possible yet to specify patterns containing two separate interactions that can be shifted independently of each other. An example would be those positions that contain both of the attributes shown in Figure 15-12.

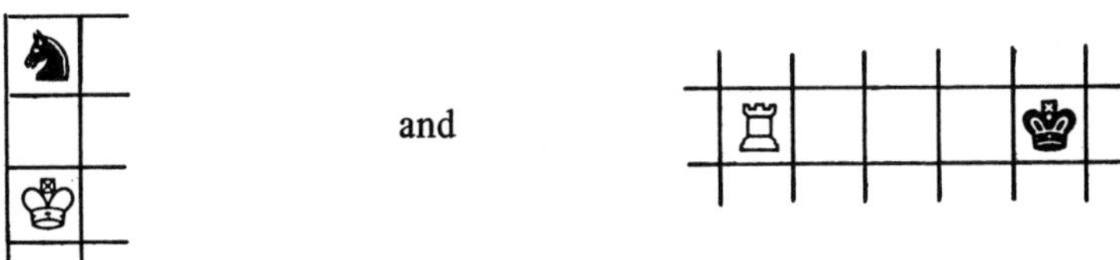

Figure 15-12: Possible disjunctive generalization.

Finally, the attributes of this pattern-based kind used in the 2-ply and 3-ply work were each built up of a number of alternative patterns of the above kind. No way has yet been devised of deciding that a set of discovered patterns are all relevant to the same mechanism and thus ought to be amalgamated into a single attribute.

15.6 CONCLUSION

The long-term goal for all this work is the discovery, with as little human intervention as possible, of a very high-performance rule for a complex relation. This process will commence with the derivation of powerful and relevant attributes from an inspection of examples, and proceed to the development of an exact decision tree couched in terms of these attributes. If the resulting tree can be shown to provide a classification method that is orders of magnitude faster than any alternative mechanism, these experiments will have established the feasibility of a machine learning approach to at least some aspects of automatic programming.

ACKNOWLEDGMENTS

I gratefully acknowledge the importance of suggestions made by Donald Michie, and of the resources provided by Stanford and Sydney Universities.

REFERENCES

Bratko, I. and Mulec, P., "An experiment in automatic learning of diagnostic rules," *Informatika*, 1981.

Dietterich, T. G. and Michalski, R. S., "Learning and generalization of characteristic descriptions: evaluation criteria and comparative review of selected methods," *Sixth International Joint Conference on Artificial Intelligence*, IJCAI, Tokyo, Japan, pp. 223-231, August 1979.

Hayes-Roth, F. and McDermott, J., "Knowledge acquisition from structural descriptions," *Proceedings of the Fifth International Joint Conference on Artificial Intelligence*, IJCAI, Cambridge, Mass., pp. 356-362, August 1977.

Hunt, E. B., Marin, J. and Stone, P. T., *Experiments in Induction*, Academic Press, New York, 1966.

Kopec, D. and Niblett, T., "How hard is the play of the King-Rook King-Knight ending?," *Advances in Computer Chess, volume 2*, Clarke, M.R.B. (Ed.), Edinburgh University Press, 1980.

Michalski, R. S., "Pattern recognition as rule-guided inductive inference," *IEEE Transactions on Pattern Analysis and Machine Intelligence*, Vol. PAMI-2, No. 4, pp. 349-361, 1980a.

Mitchell, T. M., "An analysis of generalization as a search problem," *Sixth International Joint Conference on Artificial Intelligence*, Tokyo, Japan, August 1979.

Quinlan, J. R., "Induction over large data bases", Technical Report Report HPP-79-14, Heuristic Programming Project, Stanford University, 1979.

Quinlan, J. R., "Discovering rules from large collections of examples: a case study," *Expert Systems in the Micro Electronic Age*, Michie, D. (Ed.), Edinburgh University Press, Edinburgh, 1979.

Quinlan, J. R., "Semi-autonomous acquisition of pattern-based knowledge," *Australian Computer Bulletin*, April 1980, (also to appear in Michie, D. (ed.), *Machine Intelligence 10*, Halsted Press, 1982).

Shapiro, A. and Niblett, T., "Automatic Induction of classification rules for a chess endgame," *Advances in Computer Chess, volume 3*, Clarke, M.R.B. (Ed.), Edinburgh University Press, 1982.

Vere, S. A., "Inductive learning of relational productions," *Pattern-Directed Inference Systems*, Waterman, D. A. and Hayes-Roth, F. (Eds.), Academic Press, New York, 1978.

16

INFERRING STUDENT MODELS FOR INTELLIGENT COMPUTER-AIDED INSTRUCTION

Derek H. Sleeman
University of Leeds, U.K.

ABSTRACT

The ability to formulate students' models automatically is a critical component of intelligent teaching systems. This chapter reports current progress on inducing models of simple algebraic skills from observed student performance in the context of the Leeds Modeling System (LMS). A model consists of an ordered production system with potentially incorrect variants of some rules (called *mal-rules*). Constraining the number of plausible models that account for the observed student problem-solving behavior has proved to be a major undertaking. First, the current rule-based formulation is presented. Its shortcomings are indicated and a revised analysis is given which is demonstrated to create a complete and non-redundant set of models. Second, the related issue of generating a minimal problem template is discussed. Such a template represents the simplest type of problem that insures all rules in a model are exercised. Finally, the significance of this type of analysis for other areas of AI is indicated.

16.1 INTRODUCTION

The area of Intelligent Teaching Systems (ITS) has two major aims; the practical aim of producing teaching systems that are truly responsive to the needs of the student, and the theoretical (AI) interest involved in using algorithms to formulate this activity. Hartley and Sleeman [1973] have argued that an intelligent teaching system requires access to the following information:

- knowledge of the problem domain
- a student model

- a list of teaching operations
- means-ends guidance rules that relate teaching decisions to conditions in the student model

In this chapter, I outline the issues involved in inferring a model which describes a student's performance on a set of tasks, and then I discuss some of the problems which have to be faced if the number of models generated is not to be an exponential function of the number of rules in the model.

During the last decade a number of systems have been implemented that include some or all of the above databases. In particular, during the last five years a primary focus of ITS has been to provide supportive learning environments intended to facilitate *learning-by-doing*. These systems, which include SOPHIE [Brown *et al.*, 1982], GUIDON [Clancey, 1982], WEST [Burton & Brown, 1982], WUMPUS [Goldstein, 1982] PSM-NMR [Sleeman & Hendley, 1982], provide problem-solving and tutoring capabilities. The above systems have been developed and tested in the following areas: debugging electronic circuits; medical diagnosis; a game that draws upon the student's knowledge of arithmetic; a game that similarly draws upon his power of logical inference; and a system that gives practice with a non-deterministic (backtracking) algorithm. Each of these systems has tended to emphasize some aspects of the whole design and to neglect others. Thus it is not surprising that the designers have never been fully satisfied with the performance of their systems; the following are some of the acknowledged shortcomings:

- The instructional material produced in response to a student's query or mistake is often at the wrong level of detail, as the system assumes too much or too little knowledge.
- Most tutoring systems are capable of solving problems in only one or two prescribed ways. For instance GUIDON has to use the backchaining control structure of MYCIN, rather than following other equally valid medical diagnosis procedures. As a result of this constraint, the system coerces a user's performance into its own conceptual framework.
- The tutoring and critiquing strategies used by these systems are excessively *ad hoc*, reflecting unprincipled intuitions about the role of a tutor.
- User interaction remains too restrictive, thereby limiting the student's ability to express himself (and thereby limiting the tutor's diagnostic mechanisms).

In an attempt to design more powerful systems, researchers in the area of intelligent teaching systems are now addressing the following issues:[1]

---

[1]For a more detailed discussion of these issues please see the introductory essay to *Intelligent Tutoring Systems* [Sleeman & Brown, 1982]. Also note that many of the papers in that volume address various aspects of the student modeling problem.

- Performing detailed protocol analysis of learning and mislearning.
- Developing representations of knowledge for use with ITS's which may also provide psychological insights.
- Developing and evolving AI techniques, in particular:
  - implementing friendly interfaces,
  - handling incomplete/inconsistent databases, and
  - inferring student models by "observing" the student's responses to sets of problems.

In common with the BUGGY system [Brown & Burton, 1978], the Leeds Modeling System, LMS, addresses the issue of inferring student models and uses a generative mechanism to create hypotheses/models from primitives. Without a generative facility, the ability of a system to model complex, and possibly error-prone, behavior is severely limited; this point is well argued by Carbonell [1970]. However, the use of such a mechanism also causes difficulties as such an algorithm can readily lead to a combinatorial explosion, where given N primitives, N! models are produced.[2] BUGGY uses a collection of primitive bugs from which to generate models; LMS uses domain rules and corresponding mal-rules, (incorrect) rules, which have been observed in the analysis of earlier protocols. On the other hand, whereas BUGGY uses a series of *heuristics* to limit the size of its search space, a major feature of the LMS work has been the formulation of a *systematic* search so as to focus on particular rule(s). As will be demonstrated, this technique drastically reduces the number of models that must be considered at each stage.[3]

LMS has been implemented as two subsystems. The first, the offline phase, generates a complete set of models (using the algorithms discussed below), and retains those models which give unique results with the predefined problem sets. The second phase is the online modeling system which uses the data generated by the offline phase to determine whether the student's behavior falls within the space defined by the rules and mal-rules. (Students who display inconsistent behavior or unanticipated "bugs", are not matched by this algorithm, and are reported as exhibiting inconsistent behavior.) Usually students start at the first level, and modeling continues until the problem sets are exhausted or the number of correct solutions on a particular problem set falls below some predefined threshold. (The "results" would be, respectively, a consistent model, or a statement that the student's behavior was inconsistent. See [Sleeman, 1982] for more details of the interactive phase and the results of an experiment.)

---

[2]This assumes that each model must contain N primitives; the number is much greater if *all* models are generated.

[3]Initially, we made the assumption that the domain was hierarchical and so we have referred to the stages as *levels*; and thus modeling proceeds by first considering level 1, then 2, and so on. Further, the model at level N contains *all* the rules in the level N−1 model *and* the newly introduced rule.

LMS provides extensive data for the human teacher/tutor. Note that, initially I was concerned with implementing a diagnostic system, namely a system which provided diagnostic models, and only more recently have I asked whether these models can provide insights into the cognitive processes used by the student [Sleeman, unpublished, 1982].

In this paper I review the initial formulation of LMS-I [Sleeman & Smith, 1981], together with the results of an experiment which led to the discovery of some inadequacies [Sleeman, 1982]; the body of the paper is taken up with the reformulation of the search to accommodate these points. Before considering details of these formulations, we briefly review the production system, PS, representation which LMS uses for student models, and explain the main features of the PS interpreter used to "execute" these models.

16.1.1 A Production System Representation for Domain Knowledge

Table 16-1a gives a set of production rules which are sufficient to solve linear algebraic equations. Table 16-1b gives a set of mal-rules for this domain which have been observed in protocols analyzed earlier and Table 16-1c shows pairs of correct and "buggy" models executing typical tasks.

In this work a model is an ordered list of rules. Order is significant because the interpreter executes the action of the first rule in the model whose conditions are satisfied by the problem state. Moreover, the PS interpreter being used searches from left to right; this search is terminated and the associated action is carried out when a rule's conditions are satisfied. (Thus, if a problem state was such that ADDSUB could fire twice, the interpreter always fires on the left-hand pattern first.) In this way we are able to capture algebraic precedence. The cycle of matching patterns and executing actions continues until no further rules fire.

Table 16-1: Rules and mal-rules in student models.

RULE NAME	LEVEL	CONDITION-SET	ACTION
FIN2	1	(SHD X = M/N)	(SHD (M N)) or (SHD evaluated)
SOLVE	2	(SHD M * X = N)	(SHD X = N/M) or (SHD INFINITY)
ADDSUB	3	(lhs M +|− N rhs)	(lhs [evaluated] rhs)
MULT	4	(lhs M * N rhs)	(lhs [evaluated] rhs)
XADDSUB	5	(lhs M*X +|− N*X rhs)	(lhs (M +|− N) * X rhs)
NTORHS	6	(lhs +|− M = rhs)	(lhs = rhs −|+ M)
REARRANGE	7	(lhs +|− M +|− N*X rhs)	(lhs +|− N*X +|− M rhs)
XTOLHS	8	(lhs = +|− M*X rhs)	(lhs −|+ M*X = rhs)
BRA1	9	(lhs < N > rhs)	(lhs N rhs)
BRA2	10	(lhs M * <N*X +|− P> rhs)	(lhs M*N*X +|− M*P rhs)

M, N and P are integers, lhs, rhs, *etc.*, are general patterns (which may be null), +|− means either + or − may occur, SHD indicates the String Head, and < and > represent standard "algebraic brackets".

a) Rules for the algebra domain (evaluative form and slightly stylized).

RULE NAME	LEVEL	CONDITION-SET	ACTION
MSOLVE	2	(SHD M*X = N)	(SHD X = M/N) or (SHD INFINITY)
MNTORHS	6	(lhs +|− M = rhs)	(lhs = rhs +|− M)
M2NTORHS	6	(lhs1 +|− M lhs2 = rhs)	(lhs1 +|− lhs2 = rhs +|− M)
M3NTORHS	6	(lhs1 +|− M lhs2 = rhs)	(lhs1 +|− lhs2 = rhs +|− M)
MXTOLHS	8	(lhs = +|− M*X rhs)	(lhs +|− M*X = rhs)
M1BRA2	10	(lhs M * <N*X +|− P> rhs)	(lhs M*N*X +|− P rhs)
M2BRA2	10	(lhs M * <N*X +|− P> rhs)	(lhs M*N*X +|− M +|− P rhs)

b) Some mal-rules for the domain (using the same conventions as above).

	2X = 3 * 4 + 5		2X = 3 * 4 + 5
MULT	2X = 12 + 5	ADDSUB	2X = 3 * 9
ADDSUB	2X = 17	MULT	2X = 27
SOLVE	X = 17/2	SOLVE	X = 27/2
FIN2	(17/2)	FIN2	(27/2)

i) Shows (MULT ADDSUB SOLVE FIN2) and (ADDSUB MULT SOLVE FIN2) solving 2X = 3 * 4 + 5.

	2X + 5 = 9		2X + 5 = 9
NTORHS	2X = 9−5	MNTORHS	2X = 9 + 5
ADDSUB	2X = 4	ADDSUB	2X = 14
SOLVE	X = 2/1	SOLVE	X = 7/1
FIN2	(2)	FIN2	(7)

ii) Shows (NTORHS ADDSUB SOLVE FIN2) and (MNTORHS ADDSUB SOLVE FIN2) solving 2X + 5 = 9.

c) Pairs of correct and "buggy" models executing typical tasks.
(The first line gives the initial state and all subsequent lines give the rule which fires, and the resulting state.)

16.2 GENERATING A COMPLETE AND NON-REDUNDANT SET OF MODELS

In order to generate a concise set of student models, Sleeman and Smith [1981] developed the SELECTIVE algorithm. In this algorithm only one new rule was added to a model at each stage, and further, it was assumed that if the student used the "new" rule correctly when it was first introduced, then the student would use it correctly with all subsequent problem types. In a recent field trial using LMS [Sleeman, 1982], this assumption was often violated. Removing this assumption involves only a minor change to LMS's code but means that the search space of potential models increases substantially. Hence, I was forced to reconsider the algorithm used to generate models at each level. I refer to the revised modeler as LMS-II.

The appendix presents several examples of the SELECTIVE algorithm; although several heuristics were used, many of the models gave the same results with many of their problem set. A more detailed analysis of the rules indicated that it is possible to predict that different models will yield the same behavior, and hence, in many instances, reduce the number of redundant models generated. The following classification of the condition part of rules has been evolved.

Subsume. Rule R1 is said to subsume R2, if R1's condition set is an ordered subset of R2's conditions. The effect of R1 being placed before R2 is that the production system would act as if R2 did not occur. Throughout this analysis, the order of the conditions within the condition set is significant. For example, whereas condition set [C1 C2] would subsume [C1 C2 C3], [C2 C1] would not.[4] Condition sets for such a pair of rules from the arithmetic domain are as follows:

ADD NUM + NUM
PADD < NUM + NUM

(where < is the usual left-hand "algebraic" bracket, used to change the order of the evaluation of an algebraic expression). Similarly, in this domain ADDSUB subsumes REARRANGE (see Table 16-1 and Table 16-5).

In practice, we need more complex conditions, like:

NUMBER BUT NOT 1

Such conditions further reduce the number of models generated, and so this analysis gives an *upper* bound on the number of models to be considered.[5]

Potential Interaction Between Rules. Suppose the condition set of Rule

---

[4]Note carefully this use of "subsume". We are using "subsume" only to discuss static rule conditions, not traces of the model.

[5]These redundancies and those caused by numerical degeneracy are picked up by the off-line phase which evaluates all the generated models against the tasks for the various levels.

3, R3, is [C2 C3 C4 STR1], and the condition set of Rule 4, R4, is [STR2 C3 C4 C5] where the STRi are arbitrary strings of conditions, including null, then both rules would be able to fire if the problem presented contained a pattern of the form:

C2 C3 C4 C5

As I am dealing with production rules in which the order of the conditions is significant, the order of the rules within the model determines which rule fires first. Hence such a pattern would potentially discriminate between the models (...R3...R4...) and (...R4...R3...). Whether or not the example problem discriminates depends on the *actions* of the two rules. An example of such a pair of rules is:

ADDSUB NUM +|− NUM
MULT NUM * NUM

The discriminatory patterns, which I shall also refer to as overlap patterns, in this case are:

NUM +|− NUM * NUM
NUM * NUM +|− NUM

(As explained in Table 16-1, +|− matches either the literal '+' or the literal '−', and NUM matches any integer.) A subalgorithm, called INTERACT/SUBSUME applies the previous definitions to determine independence, interaction or subsumption between ordered sets of rules.

Non-interacting, or Order-independent, Rules. Rules do not interact if their ordered condition sets do not overlap. For example, if the conditions of R5 are C1 C2 C3 and of R6 are C1 C2 C4, then these would not fire on the same input.

Note that subsumption, and failure to interact, can be determined by inspection of the condition parts of the rules. However, potential interaction or conflict depends critically on the problem considered, and so must be decided with respect to each problem type. I will now consider the algorithm based on the above analysis.

16.2.1 An Algorithm for Generating Complete and Non-Redundant Models

The task of creating a complete and non-redundant set of models from primitives is analogous to that performed by the DENDRAL algorithm that creates a comprehensive and non-redundant set of isomers given a molecular formula [Buchanan *et al.*, 1971]. The algorithm for generating models has three parts.

1. Start with the set of rules that solve algebra problems correctly at a given level, that is, the ideal student model for that level. Then add the

mal-rule[6] variants to each rule in the model. For example, the ideal student for level 4 is:

(MULT ADDSUB SOLVE FIN2)

When all the rules are retrieved this gives:

((MULT) (ADDSUB) (SOLVE MSOLVE) (FIN2))

2. Generate all configurations from this data structure:

   (MULT ADDSUB SOLVE FIN2)

   (MULT ADDSUB MSOLVE FIN2)

3. Apply the INTERACTION/SUBSUME subalgorithm to the configurations generated in the previous step. The subalgorithm separates the rules in the configuration into those which may interact and those which cannot. Next, the subalgorithm returns a complete set of all relevant (interactive) rule orderings, to each of which is added the rules that do not interact. Finally, the models are scanned to remove subsumed rules. For the configuration we are considering, this algorithm returns four models:[7]

   (MULT ADDSUB SOLVE FIN2)
   (ADDSUB MULT SOLVE FIN2)
   (MULT ADDSUB MSOLVE FIN2)
   (ADDSUB MULT MSOLVE FIN2)

Table 16-2 demonstrates the enhanced modeler's ability to detect errors in rules first introduced at "earlier" levels. (This table is purely illustrative and so there is only a single problem per level.)

One of the major concerns in generating student models has been the size of the search space. As Sleeman and Smith [1981] pointed out, the number of potential combinations of rules is vast. In that paper we analyzed the size of the search space in some detail; I provide a summary here, before discussing the extensions. This original analysis considered all models containing from 1 to R domain rules, and assumed that each rule had M erroneous alternatives, or mal-rules. This is the basis for the EXHAUSTIVE algorithm that enumerates all possible models composed of R rules or mal-rule variants. The EXHAUSTIVE-GROUPED algorithm assumes that one knows the grouping between the rules and associated mal-rules, and hence this algorithm selects a rule, or one of the associated mal-rules, and then creates all possible orderings. In the SELECTIVE algorithm the models for the $L+1^{th}$ level are based on the model that is deemed to explain the student's behavior at level L. (Recall that this formulation as-

[6]A mal-rule is an incorrect variant of a rule which has been noted in an earlier protocol. MSOLVE is a mal-rule of SOLVE.

[7]A rule set whose order does not have any significance is referred to as a configuration; whereas a rule set whose order is significant is referred to as an ordered configuration, or model.

Table 16-2: A section of a student protocol with LMS-II where the mal-rules are "in scope" at subsequent levels. (Explanatory comments are preceded by a semicolon.)

THIS IS THE ALGEBRA SYSTEM.

THE LEVEL IS 1
**Modeling OK–AT THIS LEVEL

THE LEVEL IS 2
SOLVE (3 * X = 9)
> **X = 3/9**
IS THAT WHAT YOU INTENDED (Yes/No)> **Yes**
THANK YOU.. YOU GOT 0 OUT OF 1 RIGHT
**THE STUDENT BEHAVES AS MODEL ((MSOLVE FIN2))
;The student "inverted" the answer and hence behaved as predicted by MSOLVE.

THE LEVEL IS 3
SOLVE (5 * X = 8 + 2)
> **X = 5/10**
IS THAT WHAT YOU INTENDED (Yes/No)> **Yes**
THANK YOU.. YOU GOT 0 OUT OF 1 RIGHT
**THE STUDENT BEHAVES AS MODEL ((ADDSUB MSOLVE FIN2))
;The student "inverted" the answer and hence behaved as predicted by MSOLVE.

THE LEVEL IS 4
SOLVE (5 * X = 3 * 3 + 1)
> **X = 5/12**
IS THAT WHAT YOU INTENDED (Yes/No)> **Yes**
THANK YOU.. YOU GOT 0 OUT OF 1 RIGHT
**THE STUDENT BEHAVES AS MODEL ((ADDSUB MULT MSOLVE FIN2))
;The student appears to have both an error in his precedence rules *and* "inverted" the answer.

THE LEVEL IS 5
SOLVE (2 * X + 4 * X = 12)
> **X = 6/12**
IS THAT WHAT YOU INTENDED (Yes/No)> **Yes**
THANK YOU.. YOU GOT 0 OUT OF 1 RIGHT
**THE STUDENT BEHAVES AS MODEL ((MULT ADDSUB XADDSUB MSOLVE FIN2))
;The student "inverted" the answer and hence behaved as predicted by MSOLVE.

THE LEVEL IS 6
SOLVE (2 * X + 4 * X + 4 = 16)
> **X = 6/20**
IS THAT WHAT YOU INTENDED (Yes/No)> **Yes**
THANK YOU.. YOU GOT 0 OUT OF 1 RIGHT
**THE STUDENT BEHAVES AS MODEL ((MULT ADDSUB MNTORHS XADDSUB MSOLVE FIN2))
;The student appears to have taken a number across to the RHS *without* changing the sign *and* "inverted" the answer.

THE LEVEL IS 7
SOLVE (4 + 2 * X + 2 * X = 16)
> **X = 2**
IS THAT WHAT YOU INTENDED (Yes/No)> **Yes**
THANK YOU.. YOU GOT 0 OUT OF 1 RIGHT
**THE STUDENT BEHAVES AS MODEL ((ADDSUB MULT REARRANGE NTORHS
XADDSUB SOLVE FIN2))
;This answer can be explained if one assumes the student has processed 4 + 2 * X to give 6 * X.
;A naive explanation is that he accords ADDSUB too high a precedence.

sumes that if a student does not make an error with rule L at the level at which it is introduced, then this rule will be used correctly at all subsequent levels.) In [Sleeman & Smith, 1981] we compared the number of configurations generated by the EXHAUSTIVE, the EXHAUSTIVE-GROUPED, and the SELECTIVE algorithms. The number of configurations are not directly comparable, however, for the following reasons:

1. The EXHAUSTIVE and EXHAUSTIVE-GROUPED algorithms allow mal-rules to be in "scope"—that is, accessible at all subsequent levels, but the SELECTIVE algorithm does not.
2. In all cases the number of mal-rules for each level is assumed to be constant, that is, we quoted the number of configurations which arise when M=0, M=1, M=2, and so on, at all levels; but in practice, the value of M varies at each level.

Taking these points into consideration for the EXHAUSTIVE algorithm at level L gives:

$$(L + \sum_{1 \le s \le L} Ms)\,!\ :\ \sum_{1 \le s \le L} Ms\,! \qquad (1)$$

models, where Ms is the number of mal-rules at level s. For the EXHAUSTIVE-GROUPED algorithm at level L there are

$$\mathbf{P}_{1 \le s \le L}\ (1+Ms)\times L! \qquad (2)$$

models. (Note that in Equation (2) the first term gives the number of configurations, whereas the whole expression gives the number of ordered configurations, or models.) For the SELECTIVE algorithm at level L there are

$$L\times(1+Ml) \qquad (3)$$

models.

The ANALYSIS-OF-CONDITIONS (global mal-rule) algorithm considers all configurations in which rule order is significant and further allows mal-rules to be in "scope" at the level at which the rule is first introduced and *all* subsequent levels; the ANALYSIS-OF-CONDITIONS (local mal-rule) algorithm again considers all possible interactions of the rules, but allows the mal-rules to occur only at the level the rule is introduced. This latter variant is only really included for completeness, since it has the disadvantage of having localized mal-rules. Both the global and local ANALYSIS-OF-CONDITIONS algorithms use the complete and non-redundant model-generation algorithm; indeed the latter merely provide the appropriate data (the ideal student models, and the data on rule interaction and subsumption) for the complete algorithm.

The analysis for the global ANALYSIS-OF-CONDITIONS algorithm is somewhat more complex. From Equation (2), above we know there are:

$$\mathbf{P}_{1 \le s \le L}\ (1 + Ms) \qquad (4a)$$

or NM, configurations. To determine the number of models, the

INTERACTION/SUBSUME subalgorithm is applied to each of these configurations. The number of models generated from a configuration is a function of the number of interacting rule pairs, IP, and the number of rules involved in the interacting pairs, IR; an algebraic expression for this function can be formulated in some cases, but its value is always in the range 1 to IR!. (This formulation is very general and allows both rules and their associated mal-rules to interact with other rules or mal-rules.) The total number of models generated is thus:

$$\sum_{1 \leq c \leq NM} f(IPc,\ IRc) \tag{4b}$$

Section 16.2.2 discusses the worst and best values for the function, f. Equation (4a) corresponds to the second stage of the complete and non-redundant model generation algorithm, and Equation (4b) to the third. Table 16-3 gives the number of configurations which arise with the various algorithms.

As we can correlate the mal-rules together with the rules from which they were derived, it is unlikely that the EXHAUSTIVE algorithm would ever be required. So far, the number of configurations for the SELECTIVE algorithm is consistently the lowest at each level, but it should be remembered that this algorithm allows mal-rules only to be available at the level they are first introduced. On the other hand the global ANALYSIS-OF-CONDITIONS algorithm gives all the non-redundant rules for a particular level and so a comparison between the number of models created by the EXHAUSTIVE-GROUPED and ANALYSIS-OF-CONDITIONS algorithms is pertinent. The large difference between the number of models created by the EXHAUSTIVE-GROUPED and the global ANALYSIS-OF-CONDITIONS algorithms results from the fact that the EXHAUSTIVE-GROUPED algorithm generates many equivalent models. Two models are said to be equivalent if they predict identical behavior. Applying the INTERACTION/SUBSUME subalgorithm, we conclude that the ADDSUB and the SOLVE rule are non-interacting, and so it is quite unnecessary to consider both orderings of the rules. Such a simple observation reduces the size of the search space in half. A similar observation for the MULT and SOLVE rules reduces the search space yet again in half. At level 9, for example, the number of models is reduced by a factor of 20160. Further, we note that the second and third models for the

(MULT ADDSUB SOLVE FIN2)

configuration generated by the SELECTIVE algorithm (see the appendix) are equivalent, whereas this same algorithm does not generate any of the models containing the MSOLVE variant. On the other hand, the global ANALYSIS-OF-CONDITIONS algorithm returns a complete and non-redundant set of four models as discussed earlier in this section.

However, the number of configurations to be considered with the global ANALYSIS-OF-CONDITIONS algorithm at and after level 6 begins to be sizable, and is likely to cause difficulty in a practical online modeling system. In order to reduce the number of models further, the following approaches are suggested:

Table 16-3: Comparative size of the search space.

T1	T2
FIN2	(FIN2)
SOLVE	(SOLVE FIN2)
ADDSUB	(ADDSUB SOLVE FIN2)
MULT	(MULT ADDSUB SOLVE FIN2)
XADDSUB	(MULT XADDSUB ADDSUB SOLVE FIN2)
NTORHS	(MULT XADDSUB ADDSUB NTORHS SOLVE FIN2)
REARRANGE	(MULT REARRANGE XADDSUB ADDSUB NTORHS SOLVE FIN2)
XTOLHS	(MULT REARRANGE XADDSUB ADDSUB NTORHS XTOLHS SOLVE FIN2)
BRA1	(MULT REARRANGE BRA1 XADDSUB ADDSUB NTORHS XTOLHS SOLVE FIN2)
BRA2	(MULT REARRANGE BRA1 BRA2 XADDSUB ADDSUB NTORHS XTOLHS SOLVE FIN2)

T3	T4	T5	T6	T7	T8	T9	T10
1	0	1	1	1	1	1	1
2	1	6	4	4	2	2	2
3	0	24	12	3	2	1	6
4	0	120	48	4	4	2	12
5	0	720	240	5	12	6	20
6	3	151200	5760	24	72	36	80
7	0	1663200	40320	7	144	12	280
8	1	51891840	645120	16	188	24	2240
9	0	726485760	5806080	9	288	12	20160
10	2	70572902300	174182400	30	10368	432	16800

Captions for the column headings

T1	Rule concentrated on at this level
T2	Ideal model for this level
T3	Level number
T4	Number of mal-rules observed for that level
T5	Number of configurations generated by the EXHAUSTIVE algorithm
T6	Number of configurations generated by the EXHAUSTIVE-GROUPED algorithm
T7	Number of configurations generated by the SELECTIVE algorithm[8]
T8	Number of configurations generated by the global ANALYSIS-OF-CONDITIONS algorithm
T9	Number of configurations generated by the local ANALYSIS-OF-CONDITIONS algorithm
T10	Reduction factor for the EXHAUSTIVE-GROUPED/global ANALYSIS-OF-CONDITIONS algorithms

[8]Assumes for ease of calculation that all the rules are in different priority classes; so in practice it is likely that these figures would be somewhat reduced.

1. Ensure that the problem set is discriminatory and hence stop the comparison between the student's answer and those obtained by executing the potential models set as soon as a single model matches. (This would speed up the matching process in the online modeling phase but would not prevent the system from generating a large number of models.)
2. Introduce domain-specific heuristics such as those in the DEBUGGY system [Burton, 1982]. For instance, if two rules are known not to coexist, ensure that no model incorporates both. So far it has not been necessary to explore this possibility, but we accept that it might become necessary in domains where there are substantially more rules.
3. Investigate whether or not it is possible to prevent the generation of further models; this is discussed in the next section.

16.2.2 Further Reducing the Number of Irrelevant Models Generated

This section describes two situations where redundancy in models may be reduced further. Some of the rules that were included in the models on the assumption that algebra is a hierarchical domain are simply never used when the models are run on the problems for the particular level, but they nevertheless affect the size of the search space; this is discussed further in Section 16.2.2.1. Furthermore, because of the nature of the problems presented, rules which can potentially interact are unable to do so; yet, these rules must be present so that the problems can be evaluated. This is discussed further in Section 16.2.2.2.

The issue of irrelevant models can also be considered from the viewpoint of the analysis of the ANALYSIS-OF-CONDITIONS algorithm presented earlier. Equation (4a) gives the number of configurations and (4b) gives the number of models. From (4a) we know that the number of configurations generated can be reduced if we eliminate rules with mal-rules. (Eliminating rules without mal-rules does not affect the number of configurations generated, but it does reduce the size of the models.) On the other hand, reducing the number of interacting rules can have a major effect because the value of the function, f, is at worst IR! and at best 1. That is, in the worst case all the rules interact and so the formula reduces to that for the EXHAUSTIVE-GROUPED algorithm (Equation (2)); whereas in the best case the number of models equals the number of configurations and is given by Equation (4a).

16.2.2.1 Algebra: A Non-hierarchical Domain

A principal objective for the SELECTIVE algorithm [Sleeman & Smith, 1981] was that it should concentrate on a single rule at each stage of the modeling. However, we assumed that the domain was hierarchical in that at level L + 1 when we are concentrating on the new rule, the original L rules are present and completely unchanged in both form and order. (The significance of rule interaction is considered in Section 16.2.3.) An inspection of Table 16-2, for instance, shows that at many levels a number of rules are not activated due to the nature of the problems presented. For example, the sequence of rules that solves the level-6 problem in Table 16-2 is:

MNTORHS, ADDSUB, XADDSUB, MSOLVE, FIN2,

that is, MULT is redundant. Similar redundancies are found in many other levels. In Table 16-4 we give the minimal, non-redundant (and hence non-hierarchical) rule sets and the corresponding number of models generated with this data.[9]

16.2.2.2 Section Rules That Interact in a Predefined Problem Set

In Section 16.2, I outlined the enhanced algorithm for generating models, but I have not indicated how to determine which domain rules interact. This can be done by determining whether their conditions overlap. Interaction and other information about the domain rules are given in Table 16-5. The number of models quoted for the revised generation algorithm in Table 16-3 assumes that all potentially significant interactions take place. However, a further inspection of the problems presented in Table 16-2 shows that this is not true. For example, at level 6 the ADDSUB, MULT and XADDSUB rules are unable to interact because the problems do not contain the overlap patterns for these rule pairs. In the next paragraph, we demonstrate the effects of these newly introduced constraints.

In Table 16-4, rules not necessary for solving the particular set of problems have been deleted from the rule sets. At level 6, for example, NTORHS is being tested but as at level 8 and beyond, it is no longer necessary to solve the problems, so it has been deleted. At level 6, the non-hierarchical ideal student model is:

(NTORHS ADDSUB SOLVE FIN2)

If the problems presented permit interaction between all the rules that could potentially interact, then there would be twelve models, as NTORHS has three mal-rules, MNTORHS, M2NTORHS and M3NTORHS and the last two can interact with ADDSUB, thus giving 6 $(1+1+2+2)$ models. Further, SOLVE has an associated mal-rule, MSOLVE, thus making twelve models in all. If the problems were such that they did not allow the interaction between M2NTORHS/M3NTORHS and ADDSUB to take place, then the number of models would be eight. A second example in which the restricted interaction can reduce the number of models occurs at level 9 where the reduced rule set is:

[9] I refer to this as being the non-hierarchical algorithm, but as noted above this would be more accurately described as the COMPLETE and NON-REDUNDANT algorithm activated with non-hierarchical data (namely, the reduced rule sets given in Table 16-4), whereas in ANALYSIS-OF-CONDITIONS the same algorithm is applied to the hierarchical student models given in Table 16-3.

Table 16-4: The templates and size of the search space for the non-hierarchical algebra domain.

T1	T2	T3	T4	T5	T6	T7	T8	T9	T10
FIN2	1	0	1	1	1	1	1	1	1
SOLVE	2	1	4	2	2	2	4	2	2
ADDSUB	3	0	12	2	2	2	3	6	6
MULT	4	0	48	4	2	2	4	12	24
XADDSUB	5	0	240	12	2	2	5	20	120
NTORHS	6	3	5760	72	12	12	24	80	480
REARRANGE	7	0	40320	144	32	32	7	280	1260
XTOLHS	8	1	645120	288	4	4	16	2240	161280
BRA1	9	0	5806080	288	4	2	9	20160	2903040
BRA2	10	2	174182400	10368	12	12	30	16800	14515200

T11

(FIN2)
(SOLVE FIN2)
(ADDSUB SOLVE FIN2)
(MULT SOLVE FIN2)
(XADDSUB SOLVE FIN2)
(NTORHS ADDSUB SOLVE FIN2)
(REARRANGE ADDSUB NTORHS SOLVE FIN2)
(XADDSUB XTOLHS SOLVE FIN2)
(MULT ADDSUB BRA1 SOLVE FIN2)
(BRA2 XADDSUB XTOLHS SOLVE FIN2)

Captions for Column Headers

T1 Rule focused on
T2 Level number
T3 Number of mal-rules associated with the rule
T4 Number of models with the EXHAUSTIVE-GROUPED algorithm
T5 Number of models with the global ANALYSIS-OF-CONDITIONS algorithm
T6 Number of non-hierarchical models
T7 Number of non-hierarchical models when the interaction is reduced
T8 Number of models with the SELECTIVE algorithm
T9 Reduction ratio for EXHAUSTIVE-GROUPED/GLOBAL ANALYSIS-OF-CONDITIONS algorithms.
T10 Reduction ratio for EXHAUSTIVE-GROUPED/NON-HIERARCHICAL and REDUCED INTERACTION algorithms
T11 The reduced rule sets

Note that at level 7 it is not possible to further reduce the number of models because ADDSUB subsumes REARRANGE and because this problem template allows M2NTORHS and M3NTORHS to interact with both ADDSUB and REARRANGE.

Table 16-5:

This is a sample of the output from the program which reports the rules which interact, subsume and are satisfied by other problem templates, together with a summary of all the results from this analysis. Semantically meaningful interactions are signaled by an asterisk.

```
*   ADDSUB and MULT interact; the overlap is: ((NUM +|- NUM * NUM) (NUM * NUM +|- NUM))
*   ADDSUB and XADDSUB interact; the overlap is: ((NUM +|- NUM * X +|- NUM * X))
    ADDSUB and NTORHS interact; the overlap is: ((NUM +|- NUM =))
    ADDSUB and MNTORHS interact; the overlap is: ((NUM +|- NUM =))
*   ADDSUB and M2NTORHS interact; the overlap is: ((NUM +|- NUM !LN =))
*   ADDSUB and M3NTORHS interact; the overlap is: ((NUM +|- NUM !LN =))

    ADDSUB subsumes REARRANGE

*   ADDSUB and REARRANGE interact; the overlap is: ((NUM +|- NUM * X))

*   WARNING-RULE ADDSUB IS SATISFIED BY REARRANGE'S PT **

*   ADDSUB and BRA2 interact; the overlap is: ((NUM +|- NUM * < NUM * X +|- NUM >))
*   ADDSUB and M1BRA2 interact; the overlap is: ((NUM +|- NUM * < NUM * X +|- NUM >))
*   ADDSUB and M2BRA2 interact; the overlap is: ((NUM +|- NUM * < NUM * X +|- NUM >))
```

Rephrased Summary of Complete Output

ADDSUB subsumes REARRANGE.
ADDSUB and the following rules can interact *significantly*:
MULT, REARRANGE, XADDSUB, BRA2, M1BRA2, M2BRA2, M2NTORHS and M3NTORHS.
MULT and the following rules can interact *significantly*: XADDSUB, BRA2, M1BRA2 and M2BRA2.
REARRANGE and the following rules can interact *significantly*:
XADDSUB, M2NTORHS and M3NTORHS.
XADDSUB and the following rules can interact *significantly*: M2NTORHS and M3NTORHS.
M2NTORHS and M3NTORHS are satisfied by XADDSUB's and REARRANGE's problem templates.

(MULT ADDSUB BRA1 SOLVE FIN2)

Since MULT and ADDSUB can potentially interact and SOLVE has a mal-rule alternative MSOLVE, the reduced rule set gives rise to four models. The problem template for this level (see Table 16-9) is:

$$NUM * X = NUM * < NUM + NUM >$$

Since given this template MULT and ADDSUB cannot interact, it is only necessary to consider two models. Table 16-4 also gives the number of models generated when rule interactions are reduced to those possible for the problem set.[10]

It can be seen that these additional constraints significantly reduce the number of models to be considered. Several points should be made about the reduced interaction results in Table 16-4.

---

[10]This algorithm is referred to as the non-hierarchical and reduced-interaction algorithm. That is, the complete and non-redundant algorithm is activated with ideal student models that are non-hierarchical, and where the interaction is reduced to that appropriate for the problem set.

1. Because ADDSUB subsumes REARRANGE it is never possible to create problem sets requiring both rules where these rules do not interact.
2. Several of the problem templates,[11] including those for level 7, also contain the overlap pattern for ADDSUB and REARRANGE with M2NTORHS/M3NTORHS, and this overlap pattern increases the number of models to be considered.
3. As BRA2 partially evaluates its expressions, it is not necessary to include MULT in the rule set. For example, given the expression:

   2 * <3X − 4>

   BRA2 returns:

   6X − 8

   Similarly, the mal-rule M2BRA2 evaluates its expressions, making ADDSUB also redundant.[12]

16.2.3 The Significance of Rules Which Interact

Tasks, in which more than one rule can be applied, frequently cause difficulties for the student. (See the protocols reported in the earlier experiment [Sleeman, 1982], and Matz's [1982] and Davis' [Davis *et al.*, 1978] illustrations for more examples.) In Table 16-5, the potential interactions between all the domain's rules and mal-rules are given. In Table 16-6 we have gone one step further and created a problem template that may be used to determine whether the student has the correct precedence for particular interacting rules, such as ADDSUB and MULT. However, because of the nature of the rule actions, changing the relative order of the rules does not always produce a task which can discriminate (for example, ADDSUB and NTORHS). Those pairs of rules in Table 16-6 that are significant have been starred. The algorithm for generating problem templates for interacting rules is given in Section 16.3.2. It should be noted that in the early stages of teaching algebra, teachers frequently avoid unwanted interactions by introducing brackets. However, there are problem types which are not normally disambiguated in this way, for example:

2 + 3X = 6

---

[11]By this we mean an entity in which the variables are replaced by values in order to formulate a problem. Table 16-6 gives a problem template for the ADDSUB/MULT rules as:

NUM * X = NUM +|− NUM * NUM

One instantiation of this problem template is:

2 * X = 3 + 4 * 5

[12]Without this, the number of models generated for level 10 for both the non-hierarchical and the reduced interaction rule sets would be much greater as BRA2 and its two mal-rules potentially interact with both ADDSUB and MULT.

where in our notation it is possible for both ADDSUB and REARRANGE to apply. In such examples the source of the error could be attributed to the student having a non-standard representation for the task; for obvious reasons this has been referred to as misparsing.

Rule interactions also influence the order in which topics should be presented. For example, in this domain, examples that use the XADDSUB rule should be seen before those that require the NTORHS rule, as such an order may prevent the formation of the M2NTORHS and M3NTORHS rules. That is, by presenting problems such as:

$$2X + 3X = 10$$

which is simplified by the teacher to:

$$5X = 10$$

It is hoped that the student would realize that the integer 3 cannot be detached from the X. (Such an error is captured by the mal-rules M2NTORHS and M3NTORHS.) This also means that at the stage of testing the NTORHS rules, one must give examples for the XADDSUB rule, in order to determine whether M2NTORHS or M3NTORHS is used by the student. These inferences are based on the information provided in Table 16-5 that the problem template for XADDSUB is satisfied by both M2NTORHS and M3NTORHS.

It should also be noted that the system has pointed out a problem template for the MULT/BRA2 rules that violates the commonly-taught precedence rule for arithmetic expressions.

Further, by an extension of these algorithms, it would be possible to generate problem types that discriminate between three, four, and more rules.

In Section 16.3 we outline the algorithm that determines which rule interactions are possible. In Table 16-7 we give the (non-hierarchical) rule sets necessary to embody the interacting rule pairs reported in Table 16-5; the number of models generated, assuming all the rules that can interact do so; and the number of models generated when interactions are restricted to those that can occur with the actual templates.

16.2.4 Determining the Size of the Search Space

The type of production rules we have been considering here are very reminiscent of formal grammars.[13] Hence, the question about the size of the production system search space could be said to be equivalent to asking whether in a regular BNF grammar it is possible to calculate the number of terminal strings. Hopcroft and Ullman [1969] show how to determine whether a grammar is finite or infinite, but do not give a method for enumerating all terminal

[13] BNF rules that overlap partially are assigned to the "interactive" subgroup; all the remaining rules are scanned and those that have identical condition parts are recorded as alternatives.

Table 16-6: The rules that can interact and the problem templates that the algorithm returns. (Those that are discriminatory are starred, hence the problem template for ADDSUB/MULT is significant, whereas that for ADDSUB/NTORHS is not.)

Now looking at ADDSUB and MULT overlap patterns exist:
((NUM +|- NUM * NUM) (NUM * NUM +|- NUM))
** The resulting templates are:
((NUM * X = NUM +|- NUM * NUM) (NUM * X = NUM * NUM +|- NUM))

Now looking at ADDSUB and XADDSUB overlap patterns exist:
((NUM +|- NUM * X +|- NUM * X))
** The resulting templates are: ((NUM +|- NUM * X +|- NUM * X = +|- NUM))

Now looking at ADDSUB and NTORHS overlap patterns exist: ((NUM +|- NUM =))
The resulting templates are: ((+|- NUM * X +|- NUM +|- NUM = +|- NUM))

ADDSUB subsumes REARRANGE

Now looking at ADDSUB and REARRANGE overlap patterns exist: ((NUM +|- NUM * X))
** The resulting templates are: ((NUM +|- NUM * X = NUM))

Now looking at ADDSUB and BRA2 overlap patterns exist:
((NUM +|- NUM * < NUM * X +|- NUM >))
** The resulting templates are: ((NUM * X = NUM +|- NUM * < NUM * X +|- NUM>))

Now looking at MULT and XADDSUB overlap patterns exist: ((NUM * NUM * X +|- NUM * X))
** The resulting templates are: ((NUM * NUM * X +|- NUM * X = +|- NUM))

Now looking at MULT and REARRANGE overlap patterns exist: ((NUM * NUM +|- NUM * X))
The resulting templates are: ((NUM * NUM +|- NUM * X = NUM))

Now looking at MULT and BRA2 overlap patterns exist: ((NUM * NUM * <NUM * X +|- NUM >))
** The resulting templates are: ((NUM * X = NUM * NUM * < NUM * X +|- NUM >))

Now looking at XADDSUB and XTOLHS overlap patterns exist: ((= -|+ NUM * X +|- NUM * X))
The resulting templates are: (NUM * X = -|+ NUM * X +|- NUM * X +|- NUM)

Now looking at XADDSUB and REARRANGE overlap patterns exist:
((NUM +|- NUM * X +|- NUM * X))
The resulting templates are: ((NUM +|- NUM * X +|- NUM * X = NUM))

Now looking at NTORHS and XTOLHS overlap patterns exist: ((+|- NUM = +|- NUM * X))
The resulting templates are: ((NUM * X +|- NUM = +|- NUM * X))

strings. However, it is possible to calculate the maximum possible branching factor for such a grammar or set of production rules, but only when parsing a specific string can one calculate the actual branching factors and enumerate the total number of leaves. (An upper bound on the number of terminal strings is the maximal branching factor times the path length. Various evaluation algorithms are possible, including a depth-first search which uses only N stack cells, where N is the depth of the search tree.)

Table 16-7: These are all the significant interacting rule pairs reported in Table 16-6. The non-hierarchical rule set is used for model generation.

Rules focused on reduced rule set	# of models assuming all possible interactions	# of models assuming only interactions in PT	Corresponding Rule Set
ADDSUB/MULT	4	4	(MULT ADDSUB SOLVE FIN2)
ADDSUB/XADDSUB	72	72	(REARRANGE XADDSUB ADDSUB NTORHS SOLVE FIN2)
ADDSUB/REARRANGE	32	32	(REARRANGE ADDSUB NTORHS SOLVE FIN2)
ADDSUB/BRA2	96	48	(BRA2 REARRANGE ADDSUB XTOLHS XADDSUB SOLVE FIN2)
MULT/XADDSUB	4	4	(MULT XADDSUB SOLVE FIN2)
MULT/BRA2	48	24	(MULT BRA2 XADDSUB XTOLHS SOLVE FIN2)

16.2.5 Nature of the Rules and the Type of Tasks Encoded

The task captured by such grammars is essentially that of transforming an initial state by means of several transformations into a final state that is either specified in detail or whose characteristics are predefined. In the analysis above we have also assumed that a rule that fires modifies the state and hence is not able to fire again on exactly the same data. Further, it is assumed that the model is sufficient to evaluate all the intermediary states. (Section 16.3.1 discusses how minimal models can be generated.) Finally, we have also assumed that the matcher is deterministic and not influenced by the nature of a perceived goal.

16.3 PROCESSING DOMAIN KNOWLEDGE

We have implemented a separate program which performs the following analysis on a domain's rules and mal-rules.

1. Checks that rules and mal-rules are distinct.
2. Creates problem templates for each rule (see Section 16.3.1) and then checks that they are distinct.[14]
3. Reports subsumed and subsuming rule pairs.
4. Decides which pairs of domain rules are able to interact (see Section 16.3.2) and grows a template which discriminates between them (see Table 16-6).
5. Checks whether any of the rules and mal-rules are satisfied by templates for any of the other rules or for any of the interacting rule pairs. If so, report this; see Table 16-5 and Section 16.2.3. (Also note that if it is found that a rule which is not contained in the minimal rule set is satisfied by a problem template, then it is necessary to add the rule to the rule set since the student might (incorrectly) use it. The interaction data for that level must then be enhanced and the models regenerated.)

16.3.1 Generating a Minimal Problem Template

Generating a problem template is equivalent to specifying a problem type in which each of the rules will be activated at least once. (Note that this problem is closely related to that of generating a problem to discriminate between two models; see [Sleeman, 1981].) Here I outline a rule-based problem generator, specifically for use in this domain, but as indicated in Section 16.2.5 the approach has considerable generality.

In order to generate a type of problem that would allow a rule to fire, the rules must be used in the opposite direction to which they are used to solve a problem. For example, a slightly stylized "generative" form of the MULT rule is:

(STR1 NUM STR2) $\Rightarrow$ (STR1 NUM * NUM STR2)

When using this form, the algorithm checks if NUM is contained in the input string, and, if so, it returns separate lists for each occurrence of NUM, in which NUM is replaced by the string NUM * NUM. (STRi are strings which can be null.) To initiate the generation algorithm it is necessary to specify an initial string corresponding to the problem solution, a set of rules which can be used in *generation mode* and terminating conditions (number of iterations, rules which the final pattern must contain, and so on). Table 16-8a shows the performance

[14]By definition, a mal-rule has the same template as its "parent" rule.

of the system when given the initial state (SHD NUM),[15] rule set (MULT SOLVE FIN2), and the criterion that MULT, SOLVE and FIN2 must be activated in that order. In contrast, Table 16-8b and c illustrate the creation of the same problem type in two stages; this approach greatly reduces the number of redundant configurations generated. All the remaining templates have been created from the result of the first stage rather than the basic form (SHD NUM) for this reason. Table 16-8d shows the creation of a problem template to satisfy:

(MULT BRA1 SOLVE FIN2)

Several redundant configurations could have been avoided if this template had been created from its *immediate* predecessor, namely:

(MULT SOLVE FIN2)

Hence, a sensible enhancement of this algorithm would be to use the problem template of the immediate predecessor as the initial state.

Presently, several redundant templates must be discarded manually. This process could be automated by applying the following rejection criteria:

1. If the problem template also satisfies a rule that is not in the model. For example, the problem templates generated for (ADDSUB SOLVE FIN2) are:

NUM +|− NUM * X = NUM and NUM * X = NUM +|− NUM

   The first template also satisfies REARRANGE and hence should be rejected.

2. If the problem template contains the overlap pattern for two rules that should not interact, it can be discarded. On these grounds, too, the first model above should be rejected, as it contains the overlap pattern for ADDSUB and REARRANGE.
3. If the problems specified by the problem template cannot be solved by using only the rules in the model.

Indeed, each template generated by the algorithm should be executed symbolically and the above tests applied at *each* stage. Note that the algorithm produces a problem template with the least number of rules, as it terminates as soon as the criteria are satisfied.

Table 16-9 gives the problem templates for this domain that have been selected by the experimenter from those generated by the algorithm. Two qualifications must be made about the present implementation. First, we have not so far implemented a template instantiator for this domain. This is not a very demanding task, but neither is it a very rewarding one, as similar im-

[15]SHD is an abbreviation for String Head and is appended to the tasks to be executed in order to reduce the complexity of the domain rules.

Table 16-8: Generating problem templates

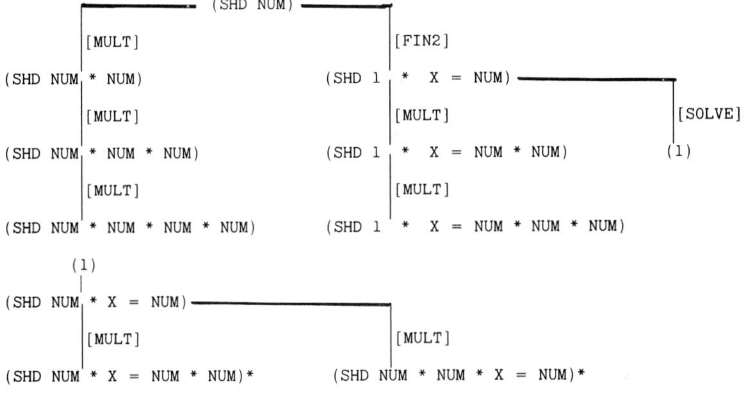

The names on the arcs show the rules used to create the next string. The starred configurations are returned by the system as ones which meet the criterion specified. (NB: a slightly simplified version of FIN2 has been used.)

a) Generation of a problem for (MULT SOLVE FIN2) starting from the basic form (SHD NUM).

```
(SHD NUM)
  |[FIN2]
(SHD 1 * X = NUM)
  |[SOLVE]
(SHD NUM * X = NUM)*
```

```
            (SHD NUM * X = NUM)
      [MULT]                      [MULT]
(SHD NUM * NUM * X = NUM)*    (SHD NUM * X = NUM * NUM)*
```

b) Generation of a problem for (SOLVE FIN2) starting from the basic form (SHD NUM).

c) Generation of a problem for (MULT SOLVE FIN2) starting from the intermediary form (SHD NUM * X = NUM).

i) Initial configuration

(SHD NUM * X = NUM)

ii) Level 1 configurations

(SHD NUM * X = < NUM >)
(SHD < NUM > * X = NUM)
(SHD NUM * X = NUM * NUM)
(SHD NUM * NUM * X = NUM)

iii) Level 2 configurations

(SHD NUM * X = < < NUM > >)
(SHD < NUM > * X = < NUM >)
(SHD NUM * X = < NUM * NUM >)
(SHD NUM * NUM * X = < NUM >)
(SHD < < NUM > > * X = NUM)
(SHD < NUM > * X = NUM * NUM)
(SHD < NUM * NUM > * X = NUM)
(SHD NUM * X = NUM * < NUM >)
(SHD NUM * X = < NUM > * NUM)
(SHD NUM * X = NUM * NUM * NUM)
(SHD NUM * NUM * X = NUM * NUM)
(SHD NUM * < NUM > * X = NUM)
(SHD < NUM > * NUM * X = NUM)
(SHD NUM * NUM * NUM * X = NUM)

iv) Level 2 configurations which satisfy the specified criterion

(SHD NUM * NUM * X = < NUM >)
(SHD < NUM > * X = NUM * NUM)
(SHD NUM * X = NUM * < NUM >)
(SHD NUM * X = < NUM > * NUM)
(SHD NUM * < NUM > * X = NUM)
(SHD < NUM > * NUM * X = NUM)

d) Generation of a problem for (MULT BRA1 SOLVE FIN2) starting from the intermediary form (SHD NUM * X = NUM) given the criterion that the MULT, BRA1, SOLVE and FIN2 rules should be activated in that sequence. "<" and ">" are the usual algebraic brackets.

Table 16-9: Stylized version of problem templates for the domain rules (the mal-rules using the problem template of the "parent" rule).

<table>
<tr><td>FIN2</td><td>(1 * X = NUM // NUM)</td></tr>
<tr><td>SOLVE</td><td>(NUM * X = NUM)</td></tr>
<tr><td>ADDSUB</td><td>(NUM * X = NUM +|− NUM)</td></tr>
<tr><td>MULT</td><td>(NUM * X = NUM * NUM)</td></tr>
<tr><td>XADDSUB</td><td>(NUM * X +|− NUM * X = +|− NUM)</td></tr>
<tr><td>NTORHS</td><td>(+|− NUM * X +|− NUM = +|− NUM)</td></tr>
<tr><td>XTOLHS</td><td>(NUM * X = −NUM − NUM * X)</td></tr>
<tr><td>REARRANGE</td><td>(NUM +|− NUM * X = NUM)</td></tr>
<tr><td>BRA1</td><td>(NUM * X = NUM * < NUM + NUM >)</td></tr>
<tr><td>BRA2</td><td>(NUM * X = NUM * < NUM * X +|− NUM >)</td></tr>
</table>

plementations have been done many times before. However, such an implementation is needed to take full advantage of LMS's online modeling capabilities. Second, the experimenter currently decides which rules need to be included in the reduced rule sets in order to activate the rules that are being focused on. However, given the analysis above, it is possible to create the reduced rule sets by growing the structure until the relevant rules have been activated. Such a search would be broad and undirected (see Table 16-8d), and it is for this reason that the algorithm has not been implemented. On the other hand, such an algorithm would sometimes generate a number of significantly different rule sets. For instance, for BRA2 there are essentially two rule sets, and hence problem templates—namely, one where the bracket is on the left-hand side and one where it is on the right-hand side of the expression. The minimal rule sets which would *both* be generated by such an algorithm are:

(BRA2 ADDSUB NTORHS SOLVE FIN2)
(BRA2 XADDSUB XTOLHS SOLVE FIN2).

In this case the experimenter selected the latter, but it could be important to present the student with problems based on the left-hand side form.

16.3.2 Problem Templates to Test Rule Ordering

Given rules R_i and R_j, and their associated problem templates PT_i and PT_j, the following algorithm generates a template to discriminate between the two rules.

1. Calculate the overlap OP_{ij} between the two rules R_i and R_j. If OP_{ij} is null, then the problem templates should already discriminate. [16]
2. If rule R_j is satisfied by PT_i go to 6; else, set RESULT to PT_i .

[16] If rule R_i has conditions C1 C2 C3 C4, and R_j has conditions C1 C3 C4, then PT_i will already discriminate between the two rules as R_i is activated by PT_i, but R_j is not.

3. Apply generate rule j to top-level elements of RESULT, store result in RESULT.
4. If at least one item in RESULT satisfies R_i and R_j independently and contains OP_{ij}, then go to 6.
5. If MAX-DEPTH is not reached, go to 3.
6. Repeat steps 2 to 5 of the above algorithm with i and j interchanged.

Table 16-6 shows the interactions that the algorithm has noted for this domain and the templates that have been generated. Not all these templates are capable of producing problems that discriminate between the order of two rules in a model because of the semantics of their actions. In Table 16-6 we have starred those templates that are discriminatory. Subsequently, we plan to use a symbolic evaluator to automate the discrimination process. At present, it is done manually.

16.4 SUMMARY

The student models generated by the revised algorithms are consistently fewer in number than the redundant and incomplete set of models generated by our earlier SELECTIVE algorithm (see Table 16-4). Moreover, the COMPLETE and NON-REDUNDANT algorithm overcomes the difficulties arising from the limitation noted in the earlier experiment by allowing mal-rules to be in "scope" at all subsequent levels. The analysis carried out in Section 16.2.3 illustrates a further assumption of the first formulation of LMS: namely, if the student accords the correct precedence to two rules R_i and R_j at level L, then the student continues to do so at all subsequent levels. More specifically, LMS-I assumes that if R_i interacts with R_j and R_j with R_k, and if the student has the correct precedence for both rule pairs, then he would be able to correctly work problems in which all three rules interact. Such an assumption is not inherent in LMS-II. Given the reduced size of the search space and the greater power of the revised algorithm, it seems reasonable to conclude that the SELECTIVE algorithm has been superseded by the newer algorithms.

In addition, this paper formulates an algorithm that reports several types of interaction that can occur between pairs of rules. A systematic investigation of the domain rules is necessary to catalogue all the interactions. Without such an investigation, one is merely considering interactions that one has happened to notice. Burton [1982] has reported another systematic approach to determining which subskills interact, but this is much more complex than the rule-based system reported here.

We expect that this analysis, and the architecture of LMS-II described in Section 16.3, could be used with any subject area in which it is possible to represent domain knowledge as an ordered set of rules and to encode errors observed in protocols as mal-rules. Indeed, this approach might also be applied to other classes of problems. For instance, if a plan is conceived of as an ordered set of rules, these algorithms can determine how many significant orderings there are. (There are analogues in the planning domain to subsumption, interaction, non-interaction and to alternatives.)

16.4.1 LMS and Related Work in Induction

LMS has been implemented as a two-stage system: first, the offline phase, in which the models are generated and evaluated against the problem set; and second, the online phase in which the student's performance is compared against those models. This separation makes it clear that the inference problem has been formulated as a search through a space predefined by rules and mal-rules, and as such conforms to Buchanan's inference paradigm [Buchanan, 1974]. Michalski [1980] has suggested that systems which perform data-driven inference may be said to perform *constructive inference* and has reported several examples in which his "enhanced" algorithm has produced composite descriptors. I wish to point out that LMS carries out another form of constructive inference, namely rule permutations based upon the domain's rules and mal-rules.

ACKNOWLEDGMENTS

I gratefully acknowledge the many helpful comments on earlier drafts of this paper from Pat Langley, Allen Newell, Michael Rychener, N. S. Sridharan, K. R. James and the editors, particularly Jaime Carbonell. In addition, I should like to thank Carnegie-Mellon University for providing a very stimulating environment in which to complete this work, and the University of Leeds for granting sabbatical leave.

REFERENCES

Brown, J. S., and Burton, R. R., "Diagnostic Models for Procedural Bugs in Basic Mathematical Skills," *Cognitive Science*, Vol. 2, No. 2, pp. 155-192, April-June 1978.

Brown, J. S., Burton, R. R., and deKleer, J., "Pedagogical, Natural Language, and Knowledge Engineering Techniques in SOPHIE I, II, and III," *Intelligent Tutoring Systems*, D. H. Sleeman and J. S. Brown (Ed.), Academic Press, New York, 1982.

Buchanan, B. G., "Scientific Theory Formation by Computer," *Proceedings of the NATO Advanced Study Institute on Computer Orientated Learning Processes*, 1974.

Buchanan, B. G., Duffield, A. M., and Robertson, A.V., "An Application of AI to the Interpretation of Mass Spectra," *Mass Spectrometry: Techniques and Appliances*, C. W. A. Miline (Ed.), Wiley, 1971.

Burton, R. R., "Diagnosing Bugs in a Simple Procedural Skill," *Intelligent Tutoring Systems*, D. H. Sleeman and J. S. Brown (Ed.), Academic Press, New York, 1982.

Burton, R. R., and Brown, J. S., "An Investigation of Computer Coaching for Informal Learning Activities," *Intelligent Tutoring Systems*, D. H. Sleeman and J. S. Brown (Ed.), Academic Press, New York, 1982.

Carbonell, J. R., *Mixed-Initiative Man-Computer Instructional Dialogues,* Ph.D. dissertation, Massachusetts Institute of Technology, 1971.

Clancey, W. J., "Tutoring Rules for Guiding a Case Method Dialogue," *Intelligent Tutoring Systems*, D. H. Sleeman and J. S. Brown (Ed.), Academic Press, New York, 1982.

Davis, R., Jockusch, E., and McKnight, C., "Cognitive Processes in Learning Algebra," *Journal of Children's Mathematical Behavior*, Vol. 2, No. 1, 1978.

Goldstein, I. P., "The Genetic Graph: A Representation for the Evolution of Procedural Knowledge," *Intelligent Tutoring Systems*, D. H. Sleeman and J. S. Brown (Ed.), Academic Press, New York, 1982.

Hartley, J. R., and Sleeman, D. H., "Towards Intelligent Teaching Systems," *International Journal of Man-Machine Studies*, Vol. 5, No. 2, pp. 215-236, April 1973.

Hopcroft, J. E., and Ullman, J. E., *Formal Languages and their Relation to Automata*, Addison-Wesley, Reading, MA, 1969.

Matz, M., "Towards a Generative theory of High School Algebra Errors," *Intelligent Tutoring Systems*, D. H. Sleeman, and Brown, J. S. (Ed.), Academic Press, New York, 1982.

Michalski, R. S., "Pattern Recognition as Rule-Guided Inductive Inference," *IEEE Transactions on Pattern Analysis and Machine Intelligence*, Vol. PAMI-2, No. 4, July 1980.

Sleeman, D. H., "A Rule-based Task System," *Proceedings of the Seventh International Conference on Artificial Intelligence*, University of British Columbia, Vancouver, BC, pp. 882-887, August 1981.

Sleeman, D. H., "Assessing Aspects of Competence in Basic Algebra," *Intelligent Tutoring Systems*, D. H. Sleeman and J. S. Brown (Ed.), Academic Press, New York, pp. 185-199, 1982.

Sleeman, D. H., and J. S. Brown, "Intelligent Tutoring Systems: An Overview," *Intelligent Tutoring Systems*, D. H. Sleeman and J. S. Brown (Ed.), Academic Press, New York, pp. 1-11, 1982.

Sleeman, D. H., and Hendley, R. J., "ACE: A System which Analyses Complex Explanations," *Intelligent Tutoring Systems*, D. H. Sleeman and J. S. Brown (Ed.), Academic Press, New York, pp. 99-118, 1982.

Sleeman, D. H., and Smith, M. J., "Modelling Students' Problem Solving," *Artificial Intelligence*, Vol. 16, No. 2, pp. 171-187, May 1981.

Sleeman, D. H., "An Attempt to Understand Pupils' Understanding of Basic Algebra", (forthcoming).

APPENDIX: AN EXAMPLE OF THE SELECTIVE ALGORITHM: LMS-I'S MODEL GENERATION ALGORITHM

The SELECTIVE algorithm added the new rule or one of its associated mal-rules in all possible places. Thus, if the student model for level 3 was:

(ADDSUB SOLVE FIN2)

and if the *ideal* model at level 4 also contains MULT, then this algorithm would create the following models:

(MULT ADDSUB SOLVE FIN2)
(ADDSUB MULT SOLVE FIN2)
(ADDSUB SOLVE MULT FIN2)

Note that no rule is added after the terminating FIN2 rule.

Similarly, if the *ideal* model for level 5 also contains NTORHS, MNTORHS, M2NTORHS, or M3NTORHS, and assuming that the student behaved "correctly" at level 4, the algorithm would generate:

(NTORHS MULT ADDSUB SOLVE FIN2)
(MULT NTORHS ADDSUB SOLVE FIN2)
(MULT ADDSUB NTORHS SOLVE FIN2)
(MULT ADDSUB SOLVE NTORHS FIN2)
(MNTORHS MULT ADDSUB SOLVE FIN2)
(MULT MNTORHS ADDSUB SOLVE FIN2)
(MULT ADDSUB MNTORHS SOLVE FIN2)
(MULT ADDSUB SOLVE MNTORHS FIN2)

and an additional eight models for the M2NTORHS and M3NTORHS rules. With this algorithm, we used the following heuristics to reduce the number of redundant models:

1. No rule should follow the terminating rule (quoted and used above).
2. If R2 is subsumed by R1 then it is possible to delete R2 in all models in which R1 precedes R2 without altering the effect of the model.
3. "New" rules can only occur before or after members of a particular class. The various domain rules were given an arbitrary priority number which determined the class; an example of such a class in the arithmetic domain is the add and subtract rules [Sleeman & Smith, 1981], and the two rules in the algebra domain which process bracketed expressions, BRA1 and BRA2. (That is, models in which the additional rule occurs between rules in the same priority class are functionally equivalent to models in which the rule occurs either before or after the class.)

COMPREHENSIVE BIBLIOGRAPHY OF MACHINE LEARNING

Paul E. Utgoff
Bernard Nudel
Rutgers University

This chapter consists of a bibliography of the field of machine learning. The sources of the references include bibliographies compiled by Saul Amarel, Dana Angluin, Ryszard S. Michalski, Tom M. Mitchell, Carl Smith, and Bruce G. Buchanan, as well as our own additions.

We define fourteen categories to classify the machine learning literature. For each category, there is a list of reference numbers indicating which references belong within that category. In addition, to the left of each reference is a list of category code letters indicating the categories to which the reference belongs.

CATEGORIES

Category **a**. Analogy: Investigation of analogical reasoning in problem solving, and the use of analogy as a learning method.

{92, 93, 94, 97, 100, 157, 274, 332, 333, 374, 472, 533, 563, 564, 565}

Category **b**. Background material: General background reading in areas of artificial intelligence, cognitive science, and related disciplines that lay the framework for many of the machine learning methods. For overviews of work on machine learning in particular, see category **o**.

{3, 4, 5, 16, 24, 29, 35, 38, 40, 51, 60, 61, 71, 75, 84, 90, 107, 111, 119, 129, 131, 132, 142, 148, 149, 153, 158, 160, 161, 166, 170, 171, 175, 176, 179, 180, 185, 205, 234, 237, 239, 252, 261, 270, 289, 292, 294, 320, 329, 330, 331, 334, 355, 358, 359, 362, 363, 369, 374, 391, 392, 393, 396, 397, 398, 400, 403, 413, 416, 429, 430, 441, 447, 448, 450, 463, 464, 467, 473, 486, 513, 523, 524, 525, 526, 544, 545, 546, 547, 559, 568}

Category **c**. Concept acquisition: Inductive inference of structural descriptions from training examples.

{11, 13, 19, 28, 30, 31, 34, 36, 37, 38, 41, 66, 69, 70, 75, 77, 78, 80, 83, 96, 97, 106, 114, 115, 116, 117, 118, 135, 140, 141, 142, 143, 144, 145, 146, 150, 152, 172, 174, 189, 207, 209, 215, 216, 217, 218, 219, 220, 221, 222, 223, 226, 242, 247, 248, 249, 250, 251, 253, 263, 264, 273, 276, 277, 278, 283, 284, 285, 303, 304, 305, 306, 307, 322, 323, 335, 340, 341, 342, 343, 344, 345, 346, 347, 348, 349, 350, 351, 352, 353, 354, 356, 357, 364, 365, 366, 367, 368, 373, 375, 376, 377, 394, 406, 412, 414, 415, 416, 420, 421, 426, 432, 439, 440, 455, 456, 457, 458, 469, 475, 476, 483, 503, 504, 506, 511, 515, 516, 517, 531, 534, 536, 537, 538, 539, 543, 562, 566, 567, 569, 571, 572}

Category **d**. Discovery and theory formation: Methods and systems that suggest new concepts and explore relationships among them.

{68, 106, 187, 210, 211, 240, 288, 296, 297, 298, 300, 301, 302, 310, 312, 313, 316, 336, 338, 428, 526, 531, 570}

Category **e**. Education and Teaching: Intelligent Computer Aided Instruction.

{72, 73, 74, 87, 88, 112, 113, 214, 327, 457, 469, 492, 493, 494, 495, 496, 497, 498, 502, 533}

Category **g**. Grammatical Inference: Inferring grammars, formal languages, finite state machines, and Turing machines from examples.

{1, 18, 20, 42, 43, 50, 52, 53, 54, 63, 89, 103, 107, 120, 121, 123, 125, 126, 127, 138, 147, 162, 163, 165, 181, 183, 185, 186, 188, 190, 191, 192, 232, 245, 246, 250, 271, 275, 326, 328, 410, 411, 479, 505, 532, 535, 550, 551, 557}

Category **h**. Learning in problem-solving and game playing: Includes self-improving problem solvers, learning of heuristics and production rules, and shifts in problem representation.

{5, 6, 14, 15, 21, 22, 23, 32, 34, 35, 49, 51, 64, 67, 69, 76, 77, 78, 79, 80, 82, 83, 84, 88, 92, 97, 104, 111, 130, 134, 151, 154, 156, 167, 169, 193, 194, 195, 201, 220, 223, 224, 226, 227, 228, 229, 254, 274, 282, 286, 287, 299, 314, 315, 316, 319, 323, 324, 332, 370, 371, 372, 378, 379, 380, 383, 384, 385, 386, 387, 388, 389, 390, 391, 392, 393, 394, 395, 399, 401, 404, 405, 409, 417, 437, 443, 451, 458, 459, 460, 461, 474, 475, 481, 485, 488, 497, 498, 499, 502, 510, 518, 519, 522, 537, 538, 539, 542, 543, 544, 548, 549}

Category **k**. Knowledge acquisition for Expert Systems: Acquiring knowledge to improve performance of Expert Systems.

{69, 78, 79, 80, 82, 83, 133, 136, 194, 196, 203, 204, 223, 224, 225, 226, 371, 372, 378, 379, 380, 427, 437, 438, 451, 452, 453, 489, 560}

Category **l**. Language learning: Acquiring grammars, vocabularies, and other aspects of natural language.

{9, 10, 12, 85, 89, 91, 93, 94, 107, 123, 129, 138, 159, 213, 219, 271, 284, 308, 407, 445, 465, 466, 471, 472, 479, 552}

Category **m**. Modeling of cognitive processes: Work in modeling human learning and inference processes.

{8, 9, 10, 11, 12, 13, 14, 15, 21, 23, 26, 61, 67, 72, 73, 74, 75, 93, 97, 102, 104, 128, 134, 159, 171, 227, 241, 242, 249, 250, 308, 309, 321, 331, 384, 385, 386, 387, 388, 389, 390, 399, 443, 447, 448, 449, 450, 465, 466, 470, 471, 473, 483, 497, 498, 553}

Category **o**. Overview: Summaries and surveys of work on machine learning.

{1, 11, 15, 17, 18, 27, 37, 38, 39, 46, 52, 60, 62, 63, 70, 71, 75, 81, 84, 95, 98, 99, 100, 101, 105, 109, 110, 118, 119, 122, 137, 142, 144, 146, 150, 168, 173, 177, 179, 181, 182, 183, 184, 189, 198, 201, 205, 206, 208, 230, 231, 234, 235, 236, 238, 239, 243, 244, 251, 252, 258, 259, 260, 266, 267, 268, 279, 290, 291, 292, 293, 294, 295, 311, 314, 315, 317, 318, 320, 325, 329, 335, 336, 337, 351, 355, 356, 360, 361, 362, 363, 366, 367, 368, 373, 376, 377, 381, 382, 394, 395, 402, 406, 408, 413, 415, 422, 425, 428, 429, 431, 433, 434, 435, 436, 442, 444, 453, 454, 467, 484, 485, 487, 490, 491, 500, 506, 507, 508, 509, 512, 514, 520, 525, 527, 529, 530, 540, 541, 558, 561}

Category **p**. Procedure learning and automatic programming: Inferring programs, functions, or procedures from input-output pairs, traces, or high-level specifications.

{2, 4, 33, 43, 44, 45, 47, 48, 49, 55, 56, 57, 58, 59, 62, 86, 130, 155, 164, 200, 202, 212, 255, 256, 257, 262, 269, 272, 280, 281, 314, 389, 418, 419, 422, 423, 424, 425, 462, 475, 477, 480, 482, 501, 521, 548, 554, 555, 556}

Category **q**. Clustering: Learning from observation, unsupervised learning, cluster analysis, and acquiring taxonomic classifications.

{7, 139, 150, 199, 353, 354, 446, 517}

Category **r**. Recognition of patterns: Inferring statistical or syntactic descriptions of classes of objects from examples.

{25, 36, 65, 66, 85, 105, 108, 124, 139, 150, 177, 178, 179, 182, 183, 184, 197, 233, 258, 259, 260, 261, 265, 282, 338, 339, 343, 363, 402, 447 449, 460, 461, 463, 468, 470, 478, 503, 504, 528, 529, 530, 541, 569}

REFERENCES

go 1. Adleman, L. and Blum, M., "Inductive Inference and Unsolvability", Technical Report, Dept. Electrical Engineering and Computer Science and the Electronics Research Lab., U. Calif. at Berkeley, 1975.

p 2. Amarel, S., "On the Automatic Formation of a Computer Program which represents a Theory", *Self-Organizing Systems*, Yovits, M., Jacobi, G. and Goldstein, G. (Eds.), Spartan Books, Washington, D.C., pp. 107-175, 1962.

b 3. Amarel, S., "On Representations of Problems of Reasoning about Actions", *Machine Intelligence*, University of Edinburgh Press, Vol. 3, 1968.

bp 4. Amarel, S., "Representations and Modeling in Problems of Program Formation", *Machine Intelligence*, University of Edinburgh Press, Vol. 6, 1971.

bh 5. Amarel, S., "Problems of Representation in Heuristic Problem Solving; Related Issues in the Development of Expert Systems", Technical Report CBM-TR-118, Department of Computer Science, Rutgers University, February 1981, (To be published in Methods of Heuristics, Groner, Groner and Bischof, Eds., Lawrence Erlbaum Associates, Hillsdale, N.J.).

h 6. Amarel, S., "Expert Behavior and Problem Representations", *Human and Artificial Intelligence*, Elithorn, A. and Banerji, R. (Eds.), Erlbaum, 1982.

q 7. Anderberg, M. R., *Cluster Analysis for Applications*, Academic Press, 1973.

m 8. Anderson, J. R. and Bower, G. H., *Human Associative Memory*, Winston & Sons, Washington, D.C., 1973.

lm 9. Anderson, J. R., *Language, Memory, and Thought*, Lawrence Erlbaum Associates, Hillsdale, N.J., 1976.

lm 10. Anderson, J. R., "Induction of Augmented Transition Networks", *Cognitive Science*, Vol. 1, 1977.

cmo 11. Anderson, J. R., Kline, P. J. and Beasley, C. M., "A General Learning Theory and its Application to Schema Abstraction", *The Psychology of Learning and Motivation*, Vol. 13, 1979.

lm 12. Anderson, J. R., "A Theory of Language Acquisition Based on General Learning Principles", *Proceedings of the Seventh International Joint Conference on Artificial Intelligence*, Vancouver, pp. 97-103, August 1981.

cm 13. Anderson, J. R. (Ed.), *Cognitive Skills and their Acquisition*, Erlbaum Associates, Hillsdale, N.J., 1981.

hm 14. Anderson, J. R., Greeno, J. G., Kline, P. J. and Neves, D. M., "Acquisition of Problem-Solving Skill", *Cognitive Skills and their Acquisition*, Anderson, J. R. (Ed.), Lawrence Erlbaum Associates, Hillsdale, N.J., ch. 6, pp. 191-230, 1981.

hmo 15. Anderson, J. R., "Acquisition of Proof Skills in Geometry", *Machine Learning*, Michalski, R. S., Carbonell, J. G. and Mitchell, T. M. (Eds.), Tioga, 1983.

b 16. Andrae, J. H., *Thinking with the Teachable Machine*, Academic Press, 1977.

o 17. Andrews, A. M., "Learning Machines", *Proceedings of the Symposium on the Mechanization of Thought Processes*, H.M. Stationary Office, London, England, 1959.

go 18. Angluin, D., "On the Complexity of Minimum Inference of Regular Sets", *Information and Control*, Vol. 39, No. 3, pp. 337-350, 1978.

c 19. Angluin, D., "Finding Patterns Common to a Set of Strings", *Eleventh Annual ACM Symposium on the Theory of Computing*, pp. 130-141, May 1979.

g 20. Angluin, D., "Inductive Inference of Formal Languages from Positive Data", Technical Report, Dept of Mathematics., U. Calif at Santa Barbara, 1979.

hm 21. Anzai, Y., "How One Learns Strategies: Processes and Representation of Strategy Acquisition", *Proceedings of the 3rd conference on AISB*, Hamburg, Gesellschaft fur Informatik, 1978.

h 22. Anzai, Y., "Learning Strategies by Computer", *Proceedings of the Second National Conference of the Canadian Society for Computational Studies of Intelligence*, pp. 181-190, 1978.

hm 23. Anzai, Y. and Simon, H., "The Theory of Learning by Doing", *Psychological Review*, Vol. 36, No. 2, pp. 124-140, 1979.

b 24. Arieti, S., *Creativity, the Magic Synthesis*, Basic Books, Inc., 1976.

r 25. Arkadev, A. G. and Braverman, E. M., *Learning in Pattern Classification Machines*, Nauka, Moscow, 1971.

m 26. Ashby, W. Ross, *Design for a Brain, The Origin of Adaptive Behavior*, John Wiley and Sons, Inc., 1960.

o 27. Asher, R. B., Andrisani II, D. and Dorato, P., "Bibliography on Adaptive Control Systems", *Proceedings IEEE*, Vol. 64, No. 8, pp. 1226-1240, 1976.

c 28. Aubin, R., "Strategies for Mechanizing Structural Induction", *Fifth International Joint Conference on Artificial Intelligence*, Cambridge, Mass., pp. 363-369, August 1977.

b 29. Banerji, R. B., "The Description List of Concepts", *J.A.C.M*, 1962.

c 30. Banerji, R. B., "Computer Programs for the Generation of New Concepts from Old Ones", *Neure Ergebnisse der Kybernetik*, Steinbuch, K. and Wagner, S. (Eds.), Oldenberg-Verlag, Munich, pp. 336, 1964.

c 31. Banerji, R. B., "A Language for Description of Concepts", *General Systems*, Vol. 9, 1964.

h 32. Banerji, R. B. and Ernst, G. W., "Strategy Construction Using Homomorphisms Between Games", *Artificial Intelligence*, Vol. 3, pp. 223-249, 1972.

p 33. Banerji, R. B., "A Data Structure Which Can Learn Simple Programs from Examples of Input-Output", *Pattern Recognition and Artificial Intelligence*, Academic Press, 1976.

ch 34. Banerji, R. B., "Learning to Solve Games and Puzzles", *Computer Oriented Learning Processes*, Simon, J. C. (Ed.), Noordhoff, Leyden, 1976.

bh 35. Banerji, R. B. and Ernst, C. W., "A Theory for the Complete Mechanization of a GPS-Type Problem Solver", *Fifth International Joint Conference on Artificial* Intelligence, Cambridge, Mass., pp. 450-456, 1977.

cr 36. Banerji, R. B., "Pattern Recognition: Structural Description Languages", *Encyclopedia of Computer Science and Technology*, Belzer, Holzman and Kent (Eds.), Marcel Dekker, New York, pp. 1, 1979.

co 37. Banerji, R. B. and Mitchell, T. M., "Description Languages and Learning Algorithms: a Paradigm for Comparison", *International Journal of Policy Analysis and Information Systems*, Vol. 4, No. 2, June 1980.

bco 38. Banerji, R. B., *Artificial Intelligence: A Theoretical Perspective*, Elsevier North Holland, Inc., New York, 1980.

o 39. Barnes, J., *Aristotle's Posterior Analytics*, Claredon Press, Oxford, 1975.

b 40. Barr, A. and Feigenbaum, E. A. (Eds.), *The Handbook of Artificial Intelligence*, William Kaufman Inc., Los Altos, Ca., 1981.

c 41. Barrow, H. G. and Popplestone, R. J., "Relational Descriptions in Picture Processing", *Machine Intelligence*, American Elsevier, Vol. 7, pp. 377-396, 1972.

g 42. Barzdin, J. A., "On Decoding Automata in the Absence of an Upper Bound on the Number of States", *Soviet Math Dokl*, pp. 1084-1051, 1970.

gp 43. Barzdin, J. A., "Prognostication of Automata and Functions", *Information Processings '71, Proceedings of the IFIP Congress 1*, pp. 81-84, 1971.

p 44. Barzdin, J. A. and Freivald, R. V., "On the Prediction of General Recursive Functions", *Soviet Math Dokl*, Vol. 13, pp. 1224-1228, 1972.

p 45. Barzdin, J. A., "On Synthesizing Programs Given by Examples", *Lecture Notes in Computer Science*, Springer-Verlag, Vol. 5, 1972.

o 46. Barzdin, J. A. and Podnieks, K. M., "The Theory of Inductive Inference", *Proceedings of the Mathematical Foundations of Computer Science*, pp. 9-15, 1973, (Russian).

p 47. Barzdin, J. A., Kinber, E. B. and Podnieks, K. M., "Concerning Synthesis and Prediction of Functions", *Theory of Algorithms and Programs*, Latvian State U., pp. 117-128, 1974.

p 48. Barzdin, J. A. and Freivald, R. V., "Prediction and Limiting Synthesis of R.E. Classes of Functions", *Theory of Algorithms and Programs*, Latvian State U., pp. 101-111, 1974.

hp 49. Bauer, M., "A Basis for the Acquisition of Procedures from Protocols", *Fourth International Joint Conference on Artificial Intelligence*, Cambridge, Mass., pp. 226-231, September 1975.

g 50. Berger, J. and Pair, C., "Inference for Regular Bi-Languages", *J. Computer and System Sciences*, Vol. 15, pp. 100-122, 1978.

bh 51. Berliner, H., "On the Construction of Evaluation Functions for Large Domains", *Sixth International Joint Conference on Artificial Intelligence*, pp. 53-55, 1979.

go 52. Bierman, A. W. and Feldman, J. A., "A Survey of Results in Grammatical Inference", *Frontiers of Pattern Recognition*, Watanabe, S. (Ed.), Academic Press, New York, pp. 31-54, 1972.

g 53. Bierman, A. W. and Feldman, J. A., "On the Synthesis of Finite-State Machines from Samples of their Behavior", *IEEE Transactions on Computers*, Vol. C-21, pp. 592-597, 1972.

g 54. Bierman, A. W., "On the Inference of Turing Machines from Sample Computations", *Artificial Intelligence*, Vol. 3, pp. 181-198, 1972.

p 55. Bierman, A. W., Baum, R. I. and Petry, F. E., "Speeding Up the Synthesis of Programs from Traces", *IEEE Transactions on Computers*, Vol. C-24, pp. 122-136, 1975.

p 56. Bierman, A. W., "Regular LISP Programs and their Automatic Synthesis from Examples", Technical Report CS-1976-12, Duke University, 1976.

p 57. Bierman, A. W. and Krishnaswamy, R., "Constructing Programs from Example Computations", *IEEE Transactions on Software Engineering*, Vol. SE-2, pp. 141-153, 1976.

p 58. Bierman, A. W. and Smith, D. R., "The Hierarchical Synthesis of LISP Scanning Programs", *Information Processing 77*, B. Gilchrist (Ed.), North Holland, Amsterdam, pp. 41-45, 1977.

p 59. Bierman, A. W., "The inference of regular LISP programs from examples", *IEEE Transactions on Systems, Man, and Cybernetics*, Vol. SMC-8, No. 8, pp. 585-600, August 1978.

bo 60. Blake, R. M., Ducasse, C. J. and Madden, E. H., *Theories of Scientific Method: The Renaissance through the Nineteenth Century*, U. Washington Press, Seattle, 1960.

bm 61. Block, H. D., "The Perceptron: A Model of Brain Functioning, I", *Rev. Math. Physics*, Vol. 34, No. 1, pp. 123-135, 1961.

op 62. Blum, L. and Blum, M., "Inductive Inference: A Recursive Theoretic Approach", Memo ERL-M386, ERL, U. California at Berkeley, March 1973.

go 63. Blum, L. and Blum, M., "Toward a Mathematical Theory of Inductive Inference", *Information and Control*, Vol. 28, pp. 125-155, 1975.

h 64. Bond, A. H. and Mott, D. H., "Learning of Sensory-Motor Schemas in a Mobile Robot", *Proceedings of the Seventh International Joint Conference on Artificial* Intelligence, Vancouver, pp. 159-161, August 1981.

r 65. Bongard, N., *Pattern Recognition*, Spartan Books, New York, 1970, (Translation from Russian).

cr 66. Bonyant, M. M., *Pattern Recognition*, Spartan Books, New York, 1970, (Translated from Russian).

hm 67. Book, W. F., "The Psychology of Skill with Special Reference to its Acquisition in Typewriting", Technical Report, University of Montana, 1908, (Facsimile in The Psychology of Skill, Armo Press, New York, 1973).

d 68. Bradshaw, G. L., Langley, P. and Simon, H. A., "BACON.4: The Discovery of Intrinsic Properties", *Proceedings of the Third National Conference of the Canadian Society for Computational Studies of Intelligence*, pp. 19-25, 1980.

chk 69. Bratko, I. and Mulec, P., "An Experiment in Automatic Learning of Diagnostic Rules", *Informatika*, 1981.

co 70. Brown, J. S., "Steps Toward Automatic Theory Formation", *Third International Joint Conference on Artificial Intelligence*, Stanford University, pp. 20-23, 1973.

bo 71. Brown, M. F. and Tarnlund, S-A., "Inductive Reasoning in Mathematics", *Fifth International Joint Conference on Artificial Intelligence*, M.I.T., Cambridge, Mass., August 1977.

em 72. Brown, J. S. and Burton, R. B., "Diagnostic Models for Procedural Bugs in Basic Mathematical Skills", *Cognitive Science*, Vol. 2, pp. 155-192, 1978.

em 73. Brown, J. S. and VanLehn, K., "Repair Theory: a Generative Theory of Bugs in Procedural Skills", *Cognitive Science*, Vol. 4, No. 4, 1980.

em 74. Brown, J. S. and VanLehn, K., "Towards a Generative Theory of Bugs", *Addition and Subtraction: a developmental perspective*, Carpenter, T., Moser, J. and Romberg, T. (Eds.), Lawrence Erlbaum Associates, Hillsdale, N. J., 1981.

bcmo 75. Bruner, J. S., Goodnow, J. J. and Austin, G. A., *A Study of Thinking*, Wiley, New York, 1956.

h 76. Buchanan, B. G., Feigenbaum, E. A. and Lederberg, J., "A Heuristic Programming Study of Theory Formation in Sciences", *Second International Joint Conference on Artificial Intelligence*, London, 1971.

ch 77. Buchanan, B. G. and Lederberg, J., "The Heuristic DENDRAL Program for Explaining Empirical Data", *Proceedings of the IFIP-71 Congress*, IFIP, 1971.

chk 78. Buchanan, B. G., Feigenbaum, E. A. and Sridharan, N. S., "Heuristic Theory Formation: Data Interpretation and Rule Formation", *Machine Intelligence*, Halsted Press, Wiley, Vol. 7, pp. 267-290, 1972.

hk 79. Buchanan, B. G. and Sridharan, N. S., "Rule Formation on Non-Homogeneous Classes of Objects", *Third International Joint Conference on Artificial Intelligence*, Stanford U., Stanford, Calif., 1973.

chk 80. Buchanan, B. G., "Scientific Theory Formation by Computer", *Computer Oriented Learning Processes*, Simon, J. C. (Ed.), Noordhoff, Leyden, 1976.

o 81. Buchanan, B. G., Mitchell, T. M., Smith, R. G. and Johnson, C. R. Jr., "Models of Learning Systems", *Encyclopedia of Computer Science and Technology*, Dekker, Vol. 11, 1978, (also Stanford report STAN-CS-79-692).

hk 82. Buchanan, B. G. and Feigenbaum, E. A., "DENDRAL and META-DENDRAL: their Applications Dimension", *Artificial Intelligence*, North-Holland, Vol. 11, pp. 5-24, 1978.

chk 83. Buchanan, B. G. and Mitchell, T. M., "Model-Directed Learning of Production Rules", *Pattern-Directed Inference Systems*, Waterman, D. A. and Hayes-Roth, F. (Eds.), Academic Press, New York, 1978.

bho 84. Bundy, A., Silver, B., "A Critical Survey of Rule Learning Programs", D.A.I. Research Paper 169, Edinburgh, December 1981, (also in *Proceedings of the European Conference on Artificial Intelligence*, Orsay, France, July 1982).

lr 85. Burge, J. and Hayes-Roth, F., "A Novel Pattern Learning and Recognition Procedure Applied to the Learning of Vowels", Technical Report, Carnegie-Mellon University, 1976.

p 86. Burstall, R. M. and Darlington, J., "A Transformation System for Developing Recursive Programs", *Journal of the ACM*, Vol. 24, No. 1, pp. 44-67, 1977.

e 87. Burton, R. R. and Brown, J. S., "An Investigation of Computer Coaching for Informal Learning Activities", *Intelligent Tutoring Systems*, Sleeman, D. and Brown, J. S. (Eds.), Academic Press, New York, 1981.

eh 88. Burton, R. R., "Diagnosing Bugs in a Simple Procedural Skill", *Intelligent Tutoring Systems*, Sleeman, D. and Brown, J. S. (Eds.), Academic Press, New York, 1981.

gl 89. Carbonell, J. G., "Towards a Self-Extending Parser", *Proceedings of the 17th Meeting of the Association for Computational Linguistics*, pp. 3-7, 1979.

b 90. Carbonell, J. G., "Δ-MIN: a Search-Control Method for Information-Gathering Problems", *First National Conference on Artificial Intelligence*, Stanford, CA., August 1980.

l 91. Carbonell, J. G., "Metaphor - A Key to Extensible Semantic Analysis", *Proceedings of the 18th Meeting of the Association for Computational Linguistics*, 1980.

ah 92. Carbonell, J. G., "A Computational Model of Analogical Problem Solving", *Proceedings of the Seventh International Joint Conference on Artificial Intelligence*, Vancouver, pp. 147-152, August 1981.

alm 93. Carbonell, J. G., "Metaphor Comprehension", *Knowledge Representation for Language Processing Systems*, Lehnert, W. and Ringle, M. (Eds.), Erlbaum, New Jersey, 1981, (also CMU Computer Science Tech. Report CMU-CS-81-115).

alm 94. Carbonell, J. G., "Invariance Hierarchies in Metaphor Interpretation", *Proceedings of the Third Meeting of the Cognitive Science Society*, Cognitive Science Society, pp. 292-295, August 1981.

o 95. Carbonell, J. G., Michalski, R. S., and Mitchell, T. M., "An Overview of Machine Learning", *Machine Learning*, Michalski, R. S., Carbonell, J. G., and Mitchell, T. M. (Eds.), Tioga, 1983.

c 96. Carbonell, J. G., "Bounded Generalization and Example Generation: Knowledge Acquisition in a Reactive Environment", Technical Report, Carnegie-Mellon University, 1983, (to appear).

ahmc 97. Carbonell, J. G., "Learning by Analogy: Formulating and Generalizing Plans from Past Experience", *Machine Learning*, Michalski, R. S., Carbonell, J. G. and Mitchell, T. M. (Eds.), Tioga, 1983.

o 98. Carnap, R., *The Continuum of Inductive Methods*, The U. of Chicago Press, Illinois, 1952.

o 99. Carnap, R., "The Aim of Inductive Logic", *Logic, Methodology and Philosophy of Science*, Nagel, E., Suppes, P. and Tarski, A. (Eds.), Stanford University Press, Stanford, California, pp. 303-318, 1962.

ao 100. Carnap, R., "Variety, Analogy and Periodicity in Inductive Logic", *Philosophy of Science*, Vol. 30, pp. 222-227, 1963.

o 101. Carnap, R. and Jeffrey, R., *Studies in Inductive Logic and Probability*, U. of Calif Press, Berkeley, Calif, 1971.

m 102. Case, J. and Smith, C., "Anomaly Hierarchies of Mechanized Inductive Inference", *Proceedings of the 10-th Symposium on the Theory of Computing*, pp. 314-319, 1978, (is an preliminary version of Case and Smith 1981, below).

g 103. Case, J. and Smith, C., "Comparison of Identification Criteria for Mechanized Inductive Inference", Technical Report 159, Department of Computer Science, SUNY Buffalo, April 1979.

hm 104. Chase, W. G. and Simon, H. A., "Perception in Chess", *Cognitive Psychology*, Vol. 4, pp. 55-81, 1974.

or 105. Chen, C. H., "Statistical Pattern Recognition- Review and Outlook", *IEEE Systems, Man and Cybernetics Newsletter*, Vol. 6, No. 4, pp. 7-8, 1977.

cd 106. Chisolm, I. H. and Sleeman, D. H., "An Aide for Theory Formation", *Expert Systems in the Micro-Electronic Age*, Michie, D. (Ed.), Edinburgh University Press, pp. 202-212, 1979.

bgl 107. Chomsky, N., *Aspects of a Theory of Syntax*, MIT Press, 1963.

r 108. Christensen, R., *Foundations of Inductive Reasoning*, Entropy Ltd., Berkeley, California, 1964, (First Edition).

o 109. Churchman, C. W., *Theory of Experimental Inference*, Macmillan, New York, 1948.

o 110. Churchman, C. W. and Buchanan, B. G., "On the Design of Inductive Systems: Some Philosophical Problems", *British J. Phil. Science*, Vol. 20, 1969.

bh 111. Citrenbaum, R., "Efficient Representation of Optimal Solutions for a Class of Games", Technical Report SRC-69-5, Systems Research Center, Case Western Reserve University, 1969.

e 112. Clancey, W. J., Shortliffe, E. H. and Buchanan, B. G., "Intelligent Computer-Aided Instruction for Medical Diagnosis", *Proceedings of the Third Annual Symposium on Computer Applications in Medical Care*, Silver Spring, Maryland, October 1979.

e 113. Clancey, W. J., "Tutoring Rules for Guiding a Case Method Dialogue", *Intelligent Tutoring Systems*, Sleeman, D. H. and Brown, J. S. (Eds.), Academic Press, New York, 1981, (also *International Journal of Man-Machine Studies*, January 1979).

c 114. Cohen, B. L., "A Powerful and Efficient Structural Pattern Recognition System", *Artificial Intelligence*, Vol. 9, No. 3, December 1977.

c 115. Cohen, B. L. and Sammut, C. A., "Pattern Recognition and Learning with a Structural Description Language", *Proceedings of the Fourth International Joint Conference on Pattern Recognition*, Kyoto, Japan, pp. 394, 1978.

c 116. Cohen, B. L., *A Theory of Structural Concept Formation and Pattern Recognition* Ph.D. dissertation, University of South Wales, 1978, (Department of Computer Science).

c 117. Cohen, B. L., "CONFUCIUS, a Structural Pattern Recognition and Learning System", *Proceedings of the International Conference on Cybernetics and Society*, Tokyo-Kyoto, pp. 1443, 1978.

co 118. Cohen, D., *Knowledge Based Theorem Proving and Learning*, UMI Research Press, AI, 1981.

bo 119. Cohen, P. R. and Feigenbaum, E. A. (Eds.), *The Handbook of Artificial* Intelligence, Kaufman, Los Altos, Ca., Vol. III, 1982.

g 120. Cook, C. M., Rosenfeld, A. and Aronson, A. R., "Grammatical Inference by Hill-Climbing", *Information Sciences*, Vol. 10, pp. 59-80, 1976.

g 121. Cook, C. M. and Rosenfeld, A., "Some Experiments in Grammatical Inference", *Computer Oriented Learning Processes*, Simon, J. C. (Ed.), Noordhoff, Leyden, 1976.

o 122. Coulon, D. and Kayser, D., "Learning Criterion and Inductive Behavior", *Pattern Recognition*, Vol. 10, No. 1, pp. 19-25, 1978.

gl 123. Coulon, D. and Kayser, D., "Construction of Natural-Language Sentence Acceptors by a Supervised Learning Technique", *IEEE Transactions on Pattern Analysis and Machine Intelligence*, Vol. PAMI-1, pp. 94-99, 1979.

r 124. Cover, T. M., "Geometrical and Statistical Properties of Systems of Linear Inequalities with Applications in Pattern Recognition", *IEEE Transactions on Electronic Computers*, Vol. EC, No. 14, pp. 326-344, 1965.

g 125. Crespi-Reghizzi, S., "Reduction of Enumeration in Grammar Acquisition", *Second International Joint Conference on Artificial Intelligence*, British Computer Society, London, 1971.

g 126. Crespi-Reghizzi, S., "An Effective Model for Grammar Inference", *Information Processings 71*, North-Holland, pp. 524-529, 1972.

g 127. Crespi-Reghizzi, S., Melkanoff, M. A. and Lichten, L., "The Use of Grammatical Inference for Designing Programming Languages", *Communications of the ACM*, Vol. 16, No. 2, pp. 83-90, February 1973.

m 128. Culberson, J. T., *The Minds of Robots*, University of Illinois Press, Urbana, Illinois, 1963.

bl 129. Cullingford, R., *Script Application: Computer Understanding of Newspaper Stories* Ph.D. dissertation, Yale University, September 1977.

hp 130. Darlington, J. and Burstall, R. M., "A System Which Automatically Improves Programs", *Acta Informatica*, Vol. 6, pp. 41-60, 1976.

b 131. Davies, W. D. T., *System Identification for Self-Adaptive Control*, Wiley-Interscience, Wiley and Sons, Ltd., 1970.

b 132. Davis, R. and King, J., "An Overview of Production Systems", Report STAN-CS-75-542, Computer Science Department, Stanford University, October 1975, (Also Stanford AI Lab Memo #AIM-271).

k 133. Davis, R., "Interactive Transfer of Expertise: Acquisition of New Inference Rules", *Fifth International Joint Conference on Artificial Intelligence*, pp. 321-328, August 1977.

hm 134. Davis, R., Jockusch, E. and McKnight, C., "Cognitive Processes in Learning Algebra", *Journal of Children's Mathematical Behavior*, Vol. 2, No. 1, 1978.

c 135. Davis, J., "Convart: A Program for Constructive Induction on Time-Dependent Data" Master's thesis, Department of Computer Science, University of Illinois, September 1981.

k 136. Davis, R., "Applications of Meta Level Knowledge to the Construction and Use of Large Knowledge Bases", *Knowledge-based Systems in Artificial Intelligence*, Davis, R. and Lenat, D. (Eds.), McGraw-Hill, New York, 1982, (also Stanford Technical Report STAN-CS-76-552).

o 137. de Finetti, B., *Probability, Induction, and Statistics -- The Art of Guessing*, John Wiley and Sons, New York, 1972.

gl 138. Derwing, B. L., *Transformational Grammar as a Theory of Language Acquisition*, Cambridge U. Press, Cambridge, England, 1973.

qr 139. Diday, E. and Simon, J. C., "Clustering Analysis", *Communication and* Cybernetics, Fu, K. S. (Ed.), Springer-Verlag, Berlin, Heidelberg, New York, 1976.

c 140. Dietterich, T., "Description of Inductive Program INDUCE 1.1", Internal Report, Department of Computer Science, University of Illinois, October 1978.

c 141. Dietterich, T. G., "The Methodology of Knowledge Layers for Inducing Descriptions of Sequentially Ordered Events" Master's thesis, University of Illinois, October 1979.

bco 142. Dietterich, T. G. and Michalski, R. S., "Learning and Generalization of Characteristic Descriptions: Evaluation Criteria and Comparative Review of Selected Methods", *Sixth International Joint Conference on Artificial Intelligence*, Tokyo, Japan, pp. 223-231, August 1979.

c 143. Dietterich, T. G., "Applying General Induction Methods to the Card Game Eleusis", *First National Conference on Artificial Intelligence*, Stanford University, pp. 218-220, August 1980.

bco 144. Dietterich, T. G. and Michalski, R. S., "Inductive Learning of Structural Descriptions", *Artificial Intelligence*, Vol. 16, 1981.

c 145. Dietterich, T. G. and Buchanan, B. G., "The Role of the Critic in Learning Systems", Report HPP-81-19, Stanford University, December 1981, (also STAN-CS-81-891).

co 146. Dietterich, T. G. and Michalski, R. S., "A Comparative Review of Selected Methods for Learning Structural Descriptions", *Machine Learning*, Michalski, R. S., Carbonell, J. G. and Mitchell, T. M. (Eds.), Tioga, Palo Alto, 1983.

g 147. Doucet, P. G., "The Syntactic Inference Problem for DOL-Sequences", *L-Systems., Lecture Notes in Computer Science*, Springer-Verlag, Vol. 15, pp. 146-161, 1974.

b 148. Doyle, J., "A Truth Maintenance System", *Artificial Intelligence*, Vol. 12, No. 3, 1979.

b 149. Dreyfus, H. L., *What Computers Can't Do: A Critique of Artificial Reason*, Harper & Row, 1972.

coqr 150. Duda, R. O. and Hart, P. E., *Pattern Classification and Scene Analysis*, Wiley, New York, 1973.

h 151. Elcock, E. W. and Murray, A. M., "Experiments with a Learning Component in a Go-Muku Playing Program", *Machine Intelligence*, Oliver & Boyd, Vol. 1, pp. 87-103, 1967.

c 152. Ernst, G. W. and Sherman, R., "Recognizing Concepts in Terms of Other Concepts", *Pattern Recognition*, Vol. 2, pp. 301, 1969.

b 153. Ernst, G. W. and Newell, A., *GPS: A Case Study in Generality and Problem Solving*, Academic Press, New York, 1969.

h 154. Ernst, G. W., "Mechanical Discovery of Certain Heuristics", Report 113, Jennings Computer Center, Case Western Reserve University, January 1974.

p 155. Ernst, G. W. and Hookway, R. J., "Formulating Inductive Assertions for Program Verifications", Technical Report, Case Western Reserve University, 1975.

h 156. Ernst, G. W. and Goldstein, M. M., "Mechanical Discovery of Classes of Problem-Solving Strategies", *Journal of the ACM*, Vol. 29, No. 1, January 1982.

a 157. Evans, T. G., "A Program for the Solution of a Class of Geometric Analogy Intelligence Test Questions", *Semantic Information Processing*, Minsky, M. (Ed.), MIT Press, Cambridge, Mass, pp. 271-253, 1968.

b 158. Feigenbaum, E. A. and Feldman, J. (Eds.), *Computers and Thought*, McGraw-Hill, New York, 1963.

lm 159. Feigenbaum, E. A., "The Simulation of Verbal Learning Behavior", *Computers and Thought*, Feigenbaum, E. A. and Feldman, J. (Eds.), McGraw-Hill, New York, pp. 297-309, 1963, (originally in Proceedings Western Joint Computer Conference, 1961).

b 160. Feigenbaum, E. A., Buchanan, B. G. and Lederberg, J., "On Generality and Problem Solving: a Case Study using the DENDRAL Program", *Machine Intelligence*, American Elsevier, Vol. 6, pp. 165-190, 1971.

b 161. Feigenbaum, E. A., "The Art of Artificial Intelligence: I. Themes and Case Studies of Knowledge Engineering", *Fifth International Joint Conference on Artificial* Intelligence, Cambridge, Mass., pp. 1014-1029, 1977.

g 162. Feldman, J. A., Gips, J., Horning, J. J. and Reder, S., "Grammatical Complexity and Inference", Technical Report CS 125, Computer Science Department, Stanford University, 1969.

g 163. Feldman, J. A., "Some Decidability Results on Grammatical Inference and Complexity", *Information and Control*, Vol. 20, pp. 244-262, 1972.

p 164. Feldman, J. and Shields, P., "Total Complexity and the Inference of Best Programs", *Math Systems Theory*, Vol. 10, pp. 181-191, 1977.

g 165. Feliciangeli, H. and Herman, G. T., "Algorithms for Producing Grammars from Sample Derivations: A Common Problem of Formal Language Theory and Developmental Biology", *Journal of Computer and System Sciences*, Vol. 7, pp. 97-118, 1973.

b 166. Fikes, R. E. and Nilsson, N. J., "STRIPS: A New Approach to the Application of Theorem Proving to Problem Solving", *Artificial Intelligence*, Vol. 2, pp. 189-208, 1971.

h 167. Fikes, R. E., Hart, P. E. and Nilsson, N. J., "Learning and Executing Generalized Robot Plans", *Artificial Intelligence*, Vol. 3, pp. 251-288, 1972.

o 168. Findler, N. V. and McKinsie, W. R., "Computer Simulation of a Self-Preserving and Learning Organism", *Bulletin Math. Biophysics*, Vol. 31, pp. 247-253, 1969.

h 169. Findler, N. V., "Studies in Machine Cognition using the Game of Poker", *CACM*, Vol. 20, No. 4, pp. 230-245, 1977.

b 170. Findler, N. V. (Ed.), *Associative Networks - The Representation and Use of Knowledge in Computers*, Academic Press, New York, 1979.

bm 171. Fodor, J. A., *The Language of Thought*, Thomas Y. Crowell Co., New York, pp. 124-156, 1975.

c 172. Fox, M. S. and Hayes-Roth, F., "Approximation Techniques for the Learning of Sequential Symbolic Patterns", *Proceedings of the Third International Joint Conference on Pattern Recognition*, pp. 616-620, 1976.

o 173. Fox, M. S., "On Inheritance in Knowledge Representation", *Sixth International Joint Conference on Artificial Intelligence*, Tokyo, Japan, 1979.

c 174. Fredkin, E., "Techniques using LISP for Automatically Discovering Interesting Relations in Data", *The Programming Language LISP*, Berkeley and Bobrow (Eds.), Information International, Cambridge, Mass., 1964.

b 175. Friedberg, R. M., "A Learning Machine: Part 1", *IBM Journal*, Vol. 2, pp. 2-13, 1958.

b 176. Friedberg, R., Dunham, B. and North, T., "A Learning Machine: Part 2", *IBM Journal of Research and Development*, Vol. 3, No. 3, pp. 282-287, 1959.

or 177. Fu, K. S., *Sequential Methods in Pattern Recognition and Machine Learning*, Academic Press, New York, 1968.

r 178. Fu, K. S. (Ed.), *Pattern Recognition and Machine Learning*, Plenum Press, New York, 1971.

bor 179. Fu, K. S., *Syntactic Methods in Pattern Recognition*, Academic Press, New York, 1974.

b 180. Fu, K. S. and Tou, J. T., *Learning Systems and Intelligent Robots*, Plenum Press, 1974.

go 181. Fu, K. S. and Booth, T. L., "Grammatical Inference: Introduction and Survey-Part", *IEEE Transactions on SMC*, Vol. 5, No. 1, 4, pp. 95-111, 409-423, 1975.

or 182. Fu, K. S., *Syntactic Pattern Recognition, Applications*, Springer-Verlag, New York, 1977.

gor 183. Fu, K. S., "Pattern Recognition: Discriminant and Syntactic Methods", *Encyclopedia of Computer Science and Technology*, Marcel Dekker, Vol. 12, 1979.

or 184. Fukanaga, K., *Introduction to Statistical Pattern Recognition*, Academic Press, 1972.

bg 185. Gaines, B. R., "Behavior/Structure Transformations under Uncertainty", *International Journal of Man-Machine Studies*, Vol. 8, pp. 337-365, 1976.

g 186. Gaines, B. R., "Maryanski's Grammatical Inferencer", *IEEE Transactions on* Computers, Vol. C-28, pp. 62-64, 1979.

d 187. German, S. M. and Wegbreit, B., "A Synthesizer of Inductive Assertions", *IEEE Transactions on Software Engineering*, Vol. SE-1, No. 1, pp. 68-75, March 1975.

g 188. Gill, A., "State-Identification Experiments in Finite Automata", *Information and Control*, Vol. 4, pp. 132-154, 1961.

co 189. Glanc, A., "Theory Formation by Machine: a General Framework of the GOLEM System", *IEEE Transactions on Systems, Man, and Cybernetics*, pp. 342-343, 1973.

g 190. Gold, E. M., "Language Identification in the Limit", *Information and Control*, Vol. 10, pp. 447-474, 1967.

g 191. Gold, E. M., "System Identification via State Characterization", *Automatica*, Vol. 8, pp. 621-636, 1972.

g 192. Gold, E. M., "Complexity of Automaton Identification from Given Data", *Information and Control*, Vol. 37, pp. 302-320, 1978.

h 193. Goldin, S. E. and Klahr, P., "Learning and Abstraction in Simulation", *Proceedings of the Seventh International Joint Conference on Artificial Intelligence*, Vancouver, pp. 212-214, August 1981.

hk 194. Goldstein, I. P. and Grissom, E., "Annotated Production Systems: a Model for Skill Acquisition", *Fifth International Joint Conference on Artificial Intelligence*, Cambridge, Mass., pp. 311-317, 1977.

h 195. Goldstein, M. M., "The Mechanical Discovery of Problem Solving Strategies", Report ESCI-77-1, Case Institute of Technology, Case Western Reserve U., 1977.

k 196. Goldstein, I. P., "The Genetic Graph: a Representation for the Evolution of Procedural Knowledge", *Intelligent Tutoring Systems*, Sleeman, D. H. and Brown, J. S. (Eds.), Academic Press, New York, 1981.

r 197. Gonzalez, R. C. and Thomason, M. G., *Syntactic Pattern Recognition, An* Introduction, Addison-Wesley, Reading, Mass., 1978.

o 198. Good, I., "The Probabilistic Explication of Information, Evidence, Surprise, Causality, Explanation, and Utility", *Foundations of statistical inference*, Godambe and Sprott (Eds.), Holt, Rinehart and Winston of Canada, Toronto, pp. 108-122, 1971.

q 199. Gowda, K. C. and Krishna, G., "Disaggregative Clustering using the Concept of Mutual Nearest Neighborhood", *IEEE Transactions on Systems, Man and Cybernetics*, Vol. SMC-8, No. 12, pp. 888-894, December 1978.

p 200. Green, C. C., "The Design of the PSI Program Synthesis System", *Proceedings of the Second International Conference on Software Engineering*, San Francisco, CA., pp. 4-18, October 1976.

ho 201. Griffith, A. K., "A Comparison and Evaluation of Three Machine Learning Procedures as Applied to the Game of Checkers", *Artificial Intelligence*, Vol. 5, pp. 137-148, 1974.

p 202. Guiho, G. and Jouannaud, J. P., "Program Synthesis for a Simple Class of Non-Loop Functions", Technical Report 6, Laboratoire de Recherche en Informatique., Universite de Paris-Sud, 1978.

k 203. Haas, N. and Hendrix, G. G., "An Approach to Applying and Acquiring Knowledge", *First National Conference on Artificial Intelligence*, Stanford, CA., pp. 235-239, August 1980.

k 204. Haas, N. and Hendrix, G. G., "Learning by Being Told: Acquiring Knowledge for Information Management", *Machine Learning*, Michalski, R. S., Carbonell, J. G. and Mitchell, T. M. (Eds.), Tioga, 1980.

bo 205. Hacking, I., *Logic of Statistical Inference*, Harvard University Press, Cambridge, Mass., 1965.

o 206. Hájek, P., "On Logics of Discovery", *Lecture Notes in Computer Science*, Springer-Verlag, Vol. 1, pp. 30-45, 1975.

c 207. Hájek, P. and Havránek, T., "On Generation of Inductive Hypotheses", *International Journal on Man-Machine Studies*, No. 9, pp. 415-438, 1977.

o 208. Hájek, P. and Havránek, T., *Mechanizing Hypothesis Formation: Mathematical Foundations for a General Theory*, Springer-Verlag, 1978.

c 209. Hájek, P. and Havránek, T., "The GUHA Method - its Aims and Techniques", *International Journal on Man-Machine Studies*, No. 10, pp. 3-22, 1978.

d 210. Hamacher, V. C., Langdon, G. G., Cantarella, R. G., English, W. and Losupovicz, *Theory of Adaptive Mechanisms*, Management Information Services, Detroit, 1970.

d 211. Hammond, P. H., "Theory of Self-Adaptive Control Systems", *Proceedings of the Second IFAC Symposium on the THeory of Self-Adaptive Control Systems*, Plenum Press, New York, September 1966.

p 212. Hardy, S., "Synthesis of LISP Functions from Examples", *Fourth International Joint Conference on Artificial Intelligence*, Cambridge, Mass., pp. 240-245, September 1975.

l 213. Harris, L. R., "A System for Primitive Natural Language Acquisition", *International Journal Man-Machine Studies*, pp. 153-206, 1977.

e 214. Hartley, J. R. and Sleeman, D. H., "Towards Intelligent Teaching Systems", *International Journal on Man-Machine Studies*, Vol. 5, pp. 215-236, 1973.

c 215. Hayes-Roth, F., "Schematic Classification Problems and their Solution", *Pattern Recognition*, Vol. 6, pp. 105-113, 1974.

c 216. Hayes-Roth, F. and Mostow, D., "An Automatically Compilable Recognition Network for Structured Patterns", *Fourth International Joint Conference on Artificial* Intelligence, Cambridge, Mass., pp. 356-362, September 1975.

c 217. Hayes-Roth, F., "Patterns of Induction and Associated Knowledge Acquisition Algorithms", *Pattern Recognition and Artificial Intelligence*, Chen, C. (Ed.), Academic Press, New York, 1976.

c 218. Hayes-Roth, F., "Representation of Structured Events and Efficient Procedures for their Recognition", *Pattern Recognition*, Vol. 8, pp. 141, 1976.

cl 219. Hayes-Roth, F. and Burge, J., "Characterizing Syllables as Sequences of Machine-Generated Labeled Segments of Connected Speech: a Study in Symbolic Pattern Learning using a Conjunctive Feature Learning and Classification System", *Proceedings of the Third International Joint Conference on Pattern Recognition*, Coronado, Ca., pp. 431-436, 1976.

ch 220. Hayes-Roth, F., "Uniform Representations of Structured Patterns and an Algorithm for the Induction of Contingency-Response Rules", *Information and Control*, Vol. 33, pp. 87-116, February 1977.

c 221. Hayes-Roth, F. and McDermott, J., "Knowledge Acquisition from Structural Descriptions", *Fifth International Joint Conference on Artificial Intelligence*, Cambridge, Mass., pp. 356-362, August 1977.

c 222. Hayes-Roth, F. and McDermott, J., "An Interference Matching Technique for Inducing Abstractions", *Communications of the ACM*, Vol. 21, No. 5, pp. 401-410, 1978.

chk 223. Hayes-Roth, F., Klahr, P., Burge, J. and Mostow, D. J., "Machine Methods for Acquiring, Learning, and Applying Knowledge", Technical Report R-6241, The RAND Corporation, 1978.

hk 224. Hayes-Roth, F., Klahr, P. and Mostow, D. J., "Knowledge Acquisition, Knowledge Programming, and Knowledge Refinement", Technical Report R-2540-NSF, The Rand Corporation, May 1980.

k 225. Hayes-Roth, F., Klahr, P. and Mostow, D. J., "Advice-Taking and Knowledge Refinement: an Iterative View of Skill Acquisition", RAND Paper Series P-6517, The RAND Corporation, 1980, (to appear in J. A. Anderson, *Skill Acquisition and* Development, Erlbaum, 1981, in press).

chk 226. Hayes-Roth, F., "Using Proofs and Refutations to Learn from Experience", *Machine Learning*, Michalski, R. S., Carbonell, J. G. and Mitchell, T. M. (Eds.), Tioga, Palo Alto, 1983.

hm 227. Hayes, J. R. and Simon, H. A., "Understanding Written Problem Instructions", *Knowledge and Cognition*, Gregg, L. W. (Ed.), Erlbaum, Potomac, Md., 1974.

h 228. Hedrick, C. L., *A Computer Program to Learn Production Systems Using a Semantic Net* Ph.D. dissertation, Carnegie-Mellon University, July 1974, (Department of Computer Science).

h 229. Hedrick, C. L., "Learning Production Systems from Examples", *Artificial* Intelligence, Vol. 7, No. 1, pp. 21-49, 1976.

o 230. Hempel, C. G., "Inductive Inconsistencies", *Synthese*, Vol. 12, pp. 439-469, 1960.

o 231. Hendel, R. J., "Mathematical Learning Theory: a Formalized, Axiomatic, Abstract Approach", *Information and Control*, Vol. 41, pp. 67-117, 1979.

g 232. Herman, G. T. and Walker, A. D., "The Syntactic Inference Problem Applied to Biological Systems", *Machine Intelligence*, Edinburgh U. Press, Vol. 7, pp. 341-356, 1972.

r 233. Highleyman, W. H., "Linear Decision Functions, with Applications to Pattern Recognition", *Proceedings of IRE*, IRE, No. 50, pp. 1501-1504, 1967.

bo 234. Hilgard, E. R. and Bower, G. H., *Theories of Learning - Third Edition*, Appleton-Century-Grofts, New York, 1966.

o 235. Hintikka, J., "On a Combined System of Inductive Logic", *Acta Philosophica* Fennica, Vol. 18, pp. 21-30, 1965.

o 236. Hintikka, J., "Towards a Theory of Inductive Generalization", *Proceedings of the 1964 Congress for Logic, Methodology and Philosophy of Science*, North Holland, Amsterdam, pp. 274-288, 1965.

b 237. Hintikka, J. and Suppes, P. (Eds.), *Aspects of Inductive Logic*, North-Holland, Amsterdam, 1966.

o 238. Hintikka, J. and Hilpinen, R., "Knowledge Acceptance and Inductive Logic", *Aspects of Inductive Logic*, Hintikka, J. and Suppes, P. (Eds.), North-Holland, Amsterdam, pp. 1-20, 1966.

bo 239. Hofstadter, D. R., *Goedel, Escher, Bach: an Eternal Golden Braid*, Basic Books Inc., New York, 1979.

d 240. Holland, J. H., *Adaptation in Natural and Artificial Systems*, University of Michigan Press, Ann Arbor, 1975.

m 241. Holland, T. H. and Reitman, J. S., *Cognitive Systems Based on Adaptive* Algorithms, Academic Press, 1978.

cm 242. Holland, J. H., "Adaptive Algorithms for Discovering and Using General Patterns in Growing Knowledge Bases", *Policy Analysis and Information Systems*, Vol. 4, No. 3, September 1980.

o 243. Hormann, A. M., "Programs for Machine Learning, Part 1", *Information and* Control, Vol. 5, pp. 347-367, 1962.

o 244. Hormann, A. M., "Programs for Machine Learning, Part 2", *Information and* Control, Vol. 7, No. 1, pp. 55-77, 1964.

g 245. Horning, J. J., *A Study of Grammatical Inference* Ph.D. dissertation, Stanford University, August 1969, (also Department of Computer Science Technical Report CS-139).

g 246. Horning, J. J., "A Procedure for Grammatical Inference", *Information Processing*, Vol. 71, pp. 519-523, 1972.

c 247. Hubel, C. U. and Rollinger, C. R., "A Sketch on Acquisition of Higher Cognitive Concepts", *NATO Symposium on Human and Artificial Intelligence*, Lyons, France, October 1981.

c 248. Hunt, E. B., *Concept Learning: An Information Processing Problem*, Wiley, New York, 1962.

cm 249. Hunt, E. B. and Hovland, C. I., "Programming a Model of Human Concept Formation", *Computers and Thought*, Feigenbaum, E. A. and Feldman, J. (Eds.), McGraw-Hill, New York, pp. 310-325, 1963.

cgm 250. Hunt, E. B., "Selection and Reception Conditions in Grammar and Concept Learning", *J. Verbal Learning Verbal Behavior*, Vol. 4, pp. 211-215, 1965.

co 251. Hunt, E. B., Marin, J. and Stone, P. T., *Experiments in Induction*, Academic Press, New York, 1966.

bo 252. Hunt, E. B., *Artificial Intelligence*, Academic Press, New York, 1975.

c 253. Iba, G. A., "Learning Disjunctive Concepts from Examples" Master's thesis, M.I.T., 1979, (also AI memo 548).

h 254. Johnson, D. L. and Holden, D. C., "Computer Learning in Theorem Proving", *IEEE Transactions on Systems Science and Cybernetics*, Vol. SSC-2, pp. 115-123, 1966.

p 255. Jouannaud, J. P., Guiho, G. and Treuil, T. P., "SISP/1 An Interactive System Able to Synthesize Functions from Examples", *Proceedings of the Fifth International Joint Conference on Artificial Intelligence*, pp. 412-418, 1977.

p 256. Jouannaud, J. P. and Guiho, G., "Inference of Functions with an Interactive System", *Machine Intelligence*, Ellis Horwood, Vol. 9, 1979.

p 257. Jouannaud, J. P. and Kodratoff, Y., "Characterization of a Class of Functions Synthesized from Examples by a Summers-Like Method using a B.M.W. Matching Technique", *Sixth International Joint Conference on Artificial Intelligence*, Tokyo, Japan, pp. 440-447, 1979.

or 258. Kanal, L. N., "Patterns in Pattern Recognition: 1968-1974", *IEEE Transactions on Information Theory*, Vol. IT-20, No. 6, pp. 697-722, 1974.

or 259. Kanal, L. N., "Current Status, Problems and Prospects of Pattern Recognition", *IEEE Systems, Man and Cybernetics Newsletter*, Vol. 6, No. 4, pp. 9-11, 1977.

or 260. Kanal, L. N., "Problem-Solving Models and Search Strategies for Pattern Recognition", *IEEE Transactions on Pattern Analysis and Machine Intelligence*, Vol. PAMI-1, No. 2, pp. 193-201, 1979.

br 261. Kanal, L. N., Leveen, N., Rosenfeld, and Azriel, *Progress in Pattern Recognition*, North-Holland, Vol. 1, 1981.

p 262. Kant, E., "A Knowledge-Based Approach to Using Efficiency Estimation in Program Synthesis", *Sixth International Joint Conference on Artificial Intelligence*, Tokyo, pp. 457-462, 1979.

p 263. Kant, E., "Efficiency in Program Synthesis", Ann Arbor, UMI Research Press, 1981

c 264. Karpinski, J. and Michalski, R. S., "A Learning Recognition System for Handwritten Alphanumeric Characters", *Papers of the Institute of Automatic Control*, No. 35, Polish Academy of Sciences, Warsaw, Poland, 1966, (In Polish).

r 265. Kazmierczak, H. and Steinbuch, K., "Adaptive Systems in Pattern Recognition", *IEEE Transactions of Electronic Computers*, IEEE, Vol. EC-12, No. 5, pp. 822-835, 1963.

o 266. Kemeny, J. G., "The Use of Simplicity in Induction", *Philosophical Review*, Vol. 62, pp. 391-408, 1953.

o 267. Kilburn, T., Grimsdale, R. L. and Sumner, F. H., "Experiments in Machine Learning and Thinking", *Information Processing of ICIP*, 1959.

o 268. Kinber, E. B., "On a Theory of Inductive Inference", *Lecture Notes in Computer Science*, Springer-Verlag, Vol. 56, pp. 435-440, 1977.

p 269. Kinber, E. B., "On Identification in the Limit of Minimal Numbers for Functions of Effectively Enumerable Classes", *Theory of Algorithms and Programs*, Latvian State U., pp. 35-56, 1977.

b 270. Klahr, P., "Partial Proofs and Partial Answers", Technical Report P-6239, The Rand Corporation, 1978, (presented at fourth Workshop on Automated Deduction, University of Texas, Austin).

gl 271. Klein, S. and Kuppon, M. A., "An Interactive Heuristic Program for Learning Transformational Grammar", Technical Report, Computer Science Dept., U. Wisconsin, 1979.

p 272. Klette, R., "Recognizing Algorithms for Recursive Functions", *Elektronicshe Informationsverarbeitung und Kybernetik*, Vol. 12, pp. 227-243, 1976, (in German).

c 273. Kline, P. J., "The Superiority of Relative Criteria in Partial Matching and Generalization", *Proceedings of the Seventh International Joint Conference on Artificial Intelligence*, Vancouver, pp. 296-303, August 1981.

ah 274. Kling, R. E., "A Paradigm for Reasoning by Analogy", *Artificial Intelligence*, Vol. 2, pp. 147-178, 1971.

g 275. Knobe, B. and Knobe, K., "A Method for Inferring Context-Free Grammars", *Information and Control*, Vol. 31, pp. 129-146, 1976.

c 276. Kochen, M., "Experimental Study of Hypothesis Formation by Computer", *Proceedings 1960 London Symposium on Information Theory*, 1960.

c 277. Kochen, M., "An Experimental Program for the Selection of Disjunctive Hypotheses", *Proceedings Western Joint Computer Conference*, pp. 571-578, 1961.

c 278. Kochen, M., "Some Mechanisms in Hypothesis Selection", *Proceedings Symposium on Mathematical Theory of Automata, N.Y. (1962)*, Polytechnic Press of the Polytechnic Institute of Brooklyn, N.Y., 1963.

o 279. Kochen, M., "Cognitive Learning Processes: an Explication", *Artificial Intelligence and Heuristic Programming*, Findler and Meltzer (Eds.), Edinburgh U. Press, 1971.

p 280. Kochen, M., "An Algorithm for Forming Hypotheses about Simple Functions", *Third Milwaukee Symposium on Automatic Computation and Control*, Milwaukee, Wisconsin, 1975.

p 281. Kodratoff, Y., "A Class of Functions Synthesised from a Finite Number of Examples and a LISP Program Scheme", *International Journal Computer and Information Sciences*, Vol. 8, No. 6, pp. 489-521, 1979.

hr 282. Koffman, E. B., "Learning Games through Pattern Recognition", *IEEE Transactions on Systems Science and Cybernetics*, Vol. SSC-4, No. 1, 1968.

c 283. Koford, T. S. and Groner, G. F., "The Use of an Adaptive Threshold Element to Design a Linear Optimal Pattern Classifier", *IEEE Transactions-Information Theory*, IEEE, Vol. 1T-12, pp. 42-50, 1966.

cl 284. Kolodner, J. L., *Retrieval and Organizational Strategies in Conceptual Memory: A Computer Model* Ph.D. dissertation, Yale University, November 1980.

c 285. Konrad, E., Orlowska, E. and Pawlak, Z., "On Approximate Concept Learning", Fachbereich 20, Informatik Technische Universitat, Berlin, October 1981.

h 286. Kopec, D. and Niblett, T., "How Hard is the Play of the King-Rook King-Knight Ending?", *Advances in Computer Chess*, Clarke, M.R.B. (Ed.), Edinburgh University Press, 1979.

h 287. Korf, R. E., "Toward a Model of Representation Changes", *Artificial Intelligence*, Vol. 14, No. 1, pp. 41-78, 1980.

d 288. Kotovski, K. and Simon, H., "Empirical Tests of a Theory of Human Acquisition of Concepts for Sequential Patterns", *Cognitive Psychology*, No. 4, pp. 399-424, 1973.

b 289. Kowalski, R., "Predicate Logic as a Programming Language", *Information* Processing, Vol. 74, pp. 569-574, 1974.

o 290. Kramer, "A Note on the Self-Consistency Definitions of Generalization and Inductive Inference", *JACM*, pp. 280-281, 1962.

o 291. Kugel, P., "Induction Pure and Simple", *Information and Control*, Vol. 35, pp. 276-336, 1977.

bo 292. Kuhn, T. S., *The Structure of Scientific Revolutions*, University of Chicago Press, Chicago, 1970, (2nd edition).

o 293. Kyburg, H., "Recent Work in Inductive Logic", *American Philosophical Quarterly*, Vol. 1, pp. 249-287, 1964.

bo 294. Lakatos, I., *Proofs and Refutations: The Logic of Mathematical Discovery*, Cambridge University Press, Cambridge, 1976.

o 295. Landan, I. D., "A Survey of Model Reference Adaptive Techniques-Theory and Applications", *Automatica*, Vol. 10, No. 4, 1974.

d 296. Langley, P. W., "BACON: A Production System that Discovers Empirical Laws", *Fifth International Joint Conference on Artificial Intelligence*, Cambridge, Mass., pp. 344-346, August 1977.

d 297. Langley, P., "BACON.1: A General Discovery System", *Proceedings of the Second National Conference of the Canadian Society for Computational Studies in Intelligence*, pp. 173-180, 1978.

d 298. Langley, P., "Rediscovering Physics with BACON.3", *Sixth International Joint Conference on Artificial Intelligence*, Tokyo, pp. 505-507, 1979.

h 299. Langley, P. W., Neches, R., Neves, D. and Anzai, Y., "A Domain-Independent Framework for Procedure Learning", *Journal of Policy Analysis and Information* Systems, Vol. 4, No. 2, pp. 163-197, June 1980.

d 300. Langley, P., Bradshaw, G. L. and Simon, H. A., "BACON.5: The Discovery of Conservation Laws", *Proceedings of the Seventh International Joint Conference on Artificial Intelligence*, Vancouver, pp. 121-126, August 1981.

d 301. Langley, P., "Data-Driven Discovery of Physical Laws", *Cognitive Science*, Vol. 5, No. 1, pp. 31-54, 1981.

d 302. Langley, P., Simon, H. A. and Bradshaw, G. L., "Rediscovering Chemistry with the BACON System", *Machine Learning*, Michalski, R. S., Carbonell, J. G. and Mitchell, T. M. (Eds.), Tioga, Palo Alto, 1982.

c 303. Larson, J. and Michalski, R. S., "AQVAL/1 (AQ7) User's Guide and Program Description", Technical Report 731, Dept. Computer Science., U. Illinois, 1975.

c 304. Larson, J., "INDUCE-1: An Interactive Inductive Inference Program in VL21 Logic System", Technical Report UIUCDCS-R-77-876, Department of Computer Science, University of Illinois, May 1977.

c 305. Larson, J., *Inductive Inference in the Variable-Valued Predicate Logic System VL21: Methodology and Computer Implementation* Ph.D. dissertation, University of Illinois, May 1977.

c 306. Larson, J. and Michalski, R. S., "Inductive Inference of VL Decision Rules", *Proceedings of the Workshop on Pattern Directed Inference Systems, SIGART Newsletter 63*, 1977.

c 307. Larson, J. and Michalski, R. S., "Inductive Inference of VL Decision Rules", *Pattern-Directed Inference Systems*, Waterman, D. A. and Hayes-Roth, F. (Eds.), Academic Press, New York, 1978.

lm 308. Lebowitz, M., *Generalization and Memory in an Integrated Understanding System* Ph.D. dissertation, Yale University, October 1980.

m 309. Lebowitz, M., "The Nature of Generalization in Understanding", *Proceedings of the Seventh International Joint Conference on Artificial Intelligence*, Vancouver, pp. 348-353, August 1981.

d 310. Lenat, D. B., *AM: An Artificial Intelligence Approach to Discovery in Mathematics as Heuristic Search* Ph.D. dissertation, Stanford University, 1976.

o 311. Lenat, D. B., "The Ubiquity of Discovery", *Artificial Intelligence*, Vol. 9, No. 3, pp. 257-285, December 1977.

d 312. Lenat, D. B., "Automated Theory Formation in Mathematics", *Fifth International Joint Conference on Artificial Intelligence*, Cambridge, Mass., pp. 833-842, 1977.

d 313. Lenat, D. and Harris, G., "Designing a Rule System that Searches for Scientific Discoveries", *Pattern-Directed Inference Systems*, Waterman, D. A. and Hayes-Roth, F. (Eds.), Academic Press, New York, pp. 25-51, 1978.

hop 314. Lenat, D. B., Hayes-Roth, F. and Klahr, P., "Cognitive Economy", RAND technical report N-1185-NSF, The RAND Corporation, June 1979.

ho 315. Lenat, D. B., "The Nature of Heuristics", Technical Report HPP-80-26, Heuristic Programming Project., Computer Science Dept., Stanford U., 1980.

dh 316. Lenat, D. B., *The Role of Heuristics in Learning by Discovery: Three Case Studies*, Tioga, Palo Alto, 1982.

o 317. Levi, I., "Deductive Cogency in Inductive Inference", *Journal of Philosophy*, Vol. 62, pp. 68-77, 1965.

o 318. Levi, I., *Gambling with Truth: An Essay on Induction and the Aims of Science*, Alfred A. Knopf, Inc., New York, 1967.

h 319. Lewis, C. H., *Production System Models of Practice Effects* Ph.D. dissertation, University of Michigan, 1978, (unpublished).

bo 320. Lindsay, P. H. and Norman, D. A., *Human Information Processing*, Academic Press, New York, 1972.

m 321. Logan, F. A. and Gordon, W. C., *Fundamentals of Learning and Motivation*, W. C. Brown Company, 1981, (third edition).

c 322. Loisel, R. and Kodratoff, Y., "Learning (Complex) Structural Descriptions from Examples", *Proceedings of the Seventh International Joint Conference on Artificial Intelligence*, Vancouver, pp. 141-143, August 1981.

ch 323. Low, J. R., "Automatic Data Structure Selection: An Example and Overview", *Communications of the ACM*, Vol. 21, No. 5, pp. 376-385, May 1978.

h 324. Luchins, A. S., "Mechanization in Problem Solving", *Psychological Monographs*, Vol. 54, No. 248, 1942.

o 325. MacKay, D. M., "The Epistemological Problem for Automata", *Automata Studies*, Shannan and McCarthy (Eds.), Princeton U. Press, Princeton, N.J., 1955.

g 326. Maryanski, F. J. and Booth, T. L., "Inference of Finite-State Probabilistic Grammars", *IEEE Transactions on Computers*, Vol. C-26, pp. 521-536, 1977, (See also Gaines 1979).

e 327. Matz, M., "Towards a Generative Theory of High School Algebra Errors", *Intelligent Tutoring Systems*, Sleeman, D. H. and Brown, J. S. (Eds.), Academic Press, New York, 1981.

g 328. McCarthy and Shannon (Eds.), *Automata Studies*, Princeton University Press, Princeton, 1955.

bo 329. McCarthy, J., "Programs with Common Sense", *Semantic Information Processing*, Minsky, M. (Ed.), M.I.T. Press, Cambridge, Mass., pp. 403-417, 1968.

b 330. McCarthy, J., "First Order Theories of Individual Concepts and Propositions", *Machine Intelligence*, Ellis Horwood, Vol. 9, 1979.

bm 331. McCulloch, W. S. and Pitts, W., "A Logical Calculus of Ideas Imminent in Nervous Activity", *Bull. Math. Biophysics*, Vol. 5, pp. 115-133, 1943.

ah 332. McDermott, J., "ANA: An Assimilating and Accommodating Production System", Technical Report CMU-CS-78-156, Carnegie-Mellon University, December 1978.

a 333. McDermott, J., "Learning to Use Analogies", *Sixth International Joint Conference on Artificial Intelligence*, 1979.

b 334. Meehan, J. R., "An Artificial Intelligence Approach to Tonal Music Theory", Technical Report 124A, Department of Information and Computer Science, University of California, Irvine, June 1979.

co 335. Meltzer, B., "The Semantics of Induction and the Possibility of Complete Systems of Inductive Inference", *Artificial Intelligence*, Vol. 1, pp. 189-192, 1970.

do 336. Meltzer, B., "Generation of Hypotheses and Theories", *Nature*, March 1970.

o 337. Meltzer, B., "The Programming of Deduction and Induction", *Artificial and Human Thinking*, Elithorn, A. and Jones, D. (Eds.), San Francisco, pp. 19-33, 1973.

dr 338. Mendel, T. and Fu, K. S., *Adaptive Learning and Pattern Recognition: Theory and Applications*, Spartan Books, New York, 1970.

r 339. Michalski, R. S., "A Variable-Valued Logic System as Applied to Picture Description and Recognition", *Graphic Languages*, Nake, F. and Rosenfeld, A. (Eds.), North-Holland, 1972.

c 340. Michalski, R. S., "Discovering Classification Rules using Variable-Valued Logic System VL1", *Third International Joint Conference on Artificial Intelligence*, pp. 162-172, 1973.

c 341. Michalski, R. S., "AQVAL/1 - Computer Implementation of a Variable Valued Logic System VL1 and Examples of its Application to Pattern Recognition", *Proceedings of the First International Joint Conference on Pattern Recognition*, Washington, D. C., pp. 3-17, 1973.

c 342. Michalski, R. S., "Synthesis of Optimal and Quasi-Optimal Variable-Valued Logic Formulas", *Fifth International Symposium on Multiple-Valued Logic*, Bloomington, Indiana, 1975.

cr 343. Michalski, R. S., "Variable-Valued Logic and its Applications to Pattern Recognition and Machine Learning", *Computer Science and Multiple-Valued Logic Theory and Applications*, Rine, D. C. (Ed.), North-Holland, pp. 506-534, 1975.

c 344. Michalski, R. S., "Learning by Inductive Inference", *Computer Oriented Learning Processes*, Simon, J. C. (Ed.), Noordhoff, Leyden, Netherlands, pp. 321-337, 1976, (Proceedings of the NATO Advanced Study Institute on Computer Oriented Learning Processes., Bonas, France, 1974).

c 345. Michalski, R. S., "A System of Programs for Computer-Aided Induction: A Summary", *Fifth International Joint Conference on Artificial Intelligence*, Cambridge, Mass., pp. 319-320, 1977.

c 346. Michalski, R. S., "Pattern Recognition as Knowledge-Guided Induction", Technical Report 927, Department of Computer Science, 1978.

c 347. Michalski, R. S. and Larson, J. B., "Selection of Most Representative Training Examples and Incremental Generation of VL1 Hypotheses: The Underlying Methodology and Description of Programs ESEL and AQ11", Report 867, University of Illinois, 1978.

cd 348. Michalski, R. S., "Pattern Recognition as Rule-Guided Inductive Inference", *IEEE Transactions on Pattern Analysis and Machine Intelligence*, Vol. PAMI-2, No. 2, 3, 4, pp. 349-361, 1980.

ck 349. Michalski, R. S. and Chilausky, R. L., "Learning by Being Told and Learning from Examples: An Experimental Comparison of the Two Methods of Knowledge Acquisition in the Context of Developing an Expert System for Soybean Disease Diagnosis", *Policy Analysis and Information Systems*, Vol. 4, No. 2, June 1980, (Special issue on knowledge acquisition and induction).

cq 350. Michalski, R. S., "Knowledge Acquisition through Conceptual Clustering: A Theoretical Framework and an Algorithm for Partitioning Data into Conjunctive Concepts", *Policy Analysis and Information Systems*, Vol. 4, No. 3, September 1980.

co 351. Michalski, R. S., "Inductive Inference as Rule-Guided Transformation of Symbolic Descriptions", *International Workshop on Program Construction*, Chateau de Bonas, France, pp. 45, September 1980, (also in *Program Construction*, Bierman (ed.)).

cq 352. Michalski, R. S. and Stepp, R. E., "An Application of AI Techniques to Structuring Objects into an Optimal Conceptual Hierarchy", *Proceedings of the Seventh International Joint Conference on Artificial Intelligence*, Vancouver, pp. 460-465, August 1981.

cq 353. Michalski, R. S., Stepp, R. and Diday, E., "A Recent Advance in Data Analysis: Conceptual Clustering", *Recent Advances in Pattern Recognition*, Rosenfeld, A. and Kanal, L. (Eds.), North-Holland, Amsterdam, pp. 33-56, 1981

cq 354. Michalski, R. S. and Stepp, R., "Learning from Observation: Conceptual Clustering", *Machine Learning*, Michalski, R. S., Carbonell, J. G. and Mitchell, T. M. (Eds.), Tioga, Palo Alto, CA, 1982.

bo 355. Michalski, R. S., Carbonell, R. S. and Mitchell, T. M. (Eds.), *Machine Learning*, Tioga, Palo Alto, CA, 1982.

cod 356. Michalski, R. S., "A Theory and Methodology of Inductive Learning", *Machine Learning*, Michalski, R. S., Carbonell, J. G. and Mitchell, T. M. (Eds.), Tioga, Palo Alto, 1982.

cod 357. Michalski, R. S., "Unifying Principles and a Methodology for Inductive Learning", *Artificial Intelligence*, 1983, (to appear).

b 358. Michie, D., *On Machine Intelligence*, John Wiley & Sons, New York, 1974.

b 359. Michie, D. (Ed.), *Expert Systems in the Micro-Electronic Age*, Redwood Burn Limited, 1979.

o 360. Michie, D., "The State of the Art in Machine Learning", *Introductory Readings in Expert Systems*, D. Michie (Ed.), Gordon and Breach, UK, 1982.

o 361. Minicozzi, E., "Some Natural Properties of Strong-Identification in Inductive Inference", *Theoretical Computer Science*, Vol. 2, pp. 345-360, 1976.

bo 362. Minsky, M., "Steps Toward Artificial Intelligence", *Computers and Thought*, Feigenbaum, E. A. and Feldman, J. (Eds.), McGraw-Hill, New York, pp. 406-450, 1963.

bor 363. Minsky, M. and Papert, S., *Perceptrons*, MIT Press, Cambridge, Mass., 1969.

c 364. Mitchell, T. M., "Version Spaces: A Candidate Elimination Approach to Rule Learning", *Fifth International Joint Conference on Artificial Intelligence*, Cambridge, Mass., pp. 305-310, 1977.

c 365. Mitchell, T. M., *Version Spaces: An Approach to Concept Learning* Ph.D. dissertation, Stanford University, December 1978, (also Stanford CS report STAN-CS-78-711, HPP-79-2).

co 366. Mitchell, T. M. and Utgoff, P. E., "Improving Problem Solving Strategies by Experimentation: A Proposal", Technical Report CBM-TR-106, Department of Computer Science, Rutgers University, December 1979.

co 367. Mitchell, T. M., "An Analysis of Generalization as a Search Problem", *Sixth International Joint Conference on Artificial Intelligence*, Tokyo, Japan, August 1979.

co 368. Mitchell, T. M., "The Need for Biases in Learning Generalizations", Technical Report CBM-TR-117, Department of Computer Science, Rutgers University, May 1980.

b 369. Mitchell, T., Carbonell, J. and Michalski, R. (Eds.), *Sigart Newsletter*, ACM Special Interest Group on Artificial Intelligence, April 1981, (Special Section on Machine Learning).

h 370. Mitchell, T. M., Utgoff, P. E., Nudel, B. and Banerji, R., "Learning Problem-Solving Heuristics through Practice", *Proceedings of the Seventh International Joint Conference on Artificial Intelligence*, Vancouver, pp. 127-134, August 1981.

hk 371. Mitchell, T. M., Utgoff, P. E. and Banerji, R. B., "Learning by Experimentation: Acquiring and Refining Problem-Solving Heuristics", *Machine Learning*, Michalski, R. S., Carbonell, J. G. and Mitchell, T. M. (Eds.), Tioga, 1983.

hk 372. Mitchell, T. M., "Toward Combining Empirical and Analytic Methods for Learning Heuristics", *Human and Artificial Intelligence*, Elithorn, A. and Banerji, R. (Eds.), Erlbaum, 1982.

co 373. Mitchell, T. M., "Generalization as Search", *Artificial Intelligence*, Vol. 18, No. 2, pp. 203-226, March 1982.

ab 374. Moore, J. and Newell, A., "How Can MERLIN Understand?", *Knowledge and Cognition*, Gregg, L. (Ed.), Erlbaum Associates, Hillsdale, N.J., pp. 253-285, 1974.

c 375. Moraya, C., "A Didactic Experiment in Pattern Recognition", Report AIUD-PR-8101, Informatik, Der Universitat Dortmund, 1981.

co 376. Morgan, C. G., "Hypothesis Generation by Machine", *Artificial Intelligence*, North-Holland, Vol. 2, pp. 179-187, 1971.

co 377. Morgan, C. G., "Automated Hypothesis Generation using Extended Inductive Resolution", *Advance Papers of Fourth International Joint Conference on Artificial Intelligence*, Tbilisi, USSR, pp. 351-356, September 1975.

hk 378. Mostow, D. J. and Hayes-Roth, F., "Operationalizing Heuristics: Some AI Methods for Assisting AI Programming", *Sixth International Joint Conference on Artificial* Intelligence, Tokyo, pp. 601-609, 1979.

hk 379. Mostow, D. J. and Hayes-Roth, F., "Machine-Aided Heuristic Programming: A Paradigm for Knowledge Engineering", Technical Report N-1007-NSF, The Rand Corporation, February 1979.

hk 380. Mostow, D. J., *Mechanical Transformation of Task Heuristics into Operational Procedures* Ph.D. dissertation, Carnegie-Mellon University, 1981.

o 381. Mostow, D. J., "Transforming Declarative Advice into Effective Procedures: A Heuristic Search Example", *Machine Learning*, Michalski, R. S., Carbonell, J. G. and Mitchell, T. M. (Eds.), Tioga Press, Palo Alto, 1982.

o 382. Nagel, E., "Carnap's Theory of Induction", *The Philosophy of Rudolf Carnap*, Schilpp, P. A. (Ed.), Open Court Publishing Co., La Salle, Illinois, pp. 785-825, 1963.

h 383. Narendra, K. S. and Thathachar, M. A. L., "Learning Automata - A Survey", *IEEE Transaction on Systems, Man, and Cybernetics*, Vol. SMC-4, No. 4, pp. 323-333, 1974.

hm 384. Neches, R. and Hayes, J. R., "Progress Towards a Taxonomy of Strategy Transformations", *Cognitive Psychology and Instruction*, Lesgold, A. M., Pellegrino, J. W., Fokkema, S. and Glaser, R. (Eds.), Plenum Books, New York, 1978.

hm 385. Neches, R., "Promoting Self-Discovery of Improved Strategies", *Annual conference of the American Educational Research Association*, San Francisco, CA., April 1979, (also report CIP 398, Psychology Department, Carnegie-Mellon).

hm 386. Neches, R., *Heuristic Procedure Modification*, Ph.D. dissertation, Carnegie-Mellon University, 1980, (in preparation, date approximate).

hm 387. Neves, D. M., "A Computer Program that Learns Algebraic Procedures", *Proceedings of the 2nd Conference on Computational Studies of Intelligence*, Toronto, 1978.

hm 388. Neves, D. and Anderson, J. R., "Becoming Expert at a Cognitive Skill", Technical Report, Carnegie-Mellon University, 1980, (in preparation, date approximate).

hmp 389. Neves, D. M., "Learning procedures from examples", *Proceedings of the Workshop on Machine Learning*, Carnegie-Mellon University, Pittsburgh, PA., July 1980.

hm 390. Neves, D. and Anderson, J. R., "Knowledge Compilation: Mechanisms for the Automatization of Cognitive Skills", *Cognitive Skills and their Acquisition*, Anderson, J. R. (Ed.), Lawrence Erlbaum Associates, Hillsdale, N.J., 1981.

bh 391. Newell, A. and Simon, H. A., "The Logic Theory Machine", *IRE Transactions on Information Theory*, Vol. IT-2, No. 3, pp. 61-79, 1956.

bh 392. Newell, A., Shaw, J. and Simon, H., "Empirical explorations of the logic theory machine: A case study in heuristics", *Proceedings of the 1957 Western Joint Computer Conference*, pp. 218-230, 1957, (Reprinted in *Computers and Thought*, McGraw-Hill).

bh 393. Newell, A., Shaw, J. and Simon, H., "Report on a General Problem-Solving Program for a Computer", *Proceedings of the International Conference on Information Processing*, UNESCO, Paris, 1960.

cho 394. Newell, A., "Learning, Generality and Problem Solving", *Proceedings of the IFIP Congress 62*, North-Holland, Amsterdam, pp. 407-412, 1962.

ho 395. Newell, A., Shaw, J. C. and Simon, H. A., "A Variety of Intelligent Learning in a General Problem Solver", *Self Organizing Systems*, Yovits and Cameron (Eds.), Pergamon Press, New York, 1969.

b 396. Newell, A., "Heuristic Programming: Ill-Structured Problems", *Progress in Operations Research*, Aronofsky, J. (Ed.), Wiley, New York, pp. 363-414, 1969.

b 397. Newell, A. and Simon, H., *Human Problem Solving*, Prentice-Hall, Englewood Cliffs, N.J., 1972.

b 398. Newell, A., "Production Systems: Models of Control Structures", *Visual Information Processing*, Chase, W. G. (Ed.), Academic Press, New York, 1973.

hm 399. Newell, A. and Rosenbloom, P., "Mechanisms of Skill Acquisition and the Law of Practice", *Cognitive Skills and Their Acquisition*, Anderson, J. R. (Ed.), Erlbaum Associates, Hillsdale, New Jersey, 1981.

b 400. Newell, A., "The Knowledge Level", Technical Report CMU-CS-81-131, Department of Computer Science, Carnegie-Mellon University, July 1981.

h 401. Newman, C. and Uhr, L., "BOGART: A Discovery and Induction Program for Games", *Twentieth National Conference of the ACM*, pp. 176, 1965.

or 402. Nilsson, N. J., *Learning Machines*, McGraw-Hill, New York, 1965.

b 403. Nilsson, N. J., *Principles of Artificial Intelligence*, Tioga, Palo Alto, 1980.

h 404. Novak, G., "Representations of Knowledge in a Program for Solving Physics Problems", *Fifth International Joint Conference on Artificial Intelligence*, Cambridge, Mass., pp. 286-291, 1977.

h 405. Novak, G. S. Jr. and Araya, A., "Research on Expert Problem Solving in Physics", *First National Conference on Artificial Intelligence*, Stanford University, pp. 178-180, August 1980.

co 406. O'Rorke, P., "A Comparative Study of Two Inductive Learning Systems AQ11 and ID3 Using a Chess Endgame Test Problem", Internal Report 82-2, Department of Computer Science, University of Illinois, September 1982.

l 407. Oakey, S. and Cawthorn, R. C., "Inductive Learning of Pronunciation Rules by Hypothesis Testing and Correction", *Proceedings of the Seventh International Joint Conference on Artificial Intelligence*, Vancouver, pp. 109-114, August 1981.

o 408. Oettinger, A. G., "Programming a Digital Computer to Learn", *Philosophy Magazine*, Vol. 43, pp. 1243-1263, 1952.

h 409. Oyen, R. A., "Mechanical Discovery of Invariances for Problem Solving", Technical Report 1168, Computer Engineering Department, Case Western Reserve University, 1975.

g 410. Pao, T. W. L., "A Solution of the Syntactical Induction-Inference Problem for a Non-Trivial Subset of Context-Free Language", Technical Report 70-19, The Moore School of Electrical Engineering., U. Pennsylvania, 1969.

g 411. Pao, T. and Carr, J. W., "A Solution of the Syntactical Induction-Inference Problem for Regular Languages", *Computer Languages*, Vol. 3, pp. 53-64, 1978.

c 412. Pao, Y. and Hu, C. H., "Methods for Manipulating Pattern Information", Technical Report MI-101-82, Case Western Reserve University, 1982.

bo 413. Pao, Y. and Ernst, G. W., *Context-Directed Pattern Recognition and Machine Intelligence Techniques for Information Processing: a Tutorial*, IEEE Computer Society Press, 1982.

c 414. Pawlak, Z., "Classification of Objects by Means of Attributes", Report 423, Institute of Computer Science, Polish Academy of Sciences, 1981.

co 415. Pearl, J., "On the Connection between the Complexity and Credibility of Inferred Models", *International Journal General Systems*, Gordon and Breach Science Publishers Ltd., Vol. 4, pp. 255-264, 1978.

bc 416. Pikas, A., *Abstraction and Concept Formation*, Harvard University Press, Cambridge, Mass., 1966.

h 417. Pitrat, J., "Realization of a Program Learning to Find Combinations at Chess", *Computer Oriented Learning Processes*, Simon, J. C. (Ed.), Noordhoff, Leyden, pp. 397-423, 1974.

p 418. Pivar, M. and Gord, E., "The LISP Program for Inductive Inference on Sequences", *The Programming Language LISP: Its Operation and Applications*, Berkeley and Bobrow (Eds.), MIT Press, Cambridge, Mass, pp. 260-289, 1964.

p 419. Pivar, M. and Finkelstein, M., "Automation, Using LISP, of Inductive Inference on Sequences", *The Programming Language LISP: Its Operation and Applications*, Berkeley and Bobrow (Eds.), MIT Press, Cambridge, Mass, pp. 125-136, 1964.

c 420. Plotkin, G. D., "A Note on Inductive Generalization", *Machine Intelligence*, Edinburgh University Press, Vol. 5, pp. 153-163, 1970.

c 421. Plotkin, G. D., "A Further Note on Inductive Generalization", *Machine Intelligence*, Edinburgh University Press, Vol. 6, pp. 101-124, 1971.

op 422. Podnieks, K. M., "Comparing Various Concepts of Function Prediction, Part 1", *Theory of Algorithms and Programs*, Latvian State U., pp. 68-81, 1974, (Part 2, 1975, pp. 35-44).

p 423. Podnieks, K. M., "Probabilistic Synthesis of Enumerated Classes of Functions", *Soviet Math Dokl*, Vol. 16, pp. 1042-1045, 1975.

p 424. Podnieks, K. M., "Probabilistic Program Synthesis", *Theory of Algorithms and Programs*, Latvian State U., pp. 57-88, 1977.

op 425. Podnieks, K. M., "Computational Complexity of Prediction Strategies", *Theory of Algorithms and Programs*, Latvian State U., 1977.

c 426. Pokorny, D., "Knowledge Acquisition by the GUHA Method", *Journal of Policy Analysis and Information Systems*, Vol. 4, No. 4, 1980.

k 427. Politakis, P., Weiss, S. and Kulikowski, C., "Designing Consistent Knowledge Bases for Expert Consultation Systems", Technical Report DCS-TR-100, Department of Computer Science, Rutgers University, 1979, (also 13th Annual Hawaii International Conference on System Sciences).

do 428. Polya, G., *Mathematics and Plausible Reasoning*, Princeton University Press, Princeton, N.J., 1954.

bo 429. Polya, G., *How to Solve It*, Doubleday, New York, 1957, (second edition).

b 430. Pople, H., "The Formation of Composite Hypotheses in Diagnostic Problem Solving", *Fifth International Joint Conference on Artificial Intelligence*, pp. 1030-1037, 1977.

o 431. Popper, K., *The Logic of Scientific Discovery*, Harper and Row, New York, 1968, (2nd edition).

c 432. Popplestone, R. J., "An Experiment in Automatic Induction", *Machine Intelligence*, Edinburgh University Press, Vol. 5, pp. 204-215, 1970.

o 433. Pudlak, P., "Polynomially Complete Problems in the Logic of Automated Discovery", *Lecture Notes in Computer Science*, Springer-Verlag, Vol. 32, pp. 358-361, 1975.

o 434. Pudlak, P. and Springsteel, F. N., "Complexity in Mechanized Hypothesis Formation", *Theoretical Computer Science*, Vol. 8, pp. 203-225, 1979.

o 435. Putnam, H., "Degree of Confirmation and Inductive Logic", *The Philosophy of Rudolph Carnap*, Schilpp, P. A. (Ed.), Open Court Publishing Co., La Salle, Illinois, pp. 761-783, 1963.

o 436. Putnam, H., "Probability and Confirmation", *Mathematics, Matter and Method*, Cambridge U. Press, 1975, (Originally appeared in 1963 as a Voice of America lecture).

hk 437. Quinlan, J. R., "Discovering Rules from Large Collections of Examples: A Case Study", *Expert Systems in the Micro Electronic Age*, Michie, D. (Ed.), Edinburgh University Press, Edinburgh, 1979.

k 438. Quinlan, J. R., "Induction over Large Data Bases", Technical Report HPP-79-14, Heuristic Programming Project, Stanford University, 1979.

c 439. Quinlan, J. R., "Semi-Autonomous Acquisition of Pattern-Based Knowledge", *Australian Computer Bulletin*, April 1980, (also to appear in Infotech State of the Art Report on Expert Systems).

c 440. Quinlan, J. R., "Learning Efficient Classification Procedures and their Application to Chess End-Games", *Machine Learning*, Michalski, R. S., Carbonell, J. G. and Mitchell, T. M. (Eds.), Tioga, Palo Alto, 1982.

b 441. Rashevsky, N., *Mathematical Biophysics*, University of Chicago Press, Chicago, IL, 1948.

o 442. Rescher, N., *Scientific Explanation*, The Free Press, New York, 1970.

hm 443. Riesbeck, C. K., "Failure-Driven Reminding for Incremental Learning", *Proceedings of the Seventh International Joint Conference on Artificial Intelligence*, Vancouver, pp. 115-120, August 1981.

o 444. Rissland, E. L. and Soloway, E. M., "Constrained Example Generation: A Testbed for Studying Issues in Learning", *Proceedings of the Seventh International Joint Conference on Artificial Intelligence*, Vancouver, pp. 162-164, August 1981.

l 445. Robinson, J. J., "DIAGRAM: An Extendible Grammar for Natural Language Dialogue", Technical Note 205, Artificial Intelligence Center, SRI International, February 1980.

q 446. Roche, C., "Application of Multilevel Clustering to the Automatic Generation of Recognition Operators: A Link between Feature Extraction and Classification", *Proceedings of the First International Joint Conference on Pattern Recognition*, Copenhagen, pp. 540-546, August 1974.

bmr 447. Rosenblatt, F., "The Perceptron: A Probabilistic Model for Information Storage and Organization in the Brain", *Psychological Review*, Vol. 65, pp. 386-407, 1958.

bm 448. Rosenblatt, F., "The Perceptron: A Theory of Statistical Separability in Cognitive Systems", Technical Report VG-1196-G-1, Cornell Aeronautical Lab., 1958.

mr 449. Rosenblatt, F., "Perceptual Generalization over Transformation Groups", *Self Organizing Systems*, Permagon Press, London, 1959.

bm 450. Rosenblatt, F., *Principles of Neurodynamics and the Theory of Brain Mechanisms*, Spartan Books, Washington, D. C., 1962.

hk 451. Rychener, M. D. and Newell, A., "An Instructable Production System: Basic Design Issues", *Pattern-Directed Inference Systems*, Waterman, D. A. and Hayes-Roth, F. (Eds.), Academic Press, New York, 1978.

k 452. Rychener, M. D., "Approaches to Knowledge Acquisition: The Instructable Production System Project", *First National Conference on Artificial Intelligence*, Stanford, CA., pp. 228-230, August 1980, (expanded version in preparation).

ko 453. Rychener, M. D., "The Instructable Production System: A Retrospective Analysis", *Machine Learning*, Michalski, R. S., Carbonell, J. G. and Mitchell, T. M. (Eds.), Tioga, Palo Alto, 1982.

o 454. Salmon, W. C., *The Foundations of Scientific Inference*, University of Pittsburgh Press, Pittsburgh, PA., 1966.

c 455. Salveter, S. C., "Inferring Conceptual Graphs", *Cognitive Science*, Vol. 3, No. 2, pp. 141-166, 1979.

c 456. Sammut, C., "Concept Learning by Experiment", *Proceedings of the Seventh International Joint Conference on Artificial Intelligence*, Vancouver, pp. 104-105, August 1981.

ce 457. Sammut, C., *Learning Concepts by Performing Experiments* Ph.D. dissertation, University of New South Wales, November 1981.

ch 458. Samuel, A. L., "Some Studies in Machine Learning Using the Game of Checkers", *IBM Journal of Research and Development*, No. 3, pp. 211-229, 1959.

h 459. Samuel, A. L., *Programming Computers to Play Games*, Academic Press, pp. 165-192, 1960.

hr 460. Samuel, A. L., "Some Studies in Machine Learning using the Game of Checkers", *Computers and Thought*, Feigenbaum, E. A. and Feldman, J. (Eds.), McGraw-Hill, New York, pp. 71-105, 1963.

hr 461. Samuel, A. L., "Some Studies in Machine Learning using the Game of Checkers II - Recent Progress", *IBM Journal of Research and Development*, Vol. 11, No. 6, pp. 601-617, 1967.

p 462. Sato, M., "Towards a Mathematical Theory of Program Synthesis", *Proceedings of the Sixth International Joint Conference on Artificial Intelligence*, pp. 757-762, 1979.

br 463. Savage, L., *The Foundations of Statistics*, Dover Publications, New York, 1972, (second edition).

b 464. Schank, R. C. and Abelson, R. P., *Scripts, Goals, Plans and Understanding*, Erlbaum Associates, Hillsdale, N.J., 1977.

lm 465. Schank, R. C., "Reminding and Memory Organization: An Introduction to MOPS", Technical Report 170, Computer Science Department, Yale University, 1979.

lm 466. Schank, R. C., "Language and Memory", *Cognitive Science*, Vol. 4, No. 3, pp. 243-284, 1980.

bo 467. Schilpp, P., *Library of Living Philosophers: The Philosophy of Rudolph Carnap*, Open Court Publishing Co., LaSalle, IL, 1963.

r 468. Sebestyen, G. S., *Decision-Making Processes in Pattern Recognition*, Macmillan, New York, 1962.

ce 469. Self, J. A., "Concept Teaching", *Artificial Intelligence*, North-Holland, Vol. 9, pp. 197-221, April 1977.

mr 470. Selfridge, O. G., "Pandemonium: A Paradigm for Learning", *Proceedings of the Symposium on Mechanization of Thought Processes*, Blake, D. and Uttley, A. (Eds.), HMSO, London, pp. 511-529, 1959.

lm 471. Selfridge, M., "A Computer Model of Child Language Acquisition", *Proceedings of the Seventh International Joint Conference on Artificial Intelligence*, Vancouver, pp. 92-95, August 1981.

al 472. Sembugamoorthy, V., "Analogy-Based Acquisition of Utterances Relating to Temporal Aspects", *Proceedings of the Seventh International Joint Conference on Artificial Intelligence*, Vancouver, pp. 106-108, August 1981.

bm 473. Schank, R. C., *Looking at Learning*, Proceedings of the European Conference on Artificial Intelligence, Orsay, France, July, 1982.

h 474. Shapiro, A. and Niblett, T., "Automatic Induction of Classification Rules for a Chess Endgame", *Advances in Computer Chess*, Clarke, M.R.B. (Ed.), Edinburgh University Press, 1981.

chp 475. Shapiro, E. Y., "An Algorithm that Infers Theories from Facts", *Proceedings of the Seventh International Joint Conference on Artificial Intelligence*, Vancouver, pp. 446-451, August 1981.

c 476. Shapiro, Ehud Y., "Inductive Inference of Theories From Facts", Research Report 192, Yale University, February 1981.

p 477. Shaw, D. E., Swartout, W. R. and Green, C. C., "Inferring LISP Programs from Examples", *Fourth International Joint Conference on Artificial Intelligence*, Tbilisi, USSR, pp. 351-356, September 1975.

r 478. Shimura, M., "Learning Procedures in Pattern Classifiers- Introduction and Survey", *Proceedings of the Fourth International Joint Conference on Pattern Recognition*, pp. 125-138, 1978.

gl 479. Siklossy, L., "Natural Language Learning by Computer", *Representations and Meanings: Experiments with Information Processing*, 1972.

p 480. Siklossy, L., "The Synthesis of Programs from their Properties, and the Insane Heuristic", *Proceedings of the Third Texas Conference on Computer Systems*, 1974.

h 481. Siklossy, L., "Procedural Learning in Worlds of Robots", *Computer Oriented Learning Processes*, Simon, J. C. (Ed.), Noordhoff, Leyden, pp. 427-440, 1974.

p 482. Siklossy, L. and Sykes, D., "Automatic Program Synthesis from Example Problems", *Fourth International Joint Conference on Artificial Intelligence*, pp. 268-273, 1975.

cm 483. Simon, H. A. and Kotovsky, K., "Human Acquisition of Concepts for Sequential Patterns", *Psychological Review*, Vol. 70, pp. 534-546, 1963.

o 484. Simon, H. A., "Scientific Discovery and the Psychology of Problem Solving", *Mind and Cosmos*, Colodny, R. G. (Ed.), University of Pittsburgh Press, Pittsburgh, pp. 22-40, 1966.

ho 485. Simon, H. A. and Lea, G., "Problem Solving and Rule Induction: A Unified View", *Knowledge and Cognition*, Gregg, L. W. (Ed.), Lawrence Erlbaum Associates, Potomac, Maryland, pp. 105-127, 1974.

b 486. Simon, J. C., *Computer Oriented Learning Processes*, Noordhoff, Leyden, Nato Advanced Study Institutes Series, Series E, 1976, (Applied Science 14).

o 487. Simon, H. A., "Models of Scientific Discovery", *Synthese Library*, Hintikka, J. (Ed.), Reidel Pub. Co., 1977.

h 488. Simon, H. A., "Artificial Intelligence Systems that Understand", *Fifth International Joint Conference on Artificial Intelligence*, Cambridge, Mass., pp. 1059-1073, 1977.

k 489. Simon, H. A., Carbonell, J. G. and Reddy, R., "Research in Automated Knowledge Acquisition", Research Proposal to the Office of Naval Research, Carnegie-Mellon Computer Science Department, 1979.

o 490. Simon, H. A., "Why Should Machines Learn?", *Machine Learning*, Michalski, R. S., Carbonell, J. G. and Mitchell, T. M. (Eds.), Tioga, 1983.

o 491. Sklansky, J., "Adaptation, Learning, Self-Repair, and Feedback", *IEEE Spectrum*, Vol. 1, No. 5, pp. 172-174, 1964.

e 492. Sleeman, D. H., "Assessing Aspects of Competence in Basic Algebra", *Intelligent Tutoring Systems*, Sleeman, D. H. and Brown, J. S. (Eds.), Academic Press, New York, 1981.

e 493. Sleeman, D. H., "A Rule-Based Task Generator", *Seventh International Joint Conference on Artificial Intelligence*, Vancouver, 1981.

e 494. Sleeman, D. H. and Brown, J. S., "Intelligent Tutoring Systems: An Overview", *Intelligent Tutoring Systems*, Sleeman, D. H. and Brown, J. S. (Eds.), Academic Press, New York, 1981.

e 495. Sleeman, D. H. and Hendley, R. J., "ACE: A System which Analyses Complex Explanations", *Intelligent Tutoring Systems*, Sleeman, D. H. and Brown, J. S. (Eds.), Academic Press, New York, 1981.

e 496. Sleeman, D. H., "Can Student Models Give Insights into Cognitive Processes?", Technical Report, Computer Science Department, Carnegie-Mellon University, 1981.

ehm 497. Sleeman, D. H. and Smith, M. J., "Modeling Student'S Problem solving", *Artificial Intelligence*, Vol. 16, No. 2, pp. 171-187, 1981.

ehm 498. Sleeman, D. H., "Inferring Student Models for Intelligent Computer-Aided Instruction", *Machine Learning*, Michalski, R. S., Carbonell, J. G. and Mitchell, T. M. (Eds.), Tioga, Palo Alto, 1982.

h 499. Smith, M. H., "A Learning Program which Plays Partnership Dominoes", *Communications of the ACM*, Vol. 16, pp. 462-467, August 1973.

o 500. Smith, R. G., Mitchell, T. M., Chestek, R. A. and Buchanan, B. G., "A Model for Learning Systems", *Fifth International Joint Conference on Artificial Intelligence*, Cambridge, Mass., pp. 338-343, 1977.

p 501. Smith, D. R., "A Survey of the Synthesis of LISP Programs from Examples", Technical Report, Duke University, September 1980.

eh 502. Smith, R. L. Jr., "Modeling Student Acquisition of Problem Solving Skills", *First National Conference on Artificial Intelligence*, pp. 221-223, August 1980.

cr 503. Sobolewski, M., "Tree Structured Attribute Pattern Recognition Systems", *Proceedings of Conference Informatica*, Bled, Yugoslavia, 1975.

cr 504. Sobolewski, M., *Classes of Languages and Models for Pattern Recognition* Ph.D. dissertation, Institute for Biocybernetics and Biomedical Engineering, Polish Academy of Sciences, 1977 (in Polish).

g 505. Solomonoff, R. J., "A New Method for Discovering the Grammars of Phrase Structured Languages", *Transactions International Conference on Information Processing*, UNESCO House, Paris, 1959.

co 506. Solomonoff, R. J., "Training Sequences for Mechanized Induction", *Self-organizing Systems*, Yovits, M., Jacobi, G. and Goldstein, G. (Eds.), Spartan Books, Washington, D.C., pp. 425-434, 1962.

o 507. Solomonoff, R. J., "A Formal Theory of Inductive Inference", *Information and Control*, Vol. 7, pp. 1-22, 224-254, 1964.

o 508. Solomonoff, R. J., "Inductive Inference Theory- A Unified Approach to Problems in Pattern Recognition and Artificial Intelligence", *Fourth International Joint Conference on Artificial Intelligence*, pp. 274-280, 1975.

o 509. Solomonoff, R. J., "Complexity-Based Induction Systems: Comparisons and Convergence Theorems", *IEEE Transactions on Information Theory*, Vol. IT-24, No. 4, pp. 422-432, 1978.

h 510. Soloway, E. M. and Riseman, E. M., "Mechanizing the Common-Sense Inference of Rules which Direct Behavior", *Proceedings AISB Summer Conference*, U. Edinburgh, 1976.

c 511. Soloway, E. M. and Riseman, E. M., "Levels of Pattern Description in Learning", *Fifth International Joint Conference on Artificial Intelligence*, Cambridge, Mass., pp. 801-811, 1977.

o 512. Soloway, E. M., *Learning Interpretation + Generalization: A Case Study in Knowledge-Directed Learning* Ph.D. dissertation, University of Massachusetts at Amherst, 1978, (Computer and Information Science Report COINS TR-78-13).

b 513. Stefik, M. J., "Inferring DNA Structures from Segmentation Data", *Artificial* Intelligence, Vol. 11, pp. 85-114, August 1978.

o 514. Stegmuller, W., *The Structure and Dynamics of Theories*, Springer-Verlag, 1976.

c 515. Stepp, R., "The Investigation of the UNICLASS Inductive Program AQ7UNI and User's Guide", Technical Report 949, Department of Computer Science, University of Illinois, November 1978.

c 516. Stepp, R., "Learning without Negative Examples via Variable Valued Logic Characterizations: The Uniclass Inductive Program AQ7UNI", Technical Report UIUCDCS-R-79-982, Dept. Computer Science., U. Illinois, 1979.

cq 517. Stepp, R., "A Description and User's Guide for CLUSTER/PAF -- A Program for Conjunctive Conceptual Clustering", Technical Report, Department of Computer Science, University of Illinois, 1982.

h 518. Stolfo, S. J. and Harrison, M. C., "Automatic Discovery of Heuristics for Non-Deterministic Programs", Technical Report 007, Courant Institute, January 1979.

h 519. Stolfo, S. J. and Harrison, M. C., "Automatic Discovery of Heuristics for Nondeterministic Programs", *Sixth International Joint Conference on Artificial Intelligence*, Tokyo, pp. 853-855, August 1979.

o 520. Strong, J., "The Infinite Ballot Box of Nature: De Morgan, Boole, and Jevons on Probability and the Logic of Induction", *Philosophy of Science Association-1976*, pp. 197-211, 1976.

p 521. Summers, P. D., "A Methodology for LISP Program Construction from Examples", *Journal of the ACM*, Vol. 24, pp. 161, 1977.

h 522. Sussman, G. J., *A Computer Model of Skill Acquisition*, American Elsevier, New York, 1975.

b 523. Trakhtenbrot, B., "On Problems Solvable by Successive Trials", *Lecture Notes in Computer Science*, Springer-Verlag, Vol. 32, pp. 125-137, 1975.

b 524. Truxal, T. G., *Automatic Feedback Control System Synthesis*, McGraw-Hill, New York, 1955, (New York).

bo 525. Tsypkin, Y. Z., "Self Learning - What is it?", *IEEE Transactions on Automatic Control*, Vol. AC-18, No. 2, pp. 109-117, 1968.

bd 526. Tsypkin, Ya Z., *Adaptation and Learning in Automatic Systems*, Academic Press, New York, 1971.

o 527. Tsypkin, Y. Z., *Foundations of the Theory of Learning Systems*, Academic Press, New York, 1973, (Translated by Z. L. Nikolic).

r 528. Uhr, L. and Vossler, C., "A Pattern-Recognition Program that Generates, Evaluates, and Adjusts its Own Operators", *Computers and Thought*, Feigenbaum, E. A. and Feldman, J. (Eds.), Mc-Graw Hill, New York, pp. 251-268, 1963.

or 529. Uhr, L., *Pattern Recognition*, John Wiley and Sons, New York, 1966.

or 530. Uhr, L., *Pattern Recognition, Learning and Thought*, Prentice-Hall, Englewood Cliffs, New Jersey, 1973.

cd 531. Utgoff, P. E. and Mitchell, T. M., "Acquisition of Appropriate Bias for Inductive Concept Learning", *Proceedings of the Second National Conference on Artificial* Intelligence, Pittsburgh, August 1982.

g 532. Van der Mude, A. and Walker, A., "On the Inference of Stochastic Regular Grammars", *Information and Control*, Vol. 38, pp. 310-329, 1978.

ae 533. VanLehn, K., Brown, J. S., "Planning Nets: A Representation for Formalizing Analogies and Semantic Models of Procedural Skills", *Aptitude Learning and Instruction: Cognitive Process Analyses*, Snow, R. E., Frederico, P. A. and Montague, W. E. (Eds.), Lawrence Erlbaum Associates, 1978.

c 534. VanLehn, K., "Algorithms for Learning by Examples", Technical Report, Xerox Palo Alto Research Center, 1980, (forthcoming, date approximate).

g 535. Veelenturf, L. P. J., "Inference of Sequential Machines from Sample Computations", *IEEE Transactions on Computers*, Vol. C-27, pp. 167-170, 1978.

c 536. Vere, S. A., "Induction of Concepts in the Predicate Calculus", *Fourth International Joint Conference on Artificial Intelligence*, Tbilisi, USSR, pp. 281-287, 1975.

ch 537. Vere, S. A., "Induction of Relational Productions in the Presence of Background Information", *Fifth International Joint Conference on Artificial Intelligence*, Cambridge, Mass., pp. 349-355, 1977.

ch 538. Vere, S. A., "Inductive Learning of Relational Productions", *Pattern-Directed Inference Systems*, Waterman, D. A. and Hayes-Roth, F. (Eds.), Academic Press, New York, 1978.

ch 539. Vere, S. A., "Multilevel Counterfactuals for Generalizations of Relational Concepts and Productions", *Artificial Intelligence*, Vol. 14, No. 2, pp. 138-164, September 1980.

o 540. Watanabe, S., "Information-Theoretic Aspects of Inductive and Deductive Inference", *IBM Journal of Research and Development*, Vol. 4, No. 2, pp. 208-231, 1960.

or 541. Watanabe, S., *Pattern Recognition as an Inductive Process, Methodologies of Pattern Recognition*, Academic Press, 1968.

h 542. Waterman, D., *Machine Learning of Heuristics* Ph.D. dissertation, Stanford University, 1968, (also report CS118, AI 74).

ch 543. Waterman, D. A., "Generalization Learning Techniques for Automating the Learning of Heuristics", *Artificial Intelligence*, Vol. 1, No. 1/2, pp. 121-170, 1970.

bh 544. Waterman, D. A., "Adaptive Production Systems", *Fourth International Joint Conference on Artificial Intelligence*, MIT, pp. 296-303, 1975.

b 545. Waterman, D. A. and Hayes-Roth, F. (Eds.), *Pattern-Directed Inference Systems*, Academic Press, New York, 1978.

b 546. Waterman, D. A. and Hayes-Roth, F. (Eds.), *Pattern-Directed Inference Systems*, Academic Press, New York, 1978.

b 547. Waterman, D. A., "Exemplary Programming in RITA", Academic Press, 1978.

hp 548. Waterman, D. A., Faught, W. S., Klahr, P., Rosenschein, S. J. and Wesson, R., "Design Issues for Exemplary Programming", RAND note N-1484-RC, The Rand Corporation, April 1980.

h 549. Wesley, L. P., "Learning Racquetball by Constrained Example Generation", *Proceedings of the Seventh International Joint Conference on Artificial Intelligence*, Vancouver, pp. 144-146, August 1981.

g 550. Wharton, R. M., "Approximate Language Identification", *Information and Control*, Vol. 26, pp. 236-255, 1974.

g 551. Wharton, R. M., "Grammar Enumeration and Inference", *Information and Control*, Vol. 33, pp. 253-272, 1977.

l 552. White, G. M., "Machine Learning through Signature Trees: Application to Human Speech", AI Memo 136 (CS-183), Stanford AI Laboratory, October 1970, (AD-717 600).

m 553. Widrow, B., *Generalization and Information Storage in Networks of Adelaine 'Neurons,' Self Organizing Systems*, Spartan Books, Washington, D. C., pp. 435-461, 1962, (Yovitz, M. C.; Jacobi, G. T.; Goldstein, G. D., editors).

p 554. Wiehagen, R., "Inductive Inference of Recursive Functions", *Lecture Notes in Computer Science*, Springer-Verlag, Vol. 32, pp. 462-464, 1974.

p 555. Wiehagen, R. and Liepe, W., "Characteristic Properties of Recognizable Classes of Recursive Functions", *Elektronische Informationsverarbeitung und Kybernetik*, Vol. 12, pp. 421-438, 1974, (in German).

p 556. Wiehagen, R. and Jung, H., "Rekursionstheoretische Charakterisierung von erkennbaren Klassen Rekursiver Funktionen", *Elektronische Informationsverarbeitung und Kybernetik*, Vol. 13, pp. 385-397, 1977.

g 557. Wiehagen, R., "Identification of Formal Languages", *Lecture Notes in Computer Science*, Springer-Verlag, Vol. 53, pp. 571-579, 1977.

o 558. Wiehagen, R., "Characterization Problems in the Theory of Inductive Inference", *Lecture Notes in Computer Science*, Springer-Verlag, Vol. 62, pp. 494-508, 1978.

b 559. Wiener, N., *Cybernetics*, New York, 1948.

k 560. Wilczynski, D., "Knowledge Acquisition in the Consul System", *Proceedings of the Seventh International Joint Conference on Artificial Intelligence*, Vancouver, pp. 135-140, August 1981.

o 561. Windeknecht, T. G., *A Theory of Simple Concepts with Applications* Ph.D. dissertation, Case Institute of Technology, 1964.

c 562. Winston, P. H., "Learning Structural Descriptions from Examples", *The Psychology of Computer Vision*, Winston, P. H. (Ed.), McGraw Hill, New York, ch. 5, 1975.

a 563. Winston, P. H., "Learning by Understanding Analogies", Memo 520, M.I.T. AI Lab, 1979.

a 564. Winston, P. H., "Learning and Reasoning by Analogy", *CACM*, Vol. 23, No. 12, pp. 689-703, 1979.

a 565. Winston, P. H., "Learning New Principles from Precedents and Exercises", AIM 632, MIT, May 1981.

c 566. Wysotzki, F., Kolbe, W. and Selbig, J., "Concept Learning by Structured Examples - An Algebraic Approach", *Proceedings of the Seventh International Joint Conference on Artificial Intelligence*, Vancouver, pp. 153-158, August 1981.

c 567. Young, R. M., Plotkin, G. D. and Linz, R. F., "Analysis of an Extended Concept-Learning Task", *Fifth International Joint Conference on Artificial Intelligence*, pp. 285, August 1977.

b 568. Yovits, M. C., Jacobi, G. T. and Goldstein, G. D. (Eds.), *Self-Organizing Systems*, Spartan Books, Washington, D. C., 1962.

cr 569. Zagoruiko, N. G., "Recognition Methods and their Application", *Sovietskoie Radio*, 1972.

d 570. Zagoruiko, N. G., "Artificial Intelligence and Empirical Prediction", Technical Report, Gosudarstviennyi Universitiet, 1975, (in Russian).

c 571. Zagoruiko, N., "Empirical Prediction Algorithms", *Computer Oriented Learning Processes*, Simon, J. C. (Ed.), Noordhoff, Leyden, pp. 581-595, 1976.

c 572. Zhuruvliev, J. I., Kuminov, M. M. and Tuliagunov, S. E., "Algorithms for Computing Estimates and their Application", *Publ. FUN*, 1974.

GLOSSARY OF SELECTED TERMS IN MACHINE LEARNING

This glossary was prepared by the editors as an attempt to systematize the meaning of some basic terms used in machine learning and closely related areas. The angle brackets "< >" indicate that a given term used in a definition is itself an entry in the glossary.

Adaptive Control Systems: Feedback control systems that adjust parameters to maintain desired performance despite external or internal disturbances.

Advice Taking: A form of learning in which the learner modifies its behavior to satisfy the advice given by an instructor. An example of <Learning from Instruction>.

Analogical Means-ends Analysis: A problem-solving process operating in the <Analogical Problem Space> akin to <Means-ends Analysis>. A new problem is solved by transforming the solution of a similar old problem into a solution for the new problem using operators that reduce differences between corresponding solution descriptions.

Analogical Inference: Mapping information from a known object or process description into a less-known, but similar one.

Analogical Problem Space: A problem space whose states are descriptions of problem solutions, and whose operators transform one problem solution into a closely-related one.

Attribute: A variable or one-argument <Descriptor> used in asserting a property of an object or situation.

Caching (Memo Functions): Storing the answer to frequently-occurring questions (problems) in order to avoid a replication of past efforts. An example of <Rote Learning>.

Causal Analysis: Tracing the probable causes of observed events, occasionally used in <Credit (Blame) Assignment>.

Composition: Grouping a sequence of <Production Rules> or <Operators> into a single rule or operator.

Computer Assisted Instruction (CAI): The study of computer-based teaching and testing.

Concept Acquisition: See <Learning from Examples>.

Concept Attainment: See <Learning from Examples>.

Concept Description (also Description, Generalization): A symbolic data structure used to describe a concept (that is, to describe a class of instances in the domain under consideration).

Concept Formation: See <Learning from Examples>.

Conceptual Clustering: Arranging objects (observations, facts, and so on) into classes corresponding to certain descriptive concepts rather than classes of objects that are similar according to some mathematical measure.

Constraint: A fact that restricts the possible solutions to a problem.

Credit (Blame) Assignment: Identifying the steps (decisions, operators, and so on) chiefly responsible for a success (failure) in the overall process of achieving a goal.

Decision Tree: A <Discrimination Network> having a tree structure.

Deductive Inference: In formal logic—the derivation of a logical consequence from a given set of premises. Informally, a mode of reasoning using <Deductive Inference Rules>, to derive new facts that contain no more information than those from which they are derived.

Deductive Inference Rule: An <Inference Rule> that, given one or more assertions, concludes a logically equivalent or more specific assertion. A deductive inference is a truth-preserving transformation of assertions.

Descriptor: A variable, function, or predicate used as an elementary concept for describing objects or situations.

Discrimination: See <Specialization>

Discrimination Network: A network encoding a set of tests to classify a collection of objects (situations, events, and so on) into fixed categories according to predetermined features of the objects.

Domain of a descriptor (also value set of a descriptor): The set of possible values that a <Descriptor> may take as part of a <Concept Description>.

Expert System: A computer program that achieves performance comparable to a human expert at solving problems in some task domain by utilizing a large amount of domain-specific knowledge. Because of the substantial amounts of knowledge required, the <Knowledge Acquisition> task assumes major proportions.

Expertise Acquisition: See <Knowledge Acquisition>.

Feature: See <Attribute>.

Generalization: Extending the scope of a concept description to include more instances (the opposite of <Specialization>). This term is sometimes also used as a noun, synonymous with <Concept Description>.

Generalization Rule: An <Inference Rule> that transforms one or more premise assertions into an assertion logically implying them.

Grammatical Inference: Inferring the grammar of a language, given a set of sentences labeled "grammatically correct", and a second (optional) set labeled "grammatically incorrect".

Heuristics: Imperfect but useful knowledge employed in many reasoning tasks, such as <Plausible Inference>, discovery, and so on, where precise knowledge is lacking.

Heuristic Search: A problem-solving method for finding a sequence of operators that transforms an initial state into a desired goal state. <Heuristics> are used to generate, test and prune operator sequences.

Incremental Learning: Multistage learning, in which information learned at one stage is modified to accommodate new facts provided in subsequent stages.

Inductive Inference: A mode of reasoning that starts with specific facts and concludes general hypotheses or theories (from which the initial facts can be rederived via <Deductive Inference>).

Inductive Learning: Learning by generalizing facts and observations obtained from a teacher or environment (that is, learning by <Inductive Inference>).

Inference Rule: A rule that concludes new facts from old, either by the application of strict logical principles or by more imperfect, plausible methods. (See also <Inductive Inference> and <Deductive Inference>.)

Intelligent CAI (ICAI): Refers to the application of AI techniques in building <Computer Assisted Instruction> systems.

Knowledge Acquisition (also expertise acquisition): A form of machine learning concerned with transferring knowledge from humans or a task environment into computers. Often associated with constructing or augmenting the knowledge-base of an <Expert System>.

Knowledge Compilation (also operationalization of knowledge): Translating knowledge from a declarative form which cannot be used directly into an effective procedural form. For example, converting the advice "Don't get wet" into specific instructions that recommend *how* to avoid getting wet in a given situation. (See also <Skill Acquisition>.)

Learning by Being Told: See <Learning from Instruction>.

Learning from Examples: Inferring a general <Concept Description> from examples and (optionally) counter-examples of that concept. This is a form of <Inductive Learning>.

Learning from Instruction (also advice taking, and learning by being told): The process of transforming and integrating instructions from an external source (such as a teacher) into an internally usable form.

Learning from Observation (also learning without a teacher, and unsupervised learning): Constructing descriptions, hypotheses or theories about a given collection of facts or observations. In this form of learning there is no *a priori* classification of observations into sets exemplifying desired concepts.

Macrooperator: An operator composed of a sequence of more primitive operators. Appropriate macrooperators can simplify problem-solving by allowing a more "coarse grain" problem-solving search.

Means-ends Analysis: A problem-solving method which at each step searches for operators that maximally reduce the difference between the current state and a known goal state.

Near-miss: A counter-example of a concept that is quite similar to positive examples of this concept. Near-misses are very useful in isolating significant features in <Learning from Examples>.

Near-miss Analysis: The process of exploiting <Near-misses> to bound the scope of <Generalization> in learning from examples.

Negative example: In <Learning from Examples>, a counter-example of a concept that may bound the scope of <Generalization>.

Operationalization: See <Knowledge Compilation>.

Parameter Adjustment: Changing the relative weight of different terms in a mathematical expression, as a function of credit (blame) for past successes (failures). A kind of incremental curve fitting.

Partially Learned Concept: In concept learning, an underdetermined concept; that is, a concept whose precise description cannot be inferred based on the learner's current data, knowledge, and assumptions. (See also <Incremental Learning> and <Version Space>.)

Partial Matching: A technique for comparing structural descriptions by identifying their corresponding components. Useful in various kinds of inference, such as <Analogical Inference>.

Path constraint: In problem solving, a <Predicate> on partial solution sequences. A type of <Constraint>.

Plausible Inference: A derivation of likely conclusions from incomplete, imperfect or indirectly relevant premises. This includes <Inductive>, approximate, default, and <Analogical Inference>.

Positive Example: In <Learning from Examples>, a correct instance of a concept that may result in <Generalization>.

Predicate: A statement that is either true or false; a basic building block of predicate logic.

Problem Reformulation: Translating a problem statement into an alternative statement so that an appropriate solution method can be applied. This may include reformulating data representations and restating problem constraints.

Production Rule: A condition-action pair, where the action is performed if the condition is matched.

Production System: An inference system comprised of a large set of <Production Rules>, a working memory against which productions are matched, and the control structure to apply the productions to working memory.

Proceduralization: Converting declarative knowledge into procedural form (see also <Knowledge Compilation>).

Rote Learning: Learning by direct memorization of facts, without generalization (see also <Caching>).

Schema: A symbolic structure that can be filled in by specific information ("instantiated") to denote an instance of the generic concept represented by the structure.

Similarity Metric: Either *(i)* a context-free mathematical measure on properties of object descriptions used in clustering—minimized for objects within a cluster and maximized for objects spanning clusters, or *(ii)* a context-sensitive symbolic expression capturing relevant similarities between two object or process descriptions—used to establish mappings in <Analogical Inference>.

Skill Acquisition (and refinement): Acquiring or improving a procedural skill (such as touch typing) by <Knowledge Compilation> and repeated practice.

Specialization: Narrowing the scope of a <Concept Description>, thus reducing the sets of instances it describes (opposite of <Generalization>).

Structural Description: A symbolic representation for objects and concepts, based on descriptions of their parts and the relationships among them.

Unsupervised Learning: See <Learning from Observation>.

Version Space (of a concept): The set of alternative plausible <Concept Descriptions> that are consistent with the training data, knowledge, and assumptions of the concept learner. This set defines a <Partially Learned Concept>, and can be represented in terms of its maximally general and maximally specific members.

Weak Methods: General methods useful for problem solving in the absence of specific knowledge required for more direct or efficient algorithmic solutions. For example, see <Means-ends Analysis> and <Heuristic Search>.

ABOUT THE AUTHORS

John Anderson is a Professor of Psychology and Computer Science at Carnegie-Mellon University. He received his B.A. from the University of British Columbia in 1968 and his Ph.D. from Stanford University in 1972. Before joining the faculty at CMU, Dr. Anderson was a Professor at Yale University. His research interests are in human learning and memory, computer simulation, and artificial intelligence. He is author of numerous journal articles and chapters. His books include *Human Associative Memory* (with G. Bower, Erlbaum, 1973), *Language, Memory, and Thought* (Erlbaum, 1976), *Cognitive Psychology and its Implications* (Freeman, 1980), *Cognitive Skills and Their Acquisition* (Erlbaum, 1981), and *The Architecture of Cognition* (Harvard, 1983). His current address is: Department of Psychology, Carnegie-Mellon University, Pittsburgh, PA 15213.

Ranan B. Banerji is a Professor of Mathematics and Computer Science at St. Joseph's University. He received his Ph.D. from the University of Calcutta in Physics and has worked on Ionospheric Physics and Propagation, Coding Theory, Languages and Automata Theory prior to his present research in AI. His major interest is in mathematical models of problems and inductive logic involved in learning heuristics for problem-solving. He is the author of two books on the subject. His current address is: Department of Mathematics and Computer Science, St. Joseph's University, 5600 City Avenue, Philadelphia, PA 19131.

Gary L. Bradshaw is a graduate student in Psychology at Carnegie-Mellon University. He received his B.A. and M.A. degrees in Psychology from the University of Missouri, Columbia. His interests include Cognitive Psychology, Artificial Intelligence, and Cognitive Science. Current work centers around three research projects: psychological investigations of human inference processes and memory retrieval phenomena, learning and discovery mechanisms in machine speech recognition, and computational models of scientific discovery (e.g., the

BACON project). His current address is: Department of Psychology, Carnegie-Mellon University, Pittsburgh, PA 15213.

Jaime G. Carbonell is an Associate Professor in Computer Science at Carnegie-Mellon University, where he has taught since 1979. Born in Montevideo, Uruguay, he was educated at the Massachusetts Institute of Technology (B.S. Mathematics 1975, B.S. Physics 1975) and Yale University (M.S. Computer Science 1976, Ph.D. Computer Science 1979). Dr. Carbonell's research interests span several areas of Artificial Intelligence and Cognitive Science, including: Natural Language Processing, Machine Learning, Analogical Reasoning, Man-Machine Interfaces, Expert Systems, and Knowledge Representation. He has authored or co-authored some 50 technical papers, reports and monographs, including a book titled *Subjective Understanding: Computer Models of Belief Systems.* His current address is: Computer Science Department, Carnegie-Mellon University, Pittsburgh, PA 15213.

Thomas G. Dietterich is a doctoral candidate at Stanford University pursuing research on machine learning and the formalization of scientific inference. He received his A.B. from Oberlin College in 1977 and his M.S. from the University of Illinois in 1979. His M.S. thesis included the construction of a program for playing the induction card game Eleusis, a game that simulates the scientific discovery process. He has written a number of articles on machine learning including a survey entitled "Learning and Inductive Inference," which constitutes Chapter XIV of Volume III of the *Handbook of Artificial Intelligence* (Kaufmann, 1982). His current address is: Department of Computer Science, Stanford University, Stanford, CA 94305.

Norman Haas is a Senior Computer Scientist at Symantec, Inc. He received his M.S. in Computer Science in 1978 from Stanford University and his B.S. in Physics from the State University of New York at Stony Brook in 1970. He was a member of the robotics group at the Stanford Artificial Intelligence Lab., and later joined the natural language research program at SRI. His current address is: Symantec, 306 Potrero Avenue, Sunnyvale, CA 94086.

Frederick Hayes-Roth is Executive Vice-President of Teknowledge, Inc. He received his Ph.D. from the University of Michigan. Prior to joining Teknowledge, he was on the Computer Science faculty at Carnegie-Mellon University and a scientist at the Information Science Department of the Rand Corporation. He was one of the designers of Hearsay-II, the first 1000-word continuous speech understanding system, the ROSIE system for programming knowledge systems, and many knowledge systems for military decision-making. He is the co-editor of *Pattern-Directed Inference Systems.* In addition, he has published numerous articles and technical reports. His current address is: Teknowledge, 525 University Avenue, Palo Alto, CA 94301.

Gary G. Hendrix is the President of Symantec, Inc. Dr. Hendrix attended the University of Texas at Austin (B.A. 1970, M.S. 1970, Ph.D. 1975). Prior to founding Symantec, he was Director of the Natural Language Research Program at SRI International and Manager of Natural Language Research Development at Machine Intelligence. His research efforts include investigations of natural language semantics, parsing systems, pragmatic and linguistically motivated grammars, knowledge representation structures (particularly semantic networks) and computational systems for knowledge acquisition and question answering. His current address is: Symantec, 306 Potrero Avenue, Sunnyvale, CA 94086.

Patrick W. Langley is a Research Scientist in the Robotics Institute at Carnegie-Mellon University. He received a B.A. in Mathematics and Psychology from Texas Christian University in 1975, and an M.S. (1976) and Ph.D. (1979) from Carnegie-Mellon in Psychology. Dr. Langley's research focuses on the ways in which intelligent systems acquire knowledge through interaction with their environment. He has done work in the areas of scientific discovery, language acquisition, strategy learning, and concept formation in the framework of adaptive production systems. He has authored or co-authored some 20 technical papers on these topics. His current address is: Robotics Institute, Carnegie-Mellon University, Pittsburgh, PA 15213.

Douglas B. Lenat is an Assistant Professor in the Computer Science Department at Stanford University. He was born in Philadelphia (Sept. 13, 1950), and attended the University of Pennsylvania, where he received B.A. degrees in mathematics and physics, and an M.S. in applied mathematics. His graduate training was in computer science at Stanford University, where he received his Ph.D. in 1976. His thesis was a demonstration that certain kinds of "creative discoveries" in mathematics could be produced by a computer program (a theorem proposer, rather than a theorem prover). Prior to joining the faculty at Stanford, Dr. Lenat was an Assistant Professor of Computer Science at Carnegie-Mellon University. In August, 1977, he was awarded the biannual Computers & Thought Award by the International Joint Committee on Artificial Intelligence. His current research deals with the question of how to discover not merely mathematical conjectures, but informal rules of thumb as well. His current address is: Department of Computer Science, Stanford University, Stanford, CA 94305.

Ryszard S. Michalski is a Professor of Computer Science and Medical Information Science, and the Director of the Artificial Intelligence Laboratory at the University of Illinois at Urbana-Champaign. He studied at the Cracow and Warsaw Technical Universities, received his M.S. degree from the Leningrad Polytechnic Insitute and his Ph.D. degree from the University of Silesia. Prior to coming to the U.S.A. in 1970, he was a Research Scientist at the Polish Academy of Sciences in Warsaw. His research interests include inductive inference, knowledge acquisition, expert systems, databases, modeling of human plausible reasoning, automated pattern discovery, classification theory, many-valued logics and application of computer science to life sciences, particularly to medicine and agriculture. Dr. Michalski has published some 70 research and technical papers on these topics. In 1982 he was appointed as an Associate in the Center of Advance Study at the University of Illinois. His current address is: Department of Computer Science, University of Illinois, 1304 W. Springfield, Urbana, IL 61801.

Tom M. Mitchell is an Associate Professor of Computer Science at Rutgers University. He received his B.S. degree (1973) in Electrical Engineering from Massachusetts Institute of Technology, and his M.S. (1975) and Ph.D. (1978) degrees in Electrical Engineering from Stanford University. Dr. Mitchell's current research on learning focuses on machine learning of heuristics and problem-solving strategies, and on knowledge acquisition for expert systems. In addition, his current research interests include applications of artificial intelligence to computer-aided circuit design, and applications of VLSI technology to problems in artificial intelligence. His current address is: Department of Computer Science, Rutgers University, New Brunswick, NJ 08903.

Jack Mostow is a Research Scientist at the Information Sciences Institute, University of Southern California. He received his A.B in Applied Mathematics from Harvard College in 1974 and his Ph.D. in Computer Science from Carnegie-Mellon University in 1981. Dr Mostow is interested in heuristic program synthesis (in both senses: synthesizing programs heuristically, and synthesizing heuristic programs). His dissertation, *Machine Transformation of Task Heuristics into Operational Procedures*, models the domain-knowledge-intensive process by which problems are reformulated in terms of AI methods. He is currently working on machine transformation of behavioral specifications into register-transfer level VLSI designs. His current address is: USC Information Sciences Institute, 4676 Admiralty Way, Marina del Rey, CA 90291.

Bernard Nudel is a doctoral candidate in the Department of Computer Science at Rutgers University. He received a B.Sc. Honors degree in Physics from Monash University, Melbourne, Australia, and an M.Sc.. in Bio-Engineering from the University of Tel Aviv. His interests in artificial intelligence include learning theory and designing algorithms for general constraint satisfaction problems. His current address is: Department of Computer Science, Rutgers University, New Brunswick, NJ 08903.

J. Ross Quinlan is the Head of the School of Computing Sciences at the New South Wales Institute of Technology in Australia. He obtained his B.Sc. from the University of Sydney in 1965, and his Ph.D. from the newly-formed Computer Science Group at the University of Washington in 1968. Dr. Quinlan spent the 1968-69 academic year as a Visiting Assistant Professor at Carnegie-Mellon University and the 1970-80 period in the Basser Department of Computer

Science at the University of Sydney. Prior to his current position he was a Computer Scientist in the Information Sciences Department of the Rand Corporation. Dr. Quinlan has worked in the area of artificial intelligence since 1965, first in problem-solving and learning, and more recently, in expert systems, inductive inference and plausible reasoning. His current address is: School of Computing Sciences, New South Wales Institute of Technology, New South Wales, Australia.

Michael D. Rychener is a Research Associate in the Department of Computer Science at Carnegie-Mellon University. His current research interest is in artificial intelligence systems that can adapt to changing environments and learn from instruction. He holds degrees from Oberlin College, Stanford University, and Carnegie-Mellon University. His doctoral research included design of, and experimentation with, production-rule systems. Applications for such systems include intelligent (personalized) user interfaces to computer systems, computer-aided engineering design, knowledge-based expert systems, and intelligent computer-aided instruction. He is author or principal co-author of ten reports and articles. His current address is: Design Research Center, Doherty Hall, Carnegie-Mellon University, Pittsburgh, PA 15213.

Herbert A. Simon, born (1916) in Milwaukee, Wisconsin, is a Professor of Computer Science and Psychology at Carnegie-Mellon University, where he has taught since 1949. Educated at the University of Chicago (B.A. 1936, Ph.D. 1943), he is a member of the National Academy of Sciences, and has received awards for distinguished research from the American Psychological Association, the Association for Computing Machinery, and the American Economic Association. In 1978, he received the Alfred Nobel Memorial Prize in Economics. His books include *Administrative Behavior*, *Human Problem Solving* (with Allen Newell), *The New Science of Management Decision* (rev. ed.), *The Sciences of the Artificial*, and *Models of Thought*. His current address is: Department of Psychology, Carnegie-Mellon University, Pittsburgh, PA 15213.

Derek H. Sleeman is a Senior Research Associate in the Department of Computer Science at Stanford University. Prior to his current position he was a Professor of Computer Science at Leeds University where he co-founded the Computer Based Learning Project. Recently he has been involved in applying/evolving AI techniques to intelligent teaching systems and expert systems set within the physical sciences. His current work involves the analysis of pupils' solving of algebraic problems, with a view to understanding the processes involved, and producing a practical micro-based system to diagnose pupils' difficulties. During the 1980-81 academic year he was a Visiting Scientist at Carnegie-Mellon University. Dr. Sleeman is the author of numerous papers, and co-editor (with Dr. John Brown) of *Intelligent Tutoring Systems*. Currently he is Secretary of the European Artificial Intelligence and Simulation of Behavior

(AISB). His address is: Computer Science Department, Stanford University, Stanford CA 94305.

Robert E. Stepp III is a doctoral candidate in the Department of Computer Science at the University of Illinois, Urbana-Champaign. He received his A.B. and M.Sc. degree from the University of Nebraska, and is expected to receive his Ph.D. in 1983. Mr. Stepp authored or co-authored several publications in the area of inductive learning, conceptual data clustering and distributed networks. His interests include machine learning, conceptual data analysis, software systems and applications of personal computers for helping the blind. His current address is: Department of Computer Science, University of Illinois, 1304 W. Springfield, Urbana, IL 61801.

Paul E. Utgoff is a doctoral candidate in the Computer Science Department at Rutgers University. His dissertation is being written under the direction of Dr. Tom Mitchell, with whom he has co-authored several publications. His dissertation, in the area of machine learning, explores methods for improving the bias which drives a generalization process. He received his B.Mus. from Oberlin College in 1974, and an M.S. from Rutgers University in 1979. His current address is: Siemens Corp., 105 College Rd. East, Princeton, N.J. 08540.

AUTHOR INDEX

Abelson, R. P., 147, 149
Abrahamson, S., 302
Amarel, S., 85
Anderson, J. R., 155, 192, 202, 205, 206, 208, 431, 442, 446
Anzai, Y., 138, 139, 164, 430, 436
Aristotle, 83
Arkadev, A. G., 15
Arons, A. B., 319
Ashby, W. R., 14

Balzer, R., 375, 396
Banerji, R. B., 85, 95
Barstow, D., 286, 292
Berliner, H., 156
Biermann, A. W., 77, 86
Block, H. D., 14
Bobrow, D. G., 33
Bongard, N., 15, 85, 90
Brachman, R. J., 84
Bradshaw, G. L., 18, 312
Bratko, I., 464
Brown, J. S., 265, 484, 485
Bruner, J. S., 85
Buchanan, B. G., 15, 42, 49, 66, 69, 85, 164, 308, 431, 489, 508
Burstall, R. M., 86, 373
Burton, R. R., 484, 485, 495, 507

Carbonell, J. G., 137, 142, 146, 155, 407, 485
Carlson, S. S., 301
Carnap, R., 88
Case, J., 86
Chang, C., 109
Chase, W. G., 218
Chilausky, R. L., 84, 85
Clancey, W. J., 484
Cohen, B. L., 77, 90
Collins, A., 456
Coulon, D., 102
Culberson, J. T., 14
Cullingford, R., 147, 149, 152

Darlington, J., 86, 373
Davies, W. D. T., 15
Davis, R., 32, 84, 93, 164, 252, 286, 407, 499
Diday, E., 347
Dietterich, T. G., 42, 90, 116, 138, 152, 407, 464
Donnelly, A. J., 195, 201
Doyle, J., 157
Duda, R. O., 15
Duncan, R., 299

Erman, L. D., 432

Feigenbaum, E. A., 15, 31, 32, 85, 244, 247, 301
Feldman, J., 86
Fikes, R. E., 95, 138, 139, 141, 151, 183
Fodor, J. A., 408
Fogel, L., 290
Forgy, C. L., 309, 431, 436, 440
Friedberg, R. M., 14, 289
Fu, K. S., 15, 32, 86
Fukananga, K., 15

Gaines, B. R., 86
Gaschnig, J., 84
Gilmartin, K., 218
Goldman, N., 396
Goldstein, I. P., 484
Gould, S. J., 299, 301
Gowda, K. C., 333

Green, C. C., 286, 291, 412
Greeno, J. G., 155
Greiner, R. D., 303

Hájek, P., 85, 86, 91
Harris, G., 393
Hartley, J. R., 483
Havránek, T., 86, 91
Hayes, J. R., 33
Hayes, P. J., 264, 412
Hayes-Roth, F., 15, 42, 47, 60, 61, 85, 90, 93, 138, 152, 183, 228, 235, 392, 464
Hedrick, C. L., 95, 107
Hendley, R. J., 484
Hendrix, G. G., 409, 413
Highleyman, W. H., 14
Hilgard, E. R., 15
Hintzman, D. L., 94
Hoff, B., 116
Holland, J. H., 14
Hopcroft, J. E., 500
Hovland, C. I., 15, 85
Hunt, E. B., 15, 47, 71, 85, 95, 465

Iba, G. A., 60, 176

Jouannaud, J. P., 86
Jurgenson, R. C., 195, 201

Kanal, L., 15
Karpinsk, J., 15
Kayser, D., 102
Kazmierczak, H., 14
Kemeni, T. G., 102
Klahr, D., 456
Klahr, P., 392
Kline, P. J., 192, 210
Kling, R. E., 137, 159
Knapman, J., 52, 54
Kochen, M., 85
Kodratoff, Y., 86
Koford, T. S., 14
Kolodner, J. L., 155
Konolige, K., 399
Kopec, D., 464
Korf, R. E., 137
Kotovsky, K., 85, 90
Kowalski, R., 412
Krishna, G., 333

Lakatos, I., 222
Langley, P. W., 98, 308, 309, 313
Larson, J. B., 45, 47, 49, 70, 75, 85, 86, 93, 97, 98, 109, 114, 116, 336, 352
Lea, G., 15, 85, 308
Lebowitz, M., 155
Lee, R. C., 109
Lenat, D. B., 16, 31, 44, 49, 84, 86, 91, 93, 107, 111, 138, 159, 234, 252, 286, 303, 308, 310, 391, 393, 400
Lesser, V. R., 432
Lindsay, P. H., 414

McCarthy, J., 264, 411
McCullough, W. S., 14
McDermott, D. V., 157
McDermott, J., 15, 60, 61, 90, 93, 138, 152, 228, 431, 440, 448, 454, 464
Maier, J. E., 195, 201,
Matz, M., 499
Meehan, J., 396, 397
Mendel, T., 15
Michalski, R. S., 15, 42, 45, 47, 49, 70, 72, 75, 84, 85, 86, 89, 90, 91, 93, 95, 97, 98, 102, 109, 114, 116, 123, 138, 152, 333, 336, 338, 340, 343, 345, 346, 352, 360, 407, 464, 508
Michie, D., 94
Minsky, M., 11, 14, 15, 94
Mitchell, T. M., 15, 43, 47, 48, 69, 85, 89, 90, 138, 152, 164, 170, 176, 177, 181, 229, 469
Moore, J., 137, 369, 436
Moore, R., 412, 413
Moraga, C., 85
Morgan, C. G., 95, 109
Mostow, D. J., 230, 232, 235, 368, 369, 373, 374, 383, 390, 392, 399, 400, 441
Mulec, P., 464

Negri, P., 84
Neves, D., 164, 202, 205, 206, 208
Newell, A., 6, 29, 85, 137, 138, 139, 140, 270, 368, 369, 374, 392, 411, 430, 431, 436, 445, 447, 450, 454, 455, 456,
Niblett, T., 84, 464
Nilsson, N. J., 14, 103, 138, 139, 141, 151, 186, 350, 399
Norman, D. A., 414
Novak, G. S., 32

O'Rorke, P., 84, 97
Owens, A., 290

Papert, S., 14, 15
Pettorossi, A., 86
Pitts, W., 14
Plotkin, G. D., 44, 95

Pokorny, D., 86, 91
Politakis, P., 164
Polya, G., 88, 254
Pople, H., 32
Popper, K., 87, 102
Post, H. R., 102
Poveda, P., 358

Quinlan, J. R., 48, 84, 85, 90, 95, 464, 469

Rashevsky, N., 14
Reddy, R., 72
Riseman, E. M., 91
Rising, G. R., 195, 201
Robinson, J. A., 412
Robinson, J. J., 418
Rosenblatt, F., 11, 14, 32
Rosenbloom, P., 6, 138
Rubin, S. M., 72
Russell, B., 87
Rychener, M. D., 430, 431, 433, 440, 445, 448, 451, 454, 455

Sacerdoti, E. D., 70, 139, 145, 392
Salzer, F., 396
Sammut, C. A., 77, 95, 110
Samuel, A. L., 14, 30, 157, 291
Schacter, C., 396
Schank, R. C., 137, 147, 149, 152, 155
Schimke, R. T., 296
Schwenzer, G. M., 69
Sebestyen, G. S., 14
Selfridge, O. G., 14
Shapiro, A., 84, 464
Shapiro, E. Y., 86
Shaw, D. E., 86
Shortliffe, E., 32, 84
Simon, H. A., 15, 29, 33, 85, 90, 138, 139, 140, 218, 270, 294, 308, 347, 369, 411, 430, 431, 436, 456
Sleeman, D. H., 483, 484, 485, 486, 488, 490, 492, 495, 499, 503, 510
Smith, C., 86
Smith, D. R., 86
Smith, M. J., 486, 488, 490, 492, 495, 510
Solomonoff, R. J., 86
Soloway, E. M., 47, 91
Stepp, R. E., 48, 90, 93, 333, 345, 360
Stoffel, J. C., 85, 90
Suppes, P., 105

Tappel, S., 369, 391, 399
Truxal, T. G., 15
Tsypkin, Y. Z., 15
Tuomela, R., 310

Uhr, L., 14, 15
Ullman, J. E., 500
Utgoff, P. E., 164, 181

VanLehn, K., 265
Vere, S. A., 15, 42, 47, 63, 65, 85, 90, 93, 95, 176, 228, 229, 464

Walsh, M., 290
Watanabe, S., 15
Waterman, D. A., 85, 95, 138, 152, 164, 448
Weston-Smith, M., 299
Weyhrauch, R. W., 412
White, T. J., 301
Widrow, B., 14
Wilson, A. C., 300, 301
Winston, P. H., 9, 15, 16, 42, 44, 45, 51, 52, 54, 55, 60, 77, 85, 90, 93, 107, 137, 138, 139, 152, 153, 159, 350, 407

Yau, K. C., 86
Young, R. M., 431
Yovits, M. C., 14

Zagoruiko, N. G., 86, 91, 95

SUBJECT INDEX

Accommodation, 440, 447
ACT, 191-218
  human behavior versus, 201
  search strategies, 195-200
Adaptive control systems, 15
Adelaine, 15
Adding alternative rule, 105-106
Additive successive approximations (ASA), 447, 448
Advice taking
  see Learning from instruction
AM, 246, 249-263, 308, 310
  constructive induction in, 98
  discoveries, 252-254, 256-261
  goal criterion, 257
  representation, 250-252, 279
  research conclusions, 261
ANA, 448
Analogical problem solving, 137-159
  evaluation of, 149-151
  means-end analysis in, 148-149
  planning in, 147, 151-155
  similarity/difference metric, 142, 145-146, 153-154, 156-157
  transform-operators, 144-145, 146, 157-159
  transform-space, 143-146
Analogy, 137-159, 209-211, 278, 441, 448
  see also Analogical problem solving
AQ11, 93, 97
AQVAL/1, 93
Archimedes' law of displacement, 315-317
Artificial intelligence, goals of, 27-28
Assurance (heuristic learning method), 226, 229, 232-233
Attribute descriptions, 42, 70-71
Attributes, automatic discovery of, 187-189, 477-481
Automatic programming, 30, 288-292
Avoidance (heuristic learning method), 225-226, 228-229, 231-232

Backward search, 201
  combined with forward search, 194-201
Bacon, Sir Francis, 309
BACON.4, 307-328
  constructive induction in, 98
  defining new terms, 310-312
  discoveries, 312-318, 322-326
  earlier versions, 308
  formulating hypotheses, 309-310
  postulating properties, 311-312
BASEBALL system, 47
Beam search, 72-73
Black's specific heat law, 317-318
Bottom-up methods
  see Data-driven methods
BUGGY, 265, 485
Bugs in modelling students, 485-500

Caching, 391
Cantus firmus, 396-398
Characteristic description, 44-45, 90, 92, 122-123
Checker-playing program, 14, 30-31, 291
Chemistry, discovery in, 307-328
  history of, 319-321
Chess endgame, 84, 470-474
  approximate decision trees, 474-477
  automatic discovery of attributes, 477-481
  benefit of decision tree, 470-474
Climbing generalization tree rule, 53, 107, 340
Closing the interval rule, 106-107, 340
CLUSTER/2, 331-362
  classification of folksongs, 358-360

full search algorithm, 346-349
hierarchy building algorithm, 357-358
path-rank-ordered search, 349-352
suggested extensions, 360-362
Clustering
see Conceptual clustering
Common divisors, 321-322, 327-328
Composition of production rules, 12, 141, 205-207, 215-217
Concept learning, 15
application of incompletely learned concepts, 171-172
multiple concept learning, 93
representation of incompletely learned concepts, 168-170
see also Learning from examples
Conceptual clustering, 45, 158, 331-362
algorithm for, 340-344, 345-352
criteria for clustering quality, 344-345
definition, 333
examples, 352-357, 358-360
generalization rules, 340-341
hierarchy building in, 357-358
Conjunctive generalization, 42-43, 62-63, 331
maximally general, 168-170
maximally specific, 43, 51, 60, 63-65, 70-73, 92, 168-170
Constructive induction, 46, 47-48, 60, 78, 98, 508
rules for, 74
Counting arguments rule, 110-111
Credit assignment, 172-173

Data base management systems
KLAUS and, 405-406, 418
machine learning in, 405-427
Data-driven methods, 48, 51-65, 308-309, 327
Data-flow graphs, 374
transformations on, 391-392
Decision-theoretic approach to learning, 14
Decision tree, 11, 463-481
approximate trees, 474-477
relationship to training set, 474-477
versus other search methods, 471-472
Descriptive discovery, 308
Descriptive generalization
see Learning from observation
Descriptors
relationships among, 99-100
types of, 99
Detecting descriptor interdependence rule, 111-112
Difference metric
see Similarity/difference metric
Discovery and learning, 10-11, 29, 234
Discovery of attributes
see Attributes, automatic discovery of
Discovery systems, 10-11, 249-263, 276-282, 307-328
control structure, 247-249
data-driven, 308, 327
descriptive, 308
theory-driven, 308, 327
Discriminant description, 45, 90, 92
in STAR, 122
Discrimination, 214-215
see also Specialization rules
Discrimination network, 31-32
see also Decision tree; Taxonomic description

Divisors of a number, 259-261
DNA as program, 286-292
heuristics in, 292-302
Dropping condition rule, 46, 59, 63, 65, 105, 340-341

Eight Queens problem, 375-376
Episodic memory
organization, 155
reminding process in, 142, 155-157
restructuring, 155-157
EURISKO, 276-282
Evolution, simulation of, 14
as heuristic search, 286-302
Exclusion (heuristic learning method), 225, 228, 230-231
Exemplary programming, 448
Expectation-driven learning, 221-239
Experimenter and bananas problem, 139, 148-149
Expert systems, knowledge acquisition for, 6, 84, 164, 244, 369, 405
Expertise acquisition
see Knowledge acquisition
Extending reference rule, 106
Extending the quantification domain rule, 108
Extension against rule, 109

Find extrema of partial orders rule, 46-48
First order logic, 12, 70-73, 95-96, 130-134, 410-412
history of use in intelligent systems, 411-412
FOO, 367-403
altering the search space, 392-393
domain knowledge in, 370-373
future work, 399-400

heuristic search in, 374-400
problem representation, 370
problem transformation rule, 373, 403
search refinement methods, 378-400
Forward search, 171-172, 195
combined with backward search, 194-201
Frame-like representation, 12, 250-252
see also Schemas

Generalization rules, 46-47, 59, 104-112
constructive, 46, 109-112
selective, 46-47, 105-109
Generalizing from examples
see Learning from examples
Generate and test algorithms, refinement into heuristic search, 375-377, 384-396
Generating chain properties rule, 111
Geometry proofs, 191-218
knowledge schemas for, 203-205
learning strategies for, 201-203, 217-218
stages in generation of, 193
Goldbach's conjecture, 258, 261
Graph-matching, 12, 54

Hearts game, 229-234, 367-396
Heuristic problem solving, learning in, 151-159, 163-189, 201-218, 221-239, 249-285, 367-396, 429-456
Heuristic search method
automatic refinement of, 378-400
definition, 374-377
instantiating, 378-384
problem mapping, 378-379
use in discovery systems, 243-305, 307-328
Heuristics
attributes of, 277-278
shallow tree problem, 273-274
space of, 271-275
theory of, 263-275
utility of individual, 266-271
Human learning, computer modelling of, 192

ID3, 463-481
automatic discovery of attributes, 477-481
classification rule, 465-467
compared to other inference systems, 463-464
decision trees in, 463-481
experimental results, 470-474
rule forming procedure, 465-470
selective induction, 97
Ideal gas law, 309-311
Inclusion (heuristic learning method), 226, 229, 233
INDUCE-1, 47-48, 49, 114-116, 464
INDUCE 1.2, 70-75
compared with other learning methods, 76-77
constructive induction in, 98
evaluation, 73-75
generalization process, 70-73
representation, 70-73
Induction methods, 48-51
evaluation criteria, 49-51
general versus specific, 49
Inductive inference
completeness condition, 91-92
consistency condition, 91-92
definition of, 88-90
Inductive learning, 83-124
definition of, 84
description languages, 94-96
types, 85-93
Inductive resolution rule, 108-109
Information management
see Data base management systems
Instructable Production System, 429-457
dialog constraints, 431
explanation capability, 439-440
functional components, 436-443
kernel systems, 443, 445-453
learning research, relationship to, 431-433
planning in, 435-436
summary table, 454-455
terminology, 433-436
Intelligent CAI, 433, 483-508
aims, 483-484
research issues, 485-486
shortcomings, 484
Interference matching, 61-62
Intrinsic properties
common divisors in, 321-322
discovery of, 311-312, 315-317
Introducing exception rule, 47, 59
IPMSL, 451
ISA hierarchies, 52-53, 166, 337, 413-415, 427
see also Semantic network
ISAAC, 32-34

KLAUS system, 405-427
data base management systems and, 405-406, 418
requirements, 406
research problems, 406-407
Knowledge acquisition, 6, 84, 164, 244, 369, 405
dialogues for, 406-407, 412-413
research plan for automatic, 244-246

Knowledge compilation, 202-217, 235, 367-403, 442-443
  review of previous research, 368-369
Knowledge intensive learning, 15, 181-189, 221-239, 370-374
Knowledge refinement learning paradigm, 221-239, 368
Knowledge representation
  see Representation

Law of conservation of momentum, 317
Law of gravitation, 317
Learning
  basic forms, 4-6
  definition of, 28
  discovery and, 29
  research priorities, 3-4, 35-36
  see also Machine learning
Learning Blocks World Concepts (Winston), 15, 51-60
  compared with other learning methods, 76-77
  evaluation, 57-60
  learning algorithm, 53-57
  network representation, 52-53
Learning by analogy, 8, 137-159, 209-211, 278, 441-442
Learning by being told
  see Learning from instruction
Learning by doing, 430
Learning by experimentation, 10-11, 163-189, 249-285, 503-507
Learning from examples, 9-10, 43-78, 85-86, 90, 168-170, 173-178, 463-481
  comparison of methods, 76-77
  descriptions, 44-45, 90
  generalization rules, 46-47
  in plan generation, 151-155
  representation in, 44
  sources of examples, 9
  types of examples, 9-10
Learning from instruction, 8, 367-403, 405-427, 429-457
  compared to other research, 407
Learning from observation, 10, 45, 86, 91, 331-362
Learning in problem solving, 151-155
  see also Heuristic problem solving, learning in
Learning to plan, 137-159, 221-239
Learning without teacher
  see Learning from observation
Leeds Modelling System, 483-508
  model generation algorithm, 488-502
  model representation, 486-487
Lemma incorporation, 234
LEX, 85, 163-189
  credit assignment (PosInst), 164, 171, 172-173, 181-187
  critic, 167, 172-173
  experimental results, 176-178
  generalizer, 168, 173-178
  knowledge driven learning in, 181-189
  limitations, 180-181
  major components, 167-168
  problem generator, 168, 178-180
  problem solver, 167, 171-172
  representation languages, 165-166
  vocabulary extension, 187-189
LMS
  see Leeds Modelling System
Logic Theorist, 29, 369

Machine learning
  application domains, 13
  comprehensibility postulate, 94
  history of research, 14-16
  objectives, 3-6
  taxonomy of systems, 7-13, 87-93
Macrooperators, 12, 141, 205-207, 215-217
Mal-rules, 489-490
Mathematical discovery, 249-263
Maximally-specific conjunctive generalization, 43, 51, 60, 63-65, 70-73, 92, 168-170
Means-ends analysis, 139-141, 148-149, 445, 453, 456
MERLIN, 369
Meta-DENDRAL, 66-69, 85, 170, 308
  compared with other learning methods, 76-77, 308
  evaluation, 68-69
  generalization process, 67-68
  INTSUM algorithm, 67, 69
  RULGEN algorithm, 67-69
  RULMOD algorithm, 67-68
Meta-knowledge, 182, 247, 276-277
Minimal discriminant descriptions, 92
Minimax search, decision tree versus, 471-472
Model-driven methods, 48, 65-75
Monkey and bananas problem, 139, 148
Monster-barring, 231
MSC-generalization
  see Maximally-specific conjunctive generalization

NANOKLAUS
  knowledge acquisition, 412-413

knowledge organization, 409
knowledge representation, 410-412
limitations, 413
natural language component, 409-410, 413-418
seed concepts, 408-409
seed vocabulary, 408-409
sort hierarchy, 413-415
verbs, 415-418
Natural language processing
in IPS, 431
in NANOKLAUS, 409-410, 413-418
"Near-miss" negative examples, 52, 153
Neural modelling, 14-15
Neural nets, 14-15

Ohm's law, 313-314
Operationalization
see Knowledge compilation
OPS language, 309, 431

Pandemonium, 14
Parameter learning, 11, 156-157
Pattern recognition, 14-15
Perceptrons, 14, 32
Physics
discovery in, 309-318
problem solving in, 32-34
Plan generalization, 151-155
Planners Workbench, 236
Planning, 147, 151-155, 222-225, 435-436
PLANTS/DS, 84
Predicate calculus
see First order logic
Prime numbers, 259-261
Problem net, 195-197
Problem solving, 139-140
see also Analogical problem solving; Heuristic problem solving, learning in
Problem spaces, 450-451
Proceduralization, 205, 207-209
Production rules, 11-12, 196, 434-436, 486-487
Production systems, 309, 429-457, 486-487
recognize-act cycle, 431, 456
Proof tree, 193-195
PSI system, 292
PW1, 291-292

Reducing search depth, 390-391
Representation, 44, 49, 75-78
classification according to types of knowledge, 11-12
of incompletely learned concepts, 168-170
self-modification of, 187-189, 282-285, 310-312, 407, 477-481
see also specific kinds of representation, e.g., Production rules
Retraction (heuristic learning method), 225, 228, 230
RLL, 303
Rote learning, 8

Samuel's checker-playing program, 14, 30-31, 291
Schemas, 203-205, 250-252, 451-453
for heuristic search, 374-377
Search
see Heuristic search method
Selective induction, 46-47, 97
Self-monitoring, 248, 442, 448
Self-organizing systems, 14-15
Semantic network, 52-53, 451
see also ISA hierarchies
Shallow tree problem, 273-274
Similarity/difference metric, 142, 145-146, 153-154, 156-157, 332, 333-335
tuning, 156-157
Skill refinement, 6
Snell's law of refraction, 317
Sort hierarchies, 413-415
Spanish folksongs, classification for, 358-360
Specialization rules, 47
Specialized search, 471
decision tree versus, 471-472
SPROUTER, 60-63
compared with other learning methods, 76-77, 464
evaluation, 62-63
STAR methodology, 49, 112-124, 341-343
algorithm, 113-114
definition of, 112-113
example, 116-123
problem background knowledge, 96-103
STRIPS with MACROPS, 141
Structural descriptions, 42, 70-71
STUDENT, 33
Student modelling in CAI, 483-508
model generation algorithm, 488-502
model representation, 486-487
Symbolic integration, 164-166
Syntactic distance, 336-338

Tabula rasa approach, 14
Taxonomic description, 12-13, 45, 67
algorithm for inferring, 357-358
TEIRESIAS, 32

Theory-driven learning methods, 181-189, 221-239, 308, 327
Theory rectification
heuristics (general), 225-226
heuristics in TL, 228-229, 230-234
Thoth, 63-65
compared with other learning methods, 76-77, 464
evaluation, 64-65
representation, 64-65
TL, 221-239
computational problems, 234-238
heurisitcs for learning, 225-234
learning cycle, 222-225
planning in, 222-225
Top-down methods
see Model-driven methods
Transform operators, 144-145, 146, 157-159
Trend detectors, 310-311
Triangle table, 141
Tuning of search strategies, 156-157, 209-217
Turning conjunction into disjunction rule, 108
Turning constants to variables rule, 63, 65, 107-108

UNDERSTAND, 33-34, 369
Unsupervised learning
see Learning from observation

Version space, 168-172, 469
refinement of, 173-178
representation of, 168-170
Vocabulary extension, 187-189, 477-481
VL_{21}, 70